THE FUN ENCYCLOPEDIA

An All-Purpose Plan Book for Those Interested in Recreation
for Clubs, Schools, Churches, and the Home

The *Fun* ENCYCLOPEDIA

A Comprehensive, All-purpose, Entertainment Plan-book for the Home, Club, School, Church, and Playground

E. O. HARBIN

ABINGDON PRESS
Nashville New York

THE FUN ENCYCLOPEDIA

ISBN 0-687-13714-4
Library of Congress Catalog Card Number: 40-27572

SET UP, PRINTED, AND BOUND BY THE
PARTHENON PRESS, AT NASHVILLE,
TENNESSEE, UNITED STATES OF AMERICA

DEDICATED TO TOMMY
WHO WAS CHEATED OF MANY AN HOUR
OF PLAY WITH HIS DADDY WHILE THIS
BOOK WAS BEING WRITTEN

PREFACE

THIS book is an attempt to provide in one volume a wide variety of ideas of interesting things to do in leisure. Suggestions are offered for home recreation, for clubrooms, for hobbies, for banquets, for sports, for picnics, for outings, for camps, for campfires, for hikes, for indoor and outdoor games, for parties, for music and musical games, for dramatics, and for puppetry. There are stories, stunts, tricks, writing contests, quizzes, nature games, party plans, and suggestions for almost every conceivable kind of recreation.

No idea is of use to you until you have appropriated it, put something of yourself into it, and put it to work. It is the hope of the author that every reader of this book will find some ideas that he can make his own, and that thereby he may enrich his own life and the lives of others. Try out some of them. Improve on them. Breathe the breath of life into them. And see what fun it is!

It is only a partial truth that "the good things in life are free." Most of the good things and good times of life must be earned. This seems to be one of the laws of life. John Ruskin said that a long time ago when he wrote: "The law of nature is that a certain amount of work is necessary to produce a certain quality of good. If you want knowledge you must toil for it; if food, you must toil for it; if pleasure, you must toil for it."

Capacity for the full enjoyment of life has to be developed. It involves attitudes, appreciations, interests, and skills. These do not come by happenstance or wishful thinking. They require time, patience, planning, and effort. You increase your capacity for enjoying life as you broaden and deepen your range of interests and skills. That man lives most who responds to most of the fine things about him—music, drama, art, literature, religion, creative activities, games of skill. These things need cultivation to permit proper growth. Thus one builds what L. P. Jacks refers to as "inner resources"—a sort of bank deposit of good times, a sinking fund laid up against dull moments, a reserve that is assurance that we will not be poverty-stricken in ideas of what to do in free time.

Four important trends among an increasing number of leaders

and institutions should be noted. We mention them briefly. (1) *The trend toward freedom of choice.* This is reflected in the increasing popularity of the open-house program where a wide variety of activities is provided. (2) *The trend toward co-operation rather than competition.* There is a feeling among a considerable number of educators and other persons interested in human welfare that the importance of competition as a factor in play has been considerably over-emphasized. Some even go so far as to charge that highly organized competitive programs are deterrents to the emergence of proper social attitudes. They insist that there should be larger use made of co-operative activities and that when competitive games are used they should be promoted without the harmful stimulation that comes from tournaments, championships, and awards. "Play the game for the fun of playing" is their slogan. (3) *The trend toward creative and cultural activities.* The meaning of recreation has been broadened to include other than mere physical activities— reading, meditation, discussion, drama, music, crafts. An increasing number of clubs, schools, and churches are making use of workshop idea, interest groups, hobby guilds. (4) *The trend toward rhythmic expression through folk games.* The growth in popularity of these games is well deserved. They are glorious fun. They are unequalled for the purpose of socializing a group. And they root back in the culture patterns of the people of many nations. This latter value is an item of no small moment in a world where there is so great a need for better understanding between peoples and races.

The writer is deeply grateful to the thousands of recreation leaders who have so profoundly influenced his own ideas of recreation and who have added to his fund of information about ways to have good times. Especially does he feel indebted to those leaders with whom he has had the privilege of sharing at the old Waldenwoods Conference, the Minnesota Recreation Leaders' Laboratory (Ihduhapi), the South-wide Leisure Time Conference, and at Lake Junaluska and Mount Sequoyah.   E. O. HARBIN.

CONTENTS

CHAPTER I
HOME FUN

HOME FUN

"The family that plays together will be more likely to stay together."

"Home, sweet home," the poet sang
In days that were of old,
But now the home has just become
A parking place, I'm told.
We park to eat, a bit to sleep,
And then we're on the run—
The office, movies, clubs, and dates;
No time for family fun!

THERE is no better place to have fun than the home. It makes good times inexpensive. It can save us from the tyranny and inanity of commercialized and stereotyped recreation. It develops skill among the members of the home in the handling of leisure. It helps to make "the house a home."

The Basement Playroom

Many families are making basements into attractive playrooms. One hostess I know had an attractive dinner party in her basement recreation room. The floor was painted in red and black one-foot squares, looking like a huge checkerboard. In another home they covered the basement walls with pine panels—stained, waxed, and polished. An unusual ceiling lighting fixture was achieved by the use of an old wagon wheel. Rag rugs decorated the floor. Games of all sorts can be provided, many of them being homemade. (See Chapter II, "Fun in the Clubroom," for suggestions.)

The Back-yard Playground

The equipment for a back-yard playground can be elaborate or simple, as desired—a slide or a sand pile for the children, a croquet court for the entire family; a basketball court; tennis and volleyball court; miniature golf course (one family arranged an interesting nine-hole course on a small front and side lawn using broken tile

(15)

pipe and mounds for hazards) ; an outdoor oven; swings; seesaws; and other playground equipment. One shuffleboard enthusiast built a concrete shuffleboard court, 60 feet long and 8 feet wide, in the back yard. (See Chapter XI, Fun with Sports, for diagram.) The family and neighbors keep the court busy. A croquet enthusiast sank two tomato cans near the center wicket and players were required to hole the ball in one of them going and the other coming, before being eligible to shoot for the center wicket.

A Back-yard Recreation Room

One family built a back-yard recreation room at a total cost of $60, plus some hard labor, that proved to be lots of fun. Discarded lumber, second-hand garden tiles for the floor, a batch of hollow tile for a two-foot foundation set upon a firm footing of crushed rock and cement, some knotted-pine paneling, a few finishing boards, some cement, sand, and paint were the materials used. There were two five-foot bay windows, a fire place and chimney made with some discarded bricks. It was furnished with made-over second-hand furniture. Many uses were found for this attractive room. The young people and parents entertained their company there informally. Often the family dines there. Sometimes it is used for an extra bedroom.

Things for the Family to Do Together

1. *Hobbies.* Nature collections, stamp collections, painting, sketching, gardening, raising chickens, pigeons, rabbits, starlore, creative hobbies—making things, writing stories, writing poetry, spatter printing—and a hundred different things.

Theodore Roosevelt always insisted on every member of the Roosevelt family having some leisure-time hobby. Hobbies to share make a happy family group.

Lord Chesterfield said that he had a hundred interests that enriched life for him. These he traced back to the many fascinating hobbies of his father. (See Chapter III, "Fun with Hobbies.")

2. *Workshop.* A workshop in the basement, garage, or shed can be a source of great happiness to all the family. Making games, toys, furniture, and bric-a-brac for the home! Making presents for friends!

If satisfaction is to be gotten out of making things, then interest must be aroused in good workmanship. The fun comes as skill and finesse are acquired. Fine character values also repay these adventures in creativity. It was Michelangelo who said, "Nothing makes the soul so pure, so religious, as the endeavor to create something perfect; and whoever strives for it strives for something Godlike.'' (See Chapter II, Fun in the Clubroom, and Chapter III, Fun with Hobbies.)

3. *Telling stories.* A storyteller's night once a month could be made lots of fun. Each member of the family should be responsible for a story—jokes, "tall" stories, "catch" stories, fairy stories, folk stories, and stories of experiences. See Bibliography for suggested sources. Note "Stunt Stories" in this chapter.

4. *Reading.* Occasionally read something together—a good play, a good story, a short excerpt from a good book, a lovely poem. Care will have to be exercised to select something that will be of general interest. If all of the members of the family are of reading age, there could be a once-a-week book chat at the table, each member of the family reporting briefly on something read during the week —a book, a poem, an article, a story.

5. *Dramatics.* Charades, stunts, Bible stories, fairy stories, Mother Goose rhymes, and everyday happenings—what fun to act them out. (See Chapter XIV, Fun with Dramatics, for suggestions.)

6. *Music.* This writer still remembers with joy those boyhood days when Mother, Dad, and two sisters gathered around the piano to sing. Occasionally there was a solo from one or the other of us. But usually we all sang together. And what fun it was!

Maybe a family orchestra is possible—an orchestra that plays just for the fun of playing.

These family music hours should be used to acquaint the family with *good* music. (See Chapter XII, Fun with Music.)

7. *Games.* Perhaps a special night can be set aside as "Game Night." Table games like logomachy, anagrams, lotto, dominoes, parchesi, pick-up sticks, ping-pong, checkers, crokinole, caroms, chess, wari, runa, helma, and the like. Social games like bug, battleship, tit-tat-toe, hangman, and hundreds of others. Occasionally invite in friends and play musical games.

8. *Marionettes and puppets.* This can be made a creative activity in which the whole family can co-operate. An occasional show for the family would be fun. In our family even the five-year-old wants to take his turn at presenting a performance. And he does surprisingly well. (See Chapter XV, Fun with Puppets, for suggestions.)

9. *Sharpening the wits with conundrums.* Every now and then have a round of conundrums. See this chapter for some suggestions.

10. *Tricks and brain teasers.* Encourage an occasional sharing of brain teasers in the family circle.

A Good Home Will Provide

1. *Social life.* Family nights. Inviting in of friends. **Home** parties. Guests for meals.

2. *Literature.* Good books and a taste for same. Good magazines. Stories. Wholesome conversation. Exchange of ideas about things read.

3. *Family fellowship.* Trips together. Outings. Picnics.

4. *Music.* Instruments from harmonica to piano. Family "sings." Family orchestra. Family "listen to good music" occasions.

5. *Drama.* Charades, stunts, acting out stories, shadow shows, puppets, marionettes, play-reading, writing.

6. *Creative activities.* Wood and soap carving, weaving, modeling, painting, sketching, paper cutting, gardening. Workshop, tools.

7. *Activity.* Play yard—slides, sand, trapeze, swings, athletic equipment. Bicycle, skates.

TRICKS

The magic candle.—Offer to light a candle without touching fire to the wick. First, light the candle and let it burn a moment, as you explain that anyone can light a candle that way. Now blow out the flame and light a match. The smoke from the extinguished candle will rise upward. Hold the lighted match in this smoke about 3 inches above the wick. The flame will travel down the smoke lighting the wick.

Calling "heads" or "tails."—Cut a small notch in the edge of a coin on one side. Be sure you remember which side. When the notched coin is coming out of a spin it will give a whirring sound if coming out on the notched side. Thus you can call "heads" or "tails" correctly every time, with back turned or blindfolded, simply by being a good listener. Try it.

The floating needle.—Secrete a small bit of candle wax under the finger nails. By drawing the needle through the wax, thus coating it with wax, you can drop it in a tumbler of water, and it will float. Drop the unwaxed needle into the water first. It will sink to the bottom. Take it out, dry it, and pass it across the finger tips as you use some magic words and the needle is ready to float.

Penny wise.—Place a penny or other coin on top of an inverted tumbler. Leave the room, after telling the group that if anyone will take the penny and conceal it about his person you will be able to tell who has it. As soon as you return, ask that all persons in the room, one at a time, put their fingers on the tumbler and then remove them after a moment. After each person has done this you look into the tumbler, feel the rim, hold it to your ear, and then point out the person that has the penny.

The trick is that your secret confederate touches the tumbler immediately after the person who has the penny.

Pairing nickels.—Place ten nickels in a row. The job is to stack them two deep without in any move passing over more or less than ten cents. The set-up will be as follows, the nickels being numbered in your mind: 1 2 3 4 5 6 7 8 9 10.

Place 4 on 1, 7 on 3, 5 on 9, 2 on 6, and 8 on 10.

Magic candles.—Make a hole in each of five candles, cutting through until the wick is severed. The holes will be at various distances from the top. Fill up the hole with candle grease and smooth the surface.

Place the candles in a row, in order. Begin a story about a little boy who went to his room all alone. In the room were five candles. He had asked his mother to leave them lit because he was afraid. Just as his mother left the room the first candle *went out*. Well, there was no use to worry for there were four more. He heard a scratching noise and another candle *went out*. But still there were three left burning. Then there was a sound as if someone blew and *out went* another candle. He was beginning to worry now for only two lighted candles were left. And then, sure enough, another candle *went out*. But there was still one burning, and he was thankful for that. When swish! and *out went* the last candle. OH MAMMA!

Practice this stunt so you can time your story just right. Point to the candles that are going out. And as you point, the light should flicker and go out. You may embellish your story as much as you please.

Swimming snake.—Lots of fun can be had with this simple device. Soak a short piece of heavy cord in molten candle grease until it is uniformly coated. Press a short piece of iron wire in the end of the cord. Put the cord in a pan of water and use a magnet. The iron wire will be attracted by the magnet and it will swim after it, looking for all the world like a snake.

The magic plate.—Explain that you have a magic plate that will allow you to pick up a nickel that is immersed in water without getting your finger wet. Set up a candle stub in the center of the plate. Place the nickel at the side of the plate. Pour in a bit of water so that the nickel is just covered. Light the candle and put a glass tumbler over it upside down. Directly then there will be a hissing sound and the water will rush into the tumbler leaving the nickel high and dry. Then pick up the coin. The candle heat creates a partial vaccum in the tumbler and the water rushes in to fill it.

The magic milk bottle.—*Equipment*—a milk bottle and a soft-boiled egg. Peel the egg. It must be soft, but not too soft. Set the milk bottle on the table. Light a match and drop it into the bottle. Place the small end of the peeled egg in the mouth of the bottle and hold it there. The suction will draw it into the bottle. The heat has created a partial vacuum.

After the egg is in the bottle, hold the bottle up to your mouth, with the small end of the egg in the neck of the bottle ready to come out. Force all the air possible into the bottle by blowing, using the egg as a sort of valve to let the air in and hold it in the bottle. When you release your mouth from the milk bottle the egg is forced out by the air pressure. Unexplained, this stunt will mystify the group.

—Don Schooler
Cape Girardeau, Missouri

Home-made post card projector.—With this arrangement song slides typed on slips of heavy paper and magazine pictures can be thrown on the screen.

For a quick start to get the principle of the projector take a paper carton approximately the size suggested and hang two extension cords, with whatever size bulbs are available, inside the box on either side. A fair degree of success can be secured without the bent tin reflectors. A two or two and a quarter-inch magnifying lens can be secured in almost any ten-cent store for ten or fifteen cents. A cardboard mailing tube the size of your lens makes a satisfactory holder. The holder is inserted in a hole in the projection box and is left free so it can be moved for focusing. Hold pictures or objects outside the box against the opening cut in the back.

After you see how much fun can be had with such a projector make one out of wood. Paint the inside black and use either curved

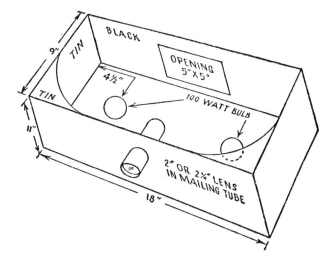

tin or mirrors for reflectors; mount bulbs in porcelain sockets and if you want best results fix your lens in a tin can the proper size and enamel it black on the inside. Ventilators can be put in the top.

The picture projected will be reversed. To correct this, project the picture on the back of a sheet with audience on the other side. Tilt the projector and sheet at approximately the same angle. Between the bottom of the picture on the sheet and the floor have some opaque object (table, heavy blanket, etc.) to cut off the light. By mounting the projector with the back on the edge of a table, pictures may be shown from any size book.

—David Cathcart, Miami, Florida

TONGUE TWISTERS

How much wood would a woodchuck chuck if a woodchuck could chuck wood? He would chuck, he would, as much as he could, and chuck as much wood as a woodchuck would if a woodchuck could chuck wood.

Bill had a billboard. Bill also had a board bill. The board bill bored Bill, so that Bill sold the billboard to pay his board bill. So after Bill sold his billboard to pay his board bill the board bill no longer bored Bill.

The swan swam the sea. We shouted, "Swim, swan, swim." The swan swirled and swam back again. "What a swim, swan, you swam."

Villey Vite and his wife went to Vinsor and Vest Vickham von Vitsun Vednesday.   (Repeat rapidly five times.)

> If a Hottentot tot taught a Hottentot tot
>   To talk ere the tot could totter,
> Ought the Hottentot be taught to say aught?
>   Or, what ought to be taught her?

> If to hoot and toot a hottentot tot
>   Be taught by a Hottentot tutor,
> Should the tutor get hot if the Hottentot tot
>   Hoot and toot at the Hottentot tutor?

Quizzical Quiz, Kiss me quick.   (Repeat rapidly six times without drawing a breath.)

Bandy-legged Borachio Mustachio whiskeyjusticus the bold and brave Bombaretino of Bagdad helped Abomilique Bluebeard Bashow of Barbad Mandab to bed down a Bumble Bee at Belsore.

The editor of *Pathfinder* got the following bit of advice from one of the readers of that magazine:

"In your frolicsome, fructiferous fulminations, eschew execrable ejaculatory equivocations; jettison juvenescent jejune babblement; palliate pragmatical prating and mitigate Machiavellian, marcescent, metetricious metaphors. Sedulously avoid thrasonical, bombastic prodigality; yield not to yearning zetetic zealotry. Elude ancephalic eructation, frigorific friction, gallimaufrious gurgitation and, above all, shun querulous quadrumanisms!"

Theophilus Thistle, the thistle sifter, in sifting thousands of unsifted thistles thrust thrice three thousand thistles through the thick of his thumb.   Now if Theophilus Thistle, the thistle sifter, in sifting thousands of unsifted thistles thrust thrice three thousand thistles through the thick of his thumb, how many wouldst thou, in sifting thrice three thousand thistles, thrust through the thick of thy thumb?

—From W. H. ALDERSON, Hempstead, L. I.

CATCHES

Jaw aches.—Pronounce J-a, w-a, c-h-e-s. Of course, it is jaw aches, but you will be surprised at the number of people who will answer, "Jay watches" or something else of the kind.

G-U-R-E-Z.—Pronounce "J-u-a-r-e-z."   Many will know of the Mexican city by that name and will answer "War-ez."   Now pronounce G-U-R-E-Z.   There will be numerous answers—"Guray,"

"Gurez." The leader will keep repeating G-U-R-E-Z until it finally dawns on them that the leader is charging them with being E-Z. G-U-R-A-J may also be used.

How many stamps?—How many eggs in a dozen? Twelve. How many stamps in a dozen? Twelve. How many two-cent stamps in a dozen? How many three-cent stamps in a dozen? You will be amazed at how many people will answer that there are six two-cent stamps, or four three-cent stamps, in a dozen.

Read the following:

$$\frac{John}{Ton} \quad \frac{Wood}{Sam} \quad 12+14=26 \quad limburger\ cheese.$$

The answer is, of course, John Overton sent Sam Underwood some (sum) limburger cheese. Someone is sure to ask where you get the "sent" (scent). "That's in the limburger cheese."

An economical telegram.—The following economical telegram was sent to describe an accident: "Bruises hurt. Erased afford. Analysis hurt too. Infectious dead." Translated it reads: "Bruce is hurt. He raced a Ford. And Alice is hurt too. In fact, she's dead."

STUNT STORIES

Ten sons or more.—This story is begun by the leader, and members of the group begin to participate in the telling of it as soon as they catch the idea. The ten sons may grow into a dozen or twenty.

Once there was a man who had ten sons. The first one was a banker, and the second had financial difficulties also. The third one was a salesman, and the fourth one couldn't sell anything either. The fifth one was a lawyer, and the sixth one handled the truth recklessly too.

By this time the others have caught on and they begin offering suggestions such as, "The seventh one was a school teacher, and the eighth one didn't know anything either." Someone suggests that the ninth one was a doctor, and the tenth one buried his mistakes too."

Other suggestions: The eleventh one was a dentist, and the twelfth one pulled a lot of things too. The thirteenth one was an elevator operator, and the fourteenth one had his ups and downs also. The fifteenth one was a stenographer, and the sixteenth one couldn't spell either. The seventeenth one was a preacher, and the eighteenth only worked one day a week too. The nineteenth one called a lot of committee meetings, and the twentieth wasted a lot of people's time also. The twenty-first one argued with his wife, and the twenty-second got struck by lightning too. The prize was taken by the fellow who suggested that the twenty-third was a milkman, and the twenty-fourth one got his living from "udders" also.

Fake ghost story.—Build up a thrilling ghost story something after this fashion: The night was dark and cold. A drizzling rain was falling. It was near midnight and Jack and Sue were returning from a friend's home where they had enjoyed a party. As they drove along the lonesome road, the engine of the car sputtered and the car stopped. One look at the meter told Jack they were out of gas. He had forgotten to get some earlier in the evening and now here they were miles from a gas station and not a building in sight except a dark, foreboding looking house across the road.

Jack got out of the car and rang the doorbell. There was no answer. He tried the doorknob and the door opened. Thinking there might be a telephone inside he stepped into the hallway. A heavy wind blew the door shut with a slam. In searching for the 'phone Jack fell over a chair and hit his head on a table, knocking him out.

Sue waited awhile and when Jack didn't reappear she tried the door and she too entered the house calling to Jack. Thinking she heard him upstairs she went to the second floor, using a tiny flashlight she had in her pocketbook. Then she heard the shuffling of feet near her, called Jack's name, and when no answer came, she screamed.

For the first time she realized that this was the famous haunted house. Jack came back to consciousness just in time to hear Sue's scream. He got to his feet and hurried upstairs to Sue's side. The shuffling feet kept coming, but neither Jack nor Sue could see anything. They kept backing away into the long hall. The shuffling feet kept coming closer and closer. They finally bumped against a wall and knew that they were at the end of the hall. The shuffling feet kept coming, and now there seemed to be a group of shuffling feet. Closer and closer they came.

Jack fumbled around the wall and finally felt a doorknob. He opened it and dragged Sue in with him. However he could not shut the door. Some unseen power seemed to hold it open. The shuffling feet seemed to be coming through the door. Jack and Sue backed away. Again a wall and again a doorknob. The door was opened and they stepped through only to find themselves trapped in a closet. The shuffling feet now seemed to fill the room. There seemed no hope.

Jack began to feel around for something with which to fight. Suddenly his hand touched a familiar instrument. "It's a drum," he whispered to Sue. "That's great," shouted Sue. So they picked up the drum and beat it.

The animals and the circus.—The animals went to the circus. They had to have some money to get in. The duck got in. Why? Someone will be sure to give the correct answer. "He had a bill." The frog got in. "He had a green-back." The deer got in. "He had a buck (or the doe)." The hog got in. "He had four quarters." But the skunk did not get in. "But he had a (s) cent," says someone. "Yes, but it was a bad one," explains the leader.

The ranch story.—A father bought a ranch and presented it to his two sons. They planned to raise cattle for the market. So they called the ranch "Focus." Why was that an appropriate name? Try to get the members of the group to guess. Ask them to think of the meaning of focus. What is it? Someone will say, "It is the bringing of the rays of light together." "That's rather warm," encourages the leader. Finally someone will see it. "Focus—that's where the sun's rays meet" (the sons raise meat).

How's your dog?—This is one of those catch stories. A lawyer was in the habit of walking to his office. One morning, as he passed the home of a certain woman, her vicious bulldog attacked him. The lawyer kicked the dog to protect himself and fortunately for him he landed his foot squarely beside the dog's head and laid it out, cold.

The next day he stopped by this same home and rang the doorbell. When the lady came to the door he said, "Lady, house your dog." She answered, "I did." The trick lies in the fact that nine out of ten people will think the question is, "Lady, how's your dog," if the build up has been well done.

The three condemned men.—A penitentiary warden, seeking pardons for three men condemned to death, was told by the governor only one could be pardoned, the decision as to which one being in the warden's hands. Wishing to give all three men equal chances, the warden called them in and explained the situation. "I shall seat you around a table and blindfold all three of you," he said. "Then

I shall place on the forehead of each either a black or a red mark. When I remove the blindfolds you are to start rapping on the table if you see black on either or both the foreheads of the other two men. The first man who can name his own color and give his reasons satisfactorily will be the one who is pardoned."

He blindfolded the men and placed black marks on all their foreheads. When the blindfolds were removed, all three men naturally began rapping. After an interval of two or three minutes, one man stopped. "Warden, my color is black," he said. He explained his reason for knowing his color, and was freed.

How did he know his color was black?

Solution—He reasoned in this way: If my color were red, we would still all three be knocking as the other men would be knocking for each other. But they could see I was black, and one or the other would realize immediately that the third man was knocking for him. If I were red, one of the other two men would have announced immediately that he was black. Since neither did, they must be mystified, and I am obviously black."

—Contributed by Lydel Sims, Nashville, Tennessee

Dollar, dollar, who's got the dollar?—Three men spent several nights in a hotel. When they were ready to check out they found that their bill was thirty dollars, ten dollars each. They sent the thirty dollars down to the desk by a bellboy. When he paid the cashier, he was told that since the hotel was run on the co-operative plan the men had five dollars coming back to them. The bellboy kept two dollars and handed to each of the men a one-dollar refund. That made each man pay nine dollars. Three times nine is twenty-seven. Add this to the two dollars retained by the bellboy and you have twenty-nine dollars. Where did the other dollar go?

Of course, the catch in this is that the men paid $25.00 to the hotel and $2.00 to the bellboy. That is $27.00. The $3.00 that was refunded to them makes $30.00.

August.—August was a hound pup who was always jumping at conclusions. One day he jumped at the conclusion of a stubborn mule. And the next day was the first of September. The leader may pause here to ask how we know the day. Finally someone will shout the answer: "Because that was the last of August."

Masticate!—The leader explains to the members of the group that they are to say, "I'm in" as soon as they catch the point of this story, but they are not to give the answer until he asks for it.

A little boy, son of a college professor, was taken to the railroad station. He was greatly thrilled by what he saw, and when a big mogul came roaring into the station, he jumped up and down in his excitement and yelled, "Masticate! Masticate!"

When the leader thinks a sufficient number are "in" he suggests that they all shout the answer together. "One, two, three!" And the "inners" shout "Chew chew!" (choo-choo).

What's wrong with this story?—A man and his wife were sitting by the fireplace. He had been reading about the French Revolution. He dozed and dreamed that he himself was in Paris and in the midst of the Revolution. He was arrested and carried before the tribunal where he was condemned to death. He was taken from the death cell and made to kneel before the guillotine. The executioner raised the terrible knife. At this point in his dream the wife, noting that he was asleep, sought to waken him by tapping him gently on the back of the neck with a paper knife. Instead of waking, the husband dropped forward, dead!

Note: The point is that if the man died before waking no one would have ever known about his dream.

A crossword puzzle.—Sixteen squares. Horizontal. 1. Four-letter word that describes what dogs do. 2. What cats do. 3. What lions do. 4. What fleas do. Vertical. 1. Insects. 2. Parts of the head. 3. What bad boys like to do. 4. Comfort. The answer, of course, in each case horizontal is B-I-T-E. That gives you B's for insects. I's for parts of the head, T's for the favorite activity of bad boys, and E's for comfort.

Too Wise.—
YY U R, YY U B;
I C U R YY 4 me.
(Too wise you are, too wise you be,
I see you are too wise for me.)

Pronounce "To."—Pronounce "to." Now "Too." Now "two." Now the second day of the week. Almost invariably the response will be "Tuesday," whereupon the leader explains that the second day of the week is Monday.

A series of Macs.—Pronounce M-a-c-d-o-u-g-a-l. Now pronounce M-a-c-d-o-n-a-l-d. Now pronounce M-a-c-h-i-n-e-r-y. After several trials the leader explains that it is machinery. In each case spell out the word.

Four nines.—Write four nines so they will make an even hundred. It is really easy. Here it is—99 9/9.

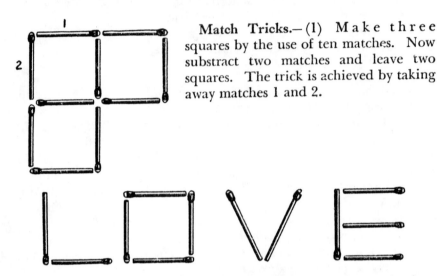

Match Tricks.—(1) Make three squares by the use of ten matches. Now substract two matches and leave two squares. The trick is achieved by taking away matches 1 and 2.

(2) *Of what matches are made*—Place sixteen matches in four squares. Move three, and substract four, and spell the word that indicates of what matches are made. The answer is LOVE.

(3) *Four triangles*—Make four triangles out of six matches. One is made flat on the table. The other three matches are held pyramid-like about this triangle, making four triangles.

(4) Take twelve matches and form six triangles with them. Form a hexagon with six of the matches. Then use the other six matches from the center of the hexagon to form the sides of the triangles.

(5) Arrange twelve matches in 4 squares as shown in the diagram at left on opposite page. Rearrange the matches, using them all but moving only three of them and change the four squares to three. This is done by removing the two matches from the upper left-hand corner and the lower match in the lower right-hand corner. Use these three matches to form a new square at the lower right, thus:

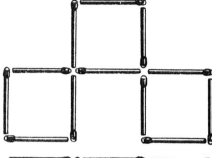

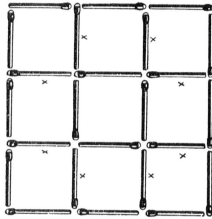

Match squares.—Use twenty-four matches arranged in nine squares, making one big square. The trick is to remove six matches and leave three complete squares. Any amount of experimenting is permissible. The solution is to take any six consecutive matches marked with an "X." That will leave the center square, one corner square, and the large square.

Variations—(*a*) Remove four matches and leave seven squares. *Solution*—Take any four outside corner matches. (*b*) Remove four matches and leave six squares. *Solution*—Remove two matches from the center square and two adjacent matches from a corner square. (*c*) Remove four matches and leave five squares. *Solution*—Remove all four center square matches.

What Relation Is

1. Your sister-in-law's father-in-law's granddaughter related to you? Niece.
2. Your uncle's father's father's wife? Great-grandmother.
3. Your mother's aunt's brother's wife? Great-aunt.
4. The grandson of the only son of your mother's mother-in-law? Son or nephew.
5. Your brother's mother's stepson's father? Stepfather.
6. Your sister's son's brother's father? Brother-in-law.
7. Your aunt's father's only grandson? Yourself.
8. Your mother's mother's son's son? First cousin.

9. Your sister-in-law's husband's grandfather's wife? Grandmother.
10. Your nephew's father's father's wife? Mother.
11. Brothers and sisters have I none
    But this man's father is my father's son. Son.
12. Your sister's father's stepson's mother? Stepmother.

Mathematical curiosities.—Figures often play pranks. Note the following freak mathematical results:

That's one on you—

      1 times 9 plus 2 equals 11
      12 times 9 plus 3 equals 111
      123 times 9 plus 4 equals 1111
      1,234 times 9 plus 5 equals 11111

Continue to figure in this same manner on up to 12345678. You will find that this number times 9 plus 9 equals 111,111,111.

What's 8-ing on you?—

      9 times   0 plus 8 equals 8
      9 times   9 plus 7 equals 88
      9 times 98 plus 6 equals 888
      9 times 987 plus 5 equals 8888

Following this same system you finally come to 9 times 98765432 plus 0 which equals 888,888,888. And then you will find that 9 times 987654321 minus 1 equals 8,888,888,888.

The winning nine—

      9 times   9 equals 81
      99 times   99 equals 9801
      999 times   999 equals 998001
      9999 times 9999 equals 99980001
      99999 times 99999 equals 9999800001

Sequences—

      1 times 8 plus 1 equals   9
      12 times 8 plus 2 equals 98
      123 times 8 plus 3 equals 987

And thus it will go until 123,456,789 times 8 plus 9 equals 987,654,321.

Six numbers six times.—This one demonstrates the point that not whether you stand, but where and how are the important considerations. Note that the same numbers are used each time. Note also their sequence. Take the number 142,857. Multiply by 2 and you have 285,714. Multiply by 3 and you get 428,571. Multiply by 4 and the result is 571,428. Five times the number gives you 714,285. Six times the number makes 857,142. Note that when you multiply by 6 the two sets of numbers are transposed. Multiply by 7 and note the result.

Take a number.—Suggest that any person or group select a number. This number is not to be told to the leader. He proceeds to find out what the number is. Suppose the number is 23.

Number selected	23
Double it	46
Add 1	47
Multiply by 5	235
Add 5	240
Multiply by 10	2,400

The leader now subtracts 100 from the result without saying anything. Thus 100 from 2,400 is 2,300. Strike off the last two digits and announce the number is 23.

Your pocket change.—Think of a number (your age, perhaps). Double it. Add five. Multiply by 50. Add the change (less than a dollar) that you have in your pocket. Substract the number of days in a year—365. Add 115. The number will be the first two digits. The amount of change will be indicated by the last two digits.
Thus:

2 times the person's age	38
Add 5	43
Multiply by 50	2,150
Add the 21 cents in the pocket	2,171
Subtract 365 days in the year	1,806
Add 115	1,921

You announce that the age is 19 and the amount of change in the pocket is 21 cents.

Number, please!—Select a number or use your age. Then follow the suggested procedure.

Number selected	27
Multiply by 3	81
Add 1	82

Multiply by 3 246
Add original number 273
Strike off last digit 27

Age and month of birth.—Write down the number of the month of birth.   Then go through the following routine:

Number of month or birth (April) 4
Double it 8
Add 5 13
Multiply by 50 650
Add your age (21) 671
Substract 365 306

The leader calls for the result.   Then he secretly adds 115, making the total 421.   He immediately announces April as the month of birth and 21 as the age.   The first one or two digits indicate the month and the last two indicate the age.

I've got your number.—Write the number 1,089 on a slip of paper and hand it to someone to hold.   This person must not look at it until asked to do so.   Ask the group or one person to write down any number of three different digits.

(1) Reverse the number and subtract the smaller from the larger.   If only two digits result, add a cipher to make three."

(2) Reverse the number which results and add it to the result.

(3) Look at the slip of paper and read the number on it.

(1) The number chosen 456
(2) Reversed 654
(3) Smaller subtracted from larger 198
(4) Reverse this result 891
(5) Add (3) and (4) 1,089

Secret number.—This simple trick furnishes fun as folk try to figure it out.   Ask someone to select a number, keeping it a secret.   Now ask them to double it, then to multiply by five, and then to tell you the total.   Immediately you are able to tell them the secret number.   All you have to do is to knock off the final digit for what you have really done is to get the number multiplied by 10   Example: The number selected is 13.   Multiplied by 2 it is 26.   Multiplied by 5 it is 130.   Knock off the last digit and it is 13, the secret number.   This may be worked on a crowd, the teller staying outside the room while the group decides on the secret number.

What's your number?—This one will mystify the uninitiated. Take a number. Double it. Add 9. Subtract 3. Divide by 2. Subtract the number you first had in your thinking. You can tell them that the answer is three. It will be three invariably.

Or suggest that someone take a number. Double it. Add twelve. Subtract four. Divide by two. Subtract the secret number. You announce that the resulting number is four.

The number in each case will always be one half of the difference between the number added and the number subtracted. If the number added is smaller than the number subtracted in steps three and four the resulting number will be a minus.

How many apples did Adam and Eve eat?—A group was discussing this question. The first person speaking, being matter-of-fact, said it couldn't have been more than 1. A second person asserted that Eve 8 and Adam 2—a total of 10. The third person said there was something wrong about that because Eve 8 and Adam 8 also, making 16. "But," said another, "if Eve 8 and Adam 82, that would be a total of 90." Still another chimed in: "According to antedeluvian history, Eve 81 and Adam 82. That would total 163." "But," contended another, "don't you see that if Eve 81 and Adam 812 that would be a total of 893." "According to my figuring I calculate that if Eve 814 Adam and Adam 8124 Eve, that would total 8938." "Yes," said the remaining member of the group, "but the best mathematicians agree that if Eve 814 Adam and if Adam 81242 oblige Eve, the total would be 82,056." "Meeting adjourned," announced the chairman.

A digit fit.—A card was given to each person. On it was printed (or mimeographed) the following:

Leader's program—Well! Well! here we are all together again! Everybody happy?

And now we are going to throw "a digit fit."

Everybody is in on it. When you have the answer shout it out. The answers must contain digits. Is everything clear?

Well, let's go!

Here's the first one—just a minute! We had better give an example. All right, here it is:

Question: "What made Willie sick?"

Answer: "While eating apples he 8-1-2 green."

Now, that you've got the idea, let's go.

1. Why did you come here tonight? Two answers were offered: "Just 4 fun," and "We came 2-8-10 the party."

2. How do you know that Noah was preceded from the ark by at least three people? Answer: "Because the Bible says that Noah came 4th (forth)."

3. Why is there so little cake left? Answer: "You 8-2 much," or "You 8-2 be 4 I 8-1."

4. How old are you? Answer: "That's 0-2 you."

5. What digit rhymes with frauds? Answer: "6, because it rhymes with tricks."

6. Who is the victor? Answer: "The 1 who 1."

7. When do we eat? Answer: "That remains 2 be seen."

BRAIN TEASERS

The dog and the rabbit.—A dog chasing a rabbit makes two jumps of ten feet each every second. The rabbit makes three jumps while the dog makes two. The dog would have caught the rabbit in just ten minutes had nothing prevented.

But ten seconds before the dog would have caught the bunny, a shot from the hunter's gun killed the hare. At the time of the shot the rabbit was only twenty feet ahead of the dog.

What was the distance between the dog and the rabbit at the start of the chase?

Answer: "1,200 feet." The dog gained two feet per second on the rabbit. That is 120 feet a minute and 1,200 feet in ten minutes, in which time you are told the dog would have caught him.

The fish tale.—A big city fish merchant once offered a 20 per cent reduction on a fish that weighed "ten pounds and half its weight," if the buyer could tell him how much the fish actually weighed. What *did* it weigh? Answer. "Twenty pounds."

The pawn shop brain teaser.—Mr. A owed Mr. B $10.00 and had only $7.00 to pay the bill. The debt had to be paid. Mr. A decided to do some juggling. So he took a $5.00 bill to the pawn shop. It being very good security he obtained a $4.00 loan. Next, he took the pawn ticket to Mr. C, who knowing the ticket represented $5.00 in currency purchased it for $4.00. Now Mr. A had the necessary $10.00 to pay his debt. Who lost in the transaction? Answer: Mr. C. He overlooked the fact that he would have to pay $4.00 to the pawn broker to redeem the $5.00 bill. Thus he paid $8.00 for the $5.00 bill, losing $3.00.

The monkey teaser.—Four monkeys can eat four sacks of peanuts in three minutes. How many monkeys will it take to eat 100 sacks of peanuts in 60 minutes. The correct answer is five.

Proof: If four monkeys can eat four sacks of peanuts in three minutes, one monkey can eat one sack of peanuts in three minutes. In sixty minutes one monkey could eat 20 sacks of peanuts. Thus it would take five monkeys to eat 100 sacks of peanuts in 60 minutes. It is, of course, taken for granted that the monkey has the capacity for consuming 20 sacks of peanuts.

The king's arithmetic problem.—Once there lived a clever king. One day there came to his court a professor who delighted the King with his knowledge. He entertained the ruler with many things that were new and interesting.

Finally, the King came to the point where he wanted to know the age of the professor, but he hesitated to ask him. So he propounded a mathematical problem.

"Professor," said the King, "I have an interesting problem for you. It is a test in mental arithmetic. Think of the number of the month of your birth, but don't tell me." Now the professor was 60 years old, and his birthday came in December. So he thought of 12.

"All right," he said.

"Multiply it by 2," said the King.

"I have."

"Add 5."

"I have."

"Now multiply by 50."

"Yes."

"Add your age."

"Yes."

"Subtract 365."

"Yes."

"Add 115."

"Yes."

"And now," said the King, "tell me the result."

"Twelve hundred and sixty," replied the professor.

"Thank you," said the King. "You were born in December sixty years ago."

"But how do you know that?" cried the professor.

"From your answer," replied the King. "You said it was 1,260. The month of birth was 12 and the last two figures gave your age."

"Well," laughed the professor, "that is a polite way to find out one's age."

Fun with anagrams.—Besides the regular game of anagrams, note the variations suggested in Chapter V, Fun with Games for Small Groups. These will provide endless fun for the members of the family.

Fun with dominoes.— (1) Play the regular game, allowing no playing on spinners except when the player can score a five or multiple of five.

(2) *Forty-two.* This comes near to being the national game of Texas. Four players. Each player draws seven dominoes. Players bid in turn, 30, 32, or the perfect score 42. The player who gets the bid names trumps—that is, the dominant number. Doubles take any trick of their kind. Points are made by taking the 5 + 5, the 6 + 4, the 5 + 0, the 4 + 1, and the 3 + 2. That totals 35. One point is allowed for each trick. Since there are seven possible tricks, that makes a total of 7 points; forty-two, thus, is the perfect score.

Bible conundrums—

1. When is money first mentioned in the Bible. Answer: When the dove brought the green back to the ark.

2. Who is the first man mentioned in the Bible? Answer: Chap I.

3. When is high financiering first mentioned in the Bible: Answer: When Pharaoh's daughter took a little prophet (profit) from the bull-rushes.

4. When was radio first mentioned in the Bible? Answer: When the Lord took a rib from Adam and made a loud speaker.

5. At what time of day was Adam born? Answer: A little before Eve.

6. Why couldn't Eve take the measles? Answer: Because she'd Adam.

7. How were Adam and Eve prevented from gambling? Answer: Their paradise (pair-o-dice) was taken away from them.

8. Why couldn't Noah play cards? Answer: Because Mrs. Noah sat on the deck.

9. What evidence have we that Adam and Eve were rowdy? Answer: Because they raised Cain.

10. When is an express company first intimated in the Bible? Answer: When Eve was made Adam's express company.

11. To what church did Eve belong? Answer: Adam thought her Eve-angelical.

12. What animal took the most baggage into the ark? Answer: The elephant. He took his trunk, while the fox and the rooster only took a brush and a comb between them.

13. What did the cat say just before the ark landed? Answer: Is that Ararat?

14. When did Moses sleep with five people sleeping in one bed? Answer: When he slept with his forefathers.

15. What man has no parents? Answer: Joshua, the son of Nun.

16. Who is the smallest man mentioned in the Bible? Answer: Bildad, the Shuhite. (Job 2: 11.)

17. Why ought one to be encouraged by the story of Jonah? Answer: He was down in the mouth, but he came out all right.

18. When was baseball mentioned in the Bible? Answer: When Rebecca walked to the well with the pitcher and when the Prodigal Son made a home run.

19. When were automobiles first mentioned? Answer: When Elijah went up on high.

20. Who was the first woman in the Bible? Answer: No, it was not Eve. It was Genesis (Jenny Sis).

21. Who was the straightest man in the Bible? Answer: Joseph, Pharaoh made a ruler out of him.

22. Who was the best financier in the Bible? Answer: Noah. He floated his stock while the whole world was in liquidation.

23. Who was the most popular actor in the Bible? Answer: Samson. He brought down the house.

24. What simple affliction brought about the death of Samson? Answer: He died of fallen arches.

25. Who was the most successful physician in the Bible? Answer: Job. He had the most patience (patients).

26. What confection did they have in the ark? Answer: Preserved pairs (pears).

Flower riddles—

27. What is a pretty girl who has had a falling out with her lover? Answer: A blue-bell (e).

28. What did the bull do in old Mrs. Grundy's china shop that reminds you of a flower? Answer: Buttercups.

29. What flowers do we all have. Answer: tulips.

30. What do unmarried men often lose? Answer: Bachelor's buttons.

31. Of what are stage walls made? Answer: Shamrocks.

32. What did the teacher do when he sat on a tack? Answer: Rose.

33. When buying a clock for what do you ask? Answer: Four-o-clock.

34. My first is a kitchen untensil;
    My second is a big body of water;
    And my whole is a flower. Answer: Pansy (pan-sea).

35. My first is a vehicle;
    My second is a nation;
    And my whole is a flower. Answer: Carnation.

36. What flower reminds you of a lot of birds. Answer: Phlox.

General conundrums—

37. My first is what,
    My second is not;
    And my whole is a piece of furniture. Answer: What-not.

38. My first some gladly take
    Entirely for my second's sake;
    But few, indeed, ever care
    Both together e'er to bear. Answer: Misfortune.

39. Why is a man looking for something that never existed like Neptune? Answer: Because he's a-seeking (sea-king) that never was.

40. If a young lady wishes her father to row her on the lake what classical name could she use? Answer: You row, pa (Europa).

41. Round as a biscuit, busy as a bee,
    Prettiest little thing you ever did see. Answer: A watch.

42. What song did Edward VII sing when abdicating the throne of England to marry Mrs. Simpson? Answer: "Ain't Gonna Rain (reign) No More."

43. What salad is liked by newlyweds? Answer: Lettuce alone.

44. What would happen if a colored waiter tripped and fell with a platter of turkey? Answer: The humiliation of Africa, the downfall of Turkey, the breaking up of China, and the overflowing of Greece.

45. How many young ladies would it take standing single file to reach from Fort Worth to Dallas? Answer: About thirty. Because a miss is as good as a mile.

46. Why is a kiss over the telephone like a straw hat? Answer: It's not felt.

47. Why is a pair of skates like an apple? Answer: Because they both occasioned the fall of man.

48. Why is a very young favorite dog like a doll? Answer: Because it is a pup-pet.

49. What is the difference between the death of a beautician

(beauty operator) and the death of a sculptor? Answer: The beauticians curls up and dyes, while the sculptor makes faces and busts.

50. Of what trade is Old Sol? Answer: He's a tanner.

51. When does a boat show affection? When it hugs the shore.

52. Why is a dog's tail like the heart of a tree? Answer: Because, it's farthest from the bark.

53. When the doctor operates on a dog and comes to his lungs what does he find? Answer: The seat of his pants.

54. Upon what does the moon have more effect than on the tide? Answer: The effect it has on the un-tied.

55. What is the difference between a piano, a ship on a stormy sea, and you? Answer: The piano makes music. The ship makes you sick, and you make me sick.

56. Why is a man who runs a fish market likely to be self-centered? Answer: Because his business makes him sell fish (selfish).

57. What paper is most suitable for aeroplanes? Answer: Fly-paper.

58. Why is a good architect like a popular actor? Answer: Because they both draw good houses.

59. Why should you be careful about making love in the country? Answer: Because the corn has ears, the potatoes have eyes, and the beans talk.

60. A man named Bigger married. How did he compare in size with his wife? Answer: He was larger, for he was always Bigger.

61. They had a child. Now who was bigger? Answer: The baby, for it was a little Bigger.

62. Mrs. Bigger died. Now who is bigger? Answer: Mrs. Bigger for she's Bigger still.

63. Why does a duck go in the water? Answer: For diverse (diver's) reasons.

64. Why does he come out? Answer: For sun-dry reasons.

65. Why does he go back in the water? Answer: To liquidate his bill.

66. Why does he come out again? Answer: To make a run on the bank.

67. What is the difference between some people and a mirror? Answer: They talk without reflecting, while a mirror reflects without talking.

68. When is it dangerous to enter the church? Answer: When there is a big gun in the pulpit.

69. What is the smallest room in the world? Answer: A mush-room.

70. What is the largest room? Answer: Room for improvement.

71. If a chicken could talk what language would it speak? Answer: Fowl language.

72. What shape is a kiss? Answer: A lip-tickle (elliptical).

73. Why is a mouse like hay? Answer: Because the cat'll (cattle) eat her.

74. A sailor and a goose are on top of a tall monument. What is the quickest way for the sailor to get down? Answer: By plucking the goose.

75. When is a lady not a lady? Answer: When she turns into a drug store.

76. Why is it unnecessary to import any dudes from other countries? Answer: Because a Yankee Doodle Do.

77. Why are some girls like arrows? Answer: Because they are all in a quiver till the beaux (bows) come and can't go anywhere without them.

78. Why will a dyspeptic likely live a bit longer? Answer: Because he can't digest yet.

79. Why may we well doubt the existence of the Blarney Stone? Answer: Because there are so many shamrocks in Ireland.

80. What remedy does a cave man use on a scolding wife? Answer: He takes an elixir.

81. In what does a sick one take her medicine? Answer: In cider.

82. Why is there always plenty of food in the desert? Answer: Because of the sand which is (sandwiches) there.

83. Why is a small boy who ripped his trousers on a nail like the preacher who is saying, "Finally, my brethren?" Answer: Because he's "tored" his clothes (toward his close).

84. Where would Satan go if he lost his caudil appendage? Answer: To a saloon where they retail the devil's own spirits.

85. Why is love like a heavy baggage you are taking on a train trip? Answer: Because if you don't check it you'll have to express it.

86. Why wouldn't mother let the doctors operate on father? Answer: Because she didn't want them to open her male (mail).

87. What kind of shoes are made out of banana skins? (Answer: Slippers.

88. What is the best way to raise cabbage? Answer: With a fork.

89. If butter is fifty cents a pound in Chicago, what are window panes in Detroit? Answer: Glass.

90. Why is a woman like an angel? Answer: Because she's usually up in the air; she's always harping on something; and she never has anything to wear.

91. When is a sailor not a sailor? Answer: When he is abroad.

("a broad" is slang for woman, growing out of the slang expression "a skirt." Skirts are often made of broadcloth. Thus the expression "a broad" became synonymous with "a skirt" or "a woman.")

92. What is the difference between a doe, an over-priced article, and a donkey? Answer: A doe is a deer, an over-priced article is too dear; and a donkey is you, dear.

93. The bishop's puzzle. This riddle is credited to Bishop Wilberforce (1759-1833). He was an English philanthropist associated with the abolition of the slave trade. Here is the riddle:

I am a wonderful trunk to which belong the following articles: (1) I have a chest; (2) two lids; (3) two musical instruments; (4) a number of articles indispensable to the carpenter; (5) two tropical trees; (6) two good fish; (7) a number of shell fish; (8) a fine stag; (9) a number of small animals, swift and shy; (10) two playful animals; (11) weapons of warfare; (12) steps of a hotel; (13) some whips without handles; (14) two learners; (15) the upper edge of a hill; (16) a number of weathercocks; (17) two established measures; (18) two sides of a vote; (19) fine flowers; (20) a fruit; (21) two places of worship; (22) a probable remark of Nebuchadnezzar when eating grass; (23) ten Spanish noblemen to wait on me; (24) a desert place; (25) part of a bell; (26) a garden vegetable; (27) an isthmus. Answer: The human body is the trunk. The articles are: (1) chest; (2) eyelids; (3) eadrums; (4) nails; (5) palms; (6) soles; (7) muscles; (8) heart (hart); (9) hairs (hares); (10) calves; (11) arms; (12) insteps (inn steps); (13) lashes; (14) pupils; (15) brow; (16) veins (vanes); (17) feet, hands; (18) eyes and nose (ayes and noes); (19) tulips; (20) Adam's apple; (21) temples; (22) eyebrows (I browse); (23) tendons (ten dons); (24) waste; (25) tongue; (26) pulse; (27) neck.

94. What relation is a doormat to a doorsill? Answer: A step farther.

95. What is it that you ought to keep after you have given it to someone else? Answer: A promise.

96. What can go up the chimney down, but cannot go down the chimney up? Answer: An umbrella.

97. Why does an old-fashioned Model T Ford remind you of a schoolroom? Answer: Because it has a lot of little nuts with a crank up front.

98. What is the longest word in the English language? Answer: Smiles, because there is a mile between the first and last letters.

99. What starts with T, ends with T, and is full of T? Answer: Teapot.

100. What asks no questions but requires a lot of answers? Answer: A door bell.

101. Why does an elephant hesitate about going visiting? Answer: Because he always has to carry his trunk with him.

102. How does a bird eat fruit? Answer: By the peck.

103. Why is a defeated team like wool? Answer: Because it is worsted.

104. Why do maiden school teachers like to go to Colorado Springs? Answer: Because there is a Manitou out there.

105. Why are women like umbrellas? Answer: Because they are made out of ribs, you have to dress them up in silk to make them look their best; at the least bit of storm they go right up in the air; it is usually your best friend who takes them away from you; and they are accustomed to reign (rain).

106. In what respect is a person who buys his clothes on the installment plan dynamic? Answer: Everything he has on is charged.

107. Why is a bald head like heaven? Answer: Because there is no parting there.

108. Why is biscuit dough like the sun? Answer: Because it rises in the (y) east and sets behind the "vest."

109. What is most like a hen stealing? Answer: A cock robin.

110. What is the oldest piece of furniture? Answer: The multiplication table.

111. How was the blind man's eyesight returned at the breakfast table? Answer: He took a cup and saw, sir (saucer).

112. What is full of holes and yet holds water? Answer: A sponge.

113. What is the richest country in the world? Answer: Ireland. Its capitol is always Dublin.

114. What runs, but does not walk,
Has a tongue, but cannot talk? Answer: A wagon.

115. What is black and white and red (read) all over? Answer: A newspaper.

116. What has four legs but cannot walk? Answer: A chair or a table.

FUN WITH PAPER

The spook train.—Two men were on the Spook Train bound for Eternity Station. One of them had been a very wicked man. The other had been a good man. When it was about time for the conductor to take up their tickets the wicked man got increasingly nervous. Finally, he said to the good man, "I have no ticket. Can you not help me?" The good man answered, "Yes, I think I can."

He tore off part of his ticket and one side and then on the other, after folding it. "But this isn't enough ticket for me," said the evil man. "Why not give me more?" So the good man tore off two more pieces and gave them to him. The conductor came by, opened the folded tickets, and this is what he saw: the good's man's ticket was in the form of a cross. The bad man's ticket spelled "H-E-L-L."

The manner of folding and tearing—Take a piece of paper about a third as wide as it is long. Fold over one-third. Now fold over the ends to a point at the middle of the double thickness part of the paper. Then fold back the top end (single thickness). Holding the pointed piece tear off a strip about 1/5 of the width. Repeat on the side. Then repeat the action and unfold.

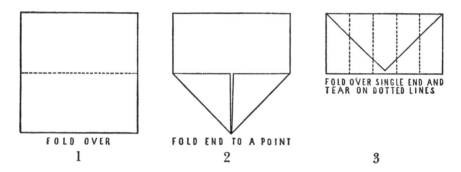

FOLD OVER 1   FOLD END TO A POINT 2   FOLD OVER SINGLE END AND TEAR ON DOTTED LINES 3

Paper tree.—To make a paper tree take two double pages of the comic section of a newspaper, and cut in two parallel with the top of the page. This gives four pieces half the width of the paper, and two widths long.

Roll up one piece three-fourths of the way with a space in the center large enough to place two fingers. Start in another piece on top of the one-fourth of the first piece not rolled and continue to roll. Start in the third piece and the fourth piece in the same manner, starting each one on the top of the one-fourth of the piece not yet completely rolled up.

Now take a scissors and cut down about halfway from one end four times. The best way is to cut down once, then cut down just across from that cut, then cut equidistant between those cuts.

Then take hold of the center piece on cut end and pull up.

Jacob's ladder.—The Jacob's Ladder is made from the same number of papers as the paper tree. Cut the papers across the same way to have four strips, one-half the width of the paper, and twice the width long.

One end of the first piece now is folded over to the first crease, or to the middle of the strip. Fold this over three more times and the folded part will be about three-fourths of an inch wide. Then roll, with this folded part in the center, just as for the tree; keeping the hole in the center about large enough to place your two fingers in it. Continue rolling in the other strips of paper.

Then put a round-shaped piece of stick in the center of the roll, with the folded part of the paper underneath this stick. Cut through the paper above this stick with a sharp pocket knife in two places, dividing the paper into thirds. Cut through to the stick and down the sides, being careful not to cut through to the folds. Take out the stick and break the ends over so that the top part is cut down the sides, and the bottom part is only slightly wider than the folds.

Then take the scissors and cut across the center piece of the three parts, parallel with the roll.

To complete the ladder take hold of the top fold with the right hand and hold the other two ends with the left hand, and pull out to the full length of the ladder.

Books

Fun with Paper Folding, by W. D. Murray and F. G. Rigney (Revell). Diagrams and paper sheets in pockets. Boards.
Paper Tearing, L. O. Brown (Meigs).
How to Cut and Fold Paper, Bamberger (Flanagan).
How to Teach Paper Folding, L. R. Latter (Flanagan).

A "Hanging of the Greens" ceremony for the home.—Provide a sufficient quantity of twigs of evergreens. Plan to place them over doorsills, windows, and mantel. The fuel should be gotten ready in the fireplace. Each member of the family should be informed on what his particular duty is. Everyone should take part in hanging the greens.

Program—
1. Singing of carols.
2. Hanging of the greens.
3. Lighting of the Yule log or fire. This duty should be assigned some member of the family, an old English poem (A.D. 1500) would be appropriate.

"Kindle the Christmas brand and then
  Till sunset let it burn;
Which quenched, then lay it up again
  Till Christmas next return.
Parts must be kept wherewith to tend
  The Christmas log next year.
And where 'tis safely kept, the fiend
  Can do no mischief there."

4. Lighting of Christmas tree.
5. Reading of the Christmas story, Luke 2: 1-14.
6. Singing of Christmas carols.

A ceremonial for home dedication.—The idea of dedicating the home seems to have originated with H. Augustine Smith back in 1926. It may be used for a new house or after moving into a different one.

The lighting of the candles of hospitality—

"We have three candles in our room,
  Slender, and tall and white;
Their tips are buds of fire bloom
  That blossom in the night.

And one I light for memory,
  All steady as a star,
And one burns clear for days to be,
  And one for days that are.

We have three candles in our room,
  Slender and tall and fair;
And everyone a fire bloom,
  And everyone a prayer."
—Arthur Ketchum in the *Churchman*. By permission.

(The lady of the house lights the three candles in different places about the room while repeating the second verse.)

Prayer for neighborliness.—Solo—Samuel Foss's "Let Me Live in a House by the Side of the Road," to the tune, "A Perfect Day."
  The ceremony followed with the dedication of various parts of the house—the doorbell (using Rachel Fields poem, "You never know with a doorbell who may be ringing it"); the library or study (Emily Dickinson's "There is no frigate like a book"); the dining room (Grace Noll Crowell's "The Shared Loaf"); the kitchen (Grace Noll Crowell's "I never knew a man who did not like a

kitchen fire" and Maltie Babcock's "Back of the loaf is the snowy flour") ; the baby's nook (reading "Children" from the "Prophet," by Christian Burke) ; the boy's room (picture, "The Appeal to the Great Spirit" and the Navajo Indian Prayer, "Lord of the Mountain," from "Prayers from an Indian College") ; the guest room (Sleep sweetly in this quiet room") ; the living room (Daniel Henderson's "Hymn for a Household" in *Quotable Poems*) ; and the whole house (Arthur Guiterman's "Bless the four corners of this house") .

Other poems that might be useful are "My Little House," by May Byron, in *Quotable Poems*, Volume II, and "Prayer for a Little Home," in the same volume.

CHAPTER II
FUN IN THE CLUBROOM

FUN IN THE CLUBROOM

Running the clubroom, whether it be for the community center, the church, or what not, is comparatively easy if there is system. Included in that system, very likely, would be the following items:

1. Someone should be in charge to see that all visitors to the clubroom find interesting things to do.

2. A wide variety of equipment games should be provided.

3. When the clubroom is patronized by the same group week after week some of the games should be withdrawn from circulation every once in a while. After giving them a rest for a few weeks or months, bring them out for use once more. This will prevent staleness.

4. Introduce a new equipment game to the clubroom every now and then.

5. Check in all equipment at the close of a session and put it away. Arrange a special place to store or place your games.

6. Work out schedules for the use of the clubroom by the different age groups.

7. Wherever practical encourage the group using the clubroom to make the equipment for it.

Equipment

Table Games

1. Checkers
2. Caroms and Crokinole
3. Dominoes
4. Lotto
5. Chess
6. Parchesi
7. Card Games (Like Old Maid, Flinch, etc.)
8. Kanugo (Crossword Lexicon)
9. Logomachy
10. Table Tennis (Ping Pong)
11. Hearts
12. "Bug" tops
13. Traditional Games like **Wari,** Helma, Ruma.
14. Chinkerchex or Chinese Checkers
15. Pick-up Sticks

Board Games

1. Dart Baseball. Excellent heavy darts with spikes that will not pull out easily; obtainable from Apex Manufacturing **Company.** Norristown, Pa.

2. Dodo Board.   One dozen Mason jar rings.
3. Bean Bag Board.
4. Bean Bag or Disc Baseball.
5. Table Shuffleboard.   (Miniature. Use checkers for discs.)
6. Table Soccer.
7. Skittles.
8. Dart Football.

Floor Games

1. Shuffleboard.
2. Bull Board.
3. Box Hockey (broomsticks) .
4. Disc Baseball.

Table soccer.—A most interesting game for four to eight persons to play is this one. It consists of a box with sides, ends, and bottom. Eight movable dowels are placed crosswise—each dowel with one to four paddles so placed to just miss touching the floor of box and when the paddles of any two adjoining dowels are held horizontally they must miss touching each other. An incline board is in each lower corner to keep the ball from lodging in the corners. An opening (the goal) is in each end and is made just large enough to permit the ball to easily pass through.

Five-ply board for sides and ends is preferable—you may use ¾-inch clear white pine of 3-ply if you are careful in handling. The floor of the box can be one piece of 3-ply. Dowels (hardwood) 36 inches long and ⅜ inches wide can be purchased at a lumber yard or hardware store. Old mop handles make excellent dowels. Be sure and get straight sticks. Sixteen washers large enough to go over the dowels and sixteen cotter pins about one inch long are needed. Four pieces ½x½x46 inches (or ½-inch quarter round) are for side strips. The incline boards in corners may be made from 3-ply of ½-inch board. The paddles are 3/16-inch 3-ply board, cigar box, or other durable thin material.

Prepare the sides—To make the ½x2½ -inch cut-out, bore a hole through side piece at bottom of the cut-to-be then saw out the part above the hole. Do this for each of the sixteen openings. Nail one of the 46-inch strips just below the 2½-inch openings on what will be the outside of each of the two side pieces.

Prepare the ends—Smooth and sandpaper all parts. Assemble sides to ends and then to the bottom. Make four incline board units and nail them in the corners. Place a dowel in position in the

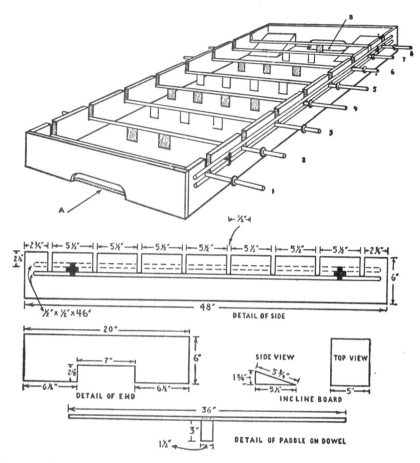

DETAIL OF SIDE

DETAIL OF END

SIDE VIEW   TOP VIEW

INCLINE BOARD

DETAIL OF PADDLE ON DOWEL

box and measure distance from under side of dowel to floor of box; add half the thickness of the dowel—this total will be about the length of the paddle (you can always trim it). With a circle saw, dado, or chisel, cut the grooves into the dowels at least half the thickness of the dowel. Be certain the grooves in each dowel are all cut in line and toward the center of the dowel. Fit the paddles to the grooves. Glue and nail (short brads) the paddles into dowel as shown in detail. Dowels 1 and 8 have only one paddle; Dowels 2 and 7 each has two paddles which are 3 inches from the center; Dowels 3 and 6 each has three paddles with one in the center and others are each 4½ inches from center paddle; Dowels 4 and 5 each has four paddles which are 3 inches apart, making the inside paddles each 1½ inches from center of dowel. Place the dowels in position in box and see that they move and turn easily. Place the other 46, inch strips one on each side above the dowels and fix some kind of wooden buttons or fasteners to hold them on.   Next put the washers over the dowel ends.   On Dowel 1 (and 8) with paddle pointing downward push dowel across box until the paddle almost touches the incline board.   At that position put a mark on dowel just outside the washer.   Bore a hole through dowel large enough for the cotter pin to be inserted and fastened.   Put in and fasten the pin. Go to the opposite end of the same dowel and repeat process.   This same thing shall be done for Dowels 2, 3, 4, 5, 6, 7, allowing each dowel to move to the side until the outside paddle on each dowel *almost* touches the opposite side of the box; then place the pin. You may desire to glue some felt or soft leather to the inside of each washer before inserting it on the dowels to cut the noise in playing. Cut out a slight recess at each end in the bottom just below the paddles of Nos. 1 and 8 when those paddles are centered.   Do you notice that all paddles can be turned completely around *except* the one on Nos. 1 and 8?   Check over the outfit.   If the openings are not large enough, cut away a little of the floor at the opening. You may desire to nail some rubber silencers and protectors under- neath the box.   For 10 cents you can purchase a small plain glass bubble level, used in carpenter's level; some persons may desire to put one in the top in one end and another in the side.   To do so, cut out a portion very slightly larger than the size of the bubble tube.   Insert the tube, curve up, and glue or cement it in place making sure that the level is below the wood surface.   To finish, shellac and varnish.   Use a ping-pong or table tennis ball.

To play—Put box on a table.

Dowels 1, 3, 5, and 7 play together with goal being B end of field.

Dowels 2, 4, 6, and 8 have goal at A end.

When four people play, one person takes hold of the ends of Dowels 1 and 3; his teammate standing on same side takes hold of 5 and 7.   On the opposite side of the box are the opponents, one having hold of 2 and 4, the other holding 6 and 8.   Each one can turn and push or pull his dowels across and back at will.   (Don't try to break them.)   Let's let the even's kick off by putting the ball in that recess in the B end.   The No. 8 paddle gives the ball a swat and the game is for the even's to work the ball on down through the field and out the opening at the A end.   The game for the opponents (holding the odd numbered dowels) is to not let the ball go down to the A end, but to change its course back and out the B end opening.   When the ball goes through the goal it's a point for the team putting it out.   Note that players of No. 1 and 8 are not only kick-off players but goal tenders.   Should the ball be hit out of the field, throw it back into play about where it was sent out.

When more than four play, some players handle only one dowel. It's exciting to play with eight different people. Try it.

If ball gets dented, hold it in the steam coming out of the spout of a teakettle, usually the dents will come out.

Decide on some figure such as 11 or 15 points to constitute a game. The side which first secures that many points wins the game.

Dart football board.—This game is played by football rules. Each dart stuck in the board counts one down. Each player throws dart or darts until a first down is made or they are required to punt. All kick off and punts are made with dart on upper chart.

This board can be made of fir panel board, beaver board, or of white pine. A piece of screen stop about two feet long should be

G 10 20 30 40 50 40 30 20 10 G

BLOCKED PUNT

(measurements: 6", 2', 4', 3', 4')

TD	FOR	3	9	15	FG	2	1	4	2	FG	9	15	3	FOR	TD
R	NG	4	L2	00S	8	7	3	2	1	8	00S	L2	4	NG	R
12	5	NG	35	L10	3	L4	PI	FG	L4	3	L10	35	NG	5	13
2	NG	1	L5	FOR	NG	21	3	3	21	NG	FOR	L5	1	NG	2
13	7	3	L6	TD NG	L5	3	IP	6	3	L5	TD NG	L6	3	7	12
7	2	11	NG	FOR	L7	5	OR	1	5	L7	FOR	NG	11	3	7
4	7	2	16	9	4	PI	5	8	OS	12	7	16	L6	2	4
8	IP	6	OS	3	6	11	L4	PI	10	NG	5	00S	4	IP	8
FOR	L5	3	8	4	1	R	7	11	NG	2	4	6	OS	L5	FOR
TD	NG	L2	1	IP	3	20	8	FOR	15	9	IP	1	12	NG	TD

made marking the yards as on the field with a small hole drilled for each yard. With this stick and three matches you mark the position of the ball, breaking off the heads of two of the matches to be used as linesmen poles; using the other as the ball.

CODE

<table>
<tr><td>TD</td><td>Touchdown</td><td>FG</td><td>Field Goal, must be within opponents 40-yard line</td></tr>
<tr><td>NG</td><td>No gain</td><td></td><td></td></tr>
<tr><td>OS</td><td>Off side</td><td>FOR</td><td>Fumble opponent recovers</td></tr>
<tr><td>IP</td><td>Incomplete pass</td><td>OOS</td><td>Opponent off side</td></tr>
<tr><td>PI</td><td>Pass intercepted</td><td>L</td><td>Lose the No. of yards indicate</td></tr>
<tr><td>R</td><td>Roughing</td><td>OR</td><td>Opponent roughing</td></tr>
</table>

Numbers indicate yards gained on down.

—VAL SHERMAN, Robstown, Texas

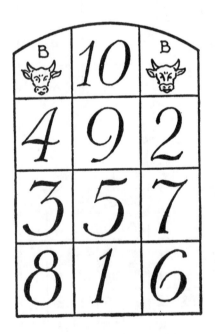

Bull board (6x3 feet).—Play as in shuffleboard. The court should not be longer than twenty or thirty feet. If a disc lands in the bull head it cancels all the score made previous to that time.

A trip around the world can be played by requiring the players to get the numbered spaces in order. A player gets three ties in this case. As long as he makes good in getting the spaces consecutively he continues to play. If a player lands a disc in the bull head, that is "mal-de-mer," or seasickness, and he must start all over.

Note that the numbers in the nine blocks represent "The Mystic Fifteen." Any way you add them they make fifteen.

This game can be played with linoleum discs three or four inches in diameter, which the players toss at the target. In this style of play the tossers stand ten to fifteen feet from the bull board.

Ciel.—This game was played aboard a ship in South American waters.

It is a combination of croquet and shuffleboard. Croquet rules are used except that only one extra play is given for playing on another and only one for making a hole. In other words, success in hitting an opponent's disc or in making the play for a "hole" only means that the player is entitled to continue playing.

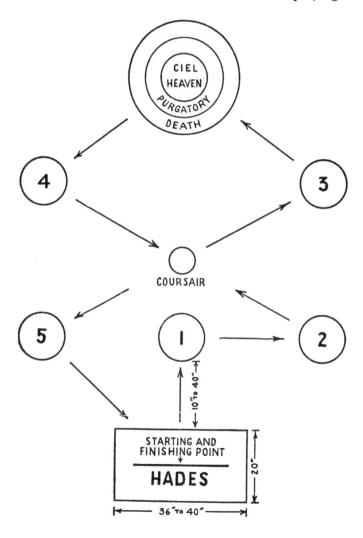

Equipment—Each player has a disc. These discs are about four inches in diameter and one inch thick. A shovel similar to that used in shuffleboard is used. The holes are one foot in diameter except that "Coursair" is about 6 inches in diameter and "Ciel" is encircled by "Purgatory" and "Death," these being 24 inches and 36 inches in diameter respectively.

The field—The game need not be laid out in any regulation manner. A hallway with several cross halls, or a series of rooms, may be used. Distances from hole to hole may vary, anywhere from 10 to 40 feet. "Hades" is from 36 to 40 inches long and 20 inches wide, with a starting line drawn at the middle.

The game.—The play starts at the center line in "Hades." The player must take the holes in turn as in croquet. These holes are painted or drawn with chalk on the floor.

A disc must be clear of the line to be considered in

Players play on one another as in croquet.

A player is "out" when he completes the course and touches the middle line in "Hades" with his disc.

Just as in croquet, a player, who has completed the course excepting for the last play, may be a rover and seek to assist his partner.

If a disc lands in "Ciel" ("heaven") the player gets a shot at No. 4. If it lands in "Purgatory" he must make No. 3 over. If it lands in "Death" he must make center and No. 3 over. A partner or an opponent may shoot him into anyone of these.

—As described by V. P. HENRY

Dart baseball.—The board should be made of soft pine, cypress, or other soft wood. Beaver board will do temporarily. Size of board, 4 square feet.

Playing rules—

1. Darts must be thrown underhand.

2. Batter may take one step forward when throwing but must not step over pitching line under penalty of being called *out*.

3. Runners advance one base on a single, two bases on a two-base hit, etc.

4. Double play—batter out. The runner nearest home is the second out. With no runners on—only one out.

5. Sacrifice out. Batter is always out even though no one is on base. All runners advance one base. A runner on third base may score on Sacrifice Out providing it is not the third out.

6. Error or hit by pitcher. Batter to first base. Runners do not advance unless forced.

7. Stolen base. Dead ball for the batter. One runner advances. With bases full runner on third scores. With runners on second

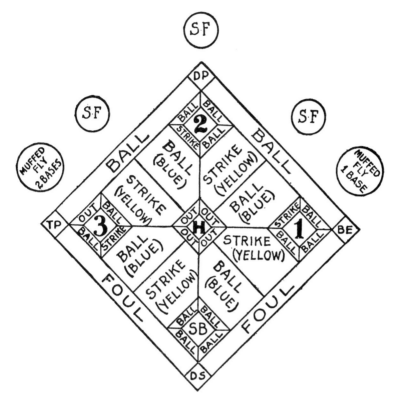

S.B. Stolen Base	H. Home Run
D.S. Double Steal	B.E. Base on Error
D.P. Double Play	1. Single
T.P. Triple Play	2. Double
S.F. Sacrifice Fly	3. Triple

and third, runner on third scores. With runners on first and third runner on first goes to second.

8. The batter is out if a dart ball fails to hit the board. If the body of the dart other than the point strikes the edge of the board and glances off, the batter is out.

9. If the dart touches the floor back of the pitching line due to interference or for any other reason, it shall be ruled a dead ball.

10. If the dart falls to the floor immediately after hitting the board, it shall be ruled a dead ball.

11. If one dart already in the board falls or is displaced by another dart and falls, the original dart shall be replaced in the board.

12. If a thrown dart sticks in the body of another dart already on the board, the last thrown dart shall be ruled a dead ball.

13. A dart which hits squarely on a line between two sections of the board shall be known as a line ball and shall be considered as in the section of least advantage to the batter.

14. If a player bats out of turn he shall be called out if the error is called to the umpire's attention before the player completes his turn at bat.

15. If a player has been replaced, he cannot re-enter the same game.

Darts may be made by using clothespins. Drive a nail in one end, file off head, and file down to a point. Insert two feathers in open end and draw prongs together with string, wire, or tape.

The board may be done in colors. All bases and home run in green; all strikes in yellow; all balls in blue; all outs in red.

Play regular baseball rules.

Box hockey.—This is a very noisy game as well as a very active one. Perhaps it should not be in the same room with other games, particularly if the play space is crowded. When going strong it

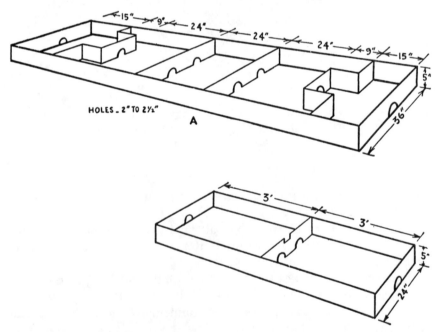

sounds like a machine gun in full tilt. If used indoors the box should be anywhere from 6 to 8 feet long and from 2 to 3 feet wide. An opening wide enough (perhaps 4 inches) to permit the easy exit of a disc 2 inches wide and ⅜- to 1-inch deep should be cut in the middle of each end of the box. A middle sector of the box has two openings of similar width, one on either side. A notch just wide enough to hold the disc is cut in the top of this middle sector. See smaller diagram. Broomsticks or shinny sticks are used. Two players oppose one another, one on either side of the box. They tip off three times (that is, they strike their sticks first to the floor and then together three times) and then each tries to knock the disc or puck off the middle sector into his opponent's side of the box. The object is to get the puck through the hole at the end of the box which the opponent is guarding. The play is fast and furious. If the puck is knocked outside the box play is started over at the middle sector. Sides of the box should be five to nine inches deep. When played outdoors a larger and heavier box may be used.

Diagram A presents a much larger game. A wooden ball the size of a golf ball would be better for this game. Play is started on the floor at center. Four players instead of two may play.

Skittles.—Skittles is a Chinese game. The only element of skill in it is the ability to spin the long-legged top. No one can predict what the top will do after it starts spinning. Nevertheless, the game has a fascination that makes it a popular one for the clubroom.

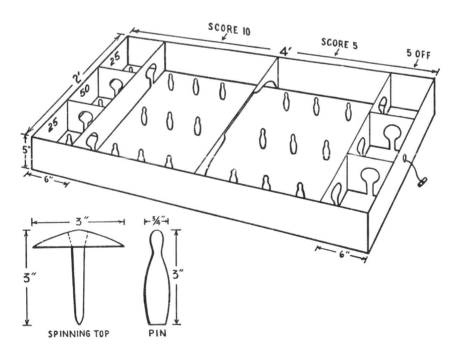

SPINNING TOP   PIN

Wind the string tightly around the spike of the top, which rests against two small braces (not shown in the diagram) in the middle section of one end of the box. Draw the string through the hole, and pull it with a snap. Pins knocked down in the near half count five points each, except that the two near corner pins take off five points each. Pins in the far half count ten points each. Far corner pins count twenty-five each, and the far middle pin counts fifty.

Bean bag boards.—Made of wood and braced. Size of No. 1, 2½x3 feet; holes 5 inches in diameter. Players get five throws for each round, 200 to 500 out. Size of No. 2, 2x3 feet; holes graduated

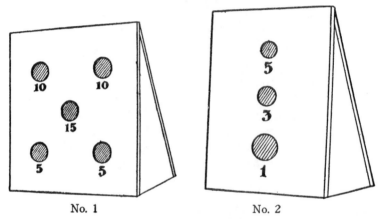

No. 1   No. 2

in size from top at 3½ inches to bottom at 5 inches. A throw over the top takes off 5 points. Players stand from ten to fifteen feet away. Bean bags about three inches square, with denim covers.

The bean bag board may be made in shape of a clown's head to add interest.

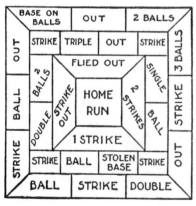

Bean bag or disc baseball.—Players stand fifteen feet away and toss bean bags or washers or linoleum discs at the diagram which is marked on the floor, or ground, or better on a beaverboard field six feet square. Any toss resting on a line is counted a "strike." Play regular baseball rules.

Target board.—This target may be painted on the back of the Dart Baseball Board. Each player gets three throws with the darts for each turn. For sides, total high score wins. For individuals, 500 points out. Players stand at a distance of fifteen to twenty feet.

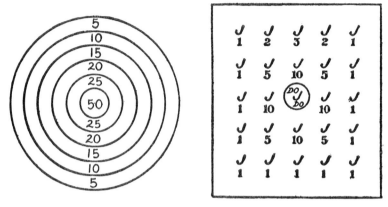

Dodo board.—Dodo is always a popular game for the clubroom. Size, 2 feet square. Twenty-five screw hooks in five rows. One dozen Mason jar rings. Each play gets twelve tosses for each turn. Ringing the Dodo (the center hood) cancels all of the score previously made by the individual or side. Score, 100 out. When played as "100 or bust" a player must make an even 100 points. If he has 98 points and gets a 3 he must start over.

Fan Mien (Fah-me).—This is a Chinese game, Fan Mien, meaning "reverses." An ordinary checker board may be used. There will need to be 64 discs—one color on one side and another color on the other. The play always starts at the center of the board. The players alternate in playing, starting with the first four plays on the four center squares. After that the two players place their discs so as to capture some of the discs of their opponent by getting on either side of them. All discs between are then turned over to show the other color. Plays must be made next to discs that have been played. The four corners are the strategic points. Therefore, skillful players try to maneuver opponents into making plays which will give them the corners. At the end of the game the player having most of his color up wins. Placing a disc between two of an opponent's disc does not turn it over. Thus a player could place a green between two reds without penalty. But if a green is on one side of a row of reds and a player plays another green on the other side of the row, all of the red discs in between the two greens are turned over with the green up. This game is sometimes called "Friends."

Chinese ping-pong.—This is a lively variation of the game of ping-pong. Players are divided into two equal sides. They line up single file at either end of the table. The first player on one side serves and the first player on the opposing side receives. Each player drops his paddle on the table as soon as he plays and the next man in line takes it up and makes the next play. Thus it continues until one side commits a fault.

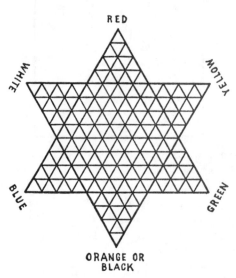

RED

WHITE

YELLOW

BLUE

GREEN

ORANGE OR
BLACK

Chinese checkers. — This game can easily be made of beaver board, c a r d b o a r d, three-ply, or, if desired, out of walnut, cherry, or pine. The game is played on a six-point star. Paint each point of the star a different color, and then shellac the entire board.

Discs can be cut from old mop handles or half-inch d o w e l s. Sandpaper to a smooth finish and paint sets in the necessary colors.

Six players may play, each having ten "men" in his point of the star. Each player's discs are of one color, and the sets are each of different color. The discs are placed on the intersections, beginning with the point, so that they are placed 1, 2, 3, and 4. Each player tries to get his men across to the opposite star point. He may move in any direction except backward. Jumps may be made of one man at a time as in checkers, but no man is removed from the board. Series of jumps may be made, of course. Often a player gets a "ladder" set up by which he jumps all the way across the board. No jumps or moves may be made back into an opponent's star point.

Three players can play the game, using alternating star points for starting points. In this case fifteen men may be used. Played in this fashion the game is the old game of Helma.

Holes may be bored at the intersections and marbles or pegs used instead of discs.

Table football.—An ordinary dining-room table or a work table not over eight feet long will do for this game. Use a ping-pong ball for the football. The ball is put in the center of the field. The players gather around the table, with chins up to the edge of the table. At the sound of the referee's whistle all players begin to blow. If the ball goes outside or over the side of the table the referee retrieves it, places it back in the middle of the field from the point at which it went out, and blows his whistle for the game to begin again. Players must not get their faces over into the field on penalty of fouling, in which case the opponents will be allowed a free blow by one player of their choice. Each ball that goes over the end of the table or goal line counts one point. Eleven points, fifteen points, or twenty-one points, as decided before play begins, constitutes a game.

Variations— (a) Play in the same fashion using a toy balloon.

(b) Use a ping-pong ball, but set up tiny goal posts eight inches apart, using spools as standards for the tiny posts. One player at a time blows, the ball being placed at center and the player blowing from behind his goal post. A ball that goes through the goal posts counts a touchdown and six points. One over the line but not through the posts counts two points. The players blow is unhindered and the sides alternate. When eleven players have blown for each side a half is finished.

(c) Use an empty eggshell instead of a ping-pong ball.

Table caroms.—Mark a spot at the center of a table (a chalk mark or a stamp). Each player is provided with two checkers. There should be an even number of reds and blacks. The blacks play first. One of their players flips his checker trying to land on or near the marked spot. Then one of the opponents flips a red checker. If the black had landed near the spot the red player probably tries to block the black away. So it continues until each player has flipped both of his checkers. Then the side with a checker nearest the target earns one point. It also gets a point for each other checker that is nearer center than any of the opponents.

Table shuffleboard.—Make a beaverboard shuffleboard five to six feet long, with a back board an inch high to stop checkers hit too hard. The discs are checkers and the players flip them by shooting with the forefinger. The same diagram (in miniature) is used as in regulation shuffleboard. Play as in regular shuffleboard.

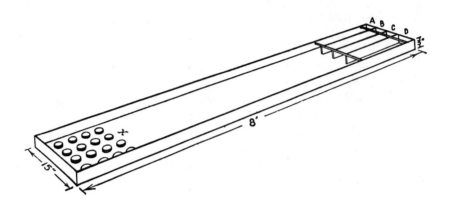

Table polo.—The object of this game is to push the discs from point (X) at the front of the board into aisles *A, B, C,* and *D.* There must be one disc in each of the pockets before one is eligible to score.

The table polo box is eight feet long and fifteen inches wide. A frame twelve inches long and fifteen inches or a little more wide, with strips three inches wide dividing it into four aisles or pockets, fits over one end of the box so that it can slide back and forth to slide the discs out after they are tossed. The discs are one and one-half inches in diameter and three-quarters of an inch thick. They are made of hardwood. Sixteen discs are used.

Each player tosses all sixteen discs. The player slides the discs from the middle of the box about twelve inches from the end nearest him. He does not begin to score until he has at least one disc in each of the four pockets. Those four score twenty points. Each complete row of four discs scores twenty. Thus a perfect score is eighty, meaning that there are four discs in each pocket. After the first complete pocketing of a row, or additional complete row, one point is allowed for each extra disc in a pocket. Thus if a player had two complete rows and three extra discs in pocket A, one in pocket B, and one in D, he would have scored forty-five points, forty for the two complete rows and five for the additional ones. A player may knock discs in with a subsequent disc. Unless a player has at least one complete row he scores nothing though he may have discs in all of the pockets but one.

Indoor shuffleboard. — The regulation shuffleboard court may be used indoors, if there is room for it. (See Chapter XI, "Fun with Sports," for diagram and description.) If this much space is not available use what you have. For a very short court a special diagram may be used. In one party the leader quickly drew with chalk four or five of these diagrams and in a jiffy he had thiry-two people playing the game.

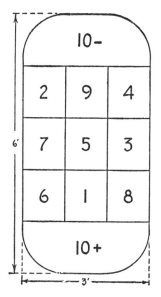

Dodo board baseball.— Make a Dodo Board eighteen inches square. Use curtain screws or label nails. Hang the diamond on the wall. Use rubber rings as in the regular game of Dodo. When a player gets on base hang a ring on that hook to indicate it. HR means Home Run; 1B, 2B, and 3B mean a single, double, or triple; SO means Strike Out; FO means Fly Out, GO means Ground Out; and W means the batter Walks.

Variation—The same idea may be used for Dodo Football.

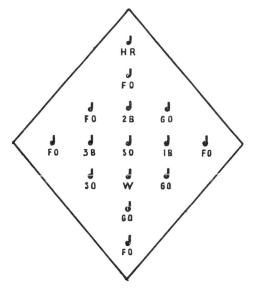

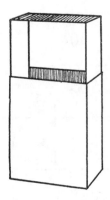

Table steeplechase.—Use six empty cardboard safety match boxes with sliding drawers. Cut the bottom out of the drawers and slip each one only part of the way back into its cover. Then arrange the partly open boxes on their ends in a row on the table. These are the hurdles.

Use tiddlywinks for "horses" and try to snap them through the hurdles. Each player must have a tiddlywink of a certain color and a shooter. In turn the players shoot, trying to make their horses fly through the openings in the drawers of the match boxes.

When a player fails to make a hurdle he gives way to another player, who has his turn. If a player succeeds in flipping his tiddlywink through the first box he shoots again, trying for the second hurdle, and so on. The hurdles must be made in their regular turn.

The game may be made more difficult by arranging the boxes in zigzag fashion rather than in a straight line.

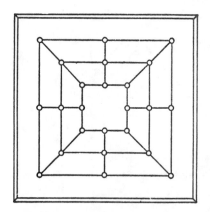

Merilles, Mill, Muhl, or Nine-Men's Morris.—This ancient game is common to a number of countries. The French call it Merilles; the Germans call it Muhl (Meal); the English call it Five-Penny Morris, Nine-Men's or Nine-Penny Morris, depending on the number of counters used. It is mentioned in *Midsummer Night's Dream.*

The game is played on three concentric squares crossed by lines at the corner and in the middle of each side, making twenty-four points or stations.

The players place their nine counters one at a time, each trying to get three-in-a-row. Three-in-a-row is any three consecutives on a line. Usually the corner line is eliminated so that a player cannot score three-in-a-row by getting three concentric corners.

When a player gets three-in-a-row he is privileged to take one of his opponent's counters off of the board excepting that he may not disturb a three-in-a-row.

After the counters are placed the players move their men, trying to move into three-in-a-row. Each player takes his turn. Moves may only be made on the line and for one space. When one player is trimmed down to three men, he is privileged to move more than one space, if he desires. Thus he may jump across the board to block his opponent and on the next play come back to a three-in-a-row.

Counters may be made of pegs (golf tees make good ones), marbles, pebbles, cardboard, or buttons. They should be in two sets of different colors so it is easy to distinguish one's own counters from an opponent's.

The board may be made of cardboard or three-ply wood.

Firms Handling Recreation Materials
Useful in Clubrooms

Apex Manufacturing Company, Norristown, Pa. (Dart games a specialty.)

Co-operative Recreation Service, Delaware, Ohio.

Milton Bradley, Springfield, Mass.

A. C. McClurg, 333 East Ontario, Chicago, Ill.

Parker Brothers, Salem, Mass.

A. G. Spalding, New York City.

CHAPTER III
FUN WITH HOBBIES

Chapter III

FUN WITH HOBBIES

"A hobby is one means for escaping institutional life."
—William G. Vinal

Why A Hobby?

Develop a hobby and beat old age," said a speaker to a convention of medical men. Well, that's one reason for urging everyone to take up some hobby.

> "Thus pleasures fade away;
> Youth, talents, beauty, thus decay,
> And leave us dark, forlorn, and gray."

A hobby, one not sufficiently burdensome to tax the strength but absorbing enough to maintain active interest in living, can stave off gloomy remembrances of happier days.

But there is a better reason for hobbies than that. One does not have to wait until "life begins at forty" to get a thrill out of a hobby. In fact, some of the most satisfying hobbies come as the result of an investment of interest early in life—an investment that pays dividends almost immediately, and continues to pay increasingly large dividends as the years pass.

So, develop a hobby or several hobbies in order to discover the joy of life. Develop an interest in hobbies in order to escape the dread monotony of a machine-made civilization. Develop an interest in hobbies so that you need not be the easy victim of the stereotyped and stale recreation that threatens those who are poverty stricken in ideas of what to do in leisure.

What Makes a Good Hobby?

Sometimes anemic, feeble, and meaningless activities parade as hobbies. "Spare-time twiddling" someone has aptly called them. Anyone who has seen some of the useless and unlovely things done in the name of handicrafts knows how meaningless such activities can sometimes become. Farnsworth Crowder (*Rotarian*, October, 1935)

(71)

insists that if hobbies are to catch on they must have "grip, entrails, and meaning." A good hobby for you is one that gives opportunity for expressing and developing your individual talents, that expands and enriches your personality, and that lures you on by ever increasing richness as you grow in knowledge and skill.

How to Develop a Hobby

The rules are simple. (1) Find a hobby that appeals to you and for which you have some aptness. This may have to be discovered by a period of experimentation. (2) Read whatever you can find on the particular activity. Saturate yourself with ideas about it. (3) Work at it. (4) Do not be satisfied with mediocre achievement. Seek continual improvement in performance and skill. A hobby becomes increasingly satisfying as one develops skill in it. Too often hobby-craft simply develops a new crop of piddlers.

Creating Interest in Hobbies

Often a leader desires to increase the interest range of a group but does not know how to begin. The following suggestions may help:

1. Bring people who have interesting hobbies before the group, not only to talk about these hobbies, but, perhaps, to demonstrate them. Or, even better, take the group to visit the hobby enthusiast.

2. Use a bulletin board to play up interesting articles, pictures, and items about hobbies.

3. Put on a Hobby Fair. Spend several months getting ready for it. See the pamphlet on "How to Run a Hobby Show," published by *Leisure*, 683 Atlantic Avenue, Boston.

4. Have a Hobby Talk Fest. Give people a chance to exchange ideas about their favorite activities.

5. Introduce hobby activities occasionally in your social gatherings. Note how this is done in a number of parties in this volume, notably the "Artisan Party" and the "Hobby Party," (see Chapter XVI, Fun with Parties).

6. Organize some Hobby Clubs in activities where there is already some interest—a Camera Club, a Book Club, a Dramatic Club, a Poetry Club, a Puppet Club.

A List of Possible Hobbies

Collections—Antiques; stamps; coins; miniatures; books; medals; dolls; glassware; rugs; quilts; post cards; Indian relics; prints; historical relics; scrapbooks; autographs.

Creative art—Drawings in charcoal, pen, pencil, crayon; painting in oil and water color; picture tinting; finger painting; prints; etchings; cuts in wood or linoleum; sculpture; clay modeling; soap carving; wood carving; designs; decorations; jewelry; metal craft; chalk talks.

Camera craft—Snapshots; portraits; landscapes; unusual snaps; movies; home developing and printing; making of slides.

Handicrafts—Beadwork; embroidery; basketry; leather work; bookbinding; plaques; masks; weaving; woodwork; paper craft; batik dyeing.

Drama—Reading plays; acting; making stage sets; costuming; lighting; make-up; collecting plays of various types; marionettes; puppets.

Music—Playing an instrument or instruments; singing; music appreciation; collecting various types of musical compositions, such as folk songs; knowing the stories of great composers, great operas; knowing and recognizing great compositions.

Literature—Poetry (reading, learning, writing) ; studying special subjects (philosophy, science, history, language, geography) ; reading fiction, non-fiction for the fun of reading; collecting books; writing.

Nature lore—Birds; insects; rocks and minerals; sea shells and fossils; butterflies and moths; pressed flowers; woods, natural or polished, leaves, seeds; trees; flowers; astronomy; gardening (flowers, vegetables) ; birdhouses.

Mechanical and technical hobbies—Chemistry; radio; microscopy; electricity; miniature railroads.

Pets and domestic animals—Birds; cats; dogs; guinea pigs; rabbits; horses; cattle; chickens; ducks; geese; swans.

Home hobbies—Cooking; interior decorating; sewing; gardening.

Sports—Archery; badminton; hiking; tennis; swimming and diving; softball; baseball; basketball; football; cricket; volleyball; horseshoes; quoits; shuffleboard.

Reading as a hobby.—Reading is a basic hobby. It enhances one's knowledge, interest, and skill in whatever activity is chosen. It is a delightful exercise that makes it possible to fellowship with the best minds of the ages. It quickens the imagination and sharpens the intellect. Therefore, no matter what other hobby a man may pursue, he should develop a taste for good books.

Reading need not be just an individual hobby. It may be shared with others. It can be made the means of developing a fine social atmosphere. There is no richer and deeper fellowship than that which grows out of shared ideas and ideals. Book Clubs, Poetry Clubs, Book Nooks, Book Discussions, Current Events, Teas, Book Hikes, reading together, conversation about interesting books and articles that have been read—all of these can do much to add to the fun of living.

Reading guideposts

(1) Read regularly. Set aside a definite time for reading. "Thirty minutes a day with the great source books of literature" was one man's rule. Arnold Bennett, in *How to Live on Twenty-four Hours a Day,* suggests an hour and a half every other day. Cultivate the habit of *regular* reading.

(2) Read discriminatingly. You cannot read everything. Therefore read the best.

(3) Read wisely. Do not allow your reading to get into a groove. Read books on a variety of subjects. Read some fiction, some poetry, some philosophy, some religion, some history, and some biography from time to time.

(4) Occasionally concentrate on a single subject over a period of time.

(5) Read thoughtfully. Spend part of your reading time in meditating on what you have just read.

A helpful 71-page pamphlet, entitled *Good Reading,* can be gotten from the National Council of Teachers of English, 211 West 68th Street, Chicago, Ill. It is a guide to 900 books.

The American Library Association, 520 North Michigan Avenue, Chicago, Ill., has some helpful suggestions to offer in its *Reading with a Purpose* pamphlet.

Yarn painting.—*Equipment*—White shellac, sheets of smooth paper, yarns of various colors.

Procedure—Block off frame for your picture. Draw or trace outline of the picture on the paper. Snip the yarn in short pieces of sizes desired. Cover the paper with white shellac. Fill in the design with the snippings of yarn and pat in place. If the shellac becomes dry, put some more on the paper where needed.

Linoleum block printing. — *Equipment* — Battleship linoleum (scraps may be obtained from the furniture store) ; linoleum block tools (inexpensive sets may be purchased or a sharp penknife may be used—umbrella ribs may be cut and sharpened to serve as gouges) ; smooth paper or cords; black printing ink or other colors, as desired; a photographer's roller. Safety razor blades may be used for fine lines.

Block printing on paper originated in Japan. India and Persia have developed the art of fabric prints to a high degree. Their hand-blocked prints are sold throughout the world.

Trace or draw the design on the surface of the linoleum. It would be well to ink the pattern with India ink so it can be seen easily. Cut out the background with block-printing tools or with a penknife. Cut away from your outline so that care can be taken not to undercut your design. The background should be cut to a depth of approximately 3/16 of an inch.

For fabric printing block out with basting thread the space where you desire the print to be. For repeats it is a good idea to lay a yardstick or ruler on the cloth. Thumbtack the material to a flat padded surface. Several layers of newspapers or old sheeting will do for padding. Oil colors or printer's inks may be used for the printing process. Care must be taken not to allow the background areas to become inked, else the design will be spotted.

Lay the painted block face down upon the fabric. This is called "direct printing." Small prints can be made by bearing down with the hands.

It would be well to tack the linoleum block to a block of wood. This makes it easier to handle.

A roller or brayer is helpful. These come in four sizes, the smallest being about four inches in length and one inch in diameter. Sometimes a photo-mounting roller is used but it is not as flexible as the brayer and does not print so well.

For printing greetings cards, announcements, program covers, use an absorbent paper.

Table and dresser scarfs, wall hangings, bedspreads, curtains, chair covers, pillows, lamp shades, screen, book covers, and wearing apparel are some of the textile possibilities.

Designs should be simple and abstract. They should have few lines, dots, or other details that will not stand impression. Finer lines should be in light against a mass of solid dark, as these will not show so much wear as lines in relief.

Bibliography—Linoleum Block Printing for Amateurs, C. D. Bone (Beacon Press, 1936); *Block Printing with Linoleum,* H. Frankenfeld (Howard Hunt Pen Company, 7th and State Streets, Camden, N. J., 1936).

Making life masks and plaques.—Here is a hobby that can bring a lot of fun and satisfaction. A life mask of a friend, baby's first shoe, the hand of a loved one, and nature lore reproductions are some of the possibilities.

For the life mask the following procedure is necessary:

(1) The subject lies down upon his back, and the entire face, or such a portion as he wishes copied, is slightly oiled by using cold

cream, Wesson oil, olive oil, or white vaseline, preferably cold cream.

(2) A pasteboard box is cut to fit closely around the face leaving a small margin to hold the plaster in place. Place this about the face, taking in a portion of the hair, which has been well oiled and combed close to the head. Also cover a part of the neck.

(3) Mix about four quarts of Plaster of Paris mixture. Pour about two quarts of water into a vessel. Add the Plaster of Paris, stirring slightly, until a thick batter is made. (Note: The person of whom the mask is to be made should be ready, face oiled and lying comfortably, before the mixing is started.)

(4) With the pasteboard shield in place, pour the Plaster of Paris over the closed eyes, and then the mouth and face, spreading it evenly so that no bubbles or wrinkles are formed near the face. Lay it carefully over the upper lips and end of the nose, leaving small holes through which the subject may breathe while the plaster sets. (Sometimes breathing tubes are placed in the nostrils. However, they may distend the nostrils. By care, the plaster may be laid about the nose and lips so breathing may continue normally.)

(5) The subject must breathe slowly through the nose, being careful not to crack the plaster while setting. A good brand of plaster will set sufficiently to be removed without cracking within a few minutes. Lift the cast from the hair and forehead first, and push slightly toward the chin, lifting it from the face.

(6) Allow the mold to set for a few minutes until firm enough to handle safely. Then correct any flaws on the inside of the mold by filling in bubbles and places not molded to the face.

(7) Oil the inside of the cast, which is the intaglio or negative, using either of the above named oils, allowing the plaster to absorb some of the oil. Then it is ready to be poured. Do not excessively oil the intaglio, nor pour too soon. Let it cool first.

(8) Mix about the same amount of plaster as before, leaving it slightly thinner than the first mixing. Pour this into the intaglio, and either by rocking or with the finger, see that the plaster forms no bubbles or flaws. When the cast is filled let it set until thoroughly hard. Do not rush. When ready, carefully break the intaglio away, leaving the cameo or life mask. This may be touched up as is necessary.

Use quick setting molding plaster. Good results can be gotten with "Red Top Pure White, Quick Setting Molding Plaster."

By using dampened buckram or papier-mache a lifelike mask can be made from the plaster casting. Paint in features with water colors or poster ink.

The casting of plaques, the hand print, the foot, leaf molds, fish, birds, and the like offer other possibilities. Put a small amount of plaster in a box large enough to contain the object to be cast. The object, well oiled, is then laid or set down into the plaster which just half covers it. When the plaster is set lift the object out. Oil the mold and the top surface of the casting. Replace the object and pour the plaster entirely over the object. When set, separate the first and second casting carefully. Remove the object. After touching up the inside cut a hole so that the thin plaster may be poured in when the two casts are tied together. Oil both well. Tie them together. Mix a thin plaster and put into the mold. Shake the plaster as it is being poured. When the object is removed from the cast, carefully trim the appendage from the cast and dress it down.

A little imagination and experimentation will enable you to make good casts of many objects.

The addition of a teaspoonful of salt to a quart of plaster will make a casting set much harder, though if it is to be painted the results may not be so desirable, as the salt will affect the paint.

—CHESTER G. NELSON
Florida City, Florida

Spray-gun painting.—If you like spatter printing you will find that spray-gun painting has a strong appeal for you.

Equipment—Some spray guns such as are used on insects. If they are the kind with glass containers so much the better. You can have several glass containers, one for each color of paint. When not in use keep the containers stoppered to keep the paint fresh.

Poster paint, thinned to the proper consistency.

Stencil paper, thin cardboard, oak tag, or heavy paper for cutting the stencils.

A sharp-pointed knife or a razor blade set in a holder, such as can be obtained from the ten-cent store, for a stencil cutter.

Procedure—Make your drawing. Trace the drawing on the stencil paper. Cut the stencil. Place it on your paper and fasten both your stencil and the paper to a drawing board or any smooth surface. Pins may be used for this purpose. Spray the design, moving the gun back and forth to get an even effect. If possible, cut the stencil out cleanly and whole, for the figure may be used to cover the design for a two-color effect. By making several stencils for the same de, sign different colors can be used. A different stencil must be cut for each color.

When you finish spraying, allow the paint a few moments to dry before removing the stencil. Be careful not to smear the design.

Posters, program covers, Christmas cards, book covers, and announcements are some of the possibilities. Much of the knack of spray gunning will come with practice.

Directions for making spatter prints.—*Leaf prints*—Materials needed: a toothbrush; green ink (dilute with equal quantity of water) ; a package of notebook paper or drawing paper; a frame covered with screen wire the size of the paper. The wooden frame should be an inch thick, so that the surface of the wire will be an inch above the surface of the paper. (A frame may be made in a few minutes from the end of an orange crate. With a hammer knock off the slats. This will leave a frame about twelve inches square. Cut a piece of screen wire to fit the frame and stretch it in place, fastening it with thumbtacks or ordinary carpet tacks.)

Place a sheet of paper on the table. On it place a leaf, or arrange several leaves that have been carefully pressed. Place the wire frame over the paper. Now dip the brush in the diluted ink, shake off surplus and rub the brush back and forth over the screen wire. The drier the brush, the finer the spattering will be. Remove the leaf carefully and allow the print to dry. Then write the name of the leaf under it. If desired, a small oblong card may be arranged on each sheet before spattering to make a blank space for writing or printing the name of the leaf.

Other prints—Leaf prints are only one of the many types of prints which may be made. Spatter printing lends itself to a variety of uses. Silhouettes may be cut from paper and used instead of pressed leaves. It is more artistic to design one's own pattern, but the beginner may cut or copy silhouettes from magazines and books. Stationery, place cards, paper napkins, book covers, posters, Christmas cards, convalescent cards, are among the articles which may be made.

With the wide range of colored inks now available there is no end to the possibilities, particularly if one is in a creative mood. White ink may be used on dark background for Christmas cards. What could be lovelier for the background of an ordinary leaf poster than a harmony of rich fall colors—brown, red, orange, green, and yellow. Stained-glass window effects may be achieved by experimenting with a combination of soft blue, violet, yellow, and red.

Two shades of one color may be used effectively. For example, a sailboat at sea furnished the inspiration for a "bon voyage" place card. A two-tone effect was produced by placing a card over the "sky section" while the ocean was spattered in. This extra card was then removed and the entire place card spattered to complete the "sky section." Naturally the ocean became a shade darker than the sky and when the tiny silhouette of the sailboat was removed a lovely two-tone blueprint with a white sailboat at sea on a deep blue ocean against a light blue sky was the result.

—ELIZABETH BROWN, Nashville, Tennessee

Art as a hobby.—"Pictures with Which I Like to Live" was the title of a series of ten art appreciation periods one cultured woman conducted for a group of young people. Learning how to enjoy the best in art, what to look for in a picture, a bit about line and color harmony, something about the great pictures and the artists who created them—these will add something to the joy of life.

Add to the capacity to appreciate art the ability to create lovely things through painting, sketching, carving, molding, or sculpturing, and you have the well-nigh perfect hobby. If you have even a little of the artistic in you give it a chance to develop. You may surprise yourself. Certainly you will find that this hobby will give you increasing satisfactions as you give expression to it. Examine the list of books suggested in the Bibliography at the end of this book. Read some of them and try your skill.

Twenty-five Famous Pictures

Bonheur, Rosa. "The Horse Fair"	Millet. "Feeding Her Birds"
Breton, Jules. "Song of the Lark"	Murillo. "Boy Drinking"
Burnand. "Go ye into All the World"	Raphael. "Madonna of Chair"
Calderon. "Ruth and Naomi"	Reynolds. "Age of Innocence"
Corregio. "Holy Night"	Reynolds. "Infant Samuel"
Ender. "Woman at the Tomb"	Sargent. "Elijah" (from friese)
Gainsborough. "Blue Boy"	Sully. "The Torn Hat"
Le Brun. "Mother and Daughter"	Taylor. "Esther"
Millais. "Boyhood of Raleigh"	Watts. "Hope"
Millett. "The Angelus"	Watts. "Sir Galahad"
Millet. "Going to Work"	Whistler. "Whistler's Mother"
Millet. "The Gleaners"	Ruisdael. "The Windmill"
Millet. "The Sower"	

Pictures and prints—Art Extension Society, Westport, Conn.; Curtis & Cameron (Copley Prints), 221 Columbus Avenue, Boston, Mass.; Edward Gross & Company, 826 Broadway, New York; Medici

Society of America, 755 Boylston Street, Boston, Mass.; Metropolitan Museum of Arts, Fifth Avenue and 82d Street, New York; Perry Pictures Company, Malden, Mass.

Artists' materials—American Crayon Company, Sandusky, Ohio; H. Reeve Angel & Company, 7-11 Spruce Street, New York (drawing paper); Binney and Smith, 41 East 42d Street, New York (paints, crayons); The Esterbrook Pen Company, 76 Cooper Street, Camden, N. J. (Drawlet pens); Favor-Ruhl and Company, 425 South Wabash Avenue, Chicago (artists supplies); C. Howard Hunt Pen Company, Camden, N. J. (Speedball pens and linoleum block printing supplies); Koh-i-noor Pencil Company, Inc., 373 Fourth Avenue, New York (drawing pencils and crayons); Henry A. Ungar, Inc., 1237 South Olive Street, Los Angeles, Calif.; F. Weber Company, Philadelphia, Pa. (paints, inks, drawing and artists materials); Winsor & Newton, Inc., 31 Union Square, New York (paints).

Finger painting.—This is an interesting hobby, holding fascination for all age groups. In addition to being lots of fun it has sound educational value, in teaching rhythm, color harmonies, color mixture, composition, designs, stimulation of the imagination, opportunity for self-expression. The essentials of art can be taught through finger painting.

You can paint with your fingers, your hands, your arms, or your elbows. Here is the procedure:

(1) Moisten a sheet of highly glazed paper (18x24 inches) on both sides by drawing it through a shallow pan of clear water. Shelf paper is an inexpensive usable paper.

(2) Spread the paper smoothly on a flat surface.

(3) Cover the surface with paint, using the palm and fingers to spread the material over the entire surface.

(4) Add color to the medium if it is not already colored when applied to the surface.

(5) Using your fingers, your doubled-up fist, your forearm, a sponge, a cookie cutter, tops of jars, corrugated cardboard pieces, potato or stick prints—anything at hand—make your design or pic·ture. If you don't like what you've done, wipe it out and begin again.

(6) Let your painting dry on a smooth surface; then press it on the back with a hot iron to smooth out the wrinkles.

(7) If you desire to preserve the picture spray it with neutral shellac.

The paint—Commercially made finger-paint may be bought from any firm handling Binney-Smith Products, or from Binney-Smith, 41 East 42nd Street, New York City.

2. An inexpensive paint may be made from gloss or elastic starch. Prepare the paste according to directions on the box. To each pint of paste add one tablespoon of glycerine to obtain a good texture and one-half teaspoon of oil of cloves to prevent the paste from souring.

Color may be added in any one of several ways: (*a*) Food coloring to be added while the mixture still is warm (this should be used especially where little children are to use the paint) ; (*b*) Alabastine or tempera powders on dry or mixed with water and applied to the paper after the surface has been covered with paste; (*c*) drops of show-card color may be placed on the paste covered surface.

3. Wallpaper paste with enough water to make it the consistency of batter can be used in the same fashion as starch.

4. Kalsomine which has been mixed with hot water and allowed to jelly may also be used.

The paint comes off the hands easily with the use of hot water and soap. Try your hand at finger painting. Get the family to try it. It's plenty of fun.

Books.—*Finger Painting*, by Ruth Faison Shaw (Little, Brown Company) ; *Finger Painting as a Hobby*, Stephen V. Thach (Harpers) .

The Workshop.—A workshop could be fitted up for the home, the club, the school, or the church. Here hobbies and crafts of all sorts could be pursued. Wood carving, plaster casting, kite making, marionette making, furniture making, the making of scenery, weaving, pottery—the possibilities for creative effort are limitless.

Materials and supplies for the woodworking shop—J. and H. Metal Products Co., 478-486 St. Paul Street, Rochester, New York. Woodworking shop complete including drill press, sander, turning lathe, jig saw, line shaft, hangers, belts, and pulleys requiring one small motor to operate.

Any small second-hand motor, 1/10 H.P. or larger, will run the complete set-up. A motor may be purchased for two or three dollars locally.

Woodworking equipment may be supplied by the following. Write for catalogue.

Sears-Roebuck and Company, Chicago, Philadelphia, Atlanta, Memphis, and local stores.

Montgomery Ward and Company, Chicago, Baltimore, and local stores.

Delta Manufacturing Company, 3775 North Holston Street, Milwaukee, Wis.

Driver Power Tools, Walker Turner Co., Inc., Plainfield, N. J.

The Ten-Cent Stores have valuable books on crafts and hobbies, such as: *How to Make It; How to Use Tools; Wood Craft; Some Things to Do; Seeing Stars; Leaves, Flowers, Birds.*

Newsstands have many magazines and helpful materials on Crafts and Hobbies: *Popular Mechanics, Science and Invention, Home craft Hobbies, Leisure, Hobbies,* handbooks of all kinds.

The Superintendent of Documents at the Government Printing Office, Washington, D. C., offers for sale at a very reasonable price publications on a large variety of hobbies, crafts, etc.   Their List No. 73, *Handy Books,* may be had free upon request.   Such books as the following may be obtained in many areas of craft work:

*You Can Make It—*Vol. I, (58 pages).

*You Can Make It for Camp and Cottage—*Vol. II, (56 pages).

*You Can Make It for Profit—*Vol. III, (52 pages).

Dealers of craft materials: Catalogues will be sent on request.

Foley-Tripp Company, 193 William Street, New York City. Leathercraft.

Ester Leather Company, 82 St. Paul Street, Rochester, New York. Leathercraft.

Craftman's Model Co., 2030 North 41st Street, Milwaukee, Wis. Woodwork models.

Craft Service, 350 University Avenue, Rochester, New York. Craftene, Beadwork, Celluloid, Boondoggle, Train Models, Airplane Models, Leathercraft, Metalcraft, Metal Tapping, Block Printing, Electric Woodburning, Archery, Sponges, Tents, Basketry, and many other crafts, and supplies.

Talens School Products, Inc., 320 East 21st Stret, Chicago, 36 West 24th, New York.   Leathercraft, Sponges, Metalcraft, Raffia Work, Fibercraft, Clay Crafts, Petricraft, Block Printing, Finger Painting, Batik Dying, Celluloid Work, and other arts and crafts.

Fellowcrafters, 64 Stanhope Street, Boston, Mass.   Leathercraft, Birchcraft, Braiding and Knotting, Fibre Crafts, Weaving Crafts, Beadcraft, Amberol Craft, Metal Craft, Block Printing, Craft Work with Wood, etching, Art Veneer Craft, Model Building, Pottery, Finger Painting, Sponge.   Their catalogue contains a splendid bibliography of late books on practically every modern craft.

HandiKraft, Inc., 217-233 West Huron Street, Chicago, Ill. Pyro-Kraft (woodburning) Tap-Kraft, Flower-Kraft, and accessories.

Carron Manufacturing Company, 415 South Aberdeen Street, Chicago, Ill. PyroKraft, Plaques, Wood Novelties, Tap-Kraft, etc.

Dennison-Craft Service, Farmingham, Mass. Paper Craft, Basketry, Flowers, Marionettes, and many related paper crafts.

H. L. Wild, 510 East 11th Street, New York, N. Y. Patterns and supplies for wood workers. Wood novelties, etc.

The Handcrafters, Waupun, Wis. Everything in crafts.

Books—

Leisure League of America, 30 Rockefeller Plaza, New York, N. Y. Series of booklets on Leisure-Time Activities.

Care and Feeding of Hobby Horses	*How to Design Your Own Clothes*
You Can Write	*Stamp Collecting*
What to Do About Your Invention	*Hiker's Guide*
Tropical Fish	*Interior Decorating*
Photography for Fun	*Discover the Stars*
Quilting	*Crochet Book*
Music for Everybody	*Friendly Animals*
Drawing for Fun	*Creative Crafts*
A Garden in the House	

and many others in this series on hobbies.

Treasure Chest Publications, 62 West 45th Street, New York.
Hobbycraft Points on Sketching and How to Draw.
Hobbycraft Points on Cartooning.
Hobbycraft Designs Planned for You to Build.
Hobbycraft Toy Designs.
Marionette Hobbycraft (series of four booklets).
Ventriloquism.
Punch and Judy (making and production).
Masks.

Boy Scouts of America, 2 Park Avenue, New York, N. Y. Merit Badge Series.

Archery	*Botany*	*Leather Work*
Art	*Carpentry*	*Metal Work*
Astronomy	*Cooking*	*Photography*
Basketry	*Handicraft*	*Stamp Collecting*
Bird Study	*Hiking*	*Wood Carving*
Blacksmithing	*Journalism*	*Wood Turning*
Bookbinding	*Leathercraft*	*Wood Work*

and about 100 other items in this Merit Badge Series.

The **Crowell-Collier** Publishing Company (*Woman's Home Companion,* Service Bureau), 250 Park Avenue, New York City. Handicraft booklets on the following and many other interests:

Basketry.	*Tire Tube Toys.*
First Lessons in Weaving.	*Craft Jewelry.*
Knitting and Crochet.	*Stuffed Toys.*
Tied and Dyed.	*To Make of Wood.*

The Modern Handy Book for Boys, Bechdolt (Greenburg).

The Complete Book of Modern Crafts, H. Atwood Reynolds (Association Press).

Handbook on the Use of Crafts, Perkins,

Handicraft, Lester Everett Griswold (Colorado Springs, Colo.). Covers entire field.

Nature Crafts, Emily A. Veazie. The Woman's Press, 600 Lexington Avenue, New York City.

Orange Book of Designs and Patterns, Charles E. White, Jr., Fellowcrafter, Boston.

Work Night, The Church Handcraft Service, Box 24, Hollis, New York.

Soap Culture—Proctor and Gamble, Education Department, Cincinnati, Ohio.

One-Evening Projects (40 Things to Make). The Home Craftsman, 63 Park Row, New York City.

A great variety of Home Workshop Books—from *Illustrated Mechanics,* Kansas City, Mo.

Practical Delta Projects. Delta Manufacturing Company, 600-634 Vienna Avenue, Milwaukee, Wis. (32 pages).

Amateur Movies—

Amateur Movie Craft, Cameron (Cameron).

Film Play Production for Amateurs, Sewell (Pitman).

Radio—

Radio Amateurs Handbook, Handy and Hull (American Radio Relay League),

Radio Amateurs Handbook, Collins (Crowell),

Printing—

The Practice of Printing, Polk (Manual Arts Press).

Elementary Platen Press Work, Polk (Manual Arts Press).

Editing the Day's News, Bastian (Macmillan).

Typography and Mechanics of the Newspaper, Olson (Appleton).

CHAPTER IV
FUN WITH BANQUETS

Chapter IV

FUN WITH BANQUETS

BANQUETS and suppers can be made excellent agencies for socializing a group and developing in it a spirit of fellowship and *esprit de corps*.

Pointers

(1) A good theme helps. "A Mother Goose Banquet," "A Rainbow Banquet," "A Circus Banquet"—the very mention of these themes sets the mind to working with the idea.

(2) Decorations in keeping with the theme add interest.

(3) Informality, spontaneity, surprise, variety, verve, fun, and good fellowship are basic necessities for the highest success.

(4) If speeches are included in the program they should be pithy, brief, and a happy combination of the humorous and serious.

(5) Check carefully on the probable attendance at least the day before the banquet. Don't guess. Know.

(6) Check carefully on all arrangements.

(7) Organize so that the work can be distributed. There should be a general committee and subcommittees on program, menu, decorations, table arrangements, and attendance.

A college banquet.—Annual meeting of Defunct and Debunk Colleges in Economics (home variety); Literature; Athletics; Mathematics; Music; and Sociabilityology.

1. *Assembly singing*—"We're Here for Fun." (Tune: "Auld Lang Syne.")

> We're here for fun right from the start
> So drop your dignity—
> Just laugh and sing with all your heart
> And show your loyalty;
> May all your troubles be forgot,
> Let this night be the best;
> Join in the songs we sing tonight,
> Be happy with the rest.

Other songs—"Vive L'Amour," "Alouette," "Let Me Call You Sweetheart," "The Sweetheart of Sigma Chi."

2. *Economics meet*—Millinery Class (combined forces of both colleges).

3. *Literature meet*—Lecture by Anglish Gremmar, D.D. (Deadly Dull). Two-minute Debate—subject: "Resolved, that College Professors Are Human." (Representative from each college, aided and abetted by classmates.)

4. *Special music*—Selections by College Glee Club—Songs by quartet or chorus—"The Bulldog on the Bank," "Love's Old Sweet Song."

5. *Athletic meet*—Basketball (combined forces of both colleges). Rowing—Single-oared skulls (?) of light draught only permitted to be manned and womanned by one male and one female representative from each college. Tennis—Racket Club Kind (four representatives of either sex from each college).

6. *Assembly singing*—(On the square now, the following are rounds): "O How Lovely Is the Evening," "Row, Row, Row Your Boat," "Tommy Tinker."

7. *Mathematricks meet*—Lecture by A. Rithmetock, LL.D. (Little Less Dull). Test: (And How?).

8. *Sociabilityology meet*—Booby Boo.

9. *Closing songs*—"Juanita," "Old Folks at Home," "Sure, We'll Love You." (Tune: "Mother Machree.")

> Sure, we'll love you, ————,
> Forever and aye
> And fond mem'ries we'll cherish
> For many a day;
> Of hours that we've spent here
> With friends, old and new.
> O, God bless you, ————,
> To you we'll be true.

Benediction.

MENU

Discus (Rolls)

Half-Back (Baked Ham)   From the Gridiron ('Tatoe Chips)

Baseballs (Candied Apples)

Scrimmage (Fruit Salad)

Ink a la Java (Coffee)

Eta Bita Pi (Boston Cream Pie)

Explanation of program—Ages ranged from 16 to 30 at this banquet for our Young People's Department, held in the Sunday school assembly room. As the girls and boys wore their best clothes, games were avoided that were strenuous.

When the crowd filed into the dining room each person found the printed program at his plate, together with a sheet of newspaper. Before they sat down a brief explanation was made concerning this program for the "Annual Meeting of Defunct and Debunk Colleges." The crowd was evenly divided, one side being given the name of the "Defuncts," and the other the name of "Debunks." Cheer leaders were appointed and mimeographed copies of cheers for both sides were distributed by the cheer leaders to students of their "college."

DEBUNK CHEERS

Stand 'em on their heads
Stand 'em on their feet
Debunk, Debunk can't be beat.

Had a lil' rooster
Put him on a fence
Crowed for Debunk
'Cause he had some sense—
Cocke-a-doodle-dooo.

Three six seven nine,
Whom do we think is fine? ———

We may be ruff and we may be rude
But we're not forgetting our
    gratitude to ———.

DEFUNCT CHEERS

Sic 'em bull dog, bite 'em pup,
Defunct, Defunct, chew 'em up.

Rome, Caesar, Cicero, Gaul,
Defunct, Defunct, beats 'em all.

Two four six eight,
Whom do we appreciate? ———

We are young and our complex swanks
But we can't be happy without
    giving thanks to ———.

"Assembly singing"—This followed the asking of the blessing, after the crowd was seated.

"Economics meet"—Millinery Class explained the presence of the newspaper and two pins at each seat. Each person had to make a hat for himself from this sheet and the two pins. The songs and this hat-making helped fill up the time while plates were being placed on the table, and with their hats on, those present entered more into the spirit of fun.

"Literature meet"—This came toward the close of the main part of the meal. One of the boys went to a blackboard, placed where all could see it. After explaining that the research department had recently unearthed some hieroglyphical writings, he proceeded to place them upon the board, one after another, for the assembly to decipher. They were as follows:

(*a*) YY U R, YY U B, I C U R YY for me.   (Too wise, you are, too wise, you be, I see you are too wise for me.)

(*b*) A B C D Goldfish; M N O Goldfish; O S A R 2.   (Abie, see the goldfish, them 'n' no goldfish; O yes they are too.)

(*c*) If the B MT put: If it B full. putting: (If the grate be empty put coal on. If it be full stop putting coal on.)

Then the professor expressed a desire to have the assembly test its ability to punctuate correctly and placed the following sentences on the board with request for the assembly as a whole or any member of it, to point out where the punctuation should be and what it should be:

(*d*) I saw a five-dollar bill blow around the corner.   (After waiting a suitable length of time and receiving little help he stated that if he saw a five-dollar bill blow around the corner he would make a dash after the five-dollar bill.)

(*e*) The cat's claws were very sharp.   (It was explained that we usually set off a clause by punctuating.)

"Two-minute Debate" explains itself on the program.

Of course toasts to the girls, by a boy, and toasts to the boys, by a girl; and things of that nature were interspersed with this program, but a strict limit of three minutes was put on every speech.

"Athletic meet"—Volleyball.   Everyone remained seated as they were. Several toy balloons were provided at each table. Each table was expected to keep the balloons in the air as long as possible, batting them with their hands. When a balloon fell to the floor or table it was out of the game.

"Rowing"—was a relay.   Two couples from each college were given two spoons and two glasses of water, which, one from each couple has to feed to his partner (who knelt on the floor with a bib around his neck to protect his collar) spoonful by spoonful. The firt college having both its couples empty their glasses won. The cheer leaders kept everybody occupied with cheer after cheer throughout the program, and especially during the "athletic meet," and it kept everybody interested and occupied.

"Tennis of the Racket Club kind" turned out to be a balloon relay. Ten representatives from each college lined up opposite to each other and each was given a rubber balloon. These were blown up until they popped by each man in the line, each starting to blow up his balloon as soon as the man next to him on his right had popped his.

"Mathematricks meet"—"Lecture by A. Rithmetock" was another blackboard stunt pulled by the leader. He questioned the assembly concerning knotty mathematical problems and then showed them the solution. There were as follows:

(a) How can we show that half of 12 is 7? This way, X̶I̶I̶ = VII.

(b) It is not generally known but two-thirds of six equals nine. This is how S̶I X = IX.

(c) Also that a half of five equals four—and how! F̶I V E̶ = IV.

(d) From what number of 3 digits can you remove one and have 9; or remove 2 and have 10? S̶I X = IX; S̶I̶X = X.

(e) What two numbers multiplied together give us 7—fractions not allowed? Most of 'em knew that this was $7 \times 1 = 7$.

(f) Prove that 8 eights added together give us 1,000 ......

$$
\begin{array}{r}
888 \\
88 \\
8 \\
8 \\
8 \\
\hline
1,000
\end{array}
$$

(g) Seven will go into 28 thirteen times—here's how:

$$
\begin{array}{r}
7/28/13 \\
\hline
7 \\
\hline
21 \\
21 \\
\hline
\end{array}
$$

Let's prove it by multiplication ....

$$
\begin{array}{r}
13 \\
7 \\
\hline
21 \\
7 \\
\hline
28
\end{array}
$$

"Test" was a pencil and paper game, mimeographed copies of the questions with the answers left blank passed around—face down—together with pencils. At the signal, everyone turned over the sheet and worked to get as many answers as possible. At the end of several minutes, the director called time up, read aloud the correct answers, and the college having the most correct papers, won. The answers were as follows:

Arithmetrick Test

(1)　　500 plus a large boat equals without light—D+ARK.
(2)　1,000 plus a poem equals manner—M+ODE.
(3)　1,000 plus help equals an unmarried woman—M+AID.
(4)　　500 plus a preposition equals a great noise—D+IN.
(5)　　500 plus uncooked equals to pull—D+RAW.
(6)　　　50 plus a kind of tree equals part of a whip—L+ASH.
(7)　　　50 plus a finish equals to loan—L+END.
(8)　　100 plus competent equals to a heavy rope—C+ABLE.
(9)　　　1 plus to scold equals angry—I+RATE.
(10)　　　5 plus frozen water equals wickedness—V+ICE.

"Sociabilityology meet"—"Booby Boo" was simply the old game Looby Loo, meant to take the place of the usual college prom. The circle was formed around the table and the chance to move around was appreciated by everybody.

The remainder of the program explains itself. Note that the collegiate idea was carried through even to the menu. Approximately fifty people enjoyed this meal and program at a cost of $15.00—total.
—Adapted from ideas furnished by L. V. BROWDER, Danville, Va.

Treasure hunt banquet.— (This banquet was 97th Annual Young People's Banquet of the Dallas District. With adaptations it could be used in other cities.)

Publicity—Mimeographed sheets may be sent to each young people's organization, with a drawing such as two pirates carrying a treasure chest in one corner, and a "skull and cross bones" in the other; in the center may be used these lines from Robert Louis Stephenson:

> If sailor takes to sailor tunes,
> 　Storm and adventure, heat and cold,
> If schooners, islands, and maroons,
> 　And buccaneers and buried gold,
> And all the old romance, retold
> 　Exactly in the ancient way,
> Can please, as me they pleased of old,
> 　The wiser youngsters of today:
>
> So be it, and fall on!

Decorations—These are very important and will add immensely to the "motif" if properly carried out. Black and red crepe paper make a good combination for streamers. Large "cut-out" pirate heads are good if they can be secured. Toy balloons are fitting for souvenirs. Imitation gold money (chocolate candy wrapped in foil) can be scattered on the tables, representing "pieces of eight." One or two ship models should be placed on each table. The speakers' table can be cleverly arranged with a large mirror for water, with a small sand island, on which may be placed a few trees, small pirate (chocolate) figures, near a ship model.

Menu—The menu may be labeled "The Treasure Chest" and may be appropriately given such terms as these: "Pirates' Delight," "Treasure Island," "Candied Skeleton," "Doubloon Salad," "Fifteen Men on a Dead Man's Chest," "Pie-rates' Cove," "Yo-ho-ho," "Skulls," "Crossbones," etc.

The program—The program may be called the "Log"; the invocation entitled "Bon Voyage." Group singing may be listed as "Mutiny of the Crew," using such improvised ditties as these:

> Sing, sing, the pirates' chant:
> "Who will be the victim?
> Who will be the victim?"
> Yell as though you've "seen a hant"!
> Come and join our pirate band.

(*Tune*: "Hail, Hail, the Gang's All Here.")

> Sail, sail, sail your ships,
>   Grandly o'er the sea,
> Merrily, merrily, merrily, merrily,
>   Pirates all are we.

(*Tune*: "Row, Row, Row Your Boats.")

"Important personages" may be introduced under the heading, "Ships Ahoy!" Suggestive titles for talks are these: "Latitude and Longitude," "S O S" "Powder and Arms," "Ships That Pass in the Night." Musical numbers may be chosen from such as: "The Volga Boatman," "Sailor, Beware!" "The Pirate," and "The Road to Mandalay."   —Walter Vernon, Jr.

Celebrating the birthday of George Washington—A Progressive Dinner Party.

Invitation:

> "Next Friday night at six o'clock
> To ——————— house we all will flock
>   To celebrate
> Great George and the Immortal Tree
> His gift to all posterity."
>   February 22.

First home—Game—"Be Truthful."

Have two sets of numbers. Give one set out to players. Leader has other set in a hat. Leader starts game by asking a question such as "Who has biggest ears?" then pulls any number out of hat. Whoever has that number stands up and says, "I have." Then *He* asks a question answered by the one whose number is next called by the leader. (See "Number Answer"—page 282, *Phunology*.)

Course—Fruit cocktail or soup. Then to—

Second home—Game—"Cherry Race."

A bowl is filled with cherries (cranberries) and each player thrusts his hand, palm down, into the bowl to see how many cherries he can catch up on the back of his hand. Without spilling a cherry, he must circle the room three times in two minutes. If two or more have similar scores, they continue to compete until one is victor. You can divide crowd into sides, competing against each other to see how many cherries both sides have, the side having the largest number being the winner.

Course—Hot beef sandwiches and potatoes. Then to—

Third home—Game—"Declaring Independence."

Make out following list and give one to each player:

1. I declare myself free of _____

2. Because _____

3. And I resolve to _____

4. At _____

5. On _____

Let each person write of what he declares himself to be free. Then fold over his answer and pass paper on to the next one in line. After all of the papers have been passed five times and all questions have been answered, have the declarations read aloud.

Course—Baked beans, rye bread, relish. Then to—

Fourth home—Game—"Cherry Cube."

Make cubes with the letters C-H-E-R-R-Y on them. You will need six cubes for each game. If a player turns up C-H he gets 5 points. For C-H-E he gets 10, and so on. For the complete word he scores an extra 5 points.

Course—Vegetable salad. Then to—

Fifth home—Game—"A Famous Washington." Give out following verses to guess. Each one describes a famous Washington.

1. I threw a dollar across the river
   I cut down a cherry tree
   But that any one would remember these
   Just never occurred to me. (George Washington)

2. My place in the sun
   Is a very small one,
   I loved him, that's all
   And our two lives were one. (Martha Washington)

3. I might have lived and died unknown
   Had fate not given me a son,
   The cherry tree belonged to me
   And that is why I'm famed, you see. (Washington's Father)

4. I make no claim to wealth or fame,
   Nor to position high
   I only taught him 'twas a shame
   For a gentleman to lie. (Washington's Mother)

5. They come and go within my gates
   The Senators, Diplomats, Presidents,
   I'm the center of politics, of nations' fates,
   U. S. workers are my residents. (Washington, D. C.)

6. I am the largest Washington
   That ever bore that name
   So my native sons and daughters
   To its glory have a claim. (Washington State)

7. I lift my granite grandeur high
   Telling of fame that will not die,
   Bearing aloft in rain or sun
   The deathless name of Washington. (Washington Monument)

8. I settled the Alabama claim,
   That is all that gives me fame.
   In 1871 was written
   To make amends for Great Britain. (Treaty of Washington)

9. Though my race was not the same
   I bore the illustrious name,
   And tried to teach my people
   That to labor is no shame. (Booker T. Washington)

10. They gave me his name
    Hoping it would bring fame,
    But my only claim to glory
    Is that I could tell a story. (Washington Irving)

Course—Dessert.

Group singing of patriotic songs. The hostess at each home can work out own ideas in decorations and favors.

—Adapted from suggestions by Mrs. J. R. Renken, Kansas City, Mo.

April Fool banquet—

1. *Decorations*—Toy balloons, cut-out clowns, clown dolls, etc.

2. *Menu*—Give the articles on the menu names that are appropriate, but do not disclose their identity. Have delightful surprises in the menu. Be sure that all of them are palatable. It will not be a great deal of fun to furnish cotton biscuits or soap confections. The ladies can think of some interesting and palatable surprises that will please everyone. For instance, beside each plate there could be a cup and saucer with the cup turned down. Naturally everyone will think this is intended for coffee, but instead when they lift the cup they find under it a molded fruit gelatine salad, or something of that sort.

3. *Program*—The chairman should introduce someone as toastmaster. That person should immediately arise and protest that there has been some mistake; that it is true that they had talked with him about it but he had not agreed to serve. He suggests that John Smith is the one who was elected. John Smith gets up and also begs to be excused, saying that there is some misunderstanding. He insists that Arthur Jones was to be toastmaster and so on it goes until they finally do get someone who serves.

Program mix-up—After the toastmaster has been finally corralled he introduces the various items on the program. However, nobody does what the toastmaster announces they are to do. For instance, he announces that Miss Brown will play a violin solo extolling her skill on the violin. Miss Brown gets up and plays a piano solo or some other instrument. Someone is introduced to sing and instead of singing gives a reading, or a poem, or a dramatic skit. Another person is introduced to make a talk on some announced subject but instead of making a talk he sings. Some person who is introduced to sing makes a brief talk, and so on. The toastmaster proceeds with the program as if nothing is amiss. Much will depend upon him.

Ship banquet.—*Decorations*—Borrow some ship models of the "Santa Maria" type. There will probably be several people in your community who have them.

Use cardboard ships on standards for table decorations.

A blue and white crepe paper color scheme would be fitting.

Place-cards decorated with "life-savers."

Talks—Select three or four subjects from the following list: (1) "What's Your Port?" (2) "The Set of the Sails." (3) "The Pilot." (4) "Anchors." (5) "The Light House." (6) "Stowaways." (7) "Mutiny." (8) "Derelicts."

Songs—"Sailing, Sailing," "Santa Lucia," "A Capital Ship," "Nancy Lee," "Song of the Volga Boatman," "My Bonnie," "Sweet and Low," "Anchors Away."

Special music—Bass solo—"Rocked in the Cradle of the Deep." Male Quartet—"My Anchor Holds," "I'll Stand By Until the Morning," "Jesus, Saviour, Pilot Me," "Remember Me, O Mighty One," "The Owl and the Pussy Cat."

Stunts—"Columbus Discovers America" (in *Successful Stunts*, Rohrbough), "The Mayflower" (in *Stunt Night Tonight*, Miller)

Book fair banquet.—*Decorations*—The various tables can be decorated to represent certain types of books.

Fairyland—Gray moss, balloons, wishing well, mirror lake, fairy characters (cut-outs from ten-cent store books). Fairy books or book covers.

Travel—Dolls of various lands. Airplanes, autos, wagons, and other toy means of transportation. Books or book covers on travel, customs of other peoples, missions.

Tales of the sea—Ships, books, book covers.

Romance—Hearts, books, book covers.

Poetry—Books and book covers.

Nature—Animals, flowers, tiny trees. Books, telescope, stars, book covers.

Programs—In shape of book. Decoration on the back appropriate to the particular table, e.g., stars on program at the Star table, hearts at Romance table, poem at Poetry table, etc.

Entertainment features—(1) The Songbook. Everyone sing.

(2) "Cross My Palm." Scene: A Gypsy Camp. Action: Book characters, "Lorna Doone," "Jean Val Jean," "Don Quixote," and others appear and have their futures told by gypsy fortune teller.

(3) Stunts by different tables. Star table trains telescope on various "stars" in the room. This is a clever way to introduce celebrities and leaders. The Fairy table gives a brief dramatization of a fairy story. The Romance table leads the entire group in singing "Love's Old Sweet Song." Someone at the Sea table tells a fish story. The Poetry table produces a rhyme, perhaps about people present.

(4) The Songbook Quartet. Four singers back of a huge book cover made of cardboard.

(5) Book Magic. If you have a magician in your group he can probably do some clever stunts with books.

Talks— (1) Snappy Reviews of books never written. Several people give one-minute reviews of imaginary books. Here are some suggestions: "A Treatise on Making Announcements," by the Assembly Dean; "Emulating the Northwest Mounted," by some girl who has recently married or who is engaged; "Perpetual Motion," by one who exemplifies it. These reviews can be made a lot of fun.

(2) Books I Have Enjoyed—A Symposium. Have several people primed to give sparkling remarks about best books they have recently read, with the idea of encouraging others to read the same books. Limit speakers to one or two minutes.

(3) The Greatest Book—Climax the program with a five- or ten-minute talk on the Bible.

> "Books are keys to wisdom's treasure;
> Books are ships to lands of pleasure;
> Books are paths that upward lead;
> Books are friends. Come! Let us read."

Barnyard banquet.—Here is a clever idea that comes to us from the Hillsborough County (Florida) Methodist Young People's Union. It's a Barnyard Banquet.

The program was mineographed with a cover of checked gingham. This enlightening verse was on the first page:

> Backward, turn backward!
> Oh! Time in your flight
> Back to the time of the
>   gingham tonight;
> Back to the time of the bonnets
>   all gay,
> When red-striped suspenders
>   were the fad of the day.

Under the title of "Vittles" was listed "termater cocktail," "Baked chicken," "dressin'," "string beans," "Sweet pertators," "pickles," "olives," "nervous puddin' and beat cream."

Under "doins" there was the "blessin'," "howdy-do's and meetin' the folks," "spechul quartette," "recitin'," and "barnyard shindig under the directshun Sister Eulalie Ginn." At that time such old favorites as "Brown-eyed Mary," "Jennie Crack Corn," "Pig in the Parlor," and "Old Brass Wagon" were enjoyed by the crowd.

Windows of the world.—At one banquet the theme was "Windows of the World." Excerpts from certain plays were presented, the toastmaster weaving the program together by telling of the program presented by the particular play and something of the events in it leading up to the action presented. This program offers opportunity for effectively presenting certain problems. The portions of the plays used were as follows:

John Withered's Hand, by H. E. Mansfield, published by the Dramatic Publishing Company, page 13, beginning with "Mother, I've been wanting to ask you," and ending with page 15, "the power he generates in struggling to be free." This is a play on the industrial problem, well worth producing.

The Two Gifts, by A. C. Lamb. In volume of *Grinnell Plays,* Dramatic Publishing Company. From page 40, "Dem chillun's singin'" to page 43, "You's bofe gwine be sorry you' fo'sook Gawd, fo' de end!"

Color Blind, by Margaret Applegarth, published by Doran. Tell action, pages 29-31. Close with speech of Artist on page 31. Presents idea of world brotherhood.

The Eleventh Mayor, Frantz. Published by the Board of Education, Church of the Brethren, Elgin, Ill. Use from point where the eleventh mayor has taken charge to end of play. A powerful peace play.

These plays were done without any effort at stage-setting or costuming. The lights were turned off at the end of each episode.

A kid banquet.—All of the guests come dressed as children. The toastmaster is designated as "Chief Kidder."

Decorations—Flowers, toy balloons, toys, dolls, etc.

Speeches— (make selection from this list).

(1) School Days.

(2) Puppy Love, or Sweetheart Days.

(3) Doll Baby Days.

(4) You Can't Slide Down My Cellar Door.

(5) Building Air Castles.

(6) The Old Gang.

Songs—"School Days," "The Barefoot Trail," by Wiggers, "The Farmer's in the Dell," "Johnny Schmoker," "Old McDonald," "That Old Gang of Mine," etc. Place song sheets at each plate.

Readings—"Little Mary's Essay on Husbands," *Phunology.* "The Old Swimmin' Hole," Riley.

Pianologues—"The Boy Who Stuttered and the Girl Who Lisped," "Spring Fever," "I Got a Pain in My Sawdust." These pianologues may be obtained from Walter H. Baker and Company, 178 Tremont Street, Boston, Mass.

Stunts— (1) Balloon blowing contest. Contestants blow balloons until they burst.

(2) Bubble blowing contest.

(3) Spoon dolls. Provide paper spoons for each guest. Also crepe paper, red crayon, pencil, and paste. Each one makes a spoon doll.

A banquet speech contest.—This contest was used at a banquet. The toastmaster eulogized a leading citizen without stating his name and concluded by saying, "You all know the man to whom I refer. We will for a moment be glad to have a few words from him." Two men stand up, glare at each for a moment and each at first politely and later rather heatedly insists that he is the man for whom the introduction is meant. Finally one man says, "I know I am the man intended because I was asked to make this talk and have my speech written out. And I am going to read it." Whereupon he reads his speech while the other man stands and glares at him. At the end of his speech the other man starts reading his speech. The first man in turn stands and glares at him while he reads his nine sentences. Just at the end he objects to the toastmaster regarding the interruption. A little argument follows, after which the toastmaster states that the only plan he can see is for each to read one sentence at a time. The first sentence of the first speech is given, followed by the first sentence of the second speech and so on. The two speakers glare at one another and sit down.

First speech—

1. To be called upon to speak on this occasion gives me great pride.

2. I presume you do not want me to talk long.

3. Therefore, I will keep you but a few moments.

4. After the fine meal you are all probably in a mood for something more entertaining than I can give you.

5. I am at a loss to know as to just what I can say.

6. I know I have done very well on previous occasions.

7. Some people wonder why figuring out my eloquent speeches does not make my head ache.

8. The reason is that my mind runs on and on.

9. My tongue has difficulty in keeping up.

Second speech—

1. Pride goeth before destruction, saith the Bible.

2. It is the truth.

3. There is something about that statement that appeals to me.

4. These few words express my feeling perfectly.

5. It is a pleasure to hear such a plain statement of an easily recognized fact.

6. However, some people are willing to make an emphatic statement to the contrary.

7. There is not a thing in it.

8. It shouldn't go any further; it has done enough damage already.

9. The sooner we can put an abrupt stop to it the better we will be satisfied.

Collegiate banquet (used by a business college) .—*Decorations*—School colors and symbols.   Pennants.

Stunts: The stunts and the entire program would fit into the theme.   Most of them could be introduced as college courses or demonstrations of certain subjects.

Millinery—This would probably be a new course for a college, but it would be a very practical one.   As each person arrives he is given a long strip of crepe paper in the school colors, two pins, and a short piece of twine.   Out of this he must make a hat to be worn during the evening.   This can be done easily by fitting the crepe paper about the head, pinning it together, gathering it together at the top, and tying it with the twine.   Some may care to work out more elaborate designs.

Reading—Arrange some tongue twisters and call on several prominent people to read them rapidly.   There are some good ones in this book.

Dramatics—Some such stunt as "The Saga of Little Nell" ought to go over big for such an occasion.   Or everyone may be asked to do "Paying the Rent" in Chapter XIV, Fun with Dramatics.

Art—At each plate is a paper spoon, a small piece of crepe paper, one or two pins, a black pencil, and a red one. If desired there may be one red pencil for every four or five people. Each person is requested to make a (*name of college*) Flapper.

Spelling—Use "Dumb Spelling" where they have to indicate the vowels by dumb motions—raising the right hand for *A*, the left for *E*, pointing to the eye for *I*, puckering the lips for *O*, and pointing to someone for *U*. Select several prominent people and conduct a spell-down in this fashion. Have a good list of words ready with some of them containing plenty of vowels.

Songs and music—Song sheets at each plate would carry school songs. "School Days" would also be appropriate.
A school orchestra would help, but don't let them play all during the time the group is eating. There ought to be spontaneous outbursts of song. Give the orchestra a definite place on the program, and when it has finished there it is done.

Geography—The group could sing the State song back and forth.

Speeches and toasts—These could be introduced as a demonstration of the "Public Speaking Department." The following suggestions are offered:

Humorous debate—Resolved, "That Men are more vain than Women." One speaker for each side. Limited to two or three minutes each.

Serious debate—Resolved, "That the abolition of the installment plan of buying and selling would eventually prove helpful to our business and economic conditions."

The value of courtesy in business.

"Please copy!" A speech that sets up the characteristics of the ideal stenog.

Divine arithmetic—If you desire a speech of this sort. It would be built on the Scripture, "Add to your patience courage, etc."—2 Peter 1: 5-8.

A musical banquet.—*Decorations*—Black and white color scheme. Crepe paper streamers, bowers, etc. Black candles with white tulle bows. Menu served by candlelight. Large cut-out notes on tables and hanging from overhead.

Programs—Hand made. Black covers, hand printed in white ink. First few bars of "Auld Lang Syne" ("Should old acquaintance be forgot?"). Use some of the following quotations on the program:

> "Music waves eternal wands,
> Enchantress of the souls of mortals."
> —STEDMAN

> "O music, sphere-descended maid,
> Friend of pleasure, wisdom's aid."
> —COLLINS

> "Music so softens and disarms the mind,
> That not an arrow does resistance find."
> —ANON.

> "Let me have music dying, and I seek no more delight."—KEATS

> "There is music in all things, if men had ears."—BYRON

> "Music is well said to be the speech of angels."—CARLYLE

> "Music is the universal language of mankind."—LONGFELLOW

> "The man that hath no music in himself,
> Nor is not moved with concord of sweet sounds,
> Is fit for treasons, stratagems, and spoils."
> —SHAKESPEARE

Stunts—The following stunts would be suitable for a Musical Banquet: (Where only the page number is given it indicates that the stunt is in *Phunology*):

Human Organ (page 311). Upside Down Sing (page 312). Victrola Stunts (page 315). Singing Backward (page 317). Animated Music Sheet (page 325). Sunflower Minstrel (pages 147,

326). Midget Ladies (page 327). The Maid O' the Mandolin (page 185 in *Stunt Night Tonight*). The Song of the Shoes (page 101 in *Successful Stunts*). See Chapter XII, Fun with Music.

Talks—Some suggested themes. Pick the ones that suit your purpose best. Don't try to use all of them. The speeches ought not to be longer than from three to five minutes.

(1) "The Staff of Life" (Key of B natural). Theme—"The Melody of Love." This may well be the climax speech of the evening.

(2) "Harmony." (Teamwork.)

(3) "Rhythm." (Keep step.)

(4) "Discord." (Sour notes.)

(5) "B Natural." (A plea for sincerity.)

(6) "C Sharp." (Be circumspect, alert, observant.)

(7) "Grace Notes." (Tribute to workers.)

(8) "Ties." (Fellowship. The spirit of friendship. Close talk with singing of "Blest Be the Tie That Binds.")

(9) "Melody Makers." (How to bring the song of joy into your own heart and the hearts of others.)

(10) "Scales." (Steady, regular growth. Minor and major scales and their significance.)

Songs—Have song sheets at each plate containing folk songs, stunt songs, greeting songs, rounds, etc.

A jolly tar banquet.—*Decorations*—Each table represents a sailing ship. This effect can be gotten with sheets or white cloth or paper. The sail would decorate the middle of the table.

A few "lifesavers" at each plate.

The speakers' table could be decorated with a miniature ship, which you ought to be able to borrow.

Favors—White sailor hats. (Buy in quantities.) They could be used for autographs.

Talks—"Ship Ahoy!" (Greeting.)

"Barnacles." (Things that hinder.)

"Sail On!" (Achievement no matter what the difficulties. Sail on until the object of our quest is attained.)

Stunts—(1) *"The Jolly Tars."* A male chorus with some sea songs. "Sailing, Sailing," "He Was a Sailor (a Harry Lauder song for solo), "Asleep in the Deep" (a bass solo). There are several good songs that would be suitable in *The Orange Book,* published by C. C. Birchard and Company, 221 Columbus Avenue, Boston, Mass. Here is a list of them: "A Sea Picture" (14), "A Sailing Song" (20), "The Three Sailor Boys" (27), "The Volga Boatman" (38), "The Cat and the Cat Boat" (81), "The Bold Fisherman" (95), "The Cautious Cat" (100).

(2) *"Six sweet sailorettes"*—Six girls dressed in middy costumes singing appropriate songs. "Santa Lucia," "Sweet and Low," and "Sailing" are in the *Rose Book* (arranged for girls' voices).

(3) *"Mayflower memories"—Stunt Night Tonight,* Miller, page 141.

(4) *"Midget ladies,"* in *Phunology,* page 327, could be adapted to "Midget Sailors" idea.

Poems— (1) "The Sea Is Great, Our Boats Are Small" (Van Dyke, in *Quotable Poems*).

(2) "We Break New Seas Today" (Oxenham, in *Quotable Poems*).

(3) "Columbus" (Joaquin Miller, in *It Can Be Done*).

(4) "Roadways" (Masefield, in his *Collected Poems*). Adventure.

Jolly tar banquet No. 2.—Another type of program could be built around the idea of sailing into various interesting ports. For instance, at Honolulu you could have some interesting Hawaiian music. In Japan, some Japanese song or stunt. Selections from "The Mikado" or "Madam Butterfly." Mexico—"La Paloma.' France—Everyone sing "Alouette."

A talk on "Parlez Vous Francais?" The speaker could spring the question, "What language do you speak?" after quoting the oft used statement, "Actions speak louder than words."

Italy—Italian music—"Sole Mio," operatic arias, etc. All could sing "Funiculi, Funicula."

Stops could be made at other ports with some appropriate speech or entertainment feature.

May Day banquet.—*Decorations*—Maypole streamers of crepe-paper—ends of which are held by tiny dolls.

Entertainment—A Maypole dance. Musical games like "All Around the Maypole."

Toasts— (1) Spring is Here.

(2) Sap and Saps.

(3) A Young Man's Fancy.

(4) An Old Maid's Whim.

(5) May Flowers.

(6) Debate—Resolved: "That the use of cosmetics should be abolished."

(7) Spring Fever.

Cowboy banquet.—The program was in the shape of a cowboy boot. An old cowbell was used to warn all the cow-hands to get ready for the "feed." When ready for the banqueteers to enter the diningroom a cowboy "cook" opened the door and yelled:

> "Chuck, chuck, come and get it,
> So we can wash the skillet."

Program

Stampede—Seating group at tables.

Feedin'—Masticating the food.

Foreman—The toastmaster.

The Round-up—Singing cowboy songs.

Cowboy of the range—Each person introduces person to his right giving the Range (town), Herd (state of birth), and Mount he prefers to ride (hobby).

Rangers' quartet—

Stunt riders—Impromptu stunts by individuals or groups. Charades.

Ranger tunes—Everybody sing !

Rodeo—Prepared stunts by special groups. See "Precious Priscilla."

Basketball banquet.—*Decorations*—Crepe-paper streamers in the team colors. Basketballs hanging. A basketball goal or basket at either end of the room made out of crepe paper. An ordinary hoop could serve. Strips of crepe paper in the team colors make the net.

Talks—"Pass the Ball." (A talk on teamwork.)
"Shooting a Goal." (A talk on high ideals—you've got to shoot high to make a goal.)
"Rooting for the Team." (A booster speech.)
"Shoot!" (Do it now. Time for action.)
"Here's to Our Girls." (Long may they wave.)

"And Here's to Our Boys." (May they always be winners in the game of life.)
"The Tip-off."
"The Coach."
"Dribbling." (Getting to your goal.)
"Time Out." (Stunts and entertainment.)

Toastmaster—"The Referee."
"Time Out."

Stunts—Making own crepe-paper caps. Give each one a strip of crepe paper, a piece of string, and a pin. Pin size of head, draw top together in a twist and tie with the string.

Burlesque basketball game—Ten girls dressed up in party frocks, and wearing hats. Use toy balloon for basketball. Tip-off. One girl gets the ball, calls "Time out." Referee blows whistle. She hands him the ball to hold for her, gets out the necessary paraphernalia from her handbag, which she carries with her, and begins to powder her nose. She then takes the ball, the referee's whistle blows, and she tosses it or hands it to a teammate who is standing near the goal. This player takes it with a dignified "thank you" and proceeds to mount a ladder which is placed by the goal. The rest of the players stand by as if unconcerned, powdering their noses or rouging their lips. As soon as the player with the ball gets to where she can reach the basket, she first stops to powder her nose and then nonchalantly drops the ball in the basket. The referee's whistle blows, and the teams gather in two groups and yell for one another in rather dignified and pepless manner.

> Baby in the high chair,
> Who put him there?
> Ma, Pa, Sis, Boom, Ah!
> .... Rah! Rah! Rah!

> Some games we win
> Some games we lose
> But we have a smile we always use.
> .... ! .... !

> Sunflower! Cauliflower! Wallflower! Roses!
> Please give us time to powder our noses!

Song sheets—Have at each plate mimeographed song sheets to stimulate singing.

Balloon burst—Ten or more persons are furnished with large balloons. They stand before the crowd and blow until they burst them, each trying to be first to burst his balloon. It adds to interest if faces are painted on the balloons.

Football banquet.—*Decorations*—School colors. Big yellow cardboard football hung on speakers' table. Miniature football field on speaker's table as centerpiece. Goal posts and players made out of peanuts.

Stunts—

(1) Girls' Football Game. A burlesque. The girls stop at unexpected moments to powder noses, use lipstick, arrange hair, etc.

(2) Songs and yells.

Talks—

(1) "The Kick-off." The idea of getting set for the game of life.

(2) "Blocking and Tackling." Tackling the problems of life. Hitting them hard.

(3) "Kicking." Speaker could show how "kicking" in life is not as valuable as in football game.

(4) "Good Sports." Speech on good sportsmanship. A good loser and magnanimous winner.
"When the last great Scorer comes
to write against your name,
He will not write that you lost or won.
But how you played the game."

(5) "Touchdown." The goal of life. Value of some aim or purpose in life.

(6) "The Daily Grind." Daily practice. Scrimmage. Preparation for the game of life.
There could also be brief speeches on "Teamwork," "Rooting," "Keeping Fit," "The Coach."

One speaker, using as his subject, "Football and the Game of Life," built his talk around the idea of tackling and interference. In the game of life, as in the game of football, there are opponents who try to throw you for a loss. He enumerated these—bad habits, evil companions, etc. But there are teammates blocking for you and clearing the way. And then he listed some such teammates—ambition, hard work, honesty, etc.

Circus banquet.—*Spielers*. When you are ready for the crowd to enter the banquet hall spielers should begin shouting, "Right this way folks! The greatest show on earth," etc., etc., etc.

Toastmaster—"The Ringmaster."

Decorations—It would be fine if you could have the entrance to the dining room made to represent the entrance to a circus tent. Some brown crepe paper, or a large piece of canvas would do the job.

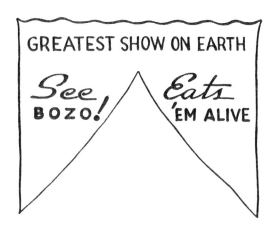

A profusion of toy balloons ought to be used in the decorations. They can be bought in quantities rather cheaply. Maybe you'll find some novelty house that will sell them to you at wholesale prices. See "Favors."

The corners of the room could be decorated to represent sideshow entrances. As banqueteers enter the dining room spielers can be shouting the merits of their shows. You need not have performers for these side shows unless desired. The spielers and entrances are simply for atmosphere. (See illustration.)

Tiny show tents could be improvised for table decoration, one to each table. These could be easily made.

Talks— (It is possible to eliminate speeches entirely from this program.)

"The animal trainer"—A toast to the dean, or principal, or teacher, or manager. This speaker could do some clever classifying of persons. The bears (grumblers), the elephants (slow), the monkeys (trouble makers), the donkeys (recalcitrants), the love birds (the sentimental), etc.

"The bandmaster"—Getting harmony.

"Hey Rube." This is the famous circus call for help. At the sound of it all circus hands rally. The speaker could point out some objectives and sound the call for a rallying to the task.

"Side shows." The speaker might mention a few of the things that divert from the main business in hand.

"The main tent." This ought to be your climax speech of the evening. It is a sort of "Seek ye first" talk. What is the main purpose in life? Don't miss the real show.

Note: If this happens to be too many talks for the time you have, you might eliminate the one or ones you feel least important.

Favors—Animal crackers. Clown hats, paper hats and balloons can be ordered of Rubenstein's, 180 Park Row, New York City, or The Slack Manufacturing Co., 124 West Lake Street, Chicago, Illinois.

Stunts and entertainment—Each table should be labeled with the name of some animal. Groups should be encouraged to give impromptu and spontaneous yells, stunts, and songs appropriate to the group name. The "Cats" could sing "What a long, long tail our cat's got," or "Pussy Willow," for instance. The "Dogs" could respond with "O Where, O Where Has My Little Dog Gone," or "I Know a Little Puppy." The "Donkeys" could sing "Hee Haw, Hee Haw, Has Anybody Seen Our Mule?" or "Sweetly Sings the Donkey." You might have some suggestions on hand to slip to someone at each table.

Circus parade—A circus band, some circus performers, etc., could put on a thrilling parade, either out in the hall before the crowd goes into the banquet room, or while the crowd is seated at the tables.

Trapeze performance—Vocal music. The ringmaster should explain that they jump from note to note. It ought to be possible to get some songs that are particularly appropriate to the circus, though that won't be absolutely necessary. "Laugh, Clown, Laugh" would be one song that might be used. "Vesti la giubla" (on with the play) from "Pagliacci" would make a suitable number.

Circus stunts—Some circus stunts might be performed. "See "Great Grinmore Circus" and "Clown Party" in this book. See "The Great Jamboree," "Circus Party," "High Class Vaudeville," pages 307-309 (*Phunology*), "Freak Exhibit," pages 321, 322, 333 (*Phunology*).

Rose banquet.—

> The rose that lives its little hour
> Is prized beyond the sculptured flower.
> —BRYANT

Decorations—Rose bowers at each table. Festooning of roses. Rose trees at corners of room. Rambler festooned over doorway.

Stunts—1. *Rose Bud Minstrel.* (Not blackface.) A five- or ten-minute performance built after the fashion of the "Sunflower Mintrel" in *Phunology*, pages 147 and 326.

Equipment—A sheet or large piece of unbleached muslin. Holes at height suited to size of participants.
The sides to be bordered in real roses.

Program.—A girl suitably garbed appears with sprinkling can and seems to be watering the roses. She may sing, as she does it, some such song as the chorus to "Moonlight and Roses" or any other "rose" song.

Chorus.

Joke.

Solo—"Roses of Picardy."

Joke.

Solo—"Roses Bring Memories of You."

2. *"Grandmother's rose jar"*—a gigantic beaverboard jar from behind which came girls dressed as roses to sing or dance.

A suitable song would be "The Violet and the Rose," by Meyer-Helmond-Page, a three-part song for treble voices, published by C. C. Birchard.

3. *Suprise buds*—This should be the first stunt. As soon as the program gets started someone interrupts with something like this:

> "Mr. Toastmaster, stop this show!
> We've got something you ought to know,
> Just watch this wand and see the fun,
> Good fairies come out one by one."

She waves her wand over one of three giant rosebuds on a table at the back. Out of this rosebud steps a girl who approaches some person previously selected, and says,

> "Where's ————? I want to know,
> Roses in the garden where I grow
> Say he's a mighty good scout to have about
> So now as I pin this rose on him
> I wish him luck full to the brim."

And so for each of the buds. Thus is honor done to certain ones at the banquet.

The buds are large enough to permit a girl to hide in each of them.

> "Lovely flowers are the smile of God's goodness."
> —WILBERFORCE

Talks—1. *Tea Roses*—This speaker could play up words beginning with the letter *T*—tact, teachableness, trustworthiness, talk, training.

2. *Garden hints*—A good chance to speak on growing—rules for growth in our personal lives.

3. *"It Never Rains Roses."*—Built on George Eliot's "It never rains roses: when we want more roses, we must plant more trees." Cause and effect. Plans and work makes results.

4. *"Moonlight and Roses"*—Romance. Well, what do you know?

5. *Buds*—Budding talents. Budding poets, etc.

6. *Thorns and roses*—

> "There is a thorn on every rose,
> But ain't the roses sweet?"

The speaker may mention some thorns and then sound note of optimism.

7. *"The Rose of Sharon."*

8. *Ramblers*—The importance of being on the move. Growing.

9. *American Beauties*—Some of the good things in America for which we should be thankful.

Select such of these speeches as seem best suited to your group. Don't try to use all of them.

Song sheets—"Rose" songs—"Moonlight and Roses," "Rose of Killarney," "When You Wore a Tulip and I Wore a Big Red Rose," etc.

Campfire banquet.—*Decorations*—Outdoor decorations. Campfire. Tepee. Miniature campfire and tepee on speakers' table.

Entertainment—Songs for everyone—"Okoboji Tribal Song" (*Parodology*), "Home On the Range" (*The Cowboy Sings*), "My Little Mohee" (*Keep On Singing*), "Sourwood Mountain" (*Songs Easily Learned and Long Remembered*), "Down in the Valley" (*The Cowboy Sings, Handy II*), "Long, Long Trail."

Special music—"Indian Love Call," "By the Waters of Minnetonka," "Pale Moon."

Possible stunts—"Pokyhuntus" (*Handy*), "An Indian Massacre" (*Stunt Night Tonight*, page 179—shadow pantomime), "Wild Nell of the Plains."

Campfire meditations—1. "The Story Teller of the Tribe"—"How the Sun, Moon, and Stars Got into the Sky." See Chapter XVIII, Fun with Children.

2. *The law of the Council*—The Indian Council Ring was a solemn occasion. Here the law of the tribe was invoked. This offers opportunity to get over to the group the seriousness of the business at hand. The Law of the Council is threefold:

(*a*) The Law of Regard for the Other Fellow's Right and Comfort.

(*b*) The Law of Participation.

(*c*) The Law of Carry-Over. This law has to do with what happens after the camper gets back home.

3. *"Follow the trail"*—What marks the trail?

(*a*) Infinite worth of human personality.

(*b*) Love.

(*c*) Sacrifice.

Or the campers may be made acquainted with camp traditions.

4. *Omaha tribal prayer*—(*Birch Bark Roll*).

Taps.

Athletic banquet.—*Decorations*—Tennis rackets, bats, footballs, basketballs, etc.

Talks—1. *"Keeping Fit."* The necessity for keeping physically, mentally, and spiritually fit for the game of life. (Five minutes.)

2. *"The Spirit of the Team"*—A tribute to the team or teams. Stress the necessity for co-operation. Regard for others. If in a camp or school show how this regard will make one careful of other people's comforts, rights, personalities, best interests. Co-operation in activities. Co-operation in big projects. (Five minutes.)

3. *Life's goal*—Life is like a race. Note Philippians 3: 13, 14. The necessity for a goal in life.

Stress the goals of the organization and inspire the group with enthusiasm for their attainment. (Ten minutes.)

Entertainment—The song, "Take Me Out to the Ball Game," would be appropriate.

"Hits and Runs"—The musical program could be built around this title. Use "hits" of the ages like "Berceuse," "Liebestraum," "Ave Maria," "Souvenir," "Moonlight Sonata," for instrumental numbers. Vocal "hits" might include "Ah, Sweet Mystery of Life," "Sylvia," "When You and I Were Young, Maggie," "Love's Old Sweet Song," and some of the lovely folk songs available.

Readings from which to select—"A Football Fan," L. A. Alexander. Eleven minutes. A girl attends a football game.

"A Football Romance," L. A. Alexander. Eight minutes. Listening in at the radio.

"Freshie's Big Game," C. L. Seeman. Ten minutes. A college freshman attends the game and has some exciting moments.

"Gladys Goes in for Baseball," L. S. Alexander. Eight minutes.

"Her First Football Game," M. Baron. Nine minutes. Lisping girl.

"Ma at the Basketball Game," L. H. Black. Eleven minutes.

"Mr. Dooley on Football," F. P. Dunne. Seven minutes. Irish dialect.

All of the above readings are available from Wetmore Declamation Bureau, 1631 South Paxton Street, Sioux City, Iowa.

Stunts—Some such stunt as "Sissy Basketball," where the players call time to use their compacts, lipsticks, etc.

Birthday banquet.—*Decorations*—Tables to represent months.

January—White. Father Time. White bell. Snow, etc.

February—Heart decorations.

March—Green.

April—Umbrella decorations, and crepe paper.

May—Maypole.

June—Wedding bells. Bride and groom. Roses.

July—Patriotic.

August—Tennis rackets, bathing beach, celluloid bathing beauties.

September—School, school dolls.

October—Halloween.

November—Football, turkey, autumn leaves.

December—Red and green. Christmas decorations.

Stunts—1. Months presented in dramatic stunts.

   2. Feature number for each month:

   January— Everyone sing "Jingle Bells."

   February— "Let Me Call You Sweetheart," by everybody.

        Some love song in solo.

   March— Some Irish jokes—"Wearing of the Green."

   April— "I'm Always Chasing Rainbows," by all.

        April Fool stunt.

   May— Violin song. "Welcome, Sweet Springtime."

        Solo—"Howdy Do, Miss Springtime," Guion (Wetmark).

   June— Short humorous debate: "Resolved, That Married Men Live Longer Than Single Men." (Speeches, one minute each.)

        Solo—"O Promise Me" or "At Dawning."

July—　　July table suddenly produces sparklers and lights them as all lights are turned out.

August—　All sing "In the Good Old Summertime."

September—Everyone sings "School Days." Short spelling bee.

October—　A short ghost story with lights low. Candles burning.

November—"Sweetheart of Sigma Chi," by all. "Sissy Football" stunt.

December—Santa Claus arrives and gives gifts to certain members. Ten-cent store purchases. Humorous. A "horn" to someone so he can "toot" his own. A toy gun to the dean so he can shoot down offenders, etc. Sing "Silent Night."

Talks—1. *"Ruby Rhymes."* Some clever rhymester could work out some appropriate rhymes in honor of leaders and members of the faculty. For instance:

> You could search from Maine to Kentucky,
> And farther, but you sure would be lucky,
> If a president you found,
> In all of that round,
> Who compared with our Nellie Buckey.

2. *"Bigger and Better Birthdays"*—A plea for a growing life for the individual and a growing program for the organization.

3. *"What Is Your Age?"*—

Is it—the bang age?
　　　the slang age?
　　　the gang age?
Is it—the go age?
　　　the show age?
　　　the beau age?
Is it—the true age?
　　　the do age?

Or this speech could be made out of words ending in "age," such as "scrimmage." ("Are you having a hard struggle?")

Season banquet.— (A co-operative affair.) *Purpose*—(1) To develop a spirit of good fellowship. (2) To promote interest and enthusiasm. (3) To present several definite challenging projects.

Program committee—Three young people from each of the participating organizations. This committee shall decide what further committees, if any, are needed. It shall elect its own chairman.

Decorations—The four corners of the room should be decorated to represent the four seasons of the year. Japanese lanterns, flowers, and pink streamers for *summer;* snow, icicles, tiny igloos, snow-covered evergreens for *winter;* flowers, green and white streamers for *spring;* Halloween decorations, black and orange streamers, colored leaves for *autumn.*

Program—Talks. 1. *"In the Good Old Summertime."* This speaker could make the following points, among others:

(*a*) Youth is the summertime of life. Implications.

(*b*) Let us "warm up" in our friendships.

"Who loves not more the night of June than cold December's gloomy moon?"
—SIR WALTER SCOTT

2. *"Winter Tales"*—

"Take winter as you find him and he turns out to be a thoroughly honest fellow with no nonsense in him, and tolerating none in you, which is great comfort in the long run." —LOWELL

"O wind, if winter comes, can spring be far behind."
—SHELLEY

This speaker could build his talk around the idea of overcoming difficulties.

3. *"Autumn Leaves"*—"The year's last loveliest smile" is the way Bryant describes autumn.

This could be a speech on "Putting color into life." The idea of adventures in living. Living the full life.

4. *"Spring Fancies"*—

"In the spring a young man's fancy turns lightly to the thoughts of love."
—TENNYSON

(*a*) Boy and girl friendships.
(*b*) Objectives.

5. *"Ring Out the Old"*—Outworn practices and ideas.

6. *"Ring Out the False"*—False notions about young people. False notions about our organizations.

Stunts—Gypsy camp—The musical program, readings, and "prophecies" could be worked out around the gipsy camp idea. See Chapter XII, Fun with Music.

Seasonal dramatics—Require the people in each section of the dining room to present a brief stunt representing the particular season. For instance, *Autumn* could be watching a football game. Yells, Tense moments. Or eleven of their number could line up and run through signals. *Winter* could turn up coat collars, shiver, skate, throw snowballs, sing "Jingle Bells." *Spring* could look up to see if rain is falling, play baseball in pantomime, hum Mendelssohn's "Spring Song." *Summer* could fan, swim, sing "In the Good Old Summertime."

Music—One group in its "Seasonal Dinner" used the following musical numbers:

Spring—"Spring Song" (Mendelssohn), "To a Wild Rose" (MacDowell), "Rustle of Spring" (Sinding).

Summer—"Take Me Out to the Ball Game," "In the Good Old Summertime," "Trees" (Rasbach), "Summer Is a-comin' In" (*Set I, Folk Songs and Ballads*, E. C. Schirmer, or *Songtime*, Paull-Pioneer Music Corporation).

Autumn—"Indian Love Call" (Friml), "Shine On Harvest Moon," "Brown October Ale" (De Koven).

Winter—"Auld Lang Syne," "Jingle Bells," "Silent Night," "O Holy Night."

Mother Goose banquet.—*Decorations*—Cut out Mother Goose characters. Mount them. Use them as table decorations. Inexpensive pictures may be found at the ten-cent store.

Mary, Mary, Quite Contrary

Mother Goose

Denison Crepe Paper Company prints some Mother Goose crepe paper. Use for table, for borders, or for panels.

Costumes—Guests may be asked to come representing Mother Goose characters. The toastmaster and waitresses may be costumed. It would be appropriate for Mother Goose to be toastmistress.

Program— (1) *"Old Mother Hubbard"*—In this speech the needs of the organization could be presented, for "when she got there the cupboard was bare."

(2) *"Little Jack Horner"*—Here should be presented the ideas of selfishness and self-satisfaction with a view to putting them on the grill.

> *Little Jack Horner sat in the corner*
> *Eating his Christmas pie;*
> He was unsocial. He was selfish.

> *He stuck in his thumb and pulled out a plum,*
> *And said, "What a great boy am I!"*
> He was uncouth. He was egotistical and self-satisfied.

(3) *"Hey-Diddle-Diddle"*—Attempting big things. Doing the impossible.

"The cow jumped over the moon." *Some* jump. But there are people and organizations that ought to be attempting some moon-jumping instead of running around in circles and stumbling over straws or allowing their way to be blocked by ten-inch barriers.

Use these suggestions merely as starting points.

Other themes that could be developed, should you need others, are as follows:

(4) *"Jack Spratt"*—Teamwork.

(5) *"Jack and Jill"*—Influence. Would Jill have fallen if Jack had kept his feet?

(6) *"Old King Cole"*—True happiness.

(7) *"The Old Woman in the Shoe"*—Building the membership.

(8) *"Humpty Dumpty"*—Falling down and getting up.

(9) Then there are "Tom, Tom, the Piper's Son," "Mary, Mary, Quite Contrary," "Little Miss Muffett," etc.

"Peter, Peter, Pumpkin Eater." "Mary Had a Little Lamb."

Have song sheets at the plates to stimulate singing. "Throw **It** Out the Window" would be appropriate, since it uses the nursery rhymes as a basis.

Little Boy Blue

Little Bopeep

Stunts—Work up some good Mother Goose stunts. Or various groups could present in dramatic action some Mother Goose rhyme, and the rest of the crowd could be required to guess the rhyme represented.

In one group they dramatized "Peter, Peter, Pumpkin Eater." Act I gave Peter's version of why he couldn't keep his wife. He returned home from work, tired and hungry. No one was home. He took off his coat and hat, seated himself in a chair, and started to read the newspaper, after looking about for the wife and calling for her. Finally, in she came. She had been to a club meeting. She was rushing away in a few minutes to meet with a committee of club women. Would he mind running out to get a snack to eat at the lunch wagon? And out she flounces.

Act II gave her version. The scene was the breakfast room. She was busy getting things ready for breakfast. The husband comes in, seats himself, and opens the morning paper. He scarcely says anything except to sharply comment on the burnt toast and the egg that's fried too hard. Directly he looks at his watch and then gets up from the table in a hurry. He grabs his hat and starts for the door. Mrs. Peter calls to him as he reaches the door. "Dear, didn't you forget something?" He fumbles in his pockets, looks puzzled, and then says, "What?" "Our goodbye kiss," replies Mrs. Peter. "Those days are gone forever," shouts Mr. Peter as he leaves.

Music—See the "Mother Goose Party" for suggestions for entertainment, especially for special musical numbers.

Menu—The menu should use Mother Goose names for each article. For instance, "Chicken a la King Cole," "Jill," pickles, "Humpty Dumpty" salad, "Jack and Jill" rolls, etc.

Aviation banquet.—*Decorations*—Red, white, and blue (the air mail colors). Toy balloons and toy airplanes.

Talks—(1) *Excuse our star dust.* A breezy retelling of achievements, with, perhaps, a prophecy for the future.

(2) *Fly high*—An exhortation to high thinking and ambitious effort.

(3) *Dead engines tell the tale*—Soul power makes achievement possible. The inner man. Dead engine means disaster. So with the group or individual unless there be inner power.

(4) *"Non-stop Flight"*—If a fourth talk is wanted this topic might be used, with the idea of putting before the group some enterprise or project that you want done.

Entertainment—*The take-off.* Some clever mimic could take off certain well known people. Or work out a dramatic skit in which there are take-offs of certain dignitaries, *a la* The Gridiron Club.

Solo flight—Special music.

You could vary from the program suggested by landing at various interesting points. For instance, you might make a landing in Hawaii and while there you could have some Hawaiian music. Then you could come down in Japan, and some Japanese song or stunt or reading could be given—something from "The Mikado" or "Madame Butterfly," maybe. Stops might be made in Mexico with some music like "Estrellita" or "La Paloma." Ireland, sing Irish songs and have a greeting, "Good Avenin'."

All your musical stunts and speeches could be introduced in this way. Negro spirituals, Italian arias, German songs, Russian music ("Volga Boatman"), and most any idea you want to expound in your speeches could be made to get into this theme.

Mother and daughter banquet.—

It may rain, it may hail,
But our MOTHERS never fail.
It may snow, it may sleet,
But our DAUGHTERS can't be
beat.

Program—Toastmistress.
Invocation.
A Tribute to Our Mothers.
A Response from the Mothers.
Solo—"Mother O' Mine."   (Kipling-Tours.)
The Girls of Yesterday.
The Girls of Today.
Debate:
Resolved, "That the Use of Cosmetics Should be Abolished,"
Affirmative.
Negative.
Beauty Secrets.

Songs—

Tune: "How Do You Do?"

How do you do, Mother dear, how do you do?
Is there anything that we can do for you?
We'll do the best we can, stand by you like a man,
How do you do, Mother dear, how do you do?

Tune: "Shine Song."

Mothers will shine tonight, mothers will shine,
Mothers will shine tonight, all down the line.
Mothers will shine tonight, they're mighty fine.
When the sun goes down and the moon comes up,
Mothers will shine.

Tune: "That's How I Need You."

Like the roses need their fragrance,
Like a milk-maid needs a pail,
Like a doctor needs his patients,
Like a hammer needs a nail:
Like the corn beek needs the cabbage,
Like the oyster needs the stew,
Like the flowers need the sunshine,
Mothers, so do we need you.

Tune: "Sweet Adeline"

Sweet Mother Mine, dear Mother Mine,
At night, dear heart, for you I pine.
In all my dreams, your fair face beams—
You're the flower of my heart,
Sweet Mother Mine.

"Blest Be the Tie That Binds."

Blest be the tie that binds,
Our hearts in friendly love,
The fellowship of kindred years
Is like to that above.

The Toastmaster's Introductions—

Every rose has its thorn,
There's fuzz on all the peaches.
There never was a banquet yet
Without some lengthy speeches.

The first speaker on our program
Will make some very true remarks.
So let me introduce to you
Our friend, Miss Billy Sparks.
    (A Tribute to Our Mothers)

And now to every tribute paid,
Some response is usually made.
For that there is no better one
Than our own Mrs. Overton.
    (A Response from the Mothers)

Music hath its charms, we're told
To fascinate the throng,
So we're having Helen O'Callaghan
To sing for you a song.
 (Solo)

The girls of yesteryear were great,
As girls have always been.
Maybe Mrs. McCord can tell
Just how *they* fooled the men.
 (Girls of Yesterday)

The girls of today are sure O.K.
Both homely maid and belle
Just what they say, how they get that way,
Well, listen to Mary Bagwell.
 (Girls of Today)

And now we come to a debate,
The question's clear and quaint,
A maiden sighs, a maiden cries
Shall she hang a sign, "Wet Paint"?
Shall lipstick be debarred?
There are some say "yes," and some say "no,"
It's puzzled sage and bard.

The affirmative gets its chance
When Mrs. Currin speaks.
She's plumb against the dreadful sin
Of powdering shining beaks.
So let Mrs. Currin now rise and make her bow.
 (Mrs. Currin—Affirmative)

Her daughter holds the negative
She defends the right to paint.
It makes the women happier
To look like what they ain't.
So Bibber Currin now speaks
On "Ruby lips and Rosy cheeks."
 (Julia Elizabeth Currin—Negative)

More music of the kind that wins
Hear Mrs. Overton and Mrs. Binns.
 (Duet)

Shh-h-h girls! Secrets! Beauty secrets!
Miss Perkinson will tell us now.
Just what they are and where they are,
And then she will tell us how.
 (Miss Perkinson—"Beauty Secrets")

Let's smile tonight as we all say "adieu"
It's been a happy time for me, for you.
To the vision we'll be true,
All our skies will be more blue.
Mother, daughter, teacher, friend,
Pledge tonight a love that knows no end.
We pledge our heart, we pledge our hand,
Till we meet again.

Phaith, Phun, and Phood Pheast.—The newspaper reports on this one said that it "proved to be a phunney phrolic and phurnished plenty of phasionable pheatures phor pleasure-loving pholks." Page Pop-eye's "Oldtopia"!

Menu—Pesky phruit (grapefruit), Pullet (chicken), Pounded potatoes (you guess!), Petite peas (you know!), Powder puffs (hot rolls), Putty paste (butter), Paradise phood (fruit salad), Palatable progeny (celery), Polar pudding (ice cream), Perfect peace (Angel Food cake), Patent pills (olives), Phinale philtration (coffee).

Program—Presiding Power, the toastmaster.

Talks—1. *"Pears"*—This speaker took a journey with Mr. Webster through a pear orchard. They saw many kinds of pairs. There was "Impair," the twin pear trees "Repair and Compare," and "Prepare."

2. *"Pals"*—Personality, amiability, love, and sincerity.

3. *Pep*—The necessity for enthusiasm.

4. *Pests*—There are plenty of them. The road-hog pest. The loud radio pest. You go on and name your own!

5. *Proposals*—Well, why not! Perhaps some projects could be proposed here.

Entertainment—There was a "Psolo" and some "Phoolishness."

The officers were listed as follows: President, Possible Presider, Pencil Pusher and Pen Punisher, Power Promoter, Philanthropist, Play Planner, Pagan Partner, Penny Picker, Paper Pedler, and Pal Phurnisher (the organization was furnishing big brothers and sisters for children in an institution).

Magic banquet.—

Menu—Roast Turkey and Dressing, Cranberry Sauce, Creamed Sweet Potatoes, Peas, Pineapple and Cheese Salad, Hot Rolls, Ice Cream, Cake, Coffee.

You will not need to be a magician to make the food disappear.

The Magic Mirror makes not nor unmakes,
Charms none to sleep nor any from sleep wakes;
It only giveth back the thing it takes.   —H. M. ALDEN

Just a trifling handful, O Philosopher!
Of magic matter; give it a slight toss over
The ambient ether—and I don't see why
You shouldn't make a sky.
                    —MORTIMER COLLINS in *Sky Making*

This banquet program will be valuable particularly where you have a person for toastmaster who knows something about magic. However, it is not necessary for the toastmaster to be skilled in legerdemain. Tricks of magic would be appropriate for the program.

Program—Toastmaster and Chief Magician.

```
???????????????????????
??                     ??
??    SINCE THIS IS     ??
??   A MAGIC BANQUET    ??
??        THE           ??
??  TOASTMASTER WILL    ??
??  PULL THE PROGRAM    ??
??   OUT OF THE HAT     ??
??                     ??
???????????????????????
```

The toastmaster may pull the program out of a hat or look into a crystal ball. Thus group singing, special music, and stunts may be introduced.

Address and discussion—"If I Had a Magic Wand."

The Old Singing School banquet.—This was a banquet without any speech of any kind. There were two stories and the rest of the time was spent in singing by the entire group. Songs from the North, South, East, and West featured "The Far Northland," "Old Black Joe," "Boys Can Whistle," "Home on the Range," "When

the Curtains of Night," and "Old Woman." "Songs Around the World," featured folk songs of other lands, such as "The Rada Song," "Alouette," "Came a-Riding," and "The Silver Moon." "Rounds and Spirituals" used were "O How Lovely Is the Evening," "Trampin'," "O Lord, I Want Two Wings," and "Stand the Storm." The banquet closed with the singing of "Taps." The program follows:

Program and personnel—

County Music Chairman.
Pianist.
Singing Teacher.
Songs from the North, South, East, and West.
A Paul Bunyan Story.
Songs Round the World.
A John Fox, Jr., Story.
Rounds and Spirituals.

A problem supper.—The Gleaners' Class had grown accustomed to expecting the unexpected. So when the announcement was made that the annual banquet would be a Problem affair they were ready for it.

The five tables were arranged to form a plus sign. Minus signs, multiplication signs, and division signs were made of nuts and candy and formed into "centerpieces."

The menu was in the form of "problems," the ingredients of each item being stated in arithmetic form. Hamburger plus eggs plus crumbs equaled veal loaf. Potatoes, minus jackets, divided by the food chopper, plus milk, plus flour, plus seasoning equaled creamed potatoes. Sugar, plus eggs, plus flour, plus milk, multiplied by baking powder was cake and cream, plus sugar, multiplied by ice, plus salt equaled ice cream.

The climax of the evening came in the toasts. The first one, "The Unknown Quantity," was rather frankly patterned after Van Dyke's book.

The second toast, "Equations," started with the axiom that things which are equal to the same thing are equal to each other. Three members, who were all lightweights, were declared equal to two of the heavy members, which they really were—in weight. From this absurd introduction the speaker shifted to the more serious strain of such equations as "Effort plus Faith, equals Results"; "Boosting plus Brains, equals Efficiency"; "Our Class plus our Leader, equals success."

The toast "Factors" recalled the old arithmetic puzzle in which the answer is reached by crossing out figures. "Not so with the Gleaners. They'll never cross you out." This was the point made here. Cancellation was shown to be a way of eliminating the wrong factors of class work, which are wiped out by the right ones.

The toast on "Improper Fractions" departed entirely from any literal interpretation. It was shown that any fraction is improper in class work. There is no place here for the half-studied lesson or the half-hearted member. Completeness as a class goal was emphasized—complete organization, complete service, and complete harmony.

The last toast was "The Unsolved Problem." The speaker mentioned examples of various unsolved problems discussed in class each Sunday. "There is a fascination in the unsolved problem," he stated in closing, "and the beauty of our lesson discussion is not that it ends our thinking, but that it starts constructive thought."

Rube's Rural Re-union banquet.—

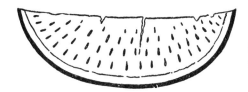

The program was printed and clipped inside a watermelon cover.

The "Food" consisted of baked ham, turnip greens, boiled eggs, potato salad, corn, sliced tomatoes, corn bread, apple pie, and coffee.
The program listed the following:
The Bullfrog Sextette
Kitten on the Keys .... Carter McClelland
Banjo Picker .... Dr. Bob Hayes
"Milk Test" .... Contest
"Cleaning the Ears" .... Contest
Home Grown Mocking Bird .... Richard Watkins

Communities

Slocum Gap ....Squire "Beet" Miller
(1) "Make Hay While the Sun Shines" .."Hayseed" Gwinner
(2) "Poultry and Produce" ....Mrs. "Egg-plant" Ragan
Bald Knob ....Squire "Onion" Claridge
(1) "Nubbins or Full Ear" ...."Roasnear" North
(2) "Sweetmilk, cream, buttermilk, butter"
"Dominecker" Dominic

Pomona Junction ....Squire "Pumpkin" Cummings
(1) "Pigs is Pigs" ...."Hambone" Will
(2) "Plowin' " .... "Beck" Russell
What Will the Harvest Be? ....Parson Stoves.

For this banquet there was no toastmaster. The various squires presided very informally from time to time. When it came his turn on the program the "squire" would get up and introduce his feature by saying, "In our community we have an expert on hay-making." Then he would introduce a speaker "to say a few words."

Heart banquet, No. 1.—

Program—
Invocation.
Toastmaster.
Vocal Solo ...."My Heart at Thy Sweet Voice."
Piano Duet ....Medley of Heart Songs.
    ("Then You'll Remember Me," "Just a Song at Twilight,"
    "Let Me Call You Sweetheart," etc.)
A Leap Year Episode .... (A dramatic skit.)
Duet ...."Will You Remember?"
Make Hay While the Sun Shines.
Debate: "Resolved, That two can live as cheap as one."
You Can't Stop Cupid.
What Is in Your Heart?

HEART BANQUET
February 12

TO WIN YOUR HEART
King of Hearts   Heart Hash
Heart Strings   Heart Beats
Broken Hearts   Light Hearts
Frozen Hearts   Sweet Hearts
    Hearts Ease

The program and menu were printed on red and white cardboard hearts. The decorations were the usual Valentine decorations.

Heart banquet, No. 2.—This banquet was held on February 22, Washington's Birthday. That explains the significance of the last toast, "America's Heart."

Program—

A Hearty Welcome.
A Heartfelt Response.
Toast to the Heart Breakers.
Response to the Heart Broken.
Solo.
Debate: "Resolved, That a Woman's Love is Stronger than a Man's."
Love Letters and Reflections.
To Our Heart of Hearts.
In My Heart.
America's Heart.

Kartoon karacters kookery and komics.—This was a funny page banquet. "Rosie's Beau" was a speech on boy and girl relationships. "Off the Record" was a report on condition of the organization. "Hambone's Meditations" dealt with one or two of the philosophic utterances of that character, such as "You never catches up with folks that you runs after" and "Some preachers runs out fo' dey runs down." "The Thimble Theater" presented a brief dramatic skit. "Bringing Up Father" was advice to fathers from a daughter (song). "The Lone Ranger" was a response from Dad, himself. "Kartoon Karacters' Blow-out" was a balloon blowing contest.

Program

Rosie's Beau.

Off the Record.

Quartet.

Hambone's Meditations.

The Thimble Theater.

Bringing Up Father.

Cartoonist.

Solo.

The Lone Ranger.

Kartoon Karacters' Blow-out.

Solo.

Characters that Stand the Test.

A garden banquet.—*Decorations*—Flowers, palms. Make a crepe-paper lattice around the walls of the room. Twine artificial or real roses about this lattice. If real lattice is obtainable so much the better. Flower mound at center of speakers' table or miniature rock garden. Japanese lanterns.

Entertainment—

(1) Sunflower Minstrels, ten or fifteen minutes. Pages 147, 326 in *Phunology*.

(2) Reading (Pianologue) in costume. *An Old-Fashioned Garden,* Music Publishers Holding Corp.

(3) See Chapter IX, Fun with Mental Games, for games.

(4) Music from which to select:

Vocal Solos from Which to Choose

"Ah Moon of My Delight," from *In a Persian Garden,* Lehmann.
"The Last Rose of Summer," Moore.
"Thank God for a Garden," Del Riego.
"I Look into Your Garden," Wood and Wilmot.
"Rose in the Bud," Massey.
"In Her Kitchen Garden," Russian Folk Song, in *Keep On Singing.*

Instrumental

"Country Garden," Granger (piano).
"Do You Know My Garden?" Haydb-Wood (violin).
"Love's Garden of Roses," Wood (violin).

"In a Chinese Temple Garden," Ketelbey (orchestra or piano).
"In a Monastery Garden," Ketelbey (orchestra or piano).
"Waltz of the Flowers," Tschaikowsky.
"Narcissus," Elthelbert Nevin (piano).

Songs for Everyone to Sing
"Bendemeer's Stream," in *Keep On Singing.*
"My Wild Irish Rose."
"In the Time of Roses," in *The Brown Book.*
"Thy Word Is Like a Garden."

Suggested Talks from Which to Choose
1. *"The Glory of the Garden"*—A speech built around Kipling's famous poem by that title.
2. *"Weeds"*—

> "I would go back and we would arm our hands,
> And strike at every ugly weed that stands
> In God's wide garden of the world."
> —EDWARD ROWLAND SILLS

The speaker should point out "weeds" in the present social order—injustice, race prejudice, etc.
3. *"How Does Your Garden Grow?"*—

> "Mary, Mary quite contrary,
> How does your garden grow?"

How about personal growth?—attitudes? interests? sense of values? prejudices? Have you grown beyond your baby days? How big are you?
4. *Garden hints*—Some of the laws of growth that need to be taken into account in growing a healthy, happy race of men.
(1) Freedom from worry. Sense of security.
(2) Time for growth.
   Etc., etc., etc.
5. *"Bread and Roses"*—Opportunities for culture and comforts. Use poem "Bread and Roses," Oppenheim.
6. *"The Garden of Gethsemane"*—The spirit of sacrifice that will be necessary if we ever substitute social passion for selfish concern.

Quotations
"The Kiss of the Son for pardon;
The song of the bird for mirth;

You are nearer to God in a garden
Than anywhere else on earth."
—Inscription in front of Bok Fountain at Lake Wales,
Florida.

"God the first garden made, and the first city, Cain."
—COWLEY
"Flowers are love's truest language."
—PARK BENJAMIN

"Flowers preach to us if we will hear."
—CHRISTINE G. ROSSETTI

" (Flowers) —How like they are to human beings."
—LONGFELLOW

"Where flowers degenerate man cannot live."
—NAPOLEON

"Sweet flowers are slow, and weeds make haste."
—SHAKESPEARE

"Flowers are the sweetest things that God ever made and forgot to put a soul into."—BEECHER.

"It is with flowers as with moral qualities; the bright are sometimes poisonous; but, I believe, never the sweet."—HARE.

"Flowers are the beautiful hieroglyphics of nature, with which she indicates how much she loves us."—GOETHE.

"God Almighty first planted a garden."
—BACON

"Flowers have an expression of countenance as much as men or animals. Some seem to smile, some have a sad expression, some are pensive and different; others again are plain, honest, and upright, like the broad-faced sunflower and the hollyhock."—BEECHER.

Quotations for Banquet Programs

"A good digestion to you all; and
once more,
I shower a welcome on you,
Welcome, all!"
—UNKNOWN

"Soup rejoices the stomach and disposes it to receive and digest other food."
—BRILLIANT SAVARIN

"Back of the loaf is the snowy flour,
And back of the flour the mill,
And back of the mill is the wheat and the shower
And the sun and the Father's will."
—BABCOCK

"Now that you have banqueted upon these more substantial dainties, I invite you to partake of the more delicate diet of tongues."—UNKNOWN.

'Nothing comes amiss; a good digestion turneth all to health."
—HERBERT, *Temple*

"One sip of this will bathe the drooping spirits in delight,
Beyond the bliss of dreams."
—MILTON, *Comus*

"We may live without poetry, music, and art;
We may live without conscience and live without heart;
We may live without friends; we may live without books;
But civilized man cannot live without cooks.
He may live without books,—what is knowledge but grieving?
He may live without hope,—what is hope but deceiving?
He may live without love,—what is passion but pining?
But where is the man that can live without dining?"
—BULWER LYTTON

"Some hae meat and canna eat,
And some wad eat that want it;
But we hae meat, and we can eat;
Sae let the Lord be thankit."
—BURNS

"We must eat to live, not live to eat."
—FIELDING

"He was a bold man that first ate an oyster."
—SWIFT

"The proof of the pudding is in the eating."
—CERVANTES

"Now good digestion wait on appetite,
And health on both."
—SHAKESPEARE

"Bad men live that they may eat and drink, whereas good men eat and drink that they may live."
—SOCRATES

"The turnpike road to people's hearts I find
Lies through their mouths, or I mistake mankind."
—DR. WOLCOTT

"Herbs and other country messes,
Which the neat-handed Phyllis dresses."
—MILTON, *L'Allego*

"Coffee, which makes the politician wise,
And see through all things with his half-shut eyes."
—POPE, *The Rape of the Lock*

"It is not the quantity of the meat, but the cheerfulness of the guests which makes the feast."—CLARENDON.

"The chief pleasure (in eating) does not consist in costly seasoning, or exquisite flavor, but in yourself. Do not seek sauce by sweating."—HORACE.

"The tocsin of the soul—the dinner bell."
—BYRON

"All human history attests
That happiness for man—the hungry sinner—
Since Eve ate apples, much depends on dinner."
—BYRON

"A good dinner sharpens wit, while it softens the heart."
—DORAN

"It's not the menu that makes a good dinner.
It's the men u sit next to."
—UNKNOWN

The Toastmaster

Ten Commandments for the Toastmaster

1. Plan carefully what thou wouldst do. He that trusteth to the last moment for inspiration will find that moment a fickle and faithless friend.

2. Allow no moss to grow under thy feet as the banquet getteth under way. Verily, a slow-moving banquet is a vexation to the spirit.

3. Thou shalt not feel under necessity to expound on the subject before or after each speaker's speech. Blessed is the toastmaster who knoweth how to be brief.

4. Thou shalt not endeavor to embarrass persons on the program by telling allegedly humorous stories about them. Blessed is the toastmaster who can be smart without being a smart-aleck. And verily it is said that he that slingeth mud loseth ground.

5. Thou shalt inform those on the program of the limits of time and then thou shalt see that these limits are observed. For verily, there is a difference between time and eternity, and a speaker whose terminal facilities are poor needeth to be sidetracked.

6. Thou shalt pay honor to whom honor is due. For truly, words of appreciation fitly spoken are "like apples of gold in pictures of silver."

7. Thou shalt repolish thy old jokes and endeavor to dig up a few new ones. For, forsooth, an old joke many times retold doth become a pain in the neck.

8. Thou shalt exude enthusiasm with the greatest of ease. Nothing so troubleth the spirit of the banqueteers as a toastmaster who hath no spizerinktum.

9. Thou shalt know the facts about the persons that thou dost introduce—who they are, from where they come, what they do and have done. Thou shalt tell it then briefly without fulsome flattery. A poor introduction is a grievance to the flesh.

10. Thou shalt bring the program to a fitting conclusion. A good climax is to be desired more than a confused banquet crowd that looketh bewildered and sayeth, "Well, is it over?"

He that heareth and doeth these things shall bless the land in which he liveth.

A Toastmaster's Poem

Whatever troubles Adam had,
No one in days of yore
Could say when he had told a joke,
"I've heard that one before."

—ANON.

CHAPTER V
FUN WITH GAMES FOR SMALL GROUPS

FUN WITH GAMES FOR SMALL GROUPS

Battleship.—It is said that this game was originated during the World War by Russian soldiers. It was first introduced in America by a business firm that used it on an advertising card.

It may be played by two persons or two groups. Each player or side has a sheet of paper containing three charts—one to register shots at the enemy ships, one to register the opponent's shots, and one to register hits. The first two of these charts contain 100 squares each.

Each player or side locates his ship in the first chart—four consecutive spaces for a battleship, three spaces for a cruiser, and two each for two submarines. The ships may be located horizontally, vertically, or diagonally. A player is not allowed to see the location of an opponent's ships.

Each player, in turn, shoots a volley of seven shots at his opponents' ships, being allowed three shots for the battleship, two for the cruiser, and one each for the two submarines. For example, Player One calls his shots as follows: "I am shooting at A 1, B 2, C 3, D 4, E 5, F 6, and G 7." As he shoots Player One locates his shots, by volley, in the second chart by using the Number 1, meaning Volley 1. At the same time Player Two marks the Figure 1 in each place called by Player One in the chart where his ships are located. Then Player One says, "Did I hit anything?" Player Two must answer truthfully, but he does not tell where the hits were scored. He simply says, "Yes, you hit my battleship once. Nothing else." Then Player Two shoots in the same manner. On the second round the players use the Number 2 to indicate that it is Volley 2. This is important for after awhile it helps one locate the ships. If he hits the cruiser on Volleys 3 and 5 he begins looking for some section of the chart where there is a 3 and 5 in line. When a ship goes down the player loses the shots going to that ship. Thus if his battleship goes down he is allowed only four shots, losing the three that belonged to the battleship. A player is not defeated until all ships are down. As long as he has one shot left he stands a chance to win.

When played by sides use large sheets of paper or use black-boards. This writer has used it at a picnic, making two large charts on paper and pinning them to heavy cardboard. The sides stood far enough apart so that the location of the ships could not be seen.

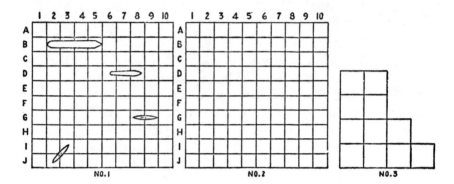

Directions—Player locates his ships in Diagram No. 1. Must locate each vessel in consecutive spaces, vertical, horizontal, or diagonal, Indicate own shots in Diagram No. 2. Score hits in Diagram No. 3. Hits are located by volley in Chart Three.

> Battleship .... 3 shots.
> Cruiser .... 2 shots.
> Submarine .... 1 shot.

Rapid-fire artists.—Each of several groups sends an "artist" to the leader. This leader whispers to these representatives some animal or other thing to draw. The representatives rush back to their respective groups and begin to draw furiously. As soon as an "artist's" group recognizes what is being drawn the members yell it, all together. The "artist" must not give them any tip except by his drawing. Each time a new "artist" must be sent to the leader.

Bug.—Make hexagon-shaped tops with letters B, H, T, E, L, F on the six sides. Or use cubes. A player spins the top. If "B" comes up he makes the body of the bug, and spins again. If he gets an "E" this time he loses his turn, for there is no head into which to fit the eye. The best second throw, therefore, is on "H" for the head. "T" is for tail, "L" for leg, and "F" for feeler. The bug must have two eyes, two feelers, and six legs in addition to its body, tail, and head before it is a complete bug. When a player tosses something he already has he loses his turn. A player cannot start drawing his bug until he gets a "B" for body.

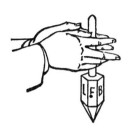

In a "Progressive Bug Party" the guests play partners. A player gets whatever his partner throws. In a party of this sort players may continue to play until one of the couples at the head table scores a complete bug, in which event they immediately bang a bell on that table. At this signal all players stop immediately. Winners at each table progress.

Electric shock.—The players stand or sit in a circle. One player is "It" and he stands inside the circle trying to discover where the electric shock is. All of the players hold hands and one player is designated to start the shock going. He squeezes the hand of either the player to the left or right of him. That player passes it on. The shock may move either direction, and at any time a player may send it back the other way. "It" watches closely the faces and hands of the players trying to detect the position of the shock. When he guesses correctly the player responsible takes his place.

Anagrams with variations.— (a) The regulation game. A set of anagram letters may be bought as cheaply as ten cents. No recreation equipment is complete without a good set of anagrams.

(b) Make a set of letters and place them face down on the table. Several alphabets should be in a set. Each player at the table turns up a letter. The first one to call a city, river, or article (as has been indicated by the leader) beginning with the letter turned up collects all of the letters turned up by the other players. Thus the leader calls "cities." Each player picks up a letter and looks at it. One of them shouts "Cincinnati," his letter being "C." He collects a letter from each player at the table and the game proceeds.

(c) *Call it*—Another way to play the game is to have one player to turn up a letter so all the players can see it. The first player to call a city, river, or article (as indicated) beginning with the letter collects the turned-up letter. The players take turn in turning up letters. Groceries, house furnishings, animals, birds, and general may be called for by the leader.

(d) *Crossword anagrams*—Players draw ten letters each. One player has been designated to begin. If he can take two, three, or four letters out of his hand and spell a word he places them on the table in order. No player can play more than four letters at one time. The next player must now build on the letters on the table, crossword fashion. Thus, the first player spells C-O-A-T. The next player builds on the "C," spelling C-R-A-T-E. After several words are down it gets harder to spell, as the players must spell both ways as in crosswords. When a player cannot spell he must discard one, face-down, and draw another from the table. The next player then proceeds to play. The first player to get rid of all of his letters scores one point for each letter left in the hands of the other players. Twenty-one points constitutes a game.

(e) *Spell it* — Each player draws four letters. One player turns up four letters from the table. He then proceeds to play. If he can take one letter from his hand and two or more from the table, thus spelling a word of three letters or more, he takes those letters and places them in front of him. If he cannot spell he discards one letter face-up, adding it to the other face-up letters on the board. If a player takes all of the letters on the board in spelling a word with the one letter from his hand he scores a "slam" and marks up a point for himself. When the players are all out of letters, they proceed to draw four more until all the letters have been drawn. On the last round, if there are not enough letters to go around so that each player will have the same number, the extra letters are placed on the table face-up with those already on the board. Thus if there are five players and eighteen letters, each player gets three letters and three are added to the turned-up letters already on the board.

The player with the largest number of letters scores two points. One point is allowed for every "slam."

Fifteen points constitutes a game.

The player who starts the game continues to lead until all letters have been drawn. Then the next player to his left leads.

Categories.—Have each player write the same name at the top of a sheet of paper, each letter the head of a column, thus:

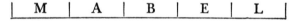

| M | A | B | E | L |

The leader now calls "Animals" and each player writes the names of as many animals as he can in each column, the names being required to begin with the letter heading the particular column. Under the direction of the leader players begin calling the animals column by column. A player scores one point for each animal listed, plus one point for each player who does not have that particular animal. The leader may call for "flowers," or "vegetables," or "trees," or "cities," or "rivers," or any category that suggests itself.

What is it?—One player goes out of the room. The others select some article or thing. The player returns and tries to discover by questioning what it is. He is allowed twenty questions. He probably will first try to locate it. "Is it in this room?" "Is it in this town?" When he gets it located he tries to find out something of its nature. "Is it human?" "Is it inanimate?" When he thinks he has it he names it. If he is correct another player, perhaps the one who gave him his cue, goes out and the game continues. If he is wrong and he has some questions left before he has used his twenty, he proceeds to ask some more questions. This is a great game for a mentally alert group.

Percolate.—One player leaves the room. The others decide on a word denoting some action, such as "walking," for instance. The player who is "It" endeavors to discover what the word is by asking questions. The players are permitted to answer only "Yes" or "No." "It" may ask any player as many questions as he desires, or he may be limited to three questions per person. "Do you percolate?" "Do you percolate in the evening?" "Do you percolate with your hands?" A clever questioner will soon locate the word selected.

Murder.—Each player is given a slip of paper which he is not to show to others. He rolls the slip up in a ball and throws it in the wastebasket after reading what is on it. Only two slips have anything on them. One of them reads "Murderer" and the other, "District Attorney." The District Attorney leaves the room. The lights are turned out and the crowd mills around in the center of the floor. Finally the murderer puts his hands to someone's throat. That person screams and falls to the floor. The lights are flashed on and the District Attorney takes charge. All persons must answer truthfully any question put to them by the District Attorney, except the Murderer, who is privileged to tell an untruth if he desires. The District Attorney tries to discover who the Murderer is. Everything depends on the cleverness of the District Attorney in cross-examining witnesses. Sometimes it is advisable to select the District Attorney arbitrarily, not depending on chance.

I have an idea.—The crowd decides on some article in the room in the absence of the person who is "It." When "It" returns some player says, "I have an idea." "What is it like?" asks "It." "It's like you," is the answer. "Why?" "Because it shines." Another player chimes in, "I have an idea." "What is it like?" "It's like you." "Why?" "Because it stays out all night." Perhaps that gives him his cue and he says, "It is the lamp."

Who am I?—A group of sophisticated adults on a west-bound train observation car had a great time with this one for more than an hour. "Who am I?" chirps one of the players. "Are you dead?" "No." "Alive?" "Yes." "Are you a man?" "Are you a political figure?" "Are you in the United States?" etc. Finally some player guesses that the person is "Franklin Delano Roosevelt," perhaps. The player who guesses correctly calls out, "Who am I?" and the game continues. Characters dead or alive may be used. Historic figures, characters in fiction, drama, or present-day personages may be used.

Grocery store.—Two lines of players of equal number. One player from each side steps forward and the leader calls out a letter. The player who first calls the name of some grocery article beginning with that letter scores a point for his side. Prompting from the sidelines subtracts a point for each infraction.

Numbered chairs.—Players are seated and numbered off. The space retains the same number throughout, though the players may change. Number One calls "Five." Immediately "Five" must respond with another number. When a person whose number is called does not respond immediately he must go foot. All players below him move up one space and change their numbers in doing so. Thus "Six" becomes "Five," and so on down the line. Numbers are called rapidly and special effort is made to send the top players to the foot.

Birds have feathers.—One player leads. The others flap their arms flying fashion when the leader names something with feathers. If a player flaps his wings on the calling of something that does not have feathers he drops out. The leader may flap his "wings" any-time to confuse the others. He makes his calls rapidly. "Birds have feathers. Geese have feathers. Ducks have feathers. Frogs have feathers. Goats have feathers. Swans have feathers."

The queen's headache.—Blindfold one player and seat him at one end of the room. Place three empty chairs on either side of him. Then announce that the queen has a headache and doesn't want to be disturbed. Ask anyone to try to walk up to the empty chairs without disturbing the queen, as the queen will groan as soon as she hears footsteps approaching and the one who is walking must sit down wherever he is. Keep up the game until six players have succeeded in getting to the empty chairs, or if this is not possible, until interest wanes.

Another way to play the game is to have all players seated in a circle. The queen is seated at center. Players try to cross the room to the opposite side. Any player may cross and demand any seat he desires. The player in the chosen seat must move to another. Whenever the queen groans players standing must sit on the floor until the queen stops groaning.

I am very, very tall.—One player shuts his eyes. The other says, "I am very, very tall, I am very, very small; sometimes I'm tall; sometimes I'm small. Guess what I am now." He stands or stoops. The player with his eyes shut guesses whether he is tall (standing) or small (stooping). He continues until he guesses correctly. Then the other player tries to do the guessing. When played by a group "It" stands in the center. The whole circle stands or stoops. If "It" guesses correctly he chooses someone to take his place.

Who's the leader?—Players stand in circle. One player goes out. A leader is appointed. The whole group starts clapping and continues until the player sent out returns and takes the center of the ring. It is his business to discover who is leading the crowd in its actions. The leader changes from clapping, for instance, to patting his head, twirling his thumbs, jumping up and down, etc. All the crowd does the same thing immediately. All players should not watch the leader. It's amazing how quickly the action goes around the circle, and how difficult it sometimes is to discover the leader. When finally discovered, the leader goes out and a new leader is selected. A good game to give the timid a chance to develop initiative. It adds to the fun if the game is played to music.

Stone, paper, scissors (Japanese game).—Players line up facing opponents in equal number. Opponents facing one another, advance, one at a time, with hands behind them. The leader counts, "One-two-three." On "three" the two players bring their hands forward in the position they choose, according as they decide to be stone, paper, or scissors. The stone is represented with clenched fists; the paper with open hands, palms down; the scissors with the extending of the index and middle fingers. The stone beats the scissors because it dulls them. The scissors beat the paper because it can cut it. The paper beats the stone because it wraps up the stone. Points are counted as the opponents contest. Another way to conduct this contest is to have all players advance to middle, face opponents hands behind them. At "three" all players bring forth hands to represent stone, paper, or scissors. Instead of "one-two-three" the Japanese say, "Jan-Kem-Po" (stone-paper-scissors).

Another way is to have all players advance and at "three" all players put forth hands, but this time all players on a side are representing the same thing. A mistake by any player on the side disqualifies his team and scores a point for the other side. Therefore, the players must get together to decide what they shall represent. The first side to make ten points in this manner wins. Variations— (a) Man, Gun, Rabbit, or Bear. (b) The Koreans play a variation in which they represent Man, Gun, and Tiger. The man holds fingers up to represent long, flowing mustaches, aims for the gun, and growls and holds claws out for the tiger. (c) "Jan Kem Po" relay. The Japanese have a relay race built on this game. The course is square or rectangular in shape. It can be marked off by stones, sticks, or trees at the four corners. Runners line up at opposite corners at the same end of the field. The first man on each team starts running around the square at the signal to go. When these two runners meet they stop, put their hands behind them, and say "Jan-Kem-Po." On "Po" they hold out their hands, representing stone, paper, or scissors. The winner continues on his way. The loser drops out and a new man starts out from his side to meet the opposing runner. Each time two runners meet they stop to do "Jan-Kem-Po," the winner always proceeding. The first team to get a runner to the opponent's corner wins.

Flying feather.—Not more than ten players in a group. The players join hands and try to keep a downy feather up in the air by blowing. A leader, or one of the group, may toss the feather into the air. Often players can keep the feather up for a long time. Players must not break hands.

In a large crowd divide into small groups and see which group can keep its feather up longest. In this case the feather would be tossed into the air when the leader blows a whistle.

Variation—Music may be played and players move in rhythm as they endeavor to keep the feather flying.

Poisoned bean bags.—Players form circle. Bean bags distributed in the group. When music starts players pass bean bags to the right. When the music stops, or leader blows whistle, players having possession of bean bags or throwing them down are poisoned and must drop out of the circle. As players drop out the circle contracts so that the players may easily hand the bean bags around.

As group gets smaller fewer bean bags should be used until only one is left for the last four or five players. The last player to stay in the game is winner.

Spell down (Baa-aa-aa).—Players in a circle. One player starts a word by giving the first letter. The next player adds a letter, though he may have another word in mind. The player finishing a word has to imitate a goat. Players have a right to challenge the player who precedes them if they doubt that player has a word in mind. If he has a legitimate word in mind the challenging player becomes a goat. If he hasn't, the challenged player is the goat. When a player once becomes a goat he must "baa-aa-aa" each time his turn comes instead of offering a letter.

You have a face (small group).—Seated in circle one player turns to neighbor to the right and says, "You have a face." The neighbor responds, "What kind of face?" The leader has announced that all answers must be made with words beginning with the letter C, and that no word once used, may be used again. "Cheerful face," says the first player. This player turns to the player on his right and the game proceeds from one to the other. "Cherub face," "calm face," "comical face," "cosmetic face," etc. It's fun sometimes to see just how long one letter can be used. The leader may change the letter to B or D, or any other letter.

My grandmother.—The leader announces, "My grandmother doesn't like tea, but she likes coffee." It goes from player to player, each saying, "My grandmother doesn't like tea, but she likes ——." If a player calls any word with the letter T in it, the leader says, "No," she doesn't like that. "She likes pears, but she doesn't like grapefruit." She doesn't like tea. Therefore, she doesn't like anything with the letter T in it. It will begin to dawn on some of them as the game proceeds.

Crossed and uncrossed.—Pair of scissors. Players seated in circle. Someone passes the pair of scissors. That player passes them on saying, "I have received them crossed and pass them uncrossed." The crossed and uncrossed refer to the passers' legs or feet, though the uninitiated invariably think it has reference to the scissors. If the receiver's feet were crossed when the scissors are passed, and also crossed as he passes them, he says, "I received them crossed and pass them crossed."

Contrary.—Two players sit facing one another. Each has a hat. The leader announces that the player opposite him is to try to do the contrary thing to the thing he does. If the leader sits down, the player is to stand. If the leader has on his hat, the player is to take his off, etc. The leader makes it difficult by doing exactly what the player does. At the same time he talks to him trying to get his attention off what he is trying to do.

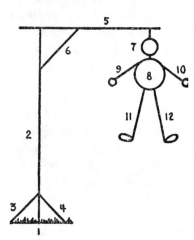

Hangman.—A player has a word in mind and puts down as many dashes as there are letters in the word. A letter is called. If the guess is correct, the writer must put the letter in all the spaces wherever it appears in the word. If the guess is wrong, the writer begins to draw the scaffold and man, as suggested in the diagram. The object is to hang the whole man. Eyes, nose, and mouth may be added, if desired. A skilful player usually calls the vowels first. Some difficult words are sylph, tryst, way, and wax.

With a large crowd, divide into two teams. Use blackboard. One side chooses a word and tries to hang the other side. Any player can call a letter.

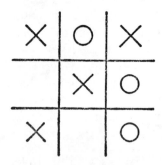

Tit-tat-toe.—Two players. Each tries to get three marks in a row. The players take turn about in marking. One used an "X," the other an "O." X got three in a row and wins. May be used as team game, players running to blackboard and marking.

Dumb spelling.—Players indicate vowels by signs. Right hand raised means *A*. Left hand raised means *E*. Pointing to eye means *I*. Puckering lips as if to say "O" means *O*. And pointing to someone is *U*. Players line up in two sides. Leader calls word to be spelled and indicates players to spell. The player must say all the consonants but must be dumb on the vowels, only giving the proper sign. Thus *C*—raise right hand, *T* in answer to

"Cat," called by the leader.   Other letters may be added to the dumb list, at will—whistle for *R*, hiss for *S*, shading eyes for *C*, stutter for *K*, "humph" for *H*, growl for *G*.

The ghost walks.—All persons except the director and one person leave the room.   The latter may be chosen by lot to remain.   After a pause the director claps his hands sharply, and a figure entirely covered by a sheet enters.   The sheet should trail the floor, and should be hung over a broom carried by the person inside, so as to disguise the height.   On top where the face is supposed to be, should be pinned a piece of black cloth to represent a mask.   The "ghost" should walk slowly and solemnly across the room and back.   The person who remains in the room must guess who the "ghost" is.   If he does then the "ghost" must take his place.   If not, he must pay a forfeit.   Another is chosen and the game proceeds.

The guessing blindman.—The players are seated in a circle.   One player is blindfolded, after which he is turned three times.   During this procedure all of the players may change seats.   The blindman next walks forward and touches someone in the circle with a wand, speaking the words: "Can you guess?"   The player touched must repeat this question three times, endeavoring to disguise his voice. Should the guessing blindman succeed the person discovered must take his place.   Otherwise, he continues until successful.

The old soldier.—The leader tells the group of an old soldier that needs assistance.   His clothes are ragged and his feet bare.   "What will you give this poor old soldier?" the leader asks different people in turn.   Each person offers some article of dress.   No two can give the same article and the words *Yes, No, Black,* and *White* are strictly banned.   The leader tries to trip players into the use of one of these words.   "Can you give him a white shirt?"   If the player slips and answers "Yes," or "No," he pays a forfeit.   He may save himself by saying, "I'm sorry.   I have all my shirts in the laundry."   Forfeits may be collected of persons making mistakes or stunts required of them without the formality of forfeits.

Bible basketball.—This game was devised and used by a California group.   They are rather enthusiastic about it.   A letter said, "We experimented with a variation of Bible basketball last night, and it was quite a 'go' for a group needing just that type of game.   Here was the layout: Mark center circle, foul line, X's for positions of players, and the baskets.   Six players, or even less with 'roving centers," will work O.K.   Ten or twelve would be the maximum for a fast game."

The referee, who asks the Bible questions, "tosses up" the ball at center.   The first of the centers to answer correctly "shoots" the ball toward his basket, pointing to the forward on his team to receive the next question.   The referee then tosses up another question for the forward and guard.   If the forward wins he scores a goal and two points.   If the guard wins, the next try goes to the forward he indicates on his team.   If the guard wins this time the play goes back to center.

Anyone "telling" allows the opposing player a free throw for a possible correct answer and one point.

It is important that the referee have a well-prepared list of questions.   Much depends on his ability to keep the game moving.

To speed up the game a time limit may be used, in which case the ball goes "out of bounds" and back to the centers with a new question.

Chicken market (a game from Italy).—All the children pretend they are chickens, except one who is the buyer, and another the market woman.   The child who is the market woman says to the children: "Stand in a row, little chickens.   Stoop down and clasp your hands under your knees.   Don't unclasp your hands and don't laugh, or even smile, no matter what happens."

The buyer then comes up and asks, "Have you any chickens?" "Yes, I have very nice chickens," answers the market woman.   "Would you like to try them?"   "If you please," says the buyer.   Then the buyer goes behind the rows of chickens.   She places her hands upon the first little chicken's head.   "This," she says, "is too tough."   She tries the second.   "This is too old," she says.   She tries the third. "This chicken is too skinny."   At last she says, "This one is just right."   Then the buyer and the market woman take hold of the little chicken's arms and swing it.   "One, two, three," they count as they swing it.   "You are a good little chicken.   You kept your hands clasped and you did not laugh."   If the chicken laughs, he is put out of the game!

Do you know Jim Crow?—Players are seated in a circle.   One player turns to his left-hand neighbor and asks, "Do you know Jim Crow?"   That player answers, "No!   How does he go?"   The first player replies, "SO," and starts patting his knee with his right hand.

The second player now turns to the person to his left, and goes through the same process. So it continues until it gets back to the leader.

The leader starts all over again with the same series of questions, this time patting the left knee with the left hand. The next time he lifts the right knee and taps the floor rhythmically with his foot. Then the left knee and the left foot. Next he gets up and begins jumping up and down. All players keep up all movements after once starting them. When the leader shouts, "Jim Crow's No Mo'!" everyone stops. If this doesn't loosen up your crowd they are hopeless.

FIVE CUBAN GAMES

One summer I had the pleasure of teaching a course in recreation in Havana. One evening the class put on a party in which they played some Cuban games. Note what variations they make to certain games that are familiar to American young people.

The priest's hat (Cuban version of "The Prince of Paris lost his hat").—Those who are to take part in this game are seated in a circle. The person acting as leader stands in the center of the circle and says: "The priest has lost his hat, and they tell me that someone in this room found it and hid it." (This may be elaborated by a clever leader.) "I do not know who it is, but I think it is ————." At the same time he points at someone in the circle. This player must not speak or smile, but with vigorous motions of the head must deny the charge, point out someone else, who in turn denies and points to another. The point of the game is to make some player laugh or smile. Players guilty of this offense must pay a forfeit. The looks of mock surprise on the faces of players charged with the offense, and their solemn protestations in pantomime are exceedingly funny and it won't be long before a number of forfeits will be surrendered. When a player is guilty of smiling or laughing, the forfeit is paid, and the leader starts the game again.

The dogs and the chickens.—The players sit in a circle. Each player is given the name of some city or town. The leader says: "In ———— the dogs crow and the chickens bark." The player with the name the leader calls must reply quickly, "No, sir, in ———— the dogs do not bark and the chickens do not bark. Where the dogs crow and the chickens bark is in ———— etc." The player who makes a mistake or does not speak must pay a fine.

The nuts.—The players sit in a circle. The leader gives the following phrases to certain of the players: "How many?" "How?"

"How cheap?" "What do you say?" and "How expensive?" To the other players he gives numbers, five and multiples of five. The leader begins by saying, "How many?" The person with this name must answer, "Sir." Then the leader says, "How many nuts did they give you at the store for a dime?" "How many" must answer with the number five or a multiple of five. The leader must repeat the number or say, "How expensive" or "How cheap" or any of the other phrases given as names to the players. The players must listen and respond accordingly or pay a fine for inattention.

The flower garden.—The leader gives names of flowers to all the players seated in a circle. Then the leader says: "In a garden of flowers that I saw, nothing but the rose was lacking." The rose must say: "The rose was not lacking, because I saw it in the garden." Then the leader says: "What was it that was lacking?" The rose answers, "The violet was lacking." The violet must respond, "The violet was there because I saw it, it was the pansy that was lacking." The game proceeds thus very quickly until some flower fails to respond. This player must pay a fine or forfeit.

"Chocolonga."—A player is selected from the crowd, and stands at arm's length before a circle placed on the wall. He is told to touch the circle as near the center as possible while he is blindfolded. While he is being blindfolded and turned around three times someone stands in front of the circle so that the player's finger goes into the mouth of the one standing against the wall. This player catches the finger between his teeth and bites it gently. If preferred, some sort of pinching instrument may be used.

Detectives.—Two or three persons go out of the room. The players remaining in the room select some object as the object they want the detectives to locate. This object may be a button on a coat or dress of a certain person, or a vase on a table, or anything in the room the group decides. The detectives come back and begin quizzing the individuals in the group. It is not allowable to ask a player if he has the object on his person, though a detective may ask someone else if a certain player has the object. The detectives are allowed only three questions per person. By clever questioning they will soon discover the secret object. It is a good idea to discover first the location. Then the rest should be easy.

Nine pins.—Line up nine snap clothespins in a row with about three inches space between each pin. Use three large marbles. Mark a line from five to six feet from the row of pins. Each player must turn with his back to the pins, kneel on one knee, and looking back over his shoulder, endeavor to knock the pins down. Three shots are allowed. A point is scored for each pin bowled over.

Variation 1—Paint the clothespins different colors. If a player calls a color and hits it he gets five points. However, if he misses, one point is subtracted even if he knocks down a pin of some other color.

Variation 2—Line the pins up, ten-pin fashion. Allow two tries. Strikes and spares would be called and scored just as in bowling. In this case it would be better to have ten pins instead of nine.

Proverb parodies.—For a mentally alert group this offers fine possibilities for keen fun. Each player is asked to write a parody of a well-known proverb. For instance: "Make way for the son to shine."—By A Backfield Star's Mother. "All that titters (or jitters) should be told."—Serious. "A fool and his money make easy pickings."—A Gold Digger.

Perhaps you could speed up the thinking of the players by providing the players with a list of proverbs, such as:

"A stitch in time saves nine."
"Money makes the mare go."
"You can lead a horse to water but you cannot make him drink."
"A bird in hand is worth two in the bush."
"One swallow does not make a summer."
"A rolling stone gathers no moss."
"A burnt child fears the fire."
"Marry in haste and repent at leisure."
"Fine feathers make fine birds."
"Happy the wooing that's not long a-doing."
"Handsome is that handsome does."
"If at first you don't succeed, try, try, again."

Word building.—A word is selected. Each player writes it at the top of his sheet of paper and makes as many words as possible by using the letters in the foundation word, being allowed to use no letter more times in a given word than it appears in the head word.

Players begin with the first letter in the foundation word. When a player has exhausted the possibilities of words beginning with that letter he starts with the next letter, and so on until he has made as many words as he possibly can.

The player whose list is longest now reads aloud his words, pausing after each word to note the number of players who do not have that word. He gets one point for each of those who fail to have it. So does every other player who has the word. Players check words called that they have on their lists.

Thus if the basic word is "Caricature." All players have "car" and no point is awarded. But six players do not have "cure" and so each player having that word scores 6 points.

The next player now reads the words that remain unchecked on his list, and so on until all words have been called.

Variation in this method may be introduced by having one player read all of his words beginning with the first letter in the main word, another player all he has beginning with the second letter, and so on.

Players count checked words and total them at the bottom. They also total points made on words some of the other players did not have. They likewise total unchecked words.

Definitions.—A small list of words is given out. The players, without conferring, write definitions on slips of paper and turn them in or pass them to the right. The definitions are read aloud for one word at a time. A dictionary is used as authority on correct definitions. This game will sharpen up the thinking of the players and will prove a good vocabulary builder.

Proverb hangman.—This game is played exactly as is "Hangman" excepting that a proverb is used instead of a single word. Players try to discover the proverb by calling letters of the alphabet they think in it. These must be written in the proper space, when they are correct.

As soon as a player recognizes the proverb he calls it. When the wrong letter is called the hanging proceeds as in "Hangman."

Wagging mandarin.—The players stand in a circle. The leader says to the person to his right, "My ship has come home from China!" That person asks, "What has it brought?" "A fan," the leader replies. Forthwith, he pretends to fan himself with his right hand. Everyone in the circle imitates the leader's motion. The next player then says to the neighbor to his right, "My ship has come home from China." Again the question is, "What has it brought? "Two fans," is the reply. Whereupon, the player fans himself with two hands, while everyone follows the gesture. The statement, "My ship has come from China," and the question, "What has it brought?" continues from one player to another. The third player, announcing that his ship has brought three fans, moves his right foot as well as the two hands, everyone else doing the same thing. At "four fans" all move both hands and feet, stepping in place. At "five fans," the hands, feet, and right eyelid; at "six fans" the hands, feet, and both eyelids; at "seven fans," the hands, feet, eyelids, and mouth; at "eight fans," the hands, feet, eyelids, mouth, and head. By this time the whole company is a group of wagging mandarins. Persons who fail to keep up with the movements must pay forfeits.

What am I?—Pin on back of each guest the picture of some well-known product (soap, chewing-gum, soup, vegetables, etc.). From hints given by others each person must guess what he is.

Variation—Names of prominent people may be used in the same manner.

Alliterative travelers.—The leader announces that everyone is going on a trip. They can go any place they choose, but when they tell what they are going to do there they may only use words beginning with the initial letter of the place to which they are going. The leader there says to some player, "Traveler, where are you going?" This person answers, "California." "What are you going to do there?" "Can corn, carrots, cucumbers." Or the answer may be, "Court cinema contract." If the answer is Boston then the player might answer, "Bake beans" or "borrow baloney."

Co-operative art.—Each player draws a head and neck, not allowing any others to see what he has drawn. The player then folds the paper over and passes it on for another player to draw the body or trunk. Again the paper is folded so what has been drawn cannot be seen, and the next player draws the legs and feet. No player allows others to see what he has drawn. After the "work of art" has been finished the paper is unfolded and the "marvelous" creation is put on display.

What is my thought like?—One player announces that he has a thought in mind which he will disclose later. In the meantime, each player, in turn, must tell what he thinks the thought is like. "It is like a piano," says one. "It is like a hot potato," says another. "It is like the deep blue sea," says still another. And thus each player responds with some analogy. The leader writes down each answer.

After the last player has answered the leader announces that he was thinking of a baseball game. Now each player, in turn, must tell why it is like what he said it was like. "It is like a piano because the pitch is important." "It is like a hot potato because the hotter it is the harder it is to handle." "It is like the deep blue sea because sometimes it is pretty rough." So each player must answer. Sometimes some "tall" stretching has to be done to bear out the analogy. There will be some side-splitting analogies in most any company.

Number call.—Players are numbered. "It" is blindfolded. Players may now change seats. "It" calls from two to four numbers and they must change seats. "It" tries either to tag a player or to get a vacated seat. Players, whose numbers are called, proceed immediately to exchange seats, moving quietly, dodging or moving stealthily as may be required to keep from being tagged. If caught, the player must take "Its" place and the game proceeds, "It" taking the number of the caught player.

Sardines.—One player hides in a closet, behind a door, under the steps, in a cavern, behind a big rock, in a clump of trees or bushes. The rest scatter and hunt, each player hunting singly. As a player finds the hidden player he hides with him. However, he is careful not to tip off the hiding place to others so, if he observes others near at the time, he may go on as if still seeking, and come back at a favorable opportunity. Imagine the fun when ten or more players crowd into the same hiding place. The hunt continues until all the players find the hiding place. The game is good fun either indoors or outdoors.

Sky writing.—One player leaves the group. The rest select a verb to be acted, such as sing, speak, dance, snore, bat, pitch, hop, jump, or race. The player is called back. The leader using his hand pretends to write the word in the air in a mysterious chirography. Occasionally he accents his writing by clapping his hands together. When he is through the player who went out does what the group decided for him to do. The leader's tips are contained in what he says and in the hand-clapping. The first consonant in a sentence indicates the consonant the leader is conveying to his accomplice. The vowels are indicated as follows: One clap for A, two claps for E, three claps for I, four claps for O, and five claps for U. Suppose the word is snore. The leader makes mysterious passes in the air as he says, "See if you can follow me." There is the S. "Now do you see." There is the N. He claps sharply four times. That is the O. "Rather easy, isn't it?" That gives the accomplice the R. Two claps, and that is E. The accomplice snores.

This is a variation of *Mysterious Chinese Writing,* where the leader uses a cane and taps out the vowels.

It is a useful stunt for campfire and picnic occasions. It may be further varied by not requiring the accomplice to act out the word spelled, but only to call it.

Musical telepathy.—One player leaves the room. The rest decide on some action he is to perform. The player returns to the room. He is told that the music played will be his only clue to the action required of him. When he approaches the spot where he is to perform the piano will play loud and fast. As he gets away from it the piano will play soft and slow. As he does the wrong thing it will play soft and slow. When he does the right thing it will play loud and fast.

This is very similar to "The Organ Grinder Man," in Chapter XIII, "Fun with Musical Games." Typical actions required are as follows: Remove a book from the table and give it to some certain person; shake hands with a certain person; take a flower from the table and give it to someone.

Making squares.—This is a good game for two people. Mark five or more rows of dots on a piece of paper. Players take turns in connecting any two dots with a straight line, except that diagonals are not permitted. Whenever a player can finish a square by adding a line he places his initial in the enclosed space. At the end when all dots have been connected a player's score is indicated by the number of squares bearing his initial.

Hearts.—Get wooden cubes and mark the sides with the letters H-E-A-R-T-S. It requires six cubes for a set. When used for a Progressive Heart Party there should be one set on each table. Each player, in turn, throws these cubes out on the table. The following is the score:

H	5 points
H-E	10 points
H-E-A	15 points
H-E-A-R	20 points
H-E-A-R-T	25 points
H-E-A-R-T-S	35 points

If the player turns up two H's he is not entitled to score 10. Nor is he entitled to 20 points if he turns up two H-E's on one throw. However, if he turns up three H's he cancels all the score he has made up to that point.

Broken hearts.—Make a spool top with six flat sides. On each of these sides print one of the letters in H-E-A-R-T-S. Each player has a cardboard heart cut into six sections. Play as you play "Bug" or "Cootie." A player must throw "H" to begin to put together his heart. He must get the other letters in order. He continues playing until he misses. Each time he makes good he places a section of the heart in place. When he misses the next player plays. Illustration: Player One throws "E" on his first turn. He has missed so player Two throws. He throws an "H" and puts one section of his broken heart before him. He then throws "E" and, since that is the next letter in the word, he continues, placing another section of the heart in place. The third time he throws "S" and loses his turn. A player throws by spinning the top, turning it with his thumb and second finger, usually.

Wink.—This is an old-timer. In the writer's boyhood days this was one of the favorites. A party was hardly complete without it.

Chairs are arranged around the room with a man behind each chair. In all but one of the chairs set young ladies. Each man keeps his hands on the back of his chair, except when trying to prevent the lady sitting there from leaving him for the winker. The man with the empty chair makes an effort to get a partner. This he does by winking. When he winks at a lady she must immediately make an effort to get up and move to his chair. The man in whose chair she is sitting tries to prevent her from getting up. If he puts his hands on her shoulders before she arises she must stay. The winker keeps at it until he succeeds in getting someone's partner.

Hunter.—Players stand or sit in a circle. Or they may be seated about a table. A small pebble, a coin, or other counter is used. The players start it around the circle, alternately clasping their hands together and stretching them to their neighbors, as they chant:

Around and round and round I go,
From hand to hand I wander so;
I'm here, I'm there, I'm not, I vow!
Pray, tell which hand enfolds me now?

One player, who is "It," tries to guess who has possession of the pebble. If he guesses correctly, that player takes the hunter's place.

Results.—One leader goes around and whispers to each person the name of some object. Another whispers something they are to do with the object. A third person whispers the consequences of such action. The fun of it arises from the fact that neither of the three knows what the others have said. Therefore, some ridiculous combinations result, such as, "I was told to take a piano and hit Mr. Brown with it." The result—"All's well that ends well."

My ship came in.—The players are seated about the room or camp-fire. The leader says to the one seated next to him, "My ship came in." "What did it bring?" asks the second player. "A fan," replies the leader, whereupon he begins a fanning motion with his hand. The second person turns to the third and the conversation is repeated. And so it goes all the way around the circle.

When it gets back to the leader he repeats, "My ship came in." "What did it bring?" this time brings the response, "A pair of scissors," and the leader uses the middle and index fingers of the other hand to imitate a pair of scissors. Next comes a pair of shoes with the feet being set in motion. Then a pair of glasses with the eyes blinking, followed by false teeth with an opening and closing of the mouth, the teeth being displayed. Finally, a hat with the head bobbing back and forth. That will probably leave the group limp, for all motions, once started, must be continued.

GAMES FOR THE TRIP

On the hike or on an auto trip there are certain things that can be done to add to the fun. Here are a few suggestions of things that will help make the trip a gay adventure:

Finish the alphabet.—The object of this game is to complete the alphabet by picking the letters in sequence from the signboards along the way. The game is played in two ways. One player takes only the signs on one side of the road. The other takes those on the other side. He calls his letters as he sees them. The second way to play it allows the players to use both sides of the road. The first player to call a letter from a particular word is the only player who can use that letter from that word. Any other player is privileged to call another letter from the same word, however. Thus one player calls "Quaker—a." Another may call "Quaker—e," if "e" is the letter he needs. The player finishing the alphabet first wins.

Variation—The players may decide to spell some word. Short words may be used first, such as cat, dog, or cow. The names of people, or cities, or rivers may be used.

Burying white horses.—The car is divided into two sides. The players on each side look for white horses on their side, counting them. If a cemetery is passed and a player on the opposite side sees it and calls it first his opponents must bury all the horses they have counted. That means that they have to start all over at one in their counting. Thus, if a player on the right sees a cemetery on the left, and calls it the left side cancels all their score up to that time. The left side may prevent such a catastrophe from happening by seeing the cemetery first and calling, "Cemetery! Alley Oop!"

Variations— (*a*) The cemetery idea may be eliminated. The first player to reach 25 or 50 or any agreed number is winner. (*b*) Counting jersey cows or any kind of cows. (*c*) One group touring through a mountainous section had a lot of fun counting beards and mustaches.

Checking mailboxes.—Teams count only on their side of the road. A mailbox counts one. A post office counts five.

SOME QUIET GAMES

The Prince of Paris.—Players stand or sit in a line or circle. They number off consecutively. One player who is "It" says, "The Prince of Paris lost his hat and I think Number Two has it." Before "It" can add, "Number Two, go foot," that player must respond with, "Who sir? I sir?" "Yes sir! You sir!" replies "It." "No sir! Not I sir!" says Number Two. "Who then, sir?" asks "It." Number Two then calls some number, such as "Number Ten, sir!" Number Ten must call, "Who sir? I sir?" before Number Two can say, "Number Ten, go foot." And so it goes until some player is caught napping. Then that player takes the place of "It," who goes to the foot of the line while all players back of the player caught move up one. In moving up they change their numbers. That complicates things and makes it easier to catch players off guard. Of course, effort is made continually to catch the players who are at the head of the line.

Buzz.—Five to thirty players. One of the players starts the game by saying, "One." The others, in turn, say, "Two," "Three," "Four," "Five," and "Six." But when "Seven" is reached that player must say, "Buzz." The counting goes on, but each time there is a multiple of seven or any number with seven in it the player must substitute "Buzz" for the number. Thus 14, 21, 28, and others that are multiples, and 17, 27, 37, and others containing the number seven must not be repeated. "Buzz" is repeated in their stead. Penalty for infraction of this rule is dropping out of the game or paying a forfeit.

Variations—Players may call the "Buzz" number, making it 3, or 5, or 8. In this case the "Buzz" would come on the number called and on its multiples.

Laugh.—Players are seated in a circle. The first player starts by saying, "Ha." The second player says, "Ha, Ha." The third says, "Ha, Ha, Ha." And so it goes around the circle with each player adding another "Ha." In each case the "Ha's" must be pronounced solemnly, or pain of dismissal from the circle. The chances are, however, that it will not get around the circle before the entire circle is responding with gales of laughter.

Beast, bird, or fish.—The players stand or sit in a circle. One player at the center has a bean bag or ball. He tosses this to a player in the circle and says quickly, "Beast, bird, or fish! Beast!" The player to whom the bean bag has been thrown must answer immediately with the name of a beast, such as, "Fox" or "Dog" or "Mule." If the center player counts to ten before a proper response is made the player must change places with him.

Variation—Instead of throwing an object the center player may simply point his finger.

Up, Jenkins.—The players sit on opposite sides of the table, a team on each side. Each team selects a captain.

An object (coin, button, pebble) is given to one team. The members of that group put their hands beneath the table and pass the object back and forth among them.

At the command, "Down, Jenkins!" from their captain the players on the team, having the object, place their hands on top of the table palm down and hand flat against the table.

The other side consults awhile and then their captain calls "Up, Jenkins!" pointing to one hand. The player whose hand it is must lift the hand and put it under the table. The object of the opposing side is to guess under which hand the object is located. Then they call all other hands up, one at a time, endeavoring to leave that one until last. If the captain of the guessing side happens to call the hand that covers the hidden object, the side in possession scores as many points as there are hands left on the table. No one but the captain may order up hands.

Then the object is given to the other side and the game continues.

Variation—"Who's got the button?" The hiding group, on command of their captain, put their closed fists on top of the table. It is the business of the opposing side to guess the location of the button in three guesses. Again only orders from the captain are obeyed. He may point to a hand and say, "Open." Or he may require all but one removed from the table and then order that one to open. If he is successful in three guesses his group gets possession of the button, and no point is scored. If he is unsuccessful the winners score a point and continue to hide the button. Twenty-one points might be considered a game.

Hul Gul.—Three or more players stand in a circle. One of them addresses his right-hand neighbor, and the following dialogue takes place:

First Player: "Hul Gul."
Second Player: "Hands full."
First Player: "How many?"
Second Player: Makes some guess as to the number of counters in the first player's extended hand.

The hand is clenched to hide the counters from view.

If the guess is four, for instance, and the first player has seven counters in his hand, the first opens his hand and says:

"Give me three to make it seven." And so it continues for a definite period of time or until one player has all of the counters.

Each player starts out with ten counters. These counters may be beans, corn, marbles, nuts, or tiny pebbles.

An equivalent of this game was played two thousand years or more ago. Xenophon makes allusion to it.

Secret word.—Guests are divided into groups of four or five each.

Each group selects a word with as many letters as there are persons in the group. Each person takes a letter in the word and these are acted out, in turn, the player acting out some word beginning with the letter assigned him. For instance, if "Slow" were the word, one player might act out "Sleepy" (yawning and stretching), another "Lying" (either lying down or telling a whopper), another "Open" (opening a book or box or door), and the fourth "Washing" (washing hands and face or clothes). The others try to guess what each is doing and then what the secret word is.

Magic music.—Something is hid around the room or grounds—a book, a coin, a peanut. The hunter returns to the room. As he hunts he gets clues from the music of the piano. When he gets farther and farther away from the object hidden, the music gets softer and softer. As he gets nearer, it becomes louder. When he is very warm (close to the object) the piano fairly bangs.

Variation—The game may be played out of doors. In this case the players would hum or sing. "She'll Be Comin' 'Round the Mountain" or any familiar tune may be used.

Blindman's buff (small group).—A blindfolded player holding a wand stands in the center of a circle of players. The circle, hand-in-hand, moves around singing some song such as "She'll Be Comin' 'Round the Mountain." When one verse is finished they stand still. The blindfolded player now points his wand in the direction of the circle. The player to whom it points must take hold of it and repeat three sounds indicated by the blindfolded player, such as "crow like a rooster," "meow like a cat," "bark like a dog," "call hogs," "laugh out loud," "sneeze," or "cry like a baby." The performer may make every effort to disguise his voice. The blindfolded player tries to identify the noisemaker. If successful, they exchange places.

Mumblety-peg.—This ancient game is played on soft turf. A pocketknife is used. The knife must stick in the earth, being thrown from various successive positions, as follows: (1) The knife, small blade open, is held in the palm, first of the right and then of the left hand, point up toward the thumb. The player brings the hand up and over toward the body, turning it so that the back of the hand is toward the body, with thumb and knife point down. (2) The knife rests successively on the right and left fists, point upward, and thrown sideways. (3) The point is pressed against each finger and thumb in succession, and cast outward. (4) After this it is held by the point and flipped from the breast, nose, cheeks, eyes, and forehead. (5) From each ear, arms crossed, and taking hold of opposite ear with the free hand. (6) Over the head backward. (7) Holding point downward and dropping through circle made by thumb and forefinger of free hand. (8) Tossing knife into the air and tipping the handle up with the finger to give it an end-over-end motion. (9) Putting free hand down as a barrier and placing the knife at a slant, point touching the turf. Flip knife over barrier and make it stick on the opposite side. (10) The blade between the first and second fingers of one hand while the handle is between the same fingers on the other hand. Flip blade over and make it stick. (11) Point of blade held between forefinger and thumb. With a sweeping motion the player hits the turf with his hand, releasing the knife as he does it.

If the knife does not stick, the next player takes his turn. The first to conclude the series wins. The winner is given six blows of the knife handle to drive a match peg into the ground, three with eyes shut and three with eyes open. The loser must extract the peg from the earth with his teeth.

GAMES OF MAGIC

C-a-r.—One player goes out of the room. The leader asks that someone touch any one of three articles in a row, announcing that the player who left the room can tell which one was touched. He calls, "Come on back" and the confederate makes a few mysterious passes over the three articles and then selects Number One. That happens to be correct. The tip-offs come in the leader's manner of calling the mind reader back. If he uses a word beginning with the letter "C" the confederate knows it is Number One—"Come back"; "Can you come now." If he uses the letter "A" he knows it is Number Two—"All right." If he uses the letter "R" it is Number Three—"Ready?" To make it more confusing the confederates may decide that one is any consonant up to "L." Two is any vowel. Three is any consonant from "M" to the end of the alphabet.

Five-in-a-row.—Five books or other articles. Someone touches one of the articles. The mind reader returns. The leader points to one of the books and says, "Is it this one?" "No," answers the mind reader, "it is that one," pointing to the article touched. The tip-off is given in this fashion. If the leader touches the upper left-hand corner of any one of the five articles the mind reader knows

Number One has been touched. The upper right-hand corner means Number Two; lower left, Number Three; lower right, Number Four; center, Number Five.

Nine squares.—Mark nine squares on the ground, blackboard, or floor. Or use nine articles in rows of three each. Some player touches one of the squares or indicates it. The player who has been out of the room returns and tells when the chosen square is touched by the leader. The secret is that all of the squares are numbered in the minds of the leader and his confederate. The leader is careful to touch the chosen square only in its regular turn. Thus if three (upper right corner) is touched he must touch three on the third time and he must be careful not to touch one or two in their regular order. Thus, he begins at the lower right (9) saying, "Is it this one?" "No," says the confederate. He touches the center square (5). "Is it this one?" "No." Now on the next turn he touches the upper right corner square (3). "Is it this one?" "Yes," answers the mind reader correctly. If a square in the bottom row is selected, the leader and his confederate may have some signal for indicating the numbering, 1, 2, 3, begins at the bottom, in order to avoid touching most every square before coming to the correct one. For instance, it may be understood that whenever the leader begins by tapping or rubbing the pencil or pointer against his leg or arm that is the signal that the numbering has been changed and that the square touched is in the bottom row. The numbering is always done from left to right.

Hands over head.—The crowd sits in a circle. One person leaves the room. The leader announces that this person will be able to tell over whose head he holds his hands when called upon to do so. The leader moves around the circle, beginning anywhere. "Hands over head," shouts the leader, as he extends his hands over some player's head. "Hands over head," repeats the person outside the room. The leader continues around the circle, stopping occasionally to extend his hands over some player's head. Finally, he stops in front of one player, extends his hands and shouts, "Hands over head and rest upon," whereupon the person outside responds, "Hands over head and rests upon Sue Jenkins."

The secret: The leader, on the call, places his hands over the head of the person third to the right of the leader when his accomplice leaves the room. The second time it can be the person third to the left. Or it can be the tenth to the right or left. Or it can be the person before whom the leader is standing when the accomplice leaves the room. Or it can be the last person to speak before the accomplice leaves the room. The leader and his accomplice should have a clear understanding of the nature and order of the "tip-offs."

Spirits move.—This is played in the same fashion as "Hands over head." The leader extends his hands and says, "Spirits move." The accomplice outside, answers, "Let them move." Finally the leader says, "Spirits move and rest upon ——." The accomplice outside finishes the sentence by adding the name of the person over whose head the leader's hands are extended.

A GOOD MIXER

King and Queen of the key.—This game is deservedly popular for reasons that will be evident as you play it. A King and Queen are selected. Then someone starts the game by appearing before the royal pair. If it is a girl she goes to the King, who whispers in her ear something to do with a key that he gives her. She looks around the room and gives the key to some man. He goes to the Queen, who whispers instructions to him. He gives the key to a girl, and thus the game continues. Finally, the King and Queen call a halt, and the fun begins. The first person has to tell why she gave the key to the one whom she selected. The second tells why he gave it to the third, and so on. Sometimes the reason is complimentary; sometimes it is not. But it is always done in fun. "Because he has the most manly bearing." "Because she has the prettiest eyes." "Because he is the wittiest." "Because she has the best disposition." "Because he has the biggest feet." "Because she talks the most." "Because he has the best looking teeth." "Because she will make the best wife." These are a few suggestions.

CHAPTER VI
FUN WITH ACTIVE GAMES

FUN WITH ACTIVE GAMES

Spud.—Playball, volleyball, or tennis ball. Leader bounces the ball and calls the name of some player. That player recovers the ball while all the other players scatter about the gymnasium or playing field. From the point of recovery he attempts to hit one of the other players with the ball. Each miss counts one "Spud" against the player missing. After missing the player must recover the ball and throw again until he hits someone, except that three spuds puts him out. When a player is hit he must recover the ball and attempt to hit someone else. When a player gets three spuds against him he must bend over against a wall while all the other players take a shot at him with the ball.

Balloon goal.—At each corner of the room are stretched strings at the height of six or seven feet. Players line up in four alternating files. Two toy balloons of different colors are put in play by the leader tossing them in the air at the center of the floor. One side has been designated as the "Greens" (if you have a green balloon) and the other as the "Yellows" (if you have a yellow balloon). The idea is for each group to try to get its balloon over either of two goals in diagonal corners of the room. A point is scored each time this is done. There is no let-up in play, the ball being immediately put into play again by the leader batting it up into the air at the center of the floor. Players have the privilege of playing anywhere on the floor after the balls are first put in play.

Bottle ball.—The ideal number for this game is five for each side. Field 60 feet x 30 feet. The three end players must guard two

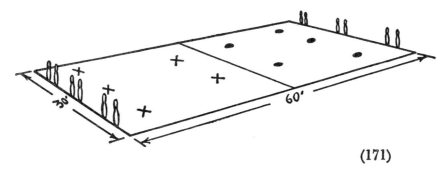

Indian clubs (or bottles) each. These clubs should be placed about 18 inches apart. The throwers try to shoot a basketball (volleyball or playball) through the opposite side, their opponents blocking the ball as best they can. Players foul when they step beyond the midway line.

Score—Five points for each Indian club knocked down. Ten points for each shot that goes between the two Indian clubs. One point for each shot rolling over the line. One point for each shot going under a string stretched across the end of the field at the height of six feet. One point off for each toss going over that string without being tipped over by an opponent.

Parlor volleyball.—A light rubber playball or water ball (ten-cent store), or a toy balloon. A row of chairs is arranged alternately as in "Going to Jersualem" across middle of floor for a net. Play as regular volleyball except—

(1) There are no out-of-bounds.
(2) A player may hit the ball as many times as he wishes.
(3) Any number of tips is allowed in getting it over net.
(4) The player may stand anywhere he desires in serving, provided that he is not allowed to stand near the chairs and hit it directly over them and down at the floor.

When played outdoors stretch a string across at waist height. Balloons must be hit over this string.

Center pitch.—Players pitch bean bags into metal wastebasket. One bean bag to a player. All line up and toss at time the leader's whistle blows. Then other side tosses. Three to five throws for each side.

"200 or Bust."—Three circles. Three bean bags. Each player gets three tosses. To go out a side must make a perfect 200. If go over then must start again. First side to make perfect 200 wins. Line counts for larger score of two.

Guarding the treasure.—Equipment—A football, volleyball, playball, or tin can.

The game—One player who is "It" guards the treasure. He may be regarded as the "miser" while the rest are robbers, or he may be considered as the "guard" while the others are the "enemy." The "guard" takes a position directly over the ball—the "treasure"—one foot on each side of it. If he prefers he can stand directly back of it, or he can keep moving around it. The rest of the players circle about attempting to get the "treasure" by kicking it away from the guard without being tagged by him. If a player succeeds, another immediately kicks it, and soon the ball is being followed by the whole crowd. They do their best to keep the guard from regaining possession of it and standing over it as before. No player but the guard is allowed to touch the "treasure" with his hands. If the guard succeeds in tagging any player before another kicks it, the tagged player becomes the guard in turn.

Spud spear relay.—Each team is provided with a fork. Potatoes are arranged on a course from four to twenty feet apart depending on the space available. Runner Number One runs to the first potato, spears it with the fork, carries it back and drops it in a basket, before handing the fork to his next teammate. Number Two gets the second potato in the same manner. The team first to get its last potato back home and in the basket wins. The hand must not touch the potato at any time.

Run, sheep, run.—Two equal sides, each with a captain. A home base is indicated. One group becomes the "sheep." They go out and hide. Their leader comes back, when they are ready, and goes with the opposing side as it hunts for the "sheep." When the leader thinks the opportune time has come he yells "Run, sheep, run!" All the "sheep" immediately rush for home base, as do the "hunters." If the "sheep" beat the "hunters" to home base, they hide again. If not, the "hunters" become "sheep" in turn.

King of the castle.—One player is chosen by lot to be King. He assumes a position on a mound, or tub, or box, or stump. He bids defiance to all his foes by shouting:

> "I'm King of the Castle;
> Get out, you cowardly rascal."

The other players assail him, everyone being a claimant for the position of eminence. He must protect his right to it, alone.

Fair pulls and pushes are allowed, but players are not permitted to catch hold of the King's clothes. Penalty for such a foul is to be set aside as a Prisoner of War—virtual expulsion from the game.

The King may have an ally, who, however, does nothing except note fouls and expel those who commit them. The ally, therefore, is nothing more than a referee.

The chances for the King retaining his throne for long are not good. The player who dethrones him becomes King for next game.

Prisoner's base.—Players are evenly divided into two sides. Zones or bases are marked off by drawing a line at either side, thirty to sixty feet apart. In back of this line a box five feet by ten feet is drawn. This is the prison.

The game begins by one side sending out a player to dare the opponents. One of the enemy starts in pursuit of him, and he runs for home. If he is touched before he can make it, he is a prisoner and must immediately go to the opposing side and take his position in prison. He goes alone for the pursuing player is himself an object of pursuit by another player from the opposite side.

A player may only tag an opponent who has left home base before himself, and he can only be tagged by the one who left home after he did.

When a player has made a prisoner, he may return home untouched, and is subject to capture only after making a fresh sally.

A prisoner may be released if a teammate runs the gauntlet of the enemy and touches him behind the enemy's line before being tagged. Such a release requires great skill, alertness, and deception. After the runner touches a prisoner the two are permitted to return unharmed to their home base.

A prisoner is required to keep only one foot in the prison. Therefore, he may stretch toward his teammate to facilitate his deliverance. When there are several prisoners, it is required that only one of them have one foot touching the prison. With the others this one may form a chain, stretching toward the rescuer. Only one prisoner may be released at a time, however.

The game continues until all the players on one side are in prison.

In a play street, the two curbings may be the safety lines. The street becomes the sallying ground.

Squirrel tails.—Players are evenly divided into two or more teams. Each player has a cloth strip (a tie or handkerchief) slipped through his belt behind. At signal all players rush to a central point where there is a treasure—peanuts or counters of some kind. Players try to get some of this treasure and return with it to their home base.

A player may be "killed" by an opponent pulling out the tail. This puts the player out of the game and makes void any treasure he has captured on that particular raid. Players are safe when home. Thus "squirrels" will be alert to protect their tails while at the same time they are trying to capture the tails of opponents and pick up some of the treasure. At the end of the game each peanut or counter counts one point. Each tail counts five points.

Stagecoach.—The players are seated in a circle. Each one is given the name of some part of the stagecoach—the wheel, the hub, the axle, the seat, the door, the harness, the brake, the horses, the driver, the passengers, the baggage, spoke, tire, step. One of the party begins telling a story about a stagecoach, bringing in all the different things related to the coach. As each thing is mentioned the player (or players) representing it gets up and runs around his chair. At some point in the story the storyteller shouts "Stagecoach!" when everyone must leave his seat and get a different one. The story-teller tries to get a seat in the scramble, thus leaving another player to begin a new story.

Auto trip.—This is similar to stagecoach. The players get the names of automobile parts. The storyteller tells a story of an auto trip. "We got out the old bus and had the 'tank' filled with 'gas.' Air was pumped into the 'tires.' A 'spare' was on the back. I put my foot on the 'starter' and we were off. The 'door' rattled, the 'engine' shook, the 'hood' came loose, etc." As the player tells the story, the parts mentioned get up and follow him. When he yells "Blowout" each player scrambles for a seat. The one left out becomes the next storyteller.

Hot cockles.—A player, kneeling down, places his face, eyes closed, in the lap of another. He places his hand on his back, palm up. Each person walks up and slaps the open hand. After each slap the kneeler tries to guess who hit him. If he guesses correctly, that player takes his places.
Variation—Instead of kneeling, the player may bend over with his head against his arm, resting against a tree or wall.

Dismounting cavalry.—Two players are needed for a team. One is the horse, the other the rider. The latter player mounts the back of his "steed," arms around his shoulders and legs wrapped around the body. The "horse" grasps the legs in his hands. Two such teams contest, the riders trying to pull one another from their mount.

Play the game on soft turf for frequently hard falls are had. The game is rough and players ought to have on old clothes.

Cavalry battle royal.—This is the same as "Dismounting Cavalry" except that there are numerous teams. The game continues until only one rider survives.

Variation—The game may be played by sides.

Sponge badminton.—Use an ordinary sponge or a rubber sponge. Use badminton rackets or ping-pong paddles. Downward strokes are not allowed. Players try to make the sponge land on the opponent's side. Each time it does a point is scored. Fifteen or twenty-one points constitute a game.

Drop the handkerchief.—This old-timer is always fun. Players form a circle. One player walks around outside the circle with a handkerchief or rag. He drops it behind some player and keeps on moving around the circle, endeavoring to walk all the way around before the player discovers it. If he does, the player becomes a "dead fish" and must stand in the center of the circle. As soon as a player discovers the handkerchief behind him he starts in pursuit of the player who dropped it. If he catches him that player becomes a "dead fish." The new runner now walks around the circle. A "dead fish" may be rescued by a player tossing the handkerchief into the circle behind him. He immediately starts in pursuit.

Variation—Play the game to music. When the music is slow the runners move slowly in time to it. When the music is fast, the runners speed up. When it stops they stop. Penalty for failing to obey instructions means becoming a "dead fish." ..

Flying Dutchman.—Players form a ring by couples. Couples hold hands. A couple stands outside the circle. They hold hands as they start around the circle. Directly they slap the hands of some couple in the circle and continue around the circle in the direction they are going. The couple touched starts running immediately in the opposite direction, holding hands as they run. When couples meet it may take some tall maneuvering to avoid a collision. The first couple back to the vacated position remains in the circle. The couple left out continues the game.

Variations—(*a*) Require that the running couples stop when they meet. The boys shake hands and the girls bow and say "Howdy." Immediately thereafter they dash madly around the rest of the circle.

(b) Require that couples perform some stunt when they meet. For instance, the boy may be required to go down to one knee, left hand over head while the girl touches the hand with one of her hands and circles around him once. Or partners may be required to take hold of hands and swing around once. Or each person may be required to put forefinger on top of his head and whirl around three times.

Chinese hop.—A row of ten sticks about one foot apart is the course. The player must hop over these sticks without touching any of them. Touching a stick disqualifies the player. After jumping over the tenth stick the player, still on one foot, reaches down and picks up the stick, and hops back over the remaining sticks. Dropping the stick, he hops over the nine, picks up the ninth stick, and returns to the starting point, again hopping the remaining sticks. This continues until all of the sticks have been picked up. A player is disqualified if he touches both feet to the ground, or if he touches a stick with his foot.

Variations—(a) The game may be used as a race. In this case, a player who fouls must start over. (b) A relay may be run. The second man would put down the ten sticks. The third would pick them up, and so on.

Bull in the ring.—The players form a ring around the "bull," holding hands. The "bull" tries to break through. He may rush, lunge, or pull, to try to break the ring. If he escapes the players chase him. Whoever catches him becomes "bull" in turn. It is not fair for the "bull" to duck under.

Bear in the net.—The formation is the same as for "Bull in the Ring." The object of the game is also the same except that the bear is allowed to duck under or plunge over the extended arms of the players in the ring.

Stormy sea.—Guests sit about the room by couples. Each couple selects the name of some fish, which they keep to themselves. There are two less chairs than there are couples. One couple, known as the "whales," walks about the room calling the names of fish. As they call "Perch," "Bass," "Cat," "Buffalo," "Porpoise," "Shark," "Mackerel," "Halibut," and other names, the couples with those names get up and follow the "Whales" around. When the "Whales" shout "Stormy sea!" each couple rushes for seats. One couple is left out and they become the "Whales" in turn.

The game may be played outdoors by assigning trees to the various couples, or by drawing small circles on the ground.

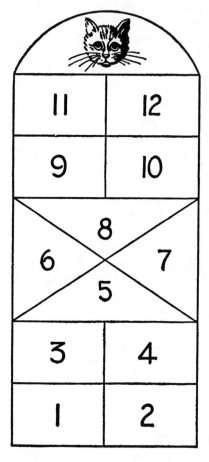

Hop scotch.—This is an old game that gives good practice in body balance and agility. Mark the diagram on the ground or walk.

Not more than three or four should play on one diagram or there will be too long to wait between turns.

A player stands two or three feet from the base of the diagram and tosses a tile or disc trying to get it in Number 1. If he succeeds he hops into Number 1, kicks the tile out, and hops out. In this performance he must not touch any line with his foot. He next throws the tile for Number 2. This is continued until he fails. Failure comes when he fails to get the tile completely in the correct space, when he touches a line with his foot, when he fails to kick the tile out, or when he touches the other foot to the ground before completing his performance. Each time he tosses the tile he stands on both feet.

Number 8 is the "resting bed." When he reaches it he may put both feet in Numbers 6 and 7 to rest himself. Before proceeding, however, he must resume the hopping position.

Before reaching "the cat's face" or "pudding" he may have as many kicks as he likes in getting the tile out. But when he reaches that point he must kick the tile through all of the divisions in a single kick. That puts him "out."

If the tile be pitched into the wrong number, or rests on one of the lines, either in pitching or kicking, or if it be kicked over the side lines, the player loses his turn. If he puts both feet down, while in the figure except in the "resting bed," or sets his foot, in hopping, on either of the lines, he suffers the same penalty. The tile may be a piece of wood, a piece of linoleum, or a flat rock.

Cat and rat.—This old game is a never failing favorite with children. The players stand in a circle, holding hands. One player inside the circle is the rat. Another player outside the circle is the cat. The cat tries to catch the rat. The players help the rat and hinder the cat by raising or lowering their arms, and by not allowing the cat to break through the circle. The game may be varied by having more than one cat and one rat at a time.

Rabbit and dog.—Players stand in a circle. Two bean bags of different colors are used, one color to represent the rabbit and the other to represent the dog. One player receives the rabbit and a player on the opposite side of the circle receives the dog. When the signal is given to start the rabbit and the dog are passed from player to player. The dog chases the rabbit. The players help the rabbit to get away and the dog to reach the rabbit. If the rabbit completes three rounds of the circle without being caught he is safe.

Lame wolf.—One player is chosen as the "lame wolf." All of the other players are the "children." A space is marked off as the wolf's den. At the other end of the playing space a place is marked off as the house for the children. The wolf goes to his den. The children run out of their house and begin to taunt the wolf, singing "Who's afraid of the big bad wolf?" or making jeering remarks, such as "Lame wolf can't catch anybody." When the wolf thinks he has a good chance to catch someone he dashes out of his den in pursuit. However, he can run only three steps when he must start hopping on one foot. Anyone caught becomes a lame wolf and must help catch the other children. When all the rest of the children are safe at home the wolf and his mates retire to their den. Again the children venture forth to taunt the wolf. The game continues until only one child remains. That player becomes the lame wolf for the next game.

The wolf and the children may return any time to the den or home to rest.

Slap Jack.—The players form a circle. There should be a distance of two feet, but no more, between players. One player is "It." With a towel or rolled newspaper he walks around outside the circle. The players stand with their hands behind them, palms up. "It" drops the towel into some player's hand and starts running around the circle. The player who has the towel runs after him and slaps him as often as he can until "It" has completed the circle and stands in the place vacated by the player who now has the towel. This latter player is "It" and the game continues.

Straddle ball.—Players stand in a circle, feet in straddle position and touching the feet of the players on either side. "It" stands in the center of the circle with a basketball or volleyball. He tries to roll the ball out of the circle between the legs of some player. The player tries to stop the ball with his hands. If successful, he rolls the ball back to the center player. If "It" does roll the ball through some player's straddled legs that player takes his place. "It" may feint at throwing in one direction and throw in another. Much depends upon his speed and his surprise moves.

Three deep.—Players form a circle, two deep, facing center. Two players on the outside of the circle and at some distance from one another begin the game as runner and chaser. The runner may save himself from being tagged by stepping in front of one of the pairs of players, thus making the circle at that point three deep. The outside player must immediately leave or be tagged. If a player is tagged he becomes the chaser, in turn. A runner may run in any direction he chooses, to the right or left or across the circle. However, he can only step in front of a player and make the circle three deep by moving from the outside into the circle and to the right.

Variations—(a) *Two Deep*—Single circle. The runner may save himself by stepping in front of another player, whereupon that player must run. (b) *Four Deep*—Where the crowd is large, players may stand in rows of three around the circle. (c) *Hook On*—Players stand about the playing space in couples, with arms linked. The outside arm is held akimbo. The runner may save himself by linking on to one of the partners, when the other must leave immediately to keep from getting caught.

Jacob and Rachel.—Circle formation. One player is blindfolded and takes the part of Jacob. Another player inside the circle is Rachel. Jacob calls, "Rachel, where are you?" Rachel must immediately answer, "Here I am, Jacob." She then darts to some other part of the circle to avoid being captured. Jacob may call as often as he desires. Rachel must answer each time.

Variations—(a) Have two Jacobs and two Rachels. Instruct Jacob to keep his hands extended all of the time to avoid head-on collisions. (b) Blindfold Rachel as well as Jacob. The hands-out rule would be advisable again.

Where posts are in the way see that blindfolded players are pro-tected from walking into them.

Poisoned circle.—Ten to a dozen players form a ring around a circle which is about five feet in diameter. The object of the game is to keep out of the poisoned circle and to try to pull some of the other players into it. When a player steps in or on the poisoned circle he is out of the game.

Variations—(*a*) Instead of a circle place Indian clubs or pop bottles in the space. A player knocking one down is out. (*b*) Place cushions in the center. A player touching the cushions is out.

Advancing statues.—All players stand in a line, except one. He stands some distance ahead of the line and covers his eyes as he counts from 1 to 10. The players try to get from one side of the room to the other while "It" is counting ten. As soon as "It" reaches ten he looks up suddenly. Any player caught in motion must go back to the starting point. The others hold whatever position they happen to have at the time, statue-like. The first player to cross the room becomes "It" or has the privilege of selecting the next "It."

Simon says calisthenics.—Players stand about with plenty of room between each player for action. The leader calls commands, such as "Simon says, 'Hands on hips and body bend.'" "Simon says, 'Hands raise.'" "Simon says, 'Position, and jump forward.'" Play-ers obey commands of the leader. However, if the command is not preceded with "Simon says," the players do nothing. Any player failing to obey a "Simon says" command immediately or any obeying a command not prefaced by "Simon says" must drop out. The leader makes it more confusing by going through the action each time.

Hill dill.—Two parallel lines are drawn near the middle of the playing space and from fifteen to thirty feet apart. This space is the tagging area. One player, who is "It," stands between the lines and calls:

> "Hill dill,
> Come over the hill,
> Or else I'll catch you
> Standing still."

The other players, who stand behind one of these lines, then run across the playing area to the other line. While running across

this area they may be tagged. When tagged they help tag the others.
The game continues until all players have been caught.

Blind pig.—Players stand in groups of ten or twelve persons. A
player who is "It" stands in the front of each group. He turns his
back and covers his eyes. Then one of the players pokes him with
his finger. The blind pig turns with uncovered eyes and tries to
name the player who poked him. After calling the name ot a player
"It" calls some penalty to be performed by the culprit, such as,
"Hop to the oak tree and back." If the guess has been correct the
guilty player must perform the assigned stunt. If the guess has
been wrong the blind pig must do the stunt himself. He then
appoints another player to take his place as blind pig, and the game
continues.

Soakey.—"Soakey, one ender!" shouts one player. "Two ender,"
shouts another. These two players place their caps or hats at either
end while the others place theirs between them in a straight line.
All players stand ready beside their caps while one of the end
players tosses or rolls a tennis ball or soft rag ball, trying to get it into
one of the caps. If he succeeds the player in whose cap the ball lands
immediately picks it up and throws, trying to hit one of the other
players. These players have scattered immediately it was apparent
that the ball would not land in one of their hats. If hit, a player
must put a counter in his hat (a match, stick, or pebble). If the
thrower misses, he must put a counter in his hat. Three counters in
any one player's hat ends the game. That player must stand bent
over against a wall or tree while each of the other players throws the
ball at him from the distance of twenty feet.

Circle touch ball.—Players form a circle around one player.
Players in the circle stand two or three feet apart. A basketball
or volleyball is passed here and there in the circle, and the center
player tries to touch it. If he succeeds the player who had it in his
possession at the time is "It." If the ball is touched while in the
air or on the ground the player who last had it in the circle is "It."
The players try to keep the ball away from the center player. They
feint, fake throws in one direction, and then throw or pass in another, and in other ways try to confuse him.

Circle catch ball.—The game is played with a smaller ball and
the center player must catch the ball instead of merely touching it.

Poisoned handkerchief.—The game is played just like "Touch Ball" except that a rag or handkerchief with a knot tied in it is used instead of a ball.

Ante over.—A shed and a ball. One team of players is stationed on one side of the building and the other on the other side. One of the players on the team that has the ball shouts "Ante Over!" as he tosses the ball over the shed. This warns the other team to be on the lookout for the ball. They try to catch it. If the ball is not caught, any member of the team may pick it up and throw it back, calling "Ante Over!" as the throw is made. If the ball is caught, the person making the catch runs around to the other side and tries to hit some player of the other team with the ball before he can get to the other side of the shed. If a player is hit he joins the other team.

Each time the ball is caught, all of the members of the catcher's team also run around the shed. Some run around one way and some the other, so as to confuse the opposing side, since it doesn't know who has the ball. As soon as a team realizes that the ball has been caught, it runs for safety on the other side of the shed. Each time the ball is caught the teams change sides. The game ends when all of the players of one team have been caught. If this seems likely not to happen, the teams decide on a number of throws before counting players to determine the winner.

Bicycle polo.—Four players make a team. Each player is mounted on a bicycle. The game is played just like regular polo except that the players use croquet mallets and the ball is a solid rubber ball. A rubber playball six to ten inches in diameter may be substituted for the solid rubber ball.

Marble golf ("Knucks").—Three holes or more, four or five inches in diameter, are dug in the ground. The distance between them is about eight or ten feet.

They may be in a straight line or not as desired.

The starting line is five or six feet from the first hole. One player starts by "knuckling down" at the starting line and shooting at Hole Number 1. If he makes good by going into this hole he plays for Hole Number 2, and so on until he has come back to Hole Number 1. When he fails to hole his marble the next player starts. If a player hits an opponent's marble he gets an extra shot. If a player holes his marble and another player's marble is near the rim of the hole ready to go in at the next shot, he may hit his opponent's marble, driving it away, before proceeding to the next hole. Some players acquire great skill in playing an opponent's marble, so that they can use it for several consecutive shots. In playing out of a hole players must knuckle with the hand at the rim of the hole from which the play is made or they may be allowed one hand's span from the rim.

The last player out must hold his clenched fist, knuckles up, at the rim of Hole Number 1 while each of the other players, in turn, plumps his marble at him, trying to hit his knuckles. Three shots are allowed at the knuckles.

Leapfrog.—The players stand in line, the first player in the line bending his back and catching hold of his ankles with his hands. The next player leaps over Number 1, putting both hands on his back and spreading his legs as he leaps. He then assumes the same position as Number 1. Number 3 goes over Numbers 1 and 2 and assumes the same position. When all players have been over, Number 1 rises and leaps over all the others. And so it continues as long as desired. Or a definite course can be marked out. Players continue until the course is covered.

One and over.—This is a variation of leapfrog. A line is marked where Number 1 bends over. The players line up in single file. The leader leaps over and makes a mark with his heel where he landed. The player who is bent over moves up to this line. The leader now calls the jump. For instance, he calls "Over." That means that each man must go over in one leap from the starting line. Players are allowed to run but the leap must be made in one bound, both feet hitting the ground at or behind the starting line. If a player fails he may call on the leader to make good. If the leader fails he goes down, and the player bent over takes his place at the foot of the line. If he succeeds the boy who has failed becomes the bender. Each time there is a failure the game begins again at the starting point with the next man in line moving up as leader.

The next call, granting that all players have made good, and the leader has marked his place of landing, may be "One and over!" That means each player is to run to the starting line, take one hop, and then go over. Whenever a player feels he can make it in less than the leader calls, he is privileged to challenge the leader. For instance, if "One and over!" is called and a player thinks he can make it in an "over" he so announces. He must make good or become "It." If he makes good the leader becomes "It."

Much depends on the skill with which the leader measures his jumps. For instance, he may make his first "over" a short one, so that his "One and over!" will be entirely too far for any player to make it in an "over."

"Hats on Davy!" (Spanish fly).—This is still another variation of leapfrog. Players need old hats or caps.

The leader calls "Spanish Fly!" as he leaps over the "bender." As he goes over he must hot hand the "bender" on the thigh.

The next call is "Spur the mule!" This time right or left heel must gently tap the "bender" on the thigh as the player goes over.

Finally, "Hats on Davy!" is the call. Each player leaps over depositing his cap on the "bender's" back as he leaps over.

If a player fails or if he knocks a hat off he is "It." It can readily be seen that as the caps stack up it becomes increasingly difficult to go over without knocking one off.

Top spinning.—Every boy should know how to spin a top skillfully.

For accuracy— (1) *Plug*—A circle about eight feet in diameter is drawn on the ground. Players spin their tops in the circle. They are allowed to spin down. When they do they are left where they stop. The top nearest the center stays in the circle. The other players spin their tops at it trying to plug it, that is dig a hole in it with their spikes. If a player's top does not run out of the circle it stays there to be the target of other tops. A top may be knocked out by a spinner. The game continues until all tops are in the circle.

(2) *Marble Plug*—Again a circle eight to ten feet in diameter is used. Fifteen to twenty marbles are gathered together at the center. The players use a top with a rounded spike. They take turns shooting at the marbles trying to knock them out of the ring. It is necessary for the top to spin for a successful shot to count. As long as a player is successful in knocking marbles out of the ring he continues.

Stunts— (1) Spin the top in the air and catch it on the palm of the hand, still spinning. Toss the spinning top into the air and catch it on the back of the hand, still spinning. (2) Pick up the spinning top on the hand between the forefinger and second finger so that it continues to spin in the palm of the hand. Toss it from the right hand to the left, catching it in the palm, still spinning.

(3) Toss the top for distance with a side sweep. The top must spin when it lands.

(4) Toss the spinning top up in the air for height and catch it in the palm of the hand, still spinning.

Ocean wave.—Players are seated in a circle. There is one vacant chair. A center player is standing. He yells, "Slide left" or "Slide right" and the players who are seated must move to the left to fill the vacant chair as it appears next to them. The player who is "It" dashes for the vacant seat and keeps on after it until he finally gets it. The location of the vacant seat is constantly changing, for the players move into it as it comes next to them. If "It" gets a seat, and the call has been "Slide left" the player to "It's" right must take his place.

Dragon tag.—From five to ten players link arms and become the dragon. They endeavor to encircle the other players one or more at a time. When they do the players thus caught add themselves to the dragon. This continues until all players are caught. Boundaries should be decided before the game begins.

Swat the fly.—The players form a circle, one player inside. A wastebasket or other suitable receptacle rests at the center of the circle. The center player has a roll of paper in his hand as he walks around the circle. He finally swats someone and immediately runs to deposit the roll in the wastebasket. The person swatted pursues, picks up the roll and tries to swat the runner before he can get back to the vacated place in the circle. The game continues with a new swatter.

Horse and rider race.—One player mounts the back of another, legs around his waist and arms around his shoulders. In this position they race to the goal. When they reach the goal they exchange positions and race back to the starting line.

Mule and rider race.—The mule goes down on all fours. The rider mounts the mule's back and they race to the finish line.

Hurdle race.—Ten players to a team. Players Number 1 and 2 on each team hold a broomstick or rope between them at a height of at least six inches from the ground. They run down the line with their teammates between them jumping the hurdle as it moves to the end of the line. As soon as they reach the end Numbzer 2 returns to the head of the line and starts down with Number 3 in the same manner. Then Number 3 runs with Number 4 and so on until Number 1 is back at the head of the line.

Dainty.—This is an old game. The "dainty" is a piece of broomstick about five inches long. It is sharpened at both ends as one would sharpen the point of a lead pencil. A piece of broomstick, from two to three feet in length, is used for a club.

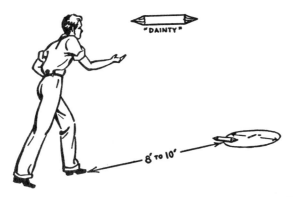

The players start the game by calling, "Dainty, One!" "Dainty, Two!" and so on. Number 1 becomes batter. Number 2 becomes pitcher.

The game starts with Number 2 standing at a line eight to ten feet away from a circle one foot in diameter. He pitches the "dainty" with an underhand swing at the circle. If the stick rests completely within the circle Number 1, the batter, loses his turn. Number 2 becomes the batter and Number 3 steps up as the new pitcher. Number 1 takes his position at the end of the line of players waiting their turn at the bat. If the "dainty" rests on the line of the circle, the batter gets one hit. If it rests completely without the circle the batter gets three licks.

The manner of striking is in this fashion: The batter holds the club in one hand and taps the end of the dainty making it rise in the air by a sharp blow. While it is in the air he endeavors to hit it with the club, driving it as far as possible. If he is to get three licks he starts the second one at the point where the "dainty" stopped after the first blow. The third blow is made from the point where the stick stopped on the second blow.

After the player has hit he estimates the distance and then calls the number of jumps (standing) that he is willing to give the player who is pitching. If that player takes up the challenge and jumps the distance in that number of jumps or less the batter scores nothing, and the next batter comes up. The last jump must clear the "dainty." If the pitcher allows the challenge to go uncontested or if he fails to jump over the "dainty" in the number of jumps called, the batter scores as many points as the number of jumps he gave. Then the next batter comes up and a new pitcher tosses the stick at the circle. Of course, if the batter hits the dainty and fails to make it rise in the air, or if he misses it as it rises, that is counted one blow. Oftentimes the batter sends the "dainty" up in the air but misses it as it comes down, thus making it possible for the pitcher to jump it in one jump. This jump must be made from the edge of the circle, the heels touching that edge.

Fifty to one hundred points, as decided, constitutes a game. The last player out pitches for each other player. Again the players get one, three, or no licks, according to where the "dainty" rests after being pitched. This time the pitcher must hop to the "dainty" after it has been hit, pick it up, and hop back to the circle, without letting the foot down. Sometimes this is a tough assignment if the batter got three good licks.

Iau Chhung.—This is an ancient Chinese game that is very similar to "Dainty." Lots are drawn to see who will be first batter, second, third, and so on. Every player except one batter scatters about in the field to try to catch the hit. Four sticks are needed. Two of them are of equal length and fat. The other two are light, usually of bamboo. They are about one foot and six inches long, respectively. The longer stick is the "club," while the shorter one is the "twig."

The batter places the "twig" across the two parallel fat sticks so that it protrudes beyond them on one side. He sharply strikes this protruding end with a downward blow so that the "twig" rises in the air. The other players try to catch it as it comes down. If it is caught the batter must take the field, and the next batter comes up to strike. If it is not caught the batter is ready for the next test.

This time he lays the "twig" crosswise on the two fat sticks, while one of the fielders throws the "club" at it. He has three tries from a position at least five yards away. If he hits the "twig" the batter is out. If he misses the batter takes the third test.

The fielder takes the "twig" and tosses it to the batter, who tries to hit it with the club. He is allowed three trials. If he misses three times he is out. If he hits the "twig" it is allowed to fall to the ground unimpeded. The batter then measures the distance from where he is standing to the "twig," using the "club" as a measuring rod. A batter continues to bat until he is put out. Each time he goes through the three tests.

The scoring is by "club" measures. Each "club" measure is a point. The players decide before the game starts whether fifty or one hundred points are "out."

There are two penalties for losing—the "hmmmmmmm" penalty and the "hopping" penalty. The players decide how many before the game begins, maybe two, three, or four. There are the same number of each type of penalty.

To impose the "hmmmmmmm" penalty the winner tosses the "twig" as far as he can. The loser must run after it and bring it back, all of the time saying "hmmmmmmm." If he should stop saying "hmmmmmmm" before returning, three more "hmmmm-mmm" penalties are levied.

In the hopping penalty the batter throws the "twig" and the loser hops to it, picks it up, and returns to the starting point without putting the foot down. If he fails three more hopping penalties are inflicted.

DUAL CONTESTS

Hand push.—Two players stand flat-footed facing one another, arm's length distance. The arms are extended, palm out. The players hit palms together, pushing, feinting, until one player loses his balance.

Hand wrestle. — Players stand with wide leg spread, with stance similar to that of a swordsman. They grasp right hands and twist, turn, and shove with the wrist, trying to throw the opponent off balance. As soon as a player moves one foot from position he has lost.

Indian wrestle.—Contestants lie side by side with feet in opposite directions. Adjacent arms are locked. At the sound of the whistle adjacent legs are interlocked at the knee. The wrestler wins who makes his opponent roll over from the position flat on his back.

Rooster fight.—Hands on ankles. Players jostle one another with the shoulder. The point is to make the opponent lose his balance or loosen his hold on his ankles.

One leg wrestle.--Players stand on one leg, grasping right hands. The wrestle consists in trying to make the opponent touch the other foot to the ground or touch the ground with his free hand. The free hand may not touch the opponent.

Chinese get-up.—Two players sit back to back with arms folded. Each tries to get up by pushing against the other.

Try the same contest with arms locked.

Brothers of the I-will-arise.—Contestants lie flat on their backs, arms folded. At signal, they rise to sitting position and then to their feet without help from their arms. If you think this is easy, try it. It is good exercise for the abdominal muscles.

Pull up.—Contestants sit on the floor or ground facing one another. The knees are straight and the feet are braced against the opponent's feet. In this position each grasps a stick between them and tries to pull his opponent to him. If a contestant bends his knees he forfeits.

Cross hand shove.—Contestants cross arms at wrist and take hold of hands. In this position they try to shove one another out of a six-foot circle. No tripping is allowed.

TAG GAMES

Cross tag.—One player may save another from capture or take the play away from him by crossing between him and the player who is "It." Immediately "It" takes out after the runner who has crossed.

Clap in, clap out.—Opposing teams line up at two ends of a playing space, being from thirty to fifty feet apart. One team sends a runner to the opposing side. The players on this side stand with both feet back of their line with one hand outstretched, palm up. The runner walks along this line. He taps each hand, in turn, until he decides which player he wants to chase him. He slaps this person's hand hard. Immediately he runs for his own line. If he gets there before the chaser can tag him he is safe. If not, he joins the other side. A runner may feint at hitting a hand hard and then hit it gently in order to throw his opponents off guard.

Maze tag (Colonade, streets and alleys).—Put the crowd through a grand march that brings them down finally in lines of eight or sixteen. Halt the march at this point and have each line space off so that all Number Ones, Number Twos, and so forth, are in straight line after they have moved so that their hands may touch the player on either side of them as they stand with arms stretched straight out from the shoulder, facing the leader. Now have them space off similarly with the player immediately behind them.

Players stand facing front with arms stretched out so as to touch the hands on either side of them. This makes a series of aisles or streets. When the leader blows his whistle all players, keeping their arms outstretched, make a quarter turn to the right. That makes new aisles. There is a runner and a chaser. Neither may break through a column, nor duck under. Each time the leader blows the whistle there is the quarter turn to the right. A leader who uses his whistle wisely will make this a very interesting game.

When a player is tagged, another couple is chosen to run.

Fish in the sea.—This is similar to "Hill Dill" and "Pom Pom Pullaway." All players but one stand behind a line. That one is "It" and stands midway between the line behind which the runners are standing and another line thirty feet or so away. He shouts:

> "Fish in the ocean,
> Fish in the sea;
> Don't get the notion
> You'll get by me."

After this challenge all the fish must leave safely and try to cross to the opposite line without being tagged.

Players who are tagged join hands with "It" and help catch the others. If the net breaks players tagged on that turn are released.

Net tag (Chain tag).—This is the same as "Fish in the Sea" except that only the end players in the net or chain may tag a runner. If the runner can get away before the end players can get to him he is safe.

Squirrel in a tree.—Players form in groups of three. Two of them take hold of hands and form a tree. The other one of the three gets inside between the two so that their arms enclose him. There are two players who are the "Dog" and the "Squirrel," respectively. The "Dog" chases the "Squirrel." It may save itself by ducking into a tree. The player in that tree must immediately leave with the

"Dog" in pursuit. The fun comes in frequent changes. When a "Dog" catches a "Squirrel" he becomes the "Squirrel" and the "Squirrel" becomes the "Dog."

Variations— (a) Instead of a "Dog" and a "Squirrel," there may be several squirrels without a home. When the leader's whistle blows every squirrel must get out of its tree and into another one. The homeless squirrels endeavor each time to get a home. This is a very lively game and a good mixer. After playing it awhile have the squirrels change places with persons forming the tree, thus giving every player a chance to run. (b) Play it with three players forming the tree.

Bird in a nest (Bird's nest).—This is similar to "Squirrel in a Tree" except that the birds are supposed to run with arms spread out straight from the side as if they were flying.

Japanese tag.—The tagger is required to hold one hand on the spot touched when he was tagged when he tags another person. It is just too bad if he was tagged on the heel.

Snatch.—Players line up in two equal sides, facing one another. About thirty feet is allowed between the two lines. The players number off from right to left. In the center of the space between the two lines is a bottle or stick with a rag or handkerchief on it. Or there may be a stool, wastebasket upside down, or stump, with a bean bag or towel on it.

The leader calls a number. The players from the two sides bearing that number rush out to the center. If one of the players is slow getting up to center the other player snatches the rag and rushes back to his side. He is safe anywhere in his line. The other player tries to tag the player who has the rag. If he does so before the runner can get back to his line one point is scored for the tagging side. However, if the runner gets to his line with the rag without being tagged he scores two points.

If both of the runners get out to center about the same time they stall around, making feints at grabbing the rag. Finally, when one of them thinks he has his opponent off balance, he snatches the rag and breaks for his own line.

Players soon learn that it is not a good idea to rush out and grab the rag immediately.

After a player has touched the rag he is liable to be tagged. It does not matter that he did not get it. The other player may tag him, or, if he thinks he can get away with it, he may snatch up the rag and rush for his line.

Mystery tag.—The players stand in a circle. Each player has his hands extended in front of him, palms together, as he faces center. The player who is "It" walks around the circle placing his hands between the hands of each player and pretending to place a pebble which he has in his possession in their hands. Each player pretends also that he has received the pebble. The player who has really received it breaks away from the circle with the other players in pursuit. The player who succeeds in catching him becomes "It."

Pick a peach tag.—The players form a line, single file. Each player has his hands on the shoulders of the person in front of him. One player stands apart. He is "It." The head player in the line is the "Gardener." The foot player is the "Peach." "It" is the "Customer."

The "Customer" approaches the "Gardener" and says, "I would like to buy a peach." "You will find one on the last tree in the orchard," replies the "Gardener."

If the "Peach" can get to the head of the line without being tagged by the "Customer" he becomes the new "Gardener." In this case the "Customer" must try again. If the "Peach" is tagged before arriving at the head of the line he becomes "It."

It can readily be seen that to stand any chance at all to tag the end player "It" must feint at running down one side, reverse and come back to the other side, thus causing the "Peach" also to reverse and probably causing him to lose a little distance.

Stealing sticks.—This game is similar to "Prisoner's Base." Players are subject to being tagged just as in that game. The player to leave home last may tag a player of the opposing side who left home before him.

If a player gets to his opponent's goal where the sticks are placed, he picks one of them up and takes it back to his own team's goal. He is free to return unmolested.

When a player is tagged he be-

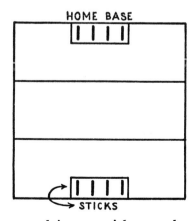

comes a prisoner. Prisoners may be rescued just as sticks may be stolen. When a side has some of its players in prison it cannot take any sticks until the prisoners are released. The first side to get all of the sticks of the opposing side wins.

Four to six sticks are used in each goal. The field is the same as in "Prisoner's Base," being thirty to sixty feet across from one goal to the other.

Dumbbell tag.—*Equipment*—A dumbbell, club, ball, or other article.

The players stand in a circle. "It" stands in the center. A dumbbell is passed from one player to another. "It" tries to tag the player who has the dumbbell. If he succeeds that person becomes "It."

Players must always receive the dumbbell when it is offered. They may move about freely, so that there will be plenty of running and chasing. Players may feint at passing the dumbbell one direction and pass it another.

Couple chair relay.—The couple links arms and runs to a designated point, the man carrying a folding chair in his free hand. At the goal, the man opens the chair, sets it up, and the girl sits down in it. Then she gets up. The man folds the chair. They link arms and he hands the chair to the man of the next couple. Four or five couples make a team.

Circle chair relay.—Two teams of ten or more players each. Chairs arranged in two circles, facing out from center. The players are seated in these chairs. At the signal to go the leader of each team starts walking around his circle. As soon as he completes the circuit and is seated the next man on his team makes the circuit. And thus it goes until every player has completed the round.

Variations— (*a*) Run around instead of walking. (*b*) Each contestant carries his chair around, puts it down and seats himself. (*c*) As soon as the first runner passes the person to his right that person gets up and follows. The third person follows the second, and so on.

Call ball.—One player bounces a ball up against a wall and calls the name or number of another player. That player endeavors to catch the ball on the rebound before it touches the ground again. If he succeeds he bounces the ball and calls some other player. If the called player fails to make the catch, the bouncer throws the ball again and calls another name. When thrown the ball must hit the floor or ground first and then the wall so that it will come looping back.

Fox and geese (Wheel tag).—This game is especially good in the snow. Clear off paths on a level surface like spokes in a wheel. See illustration. Or mark off the wheel on the ground with lime, using a liner. The game can also be played indoors by using chairs and string to mark the spokes of the wheel. The center, where the paths cross, is the goal. There may be more than one circle, one outside the other.

The player who is the fox chases the others, trying to tag someone. If he succeeds that player becomes the fox. No player must run out of the paths. Failure to observe this rule means that the offending player becomes the fox. The geese may jump across from one path to another, but the fox cannot. Neither can the fox tag a goose across the paths. Any goose who occupies the center is safe. However, only one goose is safe at a time. The last on up takes possession and all of the others must leave or be tagged.

Charley over the water.—The original Charley was Bonnie Prince Charlie who tried to be King of Scotland. It is always popular with young children. If there are more than fifteen players it may be advisable to have two or more Charleys. Charley stands in the center of the circle. The other players join hands and skip around the circle chanting:

> "Charley over the water,
> Charley over the sea,
> Charley catch a blackbird,
> Can't catch me."

As soon as they end this chant they stoop. Charley tries to tag someone before that person can get down. If he succeeds that player takes his place.

Sometimes the lines are sung to this tune:

Last couple out.—The players line up by couples. The player who is "It" stands from eight to ten feet ahead of the front couple. When he shouts, "Last couple out!" that couple must leave the rear and move forward with the idea of passing "It" and taking hold of hands in front of him. They may come swiftly or slowly as they desire. "It" may not turn his head to see them coming. He must look straight ahead. Only when they get even with him can he leave his place. But when they do get even with him he dashes after one or the other of them trying to tag one of them before they can take hold of hands in front of him. If he succeeds in tagging one of them that player takes his place, and the player who was "It" and the other member of the couple become the head couple. If the couple succeeds in getting together they become the new head couple, and "It" tries again. The two persons come up on either side of the line and not on the same side.

Jump the shot.—A stuffed sack (a volleyball or playball) is tied to the end of a long heavy string or rope. The players form a circle whose radius will be just a little less than the length of the string. A player in the center swings the sack around so that each man in the circle has to jump to keep it from hitting him on the feet. Any player who is hit must take the place of the man at the center.

Variation—Use a fishing pole instead of the string and sack.

Pin guard.—The players form a circle. One player, at center, attempts to guard a tenpin or pop bottle. The other players toss a volleyball, basketball, or playball at the pin trying to knock it down. When a player is successful in causing the pin to fall he takes the center player's place.

Can guard.—This is similar to "Pin Guard," with the players in a circle. Instead of the pin, two tin cans are set up at center, one on top of the other. When they are knocked down the center player must immediately replace them at the center spot. While he is doing this the other players may shoot at him with the ball. This they continue until he replaces the cans and yells "Cans Up!" During this procedure the players must not shoot at the cans but at the player himself. The player who knocked down the cans takes the center player's place for the next round.

Garden scamp.—All but two of the players form a circle. The space inside the circle is the garden. The "Scamp" is inside the circle. The "Gardener" is on the outside of the circle. He calls, "Who let you into my garden?" The "Scamp" replies, "I let myself into your garden." The "Gardener" then chases the "Scamp," who dodges in and out of the circle.

The "Gardener" must follow every place the "Scamp" goes, going through the same openings and doing the same things. When the "Scamp" is caught he becomes the "Gardener" and has the privilege of choosing the next "Scamp." The "Scamp" may do anything to make it more difficult for the "Gardener" to catch him, such as jump over clasped hands, play leapfrog with one of the players or go through on his hands and knees.

Water sprite.—This game is somewhat similar to "Hill Dill" and "Pom Pom Pullaway." Two lines of players are located opposite each other from 30 to 60 feet apart. The intervening space represents the river. Between the two lines is the "Water Sprite," who beckons to one of the players to leave the "bank." Immediately the "Water Sprite" must shut his eyes and count ten. The player signaled, in turn, signals to a player on the opposite "bank" while the "Sprite" has his eyes covered. These two players try to exchange positions while the "Water Sprite" tries to tag one of them. If he succeeds the player tagged takes his place.

I spy.—This ancient game never loses its appeal for children. It is nearly two thousand years old. Children in every land play it.

One player, who is "It," hides his head against a tree, post, or wall, eyes shut, and counts to 100, thus, "Five, ten, fifteen, twenty," etc. The others scatter and hide. At 100, "It" shouts, "Here I come! Ready or not! All around base are 'It.'" He then tries to find the hiders. As he finds one he shouts, "I spy Johnny" (or whoever it is) and dashes for home. If the hider gets home before the player who is "It" he is safe. The first player caught is "It" for the next time.

Throw the club (Green wolf, Hunkety, Yards off).—This game is an adaptation of "I spy." A club is leaned up against the post or wall. One player throws the club. While "It" is retrieving it and placing it back in position all of the players hide. "It" then goes out seeking to find the hiders. When he locates one of them he yells, "I spy, Charley," and dashes for the club. If he reaches it first the hider becomes a prisoner. If the hider beats "It" to the club he throws it and "It" must get the stick and replace it before hunting the other players. When a player beats "It" to the club he may select one prisoner to be free to hide again. "It" must find all of the hiders and make them prisoners.

Kick the can.—This is the same game as "Throw the Club," except that a can is used. Players kick the can instead of throwing the stick.

Pussy wants a corner.—All of the players except one occupy chairs or stand with hand against a tree or post. The player who is "It" goes around, first to one player and then to another, saying, "Pussy wants a corner." "Go to the next door neighbor," is the response. Any two players may signal one another and make an exchange of "corners." In fact, the players take great delight in tantalizing "It" by making frequent changes while his attention is directed elsewhere.

"Pussy" may feign lack of awareness of what is going on and then suddenly dash in to take a vacated "corner." When he does the player who is left out becomes "It."

If "Pussy" finds it too difficult to get a "corner" he may call "Everybody change," whereupon each player must find a new "corner." In the scramble surely "Pussy" will succeed in getting a place.

Skin the snake race.—Two or more teams of from five to ten players each stand single file. Each player stoops over, putting his right hand between his legs and grasping the left hand of the player behind him. At the signal to go the last man in line lies down on his back, putting his feet between the legs of the man in front of him. The line walks backwards, straddling the prone bodies of their teammates, each player lying down, in turn. As soon as all are flat of their backs, the last man gets up and starts back pulling up the next man after him, and so on until the players are in their original position. Players must not let go of hands.

Back to back race.—Determine the goal at 25, 50, or 75 yards. Two contestants represent each team. The members of each team are placed back to back. They link arms. At the signal to go one player runs forward while his teammate runs backward until they reach the goal line. As soon as both teammates touch the goal line they start back, reversing positions. Now the one who ran backward runs forward, while his partner runs backward. They have not finished until both runners touch the finish line.

Variation—Tie teammates together with a rope about the waist, leaving the arms free.

Animal chase.—Two corners or areas are marked off on the playground as pens. Players are named by groups—bears, dogs, cats, sheep, wolves, rabbits, etc. One person called the "Chaser" stands outside one of the pens. All others stand in the pen nearest the "Chaser." The "Chaser" calls the name of any group and all of the players bearing that name must rush for the opposite pen. Any animals caught must assist the "Chaser" in tagging animals.

Hawk.—One player is the "hawk." Another represents a "hen." The remainder are chickens. The players circle around the "hawk," chanting:

> "Chickany, chickany, craney crow,
> Went to the well to wash my toe;
> And when I came back a chicken was gone."

The "hen" then asks, "What time is it, old hawk?" The "hawk" crouches on the ground during the chanting, going through the motions of building a fire with sticks. In answer to the question he may answer anything, such as, "Five o'clock," "Ten o'clock." The players continue to circle around, repeating the chant, ending each time with the "hen" asking about the time. But if the "hawk" answers "Twelve o'clock" the entire ring stands still. Then the following dialogue takes place between the "hen" and the "hawk."

Hen: Old Hawk, Old Hawk, what are you doing?
Hawk: Picking up sticks.
Hen: Why do you want to pick up sticks?
Hawk: To build a fire.
Hen: Why are you building a fire?
Hawk: To cook a chicken.
Hen: Where are you going to get the chicken?
Hawk: Out of your flock!

The "hawk," who keeps a crouching attitude, with face downcast, during the dialogue, suddenly rises on the last words and chases the chickens.

When a player is captured the "hawk" brings him back, lays him down, and dresses him for dinner, while the rest of the players look on. The "hawk" asks the captured chicken, "Will you be picked or scraped?" He goes through the pantomime of picking feathers or scaling fish, as the recumbent victim decides. The "hawk" then asks, "Will you be pickled or salted?" and "Will you be roasted or stewed?" going through the appropriate motions each time. At the end he drags the victim to a corner, and the game continues until he has captured three chickens.

This game gives children practice in alertness, imitation, and imagination.

What did you see?—Players stand in files of from three to ten players, depending on the size of the crowd. The director, beginning with the first file, asks the leader of the file, "What did you see?" The leader suggests some activity and moves about the room demonstrating it. Each person in the row imitates the leader. For instance, the file leader responds: "I saw an eagle flying." He flies about the room with his group following him. Other suggestions: "I saw a woman sweeping," "I saw a horse trotting," "I saw a drum major strutting," "I saw a man wielding a scythe," "I saw a boy skating." Different ones should be. given opportunity to be leaders of the files.

"I say stand."—The leader shouts, "I say stand," at which command all players must stand. "I say stoop," and all players must stoop. The orders are given in rapid succession. The catch comes in the fact that the leader does not always fit his action to his command. For instance, he may say, "I say stand," and at the same time assume the stooping position. Any player who makes a mistake is out. No order should be obeyed unless the leader prefaces it by **"I say."**

Do this, do that.—This is another game of the same kind. When the leader commands, "Do this," all players must imitate him. But if he says, "Do that," players who imitate him are dropped out of the game. The leader may play a violin, a piano, a flute, or other musical instrument. He may dance, or skate, or saw, or sweep, or fly, or hammer, or bat, or kick a football, or any other action he desires.

"Have you seen my sheep?"—Players form a circle. One player acts as "shepherd." He walks around outside the circle, taps a player on the back and asks, "Have you seen my sheep?" That player asks, "What does he look like?" The "shepherd" then describes someone in the circle thus: "He wears a blue tie, a brown coat, and brown shoes." Or he may describe him as a "blonde with a good disposition, blue eyes, a square chin." The player tries to guess who is being described. When he guesses correctly, the "shepherd" says, "Right," and the guesser chases the one described. Both must run outside the circle. If the chaser catches the runner before he can get back to his position, the chaser becomes the "shepherd." If not, the runner becomes "shepherd." The "shepherd" does not run.

Pom pom pullaway.—This is an old favorite. Two lines 30 to 50 feet apart are drawn. Trees, sticks, or stones may be used to indicate the lines. Sometimes the curbings of a city street serve the purpose. All players stand on or behind one of the lines, except one player who is "It." He stands in the center of the playing field and shouts:

> "Pom Pom Pullaway!
> If you don't come I'll pull you away."

At this all players must leave the safety zone and run across to the opposite line. The one who is "It" tries to tag as many as possible before they reach the safety line. Anyone tagged joins the one who is "It" in catching other players as they dash across the open space. The game continues until all players are caught. The first one caught becomes "It" for the next game.

Duck on a rock (Boulder off).—The old gang of my boyhood days used to call this one "Boulder Off." Each player got himself a boulder or stone. A large rock was used for the "stand." Players may use bean bags instead of stones. One player is "It." He places his boulder on the "stand" and stands by as guard. Fifteen to twenty feet away is the throwing line. The other players stand at this line and toss their boulders at the "duck on the rock." When the "duck" is knocked off, the guard immediately replaces it. Players must take a position by their rocks. When a player thinks he has a good chance to get back to the throwing line without being tagged, he snatches up his boulder and dashes for safety. If he is tagged by the guard he becomes "It." Players may feint at picking up their boulders, but if a player touches his boulder he becomes liable to be tagged.

The guard may not tag a runner when his boulder is off. So when the boulder is knocked off, all players shout, "Boulder off!" and dash for home. The guard must replace his boulder before he is eligible to tag a runner who has picked up his rock.

If a player tosses his rock and it "touches" the rock of another player both players are allowed to return with their rocks without danger of being tagged.

This is a great game for developing accuracy, daring, and alertness.

Still pond.—One player is blindfolded. The others scatter about the playground. The blindfolded player is placed at the center and the leader asks: "How many horses has your father in his stable?" "Three," he replies. "What color are they?" "Black, white, and gray." "Turn around three times and catch whom you may." The blindfolded player is then spun around three times in order to confuse his sense of direction. He then says, "Still pond. No more moving." All players must now stand still, being allowed to take three steps only. The blindfolded player begins to grope around. When he catches someone, he must guess by touching the hair, dress, arm, etc., whom he has caught. If he guesses correctly, the player caught takes his place. If he guesses incorrectly he must continue his search. Players may stoop, dodge, or use any reasonable means to escape being caught, provided they do not move more than three steps. When caught a player may try to disguise himself.

Garden gate.—Two lines of players face each other, six feet apart. A leader for each line stands beside a basket. These two leaders are four feet apart. They are the posts of the "gate." Each player has an apple or bean bag in front of him.

At the starting signal the first player (the one nearest the leader) on each side runs down inside his own line, around the end player and back up behind the line and back through the gate, dropping his "apple" in the basket as he passes it and going back to position.

As soon as Number One player passes his teammate, Number Two, the second player follows. And so each in turn runs around the line and through the "garden gate."

Five points are awarded to the first team to have all players back in position. One point is taken off for each "apple" landing outside the basket.

"Stock exchange."—Give each person a number and a supply of beans. When the "stock exchange" is opened the players begin shouting their bids for numbers, so many beans for a number. After about ten or fifteen minutes of spirited buying and selling the "manager" of the "stock exchange" begins calling numbers in. The "members" of the "stock exchange" having the numbers called, surrender them to the "manager." Numbers are called in until there is but one number left. The player holding this number is awarded some prize. Up to the time the prize number is evident, players may continue to buy and sell at their discretion, quieting down long enough to hear the call that is made at intervals. In the calls suggested here fifty-nine is the lucky number. Select your number and then work out a system of calls that will leave that number. You can do this by putting the numbers down on paper and checking off on your calls. Note how the following calls are worked out:

Turn in:

3 and all multiples of 3.
All numbers having the digit 1.
All numbers in which the sum of the digits equal 13.
All even numbers.
5 and all multiples of 5.
All numbers having the digit 3.
All numbers having the digit 7.
All numbers containing a digit that is even.

This leaves fifty-nine as the lucky number that gets the prize. The person also having the largest number of beans, evidencing the fact that he has been a keen trader, wins a prize.

Players who have turned in their numbers may still continue to bid on numbers held by other players until the prize number is announced.

If desired, the "manager" may write the "calls" on the blackboard. He should allow enough time between calls for buying and selling. As the numbers on the "market" get fewer the prices will probably go up.

Square tag.—Two sides. Equal number of players. Stand at diagonal corners of square in equal files, each player with his hands on the shoulders of the teammate in front of him. Chairs, boxes, or stakes should indicate the corners of the square. Players must go around these corners.

When whistle blows the files run around outside the square, each leader trying to tag the end runner for the opposing team.

Each time this is done a point is scored, and the race starts over. Reverse directions every other time. Score best two out of three, or three out of five.

Lawn skittles.—A heavy ball suspended by a fishline or other heavy cord attached to the top of a ten-foot pole. Ninepins arranged six feet from the base of the pole. The player stands six feet away from the pole on the opposite side and swings the ball at the pins. Each player gets three trials for a turn or frame. Ten frames or thirty shots constitute a game. To get the best results the player must curve his shot around the pole.

Variation, swing skittles—Suspend golf ball or wooden ball from chandelier, doorway, or other convenient place. Place hazard in center (a candlestick, perhaps). Use toy tenpins. Play on floor or table.

Bean bag and washer baseball.—The field is marked off in nine squares, one foot square. The top squares are marked "Ball," "Second," "Foul"; the second row, "Strike," "Home Run," "Strike"; the bottom squares, "First," "Out," "Third." The batter stands about ten feet away and tries to throw the bean bag on a square that will put him on base. Each batter continues throwing until he makes a base or an out. A bean bag touching a line is a strike. When a batter gets on base he takes a position back of the base secured, not stepping on the square. Runners only advance when they are forced by the next batter.

For "Washer Baseball" use washers instead of bean bags and reduce size of squares to six inches.

Goofy-golf.—Goofy-golf, invented by George O. Crossland, a Boy Scout executive in Michigan, is a good homemade game that is becoming quite popular with boys and girls.

A course is laid out over uneven ground and horseshoes are used. Regular horseshoe pegs are set out as holes would be on golf course. The distance between them varies. Some are quite short while others are very long. Hazards such as stakes along a hillside, on top of a log, or beyond two trees that are close together, add spice to the course.

The score is kept as in golf, each throw counting a stroke. Each peg must be "rung." The player must stand behind the spot where his shoe fell for his next pitch. The far man shoots first as he does in golf.

The game is best played in twosomes or foursomes, but an unlimited number may take part.

Clock golf.—Twelve holes in a circle thirty feet in diameter. A center hole. Players start at center and hole to No. 1 in the circumference of the circle. Then he holes back to center and then to No. 2. And so it goes until he has completed the circle. The number of strokes in making the circuit are counted.

In the pond.—A good game for the picnic. Players stand in a straight line or circle with the leader giving directions. When the leader calls "In the pond" all players must jump forward one jump. If he calls "On the bank" while the group is "in the pond" they all jump backward one jump. The leader may confuse the group by jumping contrary to his own command. If the group is "in the pond" and the leader calls "in the pond" players must remain stationary. Players making mistakes drop out.

Tunnel race.—Arrange two concentric circles of players. Players face and take hold of hands forming a tunnel around the circle. One odd player is "It." He walks around the circle and taps the hands of two players. These two players immediately leave their positions, and, running in opposite directions inside the tunnel, try to get back to the position left. The tagger steps into one of the positions as soon as the runners leave. The player left out becomes "It."

Bear and guard.—The "bear" sits on a chair or stool in the center of a circle of players. A "guard" stands in back of him, or to the side, or in front of him, holding on to his chair. Players in the circle try to tap the "bear" on the knee, hand, shoulder, back, etc., without being touched by the "guard." The "guard" must keep one hand on the chair, though he can move all around it. Any player tagged by the "guard" must take the "bear's" place.

Human bingo.—Players are given sheets of paper divided into twenty squares. Each player must get a signature of someone present in each square. Names are written and placed in a hat. The leader draws these names one at a time. When a player's name is called he stands and turns around slowly. Every player with the name on his sheet checks it. When a player gets four checks in a row, horizontally, vertically, or diagonally, he yells "Bingo." A stick of candy is his reward. Continue until four or five players "Bingo." This makes a good mixer.

"Goosey-goosey-gander!"—A city street, a playground, a vacant lot, a gymnasium, or a large social room will provide a playing field for this game. Safety zones or goal lines are marked off from thirty to sixty feet apart. One player stands in the center and calls:

"Goosey-goosey-gander!"

The rest of the players are gathered behind one of the goal lines, and they shout back:
"Fox in the morning!"

The Fox calls, "How many are there?"

The Geese yell, "More than you can catch!"

Immediately they must leave safety and rush across to the opposite goal.
The Fox tags all he can. The players then catch hold of hands with him. The calls and responses are repeated. But this time the chain of players endeavor to catch some "geese." Only end players in the chain can tag, and, if the chain breaks, all catches at the time are void. The game continues until all "geese" are caught.

Pillow fight.—*Equipment*—A smooth sapling or pole about four inches in diameter mounted on a post or "horse" about four feet high.

Procedure—Two players straddle the pole. Each is given a pillow. As soon as both players are ready the fun starts. Each tries to knock the other off the pole. Players are not allowed to hold to the pole with their hands, except that when a player sees he is falling he may lighten his fall by catching hold of the pole.

If used indoors there should be a pad on the floor upon which the players may fall.

This is a great game for camp or playground.

Spot change.— (1) Players, excepting one or more designated to be "It," take positions indicated about the room or playground, standing. They are numbered consecutively. (2) The extras take positions wherever they desire. (3) The leader calls two numbers and these players have to exchange positions. (4) The extra players try to get positions. (5) When the leader calls "As you were" all players must go home to original positions except that the player who was originally "It" may take any position.

—Game invented by H. L. Longino

CHAPTER VII

FUN WITH NONSENSE GAMES AND STUNTS

FUN WITH NONSENSE GAMES AND STUNTS

"A little nonsense now and then
Is relished by the best of men."

"Thumbs Down"

$\mathbf{A}$S a steady diet nonsense is deadly. So many a group has discovered when it has built its program on that basis. The "kid stuff" and "silly doings" have sooner or later palled on the individuals engaged in it. Therefore, many leaders have placed a taboo on this type of recreation.

Nonsense Has Values

Nonsense, however, has its place in a well-rounded recreation program as an *occasional* instrument to achieve release from tension. The fun of the activity, the abandonment, the sheer silliness of it all, have values that supply an emotional catharsis that folk need every once in a while. If used infrequently it will save people from "stuffed-shirtitis" and solemncholia.

So here's for "a little nonsense now and then."

Uncle Ned is dead.—This is a good game for a small group. If you want to use it with a large crowd, either divide into small groups or have a group of about ten players play it while the rest observe the fun.

The players seat themselves in a circle. One player begins it by saying to the player to his right, "Uncle Ned is dead." That player asks, "How did he die?" "By closing his eye," is the reply, and the first player suits the action to the word by closing one eye. Then Number Two turns to the player to his right and repeats the conversation. And so it goes around the circle until all players have one eye closed. Again Number One starts it by saying, "Uncle Ned is dead." This time in answer to the question, "How did he die?" he answers, "By closing his eye, with his face a ry." When that has gone around he begins again. The third time the answer is "By closing his eye, with his face awry, and his foot up high." The fourth time all players repeat in turn, "By closing his eye, with his face awry, his foot up high, and waving goodbye." Each time the additional grimace, posture, or motion is assumed and kept to the end. After the fourth round the leader shouts, "He's buried!" and the game is ended.

Do this and more.—One player begins the game by doing something, such as putting the thumbs to the ears and wiggling the fingers. He points to another player who must repeat that action and add one of his own, such as putting his hand under his chin and wiggling his fingers. The next player may add sticking out his tongue. Each successive player must repeat, in order, all of the actions of the other players and add another. No player may be called on more than once unless he requests it.

Story mixup.—Take two short stories like "Little Black Sambo" and "Chicken Little" or "Red Riding Hood." Copy them sentence by sentence on separate slips of paper, a sentence to a slip. Mix them up in a hat and then have each player draw a slip or two, according to the size of the crowd. Indicate one person to begin the story. The person to the right of the starter reads his first sentence, and so on it goes around the circle. Naturally, there will be ridiculous combinations. That is where the fun will come in.

Shadow pictures.—Use the shadow picture idea for some interesting stunts. Here are a few suggestions:

(1) *The operation*—Have a victim on the table. Use saw, big knife, hatchet, bicycle pump for thermometer, etc. Take out a string of sausages, a can, a cabbage, a toy dog, and other things. Pretend to operate on the patient's head. Have him scream as you drive the knife into a cabbage head with a sickening sound.

(2) *Beauty parlor*—Use ridiculous-looking instruments. Curl the hair; appear to make it up in unusual shapes.

(3) *Dentist chair*—The same idea would be used here. Use coal tongs for forceps. Draw out a gigantic tooth.

Aunt Dinah's dead.—This game is particularly popular with some of the young people in Tennessee. When a group has a good sense of rhythm and exercises it in the playing of the game it adds considerably to the fun.

The players stand in a circle with one player just inside the circle so that he can be seen easily by everyone. This player starts the game by saying:

"Aunt Dinah's dead!"

All of the other players call back:
"How'd she die?"

The player answers:
"Oh, she died like this."

Having said that, he performs some action in rhythm, such as lifting the hands as if trying to ward off death's evil spirit and moving them in rhythmic motion three or four times.

All players immediately imitate the leader.

The same lines are repeated from the beginning. This time the leader does a different motion. Again the group follows suit.

Now the leader says: "Aunt Dinah's living!"

The group asks: "Where's she living?"

The leader:

"She's living in the country;
She's gonna move to town;
She's gonna shake her shoulders,
And truck on down."

As the leader says this he moves around the circle with a shuffling step and all of the players do likewise.

A new leader is selected and the game proceeds.

Poison.—Players stand in a circle. A volleyball, basketball, soft ball, bean bag, or other article is passed rapidly around the circle. When the leader's whistle blows the player who has possession of the ball, or who last touched it, is poisoned and drops out of the circle.

A player cannot refuse to receive the ball as long as it is in play. The thing to do is to receive it and get rid of it with speed.

The game may be played to music. When the music stops with a bang, the player having possession is out of the game.

The game continues until all but one player is eliminated.

When the crowd is large two plans are possible.

(1) One is to divide into small groups of from eight to sixteen players. Each circle is provided with an article to pass. The survivors in each circle may have a run-off. (2) The other plan is to provide a number of articles so that there will be from three to ten

eliminations each time. As the circle gets smaller withdraw bean bags or balls, as desired. When the group is trimmed down to five or six players only one bean bag should be used.

Pass it.—A variety of articles of varying weights is provided each team. At the signal to start, the first player picks up one article and starts it on its way down his line. Then he picks up a second article, and so on. The last player in line deposits the articles as he receives them. When all of the articles have arrived, he starts them back, one at a time. The head player must have all of the articles back in their original position before he has finished. Suggested articles are a vase, a toothpick, a ball, a teaspoon, a match box, a book, a coin, a bean bag, a comb, a rock, a pencil.

Does she cackle?—Players sit in a row or circle. Player Number One turns to the player to his right and says, "Want to buy a hen?" That player responds, "Does she cackle?" "She cackles," the first player replies. Now Number Two turns to Number Three and says, "Want to buy a hen?" Number Three asks, "Does she cackle?" Number Two then asks Number One, "Does she cackle?" Number One replies, "She cackles." Number Two turns to Number Three and repeats, "She cackles." Thus it goes all around the circle, Number Three speaking to Number Four, and so on. Each time the question "Does she cackle?" is relayed back to Number One, and the reply, "She cackles," is passed on to the last player consulted about buying a hen.

Variation—The game may be made a bit more difficult as well as a bit more helpful in acquainting players with the names of all of the others, by requiring that they know the names and use them, thus: "Margy Jones said that Tom Clark said that Pearl Brown said that Bill Sims said that May Temple said, 'Want to buy a duck?' " The relay back would also carry the names of the persons in turn.

Variations—(a) "Want to buy a duck?" "Does she quack?" "She quacks." "How does she quack?" "Quack-quack!"

(b) My dog. "Have you seen my dog?" "Does he bark?" "He barks." "How does he bark?" "Woof-woof" (the player makes an effort to imitate a dog barking). Cats and other animals may be used in the same manner.

(c) My flute. "Have you seen my flute?" "Does it toot?" "It toots." "How does it toot?" "Tweedle-weedle-weet" (the player tries to imitate a flute). Other musical instruments may be used in the same fashion.

He can do little who cannot do this.—One player holds a stick in his left hand. With this he thumps the floor, saying, "He can do little who cannot do this." Then he hands the stick to another player who tries to do exactly what the leader has done. The chances are he will fail. The trick lies in the fact that the leader holds the stick in his left hand as he thumps. He then passes it to his right as he hands it to the next player. The game continues until the secret is discovered.

Blind swat.—Contestants are blindfolded and made to lie face down on the ground or floor heads toward one another. They take hold of left hands. In their right hands they hold newspaper rolls or stockings stuffed with rags. They take turn about swatting. "Are you there, Charlie?" shouts the one who is going to do the swatting. The opponent must respond immediately with "Here!" The swatter lets fly, pronto! The swatee ducks but he must not loosen his grasp on his opponent's left hand. Hits are counted for a round of five or ten shots.

Oracles.—Children and young people are always fond of oracles, even though they may not believe in them. They count petals on a daisy, buttons on a coat or dress, or seeds in an apple.

"Who You'll Wed?"

> "Rich man, poor man, beggar man, thief,
> Doctor, lawyer, merchant, chief."

"Where You'll Reside?"

> "Brick house, stone house, frame, tepee,
> Flat boat, trailer, the shade of a tree."

The Bridal Gown:

> "Silk, satin, velvet, calico, rags,
> Cotton goods, woolen goods, burlap bags."

The Bridal Equipage:

> "Coach, carriage, wagon, wheelbarrow, blimp,
> Rattle-trap, limousine, airplane, limp."

Consequences.—Each person is given a piece of paper and a pencil. First, each one is required to write an adjective or two describing a

woman. The top of the paper is then folded down to prevent anyone seeing what has been written. It is passed to the right and the
next person writes a woman's name. This goes on until the leader
indicates the story is finished. The papers are then opened and read
aloud to the group. The following information may be required:

   (1) An adjective describing a woman.
   (2) A woman's name.
   (3) An adjective describing a man.
   (4) A man's name.
   (5) Where they met.
   (6) What she did.
   (7) What he did.
   (8) What she said.
   (9) What he said.
 (10) The results.
 (11) What the world said.

Going to Texas.—The leader announces that everyone in the group
is going to Texas and that each person is allowed to take one article.
One player starts it off by saying, "I will take my hat." Others decide to take an auto, a lamp, a suitcase, a toothbrush, a fan, a six-
shooter, etc. When each person has named an article Number One
is asked by the leader what he will do with his hat. He answers
that he will wear it. Number Two must now repeat, "I will wear
my auto"; Number Three, "I will wear my lamp"; and so on. When
it has been around, the leader asks Number Two what he will do
with his auto. He answers, "I will drive my auto." Again each
player in turn must repeat, "I will drive my lamp," etc. This is
repeated until each player has told what he will do with his article
and all players have repeated the action with the articles they have
named.

Palmistry de luxe.—Each person holds his left hand flat on a piece
of paper and outlines it with a pencil. The back of the paper is then
marked with some code so that it can be identified later. Papers
are gathered, shuffled, and then distributed. Each person writes a
description of the person to whom the hand belongs. Papers are
exhibited, identified, and the owner of a hand must stand while the
description is being read.

Blind walk.—One player is blindfolded. He stands with feet far
apart. The other players, who stand in a circle around him, toss

bean bags or other suitable objects between "It's" legs. After each player has thrown his object the blindfolded player is instructed to "Walk." When he steps on an object that was thrown, the player to whom that object belonged takes his place.

Pyramid candle bowling.—Place ten candles on a board or cardboard in the form of a pyramid, like tenpins. Put these upon the floor or upon a table. The latter, of course, would make it more comfortable for the performer. Light the candles. Place a chin rest of two or three books before the pyramid. Each player tries to blow out the candles. Two blows are allowed. Scoring is done as in bowling. Blowing all of the candles out at the first trial in a frame is a strike. The blower scores ten points plus all of the points he scores in the next two shots of the second frame. Blowing all ten candles out in the two blows in a frame is a spare and scores ten plus all that the player blows out his first turn in the next frame. (See "Bowling" in Chapter XI, "Fun with Sports.")

Teams may play or players may play singly.

This makes a good campfire or party stunt. In this case players may be given one blow to see who can blow out the most.

I saw a ghost.—The players line up in a single line, all facing the same direction. The leader says, "I saw a ghost and he went like this." He makes this sound as mysterious as possible. He then drops down to his knees. All players follow suit, doing whatever the leader does. Again the leader makes his speech. This time he extends both hands straight out in front of him. The next time he lifts the left leg in the air. The next time he suddenly shoves the next player sharply. As a result the whole crowd goes down like a pack of card.

Cross questions and silly answers.—The players sit in two rows. One person gives each player on one side a question. Another person gives each player on the other side an answer. Since neither knows what the other is doing you can imagine the results when the questions and answers begin to fall. The first player on one side asks the question assigned to him and the player opposite gives the answer that was whispered to her. "What is your hobby?" asks Number One. "No, no, a thousand times no!" comes the response from the player opposite. "Do you think the moon is made out of green cheese?" asks Number Two. "We'll fight it out on this line if it takes all summer," comes the response.

Brother Bob.—Two players are seated in chairs back to back. Each is blindfolded. The leader has displayed a book with which he explained the two players would be tapped on the head. The blindfolded players are to try to guess who has hit them with the book. The game is a "sell." One of the blindfolded players is in the "know" and he slips off his bandage and takes the book. First he taps himself on the head with the book. Then he says, "Brother Bob, I've been bobbed." "Who bobbed you?" asks the other blindfolded player. The "bobbed" player answers with some name. Then he turns and cracks the other player on the head with the book. Immediately that player must say, "Brother Bob, I've been bobbed." On "who bobbed you?" he does his best to guess the guilty party, but he will be unlikely to succeed, since the player seated in the chair backed up to his is doing all of the "bobbing." Three or four "bobs" will be enough to perpetrate on a victim.

Paddle-O.—This game is something like "Brother Bob." It is explained that two players at a time are "It." Each of them assumes a position on all fours with a blanket or sheet covering him. They are to try to identify the person that hits one of them with a paddle. When the blow is struck they lift the covering, look the crowd over,

and try to identify the guilty party. It has been explained that that person may pass the paddle on to someone else immediately after striking. When the players are ready someone slips the paddle to one of the players on the floor, who is "wise." That player taps himself gently and then pretends to try to identify the assailant, after passing the paddle back to one of the standing group. Of course, he fails. The players cover themselves again, and this time the "wise" one paddles his mate, passing the paddle hurriedly back to a standing player.

Similarities.—One person goes around the group whispering the name of some person present. Another whispers the name of some object, animal, or insect. Each person is now required to tell why the person whose name was whispered to him is like the object suggested by the second whisperer. For instance, the first whisperer tells Mary that the name is Jack Brown. The second whisperer comes along and whispers "caterpillar." At the proper time, Mary must explain why "caterpillar" is an appropriate designation for Mr. Brown. She may say, "Because he's a worm." Or she may say, "Because he can make the butterfly," and add in sotto voce, "Especially with hot biscuits." Or she may feel in a complimentary mood and say, "Because he has possibilities of beauty in him."

Blind town.—Limits are decided. All the players except one are blindfolded. They are scattered about the playing space. The player who is not blindfolded carries a bell in his hand which he must ring continuously. The blindfolded players try to catch the one carrying the bell. The person who catches him becomes the bellman. Players who are blindfolded should be cautioned to hold their hands out in front of them to avoid painful collisions.

Shadow buff.—All players but one gather in a room over the door of which a sheet has been drawn. A light is so arranged that shadow pictures can be made on the sheet. The extra player sits on the opposite side of the sheet in a dark room and tries to identify the players whose shadows appear on the screen. These players must appear one at a time. They are privileged to use simple disguise, such as false paper noses or ears, funny hats, paper curls, etc. They may make any gestures they desire. When the guesser identifies a shadow correctly the person whose identity he guessed takes his place.
Variation—This game may be used as a team game, in which case the number of correct guesses would be the score.

Poor pussy.—This old-timer wears well. The players are seated about the room. One player has a pillow. If a boy, he puts the pillow down in front of a girl, kneels on it, and meows as plaintively as he knows how. The girl must hold a solemn countenance as she pats him on the head each of the three times and say consolingly, "Poor little pussycat." If she laughs she takes the pussycat's place. The girls must kneel before boys. A player must keep on until he makes someone laugh.

Ring on a string.—Players form a circle holding a long string which is tied together at the ends. They pass their hands back and forth on the string, passing a ring from one to the other. A player in the center tries to guess who has the ring. He may stop the passing at

any time to make a player lift his hands.   If the player has the
ring he becomes "It."

Variations—"Spool on a string."   Instead of a ring use a small
spool.

"Life-saver on a string."   Use a Life-saver mint in the same
manner.

Counting apple seeds.—Name the apple and make a wish.   Cut
it open.   Take out the seeds and count them thus:

> One, I love,
> Two, I love,
> Three, I love, I say;
> Four, I love with all my heart;
> Five, I cast away;
> Six, he loves,
> Seven, she loves,
> Eight, they both love;
> Nine, he comes,
> Ten, he tarries,
> Eleven, he courts,
> Twelve, he marries;
> Thirteen, wishes,
> Fourteen, kisses,
> All the rest, little witches.

Doctoring nursery rhymes.—In a group that is mentally alert,
plenty of fun could be had by working out original endings for
well-known nursery rhymes.   The changes in the rhyme may start
after the first line.

> Mary had a little lamb,
> With green peas on the side;
> And when her escort saw the check,
> The poor boob nearly died.

> Jack Spratt could eat no fat,
> His wife could eat no lean;
> And so the question before the house
> Is "Who orders the meat, man or mouse?"

Sometimes the last line of the rhyme is changed without effort at
rhyming, as, for instance:

> Peter, Peter, Pumpkin Eater,
> Had a wife and couldn't keep her;
> He put her in a pumpkin shell—
> Well, how'd you like hobnobbing with a jack-o-lantern?

Blind rhymes.—This is fun for a small group.   Even a large crowd could be divided into numerous small groups and enjoy it. One person writes a line of poetry and folds it over so that no one can see what was written.   The next person is told what the last word is so that he can ryhme with it.   The writer may also indicate the meter to him, saying:

> "Da-da, da-da, da-da, da-da,
> Da-da, da-da, da-da, da-da."

The third person writes another line in the same meter, if possible. The fourth rhymes with the third's last word.   For nonsense rhymes this ought to score "tops."

Blind advertising.—This is similar to "Blind Rhymes."   In this case each of the four players is given a word with which to end his line.   The words may rhyme in couplets, if desired.   Thus, the four words may be *fair, rare, style,* and *smile.*   Each person writes his line and folds it over before passing it on to the next person. The rhyme must advertise some announced product, organization, or movement.

Magic animal cage.—Invite guests to view the magic animal cage in which appears any animal the person can name.   Have an elaborate build-up.   A large mirror is covered with a piano scarf so as to disguise its real identity and so that it looks like a cage.   The guests are brought in one at a time.   Each one is asked what animal he wants to see.   Whatever the answer remove the drapery and let him look in the mirror.   If he says "monkey" there is his monkey in the mirror.   If he says "bear" there is his bear.

Matchbox race.—Line up five to ten players on a side.   Provide each side with a small matchbox top (penny matchbox size).   The race starts by each team having its first man place the matchbox on his nose.   From this time on the hands must not touch the box, except to pick it up off the floor or ground if it is dropped. The players pass the box from nose to nose.   Well, you figure it out for yourself!   Sounds silly, doesn't it?   It is!

Dizzy Izzy.—An umbrella (man's size), a cane, a baseball bat, or a broomstick, thirty inches long, will be needed.   Contestants hold

the upright stick firmly on the floor, both hands on the top. Bend
ing over, they rest the head on the hands and walk around the
stick five times, without lifting the stick from the floor. Immediately
they run to a designated goal—a chair, a tree, a post—and back to
the starting point. Funny things will happen. You had better
safeguard the runners by having human buffers at danger points.
Players have been known to butt their heads into hard walls or to lose
their balance and root up the earth with a nose dive.

Novelty human checkers.—A giant checkerboard is marked out on
cloth, oilcloth, canvas, paper, floor, or court. The squares should
be at least one foot in diameter. Persons are used for checkers.
They stand in proper positions and two captains indicate the moves
to be made. When jumps are made the players do the jumps leapfrog fashion. The same rules obtain as in regular checkers. Kings
are indicated by the wearing of a hat or cap.

Obstacle race.—This is a "sell." Select two unsuspecting persons
for contestants. Obstacles of various sorts—books on end, flower
pots, pillows, Indian clubs—are distributed over a course. The
contestants are timed as they walk (not run) this course, zigzagging
in and out among the obstacles across the room. Now they are
blindfolded (or two other runners may be chosen), and, one at a
time, they are required to do the course while they are timed. While
their backers are giving them words of encouragement and counsel,
the obstacles are removed. There will be some fancy stepping,
stimulated by words of advice from the side-lines.

Blind monkeys.—Couples are blindfolded. The man shells and
feeds peanuts to his partner.

Newspaper race.—Each contestant is furnished with two news
sheets. Each step in the race must be made on the newspaper. Thus
he puts down a sheet, steps on it, puts down the other sheet, steps on
it, reaches back to get the first sheet and move it forward, and so
on until he reaches the goal line.

Brickbat race.—Each contestant is provided with two bricks. The
race is run like the "Newspaper Race," contestants being required to
step on the bricks from starting point to goal line.

Footstool race.—Each contestant is given two footstools or boxes.
These must be used just like the newspapers or bricks.

Barrel hoop relay.—*Equipment*—Four barrel hoops for each team. Be sure that all nails and snags are eliminated. Cover the hoops with crepe paper or cloth strips to insure smoothness. *Action*—Four persons to a team. The hoops are placed on the floor. At the signal to go the first man reaches down, picks up a hoop, passes it down over his body, steps out of it, passes it to his next teammate, and reaches for another hoop. The next player passes the hoop over his body, and so it continues until the last player has passed all four hoops over his body and placed them on the floor beside him. It may be required that the hoops be sent back to the head in the same fashion.

Variations—Bicycle tires or automobile inner tubes may be used instead of hoops.

Apple race.—Contestants are required to balance an apple on top of the head and walk to a goal line. If the apple falls off, the contestant must go back to the starting point and begin again.

Spooning race.—Couples are contestants. Each couple is furnished with two spoons tied together with a string six inches long. One dish of ice cream is provided each couple. Using the tied spoons they eat the ice cream as quickly as possible.

File chair relay.—Five to ten contestants to a team. Each contestant sits in a chair, the chairs being arranged in a row. The first player arises from his chair and runs around the entire row assuming his original position. As soon as he sits down, player Number Two gets up and makes the circuit. So it goes until each player has been entirely around.

Variation—As soon as player Number One passes Number Two, that player gets up and follows him. Number Three follows Two. Each makes the circuit and gets seated.

SHOT PUT

Dropping peanuts.—Contestants stand erect and drop from breast-height fifteen peanuts, one at a time. They try to make them drop into a glass fruit jar.

Dropping clothespins.—Contestants kneel on a chair. From the top of the back of the chair they try to drop clothespins into a quart milk bottle.

Tossing peanuts.—Contestants try to toss peanuts into a fruit jar or coffee can from a distance of six feet.

Pillowcase relay.—Ten players to a team. Each team is provided with a pillow. At the signal to go the first man on each team takes the pillow out of the casing and puts it back. He then hands it to his next teammate who does the same thing. So it goes down the line until each player has taken the pillow out of its casing and placed it back in the casing. Each contestant is allowed to devise his own way for getting the pillow in the casing. Some of them will show skill that has come from long practice. Others will have a terrible time.

FOUR POP SACK RACES

Run and pop.—Five to ten players on a side. As many paper bags as there are runners on chairs at the end of the room. The first player on each team runs to his chair, blows up one of the bags, bursts it, and returns to touch off his next teammate. A runner must not leave the starting point until he has been properly touched off by the preceding runner on his side.

Stand and pop.—Ten players to a team. They stand single file each holding an unopened paper bag in his right hand. At the signal to start the end player on each side blows up his sack and pops it on the back of the man immediately preceding him. As soon as the bag is popped that player blows up his bag and pops it on the back of the man in front of him. The last player pops his sack on his knee.

Right foot, left foot.—Ten players to a team stand single file with a paper bag under each foot. At the signal to go the end man reaches down, gets the sack under his right foot, blows it up and pops it. Immediately he tags the player directly in front of him. That player goes through the same performance. As soon as the top player pops the sack under his right foot, he picks up the one under his left foot and pops it, also. This is the signal for Number Two in line to pop the sack under his left foot, and so on down the line until the last player has popped the left-foot sack.

Fireworks.—Players are divided into two equal sides, the more the merrier. At a given goal there is a sack for each player. On signal there is a grand rush for the goal, where each player must blow up his sack and pop it. The first team through wins.

Hammer throw.—A paper bag is blown up and a string is tied around it. The string should be from thirty-six to forty inches long.

The contestant must catch hold of the end of the string and throw the sack as far as he can. The chances are that this will not be very far.

Apple bite. — Apples are tied on strings attached to a heavy string which is held high by standards. Each contestant has his apple arranged so that he can reach it with his mouth by standing on tiptoe. At the signal to go each player endeavors to get a bite of his apple. Perhaps, just as one player gets hold of the apple with his  teeth another player lets go of his. As a result, the apple shoots out of his mouth. The first player to get three bites wins.

Biting a doughnut.—The same thing is done with doughnuts as with apples. This time the first player to get a bite wins. No use of the hands is allowed.

Barrel hoop race.— (1) Contestants roll barrel hoops by tapping them with sticks. They must go to a given goal and back.

(2) Contestants roll the hoops by holding the sticks against them and thus pushing them along. Tapping is not allowed for the start.

Spider race.—This race is run by couples. The girl faces the goal line. The man stands with his back to the girl and they link arms. In this position they race to the goal. Immediately the man passes the goal line they start back with the girl running backwards this time. Thus they return to the starting line.

Baby marathon.—Each contestant is provided with a baby milk bottle topped with a brand new nipple, the hole of which has been enlarged. Only a little milk is put in each bottle. The contestan, must kneel with his hands behind him, while a teammate holds the bottle for him.

Honeymoon race (rainy day, costume).—Each couple is given a closed suitcase and an umbrella. At the signal to go they run arm in arm to the goal, the lady carrying the closed umbrella while the man carries the suitcase. On arrival at the goal line the suitcase is opened and the wearing apparel in it is donned. It may contain various articles—hats, pair of large man's oxfords for the lady to wear, raincoat, kimono, bathrobe, baby cap for the man. When the articles have been donned the suitcase is closed, the umbrella is opened, and the couple returns to the starting line. Arriving there they must take off the articles of wearing apparel, put them in the suitcase, close it, and close the umbrella.

Marshmallow race.—Tie a marshmallow in the middle of a string two feet long. Contestants take the ends of the string in their teeth. At the signal to go each player starts chewing the string. The first to get to the marshmallow wins.

Cracker race.—Two teams face one another. At the signal to go the first player on each team eats his cracker. As soon as he has finished he whistles. Then his next teammate may begin, but not until then. The first team through wins.

Discus throw.—Contestants are furnished with paper plates. These must be tossed like a discus.

Pushing peanuts.—Contestants are required to push peanuts across the floor with toothpicks.

Variations—Push with a pencil or with the nose. In the latter case the distance would be shortened to a few feet.

Driving the pig to market.—Contestants must push Indian clubs or pop bottles across the floor with wands. Try it and see what happens!

Potato relay.—A player must pick up a potato in a spoon, carry it back to the starting point, and deposit it in a basket. He then hands the spoon to a teammate who must get another potato and bring it back. So it goes until all members of the team have run.

Kangaroo race. — One player goes down on all fours. The second player wraps his legs about the body of the man on all fours and puts his head between his legs. He then grasps his teammate's ankles. This means that the teammates are facing in opposite directions. In this position they race to the goal line, running in the direction the player on all fours is headed.

Wheelbarrow race.—One player grasps the ankles of another player who stands on his own hands. In this position they race to a given goal. They may be required to reverse positions on a return trip.

Stilts race.—Players make stilts by nailing a piece of wood to a tall stick. After a little practice they race on these stilts.

Tin can stilts race.—Players make stilts by running wire through empty tomato cans. They race to a goal on these cans. The chances are that they will not make much speed.

Accuracy pitch.—*Equipment*—Trash basket, hat, bowl, cup, or jar.
(1) *Cards.* Players stand or sit several feet away and try to toss rook or spot cards into a wastebasket.
(2) *Checkers, coins, buttons, or clips.* Toss into series of tumblers. These tumblers can be arranged in any position desired—triangle, circle, rosebud, square, or row. Numbers on the tumblers may indicate scores. Players stand or sit six to ten feet away and toss. If a player calls his shot and makes good he doubles the points coming to him on that shot. If he fails, he loses one point.

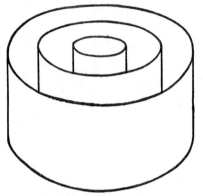

(3) *Skee ball.* Cans or boxes of various sizes set in one another. Coffee cans will do. Players toss checker counters trying to "hole" in the center can. Scoring is 10 for center, 5 for second, and 1 for outer can.

(4) *Rubber ball.* Bounce into a bucket or wastebasket.

(5) *Bean bags.* Bucket or wastebasket weighted down so that it will not upset. Two sides of five to ten players forming a circle fifteen to twenty feet in diameter. Each side has a different colored bean bag. At the signal to toss each player lets his bean bag go. Count is made of the bean bags in the basket.

(6) *Washer pitching.* Use washers or silver dollars. Players play singles or doubles. Pitching is done as in horseshoes, the winners shooting first each time. Each player pitches two washers.

Two three-inch wide holes are dug in the ground about fifteen to twenty feet apart. Count is made as in horseshoes. A washer dropping in the hole is five points. Washers nearest the hole count one just as horseshoes nearest the peg. Covering an opponents washer in the hole cancels it so that neither player scores.

Candle race.—Couples are placed so that partners face each other from opposite sides of the room. Each participant has a candle. The boy on each team also has a match. At the signal to go the boy lights his candle, crosses the room to his partner, lights her candle, and then puts out his own. She crosses the room and returns, relighting his candle. The boy then returns to his original position. If the candle goes out, it must be relighted at the starting point. Use of hands to shield the flame is not allowed.

Slams.—One player leaves the room. Each person now must make some uncomplimentary remark about the player who went out of the room. The leader writes these down. When the player returns the leader reads the "slams" and the "slamee" must try to guess who made each remark. Players whose remarks are identified must go out of the room in turn. If no correct guess is made the "slamee" has the privilege of selecting anyone he desires to take his place for the next turn.

Compliments.—This game is played just like "slams" except that compliments are substituted for "slams."

Crisscross answers.—Players sit in two rows opposite one another. One player, who is "It," roams up and down between the two rows. He asks a question pointing at a player. The player directly opposite must answer immediately. If the questioner can count five before an answer is made the person failing to respond must take his place.

DUAL NONSENSE CONTESTS

Talk fest.—Two players talk fast and furiously for thirty seconds on any subject they choose. Or a subject may be suggested by the leader.

Variations—(*a*) Whistling. (*b*) Singing. (*c*) Making a speech by repeating letters of the alphabet.

Reciting poetry dramatically.—Contestants recite Mother Goose rhymes dramatically with profuse gesturing. They may be required to recite the rhymes as tragedy, melodrama, or comedy. Imagine "Mary Had a Little Lamb" or "Twinkle, Twinkle, Little Star" done in this fashion.

Variation—Repeat the same poems using gestures only to indicate what is being said.

Campfire pantomimes.—The contestants pantomime a traffic cop at a busy corner, a lady buying a hat, a speaker delivering a Fourth of July oration, a ballgame (a la Nick Altrock—the pitch, the hit, the fly ball, the catch, etc.), a football game, a basketball game, a panhandler, a teacher trying to instruct a dumb class, etc.

Posing.—Two players stand back to back. The leader calls "You are a grouchy old man of eighty entering a room. Are you ready? About face!" The players face one another and act out the character called. Other calls may be "a girl seeing a mouse," "a superstitious person seeing a ghost," "a ballplayer protesting a decision." Instead of standing back to back players may stand with back to the crowd. They turn and act out the announced part.

Whopper's club.—Each contestant tells an exaggerated story of the Paul Bunyan type. If the story is original so much the better. Not over two minutes are allowed. If successful, the storyteller is recognized as a bona fide member of the "Whopper's Club."

Bottle balance.—Contestants must sit on top of a quart milk bottle (stood upright), put one heel on the ground, toe up, and cross the other leg over, so that the foot rests on top of the one touching the ground. In this position the player must thread a needle.

Variations—The contestants may be required to autograph a card, light a candle, or pluck a daisy ("One she loves, two she doesn't, three he loves, four she doesn't").

Ankle dizzy.—Contestants stoop and grasp their own ankles. In this position they turn around three times. Then they stand erect and try to walk to a certain goal. Protect players from injury by covering points of danger.

Sword fight.—Each contestant is blindfolded. They lie flat on the ground, face down, each holding to a handkerchief or towel between them with the left hand. In the right hand is a rolled newspaper or a stuffed stocking. The referee calls the name of one of the contestants. This player raises his "sword" and tries to hit his opponent with a downward stroke. Horizontal strokes are not allowed. The opponent holds his right hand over his head and squirms around in some position where he feels he will be safe. He has to keep hold of the handkerchief, however, which, necessarily, keeps him in striking distance of his foe. The chances are that the blow will fall harmless on the floor or ground. Then the other player gets a chance to strike. One point is allowed for a body blow and two for a head blow.

Can and glove boxing.—Each contestant has a can with a few rocks in it. This he carries in the right hand. During the contest he must continually rattle the can so his opponent may have an idea of where he is. Both contestants are blindfolded. On the left hand each wears a boxing glove. When he thinks he is near enough to his opponent to hit him he lets fly.

Variation—Instead of a boxing glove each opponent may be provided with a pillow or a stuffed stocking, with which he endeavors to hit the other contestant.

Heave away boxing.—Contestants are blindfolded, provided with boxing gloves, and tied together around the waist with a rope that leaves them six feet apart, when taut. They haul in the rope to locate one another and then whale away. When the referee blows his whistle they must go back until the rope is taut again.

Variations— (*a*) Use pillows or stuffed stockings instead of gloves. (*b*) Remove the blindfold from one contestant without letting the other one know.

Pie eating contest.—Two to eight contestants. A large piece of juicy blueberry pie or some meringue pie for each contestant. Holding their hands behind them they must eat the pie, not being allowed to push it out of the pie plate. When a contestant has finished he must take the pie plate in his teeth and deliver it thus to the leader.

Feather ball.—Two to four contestants, depending on whether you plan to play singles or doubles. A small fluffy feather is placed on the floor in the middle of a field that is ten feet long by five feet wide. The players must kneel with their hands behind them. On the signal to start each tries to blow the feather over his opponent's goal line.

*Variation—*Play the same game on a table, the players being allowed to lean over into the playing field.

Ankle throw.—Players try to throw an object (baseball, knotted rag) over the head from behind by use of the feet.

Cock fight.—The contestants have their wrists and ankles tied. The arms are then passed over the knees, and a broomstick is pushed over one arm, under both knees, and over the other arm. In this position the contestants try to upset one another.

Push 'em over.—Contestants sit facing one another, feet touching. They grasp an upright stick between them and endeavor by pressure to overthrow the opponent.

Bear stalking.—Two players are blindfolded and placed at either end of a long table. At the signal to go they begin to move around the table. The "stalker" tries to catch the "bear." Each player must stay within touching distance of the table.

Absolute silence on part of audience and stalker is essential.

Dog fight.—Contestants drop on all fours. A tied towel or buckled belt is dropped over the necks of the two players. At the signal to start they pull against each other until one of them gives way either by moving forward or by dropping his head forward and thus releasing the belt. If a leather belt is used it might be well to protect the necks of the contestants by padding with a towel.

Hat boxing.—Two contestants wear straw jimmies and boxing gloves or the kind of work gloves that can be gotten at the ten cent store. They are not allowed to pull the hats tight down over their heads. Nor are they allowed to touch the hat with either hand to hold it on the head. Each player tries to knock the hat off the opponent's head.

Balloon race.—Contestants are equipped with ping-pong or tetherball paddles and inflated toy balloons. They bat the balloons to an agreed goal and back to the starting line. The balloon must be batted through the air. If it falls to the ground the player must pick it up and bat it into the air again.

Variations—(a) Use fans instead of paddles. (b) Use brooms and propel the balloons along the floor or ground.

Rooster battle royal.—Divide the crowd into two equal groups. Herd them all within a limited space. Each person must stand on one leg, arms folded across the chest. In this position they hop around trying to force opponents to touch the floor with the other foot. All jostling must be done with the shoulders. At the end of one minute, if anyone has survived, count the lucky ones.

Modeling.—Each guest is given a card and a stick of chewing gum. He chews the gum and then models some animal, flower, tree, house, or other object on the card with it. The results may be placed on exhibit.

Human croquet race.—Eleven boys take position of stakes and arches in lawn croquet. The "arches" spread their legs. The "stakes" stand upright. Two players contest at a time. The contestants leave the opposite stakes, crawling on all fours. They go under the "arches" in the same direction that the croquet ball makes the course. The contestant has not finished until he has entirely completed the course.

Feeding the elephant.—Hang a megaphone so that it is slightly tilted with the mouthpiece down and the large end toward the tosser. Have a basket or other receptacle to catch peanuts as they fall. The tosser is given ten peanuts. He tries to toss them into the elephant's open mouth (that is, into the large end of the mega-phone). The tossers stand from eight to ten feet away.

Kiddy car polo.—This game was a feature at the banquet of the Chicago Bear's professional football club in 1938. Four players constitute a team. Each player is mounted on a kiddy car. A croquet mallet is used for the polo mallet and a volleyball or tennis ball is used for the ball. The game starts with the referee rolling the ball in the midst of the players at midfield. Play is resumed in the same manner after a goal has been made and whenever the ball goes out of bounds. Players strike the ball with the mallet and try to drive it toward the opponents' goal and between their goal posts. Two chairs six to eight feet apart may serve as these posts. Instead of the eight chukkers or periods of seven and one-half minutes each with intermissions of two and one-half minutes, except that there is a five-minute intermission between the fourth and fifth chukkers, play this game in two periods of five minutes each with a two-minute intermission. One point is scored each time the ball is knocked through the goal.

Fouls may be called for zigzagging in front of an approaching player, for blocking a player who is pursuing the ball after hitting it, and for covering the ball. The penalty is a free hit by one of the opponents from the point of foul.

This game will be as hilarious as it is strenuous.

—Suggested by MRS. SAMMIE PLASMAN, whose son, DICK, played on the Chicago Bears football team.

NONSENSE STUNTS

The lost sheep.—The leader makes an elaborate announcement introducing a soloist, who is to sing a pathetic ballad entitled "The Lost Sheep." The singer takes his position, glances at his accompanist, nods his head as a signal for the pianist to begin, stands ready as the pianist plays a prelude, and then gives a plaintive "baa-aa-aa."

A dream song.—In a camp, conference, or group where there is a notorious snorer, this stunt goes over well. The perpetrator announces that he is going to sing a new song composed by the aforesaid snorer, "a piece of sheet music entitled 'A Dream Song.'" He then snores loudly.

Gathering of the nuts.—This old one occasionally finds a group where it is not well known. Then it becomes usable. The leader announces that he is picking a cast for an impromptu play. He calls the names of prominent people in the group and asks them to form a semicircle up front. After all of them have been selected the leader announces: "I neglected to announce the title of the play. It is 'The Gathering of the Nuts.'" Exit.

The giant sneeze.—Divide the crowd into three sections. At the signal from the leader Section One is to shout "Ka-hishi," Section Two, "Ka-hashi," and Section Three, "Ka-hoshoo." "All together! One-two-three! Go!"

A fake argument.—At an appropriate time during a banquet, stunt program, or party, someone rises to protest some statement that has been made or some feature of the program. Other "instructed" persons take sides in the ensuing argument with the intention of drawing someone into it who does not know that it is a stunt. When the argument waxes warm, one of the perpetrators arises and thanks the crowd for helping in their stunt.

"Pansy."—The leader explains that the game is a test of alertness. Each player has been given the name of a flower, which he must keep secret. The leader starts to tell a story into which he weaves the names of flowers. The leader has explained that the name of one flower has been given to at least two people. When the name of a flower is called the player bearing that name must dash for the open door, each trying to get through the door first. After calling several names the leader calls "Pansy." There is a mad scene as all the rest of the players arise and dash for the door. All but about four of the players have been given that name.

Variation—The leader explains that when a player's name is called the player must dash for the door with the leader in pursuit. It is further explained that, if captured, a player must take the leader's place. The leader calls the names of two or three flowers, but he fails to catch any of them, purposely. Then when he calls "Pansy" there is a grand exodus.

"Boots without shoes."—Victims are called in one at a time. The leader goes through whatever gyrations occur to him as he commands the victim to say "Boots without shoes." The luckless individual will probably do his best to imitate the leader in saying, "Boots without shoes." The leader says, "No, you are wrong. Say it the way I tell you to say it. 'Boots without shoes,'" The victim again tries to imitate the gestures and voice inflections of the leader.

Again he is wrong. Finally, it dawns on him that the way to say "Boots without shoes" is simply to say "Boots."

The moon is big and round.—The leader stands before a group of players and repeats, "The moon is big and round. It has two eyes, a nose, and a mouth." As he repeats these words, he makes a sweeping circle with his left hand to indicate that the moon is "big and round." For the "two eyes" he dots them in with his forefinger. For "the nose" he dots it in the same manner. For the "mouth" he makes a small semicircular motion. He then invites players in the group to do the same thing. Most of the players will fail and wonder why. They will try to imitate the leader's voice inflection, his stance, his motions. A few may get it right. The secret, of course, is that the leader makes the motions with his left hand. Most persons will use the right hand.

Tom-tom-tommy-tom.—The leader taps each of his four fingers with the index finger of the other hand as he says with rising inflection, "Tom-Tom-Tom-Tom." Then with a grand sweep from the forefinger of the hand he is tapping to the thumb of the same hand, following down the finger and up the thumb, he says with a high falsetto, "Tommy-Tom!" He invites others in the crowd to attempt the same thing. They will likely fail. The catch is that he clasps his hands together as he finishes. Some players finally catch it. That makes it more mystifying to the others.

Joining the sack society.—This is a "sell." The players are brought in one at a time, and required to thread a needle with one eye closed. Be sure to use a needle with a large eye (darning needle preferred) so as to make the threading a simple matter. The leader makes sure that one eye is closed by putting his hand over the eye. The catch is that he has lampblack on his hand, thus giving the candidate a black eye. Immediately the threading is finished the leader explains that the initiation requires that all members don the society regalia. This is a large paper sack that fits over the head. It has two small holes for the eyes and may have features marked on it. All members of the society, including the leader, are wearing such regalia. This procedure prevents subsequent victims from discovering the trick before you are ready for the denouement. After all the new members have been initiated suggest that all members now remove the headgear. The looks of surprise when the black eyes are disclosed will be worth the price of admission to anybody's circus.

Blowing out the candle.—A player is blindfolded. He is moved back three steps, turned around, and permitted to take three steps before blowing. The object is to blow out a candle which rests on a table. If you think it is easy try it.

Blind feeding the blind.—Blindfold two players. Furnish them with spoons and powdered sugar or ice cream or shelled peanuts. They sit facing one another and each tries to feed the other. Protect the floor with newspapers and the players by tying aprons or towels about their necks.

The sentimentalist club.—Persons are invited to join the "Sentimentalist Club." They are taken in one at a time. The leader instructs the candidate that all questions must be answered truthfully. He may put them through some sort of intelligence test, such as "How many eggs in a dozen?" "How many two-cent stamps in a dozen?" It is amazing how many people will answer that there are six two-cent stamps in a dozen. Then, suddenly, the initiator commands: "Say, 'Whom you love.'" The victim may respond facetiously. Members of the club will protest with "I object!" The leader will explain that the candidate will please try not to be funny. Again he commands, "Say, 'Whom you love.'" The victim will respond with some name. Again the members shout, "I object! He is not answering correctly." Each time the candidate answers with some name the members shout objection. The initiator may give the victim some clues by suggesting, "Say 'I have cold feet'" or "Say 'I have a soft head.'" After a while it will dawn on the candidate that he has been asked to say "Whom you love." He repeats "Whom you love" and all the members applaud. He is now a full-fledged member. Care must be taken not to embarrass unduly any who are timid or sensitive.

Pinning the tail on the donkey.—This is an old-timer that never loses interest. The picture of a donkey is pinned on a wall. A player is blindfolded, turned around once, and told to walk to the wall and pin the tail on the donkey. Each player has a rag with a pin in the end of it. The one who gets the tail nearest the right spot wins.

Variations— (a) Pin an arrow at the center of a target. (b) Pinning horns on a cow. (c) Pinning a hook in a fishes mouth. (d) Matching colors. Seven colors on the wall. Player tries to pin paper or cloth in the corresponding color strip. (e) Pinning earring on a girl's head. (f) Pinning a rudder on a ship.

Mesmerism.—Announce that one of the persons in the group has special hypnotic powers. Ask for subjects upon whom he can work. Select one of them for the trial.

The hypnotist and the victim face one another. The hypnotist explains that the experiment requires that the subject look him squarely and intently in the eye and that he must do just what he does, using as nearly as possible the same tone of voice and making the same motions. Two saucers are handed to the hypnotist and he hands one to the subject.

> "Ready? Now, after me:
> I touch my saucer's underside,
> And then I let my finger glide
> Across my forehead, down my nose,
> Touch my chin and cheeks of rose;
> And after I have done this much,
> My saucer's inside then I touch."

Immediately present a mirror and the victim will notice that he has streaked his face with lampblack, which was smeared on the underside of the saucer handed to him.

The barnyard club.—Candidates for election to the barnyard club are brought before the club one by one. They are duly impressed with the importance of membership. "Every candidate must pass certain tests before admission to membership," explains the leader. "Face me and do as I tell you." The candidate faces the leader. There is a vacant chair immediately behind the victim. "In order to qualify for membership," says the leader, "you must imitate some animal of the barnyard, suggested by the group and satisfactory to the group." He then turns to the members and asks, "What animal shall it be?" "A hog," shouts someone. A chorus of voices protest "No! No! That is too personal!" "A donkey!" shouts another. Again there come protests on the ground that this suggestion not only is too personal but that it is unfair to the donkey. Other animals may be mentioned. When someone calls "A hen!" everyone agrees to that.

"All right," says the leader to the candidate, "cluck like a hen that has just laid an egg." The candidate clucks the best he can. While he is doing this someone slips a hard-boiled egg into the chair immediately behind him. The leader asks the candidate to turn around and look at the chair. Then he announces, "You have qualified. We recognize you as a full-fledged member of the Barnyard Club."

Silly symphony.—This one would make a good introduction to a whistling number, either with or without instrument, such as a metal bird whistle or tin tongue whistle. The artist says:

> "I bought a wooden whistle but it wooden whistle.
> So I bought a steel whistle, but steel it wooden whistle
> So I bought a lead whistle; steel they wooden lead me whistle
> So I bought a tin whistle and now—I TIN whistle!"

Knight of the blanket.—This is a good stunt for the camp or the party. An unsuspecting victim is brought into the room. At one side seats are arranged. The King and Queen are seated about two feet apart. In between them seems to be a chair. The person who is to be initiated into the rank of "Knight of the Blanket" kneels before the King and Queen. He is then told he is to arise, seat himself between them, and answer some questions before being allowed to become a Knight. When he sits down, the King and Queen arise to honor him. The Knight, as a consequence, tumbles to the ground, for there really is no chair to hold him.

The arrangement is this: Two chairs are placed with about two feet between them. Two very thin smooth sticks are placed across the chairs, one at the back and one at the front. A heavy blanket is draped over the two chairs, covering the middle space and making it look like a third chair. When the victim sits down the thin stick breaks and the "Knight" hits the ground or floor. The space under the blanket should be well padded with pillows so as to break the force of the fall.

The symphony of the desert.—A musician with great seriousness gives the following "spiel": "Most people do not get all the entertainment possible out of music because they do not recognize the story it tells. Take a symphony concert, for example. Now, the symphony is merely a series of tone pictures. Did you ever hear 'The Symphony of the Desert'? (takes a baton or a pencil). First comes the silence of the desert (beats time with great solemnity). In the midst of the desert was an oasis with three palm trees. (With the last three words she strikes three notes of a chord in the middle of the piano.) Underneath the three palm trees (repeats the three notes arpeggio) was a little babbling brook (trills one note of the chord). Away off on the edge of the desert was a little light gazelle (a rapid triplet on the three highest notes of the keyboard). This little light gazelle (repeats the triplet) scented the little babbling brook (repeat the trill) in the midst of the three palm trees (repeats the chord arpeggio) and started for a drink (rapid triplets all the way down the treble). Off at the other side of the desert was a great, fierce lion (strikes the lowest note on the piano). This lion scented the little light gazelle (repeats the triplet) and began to roar (lowest note and its octave in rapid succession—loud pedal). Then he started for the little light gazelle (repeats the triplet) to the oasis (repeats the chord arpeggio), but the little light gazelle (repeats the triplet), which was drinking at the little babbling brook (repeats the trill) under the three palm trees (repeats the chord arpeggio), heard the lion coming toward her (slow octaves up from the bass) and ran fleetly back to the outer edge of the desert (repeats the triplets up the treble). So when the lion reached the oasis (chord), there was nothing but the three palm trees (arpeggio) and the little babbling brook (repeats the trill). Angrily the lion stalked back to his lair (octaves down the bass) and roared (lowest octave alternated rapidly). And again there was nothing left but the little babbling brook (rapid trill) under the three palm trees (chord arpeggio) and the silence of the desert" (beats time silently).

If the conductor of the "symphony" prefers, the lion may devour the little light gazelle. Appropriate "tone pictures" will readily suggest themselves.

—From *Good Times for Girls*, by MARY E. MOXCEY. Used by permission.

The water stunt.—If possible rig up an old-fashioned well. On top of it, or on top of a table have a bucket, that presumably holds water drawn from the well. In fact it has only a large dipper with a bit of water in it. Several people come in and observe the well. One of the persons remarks about the good water. Another professes to be thirsty and lifts the dipper to his lips. At the taste of the water he spits it out and dashes the rest of the contents of the dipper on the floor.

"This water is terrible," he says. Thereupon he picks up the bucket and makes a motion to throw the water in the bucket right at the audience. There is a swish, screams, and ducking, and then some sheepish grins. The bucket contained some rice. As it leaves the bucket it sounds and looks like water.

Something never seen before.—Announce that you plan to show something that has never been seen before and never will be seen again. Then produce a peanut or paper-shell pecan. Crack the shell and display the kernel. Explain that this is something that has never been seen before this very moment. Now eat the kernel with the announcement, "And now it will never be seen again."

Fake pillow fight.—Two players are blindfolded. Each is provided with a pillow. They start from opposite sides of the room toward one another. The object is to see who can score the most hits. Unknown to the blindfolded players the referee is furnished with a pillow also. He hits first one and then the other blindfolded player. Each player thinks his opponent is doing the hitting.

Knot tying trick.—Provide a piece of rope or string, or use a handkerchief. Ask if anyone can tie a knot in the rope by taking hold of both ends and not letting go with either hand. After they have tried it, demonstrate how it can be done. Fold the arms, the left hand under the right elbow and the right hand over the left elbow. In this position take hold of the ends of the rope. Now unfold the arms without letting go of the ends and the knot is tied.

Balanced writing.—If you think you have a good sense of balance try this one. Stand a quart milk bottle upright. Sit down on it, crossing your legs, touching the floor only with the heel of one foot. In this position, hold a pad in your hand and try to write your name. Or hold a candle, strike a match, and light the candle. Or try threading a needle from this position. Save the pieces!

The Knott Knitter.—Tom Knott could not knit, so he invented a machine which he called "The Knott Knitter." But the "Knott Knitter" could not knot knots, so Knott invented an attachment for the "Knott Knitter" which could knot knots and which he called "The Knott Knotter." When the "Knott Knotter" was attached to the "Knott Knitter," not a knitter could knot knots like the knots Knott knot with the "Knott Knitter" and the "Knott Knotter." Knott was not married so he fell in love with a knitter who knit knots with the "Knott Knitter" and the "Knott Knotter." Knott asked her not to knit knots any longer but to become Knott forever. But the knitter was not willing to become a Knott, so she said, "Nit" to Knott.

Knott and Schott.—A man named Knott and a man named Schott had an altercation. Knott claimed that Schott was not as good a man as Knott, and Schott said that Knott was not as good as Schott. So Knott shot Schott and Schott shot Knott. Policeman Blott asked Knott if he shot Schott. Knott said he had not shot Schott. Then Blott asked Schott who shot Knott. Said Schott to Blott, "I do not know who shot Knott." So Blott told Knott and Schott that if Knott had not shot Schott and Schott had not shot Knott there was probably a plot to shoot both Knott and Schott. Therefore, Knott and Schott should not stay out on the street, else they might be shot. So Knott and Schott went home. And Blott reported that it was not Knott that shot Schott and it was not Schott that shot Knott. Who shot Knott and Schott would be an unsolved plot.

"A Tongue Twisting Romance"

"A tree-toad loved a she toad
That lived up in a tree.
She was a three-toed tree toad
But a two-toed toad was he.
The two-toed tree toad tried to win
The she toad's friendly nod.
For the two-toed tree toad loved the ground
That the three-toed tree toad trod.
But vainly the two-toed tree toad tried,
He could not please her whim.
In her tree toad bower,
With her V-toed power,
The she toad vetoed him."

Pick it up.—Stand with back against a wall, heels touching the wall. Try to pick up a coin without moving heels away from the wall. You deserve the coin if you perform this trick.

Kneeling.—Stand with toes on a line. Without using the hands or moving the feet kneel down and get up again.

Circle two.—Try moving both arms in a circle (rotary motion) in opposite directions, the right hand away from the body and the left toward the body.

Pat head and rub stomach.—Try to pat the head with one hand and rub the stomach with the other simultaneously.

Move if you can.—Stand with one side (hip, shoulder, head) against a wall. Now try to lift the free leg away from you without changing your position.

Arise.—Lie flat on the back, arms to the side, hands flat against thighs. In this position try to arise without using the hands. Come first to a sitting position and then stand, if you can.

Rising with arms crossed.—Lie flat on the back, arms crossed on chest. Try to arise without uncrossing the arms or using the elbows.

Picking up cork.—Place a cork five feet from where you are standing. Go down on all fours. Now raise one hand to the hip. Keeping it in this position lower yourself until you can pick up the cork with your teeth. Now raise yourself to your feet again without using more than one hand to do it.

CHAPTER VIII
FUN WITH ICE BREAKERS

FUN WITH ICE BREAKERS

The dummy line.—Pair off the guests through a grand march or some other plan. Now require that they carry on their conversation by signs. The leader calls the topics for conversation. A new partner must be had for each topic. Here are a few suggestions:

How do you drive a car?
What is an accordion?
What is a spiral?
What is your hobby?
Which do you like better, an electric razor or a safety razor, and why?
What are the advantages or disadvantages of bobbed hair?
What is your favorite sport?
What kind of girl (or man) do you like best? (Pointing is not allowed in this one.)

Introductions.—Each guest is given a card or slip of paper carrying the name of another guest. He must find that guest, introduce himself, and get the information called for on the slip. The men may be allowed to draw name slips first. After they have interviewed the ladies and turned in their cards, the ladies draw and then interview the men. The card would call for the following information:

Name ....
Hobby ....
Disposition ....
Color of eyes ....

After cards are turned in they may be redistributed and read aloud to the crowd.

Choo-choo.—The players form a circle. One player inside the circle stands in front of one of the circle players, introduces himself to that player, and then asks: "What is your name?" That player may say: "Stella Smith." The center player now jumps in place in front of the player to whom he has just introduced himself. This is done

in rhythm five times, first right foot and right hand extended toward
the player, then left foot and left hand, then right, left, right. On
each jump he repeats the name, thus: "Stella! Stella! Stella, Stella,
Stella!" He turns away then, the second player (Stella) puts her
hands on his shoulders, and they begin "choo-chooing" inside the
circle until they step in front of another player. Again there is the
introduction, the jumping and the repeating of the name, this time
by two people. Now player Number One and Stella turn, Number
One putting his hands on Stella's shoulders, Number Three putting
her hands on Number One's shoulders, and the three of them "Choo-
Choo" to a fourth player. Each time, now, the group reverses after
the jumping, so that a new player becomes leader.

In a large crowd the number of starters would be increased, so that
there may be from three to ten "trains" operating at one time. This
makes a good game to divide the crowd into teams for games or
stunts that are to follow.

Impromptu circus.—Guests draw slips from a hat. These slips indicate what they are to be in the circus. There will be clowns, acro-
bats, bareback riders, the circus band, animals (elephants, giraffes,
monkeys, lions, dogs). Each group is given ten or fifteen minutes to
organize its part of the show, and then the circus is on. The leader
acts as ringmaster.

A bit of previous planning can add to the effectiveness of the
performance. If the hostess or the committee can have on hand
some properties to be used by the performers it can be used to good
effect—clown suits and false faces, make-up, hobbyhorses or sticks,
kazoos and other instruments, blankets, stuffed stockings for elephant trunks, brooms for giraffe necks, paper and cardboard to
make animal heads, and other material of this sort. These materials
could be hidden about the room. Part of the fun could be that of
having each group find its own equipment.

Bumpety-bump-bump.—This makes a good get-acquainted game.
It also serves to keep the players alert. One player in the center
points to someone in the circle and says: "Right! Bumpety-bump-
bump!" The person to whom he points must shout the name of the
person to his right before the center player finishes speaking, or take
his place. In a large group there may be several center players.

Paper plate art.—Each guest is given a paper plate or a piece of
cardboard. On the table are pencils, several sets of colored crayons,
and several black marking crayons. Each person is asked to illus-

trate some nursery rhyme, or song, or book title, or some given subject, such as "Moonlight on the Beach," "Drifting and Dreaming," "A Cottage Small," and the like. One group used this idea at a banquet. Since it was a "Tree Banquet" everyone was asked to draw a scene in which trees played a prominent part. There were some really lovely creations.

A masque of months.—The group is organized by birthday months. All the January people get together, all the February, and so on. After a few moments for consultation and planning the show is on. January could stage a snowball fight with handkerchiefs. February could celebrate any one of a few birthdays—Washington, Lincoln, Longfellow. Or they could stage a burlesque of the cherry tree incident. March could march. April could play April fool jokes. May could do a Maypole dance or crown the Queen of May. June could have a wedding or the making of a flag. July could celebrate the Fourth. August could "go swimming." September could have opening day at school. October could do some Halloween pranks or tell a ghost story. November could pantomime a football game. December could sing Christmas carols.

Sack shake.—Tie a paper sack on the right hand of each guest. Request that they move about shaking hands with others, trying to keep the paper bag in good condition. Each person keeps a count of the number of people with whom he shakes hands. At the close some sort of simple prize is given to the person who has shaken hands with most people and to the one who has the least battered paper bag.

Hurly-burly.—Players are given instructions by the leader, who whispers in the ear of each one some action to be performed. One may be asked to "sing a song," another to "dance a jig," still another to "play a drum," while others may be asked to "make a speech," recite "Mary had a little lamb," with dramatic gestures, and so forth. When all have been given something to do the leader calls "Hurly-Burly" and each player performs simultaneously. Anyone failing to perform immediately is punished by being made to "walk the swamp." This is done by beginning at one end of the room and answering questions put to him by the crowd, stepping forward one step when the answer is "Yes" and backward one step when the answer is "No."

Song scramble.—Give to each guest one line of a song. It would, perhaps, simplify matters to have the slips numbered. Thus all slips of one song will be numbered "1," another "2," and so on. The players scramble around trying to get together the other members of their group and complete their song. When this is done they must render their song.

Lucky handshaker.—One or more persons in the room are secretly supplied with pennies. The tenth or thirteenth person to shake hands with this secret handshaker will receive the penny. After that, the tenth person to shake hands with the new holder of the penny receives it. Thus it goes until the leader declares an end to the handshaking. Persons who hold pennies at that time keep them. In a crowd of 100 persons it would be well to have as many as ten lucky handshakers.

I've got your number.—Give each guest a number which is to be pinned in a conspicuous place and worn throughout the game. Now give to each person a slip of instructions, such as the following: "Introduce four to three"; "shake hands with six and seven"; "go to ten and shake hands three ways—Chinese fashion (each shakes his own hand), society grip (hands held high), and good old pump-handle shake"; "kneel before twelve and meow three times"; "find out the color of eleven's eyes"; ask one what he likes best for breakfast"; ask two why good men are hard to find." It would simplify matters if odd numbers were given to men and even numbers to the ladies.

Jumbled words charades.—Write out words and cut them into single letters, giving the same number to each letter of a given word. Pass these letters out and have the players get together with the others in their particular groups. The players try to discover first what the word is and then they are to act it out for the others to guess. Thus all of the number ones get together and find that they have eight letters as follows: L, L, B, S, E, A, A, B. They put their letters down and take a look at them. Finally, someone in the group suggests that it is "Baseball." That works out all right, so they plan to act it out. Another group gets "Battle," another "Barber," another "Symphony," another "Movies," another "Newsboy," and so on.

Pantomime for dates.—Get partners by a grand march or some other plan, such as completing hearts, completing proverbs, affinities (like cap and gown, day and night, fair and warmer, Jack and Jill, sword and shield, pen and ink, bow and arrow), or old sayings like "strong as an ox," "thin as a rail," "neat as a pin," "black as coal," "white as snow," "crazy as a loon." Each couple must then stand before the whole crowd, in turn. The man must ask the lady for a date. The catch comes in the requirement that the request must be made in pantomime. The girl must reply in the same manner.

Famous people.—As guests arrive tag them with the names of famous people—Bible characters, historic personages, characters in fiction or literature, prominent present-day people (movie stars, athletes, political figures, etc.). These names they are to carry the entire evening. March in concentric circles, the men marching counterclockwise and the ladies clockwise. When the music stops each person must face someone of the opposite sex, note the name, and make appropriate greeting. They may indulge in a moment of conversation, asking questions about one another, engaging in banter, and the like. For instance, Jezebel meets David and the following conversation ensues: "How do you do, David? Where is your harp? Did you bring your sling?" "And how are you, Jezebel? How does it feel to be pitched out of a window?"

When the music starts again they yell "Goodbye!" and move on to meet some other famous person.

The names are used all evening, no matter what games are played.

Cobweb mixer.—After the guests have arrived they are led to a corner of the room where there is a giant cobweb made of strings. Within easy reach, near the center of the web, are loose strings of which the guests take hold. One color string should be for the ladies and another color for the men. Each person is to unloose his string and follow it to the  end. It will go down to the bottom of the web, then along the floor, over chairs, upstairs, downstairs, through hallways, maybe, crossing, looping, and tangling with other strings. The players stop to untangle their strings, often several players working together at the same point. When they come to the end there should be some surprise—a trinket of some sort, a fortune written on a slip of paper, directions for the next event (instructions to get together with certain others to prepare a stunt, or explanation of a game to be played, or the title of a song to be sung), or maybe two strings are tied together and when she gets to the end of her string the girl finds she has a man on the string.

What's my name?—Each guest has the name of some celebrated or well-known person pinned on his back. He is not told who it is, but must find out through the remarks of the other guests. As soon as he knows, or thinks he knows he reports to the leader. If he has really discovered his identity, the name is taken off his back and placed on his coat lapel. For example, the remarks or questions that tip off "Lord Chamberlain" as to his identity are these: "How do you see in a London fog?" "Where is your umbrella?" and "That was quite a conference at Munich, wasn't it?" "Anne Lindbergh" guesses her identity after someone has suggested that she is up in the air a good deal of the time, and someone else asks her how it feels to have a husband who is up in the air so often, and another suggests "You've listened to the wind on a trip north to the Orient, haven't you?"

Zoo.—Peanuts, paper hearts, beans, corn, or other things are hidden around the camp, or lawn, or room. Players are divided into groups. Each group is given the name of some animal and is assigned to a keeper. The players scatter to hunt the hidden treasure. When a player makes a find he cannot pick it up. He must stand by his "quarry" and make a sound like the animal he represents. He continues this noise until the keeper for his group comes and picks up what has been discovered. The dogs bark, the cats meow, the ducks quack, and the goats baa-aa-aa.

Rummage.—Guests are asked to bring along some old clothing— hats, shoes, dresses, coats, etc.—which later are to be given to the needy. They stand in a circle, each with his bundle. The music starts, and the bundles are passed to the right. When the music stops with a bang, or the whistle blows, all guests open the bundle they have at the time. They are then required to don the garments and wear them for the rest of the evening. If there is any stiffness in this party you ought to move out to the graveyard and take your place with the dead ones in the cemetery.

Secret couples.—The King and Queen of Hearts, or the King and Queen of Hunky Bunky, or George and Martha Washington preside over this affair. They draw names from a box—the King a girl's name and the Queen a boy's name. Five or six couples are thus named. The pairings are kept secret, only the King and Queen knowing who they are. It has been previously decided that these couples are to be described as:

(1) The most sensible couple.
(2) The most handsome couple.
(3) The most brilliant couple.
(4) The most thrifty couple.
(5) The most lovable couple.
(6) The most popular couple.

Guests pair off and appear before the throne to find out if they are the most of this or that couple. When properly paired they keep their partners and due announcement is made. If not properly paired, the two immediately leave one another and bring up another partner.

Shake.—When the leader blows his whistle once all players pair off and stand back to back. When he blows twice the players standing back to back face one another and shake hands according to instructions. For instance, the leader calls or holds up a sign that says "Pump handle." Partners give one another an old-fashioned pump-handle shake. At the same time they greet one another very cordially. When the leader blows his whistle again the players scurry around and stand back to back with someone else. This time, when the leader blows twice, players are instructed to give a "high-brow" shake. Hands are held high, finger-tips touching. The greeting should be blase and bored. Next players are instructed to give a "fish" shake, the hand being held lifeless and inert. The greeting is listless. The instructions the next time are "own hands." Each person greets his partner warmly but shakes his own hands.

Toy shop.—Each man draws from a box the name of some toy-shop article. He lets no one see it. The ladies draw duplicate slips from another box. The men act out their toys, each in his turn. As soon as the lady who got his slip recognizes her toy she claims it, and they become partners for the next feature. The toy dog barks. Donald Duck waddles and talks through his nose. The elephant has trouble with his trunk. The crying mamma doll puts on her plaintive act. The drum major struts and beats time. The soldier marches, gun on his shoulder. The camera takes candid shots. The hobbyhorse rocks back and forth. The player who drew "football" pretends to catch a punt and get away with it. Or he pantomimes getting off a kick. The "baseball" pantomimes a ball game. The horn toots. The gun shoots. The electric train "choo-choos" around. The automobile "chug-chugs" and blows its siren. And so it goes until each toy has found its proper owner.

Dramagrams.—The guests are divided into two teams. Each team makes up a list of short quotations, book titles, advertising slogans, proverbs, and the like. The captains of each side exchange lists. Then the fun begins. One player comes up to his captain and the captain whispers the first quotation, title, or slogan. That player then tries to convey the phrase to his teammates by acting it out. His acting must all be in pantomime. He holds up his fingers to indicate the number of words in it. Some member of his side may ask, "Is it a slogan?" He vigorously shakes his head, "No." "Is it a quotation?" He nods "Yes." Then he starts acting it out, starting anywhere in it, and indicating the number of the word on which he is starting by holding up his fingers. For instance, suppose the quotation is "Give me liberty, or give me death." The player holds up seven fingers. Then he holds up one to indicate the first word, and acts out "Give," putting on a begging act. Following that he holds up two fingers and points to himself. Then he holds up seven fingers and does a dying act. By this time his teammates will probably have guessed the quotation. If not, he acts out the other words, doing his best to tell them by his acting what the quotation is.

In one party a girl swished through the room and disappeared. It was no trouble for her group to recognize "Gone With the Wind."

On another occasion you should have seen a college student trying to convey to his group "We must hang together or we will hang separately."

Confessions.—One person whispers to each member of the group the name of a person, preferably one in the room but not necessarily so. Another person whispers to each person some location, such as, "in a tree," "on the top of the roof," "in the swimming pool," "on the beach," "in a taxi," "on the Queen Mary," "in church," and "in Cincinnati." Still a third person whispers to each one some activity, such as "singing swinging songs," "eating peanuts," "dancing the Highland fling," "listening to the Katydids," "spilling the same old romantic line," "suffering heroically."

Now each person must "confess" with whom he was, where he was, and what they were doing.

The results will naturally bring some ridiculous combinations. Imagine the uproar when one of the most sedate ladies in the group announces that she was "sitting on top of the depot smoking cigarettes with the preacher."

Blind handshake.—Boys line up on one side of the room and girls on the other. One boy and one girl are blindfolded and told to approach each other and shake hands. No coaching is permitted from the side lines. As soon as they succeed in shaking hands two more are blindfolded.

Bean quiz.—When the company begins to arrive give to each person ten beans, with instructions as to how to proceed. Whenever you trip someone into answering by saying "Yes" or "No," that person surrenders to you one bean. If you are caught, you forfeit one bean to the person catching you. At the close the winner is the person holding the largest number of beans. The idea may continue to function throughout a whole evening's program.

Bells, hearts, and the like may be used instead of beans.

Heart's desire.—Each guest must write down one thing he wants most at the particular time. Concrete things must be named. Intangibles like happiness, love, peace, and health, are not allowed. The cards are signed and turned in to the leader, who then distributes them to the members of the group, making assignments to members of the opposite sex as much as possible. The guests now have the freedom of the house and are ordered to bring back the item mentioned on the card assigned them. Where this is not possible, the nearest thing to it will do. Much of the fun comes from the clever substitutions offered.

The cards are returned to the leader at the tap of a bell or some other signal. They are read and the hunter is required to make a formal presentation of the trophy desired, or of the nearest thing to it he could find.

How do you like your neighbors?—Players sit in a circle. One player in the center points to someone and says: "How do you like your neighbors?" "Oh, not so well," comes the response. "Who would you like better?" The player must name two other persons in the room. These two must change places immediately with the undesired neighbors, the center player, in the meantime, endeavoring to get a seat. The player left out is "It" and the game proceeds. If the player to whom the question is put answers "Fine" or with some other such reply to indicate he is satisfied, there must be a general scramble in which all players change seats. In this mix-up the player who is "It" will likely get a seat.

Zip.—Players sit in a circle. Each person acquaints himself with the person to his left. The person in the center points to anyone in the circle and says: "One, two, three, four, five, zip!" The person to whom he is pointing must shout the name of the person to his left before "zip!" is called. Failing to do this, he must exchange places with the player in the center. The game must move rapidly. There may be several "zippers" in the center of the circle.

When a center player shouts "Boom-Zip!" all players must change seats. In the ensuing scramble the "zipper" may get a seat. Players must get acquainted rapidly with their new left-hand neighbor for a "zipper" may be along any moment.

Spiral handshake.—Grand march the guests into a spiral. Then have the center person start handshaking his way out of the spiral. He must shake hands with each player in turn and stand in line and wait for the rest of the crowd to come by him. As he passes the person next to him, that person follows him around the spiral. So each player shakes hands with every other person twice, once when they pass him and again when he passes them.

Blind postman.—One player is blindfolded and stands in the center of the room as postman. The leader is postmaster and has a list of cities, the names of which have been given to the players, one to each person. The postmaster calls the names of two cities, such as "New York to Dallas," for instance. "New York" and "Dallas" must immediately arise and exchange seats. The blind postman tries to catch one of them or attempts to sit in a vacated chair. The player who is caught becomes postman. Players may crawl, run, walk, dodge, or dive to escape the postman, but they are not allowed to step outside the circle of chairs. If the postman seems to have great difficulty capturing someone, the leader may call as many as four or five cities at a time, thus making it almost certain that some-one will be caught. Announcement of "Parcel Post!" means that all players must exchange seats.

Spin the platter.—Each player is numbered. A center player spins a tin platter, calling a number as he starts the spin. The player whose number is called must catch the platter before it stops spinning. Failure to do so makes him "It." If he succeeds the spinner must try again until he gets someone to miss.

Variations— (*a*) Player drops a cane by taking finger off top of cane, calling a number. Must be caught before it falls. (*b*) Bounces a ball which must be caught before it hits a second time.

Going to Jerusalem.—This is an old favorite. Chairs are set in a single row, alternately facing first one way and then the other. There are less chairs than the number of players. Someone plays a march on the piano and all players march around the chairs, keeping time to the music and keeping hands off the chairs. Suddenly the music stops and players try to sit in the chairs. It is not allowable for a player to turn a chair around. Players left without a chair drop out and the game proceeds, each time another chair being taken away. Finally two players march around the lone remaining chair. Much depends on the pianist. She should stop at unexpected intervals.

Variations— (*a*) Arrange the chairs in two rows back to back.

(*b*) Arrange the chairs in a circle facing center. This is sometimes called "Musical Chairs."

(*c*) Arrange the chairs in a circle facing out from center.

(*d*) "Jerusalem Wing Grab." Line up the men one behind another. Have each one stand with one arm akimbo, alternating right and left down the line. Thus, the first man would stand with his right hand on his hip and his arm bowed, the second with his left, and so on. The girls march around the line of boys, with at least one more girl than boys. When the music stops each girl grabs for a wing. No breaking through the line is allowed. Girls left without a wing drop out of the line. Each time one boy drops out, also, so that at the last two girls are marching around one boy.

Blind problems and answers.—Did you ever have anyone say to you, "What would you do if ———?" All right! What would you? Give to one half the crowd slips of paper on each of which is written "What would you do if ———?" They are to fill in the rest of the question.

To the other half of the crowd you give slips of paper on each of which is written "I would ———." They are to write in a proposed line of action.

The slips are all dropped in two hats, one for the problems and the other for the answers. The leader allows two people to draw at a time, one from the problems and the other from the answers. The problem is read and the solution offered.

Or the players may be numbered from one on up for the problems, and the same may be done for the answers. Number One reads his problem and Number One on the other side reads the proposed line of action.

It can be readily seen that there will be some ridiculous combinations. For instance, "What would you do if you saw Mary Jones fall off the Brooklyn Bridge?" The answer comes back "I would serve luncheon." Or "What would you do if a vicious dog attacked you?" And the answer comes back "I'd turn off the radio and go to sleep."

The talk train.—Chairs are arranged in double rows with an aisle between. Appoint a conductor, a "butch," and a porter. Couples occupy the chairs on either side of the aisle. The fun is spontaneous, the conductor and his aids doing whatever occurs to them as being appropriate in performing their duties.

The conductor calls stations occasionally. These calls are signals for the men to move up one seat. The head men go to the rear. The calls may name stations that signify some line of action. Railroad timetables will furnish plenty of ammunition for this feature. A brief glance at the index of stations in one railroad schedule indicated some of the following possibilities:

"Anchorage" (couples will discuss "Popeye, the Sailor").

"Bagdad" (pop-sack relay between two sides of the train).

"Bardstown" (each couple must write a rhyming couplet).

"Deer Range" (the man must pay some glowing compliment to his partner, addressing her as "Dear").

"Friendsville" (couples discuss the question, "What is a friend?").

"Gallaway" (girls leave men and move forward to another partner).

If desired, the station calls may simply require the changing of partners, and couples may converse on topics called by the conductor, but not necessarily related to the name of the station.

Laughing handkerchief.—All players, except one, get in a circle. That one stands inside the circle and tosses a handkerchief into the air. As he does so he starts laughing. Everyone must laugh with him until the handkerchief touches the floor, when there must be perfect silence. Anyone laughing after the handkerchief touches the floor must leave the circle.

Variation—(*a*) Players line up in two sides. Play for few mo-

ments and then count those still in line.   (*b*) Another variation is
to make the guilty one serve as leader.

Conversation circle.—Players march in concentric circles, boys on
the inside and girls on the outside. Partners march together. When
the leader blows a whistle or horn, partners stop, face each other, and
discuss whatever topic the leader calls. When they start marching
again the man moves up one partner. Some suggested topics for
conversation are as follows:
    (*a*) What is your favorite radio program?
    (*b*) What do you think of the present-day hats?
    (*c*) What do you think of the present-day fashions?
    (*d*) What do you think of the world situation?
    (*e*) What is the best book you've ever read?
    (*f*) What is the best magazine article you have read recently?
    (*g*) What good movie have you seen recently?
    (*h*) What is your favorite song?
    (*i*) What is your favorite football team, basketball team?
    (*j*) What is your favorite flower?
Variation—Players may march in opposite directions. When the
music stops the two lines stop and face one another.

Scram.—Players stand in a circle holding the left hand in toward
center. The player who is "It" starts moving around inside the
circle, counterclockwise. As he goes he takes hold of some player's
hand and that player takes hold of another hand, and so on until
most of the players are moving around inside the circle. When
"It" yells "Scram!" all players rush to get back to position. The last
player back is "It."
Variations— (*a*) "It" carries an empty suit-case. When he drops
it the players scurry back to their positions in the circle.   (*b*) "It"
carries a squawker, blown up and ready to squawk. A whistle may
be used in the same manner.

Paper bag introduction.—Each guest has a paper bag tied to his
right hand, with the hand inside and the bag tied about his wrist.
They are instructed to shake hands until they wear out the bag.
Variation—Guests are provided with crayons as well as paper bags.
Each one must draw a face on his paper bag. Noses and ears may be
added by the use of some extra paper and some library paste. Curls
may be added in the same manner, if desired. These paper bag
puppets are now tied on the right hand. Guests make these puppets
greet one another. Impromptu puppet shows may feature the pro-

gram. If this variation is used, provide a work-table where all the necessary supplies are available.

Clap in, clap out.—The men are taken out of the room and numbered. The girls form a circle standing behind chairs. The leader announces that the numbers of the men run from one to as high as they go. Now one of the girls, designated by the leader, calls a number. The man with that number enters the room. As he enters the girls clap. The man tries to sit down in the chair of the girl who called him. If he is wrong the girls applaud. He keeps on trying until he finally gets the right chair. The silence indicates to him that he is correct. He remains seated. Another man is called in. And so it goes until every man has been called in and has found the girl who called his number. This would make a good game to pair off couples for some game that is to follow.

Variation—Instead of numbering the men, allow the girls to call the men by name.

Balloon battle royal.—The guests are arranged in couples. Each girl has a toy balloon or blown-up paper sack tied to her left ankle, the string being at least a yard long. Couples must keep arms linked all during the battle, the man with the girl to his right. Each man tries to protect his partner's balloon while he, at the same time tries to step on and burst all of the others. This continues until only one couple survives, if and when they do.

As you were.—This makes a good mixer. Players get partners by doing a grand march. The group marches counterclockwise, the boys on the inside.

The leader calls directions for the group. "Girls inside, boys outside!" "Girls in front of boys!" "Halt, and face partners!" "The grand right and left!" The couples clasp right hands and pass to each other's right, the boys moving counterclockwise and the girls moving clockwise. The next player is grasped by the left hand, and players pass left shoulders to one another. So they alternate, the girls moving in one direction and the boys in another, until the leader shouts "As you were!" At this command each person must find the partner he had when the game began and line up ready to march. In the scramble the leader endeavors to get a partner. The player left out is "It."

Fashion show.—Guests are paired off. Newspapers, crepe paper, pins, library paste, scissors, and style designs are made available.

Each man dresses his partner in whatever style appeals to him. On one such occasion a clever costume was designed to represent "The Gay Nineties." The costume included hat and muff. There are all sorts of possibilities—a bridal costume, a peasant outfit, fifty years from now, colonial style. When the costumes have been finished climax this event with a grand march or a fashion show.

Ghost guess.—Two even sides. One goes out of the room and sends back one of their number wearing a sheet that covers him completely. The other side tries to guess who it is. Only one guess is allowed. As soon as a name is called, the player throws off the sheet and discloses his identity. If the guess was correct the guessing side scores one point. If incorrect, the performing side scores. Then the other side is allowed to go out and send back a ghost. The ghost may endeavor to disguise himself in any way he can devise. He may stoop, use something to make him appear taller, put on shoes belonging to another person, or anything that is likely to throw the opponents off the trail.

White elephants.—Guests are asked to bring something for which they no longer have any use. They may wrap up these white elephants in any manner they choose. On arrival they are put into wastebaskets. Guests draw numbers to determine in what order they are to choose a white elephant from a wastebasket. The last person takes whatever is left. After the guests get their packages they may open them. If not satisfied, they may wrap them up again and try to trade with someone else who is dissatisfied.

Dressing lollipops.—Provide each guest with a lollipop. Have several work-tables on which there are materials with which to dress and make up the lollipop—crepe paper, crayons, paper, library paste, scissors. Each person is to dress his lollipop, making features to represent various types of characters, the coquette, the college freshman, the handle-bar mustache villain, the old maid, the doll, Uncle Remus, Goldilocks, Red Riding Hood, Snow White, etc.

Allow from five to ten minutes for this feature and then put the lollipops on display. After the display have the guests form groups and put on some brief puppet shows with their dolls.

Millinery show.—Ask guests to bring along an old hat frame and whatever hat trimmings they might have loose around the house. Provide worktables with supplies of trimming material—ribbons, feathers, flowers, laces, buckles, crepe paper. Each person is to dress a hat and wear it. The men are included.

Laughing hat.—Divide into two sides. Toss a hat up into the air. If it lands with the top up one side laughs immediately. If it lands bottom side up the other side laughs. Any player failing to laugh drops out.

Drop the hat.—There are two teams facing one another. The hat is tossed in the air. If it comes down right side up the side designated must run to a goal line with the other side in pursuit. If it lands bottom-side up the other side runs to its goal line. Players tagged go to the opposing side.

Keyed up.—Players are seated in a circle. There are just enough chairs to seat everyone, except one player who stands inside the circle. That person has a bunch of keys on a key ring. He starts walking around the inside of the circle and crooks his finger at some player who is seated beckoning him to follow. That player gets up and follows. The second player beckons to another player who falls into line behind the other two. So it goes until a number are walking around the circle. Suddenly the leader drops the bunch of keys. That is the signal for every player to try to get a seat. The player left out becomes the leader for the next round.

Shoe scramble.—All players take off their shoes. They are stacked in a pile at center, being mixed around in the process. At the signal to go all players rush to get their shoes and put them on. The last three or four players to finish may be required to perform some stunt for the group.

Bus ride.—Players are seated in two rows of chairs, facing one another. There is six to eight feet distance between the two rows. These rows represent the seats on an old-fashioned side-seated bus.

One player is conductor; he calls various stops. If he calls a plain stop all players must get up and exchange sides. If he calls a name with "street" attached, the players do not move. If he calls a "road" each player must get up and run around the row of chairs in which he was seated and try to get a chair, any chair. The conductor also tries to get a chair. The person left out becomes the conductor.

Sample calls—Times Square, Central Park, Broadway, Belmont,

Belle Meade, Clifton—players cross over and take seats on the opposite side.

Green Street, Twenty-third Street, Plum Street, Olive Street—players remain seated. Any player who gets up must take the conductor's place.

Mockingbird Road, Peachtree Road, River Road—players get up and run around the chairs.

Ear pulling.—Guests form a circle. One player starts around the inside of the circle, moving counterclockwise. He gently pulls the ear of the person to his right and says "Hello!" He gives his name and in return receives the name of the person whose ear he pulled. He moves around the circle greeting each person, in turn, in similar fashion. As he passes the player to his right, that person falls in behind him and repeats the process with each person. The third person falls in behind the second, and so on. Soon half the circle is moving around greeting the rest. When a player completes the round he takes his position and the rest of the players come around to greet him. This type of greeting ought to break down any stiffness on the part of the guests.

Setting up.—Use the following game as a relaxing stunt or as a game of co-ordination. Repeat it two or more times increasing the speed with each repetition.

> Hands on your hips, hands on your knees,
> Put them behind you, if you please.
> Touch your shoulders, touch your nose,
> Touch your ears, touch your toes.
> Raise your hands high in the air,
> At your sides, on your hair.
> Raise your hands as before,
> While you clap one, two, three, four.
> My hands upon my head I place,
> On my shoulders, on my face.
> Then I raise them up on high
> And make my fingers quickly fly.
> Then I put them in front of me,
> And gently clap them one, two, three.
> —BRUCE TOM
> Columbus, Ohio

Professions.—Couples are formed by a grand march or by drawing numbers and then looking for the duplicate number. These couples then draw from a box a slip of paper on which is written some profession or occupation. Each couple must act out the profession given them while the rest try to guess what it is. For instance, the "dentist," pulls a tooth for the patient, or he fills one. There will likely be a lawyer, a teacher, a doctor, an actor, a radio announcer, a radio performer, a politician, a chemist, a concert artist, a grand opera star, an advertising executive, a preacher, a dancer, an orchestra leader, and so on.

GETTING PARTNERS

Hand out.—The girls stand behind a screen. One at a time they put out their hands so that nothing but the hand can be seen. As a hand appears a man steps up and takes hold of it and leads the owner of the hand away as his partner.

Athlete's foot.—The men stand behind a sheet with only their feet showing. The girls select their partners by pointing out the pair of feet wanted.

Pulling strings.—Long strings pass through a large heart (hoop, target, paper turkey, paper football) and hang down on either side. The girls take hold of the ends on one side and the men on the other. At signal they pull and thus locate their partners. Care must be taken to see that the number of strings corresponds with the number of people present.

Shadow auction.—Either the men or the girls stand behind the shadow screen and are sold at auction—beans, counters, or pennies may be used. Subjects may disguise their appearance by the use of false noses, or ears, or hair.

Matching.—Partners may be found by matching hearts, valentines, numbers, split quotations, questions and answers, states and capitals, etc.

Pet shop.—The men are herded in one room where they are given names of different pets—collie, fox terrier, wire-haired terrier, pug, scotty, parrot, rabbit, duck, etc. The girls come to the pet shop one at a time and call for the kind of pet they want. When a pet is named the person representing that pet comes to his new owner with some appropriate sound or action.

Fish pond.—The girls hide behind a screen. The men drop a fishing line over the screen. Some girl takes hold and walks out. The "poor fish" may wish she had not bitten. As far as that is concerned, so may the fisherman.

Blind choice.—They say "Love is blind," so why not try this one? Let the girls form a circle. Blindfold the men one at a time. Put the blind man in the center of the circle. Have the circle of girls march to music. When the music stops turn the man around once and then let him walk toward the circle. The girl he touches becomes his partner. No girl in the circle is permitted to move after the music stops.

Chairless couples.—Two sets of chairs are arranged as for "Going to Jerusalem." The men form a circle around one of these and the girls about the other. In each there is one less chair than there are persons. As the music starts the players march around the chairs. When it stops each person tries to get a chair. The man and girl left out become partners for the next event. Each time a player drops out a chair is removed. This continues until all the players are paired.

Riddle partners.—Each man is provided with a conundrum. The girls are allowed to draw the answers from a tray or plate, one to a person. Then each man tries to find the answer to his riddle. The girl who has the answer on her slip of paper becomes his partner for the next event.

Author and book partners.—Allow each man to draw the name of some famous author—Shakespeare, Tennyson, Kipling, Hugo, Longfellow, Mark Twain, etc.—and each girl to draw the title of some book or poem written by these authors. Each author now tries to get together with his book or poem. "Shakespeare" hunts "A Midsummer Night's Dream"; "Tennyson" looks for "The Princess"; "Kipling" locates "Gunga Dhin"; "Hugo" searches for "Les Miserables"; "Longfellow" finds "Evangeline"; "Mark Twain" seeks "Tom Sawyer"; and so on.

Famous people reminders.—The men get the names of famous people. The girls get slips that list something that reminds them of the particular character—"Moses," "the burning bush"; "George Washington," "a hatchet"; "Lincoln," "a rail splitter"; "Diogenes," "a lantern"; "Betsy Ross," "a flag"; "Frances Willard," "a white ribbon." Other suggestions may be noted in Chapter IX, "Fun with Mental Games."

Affinities.—Give to each man one word of the affinity and to each woman the other. A list follows:

Jack and *Jill*	Amos and *Andy*
Anthony and *Cleopatra*	Bread and *Butter*
Mutt and *Jeff*	Knife and *Fork*
Salt and *Pepper*	Pen and *Ink*
Ham and *Eggs*	Brush and *Comb*
Ice Cream and *Cake*	Paper and *Pencil*
Shoes and *Stockings*	Light and *Dark*
Lock and *Key*	Good and *Evil*
Fair and *Warmer*	Cup and *Saucer*
Thunder and *Lightning*	Bow and *Arrow*
House and *Lot*	Coat and *Hat*
Collar and *Tie*	Hit and *Run*
Cap and *Gown*	Army and *Navy*
Crackers and *Cheese*	Cream and *Sugar*
Soap and *Water*	Day and *Night*

Completing quotations.—Give to the women the first part of the quotation and the men the last. The woman who has "Strong as an" looks for the man who has "Ox." Other suggestions are:

"Sure as *Death*"	"Yellow as *Gold*"
"Sweet as *Sugar*"	"Slow as *Cold Molasses*"
"Sour as *Vinegar*"	"Neat as a *Pin*"
"Hot as *Blazes*"	"Heavy as *Lead*"
"Soft as *Mush*"	"Slick as *Glass*"
"Tough as *Shoe Leather*"	"Slippery as an *Eel*"
"Hard as *Rock*"	"Proud as a *Peacock*"
"Thin as a *Rail*"	"Mad as a *Wet Hen*"
"Fat as a *Butter-ball*"	"Fit as a *Fiddle*"
"Light as a *Feather*"	"Stiff as a *Board*"
"Fast as *Lightning*"	"Busy as a *Bee*"
"Cold as *Ice*"	"Straight as a *Pine Tree*"
"Still as a *Mouse*"	"Flat as a *Pancake*"
"Green as *Grass*"	"Clear as *Crystal*"
"Sly as a *Fox*"	"Dead as a *Doornail*"
"Crooked as a *Gourd*"	"Keen as a *Whip*"
"Sore as a *Boil*"	"Clean as a *Hound's Tooth*"

Definitions and words.—Write definitions on one set of slips and the words they define on another set. Let the women draw the definitions and the men the words. Each definition looks for its word. Thus "The last letter in the Greek alphabet" would look for "Omega." "A drama wholly or mostly sung, with orchestral accompaniment and appropriate costumes, scenery, and action" would pair off with "Opera." The dictionary will furnish a sufficient number of words to answer your purpose. This can be made a good mixer.

Blind date.—The girls are numbered. The boys have left the room. They are told how far the numbers range. A boy steps up to the door and knocks the number of times he desires. If he knocks three times, for instance, the girl bearing that number answers the door to meet her blind date. The two go for a short walk while the game proceeds. Or they go to another room for refreshments or for some other game.

Noah's Ark.—Use numbered slips, two of each kind, on which is written the name of an animal or bird that might be imitated. Have a duplicate numbered list of all slips given out.

Select a few players to represent Noah's family. Give out one set of slips to the men, and another to the women. Players find the persons with corresponding names for partners. Each couple is given a number.

Noah's family stands in one corner, and Noah calls a number. The couple having that number comes to the corner where Noah's family is. Before being admitted to the ark they must imitate by sound or pantomime the animal named on their slips. As soon as the animal is recognized by any of Noah's family, the couple is admitted to the ark. The variety of animals and birds possible is as broad as the universe: duck, pig, sheep, owl, bear, frog, lion, monkey, donkey, horse, elephant, cat, rabbit, dog, goose, turkey, dove, jaybird, crow, giraffe, quail, chicken, etc.

Dumb Crambo.—Two sides. One goes out while the other group selects a word that can be acted out, such as "trial." The other side is called back and told the word rhymes with "mile," for instance. After conferring among themselves they make a list of words they think might be the one selected, and decide in what order to present them. For instance they list "smile," "rile," "style." Everybody smiles broadly to enact "smile." Then they put on a "style" show. Next they get considerably "riled." Finally they try a court scene and the other side applauds for it's clear that they've guessed "trial." The number of guesses taken is counted and the other side goes out to try its hand at guessing and acting out the answer.

CHAPTER IX
FUN WITH MENTAL GAMES

FUN WITH MENTAL GAMES

How to Direct Contests

MENTAL games can be made very enjoyable. Much depends upon the attitude of the player, of course. And a good deal depends on the manner in which the games are presented. Here are a few suggestions that might prove helpful:

1. The important thing is that everyone has a good time. No one should be encouraged to take the competitive aspect of a contest too seriously.

2. Have all of the necessary materials ready. If answers are to be written have mimeographed or carbon copies of the contest prepared, pencils available, and whatever other things are necessary, such as objects properly numbered or labeled and attractively displayed.

3. One of the best ways to use contests is to read the story or questions and pause for the players to call the answers. If done by sides allow one point to the side having someone to call the correct answer first. Take off a point for an incorrect answer. This manner of using the contest is highly satisfactory because it gives everyone a sense of achievement. The player identifies himself with the group and finds pleasure in group success even though he may not individually answer any of the questions.

4. Another way to use these games is to use the same methods followed in a spelling bee.

One of the fine things about mental games is that they can be enjoyed by one person, or two, or a small group, or a large one. The popularity of the "Professor Quiz" type of radio program has demonstrated the appeal of mental play for large masses of people.

A tree romance.—Cy *Press* and Red *Wood* both loved the same girl. Her name was *Olive* and she was very *Poplar* around town. Said Cy, "*Sago* with me and I will *Orange* for you to *Cedar* world." Said she, "I am afraid *Yew* do not understand me. I don't give a *Fig* for travel. I *Pine* for love. And no matter what *Pawpaw* says I won't *Date* any *Sap* who goes materialistic on me. I want romance in my life, and by *Gum* I'm going to have it."

Plum disgusted, *Olive* strolled down to the *Beech*. She couldn't tell what the wild waves were saying, and she was anything but *Cherry*. Who should she find there but Red *Wood!* He looked as *Spruce* as you please. *Olive* had been about to *Balsam* but seeing Red changed things. He was a *Plane* man, but he was the *Apple* of her eye.

There flashed through her mind the thought that if she fell in the water Red *Maple* her out. "I *Willow* my life to him then, and maybe he will marry me." That was unnecessary, however, for Red flicked the *Ash* from his cigarette as he saw her and came immediately to her. He held her *Palm* a few moments and then pulled that old *Chestnut:* "Gee, you're a *Peach!* If you will marry me we will make a happy *Pear*." "That's a *Date*," answered *Olive*, "You may place the *Laurel* wreath on my brow. My little fox terrier, *Dogwood*, like to have you around the house, anyway. My *Red Bud Yew* are sweet!"

"*Fir* goodness sake," said Red, "let's go out on the *Bay* in my boat and talk it over."

Trees

What tree suggests:

1. The hand? Palm.
2. The seaside? Beech.
3. History? Date.
4. Neat appearance? Spruce.
5. A winter coat? Fir.
6. A valuable oil? Olive.
7. A well-worn joke? Chestnut.
8. A good-looking girl? Peach.
9. The color, black? Ebony.
10. A carpenter's tool? Plane.
11. In high favor? Poplar.
12. A parent? Pawpaw.
13. An inlet of the sea? Bay.
14. A church official? Elder.
15. Something kissable? Tulips.
16. Syrup? Maple.
17. A dead fire? Ash.
18. Sadness? Weeping willow.
19. Of a bottle? Cork.
20. Of a bouncing ball? Rubber.
21. Two? Pear.
22. A kind of grasshopper? Locust.

The botany exam.—The answers to these questions are the names of trees, flowers, and vegetables. Can you pass?

1. A body of water? Bay.
2. Shepherds watch them? Phlox.
3. A traveling Hebrew? Wandering Jew.
4. A flower that denotes time? Four O'clock.
5. They mark the march of time? Dates.
6. Found in an old boat? Leeks.
7. Has a smart, trim appearance? Spruce.
8. It is in the alphabet? Yew (U).

9. Knows "Old Man River"? Currants.
10. Necessary to a book? Leaves.

Identifying leaves.—Pin on paper or cardboard ten or more leaves of different trees. Number these and arrange them on the wall or table. Ask the guests to identify them.

Instead of the actual leaves good spatter prints might be displayed in the same way.

The following are some suggested trees:

Oak	Walnut
Maple	Hickory
Poplar	Beechnut
Magnolia	Ash
Catalpa	Elm

A vegetable and fruit romance.—A letter from a "Cabbage" Head in jail:

> You needn't *turnip* your nose at me,
> And say you do not *carrot* all;
> I'm *melon* choly you see,
> And *cantaloupe* with you till fall.
>
> In my *celery* cent days,
> It *beets* me how I pine.
> Your *radish* hair, your *cherry* smile,
> They whisper that you're mine.
>
> So *lettuce* marry when I'm free,
> My *currant* topic thou,
> No *sage* or saint will interfere;
> I love you so, and how!

Allow your guests to try their hand at making up some such romance. If it is done in rhyme so much the better, but that does not matter. Besides the produce mentioned above the following might be added: citron, mango, cucumber, pumpkin, asparagus, cauliflower, spinach, rye, cherry, peach, Brussels sprouts, artichoke, onions, parsley, broccoli, plum, corn, beans.

What berry is.—

1. Red when it is green? Blackberry.
2. Created by Mark Twain? Huckleberry.
3. On the grass. Dewberry.
4. Irritating? Raspberry.

5. A dunce? Gooseberry.
6. Used for hats? Strawberry.
7. Respected because of his age? Elderberry.
8. A beverage? Teaberry.
9. Melancholy? Blueberry.
10. Celebrates a great festival? Hollyberry.
11. Reminds you of hens? Cackleberry.
12. Furnishes an old-time ride? Hackberry.

What flower suggests.—

1. Four? Ivy (IV).
2. Gold digger's quest? Marigold.
3. A tattered bird? Ragged Robin.
4. For mother's foot? Lady's Slipper.
5. Time of day? Four O'clock.
6. A good wild beast? Dandelion.
7. A church official? Elder.
8. The rising sun? Morning Glory.
9. An amiable man? Sweet William.
10. What pa did when he proposed to ma? **Aster.**

A hiking romance.—Blank spaces are to be filled in with the names of trees and flowers. Remember that "sap" isn't a tree. It is just something in a tree or under a tree. So "sap" isn't the answer anywhere in this story. Two points off for anyone that answers "sap!" One point for each correct answer and one point off for mistakes! Does everyone understand? Let's go!

This romance began on a hike one day. It is true that he had met her once before down at the (__1__), where he was a lifesaver, but they had not been formally introduced until the day of the hike. Her name was (__2__) Budd, while his name was (__3__) Wood.

She was very (__4__) with all the boys. In fact, (__5__) of them hung around her home. Her (__6__) was afraid she would wed some ne'er-do-well. He wanted her to (__7__) so that she could have all of the comforts and luxuries she wanted. She had always said, however, that anyone was (__8__) crazy who married for anything but love.

(__9__) Wood thought that she was a (__10__) and he fell in love with her at first sight. The hike gave him his opportunity to tell her about it. "(__11__) are a real (__12__) beauty. (__13__) are the (__14__) of my eye." Thereupon he (__15__) to marry him.

She loved him but she pretended to doubt his faithfulness. "What (__16__) Slipper did I see in your possession the other day?" she parried. "Oh, that belonged to my brother, (__17__) William. It was his wife's," he replied earnestly. "Oh, (__18__) me or I'll have a (__19__). It is near to breaking now. If you only knew how I (__20__) for you."

Just then her little brother Johnny fell down. He continued to lie where he had fallen and sure did (__21__). His big sis called to him: "(__22__), you're not hurt." "Oh, sis," he yelled back at her, "How can you (__23__) that?"

(__24__) Wood resumed his courting, falling back on a little French that he had learned in his four years at college. "*Mon* (__25__), *je t'aime*." As that was all of the French he could remember he fell back on perfectly good English. "Let me press your (__26__) to mine." Johnny thought he was a big (__27__), but she thought he was wonderful. "You're a (__28__)," she said as she cuddled in his arms. "We will be married at (__29__) to-morrow."

So (__30__) performed the ceremony, and all of their days were blessed with (__31__).

(1) Beech. (2) Rose. (3) Red (Cotton or Dog will do). (4) Poplar. (5) Phlox. (6) Poppy. (7) Marigold. (8) Plum. (9) Red. (10) Peach. (11) Yew. (12) American. (13) Yew. (14) Apple. (15) Aster. (16) Lady's. (17) Sweet. (18) Rosemary. (19) Bleeding Heart. (20) Pine. (21) Balsam. (22) Johnny-jump-up. (23) Lilac. (24) Red. (25) Cherry (*Cherie*). (26) Tulips. (27) Prune. (28) Daisy. (29) Four O'clock. (30) Jack-in-the-pulpit. (31) Sweet Peas.

State flowers.—Of what states are the following flowers the state flowers? Here they are:
1. Apple Blossom? Arkansas, Michigan.
2. Goldenrod? Alabama, Kentucky, Nebraska.
3. Pine Cone and Tassel? Maine.
4. Mountain Laurel? Connecticut, Pennsylvania.
5. Violet? Rhode Island, Illinois, New Jersey, Wisconsin.
6. Sahuaro Cactus? Arizona.
7. Golden Poppy? California.
8. Wild Rose? Iowa.
9. Cherokee Rose? Georgia.
10. Orange Blossom? Florida.
11. Blue Columbine? Colorado.
12. Syringa? Idaho.

13. Zinnia? Indiana.
14. Sunflower? Kansas.
15. Magnolia? Louisiana, Mississippi.
16. Mayflower? Massachusetts.
17. Black-eyed Susan? Maryland.
18. Mocassin? Minnesota.
19. Peach Blossom? Delaware.
20. Rose? New York.
21. Hawthorn? Missouri.
22. Bitter Root? Montana.
23. Sagebrush? Nevada.
24. Yucca? New Mexico.
25. Ox-eye Daisy? North Carolina.
26. Purple Lilac? New Hampshire.
27. Indian Paint Brush? Wyoming.
28. Wild Prairie Rose? North Dakota.
29. Rhododendron? Washington, West Virginia.
30. Scarlet Carnation? Ohio.
31. American Dogwood? Virginia.
32. Mistletoe? Oklahoma.
33. Red Clover? Vermont.
34. Sego Lily? Utah.
35. Oregon Grape? Oregon.
36. Yellow Jessamine? South Carolina.
37. Pasque Flower? South Dakota.
38. Iris? Tennessee.
39. Bluebonnet? Texas.

What state.—The answers are all abbreviations of states.

1. Is used on the meadow? Mo.
2. Is religious? Mass.
3. Is important to you? Me.
4. Is Mohammedan? Ala.
5. Is a number? Tenn.
6. Is as good as a mile? Miss.
7. Was used in the flood? Ark.
8. Is an exclamation? O.
9. Is the cleanest? Wash.
10. Is sick? Ill.
11. Is a doctor? Md.
12. Is a mineral? Ore.

What city—

1. Is an improvement on Noah's boat? Newark.
2. Is a small pebble? Little Rock.
3. A good cigar? Havana.
4. A prominent surveyor? Washington.
5. A sofa? Davenport.
6. A briny body of water? Salt Lake.
7. A perfume? Cologne.
8. A hard substance? Flint.
9. A kind of paper? Manila.
10. Found in the library? Reading.

Dictionary cities.—The following cities are some recommended by Mr. Noah Webster. They represent words ending in "city." How many of them do you know?

1. An odd city. Eccentricity.
2. A lighted city? Electricity.
3. A savage city? Ferocity.
4. A fast city? Velocity.
5. A bold city? Audacity.
6. A discerning city? Perspicacity.
7. A wise city? Sagacity.
8. A quarrelsome city? Pugnacity.
9. A measuring city? Capacity.
10. A covetous city? Rapacity.
11. A truthful city? Veracity.
12. A rural city? Rusticity.
13. An advertiser's city? Publicity.
14. A beggar's city? Mendacity.
15. A happy city? Felicity.
16. A genuine city? Authenticity.
17. A resilient city? Elasticity.
18. A fast developing city? Precocity.
19. A very bad city? Atrocity.
20. A weak city? Incapacity.

Popular titles of cities.—Do you know the nicknames and popular titles of some of the cities of the United States? Try your hand at the list that follows. How do you rate?

1. The Magic City? Birmingham.
2. The City of Brotherly Love? Philadelphia.
3. Smoky City? Pittsburgh.
4. The Windy City? Chicago.

5. Gotham? New York.
6. The Rock City? Nashville.
7. The Queen City? Cincinnati.
8. The Crescent City? New Orleans.
9. The Gateway to the South or the Falls City? Louisville.
10. The City of Elms? New Haven.
11. Mound City? St. Louis.
12. Quaker City? Philadelphia.
13. The Sunshine City? St. Petersburg.
14. The Golden Gate City? San Francisco.
15. Beantown? Boston.

How many capitals do you know?—Mimeograph an outline map of the United States, including state lines. Have each guest write in the name of each state capital. Or call the names of the states and have the guests call the names of the capitals. Try it yourself. You may be surprised at the number you do not know.

1. Pennsylvania? Yes, sir, it is Harrisburg, not Pittsburgh or Philadelphia.
2. North Carolina? Raleigh.
3. Minnesota? St. Paul.
4. Georgia? Atlanta.
5. Kansas? Topeka.
6. North Dakota? Bismark.
7. Oklahoma? Oklahoma City.
8. Mississippi? Jackson.
9. Vermont? Montpelier.
10. Wisconsin? Madison.
11. Oregon? Salem.
12. California? Sacramento.
13. Nevada? Carson City.
14. Missouri? Jefferson City.
15. Maryland? Annapolis.
16. West Virginia? Charleston.
17. Illinois? Springfield.
18. Alabama? Montgomery.
19. New Hampshire? Concord.
20. Texas? Austin.
21. New Mexico? Santa Fe.
22. Iowa? Des Moines.
23. Idaho? Boise.
24. Wyoming? Cheyenne.
25. Utah? Salt Lake City.
26. Washington? Olympia.
27. Kentucky? Frankfort.
28. Arkansas? Little Rock.
29. Arizona? Phoenix.
30. Massachusetts? Boston.
31. Montana? Helena.
32. Tennessee? Nashville.
33. Maine? Augusta.
34. Nebraska? Lincoln.
35. New Jersey? Trenton.
36. Rhode Island? Providence.
37. New York? Albany.
38. Indiana? Indianapolis.
39. Louisiana? Baton Rouge.
40. Florida? Tallahassee.
41. Virginia? Richmond.
42. Connecticut? Hartford.
43. South Carolina? Columbia.
44. Michigan? Lansing.
45. Colorado? Denver.
46. South Dakota? Pierre.
47. Delaware? Dover.
48. Ohio? Columbus.

State nicknames.—How many state nicknames do you know? All right, just for an easy one, what is known as "The Blue Grass State"? "Kentucky." Right you are.

Nickname	State.	Origin of State Name
1. Cotton State	Alabama	Creek Indian for "place of rest."
2. Apache State	Arizona	Indian word meaning "place of small springs."
3. Wonder State	Arkansas	Indian for "downstream people."
4. Golden State	California	From a fabled island in Spanish romance, or from "*Caliento forno*" ("hot furnace").
5. Centennial State	Colorado	Spanish for "reddish color." First applied to the river.
6. Nutmeg State	Connecticut	Indian, "*Quonoktacut.*"
7. Blue Hen State	Delaware	From Lord de la Warr, first governor of Virginia.
8. Everglade State	Florida	From Spanish, "*Pascua Florida,*" literally, "flowery feast" for "Easter Sunday."
9. Cracker State	Georgia	Named for King George II, of England.
10. Gem State	Idaho	Indian for "gem of the mountain."
11. Sucker State	Illinois	Indian, with French ending, "*Illini*" for "men."
12. Hoosier State	Indiana	"Land of Indians."
13. Hawkeye State	Iowa	Indian for "this is the place," perhaps.
14. Jayhawker or Sunflower State	Kansas	"*Kansas,*" Indian for "wind people."
15. Blue Grass State	Kentucky	Indian, "*kentake*" for "meadow land."
16. Pelican State	Louisiana	"Land of Louis" for Louis XIV, of France.
17. Pine Tree State	Maine	Probably from name of province in France.
18. Old Line State	Maryland	For Queen Henrietta Maria, of England.
19. Old Bay State	Massachusetts	Indian, originally given to bay, "Place of great hills."

Nickname	State	Origin of State Name
20. Wolverine State	Michigan	Indian for "great lake," "great water."
21. Gopher State	Minnesota	Indian for "clouded water."
22. Bayou State	Mississippi	Indian for "gathering of all the waters," or "great river."
23. Bullion State	Missouri	Indian for "big muddy stream."
24. Treasure State	Montana	Spanish for "mountain."
25. Tree-Planter State	Nebraska	Sioux Indian for "shallow water."
26. Sagebrush or Silver State	Nevada	Spanish for "snowy."
27. Granite State	New Hampshire	From County of "Hants," or Hampshire, England.
28. Garden State	New Jersey	From Island of Jersey, England.
29. Sunshine State	New Mexico	Indian name "Mexitl, an Aztex Indian deity.
30. Empire State	New York	For Duke of York, later James II, of England.
31. Old North State or Tar Heel State	North Carolina	"Land of Charles" for Charles II, of England.
32. Flickertail State	North Dakota	Indian name for confederate Sioux tribes meaning "allies."
33. Buckeye State	Ohio	Indian for "beautiful river."
34. Sooner State	Oklahoma	Choctaw Indian for "red people."
35. Beaver State	Oregon	From first name of Columbia River popularized in Bryant's "Thanatopsis."
36. Keystone State	Pennsylvania	Latin for "Penn's woods," for William Penn.
37. Little Rhody	Rhode Island	Dutch "Roode Eylandt," for "red island."
38. Palmetto State	South Carolina	Same as North Carolina.
39. Sunshine State	South Dakota	See North Dakota.
40. Volunteer State	Tennessee	Indian name for the river.
41. Lone Star State	Texas	For Texas tribe of Indians.
42. Bee Hive State	Utah	Indian "Ute," for "high up."

Nickname	*State*	*Origin of State Name*
43. Green Mountain State	Vermont	French name meaning "green mountain."
44. The Old Dominion	Virginia	For "Virgin Queen" Elizabeth, of England.
45. Evergreen State	Washington	For George Washington.
46. Panhandle State	West Virginia	See Virginia.
47. Badger State	Wisconsin	Indian—may mean "wild rushing river," or "meeting place of the rivers."
48. Equality State	Wyoming	From Wyoming Valley in Pennsylvania.

Identifying Presidents.—Cut out, number, and post the pictures of Presidents of the United States. Ask the guests to identify them, if they can.

Historical objects.—Three methods for using this game are as follows: (1) Mimeograph copies of the contest and have guests fill in the correct names. (2) Call out the symbols and have guests shout the answers either as individuals or as groups. (3) Display objects or pictures representing them, properly numbered. Have guests move around identifying the objects and making their lists.

What persons or characters are suggested by the following:

1. A rainbow? Noah.
2. A kite? Benjamin Franklin.
3. A glass slipper? Cinderella.
4. An apple? William Tell.
5. A pound of flesh? Shylock.
6. A silver lamp? Aladdin.
7. A slingshot? David.
8. A coat of many colors? Joseph.
9. A wolf? Red Riding Hood.
10. Long hair? Samson.
11. A hatchet? George Washington.
12. A footprint? Robinson Crusoe.
13. A lantern? Diogenes.
14. A brown derby? Al Smith.
15. A cloak? Sir Walter Raleigh.
16. A spider web? Robert Bruce.
17. A key? Bluebeard.

18. A steamboat? Robert Fulton.
19. A burning bush? Moses.
20. A rail fence? Abraham Lincoln.

What president—

1. Was the first President of the United States? George Washington.
2. What President had a son who became President? John Adams.
3. What was the son's name? John Quincy Adams.
4. Fought in the war of 1812? Andrew Jackson.
5. Outlined a foreign policy with South America? Monroe.
6. What two Presidents died on the same day? Thomas Jefferson and John Adams.
7. What three Presidents were assassinated? Lincoln, Garfield, and McKinley.
8. What Presidential candidate was known as "the silver-tongued orator"? William Jennings Bryan.
9. What Presidential candidate was noted for his brown derby? Al Smith.
10. What President said "I do not choose to run"? Calvin Coolidge.

Presidential nicknames.—What Presidents answered to the following nicknames?

1. Rail Splitter of the West? Abraham Lincoln
2. Hero of New Orleans? Andrew Jackson.
3. Rough and Ready? Zachary Taylor.
4. Canal Boy? James A. Garfield.
5. Tippecanoe? W. H. Harrison.
6. Honest Abe? Lincoln.
7. Rough Rider? Theodore Roosevelt.
8. Father of His Country? George Washington.
9. The Sage of Monticello? Thomas Jefferson.
10. Old Hickory? Andrew Jackson.

Great names in history.—Provide a table on which there are a number of articles designated by numbers. The guests are to guess what great names are suggested by the displays.

1. A dinner bell? Bell.
2. A slice of bacon. Bacon.
3. A hood. Hood.
4. Picture of houses? Holmes.
5. A broken bone in two separate pieces? Bonaparte.

6. A rose on a piece of felt? Roosevelt.
7. A column of figures and a toy bus? Columbus.
8. A bit of red or yellow clay? Clay.
9. A writing pen? Penn.
10. A sea shell or empty gun shell and the letter E? Shelley.
11. Picture of a tall man? Longfellow.

Pick your country—
1. What country expresses anger? Ireland.
2. What country has a good appetite? Hungary.
3. What country mourns? Wales.
4. What country is popular on Thanksgiving Day? Turkey. •
5. What country does the cook use? Greece.
6. What country is a coin? Guinea.
7. What country is good for skaters? Iceland.
8. What country is useful at mealtime? China.
9. What country makes you shiver? Chile.
10. What country suggests a straw hat? Panama.

A college romance.—The answers are the names of colleges and universities. Try your luck at filling them in. If you do not get the answers suggested here, don't be discouraged. Maybe your answers are better than ours. All right! Here goes!

"Boy, did you get an eyeful of that *Auburn* haired peach who passed just now! And did you *Notre Dame* who was with her?"

"Yeah, that's *Agnes Scott* and her sister. She's the *Centre* of attention at the Naval Academy at *Annapolis,* a sort of *Columbia,* the gem of the ocean," answered George.

"Well," said Jack *Smith,* "She *Knox* me for a goal. You can tell it with *Penn State* it with gusto that she *Drew* me the minute she hove into sight. *Georgia* want that girl."

"Oh, yeah?" mocked George. "But she's good enough for the *Duke* of York."

"Well, I may not have as much money as *Vanderbilt* but that doesn't stop me one *Whitman. Erskine* is the skin you love to touch. She looks so good to me in that *Brown* ensemble that I would like to be her *Princeton* night and always. *Manhattan* ought to feel that way, I guess, the first time he sees a girl. But I really would like to have them fling *Rice.* at us."

"Wait a minute, pal. You can't even af *Fordham* for breakfast! And anyway, she has left her heart way down upon the *Sewanee* river. You can't expect her to be interested in two *Tufts* like us."

"Well, I guess I'll go out on the *Pacific* Coast in the *Northwestern* part of the United States. Hereafter, I am going to padlock my heart with a *Yale* lock."

After using this contest divide your guests into small groups, give each group a list of colleges, and ask them to write a story of their own. Or let each individual try it. They can, no doubt, improve on the romance suggested here. In addition to the schools already named, here is a list of colleges that offer possibilities:

Alfred	Colgate	Occidental
Asbury	Cornell	Park
Ashland	Drake	Parsons
Athens	Furman	Pomona
Baker	Fisk	Reed
Bates	Gettysburg	Skidmore
Berry	Grinnell	Southern
Bishop	Hood	Sweet Brier
Bowling Green	Howard	Temple
Byrn Mawr	Hunter	Trinity
Capital	Maine	Union
Carroll	Mills	Wabash
Centenary	National	Western
Central	Newcomb	Westminster
Citadel	Niagara	Wake Forest

IDENTIFYING ATHLETES

All sports.—Mount pictures of prominent athletes in the various sports. Newspapers, magazines, and advertising material will furnish all the pictures you need. Number the pictures and have the guests identify them. Tennis, baseball, football, track, and boxing stars would be included in the list.

Old timers.—Use pictures of athletes who have passed their prime or who have retired. *Baseball*—Ty Cobb, Babe Ruth, Hans Wagner. *Tennis*—William Tilden, Suzanne Langlen. *Football*—Knute Rockne, Jim Thorpe, Red Grange. *Boxing*—John L. Sullivan, James J. Corbitt, Robert Fitzsimmons, James J. Jeffries, Jack Dempsey. These are simply a few suggestions.

College athletes.—Mount pictures of All-American selections or of prominent football players along with other college athletes. It would be fun for the guests to select an All-American football team in the midst of football season. Each guest would make his individual selections for a first and second team. Allow two points for a selection on a first team and one point for a selection on a second team. Have a committee of judges tabulate the choices of the guests and report the All-American team.

Baseball.—Mount pictures of nationally known baseball players and have the guests identify them.

Any of the above plans would prove interesting diversion to any group interested in sports.

It's your add!—How good a mathematician are you? Here is an example of what we want you to do: "Add 1,000 to a kind of tree and get a soft damp mixture. And the answer is M—ash."

1. 500 plus a large boat equals without light ....D—ark
2. 1,000 plus a poem equals manner ....M—ode
3. 1,000 plus help equals an unmarried woman ....M—aid
4. 500 plus uncooked equals to pull ....D—raw
5. 500 plus a preposition equals to a great noise ....D—in
6. 50 plus a finish equals a loan ....L—end
7. 100 plus competent equals a heavy rope .... C—able
8. 50 plus a kind of tree equals part of a whip ....L—ash
9. 1 plus to quality equals angry ....I—rate
10. 5 plus frozen water equals wickedness ....V—ice
11. 500 plus a beam of light equals a vehicle ....D—ray
12. 500 plus a garden tool equals a male duck ....D—rake
13. 1,000 plus to inquire equals a disguise ....M—ask
14. 5 plus a valuable fur equals parasites ....V—ermin
15. 500 plus a male sheep equals one-eight of an ounce...D—ram
16. 5 plus the Scotch for own equals a weathercock.......V—ane
17. 500 plus the back of anything equals gloom ....D—rear
18. 500 plus a simple float equals a current of air ....D—raft
19. 1,000 plus a glowing fragment of fire equals a person
    who belongs to an organization ....M—ember
20. 1,000 plus similarity equals a useful liquid ....M—ilk

4	3	8
9	5	1
2	7	6

The mystic fifteen.—Ask each guest to draw a square. Then ask them to draw four lines dividing the square into nine small squares. Now each one is to put a number in each square, using the numbers from 1 to 9. No number can be used more than once. It should be explained that the numbers are to be placed so that they total 15 any way they are added—horizontally, vertically, or diagonally. The secret lies in placing 5 at the center and then working the corners with the even numbers, 2, 4, 6, and 8. See who can work it out first. Perhaps a hint regarding the placing of the number 5 may be needed.

Teakettle.—One player is sent out of the room. The rest decide on a word of the type in which the words sound alike but have different meanings. Some examples are rain, reign, rein; bare, bear (to carry), bear (an animal); in, inn; pane, pain; sore, soar; fare, fair; dear, deer; so, sow, sew; plane, plain; piece, peace; by, bye, buy.

When the player returns each person in the room is to greet him with some sentence containing one or more of the words selected. However, instead of saying the word they use the word "teakettle" wherever it appears in the sentence. Suppose the group has decided on "by, bye, and buy."

"Teakettle, the teakettle," someone says, "I went downtown today teakettle myself to teakettle something at the store."

Another player speaks up: "I never go teakettle that I don't think what a good teakettle that car would be. If I had it I would be saying teakettle."

These two are rather obvious. If the player guesses what the word is the person who gave him the tip-off is sent out.

Variation—Sometimes the guesser is permitted to ask each person one question. The answer must contain the word selected in one of its forms, at least, again the word "teakettle" being used to hide it.

Discovering nations—
1. A dreaded nation? Examination.
2. A religious nation? Denomination.
3. A political nation? Nomination.
4. A disliked nation? Abomination.

5. A fortune-telling nation? Divination
6. A fearful nation? Consternation.
7. A bright nation? Illumination.
8. The topmost nation? Culmination.
9. A leaning nation? Inclination.
10. A disrespectful nation? Insubordination.
11. A deferring nation? Procrastination.
12. A crazy nation? Hallucination.
13. A resolute nation? Determination.
14. A conniving nation? Machination.
15. A fanciful nation? Imagination.
16. A dramatic nation? Impersonation.
17. The sinner's nation? Damnation.
18. The convicted criminal's nation? Condemnation.
19. A teacher's nation? Explanation.
20. A nation that has reached its goal? Destination.
21. A nation that has come to its end? Termination.
22. A destructive nation? Extermination.

Know your alphabet?—All right! Then tell us what letter is.

1. A vegetable? P.
2. A drink? T.
3. A body of water? C.
4. A command to a horse? G.
5. Part of the head? I.
6. An exclamation? O.
7. A female sheep? U.
8. An insect? B.
9. A part of a house? L.
10. A bird? J.
11. A unit of measure in printing? M.
12. Half the width of an em? N.
13. A clew? An actor's signal? Q.
14. A query? Y.
15. A river in Scotland? D.

Can you spell?—Can you spell the following in two letters?

1. Chilly? IC.
2. Too much? XS.
3. Rot? DK.
4. Not hard? EZ.
5. Vacant? MT.
6. Jealousy? NV.
7. Composition? SA.
8. Indian tent? TP.
9. Poorly dressed? CD.
10. Surpass? XL.
11. An octogenerian? AT.
12. Results? FX.

13. Comfort? EE.
14. Much water? CC.

15. Not dumb? YY.
16. What bad boys do? TT.

Now suppose we try the following:

1. Happiness in three letters? XTC.
2. A funeral poem in three letters? LEG.
3. A poet's place of simple and quiet pleasure? RKD.
4. A small boy has lots of it—in three letters? NRG.
5. A drug in two letters and a number? OP 8.
6. Fitness in five letters? XPDNC.
7. Describe a snake's eye in two letters? BD.
8. A foe in three letters? NME.

Letter go!—The fillers in the following letter are all letters or numbers. The letter could be addressed for instance, to ME (Emmy), or LC (Elsie), or KT (Katie). Now see what you can do with it.

Dear (a girl's name in two letters—LC):

(Boy's name in two letters)—AB and I are having EZ sailing here. Really, it is XTC. No poet's RKD could B more lovely. XPDNC seemed to make it YY for us to locate here. AB's father was AT. His NRG was about gone and it was not EZ for him to overcome the FX of an attack of flu. It was EZ to 4C that he would not last long. Numerous times we had to administer an OP8 to him to relieve his suffering. Physical DK set in rather rapidly, and he died last spring.

AB likes it here and he wants to XL as a farmer. He loves to work with the CCCC (four C's) of Nature. And I too love the beauty and freshness of the countryside. The XS of noise in the city always kept me on edge. We are both taking our EE here. I don't NV you city folk one bit.

Come out 2C us when U have time.

Yours (FX) shunately,

KT.

It would be fun to have the guests try their hands at writing an ALPHABET letter or story.

An alphabet rhyme.—Fill in the blank spaces with letters of the alphabet that tell the story.

There was a man in our town,
And he was wondrous (–YY–);
He fell into a bramble bush,
And he scratched out both his (–II–).

And when old age did come to him,
He'd hoped to take his (–EE–);
Instead of that he up and died
With some dreaded di (–ZZ–).

One moral of this tale, my friend,
If moral there should (–B–),
Is watch your step and never jump
Until you really (–C–).

For man is mortal man, you know.
That theme is our (–SA–);
And when he gets the sense to live,
He meets Old Man (–DK–).

I love my love.—The players sit in a circle. The first player begins, "I love my love with an *A* because she is affectionate." The next player must say, "I love my love with a *B* because she is broadminded," or some descriptive term or word beginning with the letter *B*. The third may say, "I love my love with a *C* because she is carefree." And so it goes. When a player cannot answer appropriately he pays a forfeit or drops out. A list of words suggested by the various letters follows:

A–ardent
  amiable
  affluent
  amazing
  aristocratic
  approachable
  ambitious
  appreciative
  apt
  admirable
  adorable
  agile

B–beautiful
  baby-faced
  bashful
  beaming
  beguiling

  believing
  benevolent
  bizarre
  big
  blond
  blind

C–courteous
  careful
  cunning
  cute

D–dear
  darling
  dashing
  decent

E–energetic
  enthusiastic

  efficient
  earnest

F–fair-minded
  famous
  fashionable
  forceful

G–gorgeous
  gigantic
  gifted
  glamorous

H–happy
  harmonious
  high-brow
  honorable

I—independent
imaginative
indulgent
infallible

J—jaunty
jealous
jolly
jubilant

K—keen
kind
kingly
knowing

L—lovable
level-headed
light-hearted
loquacious

M—manly
musical
masterful
meek

N—natural
normal
novel
neutral

O—obedient
objective

obsessed
original

P—perfect
pleasant
particular
poetic

Q—quaint
qualified
quotable
quarantined

R—radiant
ready
reasonable
responsible

S—sweet
scholarly
saucy
sensible

T—tactful
teachable
thoughtful
thrifty

U—underrated
unanswerable

unadorned
understand-
able

V—valorous
valuable
venturesome
veracious

W—witty
wide-awake
warm-hearted
winsome

X—Xenophonic
Xerxesian
X-rayic
xylophonic

Y—young
yearning
yielding
youthful

Z—zealous
zestful
Zeuslike
zinclike

Variation—Require the players to use the same letter all the way around. Thus if the first player uses the letter *A*, the others must likewise respond with words beginning with *A*, such as ardent, anemic, assiduous, and the like.

The minister's cat.—This game is very similar to "I love my love." The minister's cat is an amorous cat," says the first player, perhaps. He may use any letter he desires. "The minister's cat is an artificial cat," says the second player. "The minister's cat is an annoying cat," chimes in the third. And so it goes around the circle, all of the players responding with some word beginning with the letter *A* or whatever letter is the first one used in the descriptive word called by the first player.

What to wear.—What is appropriate material for the following people to wear?

1. The artist? Canvas.
2. The dairyman? Cheesecloth.
3. The editor? Prints.
4. The banker? Checks.
5. The gardener? Lawn.
6. The Scotchman? Plaid.
7. The hunter? Duck.
8. The barber? Haircloth.
9. The fisherman? Net.
10. The government official? Red tape.
11. The prisoner? Stripes.
12. The minister? Broadcloth.
13. The bald man? Mohair.
14. The jeweler? Goldcloth.
15. The undertaker? Crepe.
16. The filling station employee? Oilcloth.
17. The inventor? Patent leather.
18. The athletic trainer? Rubber.
19. The defeated? Worsted.
20. The Floridian? Palm Beach.

What is found on a Lincoln penny?—

1. A small animal? Hair (hare).
2. A snake? Copperhead.
3. A messenger? One cent.
4. A flower? Two lips.
5. The edge of a hill? Brow.
6. A country? United States.
7. A fruit? Date.
8. Part of a river? Mouth.
9. A beverage? T.
10. Yourself? Eye.
11. A building? Temple.
12. A submarine? Under the "C."

Magazines.—What magazine is suggested by:

1. A color? Red Book.
2. Musicians? Harpers.
3. Something dear to us? Life.
4. A court? Judge.
5. A citizen of the United States? American.
6. Something not to be wasted? Time.
7. Thomas A. Edison? Scientific American.
8. Discussion? Forum.
9. Not local? Cosmopolitan.
10. An examination of conditions? Survey.
11. The good play-leader plans it wisely? Recreation.
12. A woman's pride? Good Housekeeping.
13. Mother and father? Parents.
14. An up-to-date narrative of events? Current Events.
15. The farm? Country Life.

The town newspaper.—Divide the crowd into groups and have each group edit a section of *The Daily Bugle* or *The Podunk Press*. All of the news and articles will have a personal flavor. When finished someone from each group reads the particular section of the paper allotted to it. The local news will carry startling news involving people present. General news will also be as startling and it may also concern people present. The society column will record events that stun the natives. The advertising section will be as reckless with the truth as becomes a professional advertiser. The sports page will describe such sporting events as never before graced the pages of a newspaper. Then there will be editorials—and what editorials? And of course, it would not be fair to get out a paper without Beatrice Barefax heart column. What a newspaper!

Authors.—Can you guess who the following authors are:

1. Not tame? Wilde.
2. Not alcoholic? Drinkwater.
3. An exclamation of disgust? Shaw.
4. A peaceful animal? Lamb.
5. No such word in a successful man's vocabulary? Kant.
6. Maker of barrels? Cooper.
7. A country? France.
8. For the head? Hood.
9. What fire does? Burns.
10. Nothing short about him? Longfellow.

11. The thing a bad boy sometimes plays? Dickens.
12. Living the life of? Riley.
13. The real estate man likes to sell them? Holmes.
14. A color? Gray.
15. A welcome visitor in the home? Guest.
16. Open tracts of land? Fields.
17. What the small boy said after his first taste of ice cream? Moore.
18. Make it while the sun shines? Hay.
19. Good for breakfast? Bacon.
20. Rather loud? Noyes.
21. Wind? Gale.

Blind book reviews.—Each player is furnished with a piece of paper and a pencil. At the top of the paper he writes the title of a book, real or imaginary. The paper is folded and passed to the right. The next player writes the name of an author. If the names of some of the people present happen to be used, well and good. Again the paper is folded and passed to the right. Then follow in order: the type of book (fiction, philosophy, poetry, drama, technical); a brief summary of the contents; and then a brief criticism—commending it, finding fault with it, or condemning it. It is needless, perhaps, to say that no player must see what the other players have written. Each player must fold over his contribution before passing the paper to the next player. The criticism should carry the name of some magazine or newspaper. Try this one with a small group.

Variation—With a large crowd divide into several groups of ten or more. Have each group decide on a title, write it, fold it, and pass on to the next group or hand it to the leader and let the leader pass it on to them. The second time each group decides on an author, the members of the group making suggestions. Each of the other items are given attention in the same manner. When finished each group opens the paper and appoints someone to read the resulting book review to the entire crowd.

Familiar quotations.—Familiar quotations are written on cards and read to the group. The first player naming the author is given the card. Famous sayings, familiar poems, and familiar prose may be used as sources of material.

Another plan would be to have a typed list for each guest and have individuals or couples fill in the proper sources.

A few suggested quotations will serve to illustrate what is meant.

Keep your quotations fairly within the range of interest and knowledge of your group. They must not be so difficult as to give the group a feeling of futility. As the group grows in knowledge and expertness the tests can be given wider range. They may center in some one type of quotations, such as poetry, history, drama, Bible, and the like, or they may be confined to one writer, such as Shakespeare, for instance. The guests would then be required to identify the source of the quotation. Thus, the quotation might be:

"Yond Cassius has a lean and hungry look;
He thinks too much: such men are dangerous."

The correct answer would be "Caesar" in "Julius Caesar."

1. "Give me liberty or give me death" . . . . Patrick Henry
2. "The British are coming!" . . . . .Paul Revere
3. "To be or not to be, that is the question" . . . . .Shakespeare
4. "God's in his heaven—
   All's right with the world" . . . . .Robert Browning
5. "Who gives himself with his alms feeds three—
   Himself, his hungering neighbor, and Me"
   James Russell Lowell
6. "Ring out the old, ring in the new" . . . . .Tennyson
7. "I do not choose to run" . . . . .Calvin Coolidge
8. "Blow, blow thou winter wind,
   Thou art not so unkind
   As man's ingratitude" . . . . .Shakespeare
9. "War is hell" . . . . .General Sherman
10. "Build thee more stately mansions, O my soul,
    While the swift seasons roll" . . . . .Oliver Wendell Holmes
11. "Put your trust in God, but keep your powder dry"
    Oliver Cromwell (1599-1658) to his troops
12. "Please stand out of my sunlight"
    Diogenes (412-323 B.C.) to Alexander the Great
13. "Give me a place to stand, and I will move the world"
    Archimedes (287-212 B.C.)
14. "The die is cast"
    Julius Caesar (102-44 B.C.) on crossing the Rubicon
15. "I propose to fight it out on this line if it takes all summer"
    U. S. Grant, in Civil War
16. "Know thyself" . . . . .Socrates (469-399 B.C.)
17. "I only regret that I have but one life to lose for my country"
    Nathan Hale (1751-1776)

18. "Why don't you speak for yourself, John?"

Priscilla to John Alden

19. "While there is life, there is hope"

Rev. Patrick Bronte (1774-1861) in his last words

20. "You can fool some of the people all of the time, and all of the people some of the time, but you can't fool all of the people all of the time" ....Abraham Lincoln

21. "A government of the people, by the people, and for the people" ....Abraham Lincoln

22. "It is not raining rain to me,
     It's raining daffodils;
     In every dimpled drop I see
     Wild flowers on the hills" ....Robert Loveman

23. "And only the Master shall praise us, and only the
     Master shall blame;
     And no one shall work for money, and no one shall
     work for fame;
     But each for the joy of the working, and each, in
     his separate star,
     Shall draw the Thing as he sees It for the God of
     things as they are"....................Rudyard Kipling

Variation—Give only part of the quotation and have the guests complete it.

A Shakespearean romance—

1. Who were the lovers? Romeo and Juliet.
2. What was the courtship like? A Midsummer Night's Dream.
3. What was her answer to his proposal? As You Like It.
4. About what time of the month were they married? Twelfth Night.
5. Of whom did he buy the ring? Merchant of Venice.
6. Who were the best man and the maid of honor? Anthony and Cleopatra.
7. Who were the ushers? Two Gentlemen of Verona.
8. Who gave the reception? King Lear.
9. In what kind of place did they live? Hamlet.
10. What was her disposition like? Tempest.
11. What was his chief occupation after marriage? Taming the Shrew.
12. What caused the first quarrel? The Merry Wives of Windsor.
13. How could it be described? Much Ado About Nothing.
14. What did their courtship prove to be? Love's Labor Lost.

15. What did their married life resemble?   A Comedy of Errors.
16. What did they give to each other?   Measure for Measure.
17. What Roman ruler brought about reconciliation?   Julius Caesar.
18. What did their friends say?   All's Well That Ends Well.

Do you know these commonly used foreign expressions?—Make a list of foreign expressions in common use and have each guest write beside each expression the meaning.   Or read the list and have the guests call the answers.   This will be a profitable as well as interesting exercise because these are expressions that you are meeting every day—in the newspaper, in magazines, from the platform. It may be that you will prefer using only about ten expressions at a time.

1. *ad libitum* ....at will (Latin)
2. *ad infinitum* ....endlessly (Latin)
3. *ad hominem* ....to the individual man (Latin)
4. *ad summum* ....to the highest point (Latin)
5. *ad valorem* ....according to the value (Latin)
6. *affaire d'amour* ....love affair (French)
7. *ante bellum* ....before the war (Latin)
8. *a priori* from what is before, that is, from cause to effect (Latin)
9. *argumentum ad hominem*
    an argument to the man, that is, founded on the principle of the opponent himself (Latin)
10. *auf Wiedersehen*
    till we meet again; literally, till we see again (German)
11. *au revoir* ....till we meet again (French)
12. *bete noir* ......black beast; an object of abhorrence (French)
13. *bona fide* ....good faith; freedom from deceit (Latin)
14. *bonjour* ....good day; good morning (French)
15. *bon voyage* ....good voyage to you (French)
16. *bon soir* ....good evening (French)
17. *causa sine qua non*
    cause without which nothing, that is, indispensable condition (Latin)
18. *cherchez la femme.* ....seek the woman (French)
19. *cum laude* ....with praise or honor (Latin)
20. *en rapport* ....in sympathetic relation (French)
21. *entre nous* ....between ourselves; confidentially (French)
22. *fait accompli* ....an accomplished fact (French)
23. *ich dien* ....I serve—motto of Prince of Wales (German)

24. *laissez-nous faire* ....let us be; let us alone (French)
25. *magnum opus* ....the chief work of an author (Latin)
26. *mal der mer* ....sea sickness (French)
27. *modus operandi* ....mode of operating (Latin)
28. *n'estce pas?* ....Is it not so? (French)
29. *nicht wahr?* ....Is it not so? (German)
30. *nom de plume* ..literally, a pen name; a pseudonym (French)
31. *O tempora! O mores!* ....What times! What morals! (Latin)
32. *pate de foie gras* ....a pie of fat goose livers (French)
33. *pensez a moi* ....think of me (French)
34. *persona grata*
    an acceptable person as opposed to *persona non grata*, one
    not thus acceptable (Latin)
35. *piece, de resistance*
    a piece of resistance, that is, the most substantial dish of a
    dinner. Often used figuratively to indicate the best of what-
    ever is mentioned (French)
36. *post meridiem* ....after midday; P.M. (Latin)
37. *ante meridiem* ....before midday; A.M. (Latin)
38. *pro tempore* (pro tem) ....for the time being (Latin)
39. *quod erat demonstratum*
                    (Q.E.D.) Which was to be proved (Latin)
40. *raison d'etre*..reason for being; an excuse for existing (French)
41. *sic semper tyrannis*
                    thus ever to tyrants—motto of Virginia (Latin)
42. *s'il vous plait* ....if you please (French)
43. *respondez s'il vous plait* .. (RSVP) reply if you please (French)
44. *sine die* ....without a day; indefinitely (Latin)
45. *sine qua non*....without which nothing; indispensable (Latin)
46. *status quo* ....the state in which (Latin)
47. *sub rosa* ....under the rose; in strict confidence (Latin)
48. *summum bonum* ....the supreme good (Latin)
49. *tempus fugit* ....time flies (Latin)
50. *vox populi* ....voice of the people (Latin)
51. *esprit de corps*
    common devotion of the members to an organization (French)

Cats galore—

1. A fuzzy cat? Caterpillar.
2. A cat with fits? Cataleptic.
3. A subterranean cat? Catacomb.
4. A topographical cat? Cataclinical.
5. A Spanish cat? Catalonia.

6. A tree cat? Catalpa.
7. A wildcat? Catamount.
8. A bad cat for the eye? Cataract.
9. A shooting cat? Catapult.
10. A noisy cat? Catarrh.
11. A calamitous cat? Catastrophe.
12. A violent cat? Cataclysm.
13. A grapevine cat? Catawba.
14. An electrical cat? Cathode.
15. A cat that's a dupe, a tool? **Catspaw.**
16. A universal cat? Catholic.
17. A ranchman's cat? Cattle.
18. A fisherman's cat? Catfish
19. A cat of instruction? Catechism.
20. A listing cat? Catalogue.
21. A cat with a harsh cry? Caterwaul.
22. A cat for the violinist? Catgut.
23. A church cat? Cathedral.
24. A classified cat? Category.
25. A curved cat? Catenary.

A kennel of curs—

1. A cur coming around the mountain? Curve.
2. A penman's cur? Cursive.
3. A tolling cur? Curfew.
4. A religious cur? Curate.
5. A healing cur? Curative.
6. A cur in charge? Curator.
7. A timely cur? Current.
8. A jelly-making cur? Currant.
9. A miserly cur? Curmudgeon.
10. A playful cur? Curling.
11. A college cur? Curriculum.
12. An inquisitive cur? Curiosity.
13. A cur whose caudal appendage has been amputated? **Cur-tailed.**
14. A cur that conceals? Curtain.
15. A superficial cur? Cursory.
16. A valuable cur? Currency.
17. A flying cur? Curtis.
18. A cur who handles leather? **Currier.**
19. A horse's cur? Curry.
20. A polite cur? Curtsy.

21. A cur that is a bird? Curlew.
22. A dramatic cur? Curtain-raiser.
23. A baseball pitcher's cur? Curve.
24. A prancing cur? Curvet.
25. A bending cur? Curvature.

Kinfolks—

1. Burning kin? Kindle or kindling.
2. A moving kin? Kinetic.
3. The children's kin? Kindergarten.
4. A dressmaker's kin? Manikin.
5. Similar kin? Akin.
6. Kin in the sky? Welkin.
7. Kin at the table? Napkin.
8. A pickled kin? Gherkin.
9. A football player's kin? Moleskin.
10. A clownish kin? Bumpkin.
11. A sheepish kin? Lambkin.
12. A kin that is a jar. Pipkin.
13. A kin to boot? Buskin.
14. A Halloween kin? Pumpkin.
15. A congenial kin? Kindred.

Do you know your Aunts?—

1. A hard, unyielding aunt? Adamant.
2. A calculating aunt? Accountant.
3. A ruling aunt? Dominant or Regnant.
4. A prevailing aunt? Predominant.
5. An agreeable aunt? Consonant or Accordant
6. An inhormonious aunt? Discordant.
7. An aunt who makes good jelly? Currant.
8. An uninformed aunt? Ignorant.
9. A zestful aunt? Piquant.
10. A shallow or impertinent aunt? Flippant.
11. An aunt who provides a place for you to eat? Restaurant.
12. An aunt acquainted with scum? Stagnant.
13. An angry aunt? Indignant.
14. A traveling aunt? Itinerant.
15. A notorious aunt? Flagrant.
16. An aunt that needs to be hung? Pendant.
17. A malicious aunt? Malignant.
18. A royal aunt? Regnant.

19. A sweet aunt? Fragrant.
20. A vagabond aunt? Vagrant.
21. A despotic aunt? Tyrant.
22. A school-teacher aunt? Pedant.
23. A beggar aunt? Mendicant.
24. An aunt who makes a poor finish? Anticlimax.
25. A good aunt to have around when you are poisoned? Antidote.
26. A primitive aunt? **Antediluvian.**

Meet Bill—

1. Sick? Bilious.
2. In love? Billet-doux.
3. In the army? Billet.
4. At his game? Billiards.
5. Grown wealthy? Billionaire.
6. Abusive? Billingsgate.
7. An advertiser? Billboard.
8. On the sea? Billow.
9. In a barrel? Bilge.
10. A cheat? Bilk.
11. A shipper? Bill of lading.
12. A sticker for bills? Billposter.
13. With a policeman? Billy.
14. With talent? Ability.
15. Equipped? Habilitate.

Meet Phil—

1. At the race track? **Filly.**
2. Joining? Affiliate.
3. Coming through? Filter.
4. In the movies? Film.
5. Blocking legislative action? Filibuster.
6. A nut? Filbert.
7. A son? Filial.
8. Ornamental? Filigree.
9. Stimulating, arousing, **exciting?** Fillip.
10. Unclean? Filthy.
11. Lean and without a bone? Fillet.
12. Threadlike? Filament.
13. With a parasitic blood condition? Filaria.
14. An island native? Filipino.

15. A big city? Philadelphia.
16. A stamp collector? Philatelist.
17. Generous? Philanthropist.
18. A trifling lover? Philanderer.
19. A music lover? Philharmonic.
20. Delivering an acrimonious speech? Philippic.
21. An enemy of the ancient Hebrews? Philistines.
22. Joining? Affiliate.
23. A linguist? Philologist.
24. Thinking things out? Philosopher.
25. A magic love potion? Philter.

Meet Ann—

1. A snaky Ann? Anaconda.
2. Against the law? Anarchy.
3. Unattractive? Angular.
4. A wildfire? Anemone.
5. A story? Anecdote.
6. On her birthday? Anniversary.
7. Full of life? Animated.
8. In the English Church? Anglican.
9. Holding a ship. Anchor.
10. And her forefathers? Ancestors.
11. With someone else? Another.
12. In reply? Answer.
13. Singing in the choir? Anthem.
14. Jumping to conclusions? Anticipate.
15. Showing aversion? Antipathy.
16. Quite old? Antiquated.
17. And her hobby? Antiques.
18. Bothering? Annoy.
19. At the South Pole? Antarctic.
20. Before the flood? Antediluvian.
21. Not particular? Any.
22. Plays a game? Anagrams.
23. A small fish? Anchovy.
24. Recalling a similarity? Analogy.
25. Heavenly? Angelic.

Do you know Kate?—

1. Who is sickly? Delicate.
2. Who is teacher? Educate.

3. Who is always chewing on something? **Masticate.**
4. Who predicts? Prognosticate.
5. Who oils your car? Lubricate.
6. Who roots out? Eradicate.
7. Who recommends? Advocate.
8. Who consecrates? Dedicate.
9. Who gives up the throne? Abdicate.
10. Who tells fibs? Fabricate.
11. Who points out? Indicate.
12. Who pacifies? Placate.
13. Who leaves? Vacate.
14. Who justifies? Vindicate.
15. Who incriminates? Implicate.
16. Who mixes things? Complicate.
17. Who disapproves? Deprecate.
18. Who imparts information? Communicate.
19. Who finds a definite place? Locate.
20. Who doubles? Duplicate.

Pat—

1. Hard to get along with? Incompatible.
2. Mended? Patched.
3. An inventor? Patent.
4. Needing the doctor? Patient.
5. Fatherly? Paternal.
6. Praying? Pater Noster.
7. Pitiful? Pathetic.
8. Mexican? Patio.
9. Of illiterate speech? Patois.
10. Churchly? Patriarch.
11. Aristocratic? Patrician.
12. Inheriting an estate? Patrimony.
13. On guard? Patrol.
14. Who supports? Patron.
15. Talking? Patter.
16. A model? Pattern.
17. Good to eat? Patty.
18. Expanded? Patulous.
19. Loyal to his country? Patriot.
20. Restless? Impatient.
21. Playing with the baby? Pat-a-cake.
22. With an ornamental quilt? Patchwork.
23. Head of the family? Paterfamilias.

Food for thought.—What are appropriate foods for the following persons? Want an illustration? All right! What is an appropriate food for a taxi driver? Anyone know? That's right! Cabbage (Cabage)!

1. Jeweler? Carrots (Carats).
2. Prize fighter? Punch or Duck.
3. Plumber? Leeks.
4. Teacher? Alphabet Noodles.
5. Horticulturist? Cauliflower.
6. Policeman? Beets.
7. Traffic officer? Jam.
8. Actor? Ham.
9. Sailor? Roe.
10. Shoemaker? Sole.
11. Electrician? Currants.
12. Gambler? Steaks.
13. Newly weds? Lettuce Alone.
14. Printer. Pi (e).
15. Wood cutter? Chops.
16. Real estate man? Cottage Cheese or Cottage Pudding.
17. Woodworker? Cabinet Pudding.
18. Carpenter? Hard Tack.
19. Fourth of July celebrator? Crackers.
20. Chiropodist? Corn.
21. Baseball player? Batter Cakes.
22. Chess player? Chess Pie.
23. The unemployed? Any Kind of Loaf.
24. Air condition engineer? Chile.
25. A marrying parson? Pears.
26. Stone mason? Marble Cake.

Cross word puzzle.—Horizontally and vertically:

1. A web-footed amphibian;
2. To wander from place to place;
3. Covering;
4. A micro-organism.

1. Frog; 2. Rove; 3. Over; 4. Germ.

F	R	O	G
R	O	V	E
O	V	E	R
G	E	R	M

What age is—

1. An electrician's age?　Voltage.
2. A game age?　Cribbage.
3. A spy's age?　Sabotage.
4. A human age?　Personage.
5. An aviator's age?　Fuselage.
6. A traveler's age?　Baggage or Mileage.
7. A bird's age?　Plumage.
8. A wise age?　Sage.
9. A historic age?　Lineage.
10. An idol age?　Image.
11. A plum age?　Gage.
12. An angry age?　Rage.
13. An editor's age?　Page.
14. A confining age?　Cage.
15. A war prisoner's age?　Hostage.
16. An age that is the retreat of a recluse?　Hermitage.
17. A theatrical age?　Stage.
18. A tree age?　Osage.
19. A ship age?　Steerage.
20. A ship passenger's age?　Passage.
21. A mailman's age?　Postage.
22. A liquid age?　Beverage.
23. A transporting age, especially on navigable water?　Portage.
24. A butcher's age.　Sausage.
25. An age of English nobility?　Peerage.
26. A football coach's age?　Scrimmage.
27. A ransacking age?　Rummage.
28. An old-time vehicle age?　Carriage.
29. An age for waste matter?　Sewerage.

Pans.—What pan suggests:

1. A garment?　Pants.
2. Something dramatic?　Pantomime.
3. A Roman temple?　Pantheon.
4. A constantly passing scene?　Panorama.
5. A bright, splendid covering?　Panoply.
6. A food?　Pancake.
7. A form of begging?　Panhandle.
8. Part of a door or a kind of discussion?　Panel.
9. A flower?　Pansy.
10. Greece?　Pan-Hellenic.

11. Pain? Pang.
12. A laudatory oration? Panegyric.
13. A character in Greek mythology? Pandora.
14. A wild uproar? Pandemonium.
15. A remedy? Panacea.
16. A country? Panama.
17. Overpowering fear? Panic.
18. An animal? Panther.
19. A religion? Pantheism.
20. A source of provisions? Pantry.
21. Men's wearing apparel introduced by the Venetians? Pantaloons.

A musical romance.—The fillers in this story are song titles. Several bars of each composition are to be played on the piano as they come in the narrative. Or they may be whistled or hummed. Guests fill them in or call them according to the method used. Here is the story:

There once lived on *"Ye Banks and Braes O Bonnie Doon"* a maiden fair by the name of *"Annie Laurie."* Poverty stalked in Annie's home, and so she had to go to work before her *"School Days"* were over. Her mother and brother also worked to keep the wolf from the door. In fact, *"Everybody Works but Father."*

One day while *"Comin' Thru the Rye"* Annie met *"Robin Adair."* Now Robin had never heard of *"I Dreamt that I Dwelt in Marble Halls"* but he was a dreamer nevertheless. And so he said to her *"Last Night I Was Dreaming"* of you. Won't you *"Let Me Call You Sweetheart"*?

To Annie this was *"The Sweetest Story Ever Told"* and she said, " *'Oh, Promise Me'* that you will always be true." Robin answered fervently, *"I Love You Truly."*

So they plighted their troth and one day they were married *"At Dawning."*

Then business called Robin away on a trip way down in *"Dixie."* He was gone several weeks and Annie felt *"Forsaken."* Sometimes she would go *"Down by the Old Mill Stream"* to think things through. She recalled that Robin had seemed loath to go. In fact he said *"How Can I Leave Thee?"* In her lowest moments she would feel *"The Heart Bowed Down."*

She remembered that once he had gotten a letter from a girl named *"Sylvia."* When she had asked him *"Who Is Sylvia?"* he had only smiled and said *"La Donna e Mobile"* ("Woman is fickle" from Rigoletto). Then he walked off humming, *"I Dream of Jeanie*

With the Light Brown Hair," and that worried her more than ever.

The *"Farmer in the Dell"* passed about that time and shouted: "Why so glum? You should lead '*A Merry Life.'* " She smiled back and said nothing. The letter from *"Sylvia"* had said: "If you ever come '*Way Down Upon the Suwanee River'* I hope that '*Then You'll Remember Me.'* " How could she be *"Calm as the Night"* under such circumstances?

But her fears were groundless. Robin came home and he was the same old Robin. He whispered to her *"Love's Old Sweet Song,"* *"In the Gloaming,"* and said *"Home, Sweet Home"* looked good to him.

The days that followed were indeed happy days. Many a time they rowed out on the *"Deep River"* and sang songs such as *"Juanita," "When You and I Were Young, Maggie," "Santa Lucia,"* and many others.

Every Sunday they went to *"The Church in the Wildwood."*

Soon a little stranger came into their home and then each evening she crooned *"Lullaby and Goodnight."*

Through the days and years that followed they found happiness and prosperity, and thus life moved along *"On the Wings of Song"* (Mendelssohn).

Musical terms.—What musical terms are suggested by the following?

1. An obstruction? Bar.
2. What cold molasses does with difficulty? Run.
3. A policeman's territory? Beat.
4. We want it fresh? Air.
5. Fishy? Scales.
6. A support? Brace.
7. Low down? Bass (Base).
8. Repose? Rest.
9. A brief letter? Note.
10. Shakespeare just does not do it? Repeat.
11. Delay? Retard (Ritardando).
12. General tendency? Tenor.
13. Living accomodations? Flats.
14. Swindlers? Sharps.
15. A string? Chord.
16. A reflection on character? Slur.
17. Unaffected? Natural.
18. Seen on the ocean? Swells.
19. Suggests lawyers? Bar.

20. Change one letter and it is a head cook? Clef.
21. Grace loved George. He called her letters? Grace Notes.
22. An important thing in the baseball game? The Pitch.
23. What all organizations desire? Harmony.
24. Over-exertion? Strain.

Bells.—

1. A medical bell? Belladonna.
2. A masculine bell? Bellman.
3. A Florida bell? Bellaire.
4. A high bell? Belfry.
5. An Irish bell? Belfast.
6. A noisy bell? Bellow.
7. A literary bell? Belles-lettres.
8. A warlike bell? Belligerent.
9. A European bell? Belgium.
10. A garden bell? Bellflower.
11. A pugnacious bell? Bellicose.
12. A Bible bell? Belshazzar.
13. A windy bell? Bellows.

Do you like tea.—Here you are then. See if you can recognize the very many different kinds of tea.

1. The best policy? Honesty.
2. The soul of wit? Brevity.
3. What killed a cat? Curiosity.
4. Which never faileth? Charity.
5. Mother of invention? Necessity.
6. Heat, power, and light? Electricity.
7. The Four Hundred? Society.
8. Forever and ever? Eternity.
9. A national possession? Nationality.
10. The spice of life? Variety.
11. It is only skin deep? Beauty.
12. First and always? Priority—Infinity.
13. With great speed? Velocity.
14. Brotherhood? Fraternity.
15. Where lots of people live? City.
16. An accompaniment of age? Infirmity.
17. An iced tea? Frigidity.
18. The tea of the brave? Intrepidity.
19. Slow of wit? Stupidity.

20. It is ridiculous? Absurdity.
21. It is savage? Ferocity.
22. It stretches? Elasticity.
23. It worries me? Anxiety.
24. It is generous? Liberality.
25. It is prompt? Punctuality.
26. It lasts? Durability?
27. It is proud? Haughty.
28. It is frugal? Thrifty.
29. It cannot be seen? Invisibility.
30. A happy tea? Felicity.
31. An aristocratic tea? Nobility.
32. A powerful tea? Mighty.
33. A devout tea? Piety.
34. A much-sought tea? Popularity.
35. A full tea? Capacity.
36. A thriving tea? Prosperity.
37. A nimble tea? Agility.
38. What we have been enjoying? Sociability or Party.
39. Brotherhood? Fraternity.

Do you know your cars?—

1. A martyred president? Lincoln.
2. A crossing place? Ford.
3. To grind the teeth? Nash.
4. To evade adroitly? Dodge.
5. A well known river? Hudson.
6. A Frenchman who explored the Mississippi? La Salle.
7. Across the country? Overland.
8. A kind of cracker? Graham.
9. A Spanish explorer who discovered the Mississippi? De Soto.
10. A famous rock? Plymouth.
11. Identified with Roman mythology? Mercury.
12. What the woman asked when she bought a hen? Chevrolet.
13. A diminutive fowl? Bantam.
14. An intoxicated bread-maker? Studebaker.
15. An Ottawa Indian chief? Pontiac.
16. Eliminate a letter and you have a deer? Buick.
17. The hip and ease of motion? Hupmobile.
18. A Detroit hotel? Cadillac.
19. A tall building in New York City? Chrysler.
20. A soft, gentle wind? Zephyr.

21. Ancient, a letter, and an Alabama city? Oldsmobile.
22. To compress tightly, a small stiff piece of paper? Packard.

Mary is a grand old name—

1. Mary on the sea? Mariner.
2. A puppet? Marionette.
3. A weed of narcotic effect? Mariahuana.
4. A kind of lily or tulip? Mariposa.
5. Bordering on the ocean? Maritime.
6. One of the forty-eight? Maryland.
7. A fragrant plant of the mint family? Rosemary.
8. Habitual? Customary.
9. In a desirable age? Marriage.
10. In matrimonial relations? Marital.
11. Seasoning with French dressing? Marinate.
12. A worthy Mary? Meritorious.
13. A tawdry Mary? Meretricious.
14. A plant of the genus *Tagetes?* Marigold.

Know Rose?

1. Optimistic? Roseate or Rosy.
2. Saying her prayers? Rosary.
3. A flower of the rhododendron family? Rosebay.
4. A fragrant plant? Rosemary.
5. In the Bible? Rose of Sharon.
6. An imitation? Rosette.
7. A liquid? Rose water.
8. In a valuable piece of cabinet furniture? Rosewood.
9. A member of a mystical society? Rosicrucian.
10. Don Quixote's steed? Rosinante.
11. Gloomy? Morose.
12. Ascended? Arose.
13. In a book of essays? Prose.
14. Commonplace? Prosaic.
15. In the public esteem? Heroes.
16. With an acid effect? Corrosive.

Advertising slogans.—A few years ago a writer in *Printer's Ink* (Kyle S. Crichton, of Albuquerque, New Mexico), argued that advertising slogans were futile. He contended that they meant nothing to the public they were supposed to impress. On a test, fifty of the most widely advertised slogans were submitted to sixteen veteran advertising men for identification. They averaged only 59 per cent on their guesses. The highest was 76 per cent and the lowest 40 per cent. Try out your guests on some of the slogans that follow. You can use them in various ways.

Guess these slogans—List the slogans and have the guests write in the product advertised. Or they may call them.

Act out slogans—Have various groups present certain slogans in brief dramatic skits for the other guests to guess. They may be presented charade fashion.

Getting partners—Give the slogans to the men and the products to the ladies, one to each person. Have them match up for partners. The leader had better have a master sheet at hand so as to be able to give hints to the searchers. In some cases it may be necessary to give more than hints.

Poster slogans—Number the slogans and post them around the room. Each guest will be given a numbered card on which he will identify the various slogans.

1. Keep that schoolgirl complexion. Palmolive Soap.
2. Chases dirt. Old Dutch Cleanser.
3. When it rains it pours. Morton's Salt.
4. Good to the last drop. Maxwell House Coffee.
5. Hasn't scratched yet. Bon Ami.
6. Eventually—why not now? Gold Medal Flour.
7. From contented cows. Carnation Milk.
8. The digestible fat. Crisco.
9. They satisfy. Chesterfield Cigarettes.
10. Cover the earth. Sherwin Williams Paint.
11. The flavor lasts. Wrigley Chewing Gum.
12. No metal can touch you. Paris Garters.
13. Delicious and refreshing. Coca Cola.
14. His master's voice. Victor Talking Machine.
15. Works while you sleep. Cascarets.
16. The instrument of the immortals. Steinway Piano.
17. It floats. Ivory Soap.
18. Ask the man who owns one? Packard Automobile.
19. A clean tooth never decays. Colgate Toothpaste.
20. There's a reason. Postum.
21. Time to re-tire. Fisk Tires.
22. 99 and 44/100 per cent pure. Ivory Soap.
23. It's toasted. Lucky Strike Cigarettes.
24. For economical transportation. Greyhound Bus Lines.
25. The skin you love to touch. Woodbury Soap.

26. The soap of beautiful women. Camay.
27. It beats—as it sweeps—it cleans. Hoover Vacuum Cleaner.
28. The breakfast of champions. Wheaties.
29. Everywhere on everything. Glidden Paints
30. It's dated. Chase and Sanborn Coffee.
31. Banish tattletale gray. Fels Naptha Soap.
32. Rich in dextrose. Baby Ruth Candy.
33. Look for the year mark 1847. 1847 Rogers Brothers Silver.
34. Soft as old linen. Scot Tissue.
35. 57 varieties. H. J. Heinz Company.
36. The ham what *am*. Armour.
37. Good for tender gums. Ipana Toothpaste.
38. Drink it and sleep. Sanka Coffee.
39. Not a cough in a carload. Old Gold Cigarettes.
40. Cuts the cost of better living. Kelvinator.
41. For every room in the house. Armstrong Linoleum.
42. The watch of railroad accuracy. Hamilton Watch.
43. The acid neutralizing dentrifice. Squibbs Toothpaste.
44. Candy mint with the hole. Life Saver.
45. Goes a long way to make friends. General Tires.
46. Has the strength of Gilbraltar. Prudential Life Insurance Company.
47. The name that means everything in electricity. Westinghouse.
48. The desk test. Royal Typewriter.
49. Kind to your eyes—both sides alike. Kimberly-Clark Paper Company.
50. Wrinkle proof. Botany Ties.
51. A small thing to look for—a big thing to find. Hart Schaffner and Marx.
52. Travel and sleep in safety and comfort. Pullman.
53. When better cars are made —— will make them. Buick Automobile.
54. Good for life—Drink a bite to eat. Dr. Pepper.
55. It likes you. 7 Up.
56. Watch the —— go by. Ford Automobile.

Advertising pictures.—Clip well-known advertising pictures from magazines. Mount and number them, and place them about the room. Have the guests try to identify the products advertised by the pictures. Some suggestions are Cream of Wheat, Old Dutch Cleanser, Sunkist Oranges, Van Camp's Pork and Beans, Dutch Boy White Lead, and Campbell's Soup. These and others will be found in current magazines.

Testing the five senses (a sense social).—Perhaps each guest will be expected to contribute five cents to the good of the cause.

Sight—A table is provided on which there are numerous articles—a pair of gloves, a knife, a book, a pencil, a pen, a marble, a candle, a vase, a box, a leaf, a card case, a doll, a bottle of ink, a notebook, a small flag, a perfumery bottle, a needle, a paper of pins, a spool of thread, and perhaps other articles. Guests are allowed to observe for a moment and then the table is removed. Or guests are allowed to walk past the table where the articles are displayed and then they are ushered into another room. Still another plan would be to blindfold the guests one at a time or in small groups and take the blindfold off, allowing them to observe the table for five seconds. Each person lists all of the articles he can remember having seen. Read the correct list and see who has made the highest score.

Hearing—Guests listen to certain musical selections and write down the titles of the compositions. See "The Musical Romance" in this chapter. See also Chapter XII, "Fun with Music."

Smelling—Guests are blindfolded and asked to identify certain odors. Bottles containing some of the following: Oil of cloves, oil of cedar, oil of sassafras, oil of anise, oil of bitter almonds, pennyroyal, essence of peppermint, vanilla, cinnamon, wood alcohol, valerian, bay rum, camphor, ammonia, rhubarb, arnica, spirits of niter, asafetida, turpentine, castor oil, gasoline, kerosene, linseed oil.

Feeling—Guests are blindfolded and asked to identify certain objects by feeling. A china egg, a sponge, corn silk, raw spaghetti, a soda straw, rice, navy beans, salt, sugar, flour, sand, baking powder, and face powder are some of the articles that might be used. Other possibilities are silk, satin, cotton, cellophane, oilcloth, woolen cloth, sheer, crepe de chine, and cheesecloth.

Tasting—This might be the signal for refreshments. What better way could there be for exercising the sense of taste?

If it is desired to follow the same plan as for the other senses you could blindfold the guests and have them taste and identify raw onions, carrots, salt, pepper, celery, a cereal, potato chips, and broken crackers.

Shouting proverbs.—Divide into groups. Each group selects a proverb. Each person in the group is assigned one word in the proverb. At the signal to shout the proverb each shouts his word simultaneously with the others in the group. The rest of the groups try to guess the proverb. It takes close listening to get it. The groups take turns shouting.

Split proverbs.—Part of the proverb is written on one piece of paper and part on another. Guests try to find the missing part. This would make a good mixer to get partners. Thus "A stitch in time" looks diligently for "saves nine." The searchers need not feel under compulsion of conducting a silent search.

Acting out proverbs.—Groups may present proverbs in charade fashion. For instance, a man comes up to an improvised newsstand and asks for a newspaper. The news dealer answers: "Sorry, but there are no newspapers today." "How come?" asks the man. "Well, there just ain't any news," responds the dealer. "Fine," says the man. "I'll take a magazine." He goes off whistling happily. It is easy to guess that this one is "No news is good news."

Highbrow proverbs.—Give individuals or groups a chance to doctor up any proverb they desire in extravagant phrasing. Examples: "Cast your optics carefully about previous to any attempts at taking off into space" for "Look before you leap"; "One feathered vertebrate egg-laying animal in the fingered appendage to a man's forearm is of more value than two in a thickly branching shrub" for "A bird in hand is worth two in the bush."

Mixed proverbs.—Hide portions of proverbs about the room. Require each person to find one before being seated. Now have all of the guests who have the first part of a proverb to line up on one side and all those who have the last part of a proverb to line up on the other. Have Number One on the one side to read his part of the proverb and Number One on the other side to read what he has. They are likely to be gloriously mixed. There will be such combinations as "A rolling stone is better than none," "A friend in need is the thief of time." You may have the players march in concentric circles to music. When the music stops have them read their proverb combinations.

Or you may have individuals or groups to work out their own combinations and read them to the crowd. Some clever arrangements will likely evolve out of this plan.

Improved proverbs.—Suggest that guests improve on the proverbs, if they can. There are such possibilities as "Never put off until tomorrow what you can get somebody to do for you today"; "Cosmetic fancies alter faces."

Contradictory proverbs.—Try your hand at thinking of proverbs that contradict one another. For instance, one side shouts, "Absence makes the heart grow fonder." The other side comes back with "Out of sight, out of mind." Again one side calls out: "You can't teach an old dog new tricks" and the other side, after a moment, comes back with "You are never too old to learn." "There is honor among thieves" and "Set a thief to catch a thief."

Hidden words in proverbs.—Have players try to discover words in various proverbs. The letters in the words must appear consecutively in the phrase. For instance, "Handsome is as handsome does." The words that appear here are: hand, and, an, some, so, hands, me, sash, do, and doe.

The same thing can be done with nursery rhymes, poems, famous quotations, etc.

A select list of proverbs—

1. Absence makes the heart grow fonder.
2. Out of sight, out of mind.
3. Actions speak louder than words.
4. It ought to be a good tale that is twice told.
5. Whom the gods wish to destroy they first make mad.—Latin.
6. A fool can ask questions that wise men cannot answer.
7. Appearances are deceitful.—German.
8. Disputing and borrowing cause grief and sorrowing.—German.
9. April showers bring May flowers.
10. Birds of a feather flock together.
11. One rotten apple spoils the whole barrel.
12. When about to put your words in ink,
    'Twill do no harm to stop and think.
13. It takes two to make a bargain.
14. Beauty is but skin deep.
15. Handsome is that handsome does.
16. When beauty is at the bar, blind men make the best jury.
17. Beggars must not be choosers.
18. Well begun is half done.—French, Italian, German, Spanish, Portuguese, Danish, Dutch.
19. A wager is a fool's argument.
20. The early bird catches the worm.
21. Blood is thicker than water.—German.
22. Big words seldom go with good deeds.—Danish.
23. Half a loaf is better than no bread.

24. Brevity is the soul of wit.—Shakespeare.
25. A new broom sweeps clean.—Italian, German, Dutch, Danish.
26. A penny saved is a penny earned.
27. Everybody's business is nobody's business.
28. Haste makes waste.
29. After the storm comes the calm.
30. It is better to be sure than sorry.
31. For want of a nail the shoe was lost; for want of a shoe the horse was lost; for want of a horse the man was lost.—Franklin.
32. When the cat's away the mice will play.—French, German, Spanish, Danish, Portuguese.
33. A whistling girl and a crowing hen
    Never come to any good end.
34. As the twig is bent the tree's inclined.
35. Children should be seen, not heard.
36. Like father, like son.—Portuguese.
37. If an ass goes traveling he'll not come home a horse.
38. Spare the rod and spoil the child.
39. The burnt child dreads the fire.
40. Better late than never, but better never late.
41. Circumstances alter cases.
42. Cleanliness is next to Godliness.—Wesley.
43. An ape's an ape, a varlet's a varlet,
    Though they be clad in silk and scarlet.
44. Clothes make the man.—Danish.
45. Fine feathers make fine birds.—French, Dutch.
46. The apparel oft proclaims the man.—Shakespeare.
47. The fool well dressed
    Is at his best.
48. Manners make the man.
49. Never grieve over spilt milk.
50. A guilty conscience needs no accuser.
51. Consistency, thou art a jewel.
52. A contented mind is a continual feast.
53. Convince a man against his will,
    He's of the same opinion still.—Gay.
54. Too many cooks spoil the broth.
55. A watched pot is long in boiling.
56. None but the brave deserve the fair.—Dryden.
57. A rich man's wooing is seldom long of doing.—Scotch.
58. Who the daughter would win
    With mamma must begin.—German.

59. It is too late to lock the stable door when the steed is stolen.—French, Dutch.
60. Procrastination is the thief of time.
61. Make hay while the sun shines.—German.
62. Paddle your own canoe.
63. The best physicians are Dr. Diet, Dr. Quiet, and Dr. Merryman.
64. You can't teach an old dog new tricks.
65. Barking dogs never bite.—French, German, Dutch.
66. Twin fools: one doubts nothing; the other, everything.
67. Early to bed and early to rise
    Makes a man healthy, wealthy, and wise.—Franklin.
68. What is one man's meat is another man's poison.
69. A fool may make money, but it requires a wise man to spend it.
70. Cut your coat according to your cloth.—Dutch.
71. What you do not need is dear at any price.
72. A little learning is a dangerous thing.—Pope.
73. Better an empty purse than an empty head.
74. It is never too late to learn.
75. All's well that ends well.—Shakespeare.
76. Turn about is fair play.
77. To err is human, to forgive divine.—Pope, German, Dutch.
78. A poor excuse is better than none.
79. Experience is the best teacher.
80. We learn to do by doing.
81. Easy come, easy go.—French.
82. Familiarity breeds contempt.
83. The greatest of faults is to be conscious of none.—Carlyle.
84. He that fights and runs away,
    May live to fight another day.—Butler.
85. Wherever there is smoke there is fire.
86. Fool's names as well as faces
    Are often seen in public places.
87. He who would make a fool of himself will find many to help him.—Danish.
88. No fool like an old fool.
89. Every man is the architect of his own fortune.—German, Danish.
90. Fortune sometimes favors those she afterwards destroys.—Italian.
91. A friend in need is a friend indeed.
92. The more haste the less speed.—French, Spanish, German, Dutch.
93. Marry in haste and repent at leisure.
94. Two heads are better than one.—Italian.
95. Cold hand, a warm heart.—German.

96. The road to hell is paved with good intentions.—German.
97. Plant the crab tree where you will, it will never bear pippins.
98. Honesty is the best policy.—Franklin.
99. While there is life there is hope.—Italian, Portuguese, Latin.
100. You can lead a horse to water, but you cannot make him drink.
101. Never ride a free horse to death.
102. Where ignorance is bliss 'tis folly to be wise.—Gray.
103. You can't have your cake and eat it too.
104. He robs Peter to pay Paul.
105. An idle brain is the devil's workshop.—German.
106. A stitch in time saves nine.
107. Heaven helps those who help themselves.—Franklin.
108. A little knowledge is a dangerous thing.
109. He who laughs last laughs best.—French, Italian, German, Danish.
110. Laugh and grow fat.
111. As you make your bed so must you lie on it.
112. Live to love and you will love to live.
113. Love laughs at locksmiths.
114. 'Tis better to have loved and lost
     Than never to have loved at all.—Tennyson.
115. It is best to let sleeping dogs lie.
116. Leave well enough alone.
117. Misery loves company.
118. Two things are bad: "too much" and "too little."
119. A fool and his money are soon parted.
120. He that gets money before he gets wit,
     Will be but a short while master of it.
121. Music hath charms to soothe the savage breast.—Congreve.
122. Necessity is the mother of invention.—French, German, Dutch.
123. Strike while the iron is hot.—French, Italian, German, Portuguese, Dutch, Spanish.
124. A little nonsense now and then
     Is relished by the best of men.—Holmes.
125. A wise man changes his mind, but a fool never.—Spanish.
126. Every dog has his day.
127. When passion entereth in at the foregate, wisdom goeth out at the postern.
128. All things come to him who waits.—French.
129. He labors in vain who tries to please everybody.—Latin.
130. Possession is nine points of the law.
131. A bird in hand is worth two in the bush.
132. Practice makes perfect.—German, Spanish.

133. Practice what you preach.
134. Self-praise is half slander.
135. Preachers can talk but never teach,
    Unless they practice what they preach.
136. The proof of the pudding is in the eating.—Dutch.
137. It takes two to make a quarrel,
    But only one to start it.
138. Fools rush in where angels fear to tread.—Pope.
139. A good name is sooner lost than won.
140. Be sure you're right, then go ahead.—Davy Crockett.
141. When rogues fall out, honest men come by their own.
142. A rolling stone gathers no moss.—French, German, Italian,
    Spanish, Portuguese, Dutch.
143. Easier said than done.—Chinese.
144. A miss is as good as a mile.
145. Speaking is silver, silence is golden.—Dutch.
146. Every rose has its thorn.
147. There is honor among thieves.
148. Nothing succeeds like success.
149. Everybody's business is nobody's business.—German.
150. A still tongue makes a wise head.
151. Empty wagons make most noise.—Dutch.
152. Time and tide wait for no man.
153. Jack of all trades and master of none.
154. Though the bird may fly over your head let it not make its
    nest in your hair.—Danish.
155. It is an ill wind that blows nobody good.
156. The truth will out.
157. If at first you don't succeed,
    Try, try again.
158. There is many a slip 'twixt the cup and the lip.
159. Variety's the very spice of life,
    That gives it all its flavor.—Cowper.
160. Virtue is its own reward.
161. A bad workman quarrels with his tools.
162. Never count your chickens before they are hatched.
163. Nothing ventured; nothing gained.
164. A word to the wise is sufficient.
165. Still water runs deep.
166. Every cloud has a silver lining.
167. Never put off until tomorrow what you can do today.
168. If wishes were horses, beggars would ride.

A proverb quiz—

1. What proverb is indicated by the following statement: "An inefficient artisan fumes and frets at the instruments with which he labors"? Answer—Proverb 161.

2. If wishes were horses what would beggars do? Answer—Proverb 168.

3. What is as good as a mile? Answer—Proverb 144.

4. What is the following proverb in plain English: "Sweet sounds organized toward beauty have fascinations that calm the agitated emotions of the primitive and animal-like"? Answer—Proverb 121.

5. What happens to a whistling girl and a crowing hen? Answer—Proverb 33.

6. What proverb is indicated by the following: "To depart from the path of rectitude is characteristic of the human of species, but to be tolerant, loving, and kind toward the wrongdoer is Godlike"? Answer—Proverb. 77.

7. What is "a fool's argument"? Answer—Proverb 19.

8. Finish the following: "When about to put your words in ink ————————————————————. Answer—Proverb 12.

9. What is its own reward? Answer—Proverb 160.

10. Finish the following: "Convince a man against his will ——— ————————————————————. Answer—Proverb 53.

Opera quiz.—Who were the composers of the following operas? 1. Barber of Seville. 2. Beggars Opera. 3. La Boheme. 4. Bohemian Girl. 5. Carmen. 6. Cavalleria Rusticana. 7. Chimes of Normandy. 8. Tales of Hoffman. 9. Faust. 10. Hansel and Gretel. 11. H. M. S. Pinafore. 12. Iolanthe. 13. The Mikado. 14. Lohengrin. 15. Tannhauser. 16. Die Walkuere. 17. Parsifal. 18. Lucia de Lammermoor. 19. Madame Butterfly. 20. Manon. 21. Pagliacci. 22. Rigoletto. 23. La Traviata. 24. Robin Hood. 25. Samson and Delilah. 26. The Chocolate Soldier.

Answers—1. Rossini. 2. Gay and Pepusch. 3. Puccini. 4. Balfe. 5. Bizet. 6. Mascagni. 7. Planquette. 8. Offenbach. 9. Gounod. 10. Humperdinck. 11, 12, and 13. Sullivan. 14, 15, 16, and 17. Wagner. 18. Donizetti. 19. Puccini. 20. Massenet. 21. Leoncavallo. 22, 23. Verdi. 24. DeKoven. 25. Saint-Saens. 26. Oscar Straus.

Musical quiz—

1. The composer of "Ah, Sweet Mystery of Life," was

George Gershwin,	Victor Herbert,
Franz Schubert,	Johann Strauss.

2. What lovely waltz is about a river in Germany, and who wrote it?

3. What famous lullaby was written by an Austrian, and what was his name?

4. Who wrote "The March of the Wooden Soldiers," and in what operetta does it appear?

5. "Jeannie with the Light Brown Hair" is one of the loveliest songs written by

Victor Herbert,	Irving Berlin,
Stephen Foster,	Handel.

6. *La Donna e Mobile* means "Fickle Woman" and it is sung in

Donizetti's "Lucia de Lammermoor,"	Verdi's "Rigoletto,"
Wagner's "Lohengrin,"	Mozart's "Don Juan."

7. What renowned musician was once Premier of Poland?

8. In what famous opera does a Japanese girl have a love affair with an American naval officer?

9. "Old Man River" was first sung in what musical show?

10. Who, with his flute, charmed both the rats and the children of Hamelin?

11. What opera is written about a tonsorial artist?

12. If there are eight notes of music in one octave, how many notes are there in two octaves?

13. Who was the great lover of Seville written about in opera, story, and poem by Mozart, Dumas, and Byron?

14. Who wrote "Kiss Me Again"?

15. Who composed "Moonlight Sonata"?

Answers—1. Victor Herbert. 2. "Blue Danube Waltz," by Johann Strauss. 3. "Lullaby and Goodnight," by Brahms. 4. Victor Herbert, in "Babes in Toyland." 5. Stephen Foster. 6. Verdi's "Rigoletto." 7. Paderewski. 8. "Madame Butterfly." 9. Jerome Kern's "Showboat." 10. The Pied Piper. 11. Barber of Seville. 12. Fifteen, since the last note of the first octave is the first note of the second octave. 13. Don Juan. 14. Victor Herbert. 15. Beethoven.

Nature quiz—

1. Which runs the faster, a greyhound or a whippet?

2. What baby animal is known as a pup though it has a bull for a father and a cow for a mother?

3. The most dreaded of all American snakes is (1) the cotton-mouth, (2) the bushmaster, (3) the anaconda.

4. What animal carries its home on its back and has its eyes in its horns?

5. How long would it take to drown a grasshopper by holding its head under water?

6. Do fleas have wings?

7. When Wilson Bentley photographed thousands of snowflakes what were three things that he discovered?

8. How long is a year on the planet Mercury?

9. Which of the following animals of the jungle is the largest: lion, tiger, jaguar?

10. Why does it usually seem so hot before a thunderstorm?

11. What have the cougar, panther, puma, and mountain lion in common?

12. Is a marten a bird, beast, or fish?

Answers—1. Whippet. 2. Seal. 3. Bushmaster. 4. Snail. 5. It would not drown. A grasshopper breathes through an aperture below its wings. 6. No, they hop but do not fly. 7. (1) That no two snowflakes are alike. (2) That each snowflake presents an almost unbelievably beautiful pattern. (3) That each pattern is hexagonal 8. Three months. 9. Tiger. 10. Because the evaporation of moisture from the skin, which normally cools it, is slowed down by excessive moisture already in the air. 11. In America these are all names for the same animal. 12. Beast. Slender, fur-bearing, carniverous mammal.

An astronomy quiz.—What constellation, star, or planet suggests:

1. A constellation near Vega. The Phoenicians worshiped it as a god. The Greeks called it "The Phantom" or "The Kneeler." A hero of Greek mythology noted for his strength.

2. A constellation sometimes known as "The Crab." It has a cluster of stars in it known as "The Beehive." A dread disease.

3. A planet discovered in 1846. It is not visible to the naked eye. A Greek god of the sea.

4. A constellation of six stars forming a bowl. In the spring it appears halfway up the southern sky. The opening at the top of a volcano.

5. The smallest planet and the one nearest to the sun. It is best seen in March, April, August, and September. A mythical God of the Romans who carried messages.

6. A new planet discovered in 1930. The most remote planet of the solar system. A mythological god of the lower world.

7. The largest of the planets, having a mean diameter of 87,000 miles. A Roman god of antiquity.

8. The most brilliant of the fixed stars. A planet moving in an orbit between Mercury and the earth. A goddess of beauty.

9. A planet conspicuous for the redness of its light. A Roman god of war.

10. A summer constellation known as "The Archer." Part of it is known as "The Milk Dipper."

11. A summer constellation known as "The Scorpion." It has a star (Antares) twice the extent of the earth's orbit, being 420 million miles in diameter.

12. A late summer and autumn constellation that zigzags and is sometimes called "The Lady in the Chair."

13. A winter constellation known as "The Great Hunter." It is considered the finest collection in the heavens.

14. The "dog star." It is bluish white, and to us it is the most brilliant star in the heavens.

15. A constellation that never sets and that bears a resemblance to a kitchen utensil. Twenty-three degrees away is the Pole Star. It is sometimes called "The Big Bear."

16. A constellation that includes the Pole Star (Polaris) and it is sometimes called "The Little Bear."

17. A constellation that appears nearly overhead in September and October. It is known as "The Northern Cross" or "The Swan."

18. An attractive summer star. Visible also in the fall and winter. Belongs to the constellation Lyra (the Lyre).

19. A constellation known as "The Seven Sisters" though a photographic plate reveals more than 2,000 stars in it.

20. A planet that has nine known moons. It has rings around it. First seen by Galileo in 1610.

Answers—1. Hercules. 2. Cancer. 3. Neptune. 4. Crater. 5. Mercury. 6. Pluto. 7. Jupiter. 8. Venus. 9. Mars. 10. Sagittarius. 11. Scorpio. 12. Cassiopeia. 13. Orion. 14. Sirius. 15. Ursa Major or The Big Dipper. 16. Ursa Minor or The Little Dipper. 17. Cygnus. 18. Vega. 19. Pleiades. 20. Saturn.

Bird quiz.—What bird am I?

1. I am common in all parts of the world except New Zealand and the Polar Regions. I am of three kinds—cliff, bank, and tree. My name suggests the act of taking through the esophagus into the stomach.

2. I am a songbird of value because I eat insects that destroy vegetation. My name suggests a frolic.

3. I have a crested head. As I fly I utter a loud, harsh, rattling cry. I am thirteen inches long, being considerably larger than a robin. I live along streams and feed on fish. My name suggests a royal personage on a vacation trip.

4. I am a slender bird a foot long. My tail is long. I am of a grayish brown color with dull white underneath. I am seldom seen because I hide myself in foliage. I make a peculiar sound, more like a frog than a bird. I am sometimes called a "raincrow" because I call principally in damp and cloudy weather. Some people believe that I foretell the weather. My nest is usually a flimsy creation of sticks and grass, located in low trees and shrubs. My eggs are a pale greenish-blue. My name suggests an expression for "crazy."

5. I am a gray-brown bird seven inches long. I jerk my tail nervously when perched. I am often found around bridges and buildings. My call is a "peewit" while I jerk my tail in accompaniment. I am likely to build my nest on a barn rafter, porch, gorge wall, or bridge. I feed on insects caught mostly on the wing. My name is the first name of a famous woman writer.

6. I am eight and one-fourth inches long. I am a bright, rosy red except for some black at the base of my bill and at the throat. I have a conspicuous crest. The male usually perches high and sings. My name is the title of a prominent church official.

7. I am seven and one-fourth inches long. In the summer the male is a bright scarlet, with black wings and tail. In late summer the scarlet turns to olive. The female is olive where the male is scarlet and dark green where he is black. I am rarely seen except in tall shrubs or trees. I repeat a constant "chip-chu." I am useful as a destroyer of injurious insects.

8. I am an active little bird five and one-fourth inches long. The top of my head is brick-red, with gray lines over my eyes. My breast and under parts are gray-white. The back of my neck is gray-brown. My back and wings are streaked with brown. I am remarkably tame. I repeat a monotonous "chip." I am useful as a destroyer of injurious insects. In addition, I eat small weeds, and therefore I help to control the multiplication of both weeds and insects.

9. I am ten inches long. My head is black. My upper parts are gray and my under parts are reddish-brown and white. My nest is a thick symmetrical mud bowl, reinforced with leaves and twigs, and lined with soft grass. I am considered a harbinger of spring. I have a fondness for human society and I am considered quite a singer. My name is the first name of a famous archer.

10. I am seven inches long. My upper part is a bright blue, while

my under parts are a cinnamon-chestnut and white. My wings are long and pointed. My tail is shorter than my wings and it is distinctly notched. My legs are short. My nest is located in a deserted woodpecker's hole, and it is composed of grass, weed stalks, a few bits of bark, and fine grass blades. I am a more accurate herald of spring than the robin. I like people. In our family of birds male and female mates are devoted to each other and to their young. Maeterlinck wrote a famous play about me. I am considered a symbol of happiness.

11. I am a bit smaller than the robin, with an olive-brownish back and a dully speckled breast. I build by nest on or close to the ground. It is bulky and made of small rootlets, leaves, and bits of dried moss. I am considered a lovely singer. One of my names is the last name of a famous nurse.

12. I am seven and one-half inches long. My head, neck, back, throat, and the middle of my tail are black. My wings are black and white. Elsewhere I am a brilliant orange red. I am very active in treetops and am rarely seen in evergreens. I like to balance myself on the tips of branches. I am very fond of apple trees at the time of flowering. I am useful as a destroyer of injurious insects. I have a cheerful whistle. My nest is usually from 20 to 40 feet up on the end of a slender branch. It is a hanging bag that closes with the weight of the bird, and it is made of woven plant materials. The female is brown-streaked where the male is black, and it is brilliant orange elsewhere. There is no brown on the tail of the female. The first part of my name is the name of a large American city. In fact, the professional baseball teams that have represented that city have for many years carried my name.

Answers—1. Swallow. 2. Lark. 3. Kingfisher. 4. Cuckoo. 5. Phoebe. 6. Cardinal. 7. Scarlet Tanager. 8. Chipping Sparrow. 9. Robin. 10. Bluebird. 11. Hermit Thrush or "American Nightingale." 12. Baltimore Oriole.

How many birds can you list?—It would be interesting to find out how many birds can be listed in your crowd. If the crowd is small have each person make up a list. If it is large, divide into groups and have each group make a list. After the lists are reported you might have the crowd pool its information about the various birds. A bird hike would make a good follow-up. Besides the birds listed in the previous contest, the following are suggested: Blackbird, bobolink, woodpecker, flicker, thrasher, snipe, chat, catbird, pewee, canary, bluejay, crow, cowbird, starling, wren, brown creeper, eagle, hawk, owl, quail, dove, mockingbird, nighthawk, goatsucker, peacock, grouse, pheasant, killdeer, sandpiper, plover, crane, heron, rail, gull, duck, swan, goose, hummingbird, martin, whippoorwill, purple finch, pelican.

Bird pictures.—Mount and number the pictures of familiar birds. Place them about the room and have the guests identify them. Another plan would be that of holding up the picture of a bird and having the guests call its name as soon as they can identify it. Still another plan would be that of throwing slides upon a screen and having the guests identify them. Good pictures in colors can be gotten inexpensively from The National Association of Audubon Societies, Inc., 1006 Fifth Avenue, New York City.

A literary quiz—

1. How many men rode into the Valley of Death?
2. What is the name of a sailor who was shipwrecked on a desert island? He lived there for many years with a companion whom he named after the day on which he found him. What was the companion's name?
3. What Shakespearean character demanded a pound of flesh as a forfeit? Who was his daughter?
4. What famous Dickens character was changed by a visit of spirits on Christmas Eve? In what story does he appear?
5. Who was a henpecked husband who slept for twenty years? What author tells the story?
6. Victor Hugo tells the story of a reformed convict who was persecuted because of his past. What was the name of this convict who became a respected citizen and officer, and in what novel is he the chief character?
7. What book tells the experiences of a man who was shipwrecked upon the shores of Lilliput where he dwelt for some time with the Lilliputians?
8. Who had a series of wondrous adventures as the result of going down a rabbit hole?
9. Who wrote "Alice in Wonderland"?
10. What practical reason had Shakespeare for ending most of his plays in a processional of some sort?
11. What famous American writer was born at Hannibal, Missouri? What two famous Missouri boy characters did he create?
12. What character created by J. M. Barrie refused to grow up, preferring always to be a boy?
13. What well-known poem begins, "This is the forest primeval. The murmuring pines and hemlocks. . . . .."?

14. What famous detective character was created by Conan Doyle?

15. What famous novel has a character who fights windmills?

Answers—1. Six hundred. 2. Robinson Crusoe; Friday. 3. Shylock; **Jessica.** 4. Scrooge; "Christmas Carol." 5. Rip Van Winkle; W. Irving. 6. Jean Val Jean; "Les Miserables." 7. "Gulliver's Travels," **Swift.** 8. Alice in Wonderland. 9. Lewis Carroll. 10. Elizabethan stages had no curtains. A processional made a convenient way for getting characters off the stage. 11. Mark Twain; Tom Sawyer and Huckleberry Finn. 12. Peter Pan. 13. Longfellow's "Evangeline." 14. Sherlock Holmes. 15. "Don Quixote," by Cervantes.

Sports quiz—

1. What famous baseball player holds the home run record of sixty home runs in one season?

2. Of what great outfielder was it said that the only way to stop him on the bases was to throw to third if he started for second?

3. The game of badminton was developed from tennis, handball, baseball, none of these.

4. Which of the following games originated in the United States—tennis, baseball, football, basketball, badminton, cricket?

5. What famous evangelist was once a professional baseball player?

6. Jai Lai (Hy Ly) or Pelota is a game like checkers, chess, tennis, football, handball, croquet?

7. It originated in Ireland, Italy, South America, Cuba, India, Japan, Spain. (Check which.)

8. What famous football player was known as "The Galloping Ghost"?

9. If a player of the kicking side falls on the kickoff in the opposing team's end zone in a football game, does he score a safety, a touchback, or a touchdown?

10. How many points does a football team score when it makes a safety?

11. In the ordinary game of croquet are there seven, eight, or nine wickets?

12. Who are the two most famous archers in history and legend?

13. What champion heavyweight prizefighter was known as "Gentleman Jim"?

14. What are the positions in six-man football?

15. Which is the older game, tennis or handball?

Answers—1. Babe Ruth. 2. Ty Cobb. 3. None of these. Badminton was played, though not under that name, in the Orient and in India before tennis, handball, and baseball were invented.

4. Baseball and basketball. 5. Billy Sunday. 6. Jai Lai resembles a combination of handball and tennis. 7. Spain. 8. Red Grange. 9. Touchdown. 10. Two. 11. Nine. 12. William Tell and Robin Hood. 13. James J. Corbett. 14. Center, two ends, a quarterback, halfback, and fullback. 15. Handball. Tennis was developed in the fourteenth century from the game of handball.

Hodgepodge quiz—

1. Is Phi Beta Kappa a social, professional, or scholastic fraternity?
2. The Ohio River forms the entire northern boundary of what state?
3. What colors are obtained by mixing (1) blue and yellow, (2) red and yellow, and (3) black and orange?
4. Why are pine trees less likely to be struck by lightening than any other trees?
5. What scientific principle did Archimedes discover while sitting in his bathtub?
6. How many reindeer were there in the poem, "The Visit of St. Nicholas," by Clement C. Moore? Can you name four of them? How does the poem begin?
7. What character in nursery rhyme ate Christmas pie?
8. What character in history was known as "The Father of His Country"?
9. Which letters of the alphabet are used as Roman numerals?
10. Why is it that you see the lightning before you hear the thunder?

Answers—1. Scholastic. 2. Kentucky. 3. (1) green, (2) orange, (3) brown. 4. The resin in the pine tree makes it a poor conductor. 5. Specific gravity. 6. Eight. Dasher, Dancer, Prancer, Vixen, Comet, Cupid, Donner, Blitzen. "'Twas the night before Christmas and all through the house. . . . ." 7. Little Jack Horner. 8. George Washington. 9. I, V, X, L, D, M, C. 10. Because light travels faster than sound.

Bible quiz—

1. Who caught his hair in an oak tree while fleeing from his father's soldiers?
2. Which of the twelve disciples acted as treasurer?
3. Moses' rod was turned into which of the following: a live branch, a serpent, a burning bush?
4. On what world famous road did Paul travel on his way to Rome?
5. What was Methusaleh's father's name?

6. Who is the greatest orator mentioned in the Bible?

7. What boy had a coat of many colors?

8. What was the name of Abraham's wife?

9. What Old Testament character asked permission of his king to go back to Jerusalem to rebuild its walls?

10. Who was the "weeping prophet"?

11. What prophet saw a wheel and is memorialized therefore in a Negro spiritual? What is the spiritual?

12. What Old Testament character put up a great wrestling exhibition?

13. Finish the following question: "Greater love hath no man than ————————————————."

14. What were the names of the three Hebrew boys whom a Babylonian king threw into the fiery furnace?

15. What was the name of this king?

16. Who was the king of Babylon who had a big feast at which he saw a hand writing on the wall, the writing being interpreted to him by Daniel?

17. What prophet anointed Saul as king of Israel?

18. What great warrior and king played a harp and wrote songs?

19. What famous queen came to visit Solomon?

20. What wicked queen frightened Elijah so that he fled?

21. What prophet "saw the Lord" in the year King Uzziah died?

22. Fill in the missing word in the following quotation from I Timothy 4: 12: "Let no man despise thy youth, but be thou an ———— of the believers in word, in conversation, in charity, in spirit, in faith, in purity."

23. What prophet was swallowed by a whale?

24. One of Job's "comforters" is often referred to as "the smallest man in the Bible." Who was he?

25. What is the name of the woman Samson loved?

Answers—I. Absalom. 2. Judas. 3. A serpent. 4. The Appian Way. 5. Enoch. 6. Samson. He brought the house down even though it was filled with his enemies. 7. Joseph. 8. Sarah. 9. Nehemiah. 10. Jeremiah. 11. Ezekiel. "Ezekiel saw de wheel." 12. Jacob. 13. "this, that a man lay down his life for his friend." 14. Shadrach, Meshach, and Abednego. 15. Nebuchadnezzar. 16. Belshazzar. 17. Samuel. 18. David. 19. The Queen of Sheba. 20. Jezebel. 21. Isaiah. 22. example. 23. Jonah. 24. Bildad the Shuhite. 25. Delilah.

Funny bunnies (Rime times).—After having the guests work on these "funny bunny" phrases let them try their hands at creating some new ones. Perhaps you could divide into small groups and have each group work up some "funny bunnies" for the others to guess. The idea is for the answer to rhyme.

1. A jitterbug fowl? Jerky turkey.
2. A sly hen? Trickin' chicken.
3. A fox terrier pup that has just fallen into the lake? Wet pet.
4. A rude, ill-humored high-school girl? Surly girlie.
5. A male parent in Joppa? Joppa papa.
6. A badly frightened man? Pale male.
7. A tale of much bloodshed? Gory story.
8. A rose dipped in vinegar? Sour flower.
9. The color of the sky on a bright June day? Blue hue.
10. A drinking fountain high up in the Catskills? Mountain fountain.
11. Extraordinary food at a banquet? Rare fare.
12. A sorrowing boy? Sad lad.
13. An alert head of an educational institution? Keen dean.
14. The head of a college in his home town? Resident president.
15. A fowl that has escaped from its coop? Loose goose.
16. Well-behaved rodents? Nice mice.
17. A hobo in the rain? Damp tramp.
18. A drunkard on a warm summer's day? Hot sot.
19. A very small sausage? Teenie weenie.
20. A flop who is drunk? "Stewed" dude.
21. Checkers, as some people view it? Tame game.
22. A fresh vegetable? Green bean.
23. A masculine doll? Boy toy.
24. A girl from Switzerland? Swiss miss.
25. Darning cotton of a certain color? Red thread.
26. Skilful stunt with wood? Stick trick.
27. A group of well-organized clean ships? Neat fleet.
28. A bee's abode? Live hive.
29. A person with too much zeal for Thespian activities? Dramatic fanatic.
30. A flower asleep in the field? Lazy daisy.
31. Timid insect? Shy fly.
32. Small, short foliage? Brief leaf.
33. A dejected boy? Sad lad.
34. A well-seasoned smoking device? Ripe pipe.
35. An odd fortune teller? Queer seer.
36. Two good looking girls? Fair pair.
    (Someone suggested "Double trouble" for this one.)
37. An embarrassed citizen of Moscow? Blushin' Russian.

38. A love-sick native of Tokyo? Sentimental Oriental.
39. A resident of Warsaw who is amusing? Droll Pole.
40. Hot musical instruments (or the devil's dinner gongs) ? Hell's bells.
41. A woman with an unwholesome reputation? Shady lady.
42. A rural teacher of English? Agrarian grammarian.
43. A not-so-bright sea bird? Dull gull.
44. A shady past? Checkered record.
45. A professional religious worker who is "a wolf in sheep's clothing"? Sinister minister.
46. A conceited young rustic? Vain swain.
47. Just a bit monotonous? Humdrum.
48. A foul in a prize fight? Low blow.
49. A strange, but pleasing old man of godly character? Quaint saint.
50. A queer little rabbit? Funny bunny.

Fill-ins.—The idea of the game is to fill in the missing letters of a four-letter word. The first and last letters are given. For instance, P——P may be filled in with a U and M, so that it spells PUMP.

P (AR) T			T (ES) T	
P (IN) K			T (ON) E	
H (UM) P			F (IL) L	
H (AR) D			I (NC) H	
P (IN) K			B (LU) E	
L (OV) E			L (AM) P	

The game may be made a little harder by requiring five-letter words, such as P (INC) H, H (UNC) H, T (RAI) N, C (RAT) E, R (HYM) E.

Spelling baseball.—The pitcher pitches a word to the batter. If he spells it correctly, he goes to first base. If he misses, he is out. Base runners advance only by being forced. When three outs are made, the other side comes to the bat. The pitcher may be advised by his teammates regarding words to use. This is a baseball game where the pitcher always has a lot of "English" on the ball.

Calling opposites.—The leader calls a word that has an opposite, such as "light." The first player to call out "dark" scores one point. This may also be used as a paper and pencil game, in which case each player would be given a list of words with instructions to write the opposites beside their respective words. Here is a suggested list:

tall—short	clear—cloudy	wet—dry
fast—slow	hero—villian	love—hate
strong—weak	loud—quiet	hard—soft
sick—well	gay—sad	bold—shy
fat—thin	hot—cold	sharp—dull

I pack my trunk.—One player starts the game by saying, "I pack my trunk for China, and I put in it artichokes." The second player then says, "I pack my trunk for China, and I put in it artichokes and balsam." Each player, in turn, repeats all that has gone before and adds one article of his own. The articles must be run alphabetically.

If a player leaves an article out of the sequence in which it was given, he drops out of the game.

Nursery rhyme contest.—The guests are divided into two groups. One group starts the game by repeating or singing in unison some nursery rhyme. The other group must respond with another rhyme. And so it continues until one or the other group fails to respond. If the responses are sung, the following tune is used:

Little Jack Horner sat in a corner,
Eating his Christmas pie,
He stuck in his thumb and pulled out a plum,
And threw it out the window.
The window, the window,
He threw it out the window,
He stuck in his thumb and pulled out a plum,
And threw it out the window.

Transitions.—Take a word and by one-letter steps change it into its opposite. It is important to note that only one letter may be changed at a time. Note the following examples:

For instance, try changing "poor" to "rich." You may be tempted to give up. But keep at it. It can be done. Here's how:

Poor, moor, moon, boon, born, torn, town, down, dawn, damn, dame, dime, dice, rice, rich.

Now take "slow" and make it "fast"—slow, slot, blot, boot, boat, coat, cost, cast, fast. Other examples: "sad" to "gay"—sad, say, gay; "dark" to "dawn"—dark, darn, dawn; "sick" to "well"—sick, silk, sill, sell, well; "rags" to "silk"—rags, rage, sage, sale, male, mile, milk, silk; "roam" to "home"—roam, room, boom, book, hook, honk, hone, home.

Calling all cities.—The first player calls the name of a city. The next player must call a city whose name begins with the last letter of the city just given. Thus, the first player calls New York. The next player immediately calls Kalamazoo. The next calls Orlando. Then come Oklahoma City, Yonkers, Syracuse, Evanston, New Orleans, Seattle, El Paso, Omaha, Augusta, Akron, Newport, and so on. A player must name his city before the count of ten. On failure he is eliminated. Names used may not be repeated during the round. The person wins who stays in the longest. This game may be played by sides.

Number guessing.—This is a good game for two persons. Guests may be paired off in order to play. Each player makes a diagram like the example:

1   One player holds one hand before the writing hand,
22   so that his opponent cannot see what number he is
333   writing. The other player watches closely the move-
4444   ment of the writer's hand and pencil, and then tries
55555   to guess what number he has written. If he guesses
666666   correctly, he marks that number off of his diagram.
7777777   If he misses, the writer marks the number off of his
88888888   own diagram and takes another turn. This continues
999999999   until one player has no numbers left. Only one digit
             may be written at a time, and therefore only one may
             be marked off at a time. Thus if a player writes 9,
and the opponent guesses 4, the writer does not mark off his whole
row of nines, but only one of them.

Quintuplets.—Guests are asked to list five of each in various categories. For instance: Give five girls names beginning with the letter *M*—Marjorie, Margaret, Mary, Mamie, Maxine. Give five boys names beginning with the letter *P*—Philip, Paul, Penrod, Prentice, Porter. Other lists might include five games—football, basketball, baseball, tennis, badminton; or five sports played with a large ball—soccer, volleyball, football, basketball, dodgeball; or five green vegetables—spinach, lettuce, peas, string beans; broccoli; or five fruits beginning with the letter *P*—peaches, pears, plums, prunes, pineapples; or five words of four letters ending in *mb*—dumb, numb, bomb, comb, tomb (note also limb, lamb, jamb, womb) ; or five ways to prepare potatoes—baked, mashed, boiled, scalloped, roasted; or five strokes in swimming—side, breast, back, crawl, dog-fashion; or five southern colleges that usually have good football teams— Alabama, Georgia Tech, Louisiana State University, Tennessee, Vanderbilt; or five well-known shaving creams—Palmolive, Williams, Ingrams, Mennens, Colgates; or five disagreeable things that often get into your eyes—cinders, dust, smoke, hair, grapefruit juice; or five edible roots that are common table fare—Irish potatoes, sweet potatoes, radishes, onions, turnips; or five words that rhyme with most—host, post, roast, coast, toast. And so on the lists of quintuplets might go. Try your hand at making some quintuplets of your own.

Initialed authors.—Each guest is given a list of phrases that describe certain authors. Each word begins with an initial of the author's name, the initials appearing in regular order. The players try to guess the names of the authors. Following are a few suggestions:

1. Merry tale-spinner. Mark Twain.
2. Wise stage-craftsman. William Shakespeare.
3. Courageous, lovable truth-seeker. Count Leo Tolstoi.
4. Amazing dreamer. Alexander Dumas.
5. Wrote masterful tales. William Makepeace Thackeray.
6. Versatile heroes. Victor Hugo.
7. Almost theological. Alfred Tennyson.
8. Has children's attention. Hans Christian Andersen.
9. Juveniles firmly conquered. James Fenimore Cooper.
10. Name honored. Nathaniel Hawthorne.
11. Bright humor. Bret Harte.
12. Really lasting stories. Robert Louis Stevenson.
13. Cheerful laborer. Charles Lamb.
14. Heroism wisely lauded. Henry Wadsworth Longfellow.

15. Just, gentle writer. John Greenleaf Whittier.
16. Poetry built skyward. Percy Bysche Shelley.
17. Clever delineator. Charles Dickens.
18. Weird imagination. Washington Irving.
19. Rare brain. Robert Browning.
20. Winsome writer. Walt Whitman.

Anagrams college.—This idea can be used for a progressive party. The tables are marked (1) LITERATURE, (2) GEOGRAPHY, (3) BOTANY, (4) ZOOLOGY, (5) HISTORY. Players may be paired off or they may play as individuals. Players may progress in any one of three ways: (1) The winning couple moves up, except that, at the head table, the losing couple would go to the last table; (2) All players move to another table; half at each table move up and half move back, in which case half at the head table would go foot and half at the foot table would go to the head table.

Players take turns turning up a letter. The player who turns up the letter tries to call a word beginning with that letter. The word must be appropriate to the subject to which the table is devoted. If he cannot answer immediately any other player calling a suitable word takes up the letter. Unclaimed letters lie face up on the table and they may be claimed anytime.

After players have made several progressions it can be readily seen they are likely to get their categories mixed. No penalties are required for such mistakes but, of course, a player is not allowed to pick up a *K* for shouting "Kipling" at the zoology table.

Suggested thoughts.—The leader or someone in the group suggests a word. Someone else calls out another word suggested by the first. The third word must be suggested by the second, and so on. The players may take part in rotation or as they think of suggested words. In the latter case, the leader will have to decide which word will be used, if several are suggested.

The game would begin, for instance, by the leader calling out "Nashville." Someone else immediately shouts "Parthenon," and the game is on. It might work out, as follows:

Nashville, Parthenon, Greece, Turkey, Thanksgiving, Football, College, Education, Teachers, Books, Libraries, Silence, Sleep, Lying, Lawyers, Court, Marriage, Home.

Or it might work out this way: Nashville, Tennessee, Volunteer, Army, March, St. Patrick, Ireland, Corrigan, Airplane, Lindbergh, Kidnaping, Criminals, Jails, Prisoners, Lock-step, Goose-step, Germany, Hitler, Mussolini, Italy, Rome.

Try it out. In a small crowd it would be interesting to have each player write out his own list. Mix them up and pass them out to be read aloud. Have the crowd guess who wrote each sequence of thoughts.

Guessing.—Are you a good guesser? Try yourself out on some of these. Then try them out on your guests. Arrange the displays and number them.

How many pins in a paper of pins?
How many beans in a quart measure?
How many peanuts in a glass quart jar?
How many seeds in a cup?
How many grains of corn in a glass tumbler?
How many matches in a box?
How much does a silver dollar measure in diameter?
How much does a paper bill measure in length and width?
How many seeds in a grapefruit? An apple?
How many stars in the United States flag?
What is the weight of an egg?
How many letters in the dictionary (displayed)? This one is a catch. Of course, there are just 26 letters in the dictionary.

Observation.—*Articles on a table*—Place twenty-five articles on a table and ask the guests to observe them for a few moments and then write down all they can remember having seen.

Wearing apparel—From three to five guests are asked to leave the room. The rest of the guests are now asked to describe the wearing apparel of the individuals who have left the room. It will be interesting to note how many people will not even know the color of the costume worn by any of the persons.

Another method for handling this observation test would be to give to each person the name of some other person present whose costume they are to describe. The descriptions are written, taken up, shuffled, and redistributed. Each person reads aloud the description given him and the group tries to guess who is being described. The group may also try to guess the writer of each description.

Picking up toothpicks.—This game is played in two ways. Fifteen toothpicks (matches, checkers, discs, rocks, or other counters) are needed. Players try to make opponents pick up the last toothpick. Those players who know the secret can always win. Where the secret is common property the game loses its appeal. It is best, therefore, to let players work out the skills of the game for themselves.

One row—Fifteen toothpicks are placed in one row. The players alternate picking up toothpicks. Not more than three may be picked up at a time. The secret—a player can make certain of winning by always arranging to leave a set-up of five for the opponent's turn. Then, if he draws one, you draw three. If he draws two, you draw two. This leaves him the last one to handle. Be sure to get six and ten in the draw.

Three rows—Arrange the toothpicks in three rows—seven in one row, five in the next, and three in the next. Again you are trying to make your opponent pick up the last toothpick. This time a player may take as many as he desires from any *one* row. For instance, he would take up all seven in the top row. That would make it easy for you, for all you would have to do then would be to take two from the second row, leaving a three and three set-up. Now, if he takes one from the top three, you take one from the bottom three. This leaves a set-up of two and two. If he takes one from the top two, you take the two left at the bottom, leaving him the last one to pick.

The winning combinations, as the game progresses, are: 6-4-2, 5-4-1, 3-2-1, 1-1-1, or when only two rows of toothpicks are left, the same number in the two rows.

Practice at it a bit, and see for yourself.

Progressive poetry.—This game can be played between three or four groups, or by any number of individuals.

Group Number One starts off with some such line as:

"The lark is singing. Hear his song?"

Group Number Two adds the following:
"He's been singing all day long;"

After a bit of thought Group Number Three adds:
"Why can't we be as gay as he?"

And Number Four has an inspiration that closes the quatrain:
"O what fools we mortals be."

Then Group Number Two has the privilege of starting another quatrain, and again each group gives a line at a time.

The game can be played orally between groups or individuals. Or the players may write their lines and pass them on to the next person or group. It makes a grand game for several people who are making a train trip together.

Living alphabet.—Two sets of alphabet letters are provided. The letters should be from three to five inches long on stiff cardboard. Two sides line up facing one another, the players arranged alphabetically. There should be a captain for each side. His business will be to arrange the players in proper position when they rush out in front of their line to spell a word. Thus, when a word is called, the players who have the letters in that word rush out in front of their line and try to spell the word by holding the letters up facing their opponents. In the excitement they are likely to assume wrong positions. It is the captain's job to arrange them correctly so that they spell the word. The leader decides which group first spells the word. Where a double letter occurs, the player holding that letter indicates that it is double by waving it pendulum fashion. Where a letter appears in two different places in the word, the player appears in the first position and then in the second.

The interest in the game may be increased by calling out questions on history, literature, geography, the Bible, and any other subject, the sides being required to spell out the answers. Note the following examples:

1. Who invented the steamboat? FULTON.
2. Who wrote "The Iliad"? HOMER.
3. What was the most famous river in the ancient world? NILE.
4. What city was the center of learning in the ancient world? ATHENS.
5. London is on what river? THAMES.
6. Who founded the Methodist Church? JOHN WESLEY.
7. Who is sometimes credited with writing Shakespeare's plays? FRANCIS BACON.
8. Who wrote "Pilgrim's Progress"? BUNYAN.
9. Who was converted on the Damascus highway? SAUL.
10. Who was spokesman for Moses? AARON.
11. Who succeeded Saul as king of Israel? DAVID.
12. Who was David's very devoted friend? JONATHAN.

The leader should be careful in making out the list of words to be spelled to include every letter in the alphabet. In case the size of the group will not permit the use of all of the letters, then make out a list of words to cover only the letters used in the game.

Spelldown.—*Sides*—The players line up in two equal sides. The head player on one side starts a word with one letter. The head player on the opposing side adds a letter, though he may have a different word in mind from that of the starter. The second player on the starting side now picks it up and adds another letter. He may have still a different word in mind. So the word is tossed back and forth from side to side until some player finishes a word or until one player challenges the opponent just preceding him. If a player finishes a word he is out. It does not matter that he has a longer word in mind. For instance, the first player says *F*. The player on the opposing side says *I*. If Number Two on the starting adds *N* he is out, for he has spelled *FIN*. The fact that he had *FINISH* in mind doesn't help him. A player is given until the leader counts ten to respond or challenge. In order to keep from finishing a word a player may add any letter he chooses whether he has a word in mind or not. If he fakes through and the next opponent does not challenge him he is safe as soon as that player adds another letter or allows himself to be counted out. If a player is challenged by the player whose next turn it is he must announce what word he is spelling. If he is spelling a good word and all of the necessary letters are there as far as the word has gone the challenger is out. If he has no legitimate word in mind he is out. Proper names do not count. A challenger signifies his intention by simply announcing, "I challenge you."

Whenever a player drops out, a new word is started by the player whose next turn it is.

Black sheep.—The game is played the same as the above except that there are no sides. The players in a circle or in rows take turns in regular order. Whenever a player finishes a word he becomes a "Black Sheep" and must say "Baa-aa-aa." Thereafter whenever it is his turn he must respond with a plaintive "Baa-aa-aa." You can imagine how it sounds when the "Black Sheep" family increases in size.

End pick-ups.—In this game a player spells any word he chooses. The next player must spell a word that begins with the last letter of the word just spelled. Thus, if the first player spelled "AND," the next must begin immediately with some word that begins with the letter *D*, such as "DENY." The next player must now spell a word beginning with *Y*, such as "YOU." And so on it goes. Words used once may not be used again.

Add-a-letter.—Each player is given a complete alphabet set with some extra vowels so that playing is made easier. The letters may be made on cards a half-inch square. Players may play as individuals or as partners. In this latter case partners would sit alternately.

One player puts down a letter, having some word in mind. The next player adds a letter, probably having some other word in mind. Suppose the first player has "Query" in mind and therefore puts down a Q. The next player thinks of "Quiz" and adds a U. The next player thinks of "Quota" and puts down an O, thinking that his partner can finish the word if the next player makes a slip and puts down a T. But the next player is alert and so he thinks of "Quorum" and adds an R. The next player can think of nothing else to add except U, and so the next player plays M and takes up all the letters in the word. Then the next player starts another word, and so it goes. At the end the partners with the largest number of letters win. A player must play in his regular turn. He cannot hold out a letter just to prevent an opponent from spelling a word. When a player cannot spell or when he cannot add a letter to the word being spelled he must cast off a letter face-up on the table. The player spelling the last word gets all the letters left on the table.

You know me.—One player starts the game by saying, "You know me. I am the Spanish explorer who discovered Florida. I spent much time seeking the fountain of youth." The player naming Ponce de Leon is given the right to name the next "You know me." Thus, a player thinks of some well-known character, past or present, and, assuming that he is that person, makes some statement that indicates his identity.

A few suggested "You-Know-Me's" are the following:

"I discovered the Mississippi." De Soto.
"I started the Red Cross idea." Clara Barton.
"I started the W.C.T.U." Frances Willard.
"I wrecked saloons with a hatchet." Carrie Nation.
"I became famous crossing plants." Luther Burbank.
"I wrote 'The Three Musketeers.'" Alexander Dumas.

Living numbers.—Two teams of from ten to thirteen players line up facing one another. Each player has a number of one digit— 1, 2, 3, 4, 5, 6, 7, 8, 9, 0—and, if desired, some extras such as an additional 1, 7, and 8. The leader can call out questions which can be answered by numbers. The players with the proper numbers rush out in front of their line and arrange themselves in order. Questions of historic dates, arithmetic problems, and other questions that can be answered by numbers are used. If the crowd is large they may be divided into two groups, each group to sponsor one of the teams. The sponsors may coach, instruct, and encourage their teams.

1. How many states in the Union? 48
2. How many men on a football team? 11
3. How many musical notes in two octaves? 15
4. How many days in the year? 365
5. When did Columbus discover America? 1492
6. When did the Pilgrims land at Plymouth? 1620
7. When was the Declaration of Independence signed?. 1776
8. When did the so-called World War end? 1918
9. How many days in September? 30
10. How many weeks in a year? 52
11. How many inches in a yard? 36

Odd or even.—This is an ancient game that can be traced back to early Greece and Rome. It is a familiar game in Europe. In the classic game the player won or lost as many counters as he had in his hand.

A small number of beans or other counters is held in the hand, fist closed. "Odd or even?" says the holder. If the guess is "Even," and the number really is odd, then the holder claims a counter from his opponent, saying, "Give me one to make it even," and vice versa. The game continues until one or the other of the players is out of counters.

The game can easily be adapted for sides, each time a different player representing his side.

Word calling.—Players are seated in a circle. The leader stands in the center, watch in hand. He points to a player and calls some letter. That player must immediately begin calling words beginning with that letter. Proper names are not allowed. He continues calling words until the period of one minute has elapsed. A count is kept of the words called. No words may be used twice. Before the minute is up the flow of words will likely come slower and slower. At the end of one minute the leader announces the number of words called, and then points to another player and calls another letter. X, Y, and Z are barred.

Example: B—bane, ball, ban, bar, bare, bear, etc.

Word snap.—The leader holds two or more sets of alphabet cards and draws one letter after calling some category, such as "birds," "fruits," "vegetables," "cities," and so forth. He holds the letter up in plain sight of the group of players. The first player to respond with an appropriate word receives the card. If no one responds within five seconds the cards is put back in the stack. The player holding the most cards at the close of the game wins. The game may be played by sides.

Initial information.—Slips of paper are prepared, one for each player. At the head of the paper are written the initials of some person who will be present. Under this is written a series of questions which the player drawing the paper is to answer. The papers are shuffled and handed out to the players, or they may be allowed to make a blind draw.

The answers must be written, in each case, beside the question, and must consist of only as many words as there are initials at the top of the sheet. These words must begin with the initials in their proper order. These words must begin with the initials in their proper order.
Example:

E. S. D.

1. To whom does this paper belong? (Ernest S. Doe.)
2. What is his character? (Easy-going, sweet, desperate.)
3. What is his present occupation? (Entertaining, sweet dumb-belles.)
4. What are his suppressed desires? (Evangelist, sculptor, Don Juan.)
5. What kind of hair has he? (Extinct, soft down.)
6. What books does he prefer? (Enlivening, slippery detective.)
7. What animals are his favorites? (Erratic, slim dachshunds.)
8. What does he think of the opposite sex? (Exquisite sweet darlings.)
9. What does he think of the world in general? (Execrable, sordid, dumb.)
10. What do you predict for his future? (Earning swell dividends.)

Our cook doesn't like peas.—One player starts the game by saying: "Our cook doesn't like peas. What can we have for dinner?" He points his finger at some player who must quickly answer with some article of food. To be acceptable the article must be one that is spelled without the letter *P*. Onions, garlic, cabbage, chocolate, celery, and the like are accepted, but if the player answers with peas, pumpkin pie, parsnips, or some other word having the letter *P* the leader will say: "I am sorry, but our cook will not prepare that." A player who answers incorrectly may be required to pay a forfeit. Or the game may be played until most of the players get the idea.

Rhyme guess.—Someone in the group begins the game by saying, for example, "I am thinking of a word that rhymes with *play*." The other players begin to guess the word by defining it instead of naming it. "Is it a fight?" "No, it is not *fray*." "Is it the opposite of night?" "No, it is not *day*." "Is it a beam of light?" "No, it is not *ray*." "Is it a vehicle?" "Yes, it is *dray*." The person guessing correctly starts a new rhyme guess.

"Buzz" baseball.—Players seat themselves or stand in baseball positions—catcher, pitcher, and so forth. The distance between bases need only be a few feet. A player from the opposing side comes to the bat. The pitcher calls a number, three, for instance. The batter calls "One." His teammates are arranged in line. The next one of them calls "Two." The third man must say "Buzz." Four, five, "Buzz." If the batting side gets through without an error, then the fielding side must take up the counting beginning with the catcher and then going to the pitcher, first baseman, and so forth. If a man on the batting side makes a mistake the batter is out and another man steps to the plate. If a man on the fielding team fails to "buzz" in the proper place the batter takes a base, and he advances one base for each mistake made. Another batter comes to the plate and the pitcher calls another number, for instance, "Two," this time. Then all the players must "buzz" on "Two" and another multiple of two. If the call goes completely around without any player making a mistake then the batter is out. Three outs and the fielding side comes to the bat. It must be noted that any number in which the call number appears as well as multiples of the number count as an error. For instance, when "Three" is called "Thirteen" is a "Buzz" number.

Players must count rapidly so that the game does not drag. The umpire may allow a batter a base if there is unnecessary delay in the field. On the other hand, he may call the batter out for unnecessary slowness on the part of the team at the bat. It is up to the umpire to keep the game moving rapidly.

Bird, fish, or animal.—Players seat themselves in a circle. One player stands in the center, and, suddenly pointing to some player, shouts, "Bird, fish, or animal!" Then he calls the name of one of these classes and immediately begins counting to ten. The player to whom he points must name some bird, fish, or animal, according to the class designated by the caller, before the caller can count ten. Example: The caller shouts: "Bird, fish, or animal! Bird!" The person to whom he points must name some bird before ten is counted. It is not as easy as it sounds. In the hurry to make the proper answer in the allotted time a player is likely to get his categories mixed. Repetition of anything previously named is not allowable. The use of the word "cat" is barred because there is a catbird, a catfish, and a cat.

It.—This is an old-timer that is plenty of fun where there are still people that do not know it. One or more persons, not familiar with the game, are invited to go out of the room. The rest decide that "It" is always the person to the right. One at a time, the persons who were sent out of the room come back and try by questioning to discover who or what "It" is. One question only may be asked of a player, and they must be questions that can be answered by "Yes" or "No." The answers they get will be very confusing, and the crowd will be greatly amused by the bewildered expression on the face of the questioner.

Example—"Is 'It' human?" "Yes, I think so." "Is 'It' a man?" "No." "Is 'It' a woman?" "No." "Is 'It' in this part of the room?" "Yes."

Telegrams.—Guests are asked to write ten-word telegrams. The catch is that the words of the telegram must begin with the letters of some ten-letter word announced by the leader. It will add to the interest if the messages are between widely different and incompatible people, such as Caspar Milquetoast and "Dizzy" Dean or Benito Mussolini, or Charlie McCarthy and Lord Chamberlain. Some suggested ten-letter words are: impossible, refractory, patriotism, commentary, combustion, Bolshevism.

Kings.—What king is (1) the most powerful king? WOR-KING; (2) the laziest king? SHIR-KING; (3) a king who is hard on athletes? SMO-KING; (4) the jolliest? JO-KING; (5) the quietest? THIN-KING; (6) the thirstiest? DRIN-KING; (7) the slyest? WIN-KING; (8) the noisiest? TAL-KING; (9) the most nervous? SHA-KING; (10) the most counterfeit? FA-KING; (11) the most furtive? SNEA-KING or SLIN-KING; (12) the best hunter? STAL-KING. Try your own hand at making kings. There are plenty of them, such as sinking, peeking, poking, cranking, checking, ducking, bucking, hiking, nicking, raking, creaking, squeaking, stacking, staking, baking, streaking, speaking, seeking, and so on and on.

How do you like it?—One player goes out of the room. The others decide on some one thing. The player returns. He has the privilege of asking any player three questions, which must be answered truthfully. How do you like it? Where do you like it? When do you like it? In this way he tries to get information that will help him guess what the group has in mind.

Quiz baseball.—Here is a game that can be used at the picnic or the party, with a small group or a larger one. Sides are chosen or designated. Players come to the bat as in regular baseball. The umpire, or leader shoots a question at the batter. If he answers correctly, he makes a hit and gets on base. Then another batter comes up. A side completes its inning at the bat when it has missed three questions.

Questions are designated as singles, doubles, triples, or home runs according to their difficulty. Extremely easy questions might be designated as "double-play balls," in which case, if there are men on the bases, two outs are made if the batter answers incorrectly. The leader should work out his list of questions carefully, evaluating them as singles, doubles, etc., according to the ability of his group. A few suggested questions are offered here. Others may be gleaned from the various quizzes in this chapter. When an umpire calls a question he indicates its value by announcing: "This question is a 'single' (or 'double,' or 'triple' or 'home run')," as the case may be.

1. How long is a fortnight? (Single.)
2. What aviator is called "The Lone Eagle" (Single.)
3. What is the largest ocean in the world? (Double.)
4. Who threw his cloak over a mud puddle for his queen? (Single.)
5. Do fish close their eyes when they sleep? Give the reason for your answer. (Single, if only first part is answered correctly; triple, if reason is correct.)
6. Who sold his birthright for a mess of pottage? (Single.)
7. What animal is King of Beasts? (Single; double play if missed.)
8. Who wrote a collection of maxims called "Poor Richard's Almanac"? (Double.)
9. What colors would you mix to make orange? (Double.)
10. How long did Rip Van Winkle sleep? (Double.)
11. What was the first permanent English settlement in America? (Double.)
12. Who was the father of Pocahontas? (Home run.)

13. How many senators are elected from each state? (Double.)
14. What Carthaginian general crossed the Alps with his army?
    (Home run.)
15. Why does a cowboy wear chaparajos, or chaps? (Triple.)
16. What sea animal has eight arms or tentacles? (Single.)
17. In what athletic game is a puck used? (Single.)
18. In what athletic game is a "pigskin" used? (Single; double
    play if missed.)
19. What is an unbranded calf called? (Triple.)
20. Who said "Am I my brother's keeper?" (Single.)
21. How many letters are there in the English alphabet? (Single.)
22. Who looked just like Tweedledum? (Single.)
23. What animal in America carries her baby in a pouch, like the
    kangaroo? (Home run.)
24. What year followed 1 B.C.? (Single.)
25. What Athenian drank a cup of hemlock? (Triple.)
26. What boy in a story would not grow up? (Single.)
27. What animal is called the Ship of the Desert? (Single.)
28. In the Bible, whose wife turned into a pillar of salt? (Single.)
29. Does a rabbit run faster uphill or downhill? Give the reason
    for your answer. (Single, if the first part is answered; home
    run, if the reason is given.)
30. What is a dogie? (Triple.)
31. Where did the Incas live? (Double.)
32. Who said "Give me liberty or give me death"? (Single; dou-
    ble play is missed.)
33. How many legs has a spider? (Triple.)
34. What is a baby pigeon called? (Single.)
35. What inventor was called the "Wizard of Menlo Park"?
    (Triple.)
36. What is a doe? (Double.)
37. People of what profession take the oath of Hippocrates?
    (Triple.)
38. What famous pianist and composer was once Premier of Po-
    land? (Single.)
39. How do frogs drink? (Double.)
40. What mythical giant held the world on his shoulders? (Sin-
    gle.)
41. What is the Mohammedan Bible? (Double.)
42. What President said, "All that I am or hope to be I owe to
    my angel mother"? (Single.)
43. Who wrote *Tom Sawyer?* (Single.)

44. What famous German composer was deaf during the last years of his life?　(Double.)
45. In the Bible who had a coat of many colors?　(Single.)
46. What is the oldest city in the United States?　(Double.)
47. Who wrote *Treasure Island?*　(Double.)
48. What is the largest desert in the world?　(Single.)
49. What is a broncho?　(Double.)
50. Do birds have teeth?　(Single.)

For an ordinary game the umpire would need at least one hundred questions.　When a question is missed it is not necessary to continue calling it until it is answered.　It might be good technique to save it for use later in the game, coming back to it occasionally until it is answered correctly.

Answers—1. Two weeks.　2. Charles A. Lindbergh.　3. Pacific.　It is more than twice as large as the Atlantic.　4. Sir Walter Raleigh.　5. No. They have no eyelids.　6. Esau.　7. Lion.　8. Benjamin Franklin.　9. Red and yellow.　10. Twenty years.　11. Jamestown, Virginia.　12. Powhatan.　13. Two.　14. Hannibal.　15. To protect his legs against cactus, briars, etc.　16. An octopus.　17. Ice hockey.　18. Football.　19. Maverick.　20. Cain.　21. Twenty-six.　22. Tweedledee.　23. An opossum.　24. 1 A.D.　25. Socrates.　26. Peter Pan.　27. A camel.　28. Lot's.　29. Uphill, because his front legs are shorter than his hind ones.　30. A motherless calf.　31. In Peru.　32. Patrick Henry.　33. Eight.　34. Squab.　35. Thomas A. Edison.　36. A female deer.　37. The medical profession.　38. Ignace Jan Paderewski.　39. Through their skins and not through their mouths.　40. Atlas.　41. The Koran.　42. Abraham Lincoln.　43. Mark Twain (Samuel L. Clemens).　44. Ludwig van Beethoven.　45. Joseph.　46. St. Augustine, Florida.　47. Robert Louis Stevenson.　48. Sahara.　49. A half-wild unbroken pony.　50. No.

Poetic anagrams.—In playing this game the idea is to fill in the spaces with words, all of which have the same letters in them though in different order.

1. *Landlord*
Landlord, fill the flowing (1),
Until the (2) run over;
Tonight we (3) upon the (4),
Tomorrow go to Dover.

You might tip off the guessers to the fact that each word is a four-letter word.

Answers— (1) *pots,* (2) *tops,* (3) *stop,* (4) *post.*

2. *Old Lady*

A (1) old lady, with (2) intent,
Put on her (3) , and away she went;
"Oh (4) ," she cried, "give me today
Something on which to (5) , I pray."

You might offer some tips, such as to suggest that (3) is a bit of lady's wearing apparel, infrequently worn, or that (4) is a man's name.

Answers— (1) *vile,* (2) *evil,* (3) *veil,* (4) *Levi,* (5) *live.*

STORYTELLING STUNTS

Spinning yarns.—A ball of yarn is made up of short pieces of yarn or string. The storytellers sit in a circle. One player starts the story and keeps going until he comes to the end of his string. The story is one of his own choosing and may be entirely original. As he comes to the end of his string he passes the ball to the right, and that player takes up the story, adding his bit and surrendering the ball to the player at his right. The story may be a bit disjointed, and there may be ridiculous sequences, but that will only add to the fun.

Feather pass.—The leader starts a story and then hands a feather or ball to some other player. That player must take up the story and then pass the feather or ball on to some other player. The storyteller may choose any player in the group to take up the story. Each storyteller must complete at least one sentence before handing the feather to another person. Or it may be required that he carry the story on for at least thirty seconds.

A joke-telling festival.—As part of a fireside or campfire program this would make an interesting feature. Have certain persons primed to start the fun with some good stories.

A whopper or Paul Bunyan festival.—Whoppers of the Paul Bunyan variety would make an unusual evening of fun. One group conducted such a program around the campfire after a short hike and picnic. They advertised it as "A Liars' Convention."

Embarrassing moments.—The stories could be built around such a theme as "Life's Most Embarrassing Moment" or "My Most Exciting Adventure." For the first half of the program participants would be confined to the telling of actual experiences. For the last half of the program let imagination run in whatever direction it will.

Fox and Geese.—Seventeen geese represented by checkers, marbles, pebbles, pegs, or cardboard counters, try to pen up a fox, represented by a counter that is distinguished from the geese by color or size or material. The field consists of thirty-three spots or holes, marked on sheets of paper or cardboard, or made in a wooden base or in the ground, thus:

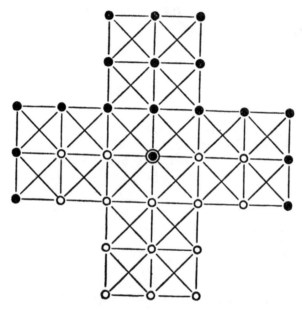

Place the fox in the center. The geese are placed at every point in the three top rows and at the end of the fourth and fifth rows. One player moves the fox, while the other player maneuvers the geese.

The fox has the first move. He tries to maneuver into such a position as to make it possible to jump the geese as in checkers, and thus capture them. He can jump backward and forward, up, down, and across. The geese cannot jump. They may move in any direction one space at a time. The fox is not forced to jump, but jumps only when he desires to do so. However, each player must make a move each time. The geese try to pen the fox so that he cannot move.

Pick-a-letter.—Some player closes his eyes. He then touches a printed or mimeographed page with a pencil point. The letter on which, or nearest which, the point rests indicates the chosen letter. The player then names one or more of the following classes which begin with that letter: quadruped, fish, bird, flower, tree, mineral, insect, country, river, city, lake, ruler, author, scientist, philosopher, book, drama, poem, poet, prophet, hero, saint, invention, fictional or dramatic character, character or book of the Bible. Try it out yourself.

Seven-come-eleven.—The players stand or sit in a circle. A leader stands at center. He points to someone in the circle and calls a number. Immediately that person must answer with the situation or event that first comes to his mind. For example, if the leader calls "Seven," the answer may be "Come eleven," or the answer may be "Dwarfs." For "Three," the answer could be "Little pigs," or "Is a crowd," or "Bears." For "Four," one might shout "Horsemen of the Apocalypse." Other suggestions: "1492," "Columbus discovered America"; "1776," "Declaration of Independence"; "Ten," "Nights in a barroom," or "Pins," or "And you are out"; "Five," "Basketball team"; "Six," "Man football," or "Pick up sticks"; "Eight," "O'clock coffee"; "Nine," "Baseball," or "Innings," or "Lives"; "Sixteen," "Sweet"; "1918," "Armistice."

Called-letter crosswords.—Each player is given a sheet of paper and a pencil. He draws a square and divides it up so that there are five small squares horizontally and five vertically. Thus there are twenty-five small squares in the large square.

Some player now calls a letter of the alphabet. Each player places the letter in one of the small squares. The player uses his own judgment about where to place a letter. However when a letter is placed it may not be removed and put elsewhere. When a player has located the called letter he says, "Right." After all players have called "Right," the next player calls a letter. He may call any letter he chooses, being allowed even to repeat a letter that has just been called. Again each player puts the called letter down in one of the vacant squares. This continues until twenty-five letters have been called, thus filling each one of the small squares.

Each player tries to arrange his letters so as to spell as many words as possible. The words may be spelled either horizontally or vertically. Proper names are not permitted to count. The letters in a word must be consecutively arranged. Points are allowed as follows: For a word of five letters, five points; for a word of four letters, three points; for a word of three letters, one point. No points are allowed for a word of two letters. Short words within longer ones do not count. Thus "T-H-I-N-E" could not count as "in," and "thin," and "thine." Five points would be allowed for "thine."

Famous names.—A letter is announced and each person jots down all of the famous people of whom he can think whose names begin with that letter. It is permissible to use first names. Characters in history, fiction, the Bible, prominent people, political figures, statesmen, athletes, movie stars, and the like may be listed. A timekeeper should be appointed and a time limit set. The game may confine its attention to a particular classification, such as athletes, Bible characters, historic names, etc.

Traveler.—One player who is "It" stops before another player, points his finger, and announces, for instance, "I am going to Chicago." The player before whom he has stopped must call the names of three things before "It" can count to ten. All three of these things must begin with the first letter of the announced destination of the traveler, for example, "Candy, cigars, and carrots." If he fails he takes the traveler's place.

Snip!—The players stand or sit in a circle. One player who is "It" tosses a knotted handkerchief and calls out some word of three letters. Immediately he starts counting to twelve. The player who receives the handkerchief must respond with three words that begin with the letters in the called word before the center player can finish his count—"ten, eleven, twelve, snip." For instance, if "It" calls "Din," the player who receives the handkerchief may shout, "Dinner, India, Now." He must get out the last word before "It" can shout "Snip."

How, when, where.—One player leaves the room. The rest decide on some one thing, such as, a "flashlight." The player is recalled and he tries to discover what the group has in mind. He may ask just three questions: "How do you like it?" "When do you like it?" and "where do you like it?" Maybe the answer to the first question is "Light and bright," to the second, "At night," and to the third, "In camp." The word selected must be a noun.

CHAPTER X
FUN OUTDOORS

Chapter X

FUN OUTDOORS

Hikes, Camps, Campfires, Picnics, Active Games, Water Games

"Follow the trail to the open air,
　　Alone with the hills and sky,
With a pack on your back and never a care,
　　Letting the days slip by.
Healing fragrance of pines in the dark
　　Glow from the camper's fire;
Starlight and shadows and music of waves,
　　While the gray smoke curls higher.
Follow the trail to the open air,
　　Letting the days slip by.
A smile on your lips and a song in your heart,
　　One with the hills and sky."
　　　　　　　　　　—Agatha Deming

Hikes

"It's the far Northland that's a-calling me away,
　As take I with my knapsack to the road,
It's the call on me of the forest in the north
　As step I with the sunlight for my load
On the trail a-windin' deep into the forest, I will go,
Where you see the loon and hear its plaintive wail,
If you're thinkin' in your inner heart there's swagger in my step,
Then you've never been along the border trail.
It's the far Northland that's a-calling me away.
As take I with my knapsack to the road."

A happy singing, hiking group swinging along a wooded lane or a border trail is a sight to warm the cockles of the heart. There's "swagger" in the step and a song in the heart. It's the joy of the open road!

A hobo hike.—This invitation suggests that everyone come dressed in ragged clothes:

"Hello, Bo! Better go on a hike you will like.
Wear old clothes; we're hoboes. Get me, Steve?
Gonna leave from this dive prompt at five."

The hoboes visit at back doors of certain designated homes where they get "hand-outs."

(351)

At the campfire a hobo convention is held. Reports are made by committees as to the largest, hungriest, etc. Other committees that may report are as follows: Committee on Complaints, Committee on the Good of the Order, and the Committee on Extension of Rest. An experience meeting can be held at which time imagination runs rife. A joke-telling contest may climax the fun.

A Captain Kidd hike.—This couplet may be used on a poster or special invitation card, along with the picture of a treasure chest or skull and crossbones:

> We're not kidding old Captain Kidd;
> We're going to find the treasure he hid.

Directions along the way indicate the route of the hike. These should be written in red ink on slips of paper decorated with skull and crossbones. They are nailed to trees, stuck on bushes, placed under rocks, and tacked on fences. The instructons may be written in verse or code, or a combination of both. For instance

> When you get to the forks of the road,
> Look for the tree where you'll find our code.

When discovered, the directions here may be written in dog Latin, "Ogay otay ethay eftlay," which every good dog-Latin scholar knows is "Go to the Left." At another point the group may be instructed to "Obey Horace Greeley." Someone will be sure to remember that Mr. Greeley said, "Go west, young man." Directions may instruct the group to sing a song, play a game, change partners, or shake hands all around. Finally the group reaches a point where they are told to dig for the treasure. It is contained in a box adorned with skull and crossbones. The box, when opened, was found to contain peanuts, or other refreshments, or trinkets of various sorts, at least one for each person.

A camera hike.—Hikers take snapshots along the way. They should be instructed to get several kinds of pictures, such as still life (landscapes, trees, flowers, houses), animal life (birds, fowls, dogs, horses), and persons (in groups or single), or the picture taking may be confined to a single kind of picture—trees, for instance. They should also be instructed to have an eye for the artistic, the humorous, and the unique. At the end of the hike have a picnic. After the pictures are developed have a Kodak Party. See the one outlined in this book.

Photography treasure hunt.—Here is an unusual kind of treasure hunt that some groups are finding intriguing. Couples go out on photographic expeditions much after the fashion of the scavenger hunt. Each has a camera and flash lamps. They are instructed to get pictures of "Tired Feet," "Cover the Water Front," "A Pullman Porter," etc. The hunters are to return at a specified time (usually an hour or two is given them). Someone develops the films while the others play games and dine. The pictures are then put on display. A Kodak Klub with some experienced camera fans can get a great thrill out of an evening's entertainment of this sort.

Hare and hound hike.—A small committee gets a half-hour start of the rest of the crowd from some designated point. This committee is supplied with an abundance of confetti or something else to mark the trail. Their destination is kept a secret, of course, and it should not be too easy for the second group to find. The committee has the "eats" so there is reason for group two to persevere in finding them. The trail should be clearly indicated by the confetti or whatever else is chosen. The committee should have a fire built and lunch ready by the time the second crowd arrives.

Observation hike.—Divide the crowd into two or more groups. Groups are told to hike to a designated point, where they are to report what they have seen along the way. Each group will take a different route. One point is allowed for every unusual object or incident seen, such as birds fighting, a man with whiskers, girls without lipstick or rouge, man fixing a puncture, squirrel and bird fighting, etc.

Treasure hunts.—Treasure hunts are always popular. They may be conducted as hikes, the group getting a map at the beginning or finding instructions along the way. Or the treasure hunt may be made in cars. One group, following this latter plan, used advertising slogans as cues for the hunters. For instance, the first instructions said simply, "Cheer up!" Everyone knew that was the advertising slogan of a well-known laundry. They went there and found their instructions in an envelope. "Say it with flowers!" To a prominent florist shop they went. Slogan after slogan, carried them about the city until at last the treasure was found. All cars were instructed that if they lost the trail they should report at a designated point after a certain hour.

A surprise hike.—Along the route arrange surprises of all sorts. At one point noise-making toys may be handed out to each hiker. At another spot some unusual sight is arranged. About midway the group should be delightfully surprised to find a bucket or tub of ice-cold lemonade. At the end of the trail there might be some unusually pleasant company, some attractive decorations, some program surprises, and some food surprises.

A lantern hike party.—Here is a beautiful evening hike for young people. Each couple is asked to bring a Japanese lantern, equipped with a candle. The committee should have ready forked sticks two and a half or three feet long, one for each couple. Or lanterns may be furnished for every four or five couples.

1. Lanterns are lighted and placed on the forked sticks. Thus they are carried by the hikers, who march two by two.

2. They hike to a spot that has previously been decorated with Japanese lanterns, if that proves practical.

3. The hikers push the forked sticks into the ground, forming a circle of lighted lanterns. This marks the play space for the games.

4. Games:

(1) *Pass the lantern relay*—Two sides of about five couples each. Head player on each side has a lantern on a forked stick. Each of the other players has a forked stick. At the signal to start the head player passes the lighted lantern from his forked stick to the forked stick of the next player. Thus it continues until the lantern has reached the end of the line.

(2) *Candle race*—Each runner carrying a lighted candle. If a candle snuffs out the player must go back and start over.

(3) *Blow and light relay*—The first player runs and blows out a candle. Runs back and "touches off" teammate. This teammate runs to the candle and relights it. So it continues until each player has run.

(4) *Blowing out lighted candle* blindfolded.

(5) *Dumb crambo, or charades*—"The light dawns."

(6) *"Jack's alive"*—"Light's out!" Corks on long sticks are burned in the campfire until they become red coals. They must then be passed to the right from player to player. The player must blow on the cork. If he gets a spark he calls "Jack's alive!" and passes it on to the next player. If he can get no spark "Jack is dead" and the player to his left has the privilege of making one smut mark on his face, using the burnt cork for purpose.

(7) *Songs*—"Long, Long Trail," "Let the Lower Lights Be Burn-

ing," and "Follow the Gleam," followed by "Taps" and the benediction.

> "Fading light dims the sight,
> And a star gems the sky, gleaming bright,
> From afar drawing nigh,
> Falls the night."

Note: In lieu of this program the hike may be climaxed by a
storytellers' convention, or a sing, or dramatics.

A book hike.—Some groups would enjoy an afternoon hike to
some shady nook, there to read together and discuss some good book.
Some good biography like Gamaliel Bradford's *Lee, the American;*
or a good play like *Green Pastures,* or Drinkwater's *Abraham Lincoln,* or Barrie's *Alice Sit by the Fire,* or Kennedy's *Servant in the
House,* or Jerome's *The Passing of the Third Floor Back;* or some of
John Masefield's poems, such as *Dauber, The Hounds of Hell, The
Widow in the Bye Street, Enslaved,* and *The Everlasting Mercy,* or
the poems of Riley, or Guest, or others; or maybe something humorous like *Pigs Is Pigs* and *Goat Feathers,* by Ellis Parks Butler. Any
of these would make a mighty interesting afternoon for many groups.

Another hare and hound hike.—This is a good one for camp. The
crowd is divided into two groups. Group One is given five minutes
to get started on a twenty-minute hike that leads wherever the leader
of the group chooses. This leader leaves one-foot-square sheets of
newspaper at head height every hundred feet. Group Two starts in
pursuit following the trail marked by newspapers. If Group One
gets home without Group Two seeing any of its members, it is considered winner. Otherwise Group Two wins.

Nature hikes.—There are numerous possibilities in nature hikes
where someone can go along who knows something about birds, or
trees, or flowers, or insects. A tree hike could be lots of fun. A
"Star Dust Trail" would make a good hike for a clear evening. Hike
to some interesting open space. There different constellations could
be identified. Star legends would add to the interest.

Hiking hints.—(1) Dress appropriately. Dress-up clothes and high-
heel shoes are taboo on a hike. (2) Keep the hiking group together
as much as possible. Discourage racing. Much of the social value
of the hike is lost if the group gets too scattered. (3) In mountainous and hill countries make frequent stops for rest. (4) At stops
occasionally provide for some quiet recreation—a story, a brain-

teaser, the swapping of stories and jokes, a song, tricks, social games, some nature lore or historical information. (5) Don't drink water along the way unless you know it has been tested and found pure. Better, carry along your own drinking water. (6) Don't destroy animal and plant life.

Picnic pointers—

1. Plan carefully the necessary details—selection and securing of place, transportation, food arrangements, entertainment plans (games, stunts, stories, etc.), clean-up.

2. Arrange numerous things for the entire group to do together. Conserve the social values of the picnic. Use games in which everyone plays, group singing, stories, etc.

3. Clean up the grounds after you are through. Burn all trash.

4. Put out whatever fire you have had. Scatter the embers. Do not leave any sparks.

For steak and fish frys, bacon bats, clam bakes, and bean holes be sure to have someone in charge who knows the art of outdoor cookery.

The picnic kit.—A picnic kit would be a handy bit of equipment for use in outings. The canvas bag should contain two softballs, two baseballs, a volleyball or playball or two, several bats, one dozen bean bags, a badminton set, deck tennis equipment, a six-inch rubber ball for zone ball and punch ball, a set of regulation horseshoes or quoits and pegs, and a tennis court liner which will come in handy for marking boundaries and circles for various games such as captain ball, zone ball, boundary ball, bombardment, and the like. Darts and dart games, bean-bag boards and other equipment games described in Chapter II, "Fun in the Clubroom," will come in handy. If all of this equipment cannot be gotten at once, get what you can, and add to it from time to time.

The Weaver Scholastic Ball, made by C. D. Webb Company, Lebanon, Pa., comes in various sizes, 5, 7, 8½, 10, and 12½ inches. It has a patented valve, and makes a good playball.

W. J. Voit, Los Angeles, Calif., also makes a good patented valve playball in the same sizes.

SPECIAL PICNIC PLANS

Mystery picnic.—Only a few members of the committee know the plans for the picnic. Even the destination is kept a secret. If some surprise in transportation can be provided, such as a truck straw-ride, so much the better. Ice-cold lemonade served from coffeepot, sandwiches done up in surprise packages, mysterious announcements and music coming from a cleverly concealed public address system, some sleight-of-hand stunts by a magician, a Punch and Judy show featuring toy balloon and paper bag puppets, and a treasure hunt are some of the interesting possibilities for such a picnic.

Bean-hole picnic.—A hole is dug in the ground. The bottom is lined with large stones. A hot fire is built and allowed to burn for a half hour or so. A pot of beans, tightly covered, is placed on the red coals and the whole is covered with stones and dirt. This is left alone for four or five hours. The pot is then uncovered and the beans served in tin cups.

Picnic roasts.—Corn roasts, potato roasts, and oyster roasts offer fine possibilities. Anyone who has enjoyed the fun of roasting and eating a big sweet potato knows what fun it is. Well, anyway, a boy would enjoy it because he wouldn't mind getting the char on his hands and face.

A peasant festival picnic.—Feature folk songs and games of other lands. Do some of the numbers in costume. Encourage all who come to attend in some colorful costume.

Other picnic plans.—See The Tree Picnic, The Hiram and Mirandy Party, The Hobo Party, and other outdoor party ideas for use on picnic occasions.

Picnic Games

Bat Ball
Badminton
Beanbag Board
Beanbag Basketball
Beanbag or Washer Baseball
Bear and Guard
Bombardment
Bottle Ball
Boundary Ball
Center Dodge
Center Pitch
Clock Golf
Dodge Ball
Goofy Golf
Goosey Goosey Gander
Hand Tennis
Human Ring Toss
Human Bingo
Indian Baseball

On the Pond
Kick Ball
Musical Games like "Daisy" and "Ach Ja"
Parlor Volleyball
Punch Ball
Sack Baseball
Safety Zone Ball
Score Ball
Spud
Stop Ball
Stock Exchange
Stop Tag
Square Tag
Sidewalk Tennis
Spot Ball
Triangle Ball
"Two Hundred or Bust"
Tunnel Race

See Chapter XI, Fun with Sports, and Chapter VI, Fun with Active Games.

OTHER PICNIC STUNTS

Women's nail-driving contest.—Some of the women will surprise you with their skill with the hammer. Others—well, that's the fun of it.

Sack race.—Each runner wears a burlap sack up to the hips, holding the sack with his hands. This is an old one but it is always a lot of fun.

Three-legged race.—Tie the right leg of one runner to the left leg of a teammate. Allow the teams to practice a bit before the race. There is some skill necessary to do a good job of three-legged running.

Spoke relay.—Ten or more players to a team. Players lie flat on their backs, feet pointing to the center of a circle about fifteen or twenty feet in diameter. Player Number One starts, leaping over each teammate in turn. When he has completed the circle he drops flat in his original position. This is necessary for as soon as he passes teammate Number Two that player gets up and follows him. Thus each runner must flop immediately he has finished in order to allow the other players to jump over him. The first team with all men to complete the circle and assume the original prostrate position wins.

Tag games.—Straight Tag, Cross Tag, Chain Tag, Pom Pom Pullaway, Goosey Goosey Gander, Cat and Rat, Maze Tag, Squirrel in a Nest, Drop the Handkerchief, Three Deep, Couple Tag, Black and White Tag, Crows and Cranes, True and False Tag, and Safety Tag games.

Couple tag.—Couples link arms. A chaser and runner weave in and out among the couples. The runner can save himself by linking arms with either player of any couple. The other player of the couple must leave, becoming the runner immediately. The fun comes when there are frequent changes in runners. When the runner is tagged he becomes the chaser.

Crows and cranes.—Two equal groups. A field fifty to ninety feet long. At either end is safety zone. The teams advance to a middle line, facing one another. One team represents the Cranes, the other the Crows. If the leader calls "Cr-r-r-r-anes," the Cranes must dash for their safety zone. The Crows pursue them and each Crane tagged must become a Crow. Of course, if the leader calls "Cr-r-r-rows," the Crows are liable to be tagged.

Black and white tag.—Played exactly as Crows and Cranes, except that the leader tosses a shell or disk up in the air. If it comes down, white side up, for instance, the Whites must dash for safety with the Blacks in pursuit. Sometimes a hat is used. If it lands crown up, one side runs for safety, while if crown down, the other side is pursued.

True and false tag.—Another safety zone game. This time the leader calls out statements which are true or false. If the statement is false, the False team races for its goal. If true, the True team is chased. It can readily be seen that the players need to be alert and informed. The leader says, "Montpelier is the capital of Vermont." This is the signal for the "Trues" to dash for "home." Should the leader call "Chicago is the capital of Illinois" or "Helen of Troy was a Queen of England" the "False" team would run.

Back to back tag.—Players arrange themselves by couples back to back. Each time the leader blows a whistle players must change partners. If there is an extra player, there will be one player left out each time.

Variations— (1) Have three players stand back to back, or as nearly back to back as they can. (2) Have players turn, face, hold hands, and get acquainted whenever the leader blows two blasts on the whistle.

Loose caboose.—Groups of three to six players. Each player in a group lines up behind one player who is the "engine," holding one another around the waist or arms. One or more extra players are left out of formation. These are the "loose cabooses." They try to catch on to end of the various "trains." When a "caboose" is successful, the "engine" of that group becomes the "loose caboose."

Spoke tag.—Groups of five to six players stand single file facing center. One player is "It." That player walks around the outside of the spoke and tags the outside player of some one spoke. That player taps the player in front of him on the back. And so it is passed to the last player in that spoke. As soon as he is tagged he yells "Hike!" All players, "It" included, run swiftly around the outside of the spoke until they have completed the circuit. They line up single file in whatever order they return. The last player back is "It," in turn.

Variation—Require each player to perform some stunt before completing the circuit, such as "Circle that tree," "Shake hands with Mr. Brown," "Spin around five times, hand on top of head."

SAFETY TAG GAMES

Safety tag games are those tag games where a player is safe as long as he meets certain requirements. The following are a few of the safety type:

Hindu tag.—No player may be tagged as long as he is on his knees, forehead touching the ground.

Nose and toe tag.—A player is exempt from being tagged as long as he holds his nose with one hand and one of his feet with the other.

Other such safety tag games require the player to touch wood, stone, stand on one foot, squat, stand in someone's shadow, or assume some striking pose.

For other tag games see Chapter VI, "Fun with Active Games."

DELECTABLE OUTING TREATS

Carrigan goulash.—1 can tomato soup, 1 pound steak, 1 onion chopped fine, butter size of egg. Put butter in frying pan over the fire. When melted add onion and fry brown. Add steak and cook well done. Pour in soup and allow it to simmer. For delicious hot sandwiches this is hard to beat.

Meal-on-a-stick or Kabobs.—A quarter pound of meat, half a potato, and half an onion for each person. Cut meat into inch squares, the onions lengthwise, and the potato in thin slices. Using a stick as a skewer, pierce first a piece of meat, then a piece of onion, then a slice of potato. Repeat until all is on the stick. Cook over the live coals, turning constantly. It would help to dip in some kind of cooking oil, such as Mazola or Wesson or peanut oil, before cooking.

Cheese dreams.—Sliced American cheese and bread. Spear on forked green stick and toast. Or drop into very hot bacon fat and fry quickly.

Tongue sandwiches.—Shred contents of can of cooked tongue. Add two tablespoons of chopped dill pickles, three tablespoons of mayonnaise. White, whole wheat, or rye bread.

Sardine sandwiches.—Remove bones of sardines and mash to paste. Add two tablespoons of chili sauce, a few drops of lemon juice, salt and cayenne pepper to taste. Add enough olive oil or melted butter to make it easy to spread between thin slices of buttered bread.

Vienna sausage sandwiches.—Slice canned Vienna sausage lengthwise and arrange on buttered bread. Mix six hard-boiled egg yolks with enough cream to moisten. Add one-half teaspoon of dry mustard, a dash of paprika, and a teaspoon of chili sauce. Spread on the sausage. Sprinkle with chopped whites of eggs and cover with buttered bread.

CAMPING

Camping is becoming increasingly popular as a recreational agency for all ages. It has become so popular, in fact, that the Day Camping idea has spread with amazing rapidity. This development came about as a result of concern for those who have no opportunity to go camping. Therefore Day Camps, using much the same kind of program as the regular camp, have been set up in many places. The group goes out to a park or camp for the day. There they conduct activities common to camp life. The campers return to their homes at night. In some instances the camping program, with some limitations, has been carried out in a gymnasium or hall. (For books on camping see the bibliography.)

CAMPFIRES

Special campfire programs.— (1) An Indian Pow Wow or Council. (2) Singing—camp songs, folk songs, stunt songs; acting out of songs; special numbers. (3) Stories—Storytellers' Convention, Paul Bunyan or Whopper Night, Fairy Tale Night. (4) Dramatic stunts—Historical Night, Story Dramatizations, Song Dramatizations, Charade Night. (5) Game Night. (6) Ceremonials—The Council, Fire-Lighting Ceremony, Candle-Lighting Ceremonies, World Friendship Night.

PROGRAM FOR COUNCIL FIRE
By M. H. Hoffman

1. *Call to Council*—This should be a call that is unique and used for no other assembly. The more "woodcrafty," or "Indian," or "campy" it is, the better. Drums, tom-toms, cowbell, fox horn, trumpet shell, etc.

2. *Entrance to Council Ring*—If there is a Council Ring, entrance should be only by recognition by the "Chief" if he is already within the ring; otherwise, not. But at no time should anyone cut across the Council Ring area. Always walk around the circle that is the outside limit of the inside area.

3. *Signal for silence*—In a properly organized Council silence is an essential part of the decorum. A Council Fire is an organized procedure, not a hit-or-miss affair. Certain formalities and decorum at certain points will in no way inhibit informality, spontaneity, and freedom at other proper points. Securing absolute silence at the beginning brings the group into coherence and co-operation. It also has the value of adding a certain mystic quality to the occasion. The Chief then says, "My friends, we are about to hold a council." Various types of opening sentences may be used, of course.

4. *Lighting of the fire*—Whether it be by matches or by friction, silence is usually observed during this mystic process so significant in the past history of mankind. Special types of fires may be built, as suggested in any woodcraft manual. Do not overlook altar and platform fires. Special types of firelighting may be introduced ranging from the bizarre "fire from heaven" on a wire, chemical stunts, etc., to firelighting with ritualistic dances. With careful planning a very high note may be struck here.

5. *Firelighting song* (sung as the flames arise) —

> Wah - ta - ho - ta - ho! Wah - ta - ho - ta - ho!
> Come (Ye Campers),
> Drums are calling thee:
> Come (Ye Campers),
> Fire is greeting thee.
> Join our Circle,
> Let us merry be.
> Council gathers,
> Let our hearts be free!
> Wah - ta - ho - ta - ho!

Music: Suni Sunrise Call. Words adapted from Camp Sequoyah, Asheville, North Carolina, opening song.

6. *Words from the chief*—This is NOT a speech but at times it may

be well for the chief to "Set the tone" of the program for the night by a few well chosen words. In the beginning of the season a few words as to the meaning of fire in the life of primitive man, the significance of the democratic "round table" circle, the mystery of fire and the dark, etc.

7. *Song* (old favorite type) —The question of camp and council fire songs is a whole subject in itself. Having a song of the "old favorite type" at this time, such as "Long, Long Trail," "Carry Me Back to Old Virginny," "My Old Kentucky Home," etc., will perhaps call for a pretty general participation, as it is well known. This will tend to make the group articulate and unified. However, some old favorites have been sung to death and may make a stifled, boresome event. Avoid such. Avoid also the use of current popular music. This will kill all "atmosphere" of mystery, adventure, perhaps of beauty, because of the associations of such music with the hectic pulse of town life. Let your songs have associations that build up the "woodcraft" or "outdoor" and mystic atmosphere, and not the atmosphere of the radio, the movie, and the theater. Old favorites may be found in any good general songbook.

8. *Challenges to wrestle, games, etc.*—The Chief calls for challenges. The group members, rising in place and giving the proper sign for recognition, say, "O Chief, I challenge John Smith to a (hand) wrestle." John Smith rises and says, "O Chief, I accept the challenge of Robert Jones to a (hand) wrestle."

There are various types of games that may be used. All sorts of dual wrestles, horse and riders, or any game that from one to three on a side may play, can be used. It should be short and snappy so that many different challenges may be made. Individual ingenuity will devise and discover a variety of challenges. The more of this unique quality that can be added to the Council Fire program, the better.

9. *Scout reports*—Here is a chance to get nature lore, Indian lore, into the program. Anybody may take part. It consists simply of making a brief (very) report of some interesting or beautiful thing one has observed that day (or recently). Examples: "O Chief, today as I was walking down the path I saw a big wasp light on a spider and carry it off." "O Chief, today I saw a blacksnake climbing the tree where the robins are nesting, and the mother bird was flying around, etc." " O Chief, I wonder how many tonight observed the perfectly glorious sunset, the wealth of deep purple, etc." This may be a real feature. The Chief may comment briefly on each or not as he pleases.

10. *Song* (stunt—extravaganza—comic—motion type)—The group is now warmed up and ready for action. Here may well come in a group of stunt songs, silly songs, motion songs, joke songs. Here, as before, there is a chance for fine discrimination and for the individual flavor. There are many "ruff-stuff" songs that are nonsensical, delightfully silly and absurd, that deal with blood and gore, that are dramatic extravaganza. Much of this is of value. It offers the needed emotional "catharsis," the escape and outlet oftentime for suppressed emotions that may break out otherwise, or fester in mere suppression. Songs of the wild, rollicking, highly imaginative type, and dealing with elemental and basic emotions of fighting, courage, conquest, blood, pursuit, etc., even though all in pseudo-emotion, are one means of healthful and mentally and emotionally sound expression. The leader will find it necessary to discriminate between what is to be regarded as coarse and vulgar, contributing a doubtful value, and what is worth using.

11. *Dramatization of themes* (silent movies)—Here a theme is set: You are lost in the desert and dying of thirst; you go to the theater with your girl and discover you have forgotten your necktie; you find yourself on the train having gone past your station, etc. These should be acted in absolute silence, no speaking on the part of actor or of group. Noise detracts from the quality.

12. *Dramatized ballads* (or songs or poems)—Here is a chance for individuals to use their dramatic imagination. Costumes should be largely improvised; e.g., turning a coat inside out, wearing a coat for a skirt, etc., or should be extremely simple. Use material that is at hand, such songs as "I'm Romeo—I'm Juliet," "There Were Three Gypsies," "Whistle, Mary, Whistle," Mother Goose rhymes, mountain ballads, etc.

13. *Playlet*—This offers a chance for a play that has been more carefully prepared. It may be of a serious type or otherwise. Generally speaking, the curve of the Council Fire should be moving toward a more serious atmosphere and toward work of a higher artistic, esthetic, and moral value.

14. *Song* (Negro spiritual or mountain ballad or folk song type)—Here a few words about the song to be used may be fitting. A bit of musical appreciation wisely spoken may add to the spirit of the Council and greatly increase not only the enjoyment of the song, but offer also a good opportunity for teaching how the songs may be sung in order more nearly to realize their musical value.

15. *Story*—A special field in itself. Stories for Council Fire should have a special flavor.

Campfire lighting stunts—

1. *Spontaneous fire*—This is a mystifying firelighting stunt. Suddenly at command of the leader the fire starts. This is achieved in the following manner: Prepare a mixture of equal parts of potassium chlorate and sugar. Mix thoroughly. Spread this mixture under the kindling of fine shavings or dry twigs, arranged wigwam fashion, which have been soaked in kerosene. Concentrated sulphuric acid (less than an ounce) is placed in a bottle with a string tied to the top of the bottle. This string is held secretly by someone in the council ring. When ready for the fire to ignite pull the string, thus tipping the bottle over so that it pours on the mixture. The moment the sulphuric acid pours out there is a slight explosion and the shavings burst into flame. Experiment a bit first. Never pour the acid on the mixture by holding the bottle in your hand. Keep all persons away from the fire for the acid spatters and it will burn holes in clothing. In some cases the string is tied to a stopper loosely placed in the bottle, when the stopper is pulled the acid touches off the mixture.

The most impressive manner for using this scheme is to build a fire on a wooden altar of logs, 3 feet high, the top boarded over and covered with sand, mud, or something to keep it from burning.

—J. D. F. WILLIAMS

2. *Colored snowballs*—Use small balls of absorbent cotton, not too thick. Place in each a teaspoon full of red, green, blue, or other color fire-powders. Toss these into the fire every now and then.

3. *Fireworks*—Fireworks snakes that come in tablet form and other fireworks of the same sort may be thrown into the fire now and then, especially if it is a small campfire and the group is enjoying the glowing embers.

4. *Fire from heaven*—Saturate the kindling and shavings with kerosene. A wire is stretched from this point to a point in a tree close by. A boy, hidden by the foliage, has a ball of excelsior, saturated with kerosene, in the tree. This ball is wrapped with a wire which hooks over the wire leading to the fire. At signal the boy in the tree lights the ball of excelsior and lets it slide down the wire.

FIRE BUILDING

Council fire.—The Council Fire gives a good light and burns steadily and long. The fire is built log-cabin style and is therefore sometimes called the "log-cabin" fire. Fill the center of the "cabin" with fine easily inflammable material—perhaps several fuzz sticks and kindling. Lay the log-cabin by using small logs about three feet long and two and one-half to three inches in diameter. Build pyramid fashion so that the logs slope upward about two feet.

Wigwam fire (Tepee fire).—This fire is made by stacking long two-inch poles wigwam fashion. It burns quickly and furnishes a bright light. It is useful for bonfire purposes where a quick-burning brilliant conflagration is wanted. This is sometimes called a Pyramid Fire.

Reflector fire.—A good all-night fire for heating and lighting purposes is the reflector fire. It is also useful for baking biscuits and other food. The log reflector is made by stacking up a single row of logs against a brace at a slight angle two or three feet high. Build a small wigwam fire in front of the reflector. If used for baking a small stone oven may be built into which the heat is reflected. This fire makes a good one to heat the tent at night.

Star or Indian fire.—This is sometimes called the "lazy man's fire" because it can burn for days. Long logs may be used, placed like spokes of a wheel. A fire is built at center and the logs are pushed in toward center, as they are consumed. This is a steady fire for slow cooking.

Hunter's or Trapper's fire.—For general usage and particularly for cooking done in stew pans and skillets this fire is unequalled. Lay two large logs parallel with as much space between them as will accommodate the cooking utensils. Place a three-inch in diameter stick under the windward log to permit a draft on the fire. Lay a small fire between the logs for each cooking utensil to be used.

Open trench fire.—This is used for the same purposes as the Hunter's or Trapper's Fire. In this case, a trench eight to ten inches wide and of the same depth, and about two or three feet long is dug. This trench is lined with rocks about fist size. The fire is built in this trench. It will need less fuel than most any other cooking fire.

Back log fire.—The back-log fire is a small fire built against a large log which serves as a sort of reflector.

Cook fire.—Two forked sticks three or four feet long driven into the ground about three feet apart. A cross stick dropped between the two forks. Some double forked sticks to hang over the cross piece on which cooking vessels may be hung or meat to be cooked may be tied with wire.

Dingle stick fire (Crane fire).—Much the same as the Cook Fire, except that only one forked stick is used and a stone is used to hold the end of the dingle stick down.

Stone fireplace.—Pile stones on two sides and build the fire between them.   This serves as a good fire for cooking eggs, bacon, pancakes, or anything cooked in a skillet.

A mound fire.—Build a mound one to two feet high of logs and mud.   On this mound build a council fire or wigwam fire.

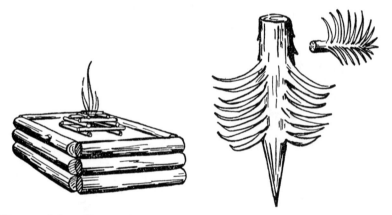

Fuzz sticks.—Fuzz sticks are made of soft wood.   They are used to kindle a fire.   Often they are sharpened to a point and driven in the ground.   Shave the first sliver as long as possible without severing it from the stick.   The first slivers are the hardest.   The following ones are easier.

FIRE WITHOUT MATCHES

Bamboo fire maker.—This is used in the Philippines.   Use a piece of bamboo about eighteen inches long.   Split it in half.   Nail one half, rounded side down, across a box (18x8x6 inches).   Notch the other half.

Place tinder in the notched half and draw rapidly back and forth. A spark will form in the notch.   Blow or fan into a flame.

Wood for firebuilding.—Dried bark of hemlock makes a good bed of glowing coals in a very short time.   Do not use, when green, basswood, ash, balsam, boxelder, black or pitch pine, white pine, yellow poplar, sassafras, or sycamore.

For a stewing fire you may use chestnut, red oak, or rock maple, when green. Always split pine to make it burn well.

Bow and spindle. — The bow is 17 inches long, ⅝-inch wide, ½-inch thick, and has a curve ½-inch high at the middle. Whittle out a 1⅛-inch wide strip. The ends need to be large enough to permit holes for the cord.

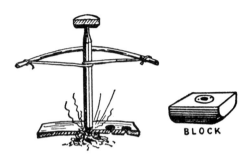

BLOCK

The thong should be a leather shoe lace. Fasten to one end of the bow and then to the other end, leaving enough slack so it can be given one turn around the spindle.

The spindle should be about ¾-inch in diameter and of the same material as your fire board. It is sharpened to a point at one end and blunt at the other.

The fire board should be about a foot long, 3 or 4 inches wide, and about ¾-inch thick. Along the edges of this piece of wood cut a series of notches about ¾-inch deep and tapering from a mere cut in the wood to about a half an inch on the lower side. Hollow out a slight circular depression deep enough to hold the blunt end of the spindle.

Place the fire board on a firm surface, and under one of the notches place a strip of bark or a shaving. Have your tinder (bird's or mouse's nest, cedar bark, dried fine grasses, charred cotton) handy. Place your left foot on the fire board so that the notched side of the board is about even with your instep.

Take the bow in the right hand and the spindle in your left. The pointed end of the spindle rests in a small wooden block or stone that protects the palm of the left hand and allows the spindle to spin.

As soon as the material in the fire board gets a spark get a ball of tinder and blow the spark into a flame.

Bow and spindle equipment may be bought inexpensively at Boy Scout headquarters.

Flint and steel.—A piece of flint, chert, quartz, or similar rock and a piece of steel, perhaps, a jackknife. Some punk or charred cotton cloth. Hold the flint so that the spark will fall on the charred cloth or piece of punk. Strike the flint with the steel and blow the spark in some tinder until it bursts into flame.

The cooking value of most common woods may be rated as follows:

Shellbark Hickory	100	Hard Maple	59
Fignut	95	White Elm	58
White Oak	84	Red Cedar	56
White Ash	77	Wild Cherry	55
Dogwood	75	Yellow Pine	54
Scrub Oak	70	Chestnut	52
Apple Tree	70	Yellow Poplar	51
Red Oak	67	Butternut	43
White Beech	65	White Birch	43
Yellow Oak	60	White Pine	30

Rotted wood does not burn well and makes a lot of smoke. However, dead timber, if not rotted, makes good fuel.

Cook-outs.—Cook-outs are enjoyable occasions. Distribute the duties incident to the affair so that everyone has something to do. In a large group it is wise to break up into small units with each unit having its own fire and preparing its own food. Steak frys, fish frys, bacon bats, weiner roasts, clam bakes, and a number of other possibilities are open to those who thrill to outdoor life. A study of the various kinds of fires will likely add to the effectiveness of your cook-out.

Delicious potatoes.—Dig a hole in the ground from six to ten inches deep and big enough to hold all of your potatoes. Line this with small stones. Build a fire in this hole and heat the stones to a white heat. When the fire dies down, cover the hot coals with about ¼-inch of earth. Then place the potatoes on top and cover them with another layer of earth about ½-inch deep. Build a fire on top of this second layer of earth and keep it burning for thirty minutes or more. Sometimes it takes nearly an hour to cook the potatoes in this fashion.

The same fire may be used to cook other food that is to be prepared.

A piece of meat can be wrapped in leaves that are not bitter and cooked in the same fashion as the potatoes.

Open-fire baked chicken.—Cut off the head and feet of the chicken. Dress, leaving "pin" feathers remaining. Draw. Season inside the chicken.

Wrap in heavy wrapping paper or pack with mud. The packing

is done by covering the chicken all over with about one inch of clay mud. The legs and the neck would be included in this packing. This is important so as to keep the fire out.

Place in hot ashes made from hardwood. Build a hot fire on top. Bake about one hour.

Remove the chicken from the fire. Break off the clay. This is food fit for a king!

—AL A. KOESTLINE
Lake Wales, Florida

Open-fire baked potatoes.—Cover the potatoes with a thick layer of clay mud. Toss them into the fire and allow them to cook for about forty-five minutes for ordinary sized potatoes. Break off the hard mud and the potatoes will be ready to eat.

A clam bake.—Dig a hole about two feet deep. Line the bottom and the sides with rocks. If practical, arrange an iron grate three or four inches from the bottom to allow the fire to draw. Build a hot fire. Allow it to burn several hours until the stones are hot clear through. Then rake out the coals and you are ready to bake the clams.

Place a six- to eight-inch layer of dampened sweet grass or clover on the grate. Be careful not to get any weeds, or the clams will have a bitter taste. Cover the grass with a piece of wet burlap to hold the dampness in. Cover all of this with a clean white cloth. Lay the clams flat on this cloth so the juice will not run out.

On top of the clams place chickens and unhusked corn. Cover with another piece of clean white cloth and then some more wet burlap. Keep the covering damp. Cook for an hour or more. Serve the clams as soon as they are opened. They get tough as soon as the juice escapes.

Corn roast.—Let the fire burn to hot coals. Wet the corn in husks and wrap in a bit of wet burlap. Place the bundle on the fire and keep it moist so it won't burn. Roast till done. Slaw and tomato salad would make a good combination to eat with the corn.

Barbecue.—Dig the pit three and one-half feet wide and six feet long by eight inches deep, the sides of the pit being perpendicular. Lay out the pit so that one end will be about eight inches lower than the other end. Lay three iron bars about half-inch in diameter, and four feet long across the pit for supports. On these lay an iron grate, and on this rest the pig or whatever meat is to be barbecued.

Distribute the hot coals of the fire throughout the pit under the cooking meat. Keep the fire just hot enough to make it uncomfortable to hold your hand beneath the meat. Keep up this regular heat until the meat is done.

Baste the meat with barbecue sauce while cooking

The sauce: For one pig use three pounds of butter, one gallon of pure apple cider vinegar, salt, red pepper in pods, and a very little black pepper. Use a mop made of a clean white rag tied to a stick and baste the meat with the sauce after it has been melted and thoroughly mixed. Use a large spoon to shift the gravy from the pig to the pan in which the sauce is kept, back and forth between the pig and the pan, wasting as little as possible.

Add one-half gallon of fresh apple cider vinegar to the sauce that is left in the pan from which the pig is basted, and pour it over the pig, which is chopped up and put in a large container, a wooden tub being preferable.

NATURE GAMES

A nature treasure hunt.—All of the directions require the identification of some specimen of nature. For instance, the first one, folded and placed in an envelope, reads: "Go to the big elm at the fork of the road." Other directions that follow may be "Stop at the first zinnia garden on the road," "Find the white pine tree that has been topped," "Walk along this road until you come to a buttercup patch," and so on. The treasure may be a box containing the leaves of different trees, which the group must identify.

Observation tour.—The group takes a short hike, each hiker making mental note of all the things he sees on the trip. At the end of the hike the group seats itself on the ground and each person reports on the things he has seen—the different kinds of trees, birds, flowers, any natural phenomenon, and any unusual incident. After the first report subsequent hikers simply report on additional things seen.

Sit and see.—Players sit facing in one direction. Each one tells what he sees—a black oak, a robin, a daisy, a cow, etc. What a player sees he points out to the others.

Nature discovery in twenty-foot radius.—Players comb a radius of twenty feet to see what they can find—a bird nest (which is left where it is found), trees, flowers, weeds, feathers, rocks, etc. When the leader blows the whistle each player returns to report what he has discovered.

Guess what.—Pictures of birds, tree leaves, constellations, and flowers are mounted on cards and held up before the group one at a time. The first player to shout the correct names scores one point for his side. The wrong answer subtracts a point. Excellent bird pictures may be obtained for a nominal sum from the Audobon Society.

A nature scavenger hunt.—This will be a much more interesting and profitable scavenger hunt than the usual one. The players are required to return with an oak leaf, a maple leaf, a bird feather, a devil's walking stick, a grasshopper, a piece of mica, soapstone, a fern, a sassafras leaf, a pine cone, a sprig of pennyroyal.

Identifying nature specimens by odor.—Blindfold the different players and have them identify, if they can, various nature specimens by their odor. The following things could be used:

pennyroyal	fresh pine	calicanthus
ragweed	mint leaf	tuberose
pepper grass	rose	magnolia blossom
elderberry	dahlia	apple
wild locust	cedar	orange

Foraging for nature specimens.—The players would scatter in groups to bring back the leaves of trees, weeds (ironweed, Queen Anne's Lace, etc.), and other specimens. They must be able to identify them.

Animal antics.—Teams line up single file. The leader calls the name of an animal, bird, reptile, or insect that is to be imitated. Immediately the first player in each line imitates the motions of the animal called for a distance of three or four feet. Then he turns and imitates the cry or call of the animal, if any. Judges decide the winner, and the two players go to the foot of the line on each side. The next players are now ready for the next call. The following imitations are some suggested ones: cow, kangaroo, elephant, duck, goose, dog, cat, frog, snake, eagle, bee, caterpillar, horse, butterfly, and rabbit.

Observation trail.—Divide into two groups and scout a bit of wooded territory. Players keep a record of what they see, checking with a leader now and then. Points are scored as follows: For each domestic animal seen, 1 point; for each wild animal, 2 points; each bird, 1 point (ability to identify the bird doubles the score) ; each snail, 2 points; Indian pipes, 2 points; wild animal tracks, 4 points; bird tracks, 5 points; each tree leaf, 2 points (ability to identify the tree doubles score) ; each small mineral, such as mica, 2 points; cultivated flowers seen, 1 point; wild flowers, 2 points (double the score for identification) .

Bird charades.—Divide into two groups. One group retires, decides upon the name of a bird, and returns to present that name in dramatic fashion as is done in "Charades." The other group tries to guess what bird is being presented. Then the second group presents a charade. And thus the game continues. It would be advisable to give to each group a list with a few suggestions of possible names to dramatize. If there are those in the group who know birds well, it would add to the interest to tell something about each bird presented, after the guessing has been done.

The following is a list of charade possibilities:

Cardinal (Car-din-all)
Crane
Brown Creeper
Chat
Crested Flycatcher (Crest-Ed-Fly-Catcher)
Bobolink (Bob-owe-link)
Canary (Can-airy)
Flicker (Flick-her)
Catbird (Cat-bird)
Duck
Brown Thrasher (Brown-Thrash-Her)
Cuckoo
Nightingale (Night-Inn-Gale\
Crow
Cowbird (Cow-Bird)
Mocking Bird (Mocking-Bird)
Killdeer (Kill-Deer)
Humming Bird
Heron (Hair-Run)
Rail
Snipe

Sandpiper (Sand-Pipe-Her)
Whip-poor-will
Bank Swallow
Scarlet Tanager (Scarlet-Tan-Age-Her)
Warbler (War-Blur)
Robin (Rob-Inn)
Martin (Mar-Tin)

Nature sounds.—The group is seated in a quiet place in the woods. Each person listens intently for two or three minutes, listing all of the nature sounds heard in that time. It may be a bird call, a rustling of leaves, a cow, a horse, a dog, a rooster, the tapping of a woodpecker, the gurgling of a small stream, or the patter of rain. After the time is up, each tells what he has heard.

Curio hunters.—This game is to be played while walking through the woods. Nature curiosities are called one at a time and the group scatters to find them. The one to discover it first gives the call and all of the others gather to observe it. As soon as one curio is found, the next hunt starts. A few suggestions follow: a robin's nest, a tree struck by lightning, a tree with branches on one side only, a tree with moss on one side, a tree with three kinds of leaves (sassafras), a tree with a woodpecker hole, a feldspar crystal, a rock with a quartz vein, a mud dauber's nest, a hornet's nest, a humpbacked tree.

1. What tree am I?—My trunk is straight, and when growing in the forest, clear of branches for many feet. I grow fifty to sixty feet tall and one to two feet in diameter.

My branches extend horizontally in whorls (i.e., arranged in a circle on the stem), marking the successive years of growth.

My bark is thin and greenish red on young trees, but thick, deeply furrowed, and grayish brown on older trees.

My leaves are needlelike, three to five inches long, bluish green on the upper surface and whitish underneath. They grow in bundles of five.

My fruit is a cone, four to six inches long, with gummy scales.

My wood is light, soft, not strong, light brown in color, often tinged with red, and easily worked. I am in demand for construction purposes, box boards, matches, and so forth.

Answer—WHITE PINE.

2. What tree am I?—I am found exclusively in deep swamps, on wet stream banks, and bottom lands.

My narrow conical outline and straight trunk make me pleasing to the eye.

My bark is silvery to cinnamon-red.

My leaves are almost one-half to three-fourths of an inch in length, arranged featherlike fashion along two sides of small branchlets. These fall in the autumn with the leaves still attached.

My fruit is a rounded cone about one inch in diameter.

My wood is light, soft, easily worked, and varies in color from a light sapwood to dark-brown heartwood. It is particularly durable in contact with the soil. Hence I am in demand for the building of houses, boats, ships, and am widely used for posts, poles, and cross-ties.

Answer—CYPRESS.

3. What tree am I?—I grow in any kind of soil from swamps to dry, rocky ridges.

I have two kinds of leaves, usually both being found on the same tree. Usually my leaf is dark green, minute, and scalelike, clasping the stem in four ranks, so that the stem appears square. My other kind of leaf, usually appearing on young growth, is awl-shaped, quite sharp-pointed, spreading and whitened.

I have two kinds of flowers at the end of minute twigs on separate trees. Male trees bloom in February and March, often assuming a golden color from the small catkins, which, when shaken, shed clouds of yellow pollen. The fruit is pale blue, often with a white bloom, one-quarter of an inch in diameter, berrylike, enclosing one or two seeds in the sweet flesh. Birds find this a favorite winter food.

My bark is very thin, reddish-brown, peeling off in long, shredlike strips.

My heartwood is red, and the sapwood is white.

I am used extensively to make chests, closets, and for interior woodwork. My wood is aromatic, soft, strong, and of even texture. I am used to make pencils. I am durable in contact with the soil, and so I am used for posts, poles, and rustic work.

Answer—RED CEDAR.

4. What tree am I?—I grow on rich bottom lands and moist fertile hillsides. In the forest I grow to a height of one hundred feet with a straight stem, clear of branches for half its height. In open-grown trees my stem is short and my crown broad and spreading.

My leaves are alternate, compound, one to two feet long, consisting of from fifteen to twenty-three leaflets of yellowish green color. The leaflets are about three inches long, extremely tapering at the end, and toothed along the margin. The bark is thick, dark brown in color, and divided rather deep fissures into rounded ridges.

My fruit is a nut, borne singly or in pairs, and enclosed in a solid green husk which does not split open, even after the nut is ripe. The nut itself is black and the shell is very hard, thick, finely ridged, enclosing a rich, oily edible kernel.

My heartwood is of superior quality. It is heavy, hard, and strong. Its rich chocolate-brown color, freedom from warping, susceptibility to a high polish, and durability make me popular for a variety of uses—furniture, cabinet work, gunstocks, airplane propellors.

Answer—BLACK WALNUT.

5. What tree am I?—While I grow in poor soil, I grow best in deep, moist loam.

I have simple oval leaves three to four inches long, pointed at the tip and coarsely toothed along the margin.

My bark maintains an unbroken, light gray surface throughout my life.

My fruit is a little, brown, three-sided nut formed usually in pairs in a prickly burr.

My wood is very hard, strong, and tough, though it will not last long on exposure to weather or in the soil.

Answer—BEECH.

6. What tree am I?—I grow in hilly and mountain sections and like sandy soil.

My leaves are pointed, with very coarse teeth. They are simple, alternates, dark green, and average five to ten inches in length.

My flowers are of two kinds on the same tree, the long, slender, whitish catkins opening in midsummer.

My fruit is a sweet, edible nut, two or three of them appearing in a prickly burr.

My bark becomes broken into light-gray, broad, flat ridges, which often have a tendency toward a spiral course around the trunk.

My wood is light, soft, not strong, coarse-grained, and very durable in contact with the soil—qualities which make it particularly valuable for posts, crossties, as well as for light building construction. The wood is rich in tannin.

Just now a bark disease is proving fatal to many of my kind, and they have been practically exterminated over much of the northeastern United States and even down into Virginia and North Carolina.

Answer—CHESTNUT.

7. What tree am I?—I am one of the most important timber trees in the United States. I grow from sixty to one hundred feet high and from two to three feet in diameter, and sometimes much larger.

In the forest I grow straight and free of side branches for over half my length. In the open I develop a broad crown with far-reaching limbs.

My leaves are alternate, simple, five to nine inches long and about half as broad. They are deeply divided into five to nine rounded, fingerlike lobes.

My fruit is an acorn maturing the first year. It is relished by hogs and livestock.

My bark is thin, light ashy gray and covered with loose scales or broad plates.

My wood is useful and valuable. It is heavy, strong, hard, tough, coarse-grained, durable, and light brown in color. I am made into ships, barrels, furniture, wagons, implements, interior finish, flooring, and fuel.

Answer—WHITE OAK.

8. What tree am I?—I usually grow to a height of eighty feet and a diameter of from one to three feet. My trunk is clear for twenty feet or more on large trees.

My leaves are alternate, simple, five to ten inches long, shallow and deeply lobed, the shape varying. When mature there are conspicuous rusty brown hairs in the forks of the veins.

My fruit is an acorn maturing the second year.

My bark is black, with deep furrows and rough broken edges. My inner bark is bright yellow and has a bitter taste, due to tannic acid.

My wood is hard, heavy, strong, coarse-grained, and checks easily. It is bright red-brown with a thin outer edge of paler sapwood. I am used for barrels, interior finish, construction, furniture, and crossties.

Answer—BLACK OAK.

9. What tree am I?—I am the famous shade tree of New England. I grow, however, from coast to coast and as far southward as Texas. I reach a height of from sixty to seventy feet and a diameter of from four to five feet.

My leaves are alternate, simple, four to six inches long, rather thick, somewhat one-sided, doubly toothed on the margin, and generally smooth above and downy beneath. The leaf veins are very pronounced and run in parallel lines from the midrib to leaf-edge.

I have a small, perfect, greenish flower on slender stalks, sometimes an inch long.

My fruit is a light green, oval-shaped samara (winged fruit) with the seed portion in the center and surrounded entirely by a wing. A deep notch in the end of the wing is distinctive of the species.

My bark is dark gray, divided into irregular, flat-topped, thick ridges, and is generally firm, though on old trees it tends to come off in flakes. An incision into my inner bark will show alternate layers of brown and white.

My wood is heavy, hard, strong, tough, and difficult to split. It is used for hubs of wheels, saddletrees, boats, ships, barrel hoops, and veneer for baskets and crates.

Answer—WHITE ELM.

10. What tree am I?—I am a small tree with large leaves crowded on the stem. I am a close relative of the large magnolia.

My leaves vary from fourteen to twenty-two inches in length by eight to ten inches wide and are borne on stout stems. They are alternate, simple, narrowly peared or ovate, pointed at both ends, smooth, and fall in the autumn with little change in color.

My flower is creamy white, ill-scented, cup-shaped, with petals six to nine inches long. A whorl of leaves usually surround the flower.

My fruit is rose-colored when ripe, from two to four inches long, cylindrical or cone-shaped, consisting of small capsules, each containing a red seed about one-half inch in length.

My bark is thin, light gray, smooth, and roughened by irregular protruding portions.

My wood is light, soft, light brown in color, and of little practical value.

I am planted for ornamental purposes and resemble a rainy-day favorite.

Answer—UMBRELLA TREE.

11. What tree am I?—I am a small, aromatic tree not over forty feet in height or a foot in diameter. I am closely related to the camphor tree of Japan.

My leaves are of widely different shape on the same tree, or even on the same twig. Some are oval and entire, four to six inches long; others have one long lobe resembling the thumb of a mitten; still others are divided at the outer end into three distinct lobes. Young leaves and twigs are quite sticky.

My flowers are clustered, greenish yellow, and open with the first unfolding of the leaves.

My fruit is an oblong, dark blue or black, lustrous berry, containing one seed, and surrounded by what appears to be a small orange-red or scarlet cup at the end of a scarlet stalk.

My bark is thick, red-brown, and deeply furrowed. That of the twigs is bright green.

My wood is light, soft, weak, brittle, and durable in the soil. The heartwood is dull orange-brown. I am used for posts, rails, boats, barrels, and ox yokes. The bark of the roots yields a rich aromatic oil used for flavoring candies and other products.

*Answer—*SASSAFRAS.

12. What tree am I?—I am considered the largest hardwood tree in North America. I often attain a height of 140 to 170 feet and a diameter of ten to eleven feet.

My leaves are simple, alternate, four to seven inches long and about as broad, light green and smooth above, and a paler green below.

My fruit is a ball about one inch in diameter, conspicuous through the winter as it hangs on its flexible stem, which is three to five inches long.

My bark is a very smooth and a greenish gray on younger trunks and large limbs. The outer bark flakes off in large patches and exposes the nearly white younger bark. Near the base of old trees the bark becomes thick, dark brown and divided by deep furrows.

My wood is hard and moderately strong, but decays rapidly in the ground. I am used for butcher's blocks, tobacco boxes, furniture, and interior finish.

*Answer—*SYCAMORE.

13. What tree am I?—I am a small tree, sometimes called Judas tree from my oriental relative of that name. I grow twenty-five to thirty feet tall and from six to twelve inches in diameter.

My leaves are alternate, heart-shaped, entire, three to five inches long and wide, glossy green turning in the autumn to a clear yellow.

My flowers are a conspicuous, bright purplish red, pea-shaped, and in numerous clusters along the twigs and branches, appearing before the leaves in early spring. In full bloom I make the hillsides and fields of the countryside a sight long to be remembered.

My fruit is an oblong, flat, many-sided pod two to four inches long, reddish during the summer, and often hanging on the tree for the most of the winter.

My bark is bright red-brown, the long narrow plates separating into thin scales.

My wood is heavy, hard, not strong, rich dark brown in color, and of little commercial value.

Answer—RED BUD.

14. What tree am I?—I grow rapidly with a very symmetrical, dense crown, affording heavy shade.

My leaves are three to five inches across, simple opposite, with three to five pointed and sparsely-toothed lobes, the divisions between the lobes being rounded. The leaves are dark green on the upper surface, lighter green beneath, turning in the autumn to brilliant dark red, scarlet, orange, and yellow.

My flowers are yellowish green, on long thread-like stalks, appearing with the leaves, the two kinds in separate clusters.

My fruit, which ripens in the fall, consists of a two-winged "samara," the two wings nearly parallel, about one inch in length and containing a seed.

My bark on young trees is light gray and brown and rather smooth. As the tree grows older it breaks up into long, irregular plates or scales, which vary from light gray to almost black.

My sap yields sugar and syrup.

My wood is hard, heavy, strong, close-grained, and light brown in color. I am used for flooring, furniture, shoe lasts, and a variety of novelties.

Answer—SUGAR MAPLE.

15. What tree am I?—I am a small tree, fifteen to thirty feet high, with a rather flat and spreading crown and a short, often crooked trunk.

My leaves are opposite, ovate, three to five inches long, two to three inches wide, pointed, entire or wavy on the margin, green above and pale green or grayish beneath.

My flowers unfold before the leaves come out. They are small, greenish yellow, arranged in dense heads surrounded by large white or rarely pink petal-like bracts, which give the appearance of large spreading flowers two to four inches across. I am a lovely sight in the spring and almost as lovely in the autumn.

My fruit is a bright scarlet "berry," one-half an inch long and containing a hard nutlet in which are one or two seeds. Usually several fruits or "berries" are contained in one head. Squirrels and birds like these "berries."

My bark is reddish brown to black and broken up into four-sided scaly blocks.

My wood is hard, heavy, strong, close-grained, brown to red in color.   In demand for cotton mill machinery, turnery handles and forms.

Answer—DOGWOOD.

A verse speaking choir for Arbor Day—

1: "All the seasons we shall see."
2: "All the seasons we shall see."
3: "All the seasons we shall see."
All: "In the planting of a tree."
1: "Where the birds shall sing at dawn."
All: "In this monument of shade."
2 and 3: "Giving beauty to our lawn."
All: "In this monument of shade."
1: "Shade."
2: "Shade."
3: "Shade."
All: "Sha——de—."

1, 2, 3, respectively: "Buds are swelling on the trees."
All: "Color comes with growing leaves."
1: "Magic blossoms then unfold."
All: "And the sunshine makes them grow."
2 and 3: "Little leaves out in the cold."
All: "And the sunshine makes them grow."
1, 2, 3, All, respectively: "Grow."

1, 2, 3, respectively: "Rain is dripping through the leaves."
All: "Silver lightning in the breeze."
1: "Down the bark the raindrops slide."
All: "Rushing to the thirsty ground."
2 and 3: "To the grass they softly glide."
All: "Speaking with a rhythmic sound."
1, 2, 3, All, respectively: "Sound."

1, 2, 3, All, respectively: "Wind is blowing through the trees."
All: "Filling sky with falling leaves."
1: "O'er the hill the red leaves fly."
All: "Like a hurricane they blow."
2 and 3: "Bare limbs bend as wind goes by."
All: "Like a hurricane they blow."
1, 2, 3, All, respectively: "Blow."

1, 2, 3, All, respectively: "Through leafless trees straight and tall."
All: "Whirling snowflakes softly fall."

1: "Clinging to the greenest pine."
All: "Winter sunset adds it's glow."
2 and 3: "Touching ev'ry little vine."
All: "Silence comes with falling snow."
1, 2, 3, All, respectively: "Snow."

The numbers refer to the groups. Light voices should be in Group 1, medium voices in Group 2, heavy voices in Group 3. "All" means that the three groups speak in concert.

Where there are repetitions the volume increases in tone to represent greater power, except in the final repetition using the word "Snow." The volume is lowered in tone until the heavier voices hush the sound as if falling snow were actually stopping their words from sounding.

—ALICE GIBSON HEAP

A Community Sing at Camp Edith Macy
Briarcliff Manor, N. Y.

Following the leader of each unit
We walked in groups, at fifteen-minute intervals,
To see a play to be given along the trail—
A winding path that led to the hillside
Where later we were to eat and to sing.

Each scene was performed four times,
And done with ease, as the stage casts
Had separate Hansels and Gretels.
Guides stationed along the footpath
Kept groups arriving according to schedule.

Before the log cabin Troup House of "Innisfree"
The first Hansel and the first Gretel hungrily ate the bread,
Their portion and that of their parents,
And were sent into the nearby forest
To gather berries for a worried mother.

In the shade of a majestic oak
Another Hansel and another Gretel,
Romped and played and ate their berries
Then fell asleep while fourteen angels
With golden haloes
Rose up beneath the oak and sang their slumber song.

Next we went to the Glen where artificial toad stools,
Gaily painted and of giant size,
Were illumined by the slanting rays of the evening sun
That also enriched the glory

Of a paper gingerbread house,
And a life-size oven with a swinging door
Into which the third Gretel
Pushed the terrible witch.

Still in small groups we arrived at our hill,
And selected flowers from a hostess basket—
Clovers and Daises, Black-eyed Susans and Queen Anne's Lace,
Each group to eat in their respective places.
We were served cafeteria style,
The food arranged along the ground
In decorative settings,
When we found our place to eat
We were still part of a large crowd
Yet never crowded and always with a little group.

As the clouds became tinted with the sunset
We found upon the sloping hillside
Our own unit campfire,
Like a blazing star. We were seated,
With each cluster of people at a point,
And the judges in the center.

At a signal from a whistle
We sang as groups,
Each unit having previously prepared
An art song and a folk tune
And the melody of a round.
Only the music of the whistle
Announced unexpectedly
The group to sing and the type of song.

Softly in the twilight of the evening,
Growing mysterious in the lengthening shadows,
Like the notes upon a Shepherd's Pipe,
Sounded songs upon the hillside.
Slumber songs, then Negro spirituals
And then the beauty of softly pitched
And well-timed rounds.

When the fires were glowing embers
And taps echoed up and down the hill
One by one their lights were quenched
And each group still a unit
Followed the trail which led back home.

—Alice Gibson Heap

Water dodgeball.—A rubber playball is used. The players for one side form a ring around their opponents. Players inside the circle may duck at will but they are not allowed to dive outside the circle. Just as in regular dodgeball the players in the ring try to hit players on the opposing side. When they are successful the player hit must get out of the circle. Players are only permitted to throw from the circle.

Center water dodgeball.—All the players but one form a circle. That one takes a position somewhere inside the circle. All of the other players try to hit him with the ball. The center player may duck, dive, dodge, or stay under to keep from getting hit. He may not go outside the circle. When he is hit the player who hit him takes his place.

Whale says.—This game is played in the water. It is similar to "Simon Says." Any order the leader gives that is prefaced with "Whale Says" is to be obeyed immediately. However, if the order is not so prefaced any player obeying it is out. To confuse the players the leader does or starts to do all actions whether prefaced by "Whale Says" or not. "Whale says 'Duck.'" All players duck under and come up. "Whale says 'Float on back,'" and players obey. The leader shouts, "Right foot in the air." Players who raise the right foot are out for the order was not prefaced by "Whale says." "Whale says, 'Left foot raised,'" and up comes the left foot. Other calls are "Sit down," "Dive and come up," etc.

Fish net haul.—This game would be better where the players can both swim and walk in the water. Boundary lines are indicated as in "Pom Pom Pullaway." All of the players but one stand behind one of these boundary lines. If one of these lines can be a dock so much the better. One player, who is "It," stands at center. He calls:

> Poor fish, poor fish, poor fish,
> Better get wet;
> I'm going to catch you
> Within my net.

As he finishes this he starts toward the line where the fish are. They dive into the water and swim or wade to the opposite line. "It" tries to tag some of them. All players caught take hold of hands and help "It" catch the others. After awhile they will have considerable of a net to stretch across the playing space. Any player caught in the net joins himself to the net to catch others.

Chinese chicken.—This makes a good game for a sandy beach. In fact, it is so used in China. Usually, bathing slippers are used.

However, the game may be played with bean bags, strips of seaweed, shells, or sticks.

Two or more players may play it. If the crowd is large divide into groups of five or six players each and have several games going simultaneously.

Place five to ten bathing slippers in a straight row and about ten inches apart. There should be a row for each group playing. Each player becomes a "lame chicken" and hops on one foot over each slipper until he reaches the end. There he kicks the last slipper with his hopping foot, picks it up, and hops back over the other slippers. When he hops over the first one this time he turns and kicks it with the hopping foot. Then he hops over the remaining shoes treating them in the same manner until all of the shoes have been picked up. In all of this he must never let the lame foot touch the ground. Nor must he touch a shoe except in its regular turn when he is supposed to kick it and pick it up. Players who fall, touch the lame foot to the ground, or touch any of the shoes out of turn drop out of the contest.

Tilting.—Contestants stand in canoes and each tries to make his opponent fall overboard or touch the canoe with his hands. The tilting pole should be made of spruce or bamboo. It should be ten feet long and well padded at the end. Thrusts only are allowed. In other words, the tilter cannot take a swing. Hitting any other part of the body than the torso and arms is a foul.

Water bucket tilting.—*Equipment*—Two water pails and two mops. Opponents stand on the water buckets and try to cause one another to lose balance and fall off the bucket. The same method of thrusting must be used as in canoe tilting.

Water rough riders.—In water waist high two players mount the backs of two teammates. The riders try to dislodge each other from their mounts. They pull, tug, and push one another in their efforts. It is unfair to push, trip, or otherwise upset the "horses." If a horse slips and falls his rider is out.

Water rough riders' battle royal.—There will be a number of mounted riders. Each rider attempts to pull the others from their mounts. The last to survive is winner.

Variation—Have two teams of riders contest with one another. The contest goes on until one side is entirely eliminated. A player once dismounted may not re-enter the contest.

Water tag games.—Various tag games are possible of adaptation in the water. Note "Cross Tag," "Straight Tag," "Fish in the Sea," "Charley Over the Water" (with the players ducking to prevent being tagged), and many of the Safety Tag games which may be adapted by requiring the players to duck, hold up one foot, float motionless, tread, hold one hand on the bottom, etc.

Water circle touchball.—The players stand two or three feet apart and toss or pass a ball around the circle. One player inside the circle tries to get possession of the ball. If he touches it at any time the player in the circle who last touched it must take his place. "It" may be given the privilege of ducking the player who is to take his place.

Variation—In a large circle have several players inside the circle.

Fish market.—Each of the players on the dock, bank, or the edge of the pool, is given the name of some fish, such as Whale, Perch, Bass, Catfish, Shark, Porpoise, Mackerel, Red Snapper, Salmon, or Trout. One player is the fish-market proprietor. Another player is "It." The names of the various players are kept secret. "It" comes to the market. "What kind of fish do you want?" asks the proprietor. "I'll take trout," may be the reply. Immediately the Trout dives off the dock and swims to an agreed safety zone with the customer in pursuit. If caught before he reaches the safety zone he is "It," and the player who was "It" takes his place in the market, being given a fish name.

Variation—A less exhausting way to play this game would be to divide into two sides. Each side names its own fish. The customers (or opponents) come in one at a time to buy fish. If a customer catches his fish he scores one point for his side. If the fish reaches the safety line he scores for his side. Then another customer calls until all of the side has had a chance to get a poor fish from the other side. Following this, after a few moments of rest, the sides change, the customers becoming the fish and the fish the customers.

Merry-go-round.—Merry-go-round makes a good game where the beach offers a good underfooting in water that is not too deep. Players form in a circle, holding hands. They number off by twos all the way around. The players move around in the circle gradually increasing their speed. When the leader thinks they are moving fast enough he yells, "Ones ride!" The Ones then lie on their backs while the Twos pull them around. Next the Twos may do the riding. If you don't think this is fun, try it.

Ring around the rosy.—Just as in the old children's game the group moves around in the circle singing:

> Ring around the rosy,
> Pocket full of posey,
> Fall down and break your nosey.

On the "break your nosey" the group ducks under the water, continuing to hold hands. When a player has stayed under as long as he can he raises his head. The last player up is winner.

Keep it ball.—Two equally divided sides. A large water ball, or a small rubber ball. One side is given possession of the ball and tries to keep it among its own players. The other side tries to capture the ball and then passes it among its players. The ball must be kept moving, the players tossing it from one to the other of their teammates. While a player is holding the ball he may be ducked and held under until he lets it go.

Swimming relay.—Two lines of swimmers, equal in number, with enough room between the two lines to allow two players to swim without interfering with one another. The head player in each line holds a handkerchief or rag. At the signal to go he swims down back of his own line, around it, and back up the space between the two lines to his original position. As he reaches there he hands the handkerchief to his next teammate. That player must swim inside around the head player, down back of his line, around it, and up the inside back to position. So each player must swim all around his own line. The first team having every player do that, wins.

"Farmer in the dell."—You've never really played this game until you play it in the water. When "The cheese stands alone" the entire circle of players close in and shower "the cheese" with water, splashing it into his face and body.

Through the water barrel.—The players all stand astraddle with legs far apart. One player takes a short run and dives under the spread legs trying to make it to the end of the line.

Folk games in the water.—In water not over waist high it is great fun to play well-known folk games. One group had a grand time doing "Weave the Wadmal" in water where there was a sandy beach.

Water pillow fight.—A smooth sapling hung from the branch of a tree overhanging the water or pillow-fighting equipment set up in water two or three feet deep would furnish worlds of fun. Canvas-covered pillows should be used. Or hand jousting could be done. In this case contestants would sit close enough so that they could easily touch hands. Hands are held breast high, palm out. Players feint, shove palm against palm, and try to unbalance their opponents.

Greased watermelon pushball.—*Equipment*—A greased watermelon. *Field*—The width of the swimming pool would make the court. In a lake the same arrangement would be observed as for "Water Basketball." The field should not be more than twenty feet long.

The game—The greased watermelon is deposited by the referee in the water midway between the two teams. Any number of players may play. The more, the merrier. When the referee blows his whistle the opposing teams dive into the water and swim for the watermelon. From then on it is one grand tussle. Each team tries to get the watermelon deposited on its bank. The melon must be completely out of the water and on the shore to count a goal. After two out of three victories the winners may cut open the melon and feast on it. They will probably share with the losers, the winners acting as hosts.

A player holding the melon may be ducked until he lets go.

Water basketball.—*Equipment*—A ten- or twelve-inch rubber playball. *The court*—The baskets can be regulation basketball goals or wastebaskets hung at a height of five feet or placed on the shore at either end of a small pool. If in a large pool or a lake, the goals may be anywhere from twenty to thirty feet apart on the same side of the swimming pool or lake.

The game—Play as in regulation basketball, except that a player may push the ball along in place of the dribble.

Boat polo.—*Equipment*—A rubber playball, six to ten inches in diameter. Each player is equipped with a mallet, similar to a croquet mallet, except that the handle is only ten inches long.

The field—The field is from twenty to thirty yards long. There is a goal fifteen feet wide at either end of the field. Anchored pennants mark these goals.

The game—Play as in regulation polo except that the players are in rowboats instead of on ponies.

CHAPTER XI
FUN WITH SPORTS

FUN WITH SPORTS

The salvation of sports will be achieved when
we play, not for championships, medals, and other
external awards, but rather for fun of playing.

Archery.—Archery is one of the most ancient of sports. Some as-
cribe its beginning to the ancient Scythians. The Greeks seem to
have learned the use of the bow and arrow from them. The Bible is
full of references to archery. Jonathan was an expert archer, as
was Ishmael. The expression "drew a bow at a venture" appears in
I Kings 22: 34.

Robin Hood and his Merrie Men and Willian Tell and his famous
exploit of shooting the apple off of his son's head lend romance to
an activity that makes an appeal in its own right.

Archery has splendid value as a health builder. The erect posture
required of the archer, the exercise of muscles without strenuous
effort, the fact that it is usually done out-of-doors—all of these
make it splendid physical exercise.

When archers make their own equipment that adds the values
that come from creative effort. Bows are made of Osage orange, yew,
lemon, hickory, ash, and ironwood.

Archery pointers.— (1) To string the bow keep the flat side toward
the body. Place the lower nock against the instep of the left foot,
the horn barely touching the ground. Hold the middle of the
bow firmly with the left hand. Bend the bow by pushing the
upper end away from the body with the right hand. At the same
time carry the loop of the string to the notch in the upper nock
with the fingers of the right hand. Allow it to drop in the notch.

(2) Keep archery tackle dry. If it gets wet, dry the bow with a
soft oily cloth. Straighten the feathers and arrows before drying.

(3) Always unstring the bow when not in use. Hang it up by
the string rather than stand it on end.

(4) Always bend the bow with the flat side out. Never try to
straighten it. Any bow has a tendency to "follow the string."

(5) Always use an arrow of correct length and draw it to a head.

(6) Never draw and loose the bow without an arrow on the
string. An overdraw will break any bow, and the drawn bow
released without an arrow usually snaps the string.

Proper arrow lengths—

    4 foot bow, 21-inch arrow.
    4 foot 6 inch bow, 21-inch arrow.
    5 foot bow, 24-inch arrow.
    5 foot 3 inch bow, 25-inch arrow.
    5 foot 6 inch bow, 26-inch arrow.
    6 foot bow, 28-inch arrow.

Some archery rules.—*Targets*—Four feet in diameter. They are usually made of straw three or four inches thick, and are supported by a tripod sloping slightly backwards. The faces are of oilcloth painted with concentric circles four and four-fifths inches in breadth.

Scoring—Outer ring, white, one point; next ring, black, three points; next ring, blue, five points; next ring, red, seven points. The bull's-eye, gold, four and four-fifths inches in radius counts nine points.

Men stand 100, 80, and 60 yards away. Ladies stand 60, 50, 40, and 30 yards away.

If an arrow cuts two rings the archer is credited with the higher one.

Rounds—York for men—144 arrows. Seventy-two at one hundred yards; forty-eight at eighty yards; twenty-four at sixty yards. (Called "Double York" when another round is shot the next day.)

Columbia, for ladies. Twenty-four arrows for each distance at fifty, forty, and thirty yards.

National for ladies. Forty-eight arrows at sixty yards; twenty-four arrows at fifty yards.

American for both sexes. Thirty arrows for each distance at sixty, fifty, and forty yards.

Team round—Men—ninety-six arrows at sixty yards. Ladies—ninety-six arrows at fifty yards.

Each archer shoots three arrows in turn. When six arrows have been shot by each one, they are drawn from the target and scored before further shooting is allowed.

Archery golf.—Mark out a course. Shoot oranges or straw sacks. Count the number of shots as you count strokes in golf. Novelty contests between archers and golfers are sometimes staged. The golfer uses his sticks and golf ball. The archer uses his bow and arrow, shooting an orange on the green.

Books and stories relating archery achievements.—*Ivanhoe,* Sir Walter Scott; *The White Company,* Sir Arthur Conan Doyle; *The Black Arrow,* Robert Louis Stevenson; *Tekla,* Robert Barr; *Robin Hood,* Howard Pyle; *The Witchery of Archery,* Maurice Thompson. There are also accounts in English histories in descriptions of the battles of Hastings, Crecy, Agincourt, Flodden Field, Poitiers, Halidowne Hill, and Shrewsbury.

Bibliography.—*Modern Methods in Archery,* Reichart and Keasey (Barnes), 1938; *Modern Archery,* Lambert (Barnes); *The Teaching of Archery,* Craft (Barnes); *Archery Simplified,* Rounsevelle, (Barnes); *The Archery Workshop,* L. E. Stemmler Co., Queen's Village, Long Island, New York; *How to Make Bows and Arrows,* Boy Scouts of America, 2 Park Ave., New York City.

Archery supplies.—Frederick A. Kibbe, Wolverine Archery, Coldwater, Mich.; L. E. Stemmler Co., Queen's Village, Long Island; Pioneer Pole and Shaft Company, Memphis, Tenn.; The Archers Company, Bristol, Conn.; The Archery Supply Company, Pinehurst, N. C.; Archery Sales and Service Company, 510 W. Van Buren St., Chicago, Ill.

Billiards.—Little accurate information regarding the origin of the game of billiards is available. It is variously ascribed to England, Spain, Italy, Germany, and Egypt. The name is probably derived from the French *bille* (English, billet) meaning a stick.

The old game of Paillemaille (Pall Mall) may have furnished the original idea for billiards. It was played on the ground or floor instead of on a table.

In Shakespeare's "Anthony and Cleopatra," Act II, scene 5, Cleopatra says, "Let us to billiards; come, Charmaine."

The game is known to have been played during the reign of Louis XI in the fifteenth century.

The game was brought to America by the Spaniards who settled in St. Augustine, Florida, in 1565.

Equipment—Regulation tables are five by ten feet in size. Standard sizes for balls are: Carom games, $2\frac{3}{8}$ inches in diameter; pocket games, $2\frac{1}{4}$ inches in diameter. Cues are of various sizes and weights according to the desires of the player.

Games—Various games are played such as "Three-ball Carom," "Four-ball Carom," "Fourteen-inch Balk Line," "Eighteen-inch Balk Line," "Cushion Carom," "Three-cushion Carom," "Bank Shot,"

"Red, White, and Blue," "Pin Game," "14-1 Continuous Pocket Billiards," "Non-Continuous Fifteen-ball Pocket Billiards," "American Pyramid Fifteen-ball Pocket Billiards," "Rotation Pocket Billiards," and others.

Bowling.—Bowling has been a pastime for centuries in Germany and the low countries. It was introduced into the United States from Holland. The Dutch inhabitants of New Amsterdam, now New York, were very fond of it. From 1623-1840 it was played on the green, the principal resort of the bowlers being the square, just north of the Battery, which is still called "Bowling Green."

Size of alley—The alley should not be less that forty-one nor more than forty-two inches in width. In length it is sixty feet from the center of Number 1 pin spot to the foul line.

Pins—Ten pins are used. They are placed with one pin at the apex, two pins in the next row, three pins in the next, and four in the last row. The pins are placed on spots two and one-fourth inches in diameter at a distance of twelve inches from the center of one spot to the next.

The dimensions of the pins are as follows.

Height—Fifteen inches.

Width— Two and one-fourth inches in diameter at the base.
Twelve and one-fourth inches in circumference, two and one-fourth inches from the base.
Fifteen inches in circumference, four and one-half inches from the base.
Eleven and five-eights inches in circumference, seven and one-fourth inches from the base.
Five and one-fourth inches in circumference at the neck, ten inches from the base.
Eight inches in circumference at the head, thirteen and one-half inches from the base.

The pins are made of hard, solid maple. They should weigh not less than three pounds, nor more than three pounds eight ounces.

The ball—Bowling balls shall not exceed twenty-seven inches in circumference, nor sixteen pounds in weight.

The game— (1) Each player bowls two balls for each frame. Ten frames make a game. (2) Pins knocked down are removed from the alley before the next ball is bowled. (3) If a player knocks all of the pins down with his first ball he scores a "strike." He does not make a second bowl that frame. But on the next frame he scores ten points plus the number of pins he knocks down with the two bowls for that frame. (4) If a player knocks down all of the pins in two shots he scores a "spare." In this case his score is ten plus the number of pins he gets on his first shot for the next frame.

Cocked hat bowling.—Only three pins are used. They are placed in triangle formation. The pins are seventeen inches high, and two and one-fourth inches in diameter at the base. The balls should not exceed five and one-half inches in diameter.

The same rules that govern regulation bowling are in force, except that if the bowler makes a "strike" he scores only three points plus the number he gets on his two shots in the next frame. On a "spare" he gets three points plus what he gets in his first bowl in the next frame.

Cocked hat feather bowling.—This game has the same set up as "Cocked hat" except that there are four pins instead of three. The fourth pin is placed one foot behind the Number 1 pin. It is the "feather." Ten innings are played. Each player bowls three balls (5½ inches in diameter). The aim of the bowler is to knock down pins 1, 2, and 3 and to leave the "feather" standing. Unless this is done the player scores nothing. If it is done the player scores one.

Bowls or bowling on the green.—This is one of the oldest of outdoor sports. It has been traced for certain as far back as the thirteenth century. It was probaby played as early as the twelfth century.

The game was banned by royal edict in England for fear that it might jeopardize the practice of archery. Later in 1455 it was repressed because it had fallen into disrepute, many of the alleys being connected with taverns frequented by the dissolute and gamblers.

In 1511 a statute proclaimed by Henry VIII confirmed previous enactments against unlawful games, of which "bowls" was one. In 1541 an act specified that "artificers, labourers, apprentices, servants, and the like" were forbidden to play "bowls" except at Christmas. This law was not repealed until 1845.

The game is played on a smooth lawn bordered by a six-inch trough. In place of the trough one may use a border of heavy cord held up by corner spikes at a height of about eighteen inches. Balls in the trough or outside the border cord are not counted.

A white ball, of smaller size than the bowling balls, is called "the jack." It is bowled first. Then each bowler, in succession, tries to land nearest the "jack." Points are made as in quoits, that is, the player nearest the "jack" scores a point. Both the bowled ball and the "jack" may be hit and knocked away. It is the final position of the "jack" after all players have bowled that decides the points.

Croquet ball bowling.—This game may be played on any smooth floor or lawn. Ten pins are set up. Three croquet balls are used, each player getting three bowls.

1. The pins are set up on a triangle, there being about six inches space between the pins.

2. Players roll balls from a distance of from twenty to thirty feet, the distance depending somewhat on the condition of the bowling surface.

3. The object of the bowler is to knock down all of the pins in three shots or less.

4. When all of the pins are down, or after the third ball has been rolled, a "turn" or "frame" has been completed.

5. Ten frames constitute a game.

6. Pins down after each bowl are to be removed from the playing area.

7. Method of scoring—(a) The number of pins down after each frame is recorded on a sheet. (b) When all of the pins are down after the first bowl, the player has scored a "strike" and it is designated on the scoring sheet by an X. It counts ten, with a bonus equal to the number of pins down on the first and second balls of the next frame. Thus, if he gets four down on the first shot of the next frame and three on the second shot, the score will be seventeen for the first frame. (c) When all of the pins are down on the second ball it is called a "spare." The score is ten plus whatever balls go down on the first shot of the next frame.

8. When the player makes a "strike" on the last frame he gets two more bowls immediately and the results are added to his score in the tenth frame. If he scores a "spare" in this last frame, he gets one more bowl.

9. The score indicated in each frame is always the score made in that frame plus the scores made in all the previous frames. Thus the score indicated in the tenth frame would be the total score for the game.

Duck pins.—The same rules obtain as in regulation bowling, with the following exceptions:

(1) The pins are smaller and lighter. The size of a duck pin is

as follows: height, nine and thirteen thirty-seconds inches; diameter, one and fifty-five sixty-fourths inches at the top, four and one-tighth inches at the middle, and one an dthree-eights inches at the base.

(2) The ball shall not exceed five inches in diameter nor three pounds twelve ounces in weight.

(3) Each player gets three rolls to a frame and bowls two frames in succession.

(4) The foul line is ten yards beyond the regular foul line. A player going over this line fouls.

Bowling skittles.—The pins are set up as in regulation bowling. Instead of bowling a ball, however, the player tosses a disc about the size and weight of a shuffleboard disc, four and one-half inches in diameter and one inch thick. This disc is tossed with an underhand swing as in horseshoes. The player may hit the pins on the fly or he may slide the disc into them. The count is the same as in bowling.

Hole bowl.—Dig five holes, one at center and the other four at the corners of a two-foot square. If possible sink coffee cans in these holes level with the ground. Players bowl a croquet ball at a distance of fifteen to twenty feet. The center hole counts five points. The two holes nearest the bowler count one point each. The two corner holes farthest away from the bowler count three points each. Each player gets five bowls for a turn. Any player who rolls into each of the five holes on one turn scores an extra ten points.

Square five bowling.—Set five regulation pins up on a two-foot square with one pin at center. Bowlers get three rolls. Each pin counts one.

Variation—Allow no scoring until the center pin is down.

Dead wood must be moved off of the court.

Curling.—It is not certain where the game of curling originated. We know that it has been played in Scotland for three centuries, at least. Some trace the game to the Netherlands.

The players prepare large rounded stones upon a rink or sheet of ice, toward a mark called a tee. This is usually a scooped-out place in the ice.

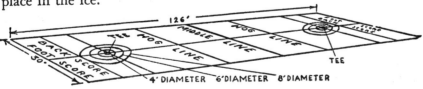

Equipment—A broom ("besom"), with which the curler keeps the ice swept ("sooped") clean; a "crampit," or piece of iron plate fitted with spikes, on which the curler stands; a stone, with two flat sides. The sides or "soles" of the stone are so shaped that one is serviceable for keen ice and the other for ice that is soft or rough.

The handle can be fitted to either side. In some places in the United States and Canada iron is used instead of stone. Curling stones should be circular in shape, of about forty-four pounds in weight, and not over thirty-six inches in circumference. It should be of less height than one and one-eighth part of its circumference.

Game—The game is practically "bowls" on ice. Each side has four players, each playing two stones.

Each team has a leader who is called the "skip." When the "skip" feels a little sweeping in front of the curling iron would be helpful he calls for a player to "soop." That removes any snow or other impediment and makes it possible for the iron to go a bit farther. The sweeper must not touch the iron with his broom. Orders to "soop" can only be called by the "skip."

Sweeping may only be done from the hog line to the sweeping line, except that when snow is falling the rink may be swept from tee to tee.

The rink is 126 feet (sometimes 96 feet) long and thirty feet wide. It is marked off as indicated in the diagram. A circle of seven feet radius surrounds the tee. There are two more concentric circles of four feet and two feet radius to aid in measuring.

A stone is of no value unless it reaches the hog line, nor if it passes out of the "parish," which is the ring of seven feet radius encircling the tee. All stones that stay within the parish are counted. The side wins which has the greatest number of stones nearest the tee, receiving a point for each stone nearest the tee. Twenty-one points constitute a game.

A set of matches is called a "bonspiel."

Variation—Curling stones are expensive. It would be possible to work out an adaptation of the regulation game where the players use such stones as are available in the neighborhood. In fact, the game originally was played in that fashion.

Cricket.—A game called "Club Ball," played in the thirteenth Century, was identical with single wicket cricket. The present game of cricket has been played in England for more than two hundred and fifty years.

The field—The wickets, each consisting of three upright wooden stumps, twenty-one inches high, are placed twenty-two feet apart.

Each wicket is eight inches in width. The stumps are wide enough so that the ball cannot pass through the wicket. The bails are four inches long, and rest on top of the wickets. These bails are short pieces of wood. When the stumps receive a lick, one or both bails are likely shaken off. The stumps are held upright by sharp points so that they can be easily knocked over when a ball hits them.

Four feet from one of the wickets and parallel to it a line is marked. This is the "popping crease" or place for the batter to take his position.

On a line with the wicket the "bowling crease," or pitcher's line, eight feet, eight inches in length, is drawn.

The game—Eleven players make a team. Two players, one at each wicket, come to bat at the same time. The members of the fielding team place themselves wherever they think the ball might be hit. The bowler takes a short run from behind one of the wickets and hurls the ball, by an over-arm swing, toward the other wicket. He tries to knock the wicket down. The batter standing at the "popping crease" defends the wicket and tries to hit the ball clear of all of the players in the field. If he succeeds he runs to the opposite wicket twenty-two yards away. At the same time the batsman at that wicket runs—the two exchanging places. When they arrive safely they have made one run. If the ball is caught before it touches the ground or if it is thrown back and knocks down one of the wickets while the runners are between wickets, the player whose wicket is upset is out.

When all of the players of one side are out the opponents have their inning at the bat.

The bowler delivers six balls from one end and then another member of his team bowls six balls from the opposite wicket. Six balls is called an "over," but they must be good bowls.

The change in bowlers does not necessarily mean a change in batters. This depends entirely on what runs have been made. Any number of runs, from one to six, or more, can be scored on one hit. The runners keep going until the batted ball is recovered. If a single run has been made, the ends will be changed. But if two runs, or any even number of runs have been made, the batsman will be back where he was before.

When a batsman is out he leaves the field and the captain sends out a new man to take his place. This continues until the last two are on the field. When one of these is "out," the inning is over and the other side comes to the bat. A single player is not allowed to go on.

Equipment—The ball weighs five and one-half ounces and measures nine and one-half inches in circumference. The bat shall not exceed four and one-quarter inches at the widest part, nor be more than thirty-eight inches in length.

Bibliography

Hobbs, J. B.: *Cricket for Beginners* (Pearson, England).

Fender, P. G. H.: *A B C of Cricket* (Barker, England) (Sanders, America).

Touch football.—Touch football has become increasingly popular. Everywhere, in season, one can find groups of boys, and sometimes girls, playing the game. Playgrounds, streets, vacant lots, back alleys, and school grounds furnish playing fields of various sizes, shapes, and conditions. The game has been a growth rather than an invention. Therefore the rules vary slightly in different localities. This writer remembers those boyhood days when we used an old cap for the ball.

Most of the risks of injury, incident to the regulation game, are eliminated in touch football.

Equipment—A football.

Field—The regulation football field, 160 feet wide and 300 feet long, or whatever space is available.

Passes—Passing is the chief offensive weapon of the game. All players are eligible to receive passes. Forward passes can be thrown from any place back of the line of scrimmage. Lateral passes may be thrown at any time and from any position in back of or beyond the line of scrimmage. In some instances, by agreement, forward passing is allowed after the ball has passed the line of scrimmage.

Blocking—Players use the shoulder block, hands at breast, elbows spread. All use of the hands or outstretched arms in blocking is forbidden. Neither can a player leave his feet to block an opponent.

Tackling—All tackling is eliminated. A player is "downed" whenever an opponent touches him on any part of his body while he has possession of the ball.

Penalties—Foul penalties of fifteen yards are called for the following infractions:

1. For tackling, tripping, pushing, holding, roughing.
2. Using hands or leaving feet to block.

A penalty of five yards is called for off-side. A player is off-side when he is in his opponent's territory before the ball is snapped from center.

Periods—The game is usually played in four periods of ten to fifteen minutes each. Between the first and second and third and fourth periods there is a rest period of three minutes. Between the second and third periods there is a five-minute rest period.

Scoring—The scoring is the same as in the regulation game, six points for a touchdown, three points for a field goal or drop kick, two points for a safety, and one point for a successful play after touchdown.

Advancing the ball—The offensive team must advance the ball at least ten yards in four downs, just as in the regulation game, or surrender the ball to the opponents.

Softball (playground ball, kitten ball, indoor baseball).—This game has become tremendously popular. It is a bit less strenuous than regulation baseball, and it requires less skill. Therefore it can be enjoyed by a larger number than the regulation game. At most points the rules of regular baseball obtain. Exceptions are noted.

A regulation game shall consist of seven innings.

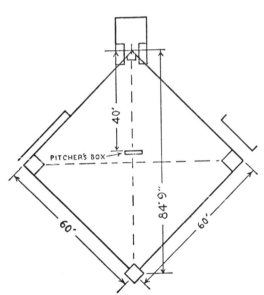

The field — The bases are sixty feet apart, the diamond shape used in baseball being in vogue. There are four bases, home, first, second, and third. Indoors and for younger players the base distance is forty-five feet.

The pitcher's plate or box is forty feet (for girls, thirty-five feet) f r o m home plate when the bases are sixty feet apart, and thirty-seven and one-half feet when they are forty-five feet apart.

Pitching—The pitcher must stand with both feet on the pitcher's plate, facing the batter. He may take only one step in the act of delivering the ball. In tossing the ball, he must use an underhand throw with a full arm swing. After he has released the ball he can take as many steps as he wishes.

Illegal pitches—The following illegal pitches entitles the base runner or base runners to advance one base and a ball is called in favor of the batter. However, if a batter strikes at the ball and *hits it into fair territory,* no penalty is called for an illegal pitch. The ball is in play as if the ball had been pitched legally, and the base runners may be put out as on any other play.

(1) Any delivery of the ball which violates the pitching rule noted above. That is, the pitcher must face the batter with both feet on the pitching rubber. He shall hold the ball in front of his body. In the act of delivering the ball he can take not more than one step, and one foot must be kept in contact with the pitcher's rubber until the ball has left his hand. The ball must be thrown underhand, and with a follow through of the hand and the wrist before the ball is released.

(2) Dropping the ball, accidentally or intentionally, when in position to pitch.

(3) Rolling the ball along the ground from pitching position.

(4) Making any motion to pitch without immediately delivering the ball.

(5) Delaying the game by holding the ball more than twenty seconds.

Base runners—A runner on third may not score on a ball that passes the batter, provided the catcher returns it immediately to the pitcher.

A runner is out if he fails to keep contact with the base to which he is entitled while the pitcher has the ball in pitching position. He must remain at the base until the pitched ball has left the pitcher's hand.

Number of players—Ten players constitute a team, one of the players acting as a roving fielder.

Softball touch football.—In this game a softball or playground ball is used instead of a football. Naturally, that eliminates kicking as a feature of the game. On the kickoff one of the players throws the ball from the twenty-five or thirty-yard line. His teammates line up at midfield and rush down the field to "tackle" the receiver. On a short field there would be suitable variation from this rule.

It is necessary for the offensive team to score a touchdown in four plays, no matter where the first play begins. If the age and skill of the players make this rule impractical, adaptations can be made, such as requiring the offensive team to make an advance of twenty yards in four plays.

In all other respects the same rules obtain as in Touch Football.

Field hockey.—This game was originated in Northern Europe. It has been a popular form of sport in England for nearly seventy years.

Equipment—Hockey sticks and a small cricket ball, covered with leather and about the size of a baseball.

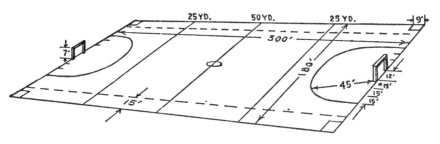

The field—Ninety to one hundred yards long and fifty to sixty yards wide.

Players—Eleven players on either side, though it is possible to use any number.

Time—Played in two thirty-minute halves.

Starting the game—The game is started by two players "tipping off" at the center of the field just as they do in "Shinney." This is called "bullying."

Outside balls are rolled in from the point at which they went outside. A ball that goes over the end boundary but not through the goal is put in play on the twenty-five-yard line by "tipping off."

Goal—The goal is twelve feet wide, marked by posts seven feet high connected by a cross bar.

Book.—*Hockey Guide,* Spalding Athletic Library. American Sports Publishing Company.

Ice hockey.—The field is 200 feet long by 85 feet or 160 feet long by 60 feet wide. The goal is ten feet from the end boundary. It is a movable cage four feet high and six feet wide. The puck is put

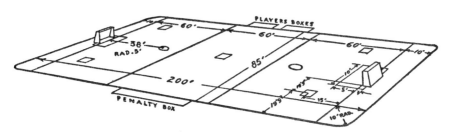

in play by the referee, who tosses it in between two center players who try to get possession.

Book.—*Spalding's Official Ice Hockey Guide* and *How to Play Ice Hockey,* American Sports Publishing Company.

Shinney.—Shinney is an adaptation of hockey. It grew up on the vacant lots and open fields wherever youngsters got together to play. In the neighborhood where this writer grew up every boy had his own shinney stick. Trees were always carefully inspected in the search for good sticks with just the right curve at the end. No golfer or hockey player with the most expensive equipment ever got more thrill out of hitting the ball or puck than the shinney player who hooked an old "crobate" (spikeless top) with a perfect swing that sent it sailing on a line through the air.

Equipment—A puck, spikeless top, or battered tin can. A shinney stick for each player. The stick should be about three feet long with a decided hook at the end.

Goals—The playing field is often determined by the available playing space. In the old days often a city street furnished the field, the curbings marking outside boundaries and the street intersections providing end boundaries. Where the space is available the field should be the same size as a hockey field.

At either end of the field a goal is marked by tin cans or stones. This goal is six to ten feet wide. A goal tender guards this goal, trying to prevent the puck from going through. Our group allowed scores for pucks hit through on the fly. Often the boys developed great skill in intercepting a line drive with the shinney stick, knocking it down, and returning it with lightning speed by a swift swing of the shinney stick.

Sometimes the entire width of the field is considered the goal. In this case a score is made whenever the puck goes across the end boundary.

Starting the game—The game is started at the center of the field by two players "tipping off." The puck is on the ground between them. They "tip off" by tapping the ground with the shinney stick and then tapping lightly each other's sticks down near the base of the stick. The two players often count as they "tip off," thus: "One, two, three!" After the third tip each player tries to hit the puck to a teammate. A favorite trick is to allow the opponent to hit first, blocking his stick by placing your own firmly on the ground in his way, and then quickly drawing the puck aside for a drive.

Advancing the puck—Players try to pass the puck on to teammates until finally a player gets it in position for a drive through the goal. One point is scored whenever the puck is driven through the goal.

Players must "shinney on their own side." In other words, they must face toward the goal for which they are driving. They cannot stand in the way, blocking an opponent.

Ice shinney—The game is played in the same fashion as "Shinney," excepting that the players all wear ice skates. A flat puck or battered tin can is used.

Pig-in-a-hole (sowbelly).—This is an inelegant name but a good game. Each player has a shinney stick. One player is counted out and he becomes "It." He digs a small hole in the ground with his stick. An old battered tin can or "crobate" is used and he rests this puck in the hole. Each of the other players digs a hole about ten to fifteen feet from hole dug by the one who is "It," making a circle of holes about him.

"It" now uses his stick to move the puck toward the circumference of the circle. Each player stands with his stick resting in the hole he has dug. If "It" drags the puck to a player's hole and rests it there in the hole that player is "It." His only hope is to hit the puck and knock it away, preferably out of the circle. In this case "It" must retrieve the puck and start again from center.

However, when a player removes the stick from his hole to hit the puck, "It" is privileged to take possession by setting the end of his stick in the hole before the hitter can get back into it. Players may leave their holes to help the attacked player by hitting the puck out of the circle. However, if a player leaves his position "It" may take possession by beating him to it. This means that "It" often fakes at being unaware of a player approaching from the back or side, only to come suddenly alive, dash past the daring player, and jab his stick in the empty hole. The puck must be within the circle when "It" takes charge of a hole if he would retain possession of it.

Badminton.—This is the old game of Battledore and Shuttlecock. It was played in India long ago. It has been popular in the Orient for at least 2,000 years. English army officers introduced it to England. In India they called it "poona." It is older than tennis. Badminton, England, the town which gave it it's present name is one hundred miles west of London.

Equipment—A racket somewhat smaller than a tennis racket. A "bird," which is a piece of cork or rubber with an even row of tiny feathers stuck into it.

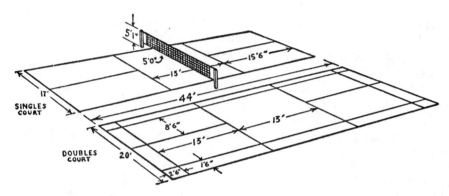

Playing field—The court is forty-four feet long and twenty feet wide. A service line six feet six inches from the middle is marked on either side of the net.

Two alleys, eighteen inches in width, extend down the two sides of the court. The inner line constitutes the boundary line when playing singles.

The top of the net is five feet one inch at either post and five feet at center.

Service—Service is made, first from the right hand court and then the left, as in lawn tennis. A server continues to serve until he loses a play.

In doubles, the player in the right hand court serves first. If the point is made his teammate serves from the left hand court.

When the server is out, the opponent or opponents serve.

The service must be made with an underhand stroke.

The "bird" on the service must be beyond the service line and within the bounds of the court served.

Fouls—(1) Touching the net with the racket or person.

(2) Reaching over the net to hit the "bird." (A racket following through a shot may go over the net without penalty.)

(3) Hitting the "bird" twice before sending it over the net.

(4) Feinting at service.

(5) Failing to stand within the proper court when serving.

(6) Failing to get the "bird" within the proper court on the serve.

(7) Knocking the "bird" outside the boundary lines.

(8) Serving overhanded.

Scoring—Points are scored as in volleyball, only the serving side scoring. A game is set at fifteen or twenty-one points. For women, eleven points constitutes a game. In a "fifteen" game, when the score is tied at thirteen-all, the side first reaching that score has the privilege of "setting" the game at five. That is, the first side scoring five points wins. If the score is tied at fourteen-all the side first reaching fourteen has the privilege of "setting" the game at three. That is the first side to score three points wins. In a game where twenty-one is out, nineteen and twenty are the scores at which the game may be set for five or three.

Pin ball.—*Equipment*—A softball, a baseball bat, two Indian Clubs, pop bottles or tin cans for pins.
Players—Any number of players for each team. The pitchers and catchers are particularly important.

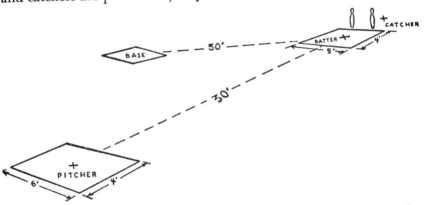

Field—A ball diamond may be used, using only one base. The distance of this base would depend on the skill and age of the players. Under any circumstances it should not be longer than thirty feet.
The batter's box at home plate should be four feet wide and five feet long. Directly behind this box set up the two pins, one foot apart.
The pitcher's box should be thirty feet from the batter's box. It is four feet wide by six feet long.
The pitcher must serve the ball underhand. The batter strikes as in baseball. The batter may be put out any time his bat is not touching the ground within the limits of the batter's box, by an opponent's bowling one or the other of the pins down. He runs for base (1) when he hits the ball, (2) when the catcher fails to catch the ball, or (3) any other time when he thinks he has a chance to get on base and back before his pins can be bowled over. He scores every time he gets to base and back without being put out.

Any opponent may bowl the pins down when the bat is not touching the ground within the batter's box. However, good team play usually calls for a throw to the catcher so he can bowl down one of the pins.

A caught fly it out. There are no strikes nor fouls. Three outs retire the side.

Tether ball.—*Equipment* —A pole ten feet above ground. It should not be over seven and one-h a l f inches in circumference at the base. Six feet above the ground paint a two-inch stripe.

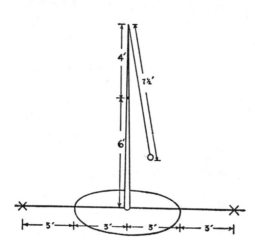

A tennis ball or sponge-rubber ball is encased in a cord mesh or a tight-fitting sack and hung from the top of the pole by a heavy fishing cord. This cord is attached at the top to a heavy screw-eye. It is 7½ feet long.

The ball is hit with a tennis racket or heavy paddle. The paddles should be about eight inches wide and twelve inches long exclusive of the handle. They should be made of five-ply wood or of two three-ply pieces glued together. The handles should be about four inches long and they need to be reinforced with eight-inch strips on either side. Smooth all rough edges.

The field—A circle six feet in diameter is marked around the pole. A straight line twenty feet long bisects this circle, dividing the court into two sections. Six feet from the pole on either side a cross is marked on this bisecting line. These two crosses mark the serving spots.

The play—The ball is put in play by one player serving from one of the serving spots. He hits it with the idea of winding the string around the pole above the six-foot stripe. The server may choose the direction in which he desires to wind the string. The opponent tries to hit the ball back and wind it in the opposite direction.

Fouls— (1) A player fouls when he steps into the circle or over the dividing line. (2) When he winds the string around the pole below the six-foot stripe. (3) When he winds the string around his racket.

The penalty for a foul is a free hit by the opponent. If he can wind the string around the pole in one unimpeded stroke he scores a point.

Score—Players set the score. Usually eleven to fifteen points make a game.

Volleyball.—This is a popular game. It provides good and not too strenuous exercise, being especially helpful in developing the muscles of the chest. It was invented in 1895 by William J. Morgan for use in the Holyoke, Massachusetts, Y.M.C.A.

The field—The field is 60 feet long and 30 feet wide. The net should be seven and one-half feet high at its upper edge and of even height throughout.

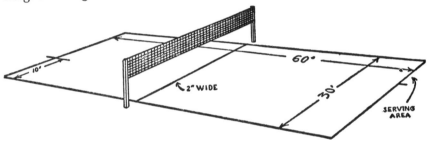

Service—The ball is served from the right-hand corner of the court just behind the end boundary line. The service, and, in fact, all hitting of the ball, must be with the open hand.

A ball that tips the net before going over on the service is a dead ball. A returned ball, however, is good if it goes over after touching the net.

A player continues serving until he makes a faulty serve or until his team fails to make good on a return.

Each player serves in turn.

The ball must go over the net on the serve without help from a teammate.

Rotation—Players rotate to the left after a service by their opponents has been "killed."

Returning—A team is not allowed to take more than three tips to get the ball over the net. (In many cases this rule is waived by agreement, allowing any number of tips. In an inexperienced group this will add interest to the game.)

Skilled players usually tip the ball to a teammate at the net, who smashes it over.

The ball may be played off of the net after the service play is made.

Fouls— (1) Catching the ball; (2) Hitting with the fist; (3) Getting into the opponent's territory; (4) Touching the net with any part of the body; (5) Hitting the ball more than once in succession.

Score—Fifteen or twenty-one points make a game. A tie at fourteen-all or twenty-all requires that one team make two points in succession to win.

Adaptations—With unskilled players it is sometimes advisable to allow a help-over on the serve. This can only be done by agreement between the two teams.

A lot of fun can be had by playing more than the regulation six players. In large groups this is preferable because it gives more people a chance to play.

Paddle tennis.—Invented about 1908 by Frank Beal, who later became Recreational and Educational Director for Judson Memorial Church, New York.

Field—One-fourth the size of a regulation tennis court—thirty-nine feet long and thirteen and one-half feet wide. For doubles, eighteen feet, adding lanes two feet three inches to either side of the court. The net is twenty-six inches high at the middle and twenty-eight inches at the posts.

Equiment—A sponge-rubber ball, a net, and heavy wooden paddles.

Rules—Play as in regulation tennis except that the server bounces the ball before serving.

Deck tennis.—A ship game now used widely on playgrounds and gymnasium floors.

Field—The court is forty feet long and twelve feet wide. For doubles add a lane three feet deep to either side. The net is four feet, eight inches high. Three feet beyond the middle, on either side of the net, a foul line is drawn. Service must be beyond this line. A middle line dividing the court is necesary for doubles.

Service—Service is underhanded from any place back of the boundary line in singles. It must be made from first the right-hand and then the left-hand court for doubles. A net serve that drops over into foul territory gives the server another try. A service topping the net and going into fair territory may be played or not at the discretion of the receiver. If not played, the server tries again. A server continues to serve as long as he scores points. Points are only made on the serve as in volleyball. Fifteen points constitute a game. At fourteen-all, a server must make two points in succession to go out.

Receiving—The receiver must stand back of the boundary line until the serve. He must catch and return the teniquoit immediately. Players often develop skill in serving and returning with varied methods, such as the spinner, the wobble, and the end over end shot.

Equipment—A net and a rubber ring six inches in diameter. The trade name for the ring is "teniquoit," obtainable from any sporting goods house.

Six-man football.—This game was invented by Stephen Epler, a teacher in Nebraska, in 1934, to meet the needs of small schools that hardly have enough players to make regulation football practical.

It calls for two ends, a center, and three backfield players. Players wear sneakers or basketball shoes, and regulation football regalia is unnecessary.

Open play, the decrease in pile-up plays, and the absence of cleats lessen the chance of injury. Strategy is at a premium.

Three men must be on the line at the snap of the ball. The man receiving the ball from center must pass it to a teammate before it can be advanced. This eliminates direct line bucks. The ball must go at least two yards through the air after leaving the passer's hand, by forward, lateral, or backward flip.

Forward passing can be done from any place back of the line of scrimmage. Any man may catch a pass except the offensive center, and there is some agitation to permit even the center to receive passes.

The kickoff is made from the twenty-yard line. The receiving team may line up anywhere it desires, except that no man can be closer than ten yards to the ball at the kickoff.

Fundamentals are the same as regulation football.

The field—The dimensions of the field are eighty yards long by forty yards wide. It is marked off in five-yard stripes. The goal posts are wider and lower than in regulation football.

ORIGIN AND FIELD DIMENSIONS OF OTHER SPORTS

Croquet.—The game originated in France. It was carried from there to Ireland and then to England. Public match games were played in England as early as 1867.

Field—A court twenty-five by fifty feet, or thirty by sixty feet is desirable. The ground should be level, with closely cropped grass.

Golf.—The Dutch claim that golf was played in Holland early in the fourteenth century. Scotland also lays claim to it and as early as 1457 we find the ruler and parliament in Scotland legislating against golf and football because they were displacing archery as a national sport.

Bibliography—How to Play Golf, Innis Brown, Spalding Athletic Library (American Sports Publishing Co.); *Golf Facts for Young People,* Frances Ouinet (Century), 1921; *Down the Fairway,* R. T. Jones and O. B. Keeler (Minton Balch), 1927; *A New Way to Better Golf,* Alex Morrison (Simon and Schuster), 1932.

Fencing.—The sword was an ancient weapon of combat. Before man knew how to make weapons of metal he learned to parry and thrust with sticks and clubs. As early as 1500 B.C. iron was used to make swords. Before that bronze had been used. Arabic culture taught the Western world how to make better steel, and swords became lighter and sharper. The French did much to develop the art of fencing. It was popular also in Italy and England.

Bibliography—Fencing, Breck (American Sports Publishing Co.); *The Art of Fencing,* Regis and Louis Senoc (American Sports Publishing Co.), 1922; *The Theory and Practice of Fencing,* Castello (Scribners), 1933.

Football.—Plato credits it to the Egyptians. There is evidence that it was known in the valley of the Nile as early as the Twelfth Dynasty. The ancient Greeks and Romans played with an inflated animal bladder. The game was played in England and Scotland from the beginning of their history. There were frequent royal edicts against it because it was "a dangerous sport." Queen Elizabeth on two occasions forbade the playing of football in London.

The present Rugby game of football had its inception when an English player named William Webb Ellis, of Rugby, England, disregarded the rules and ran with the ball. That was in 1823.

A game virtually the same as present-day football was played at Harvard University by class teams as early as 1830. The first intercollegiate game to attract public attention was played on November 6, 1869, between Rutgers and Princeton.

Field—360 feet long and 160 feet wide.

Bibliography—Practical Football, Crisler, H. O., and Wieman, E. E. (McGraw-Hill), 1934; *Football Line Plays for Coaches and Players,* B. F. Oakes (A. S. Barnes Co.).

Baseball.—Modern baseball was probably born at Cooperstown, New York, about 1839. Abner Doubleday is generally credited with being the originator. The old British game of "Rounders," town ball, tip-tap-bat, and one-old-cat are close relatives. That there was a game called baseball before Doubleday is credited with inventing the modern game is proven by the fact that Oliver Wendell Holmes played baseball at Harvard from which he graduated in 1829.

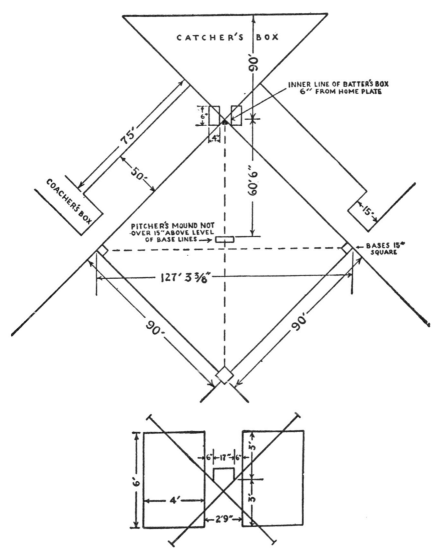

Field—Four bases. Diamond shaped infield. The bases are **ninety** feet apart. The pitcher's box or rubber is in the center of the diamond on an imaginary line drawn between first and third bases, sixty and one-half feet from the back end of home plate.

Basketball.—Dr. James Naismith, an instructor in the Young Men's Christian Association at Springfield, Mass., invented this game in 1891. He wanted a game to fill in the interval between football in the autumn and baseball in the spring. The first basket used was an ordinary peach crate and the first ball was a football.

Field—Maximum, ninety-four feet by fifty feet. Minimum, sixty feet by thirty-five feet. Ten feet above the floor at either end of the field are two metal rings eighteen inches in diameter. The free throw line is fifteen feet from the goal.

Handball.—This game was played in Ireland as far back as the tenth century. It was introduced in the United States about 1840.

Field—Single wall court, thirty-four feet long and twenty feet wide. The wall is sixteen feet high.

Four-wall court, forty-six feet long and twenty-two feet wide. The wall is twenty-two feet high.

The serving area is at least sixteen feet from the wall.

Jai Lai (Pronounced Hy-Ly) or **Pelota** (pronounced Pay-lo-ta). A Basque game introduced into South America and Cuba from Northern Spain.

Field—Court, 200 feet long and 65 feet wide. A frontis or fronton (front wall) is thirty-six feet square. In the back there is a similar wall called *la parde de rebote* or rebounding wall. On the front wall iron stripes painted red mark boundaries in which the ball must strike.

Equipment—Light wicker workbasket about eighteen inches long fastened to the hand by a glove attachment. The basket is long and narrow, about five inches wide at the end. The ball is about the size of a tennis ball. It has a core of India rubber bound with yarn and covered with sheepskin.

Service and return—On the serve a player at the middle of the floor bounces the ball, turns around swiftly, and catches it on the first bounce to throw it against the front wall. An opponent must catch it on the fly or on the first bounce and return it to the wall. There must be no holding of the ball in the basket. It must be kept in motion. Failure to return the ball scores a point for the opponent. The play is fast and furious. Singles or doubles are played. Fifty points constitutes a game.

LaCrosse.—This game was originally played by the North American Indians, who called it *crosse*. They ornamented their hoops and handles with feathers, tufts of hair, and paint or dye.

Field—110 to 125 yards long and 50 to 75 yards wide. The goal posts are six feet above the ground and six feet apart.

Polo.—The game was played in Persia before the Christian era. There are evidences that it was played in the Orient as early as the tenth century.

Field—750 feet long and 500 feet wide, when possible. A white board ten inches high borders the length of the field on both sides. The ends are open. The goal is in the middle of each end of the field, where stand two very light goal posts twenty-four feet apart. The ball is of basswood, three and one-eighth inches in diameter and weighing five ounces. The sticks are fifty to fifty-six inches long with mallet on the end.

Soccer.—See "Football."

Field—Maximum length, 130 yards. Minimum length, 100 yards. Maximum width, 100 yards. Minimum width, 50 yards. The field of play should be marked by boundary lines. Side lines are touch lines. End lines are goal lines. A flagstaff not less than five feet

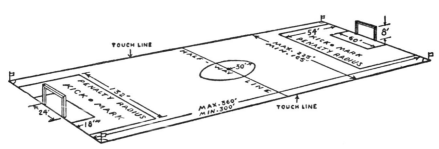

tall is placed at each corner of the field. A halfway line is marked across the middle of the field. The center of the field should be indicated by a suitable mark, and a circle with a radius of ten yards should be marked around it. The goal posts are upright posts fixed on the goal lines, equidistant from the corner flagstaffs, and eight yards apart, with a bar across them at the height of eight feet from the ground. Goal posts and crossbars should not be over five inches in width. The goal area is marked off by lines six yards from the goal posts at right angles to the goal lines and connected by a line twenty yards long and parallel with the goal line. The penalty radius is drawn around this goal area with lines eighteen yards long at right angles to the goal lines and connected by a line forty-four yards long, parallel to the goal lines. A suitable mark should be made twelve yards from the goal line. This is the penalty-kick mark.

Tennis.—Tennis was a child of handball. Not content with the necessary wall, boys began to stretch a piece of string between two poles, and then batted the ball back and forth over this first "net."

During the fourteenth century this type of handball became exceedingly popular in France and Italy. A woman, Mme. Margot, came to Paris from Rainault to compete in a tournament. She used a "battoir," a wooden frame covered with parchment, and defeated all comers. This was the first racket. The balls she used were made of soft rubber. Thus began the game of tenez, or tennis.

The popularity of the game spread quickly and as early as 1365 we find edicts forbidding the game in England.

The first lawn tennis game in America was played at Nahant, Massachusetts, in 1874. At one time the regulations called for the net to be seven feet high at the sidelines and four feet eight inches at the middle.

Field—The court is seventy-eight feet long and twenty-seven feet wide. The service line is twenty-two feet from the net. The net is three feet high at the middle and three feet six inches at the posts. For doubles, outside lines are marked four and one-half feet on either side, the length of the court.

Rackets or racquets.—Efforts have been made to trace the game back to ancient origin but the game as played today was probably not known before the nineteenth century. It is popular in England.

Field—The court is usually sixty feet by thirty feet. Players serve from service boxes about five feet three inches square at the sides of the court, about thirty-five feet ten inches from the front wall. The walls, front and side, are fifteen feet high. The back wall is seven feet high.

Equipment—A racket similar to a tennis racket, but smaller and round, is used. The ball is one inch in diameter and one ounce in weight. It is made of cloth strips wound over each other and bound with twine. This is covered with smooth white leather.

Play—Players serve the ball against the front wall and the opponent must play it on the rebound. Players develop skill in serving at such an angle as to make a return difficult.

Fifteen points constitutes a game.

Squash rackets.—This game is similar to Rackets except that the court is smaller and the ball is made of India rubber. The court is thirty-two feet by twenty-one feet. The floor in a closed court is made of wood. The open court has a cement floor. The American court is thirty-one feet by eighteen feet six inches.

The top of the play line on the front wall is nineteen inches from the floor. The service line is six feet from the floor.

The short line is fourteen feet from the back wall. The service boxes are five feet three inches square.

Fifteen points is a game.

Shuffleboard.—(1) The game of shuffleboard is played by either two persons (called singles), or by four persons (called doubles).

(2) The object of the game is to propel discs by means of a cue onto scoring diagram at opposite end of court—to score, to prevent opponent from scoring, or both.

Court—(1) The court shall measure fifty-two feet in length and

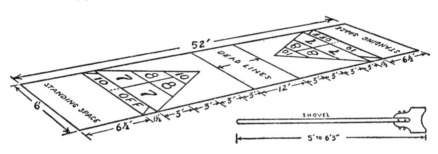

six feet in width. The playing surface shall be concrete or terrazzo —preferably concrete.

(2) The court shall be marked according to the official diagram. Maximum width of lines, one and one-half inches; minimum width, three-fourth inches. All dimensions measured to line centers. The separation line is now replaced by a triangle three inches at base running to a point. The outline of this triangle shall be one-quarter-inch lines; a clearance of one-half inch at point and base of triangle from 10-off space lines.

(3) One end of court shall be designated as Head of Court; the opposite end as Foot of Court.

Equipment—(1) Discs shall be made of wood or composition not less than three-quarter inches and not more than one inch in thickness; six inches in diameter; and not less than eleven and a half ounces, nor more than fifteen ounces in weight. Four discs shall be colored red, four colored black. These eight discs comprise a set. Care should be taken that all discs in a set shall be uniform in weight and thickness.

(2) The cue shall not have an over-all length of more than six feet three inches. No metal parts on cue shall touch playing surface of court.

Playing rules—(1) Choice of color is determined by each player (if singles), and by one of each team (if doubles), playing one disc to farthest dead line. The player whose disc is nearest this line has choice of color. In doubles, team players may change ends of court once before play begins, but at no time thereafter.

(2) To start a game, the red disc is shot first. Play alternates—red, then black—until all discs are shot. Red shall always be played from right side of Head of Court, and left side of Foot of Court. *In singles*—after all discs are played, constituting a half round, the players walk to opposite end of court, or Foot of Court, and start play, with the color lead changing to black. In doubles—after all discs are played at Head of Court, play starts at foot or opposite end—Red leading, Black following. Color lead does not change until both ends have played a "round." A "round" consists of complete play at head and foot of court—a "half-round," complete play at one end of court.

(3) Game is considered on 50-, 75-, or 100-point basis. Match play shall be on the basis of best two out of three games. The second game is started by the black at the end of court where preceding game finished play. (At that end of court where disc were being played to.) The third game is started by the Red under the same conditions as start of second game.

(4) Players shall place their four discs within and not touching lines of their respective half of 10-off area. *Penalty—5-off.* (It is common practice with players to jockey or slide the playing disc backward and forward to see if there is sand which might interfere with disc sliding evenly. No penalty to be called on this practice if lines are touched or crossed.)

Discs being played—Discs must be played from the clear from within the respective half of 10-off area—if not, *a Penalty of 10-off,* offender's disc removed, and opponent credited with any discs displaced. Discs in motion may cross diagonal line. *No penalty* inflicted if disc being played, starting in clear, should touch or cross separation triangle. *No Hesitation shots* allowed; forward motion of disc must be continuous. *Penalty—10-off,* offender's disc removed and opponent credited with score of any of his displaced discs.

(5) Players shall not step on or over base line of court, or extension of base line, real or imaginary. (Except to gather and place their discs.) *Penalty—5-off.* Players may stand in alley between courts, but not on adjoining court, making their play or sighting play on disc. *Penalty—5-off.*

(6) Players must remain seated when play is to their end of court until all discs are shot, score announced, and Official has called "Play." *Penalty—5-off.*

(7) Players shall not stand in the way of, or have cue in the way of, or interfere with, opponent while he is executing a play. *Penalty—5-off.* Players shall not touch live discs at any time. *Penalty—5-off.*

(8) Players must not talk or make remarks to disconcert opponent's play. *Penalty—10-off.*

(9) Any remark of motion to partner which indicates coaching his play is prohibited. *Penalty—10-off.*

(10) A disc, or discs, returning or remaining on court after having struck any object other than a live disc shall be removed before further play. A disc from an adjoining court is called a dead disc, and shall be immediately removed; if it displaces any disc, that half-round shall be played over. Any score lost as above noted, other than disc from adjoining court, is credited to player or players, and play continues.

(11) A disc which stops in area between farthest dead line and starting area is dead, and shall be removed before further play.

(12) A disc which stops just beyond farthest base line shall be removed at least eight inches back from base line.

(13) A disc which is more than halfway over side of court, and which rests or leans on edge, shall be immediately removed.

Scoring— (1) Scoring Diagram—one 10-point area; two 8-point areas; two 7-point areas; one 10-off area. (See diagram.)

(2) After both players have shot their four discs, SCORE ALL discs on diagram (those within and not touching lines; separation triangle in 10-off area not considered.)

(3) Play continues until all discs have been shot even if game point has been reached.

(4) If a tie score results at game point or over, two complete rounds shall be played (if doubles), and score totaled. Highest score at game point or over shall be declared the winner. If score is tied again, or is below game point, play continues again as above outlined. In singles—one round of play shall decide tie.

Officials— (1) Officials in tournament play shall be: Tournament Manager; Divisional Referees; Court Referees; Court Umpires; Court Scorers.

(2) "The Tournament Manager" shall have complete charge of all arrangements of the tournament—namely, conduct the drawings, pairings, assign the courts, officials, set time for starting games and matches, inspect all courts and equipment, etc., and all other detail which enters into tournament play.

(3) "Divisional Referee"—one or more Divisional Referees shall be appointed, number dependent on how many courts are in play and number of tournaments being run off at the same time. The Divisional Referees are the aides of the Tournament Manager, and shall carry out his orders regarding assigning officials and players to courts. He shall see that discs, indicators, pointers, chalk, score cards, and other necessary equipment are at each court. He shall inform court officials of any special rules and regulations which have been made for the conducting of the tournament. He shall collect all score cards at finish of matches and return same to Tournament Manager. He shall have jurisdiction only on the section of courts assigned to him. Divisional Referees shall be informed by Court Referees of all "Players Appeals," and if decision made by Court Referee is not justified or not according to rules may overrule same.

(4) "Court Referee" shall have complete charge of play on court assigned to him. He shall consult his Divisional Referee on all "Appeal from Players." He shall be sole authority on decisions and scores, except as above noted. He shall always officiate at Head of Court, changing position only if Head of Court changes as result of games ending. He shall determine and announce winner of color choice. He shall inform players of any rules and regulations made for the tournament. He shall give signal for start of play, shall call disc

good or no count, shall remove dead discs from play, shall announce score at end of each play at his end of court. He shall have charge of color indicator and announce color lead. He shall announce any violation of rules and instruct scorer as to penalty of same.

(5) "Court Umpire" shall take charge of play at "Foot of Court" and assume same duties of Court Referee pertaining to play only, referring any decision on rules or violations "On Appeal" to Court Referee. Officials shall not touch discs in determining whether it is good or no count, and "they shall not" gather discs for the players.

(6) "Court Scorer" shall tally clearly the score of game on scoreboard at end of court, tallying only score called by Court Referee and Court Umpire, after each round. He shall also record on the official score card the final scores of each game of the match, sign and return to the Divisional Referee.

Appeals—(1) Players in match play may appeal decision rendered by an official, if made before any live disc is touched or moved. Appeal shall be heard. (2) Players may request officials to give them information concerning location of discs. (3) Player or players making appeal without sufficient reason shall be "penalized 10 points off score." (4) A player or team may protest any one or more officials assigned to their court, provided such protest is placed before the Divisional Referee or Tournament Manager before the choice of color has been made. Tournament Manager or Divisional Referee may appoint other officials to serve in place of those protested, which appointment must stand.

Substitutes—One substitute may be registered for each team in tournament play. This substitute may, in case of physical disability of the regular player during the match, take up play. The Tournament Manager decides on the physical disability of player. Disabled player may not return.

Penalty for illegal substitution—forfeiture of match.

Wet courts—If Tournament Manager shall deem it necessary to discontinue play on account of weather conditions, any unfinished game or match shall be resumed later, at score and color lead where play ceased.

Violations and penalties—

D-4 Discs not in starting area	....	5-off
D-4 Disc touching lines	....	5-off
D-5 Stepping on or over baseline	....	5-off
D-5 Stepping on next court	....	5-off
D-6 Player not remaining seated	....	5-off
D-7 Standing in way of, or equipment in way of, opponent	....	5-off
D-7 Touching live discs	....	5-off
D-4 Played disc touching lines	....	10-off
offending disc removed and opponents credited with amount of score lost by violation.		
D-4 Hesitation shot	....	10-off
offending disc removed, etc.		
D-8 Remarks disconcerting opponent	....	10-off
D-9 Talking to or coaching partner	....	10-off
G-3 Appealing without reason	....	10-off
H-1 Illegal substitution	...........................Forfeiture of match

INTERPRETATIONS

Error in Color Lead—Error in color lead shall be corrected if discovered before half-round play is completed; otherwise, play continues in order started at beginning of game.

Correction means—half-round played over with correct color lead.

Balk—The Balk rule has been taken out, and Rule D-11 covers same.

A Mounted Disc or disc resting on top of disc, happens sometimes when players use excessive force in shooting. Scoring rules apply just the same to disc on top as to disc on court.

Disc or Discs broken in play—Play entire half-round over.

Ground Rules—May be made to meet local conditions. The use of sand is considered under ground rules.

Measurement of Disc to Line—In play for color lead center of disc to line center.

Penalty Under D-4—Penalty not applied until "after" disc is played.

—Official National Shuffleboard Rules, adopted by Florida Shuffleboard Association, revised 1934 and 1937 by P. V. Gahan, President, National Shuffleboard Association. Used by permission.

Spot ball.—Draw a circle from three to six feet in diameter. Divide it by a line drawn through the center. One-half of the players are on one side of the dividing line and one half on the other. A live rubber ball is used (a rubber playball or a volleyball will do). The server bounces the ball and then bats it with his hand so that the second bounce is within the "spot." The opponents return the ball by hitting it, trying to get it within the circle on the first bounce. This continues until one side fails to hit it within the circle. After the serve the ball is dead whenever it touches the floor or ground outside the "spot." A player must not step over the line nor on the rim of the circle. Neither may he reach over into the circle to hit the ball. Points are scored as in volleyball.

Tennis spot ball.—The game is played in similar style to regular Spot Ball except that a tennis ball is used and the players use tennis rackets. The players are not allowed to serve closer than ten feet from the rim of the circle. No smashes are allowed.

Instead of the circle the spot may be a strip six feet wide across the playing space.

Kick ball (Hit-pinball).—Four Indian clubs or long-necked bottles. A volleyball, or playball. Bases twenty to thirty feet apart—circles one foot in diameter with Indian club in circle. Full team or more, if desired. Pitcher rolls ball along floor or ground—no bounding or shooting ball through the air. Batter stands beside circle at home plate and, as ball comes, steps in front of the plate and kicks. In an enclosed field, or where there are enough players to play them all around the field, no fouls are called. Every kicked ball is fair. When the batter kicks the ball he must make the complete circuit of the bases. He cannot stop at any of the intermediate bases. A player is out when a pitched ball knocks down the Indian club at home plate or when the batter knocks it down in attempting to kick. He is out when the fielders get the ball ahead of him and the baseman knocks down the Indian club at that base, scooping it down with the ball in his possession. The fielders must start the ball at first base, and it must go around the bases in regular order—1st, 2nd, 3rd, and home. A line fly caught on the infield does not put a batter out. A fly caught in the outfield *is* out.

Score ball.—Volleyball, playball, basketball, baseball, or bean bag. Two equal sides. Toss up in center or toss coin for possession. Side obtaining possession tries to keep the ball in possession of their teammates. Each catch of the ball, either through the air or on the bounce, or rolling, counts one point for the side of the player making the catch. The players keep the ball moving and do not stop each time a score is made. May be placed in ten-minute halves. This is a variation of "Keep-It-Ball."

Punch ball.—Playball or volleyball. Bases twenty to thirty feet apart. Regular baseball positions. Pitcher "lobs" the ball to the batter who punches it with his fist, and runs for first base. A player may be put out by a caught fly, by a force out, or by being hit with the ball while anywhere between bases. No stealing of bases is allowed, and base runners must hold bases until the ball is hit. Regular baseball rules, other than the variations mentioned.

Bean bag basketball.—Two of tallest players, good catchers, hold aloft large wastebaskets or one-gallon tin cans. These are the goal posts and baskets. These players must stand flat-footed, and may not take even one step in any direction on penalty of committing a foul. They may reach as far as they can in any direction so long as they do not take a step with either foot. Regular basketball rules. Regular basketball, volleyball, or playball, may be used instead of a bean bag.

Center dodge.—Players form a circle with one man in center. Use volleyball or playball. Players throw ball at center man endeavoring to hit him. This player can take any position inside the circle to avoid being hit. When hit, he takes the place of the player hitting him and the game proceeds. Players must throw only from the circle.

Dodge ball.—Played much like "Center Dodge" only a whole team goes to center. As soon as a player is hit, he must retire from the circle. A hit scored again before he gets out scores a point for the tossing side.

When two men are hit by one throw of the ball only the first one hit retires from the circle.

Play two- to five-minute halves. Every man left at end of agreed time scores one point for that team.

Players must not step inside the circle to throw.

If desired, ruling may be made to the effect that hits above the belt do not count. This ruling would lessen likelihood of injury by being hit in the face.

Bombardment.—Divide into equal sides. Field about forty to fifty feet long and twenty to thirty feet wide. Dividing line at middle. Players scatter anywhere in their own territory, but no player must step over the dividing line into the opponents territory. At either end of field, stand in a row as many Indian clubs (or pop bottles) as there are players on a side. With a volleyball, basketball, or playball, players attempt to knock down opponent's clubs. The opponents protect clubs by catching or blocking the ball. If the ball hits something outside the field and knocks a club on the rebound it counts. No time is taken out. Game plays for fifteen minutes with ball shooting back and forth rapidly. Interest is added if two balls are in play at the same time.

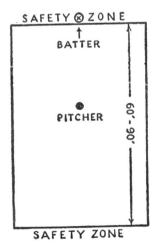

Safety zone ball.—The beauty of this game is that you can use everyone who will play, and that special skill is not needed for one to enjoy playing. I have seen a hundred or more players in the game, with about fifty to a side.

Equipment—Volleyball or heavy rubber playball.

Place—Gym or field.

Size—Two safety zones are marked off sixty feet apart. The width of the field would be either the width of a regulation baseball diamond or the width of the gym.

Procedure—Players who take the field scatter themselves so as to guard all the territory where a ball is liable to be hit. If there are enough players anything on a line with the safety zones may be called a "fair ball." The pitcher "lobs" the ball up easily with an underhand throw. "Hard" pitching is barred. If the batter chooses not to run he remains within the safety zone and steps to one side to be ready to run when some player happens to hit the ball far enough to make it safe to run. However, if this policy of choosing not to run is continued until the supply of batters is exhausted the side is automatically out.

A player is out:

(1) When he knocks a "flyball" which is caught.

(2) When the batted ball is fielded and he is hit with it while he is outside the safety zone. A player fielding the ball must throw from where he gets it. It is best, therefore, often, to relay the ball to a teammate who is in position to hit the runner.

(3) Sometimes only one out is allowed a side. This writer has found it more fun to allow three outs.

(4) Immediately a side is retired the fielding side must hurry to get past the batting safety zone. The batting side rushes out to get possession of the ball. If they hit one of the opponents before he can get to safety they stay at bat. Therefore, when a fielder catches a "fly" he shouts to his teammates and tosses the ball straight up in the air, rushing for safety and calling on all teammates to do the same. When the runner has been hit there is the same rush for safety on the part of the fielding team.

Do not introduce Rule Four until the group gets familiar with the game.

A runner scores when he goes down to the safety zone and back to the "batting" safety zone, though he does not have to make the trip down and back on one play. There is no limit to the number of runners who may occupy a safety zone at one time. A player may only run on a batted ball. There is no "stealing of bases" allowed.

Stop ball.—Use a volleyball or rubber playball. Divide into two or more groups, not over ten in a group. The fielding side scatters over the playing space while the side at the bat lines up, single file. One player "lobs" the ball up to the head man in the single file. That player hits the ball with his fist and immediately starts running around his teammates who remain standing in single file. The fielding side scurries to line up single file behind the player who fields the ball. When they have all lined up they yell, "Stop!" The base runner halts immediately. One point is scored for each complete circling of his line. The fielding side remains lined up single file at the point where the ball was fielded to become the batting side. Their opponents scatter to field the ball and the game continues. Several games may go on in the same play space simultaneously.

Hand tennis.—*The court*—The court is forty feet long and sixteen feet wide is divided in the center by a net two feet four inches high. Three feet from the net and on each side of it, there is a line called the foul line the full width of the court.

The Ball—The ball may be hit with either hand. It is permissible to turn the hand so as to cut and curve the ball.

In play—The ball is put in play by the server who must stand behind the rear line of the court and drop the ball to the ground, then hit it over the net underhand after the first bounce. The receiver must allow a served ball to bounce before returning it. After the served ball had been played it may be returned on the fly or after the first bounce.

Two serves—The only time two serves are allowed is when the first serve hits the net and goes over. If the server serves into the net or out of bounds, he loses his serve and the ball goes to the other side.

Good balls—If during play the ball hits the net and goes over, it is a good ball.

The server—The server continues to serve so long as he is scoring points. When a server fails to make a good return, he loses the serve. It is a hand-out, as in handball.

Points—Points are scored when a player fails to return the ball over the net or fails to return it so that it strikes the ground inside the opponent's court. The court runs from net to base line. Points can be scored only by the side that is serving.

Foul line—Stepping over the foul line during the game is a foul and the offender loses one point. If the server fouls, he loses his serve.

The winner—The winner is the one who first scores fifteen points.

Doubles—When playing doubles, the serve alternates between partners every time they win back the serve, which means that both members of the team serve before the serve goes to the other side.

Variation—May be played according to the above rules. Use heavy wooden paddles and a sponge ball.

Sidewalk hand tennis.—Use tennis ball or any hollow rubber ball. The line between two blocks of sidewalk is the middle line. Players take positions in the two blocks and bounce ball back and forth, hitting with the hand. A return must go over the middle line and in bounds to be good. Out of bounds would be considered any ball landing outside of the lines around the two blocks. Eleven points is considered a game. Players alternate serving.

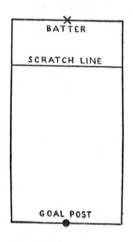

BATTER

SCRATCH LINE

GOAL POST

German bat ball. — *Equipment* — A rubber playball or volleyball.

Field—Space thirty to seventy feet. A larger or smaller area may be used. A scratch line is drawn ten feet from the batter's line. A post, tree, or other marker is used as a goal post anywhere from forty to sixty feet from the batter's line. It is placed in the middle of the base line.

The play—Any number of players may be used, the sides being evenly divided. The first batter steps up and hits the ball with his open hand. (If the playing field is crowded allow the batter to hit with his clenched fist.) No pitcher and no catcher are needed, since the batter tosses up his own ball. The batted ball must go over the scratch line before it hits the ground. If it does not, the batter is out. At the same time the ball must hit within the playing field to be fair. Three strikes are allowed, but it is not likely that any player will strike out. When the ball is hit the batter must run around the goal post and back to the batting line. He may hesitate at the goal post, but only for five seconds. The runner may duck, zigzag, and in other ways try to avoid being hit. The fielders retrieve the batted ball and try to hit the runner with it, while he is in the playing area between the goal post and the batting line. A fielder is allowed to take only one step with the ball in his possession. He may not hold the ball for longer than five seconds. Nor is he allowed to bounce it. He may pass it to another player, but two players are not allowed to pass the ball back and forth from one to the other more than twice, before passing it to a third player. A batter is out when he hits a fly that is caught, when he is hit by the ball thrown by a fielder, and when he fails to hit the ball beyond the scratch line before it hits the ground.

Three outs retire the side.

Triangle ball.—Here is a good ball game for limited space. Number of players on a side—from two on up.

Ball used—Rubber playball, tennis ball, ten-cent store hollow rubber ball.

Playing field—An equilaterial triangle, twenty or thirty feet to a side. The batter stands at the apex of the triangle and acts as his own catcher, returning to the pitcher deliveries that do not suit him. The open hand is used instead of a club in hitting the ball. The ball must be hit on the ground or directly at one of the opposing fielders. If the batter hits the ball outside the triangle on a fly he is out. This rule is designed to keep down the score. The principal opportunities for a player to reach first base are to hit the ball on the ground between the opposing players or to hit one too hard to handle. With the exceptions cited regular softball rules are observed.

Sack baseball.—A small sack filled with sand or a bean bag for a ball. Bases are about twenty feet apart. The batter places the sack or bean bag on the toe of his shoe and kicks. A fly caught is out, The base runner is also out when any baseman holds the ball in his possession while standing on the base and while the runner is between bases. When two or more runners are on bases, the runner who is farthest advanced is out if all of the runners are between bases when the bag is retrieved.

Indian baseball.—Use large rubber ball. The batter places the ball on home base and kicks. A fly caught puts the batter out. If the runner is hit by the ball while running between bases he is out. The catcher must get the ball dead on home base as soon as possible so the next batter may kick.

Water baseball.—The bases are anchored fifteen feet apart. It would be best if all of the basemen and the pitcher could stand in the water. The outfielders will probably have to tread. The batter and catcher stand on the dock or shore. A tennis ball is used and a short paddle. When the ball is hit fair the batter dives into the water and swims to first. A base runner may dive under the water to escape being tagged out. Regular baseball rules are used.

From Thomas E. Wilson and Company, Chicago, New York, and San Francisco, may be secured an official *Swimming Guide.* This book contains the official rules for swimming, diving, water polo, water basketball and baseball, international or soccer water polo, water cage ball, and life saving.

Recreative Athletics, published by the National Recreation Association, contains a chapter on water sports.

Captain ball.—The field is thirty by sixty feet or whatever space is available. A basketball is used, preferably, since this is a lead-up game to increase skill in passing. Six circles from two to five feet in diameter, depending on the skill of the players, are made, three on either side of the court. These circles are arranged in triangular fashion with the apex away from the middle line. The circles in each set are fifteen feet apart. The captain for each team occupies the circle farthest away from the middle.

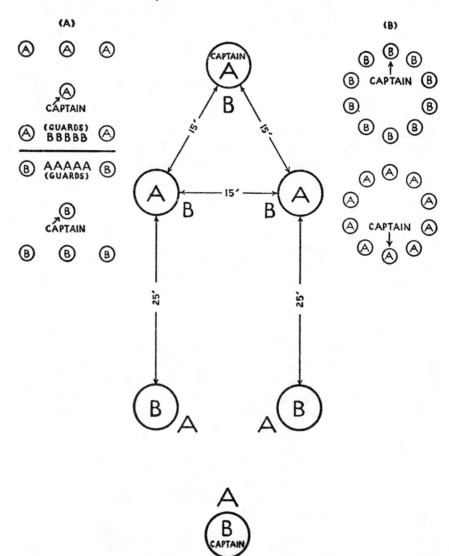

Each team has three basemen, one of whom is designated the captain, three base guards, and a fielder. Each team has a guard near one of the opponent's bases.

Each time a captain catches the ball from one of his own basemen a point is scored. The guard tries to prevent a catch from being made. No score is allowed except when a captain catches a ball tossed by a baseman. The baseman may put one foot outside the circle. If he steps out with both feet he commits a foul. A guard must not step on or over the baseman's circle. No player is allowed to touch a ball while it is the possession of an opponent. It is a foul to hold the ball over three seconds. Penalty for fouls is a free throw from one of the basemen to the captain.

The ball is put into play by being tossed up between the two fielders at center. The one who catches it gains possession for his side. He tries to toss it to one of his basemen. After that the fielder stays out of the play, except to retrieve balls that go outside. Often no fielders are used, and the ball is given to a baseman of the side that wins the toss.

The game is played in halves of ten minutes or more. If no fielders are used the play is continuous.

Variations— (a) Instead of three circles have six circles with the captain at the center. There are five guards for each side, thus making eleven players to a team. A point is scored every time the center player catches a pass from a baseman. Any time a team completes the circle with passes without losing the ball it scores three points. In this case it is not necessary to pass the ball to the center baseman. (b) Any number of players in a circle with a guard for each player. This would mean that there would be two circles. When a guard gets possession of the ball he tries to toss it over to his teammates in the other circle. A score is made every time a baseman catches a pass from a baseman. Completing the circle adds five points to the score of the side achieving that distinction. The circles are five feet apart. Two balls may be put into play at the same time, one in each circle. A toss to the one designated as captain scores two points. The captains are at opposite ends of the playing field.

Boundary ball.—Mark off a playing field approximately sixty by sixty feet, and establish a center line halfway between the ends. Sticks, stones, trees, or any other objects may be used to designate playing space. Divide the players into two equal teams and place each in opposite ends of field and facing each other. Provide each team with a soft ball (large rubber, volley, playground, or basket).

At a signal each team attempts to throw its ball so that it crosses the others' goal line. Ball must cross the goal line on bounce or roll, and be within the side limits of the playing space; throwing across on the fly does not count. After balls are put in play each team may throw either ball. The players may move freely within their playing space, but cannot cross the center line to the opponents' side. A point is gained when one team succeeds in bouncing or rolling the ball across the opponents' goal. Fifteen points constitute a game.

Corner ball.—Field about thirty by twenty feet or up to sixty by thirty feet. Basketball, volleyball, or playball. At each of the four corners is a base four or five feet square. The field is divided by a line across the middle. Two members of each team take positions in the bases on their opponent's side. Besides the corner players there are five other players on each team. Two of these players act as guards while the other three act as tossers. A toss of the coin decides which team shall have first possession of the ball. Tossers try to get the ball to a baseman or corner player of their team by tossing through the air, bouncing, or rolling the ball. The opponents try to prevent this happening and endeavor to get possession of the ball. The baseman must keep one foot, at least, in the corner base in catching the ball. A guard cannot step on the line or within one of the squares without fouling. It is also a foul for a player to touch the ball while it is in the possession of an opponent. Play continues uninterrupted. When a baseman catches a ball he immediately tries to pass it back to one of his teammates, to the other baseman on his side or to a guard or tosser. One point is scored each time a baseman gets possession of the ball legitimately. Play in ten-minute halves.

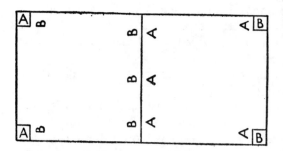

A player may not cross over the middle line.

Variation—Put two balls in play at the same time. That will speed up the game considerably.

End ball.—The field is about thirty by sixty feet. Use a volleyball, basketball, or playball. At either end of the field mark off a space three feet wide and the width of the field. Nine players constitute a team. Three of these players occupy the space in the three-foot end zone on the opponent's side. The field is divided by a middle line. The other six players on a team occupy the space between the end zone and the middle line.

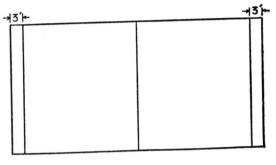

They are not permitted to cross over this middle line.

The game begins with the referee tossing up the ball between two opponents at the middle line. The one who first touches it obtains possession. He endeavors to toss the ball to a teammate in the end zone. If the end-zone player catches it or gets possession of the ball without taking more than one foot out of the end zone he scores a point.

Ten- or fifteen-minute halves are played, the teams changing sides for the last half.

Fouls are made: (1) When a player steps out of bounds in catching the ball. (2) When a player touches the ball while it is in the possession of an opponent. The penalty for a foul is to allow an unobstructed toss. When a ball goes outside the player nearest it retrieves it and puts it into play.

Keep-it-up ball.—This game is good practice for volleyball players. It offers opportunities to acquaint new players with some of the skills of the game. Players are divided into two or more teams of any number. At the sound of the whistle one player of each team tosses the ball up in the air. The ball is then volleyed (batted, preferably with two hands) from one player to another without any special order, until the ball hits the ground or some obstruction such as the wall or a tree. Players keep count of the hits scored. After a ball is dead a new game begins and the scoring starts at one. Each team reports its best score after five minutes. Players are allowed to hit as many times in succession as they desire so long as the successive hits are not deliberately planned.

Variations— (*a*) Enforce the volleying rule whereby a player may not strike the ball more than once before it is touched by another player. (*b*) Require that the ball be volleyed in a certain manner, such as above the head, from the chest, above the waist, below the waist. (*c*) Zigzag volley. Line up players in two lines, teams alternating players. Require that the volleying be to teammates across the line, zigzag fashion. (*d*) Volley to a leader who stands inside the circle.

Newcomb.—A regulation volleyball court is used. The game is played with a volleyball. Teams may consist of any number up to twenty. All rules governing the game of volleyball are used, including scoring, order of service, side out, service, and so forth, with the following exceptions: (1) The ball is thrown instead of batted. (2) Service over the net must be made with one hand, though players are permitted to pass to a teammate with two hands. (3) A player may catch the ball with one or two hands, but he must immediately release it by passing to a teammate or serving over the net.

Variation—"Mad Newcomb." The court is full of players. Three or four balls are used at the same time. When a ball hits the ground a point is scored. The game does not stop. The ball is picked up and the game goes on uninterrupted for five minutes. It will be necessary for there to be a scorer on each side of the net to keep track of points.

Catch and tag.—*Equipment*—A baseball or softball.

Two players are basemen. One player is a base runner. The bases are from thirty to ninety feet apart. The base runner may leave base whenever he desires. In the meantime the basemen toss the ball back and forth. The object of the base runner is to get to the opposite base without being tagged out. He may return to the base he has left at any time. When he leaves a base the basemen close in on him trying to tag him with the ball. The runner must stay in path. This is good practice in the technique of tagging a base runner caught between the bases. The alert player soon finds that one of the skills of putting out runners between bases is to throw the ball as little as possible. Every throw invites an error or wild throw. Therefore, basemen close in on the runner, feinting at throwing, thus causing the runner to run toward the one who has the ball, and lunging at the runner while he is off balance. The runner, too, develops skill in avoiding being tagged, learning that a daring dash often disconcerts the baseman. A point is scored each time a runner makes a base safely. On three outs the base runner changes with a baseman.

Variation—It adds to the interest and speed of the game to have two base runners, one at either base. Both of them may start at the same time.

Ping-pong (Table tennis).—*Table* nine feet long and five feet wide. The table top is thirty inches from the floor.

Net—The top of the net is six and three-fourths inches above the table.

Ball—Regulation ping-pong balls are used.

Paddle—The paddle is 5¼ inches wide and 6½ inches long, with a 5¼-inch handle.

Rules—(1) The ball must bounce once on the server's side before going over the net. The ball may be returned without bouncing.

(2) Service is similar to tennis in that the service is first from the right hand of the court and then from the left.

(3) Only one serve is allowed against two in tennis.

(4) A served ball that tips the net and goes over is a hit and the player gets another serve.

(5) A player fouls when he volleys a return, that is, when he hits the ball before it has touched the table.

(6) A ball tipping the table is good except on the serve.

(7) A point is scored each time an opponent fails to return the ball.

(8) Service changes each time five points are made by the server, except that when the score is twenty-all the service changes after each point made.

(9) Twenty-one points constitute a game.

(10) With the score twenty-all a player must score two successive points to win, as in tennis.

(11) A player fouls when his paddle touches the net.

Chinese ping-pong.—Two or more players line up at either end of the table. The server strikes the ball, drops the paddle on the table, and steps aside. The next teammate picks up the paddle and gets the return. Each player relinquishes the paddle as soon as he has made his play.

Ping-pong spotball.—The net is removed from the ping-pong table and a circle one or two feet in diameter is drawn on the table at center. The players must bounce the ball in this area on the serve and return. Failure to hit within the circle loses a point. The circle may be drawn on the floor, in which case the area should be two or three feet in diameter.

Ping-pong rounders.—This is similar to "Chinese ping-pong" except that as soon as the player makes his play he drops the paddle and runs around the table to the end of the line on the opposite side.

As a player misses he drops out of the game. It can be readily seen that as the play trims down to four or five men it becomes fast and furious.

Tug of war.—A rope twenty or thirty feet long. An equal number of players on either side.

A line is drawn at right angles to the rope and midway between the two teams. A handkerchief or white rag is tied in the middle of the rope. Players line up, taking hold of the rope. The anchor man on each side, that is, the end man, may wind the rope about his body. He may also dig a small hole in the ground against which he is allowed to brace his feet.

The leader calls "Ready! All players assume positions. "Set!" All players pull the slack out of the rope and get ready for the pull. "Go!" All players pull with all their might.

The winner may be decided in two ways: (1) A time limit may be set, such as one minute. At the end of the minute, the position of the handkerchief decides the winner; (2) The teams may continue to pull until one team is routed.

Parlor dodgeball.—Divide into two equal groups. One group forms a circle, while the other group takes the inside of the circle, standing about promiscuously. The circle group is provided with a very light rubber ball, such as you can buy at the ten-cent store. The ball is so light that it will be difficult to throw it with accuracy. Should it hit anyone or anything it will not be likely to do damage.

At the signal to start, the circle group begins to throw the ball at the group within the circle. No player is allowed to throw from any place except his position in the circle. He may toss the ball, however, to a teammate who stands in the circle and that player may throw.

Any player hit must immediately leave the circle.

Time is kept to see how long it takes to hit every player in the circle. Where the circle is big it might be well to allow it to close in as players are eliminated, because it is almost impossible to hit one player with the light ball, at any distance.

Battledore and shuttlecock.—This is the old game from which "Badminton" developed. Players are divided into two equal sides. One player from each side contests at a time. A line is drawn in the middle of the playing space, which should not exceed thirty feet by fifteen feet. It may be less. Each of the players has a badminton racket or ping-pong paddle. The shuttlecock should be an outdoor badminton bird or a home-made bird, made of cork and feathers. The players bat the shuttlecock back and forth over the line, downward shots not being allowed. Finally, when a player misses, a point is scored by the opposing side and two more players step up to play.

Barrel boxing.—Two boys are provided with boxing gloves. Each stands in a barrel close enough together so as to be able to hit one another. In this position they box until one is knocked over.

The barrels should be carefully prepared, all splinters and protruding nails being eliminated.

Variations—(a) Use pillows instead of boxing gloves. *(b)* Knock the bottom out of the barrel. Allow players to don these barrels so as to allow freedom of movement.

Blind boxing.—Blindfold the boxers. Form a ring around them and let them go to it. Smear the gloves with soot, without the boxers knowing it. Allow no slugging.

Bunt ball.—Same rules as regular baseball. The basemen are required to play at their regular positions until the ball is hit. The batter must bunt. Any ball hit beyond the infield either on the fly or on the ground puts the batter out.

Tip-tap-bat (Long ball—one-old-cat).—Only two bases are used in this game, home plate and a base back of the pitcher's position, forty-five to sixty feet away from home plate.

The game begins by players calling "Tip-tap-bat! Bat!" "Catch!" "Pitch!" "First base!" etc. Players first calling the positions get them.

Any ball touched by the bat is fair. The batter must then run to the designated base and back. He may be put out by the catcher holding the ball on home base before he can return. Or a player may put him out by throwing the ball across his path before he can make the circuit.

Variation—Where two batters are available, the runner may stop at the intermediary base. Or players may run to first base, and then to second as in regular baseball. With three batters, third base is the goal. With four batters the runners complete the circuit to home base.

Square dodgeball.—Four players stand at four corners of an imaginary square. All the other players stand inside the square. One of the four corner players has a volleyball or playball. He throws at the center players who try to avoid being hit. As a player is hit he joins one of the corner players and helps hit the center players. This continues until there is a square of players. The last four players to be hit form the corners for the next game.

Kickball.—Play on diamond where bases are forty-five feet apart. Regulation baseball rules are used except that a volleyball or play-ball is used instead of a baseball and the pitcher bowls the ball to the batter.

A "bowl" is fair that passes over the plate below the batters knees. The batter stands beside home plate. When the ball is rolled to him he steps in front of the plate and kicks. Just as in regular baseball he makes as many bases as he can.

Horseshoes.—An American cousin of the English game of "Quoits." Sometimes it is facetiously called "Barnyard Golf."

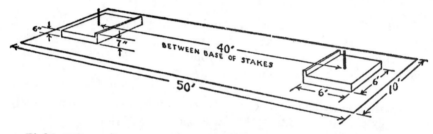

Field—The stakes should be of iron. They extend eight inches above the ground and are inclined slightly toward one another. They are forty feet apart. For women the distance is thirty feet. The dirt around each peg should be soft. Usually the peg is in the center of a box, six feet square. This box is made by setting some two-by-fours in the ground so that only about one inch appears above the surface. The ground inside the box is loose and soft. The players pitch from this box.

The shoes—Regulation horseshoes are seven and one-half inches long and seven inches wide at the widest part. The opening at the calks (or ends) should not exceed three and one-half inches. Weight, two and one-half pounds. The calks should not exceed three-fourths of an inch.

Rules—(1) A shoe farther than six inches from the peg does not count.

(2) Earth softened around peg in a circle two feet in diameter.

(3) Any shoe falling more than one foot away from the peg when

it first hits the ground does not count no matter where it rests when it stops.

(4) Each player tosses two shoes, one player beginning the game by throwing both his shoes. After that the winner always shoots first.

(5) Points are scored as follows: One point for each shoe nearer the peg than any of the opponent's. A leaner counts only one point. If the opponent also has a leaner the two are tied and no point is allowed. A ringer is a shoe that fits around the peg so that both prongs are beyond a line drawn across the circle even with the side of the peg where the prongs or calks are. A straight edge must be able to touch both calks beyond the peg. Three points are scored for a ringer.

(6) If one player scores a ringer and an opponent throws another on top of it both ringers are canceled and the other two shoes are measured to see which player gets one point.

(7) Twenty-one points constitute a game.

Variation—Often the game is played with a ringer scoring five points and a leaner three. If a player tops an opponent's ringer with another one then he scores ten points. If one player throws a leaner and another a ringer the player who throws the ringer scores eight points.

Bibliography—*How to Play Horseshoes*, Diamond Calk Horseshoe Company, Duluth, Minnesota; official rules obtainable from the National Horseshoe Association, London, Ohio.

Quoits.—This game is similar to "Horseshoes," being the original game from which "Horseshoes" was developed. The usual distance between the stakes is thirty feet. In "Quoits" the stakes are driven down in the ground so that the tops are about even with the surface of the ground.

The quoits—The quoits are circular with a hole four inches in diameter at the center. The rim is two and one-half inches wide. The weight is three pounds.

Rules— (1) The pitch must be from behind the stake; (2) A ringer counts three points; (3) If a player covers a ringer with another one he scores six points; (4) A leaner (or hobber) counts two points; (5) If there is a tie between two opposing quoits the decision as to points is decided between the other two quoits.

English rules call for the pegs to be fifty-four feet apart.

Parlor badminton.—Use ping-pong paddles and, for the birds, corks with feathers stuck in them. Set a row of chairs across the middle of the room to serve as a net.

Rubber ring quoits.—Use pieces of old hose or bicycle tires for quoits. Splice them together and tape. The rings should be about one foot in diameter.

The pegs are two broomsticks driven in the ground. They stand about two feet above the ground and are about twenty feet apart. Players toss as in "Horseshoes," though only ringers count in this game. A ringer counts one point. The first side to score fifteen or twenty-one points, as decided, wins. The quoits should be in two colors so that it is easy to distinguish them. Or they may be marked with whitewash or colored strings.

Variation—One player tosses from one end and the other from the opposite. Each throw all of the rings each time.

Bean bag toss.—Players divided into equal sides. Ten at a time for each side form a semicircle around a wastebasket or box and at signal from the referee all players throw at the same time, trying to get the bean bag in the basket. Players stand at a distance of from ten to fifteen feet away from the basket. The players for the other side have formed a semicircle opposite and now at a signal they toss their bean bags, which are of a different color. Count all bean bags that land in the basket, one point each. No points for landing on the rim.

It will be advisable to put a weight (brickbat or doorstop) in the basket so that it will not tip.

Circle ball.—Players form a circle standing four to ten feet away from one another. The ball may be a small ball (tennis, hard, soft), a playball (6, 7, 8, 10 inches), a volleyball, a basketball, or a medicine ball. Players toss the ball around the circle or across it. Quick, short passes, feinting in one direction and passing in another, throwing in a direction where one is not looking, and thus catching players unawares, will make the game more interesting.

Variation—Players may be eliminated when they miss. Or elimination may occur on missing three times.

Corner balloon ball.—Strings at six feet height are drawn across the four corners of the room. A toy balloon is put in play at the center of the room. Teams battle, endeavoring to knock the balloon over the string in a corner protected by the opponents. When they do they score a point. When the ball hits the floor in the field the referee puts it in play by batting it up in the air. Players bat the balloon with open hand.

Variations— (a) Stretch the string straight across the end of the field, one string at either end. (b) Where there is a large crowd of players put two or more balls in play at the same time.

Sit down ball.—The players of the two sides sit in two rows facing one another. The rows are close enough together so that the players of opposing sides can touch one another's hands. A toy balloon is put in play at the middle of the line. Players use the open hand in hitting the ball. The object is to knock the balloon over the heads of the opponents so that it falls to the floor on their side. That scores a point. Players are not permitted to rise from their chairs. An infraction of this rule awards a point to the opponents. Fifteen points constitute a game.

Variation—The players may be seated two rows deep. If the balloon falls to the floor between the two rows of one side a point is scored by the other side.

Hoop ball.—This game is similar to "Corner Balloon Ball," except that six hoops are hung at eight-feet height at either end of the room. A score is made when the balloon is sent through one of the hoops at an opponent's end of the floor. Several balls in play at the same time would greatly add to the interest in the game.

Basketball target.—Place a wastebasket, weighted down, on a table. Players stand at a distance of ten feet. Each player is allowed five throws. The throw must be an underhand toss. After five underhand tosses let the players try five chest shots, five shots with hands held high over head, five tosses with the right hand and five with the left.

Beat ball.—*Equipment*—A rubber playball.

Field—Four bases about thirty feet apart. Diamond shaped infield as in softball.

Directions for playing—A regulation team is ten men as in softball, but any number may play. The batter tosses the ball in the air and hits it with his open hand or closed fist. He then runs around the bases, being required to make the complete circuit without stopping at intermediate bases. The only way he can be put out is by a caught fly or by getting the ball ahead of him on any base before he has completed the circuit. The ball must be fielded to the first baseman and must proceed in regular order to second, third, and home until it arrives at one of these bases ahead of the runner.

The baseman must have his foot on the base before tossing it to the next base. If he drops the ball he must recover it and return it to the base before throwing to the next baseman. Another player may come up to cover a base in case of a fumble that gets away from the baseman. In this latter case the baseman would toss the ball to the player covering the base he has left. That player would then pass it to the next baseman.

Racket volley.—*Equipment*—Tennis ball. Racket eleven inches in diameter made of three-ply wood. See diagram.

The court—The court is fifty feet long and about fifteen to twenty feet wide. Across the middle stretch a piece of cloth six inches wide at a height of six feet.

The game—Play as in regulation volleyball.

ATHLETIC ACCURACY TESTS

Baseball.— (1) *Second base throw*—The thrower must toss on a line from behind home plate, endeavoring to hit second base.

(2) *Outfield throw*—The player must throw from right, left, or center field to first base, second base, third base, and home plate. The throws to the two nearest bases must be thrown direct to a baseman. The throws to the farthest infield base and to home plate must reach the baseman and the catcher on the first bound.

(3) *Bunting*—The batter must bunt pitched bails down the first-base line, the third-base line, and in front of the plate, and in that order.

(4) *Placing hits*—The batter must hit pitched balls to right, to center, and to left, in order.

(5) *Calling drives*—The batter must hit on the line, on the ground, and on the fly, in order.

Basketball.— (1) Throws from the foul line, mid floor, and side lines. (2) Backward toss. (3) One-handed shot from under the basket on receiving a pass. (4) Line pass and then loop pass from mid floor and then from opposite goal to player under the goal.

Football.— (1) *Kicking*. Punting outside at point marked by white paper, one yard from goal, three yards, five yards, eight yards, ten yards. Place kicking from twenty-yard line, twenty-five-, thirty-, thirty-five-, and forty-yard lines. Place kicking from side of the field. Drop kicking—same. (2) *Forward passing*. Passing through a hoop held six feet high at various distances—fifteen yards to forty yards. Passing into a barrel at various distances. (3) *Center passing*. Passing into a basket held in various positions back of the center.

Tire bowling.—*Equipment*—An old automobile tire casing of any regulation size. Tenpins. Often discarded pins may be purchased inexpensively from a bowling alley.

The play—Set the pins up as in regulation bowling. Play ten frames as in the regulation game, except that a player gets only one shot for a frame. If he makes a strike (all pins down) his next frame shot counts double. A strike on the tenth frame entitles the bowler to an extra shot. The tire is rolled at the pins. Players develop quite a bit of skill in this kind of bowling. One team sets up pins while their opponents bowl. The game is quite popular with men.

Water polo.—*Equipment*—A water polo ball, leather-covered, twenty-eight inches in circumference.

Field—An area or pool from sixty feet by twenty feet to seventy-five feet by forty feet. At either end of the playing area is a goal ten feet wide and from one to three feet above the water.

Team—Seven players constitute a team, one of whom is designated the goalie.

Play—The ball is put in play at the center of the playing area. Usually it is held in place by a long pole or by a wire cage operated on a pulley.

Players line up at their end of the playing area. When the whistle blows they swim for the ball. The player getting the ball endeavors to pass it to a teammate. Each team tries to maneuver the ball toward the goal protected by the opposing team. Throwing the ball into the net scores a goal and one point.

Two seven-minute halves are played with a three-minute intermission. Time-out is taken when a goal is scored, when a foul is made, and when the ball goes out of bounds.

Players, except the goalie, are required to handle the ball with only one hand.

Fouls—1. Handling the ball with two hands, except that the goal-keeper may use two hands.

2. The goalkeeper getting more than four yards away from the goal line.

3. Holding the ball under water.

4. Holding to the goal or side of the pool.

5. Impeding the progress of an opposing player who does not have the ball.

6. Kicking or kicking at an opponent.

7. Striking the ball with clenched fist.

8. Jumping from the bottom or pushing from the side of the pool to play the ball.

9. Throwing the ball directly at the goalkeeper on a free throw.

10. Standing on the bottom of the pool, except to rest.

Violations entitle the opponent to a free throw. On a free throw the ball may not be thrown directly to the goal but must be passed to another player. The toss to this player is to be unhindered.

The following fouls bring the penalty of ejection from the game. The ejection is enforced until a point is made, whereupon the player may re-enter the game.

1. Taking a position nearer than within two yards of the opposing team's goal.

2. Refusing to obey the referee.

3. Changing position after the referee has blown his whistle.

4. Purposely wasting time.

The goalkeeper is the only player who may stand on the bottom of the pool, while playing the ball. He may use both hands in handling the ball, but is not allowed to throw the ball more than half the length of the pool.

If the impetus to an outside ball is furnished by the attacking team, the ball is given to the opposing goaltender for a free throw. If the defenders furnish the impetus the ball is given to an opponent who gets a free throw from the corner of the playing area.

Variations—Adaptations are often made of the above rules. For instance, the playing area may be much smaller. For younger players this is highly desirable. The number of players may be increased or diminished. Players may be allowed to push the ball to the goal line instead of tossing it into the goal. In this case a score is made when a player touches the ball to the opponent's goal line, anywhere in the line. Players may be allowed, if agreed, to use both hands in handling the ball. A rubber playball may be used instead of the regulation water polo ball.

Mass deck tennis.—*Equipment*—A deck tennis ring or a piece of garden hose joined together with tape. A net across the middle of the playing area at the height of seven feet.

Playing area—From twenty to forty feet to thirty to sixty feet.

Players—From two to fifteen players on a side.

The Game—Score as in volleyball. Fifteen points constitute a game. Serve from the right-hand base line. The ring must be thrown with an underhand throw and with a minimum rise of at least six inches. Players must catch and throw with one hand. The ring must be returned immediately. A player may not take a step with it in his possession, nor may he feint at throwing it in order to confuse the opposition. The ring must not be touched at any time by both hands. Points are scored only by the serving side, as in basketball. When the ring hits the ground, or goes outside, or is illegally played, the play for that serve is over.

With the score fourteen-all two straight points must be scored to end the game.

Pinochle basketball.—One to five players on a side are used in this game. The players toss a coin to determine which side starts the ball in play from the center of the floor. There is no jump at center to start the game. The only difference from regular basketball rules is that all of the playing is done at one end of the floor around one basket. Players call their own fouls, ties, and outside balls. They toss their own tie balls. Thus there is no referee. Twenty-one points constitute a game. This is a good game for developing skill in basketball, particularly for developing play under the basket.

SOME BOOKS ON SPORTS

How to Play Handball. Charles O'Connell (American Sports Publishing Company), 1931.

How to Bowl. Pamphlet (Brunswick-Balke Collender Co.), 1934.

How to Bowl. Spalding Red Cover Series. No. 49R (American Sports Publishing Company), 1929.

Hockey Guide. Spalding Athletic Library (American Sports Publishing Company).

Volley Ball, A Man's Game. Robert Laveaga (Barnes), 1933.

Volley Ball for Women. Katherine Montgomery (Barnes), 1938.

Official Volley Ball Rules. (American Sports Publishing Company.)

Spalding Athletic Library. Booklets on golf, football, baseball, soccer, tennis, skating, wrestling, boxing, bowling, basketball, track and field sports, swimming, quoits, polo, cricket, tumbling, and every conceivable sport. (American Sports Publishing Company.)

How to Play Tennis. Mercer Beasley (Garden City Publishers), 1936.

Modern Tennis. H. H. Jacobs (Bobbs-Merrill), 1933.

Art of Lawn Tennis. W. T. Tilden (Doran), 1932.

Swimming Analyzed. G. E. Goss (Barnes), 1935.

Swimming and Plain Diving. A. A. Smith (Scribner's Sons), 1930.

Water Pageants. O. McCormick (Barnes), 1933.

Canoeing. W. B. Clausen (Boy Scouts of America), 1937.

Conditioning Gymnastics. S. C. Staley (Barnes).

Calisthenics. S. C. Staley (Barnes).

Tumbling Illustrated. L. L. McClow (Barnes).

Soccer for Junior and Senior High Schools. J. E. Caswell (Barnes).

Primitive Pioneer Sports. B. S. Mason (Barnes)—Boomerangs, rope activities, log-rolling, darts, etc.

Sports for Recreation. E. D. Mitchell (Barnes).

How to Make Devices for Outdoor Winter Sports. Popular Mechanics Press, 200 East Ontario, Chicago, Ill.

CHAPTER XII
FUN WITH MUSIC

FUN WITH MUSIC

"Music washes away from the soul the dust of everyday life."
—Averbach

THERE are various uses of music in leisure. One may listen, and there is an art in listening known only to him who listens with an imaginative mind. One may produce music by playing an instrument or by singing or whistling. One may play games to the sweet tunefulness of music, beating out the time with his feet or his hands, capturing the rhythm of it in his heart and translating it into graceful motion. No recreation gets such a universal response as music.

"The power of enjoying and loving the best music is not a rare and special privilege, but the natural inheritance of everyone who has ear enough to distinguish one tune from another, and wit enough to prefer order to incoherence."
—Sir Henry Hadow

"Give us the man who sings at his work. Be his occupation what it may, he is equal to any of those who follow the same pursuit in sullen silence. He will do more in the same time—he will do it better—he will persevere longer. One is scarcely sensitive to fatigue whilst he marches to music."
—Thomas Carlyle

"Bands or Bandits"

"Bands or Bandits" was the title of an editorial in *Etude,* in making a plea for community interest in encouraging and promoting wide interest in music. The foreword to a community chorus concert program stresses the value of music as a factor in community improvement in the following words: "There is no more elevating recreation than the practice of beautiful music, and there could be no better influence on the social life of a community than the making of, and listening to, fine music, which is ever a universal language of the soul, *helping a person keep human."*

Objectives

The Hartland (Michigan) Area Music Project sets up the following objectives:

(449)

1. The development of a music consciousness throughout the entire area.

2. Specific training in music for all of the school children in the area.

3. Development of chorus, orchestra, and choir work within the area.

4. The encouragement of a better type of sacred music in the churches.

Contemplated results are:

(1) An attainment of a music consciousness through the area, leading to an interest in co-operative chorus, orchestra, and choir work. This will apply to both school children and adults.

(2) The creating of enjoyment in participation in vocal and instrumental music by children.

(3) The gradual development of a sense of discrimination in worth-while music.

(4) The value of good music in the home as a character builder, and the enjoyment of all of its phases as an activity for leisure time.

These objectives and desired results would make worthy aims for any group contemplating the use of music in recreation.

MUSICAL ACTIVITIES

"Sing, sing, music was given
To brighten the gay and kindle the livin'."
—MOORE

Possible music projects.— (1) Glee and choral clubs. (2) Concerts and musicales. (3) Community sings. (4) Hymn study and sings. (5) Music appreciation clubs. (6) Orchestra, band. (7) Part-singing for fun. (8) Learning lovely folk music. (9) Toy rhythm bands. (10) Rhythmic games—marches, folk games, etc. (11) Presenting operas, operettas, cantatas, oratorios.

Community sings.—It is a mistake to think that people will not enjoy singing songs of merit. Anyone who has given a group a chance at a lovely song like "All Through the Night," or a lively one like "A Merry Life," or a harmony number like "Love's Old Sweet Song," knows better. The increasing popularity of folk songs is another evidence that people will respond to good music. If Theodore Thomas was right when he said, "Popular music is familiar music," then we ought to make *good* music popular by giving people frequent experiences with it. *It can be done, for good music wears well.*

Fun songs have their place in community sings, even though it is a minor one. Good stunt songs bear the same relation to songs like "Calm as the Night" that good jokes do to a great book like *Les Miserables*. But it must not be forgotten that good jokes serve a worthy end, even as do good fun songs.

Books helpful in community singing.—
Joyful Singing, section of Handy II, Folk Songs.
Folk Songs and Ballads, Sets I, II, III, and IV, E. C. Schirmer.
Get Together Songs, Lorenz.
The Brown Book, Birchard.
The Green Book, Birchard.
Keep on Singing, Paull-Pioneer.
The Cowboy Sings, Paull-Pioneer.
Sing, Birchard.
Sing Together, Girl Scouts, Inc.
Songs for Informal Singing, Sets I, II, III, National Recreation Association.
Parodology, Cokesbury.
The Universal Folk Songster, Botsford, G. Schirmer.
Folk Songs of Many Peoples—3 volumes—Botsford, G. Schirmer.

Folk songs.—Folk music comes to us out of the life of the people. We seldom can trace it back to an original composer. It is passed on from generation to generation. Some claim it is not folk music if you can identify the composer. Others hold that that is not necessarily true, and they classify many of the songs of Stephen Foster as folk songs.

The world's greatest composers have been influenced by folk music. Tchaikowsky's Fifth Symphony is built about "The Birch Tree, a Russian folk song. Gypsy music inspired Liszt, Haydn, Brahms, and Bach. German folk music is reflected in the works of Mozart, Schubert, Schumann, Wagner, Brahms, Bach, and other composers. One, therefore, is in good company when he consorts with folk music.

Folk songs have grown increasingly in popularity as recreational songs. Numerous inexpensive collections have made them available for use. This is a wholesome trend. America has made its contribution to the folk music of the world with its Negro Spirituals, its cowboy songs, its plantation melodies and work songs, and its mountain ballads. These and the hundreds of beautiful folk songs of other lands make excellent material for community sings.

Part singing.—Try part singing for fun. There is no keener delight than that which comes to the singer when his voice blends in harmony with others on some sweet chord. Glee and choral clubs are attractive forms of recreation. Note the following list of good choral numbers and the list of publishers:

Octavo Music for Chorus and Mixed Quartet—
"All Through the Night," Neidlinger (Presser).
"Anvil Chorus," from *Il Trovatore,* Verdi (Birchard) (Parks).
"Barcarolle," from *Tales of Hoffman,* Offenbach (Birchard).
"Beautiful Blue Danube," Strauss (Birchard).
"Bendemeer's Stream," Irish (E. C. Schirmer) (Parks).
"Berceuse," from *Joselyn,* Godard (Ditson).
"Calm as the Night," Bohm (Birchard).
"Ciribiribin," Pestalozza-Moore (Parks).
"Darkey Lullaby," *Humoresque,* Dvorak-Page (Birchard).
"Estudiantina," Lacome (Birchard).
"Goodnight, Goodnight, Beloved," Pinsuti (Birchard).
"Grandfather's Clock," Work-Grey (Parks).
"Kentucky Babe," Matthews (G. Schirmer).
"Listen to the Lambs," Dett (G. Schirmer).
"Love's Old Sweet Song," Mulloy-Bliss (Presser) (Parks).
"Lullaby," Clokey (Birchard) S. S. A. T. B. B.
"Massa Dear," Dvorak-Moomis (Birchard).
"Miserere" from *Il Trovatore,* Verdi (Birchard).
"The Old Woman and the Pedlar," English (Birchard).
"Pilgrims' Chorus," from *Tannhauser,* Wagner (Birchard).
"Quartette from Rigoletto," Verdi (Birchard).
"Santa Lucia," Italian (Birchard).
"Sweet and Low," Barnby (Presser).
"Swing Along," Cook (G. Schirmer).
"Sylvia," Speaks-Gaines (G. Schirmer).
"Traumerei," Schumann (Birchard).
"Wynken, Blynken, and Nod," Beale (Birchard).
"Who Is Sylvia?" Schubert (Birchard).

Collections for mixed voices—
Flambeau (Rodeheaver-Hall-Mack).
25 chorals, Bach (E. C. Schirmer).
The Parks Series.
"The Green Book" (C. C. Birchard).

Male Quartets—
Parks Concert Quartet Series (6 volumes).
Parks Program Series (6 volumes).
Parks Encore Numbers (3 volumes).
    (These published by J. A. Parks Co., York, Nebraska.)
The A Cappella Singer (E. C. Schirmer).

Humorous male quartet numbers.—

Presser
 6130 "An act of Up-to-date Grand Opera," Smith.
  184 "The Cobble and the Crow," Powell.
10333 "Listen to My Tale of Woe," Smith-Petrie.
20174 "Old King Cole," Sheppard.
15657 "One, Two, Three, Four," Alan-Earle.
20313 "The Three Clocks," Starke.
 6111 "Who Killed Cock Robin?" Watson-Scott.

Parks
   43 "The Story of the Tack," Parks.
  871 "The Male Quartet," Parks.
  383 "Jim," Parks.
   63 "Two Flies," and "De Backsliding Brudder."
  554 "Andalusia," Audran-Parks.

Birchard
  830 "Arkansaw Traveller."
  144 "Scandalize My Name," Spiritual.
   78 "The Pigtail," Bullard, a cappella.
 1007 "Just Us Chickens," O'Hara, a cappella.

Treble voices.—
The Parks Series.
The Concord Song Book for Women's Voices, Surette and Davison (E. C. Schirmer).
The A Cappella Singer (E. C. Schirmer).
The Rose Book (Birchard).

Music publishers.—
C. C. Birchard and Company, 221 Columbus Avenue, Boston, Mass.
John Church Co., Cincinnati, Ohio.
Co-operative Recreation Service, Delaware, Ohio.
Oliver Ditson, 166 Terrace Street, Boston, Mass.

Leo Feist, New York City.

Lorenz Publishing Company, Dayton, Ohio.

J. A. Parks Co., York, Nebraska.

Paull-Pioneer Music Corporation, 119 Fifth Avenue, New York City.

Rodeheaver, Hall-Mack Co., 124 No. 15th Street, Philadelphia, Pa.

E. C. Schirmer, 221 Columbus Avenue, Boston, Mass.

George Schirmer, 3 E. 43rd Street, New York City.

Willis Music Co., 137 West 4th, Cincinnati, Ohio.

Orchestra—Willis Orchestra Album, Numbers 1, 2, and 3, Willis Music Co.; Concert Album, Volumes 1, 2, Leo Feist.

"Music is perhaps the best creation in the world. It is also the best unifier in the world. It is the best bond of comradeship."—DR. FRANK CRANE.

Concerts and musicales.—Set down three rules for your concerts. (1) Nothing less than good performance will satisfy. Use only people who can give good rendition to the numbers assigned them. (2) Only good music will get a place on the program. (3) Provide variety in types of music offered and in manner of presentation. Color, drama, and surprise can be used effectively to popularize good music.

"Music is the commonest tie between races and nationalities, and recognizes no caste."—JACQUES L. GOTTLIEB

UNUSUAL PROGRAMS

One group has an annual Costume Musicale. All numbers are dramatized. Stage settings and costumes are made. One year the theme was "The Four Seasons," with each of four sections of the program representing a season. A rural group built a Music Festival Program about the Fair idea. The stage was decorated to represent a Fair. The singers were milling about on the stage singing "Come to the Fair" as the curtains were drawn. All musical numbers were introduced dramatically. A woman came on the scene with a baby in her arms. She was singing "Lullaby and Goodnight" (Brahms) while the chorus gave a humming accompaniment. An old lady came on while a quartet at one side sang "The Old Woman and the Pedlar." That famous old English folk song was acted out as the quartet sang. And so every number on the program was presented. This form of presentation lends variety and interest to concert programs.

An evening of old favorites.—

SCENE I. Outdoor setting—trees, moon. Boy and girl in old-fashioned costumes. The boy plays guitar and sings "Sweet Genevieve," or "Believe Me, If All Those Endearing Young Charms," or "How Can I Leave Thee?"

SCENE II. A sitting room, dimly lighted. Young mother rocking cradle and singing "Lullaby and Goodnight," Brahms. The young husband sits over on one side of the room reading a newspaper.

SCENE III. Same sitting room, with cradle removed, and divan and chairs added. An old woman seated in a rocking chair, stage left. Sound of voices, as if in distance, singing "Jingle Bells," or "A Merry Life." Gradually increase in volume and finally burst into the room singing gaily. Grandma greets them and asks them to sing her favorite, "Love's Old Sweet Song." They sing in harmony. As the number is finished a man's voice is heard singing off stage, "I Wandered Today by the Mill, Maggie." An old man leaning heavily on a cane appears. He crosses the stage to the opposite side where the old woman is seated in the rocking chair. He kneels beside her chair and they finish the song as a duet. Curtain.

SCENE IV. Same sitting room.

Enter little girl: "O Grandmother, I have just finished my music lesson."

GRANDMOTHER: "That's fine. And I hope you had a good lesson."

GIRL: "Oh, very good. But it gets tiresome sometimes."

GRANDMOTHER: "All good things require effort, if we would enjoy them."

GIRL: "Grandmother, sing one of your songs for me."

GRANDMOTHER: "I'm a little out of practice. What shall it be?"

GIRL: "Just anything, so you sing. Maggie sings 'Kathleen Mavourneen,' 'Annie Laurie,' and 'Juanita.' Jim sings me some pretty songs, too."

GRANDMOTHER: "Well, I'm glad they sing good songs to my darling. I'll do my best with an old favorite."

Grandmother sings first verse of "Long, Long Ago," the little girl lays her head on her grandmother's shoulder and finally both go to sleep.

Fairies enter and do a drill with rose-petaled parasols. Following in order comes "Kathleen Mavourneen" dressed in green. She sings that song. Then "Annie Laurie" enters in Scotch costume, and then "Juanita" in Spanish costume. Next a voice is heard off stage singing "I'm coming, I'm coming, for my head is bending low." "Old Black Joe," bent and weary, leaning on a cane, appears. Two of the fairies go to meet him. He sings the verse and chorus. Then they all sing the chorus softly, while the fairies tiptoe off cautiously, beckoning the "Songs" to follow them. "Old Black Joe" is the last one to disappear and the chorus is finished off stage.

The little girl awakens, rubs her eyes, and looks all around, under chairs and behind them, trying to find the fairies. She shakes Grandmother.

GIRL: "Grandmother! Wake up, quick! The fairies were here! I saw Kathleen Mavourneen, Annie Laurie, Juanita, and Old Black Joe. But they're gone! Oh, I wish you could have seen them, Grandmother."

GRANDMOTHER: "Maybe, I did, child!"

GIRL: "Sing another verse of your song, Grandmother."

GRANDMOTHER: (arising) "All right, child, but I'll have to go now."

Leave stage together, singing softly "Long, Long Ago."

Other old songs may be introduced as desired.

A night in a gypsy camp.—*Setting*—gypsy camp, costumes. One gypsy at stage right leaning disconsolately against a tree, playing "Berceuse" from *Jocelyn* on violin. As soon as he has finished the Chieftain, who enters stage left, says: "That's doleful music, Petro, but it's beautiful. I feel in a gay mood today, so I sing ————," and Chieftain sings "I Love Life." All the gypsies applaud and swing into the "Gypsy Chorus," from Balfe's *Bohemian Girl* (John Church) or "The Gypsy Song" from *Carmen*, Bizet-Remick (Birchard). Other gypsy numbers are: "Gypsy Trail," Galloway (Presser); "Gypsy Life," Schumann (John Church); "The Gypsy Camp," Russian-Pitcher (Birchard); "Gypsy-John," Clay (Birchard); "Gypsy Song," Wood, Soprano-alto duet (Birchard); "Gypsy Song," from *La Traviata,* Verdi-Mitchell (Birchard); "A Merry Gypsy Band," Barritt, Soprano-alto duet (Ditson); "Come with the Gypsy Bride," from *The Bohemian Girl,* Soprano solo part (Ditson); and "Gypsy Love Song."

The gypsies are surprised by a visit from a group of American tourists, who enter into the spirit of the occasion and help in the entertainment. Among the tourists is an Indian guide who sings "Indian Love Call." The plaintive call of this song awakens memories in one of the gypsies who has stood off to the side, back to the group, gazing off into the distance. She has not entered into any of the merriment. As the Indian guide sings she turns with a start, and then joins in singing the chorus. She turns out to be an Indian captive, and sweetheart of the guide. The Gypsy Chieftain admits that she was stolen from the Indians, and agrees for her to go with her lover.

From an Indian wigwam.—*Setting*—An Indian camp, wigwams, trees.

Program—(a) *Indian Melodies*—"By the Waters of Minnetonka," "By the Weeping Waters," "Chant of the Corn Grinders," "The Deserted Lodge," "Love Song," "Lullaby," "O'er Birch Moon Waters" (with flute or violin), "The Owl Hoots on a Tepee Pole," "My Lark, My Love," "Pakoble—The Rose," "Rue, A Pueblo Spring Song"—all of these by Lieurance and published by Presser. "In the Land of the Sky Blue Water," Cadman. "Indian Love Call," Friml. "Little Papoose on the Wind-swung Bough," Cadman. Three-part treble unaccompanied (Ditson), "Indian Mountain Song," Cadman, four-part treble (Ditson). Make a selection from these chorus and solo numbers.

(b) *Indian Dance*—See *Indian Games and Games with Native Songs*, Alice Fletcher, and *Indian Action Songs*, Densmore (Birchard).

"Sun Worshippers' Dance" in *Brown Book* (Birchard).

Suggestion for Dramatizing "By the Waters of Minnetonka"— The legend upon which this song is based deals with an old story of the Sun Tribe and the Moon Tribe, who, in the long ago, lived on the shores of Lake Minnetonka (Wisconsin). According to the story, a young brave from the lodge of the Sun Chief fell in love with a maiden from the lodge of the Moon Chief. Tribal laws made it impossible for them to mate. Rather than be separated, the young lovers met on the shores of the lake and walked, hand in hand, into its waters, so as to enter the Happy Hunting Grounds together. The song seems to relate the conversation between the two lovers as they kept their tryst. The flute-like notes of the melody and the rippling piano tones, Mr. Lieurance explains, simulate the movement of the waters and the Indian lover's wooing flute call. It would be a simple matter to dramatize this beautiful legend.

SCENE I. The meeting of the lovers.

SCENE II. The Brave tells the Sun Chief of his love.

SCENE III. The girl tells her father of her love for the young Brave.

SCENE IV. The lovers keep their fatal tryst.

A musical journey around the world.—"Aboard the Good Ship, Harmony." The program announced the chorus director as captain, the pianist as "ship's pianist," the singers as "ship passengers," and the master of ceremonies as "travel guide." A ship setting. Most of the numbers were sung from the deck of the ship, but a few of them came from the "shore" in front of the ship as it landed at certain ports. Following is the program:

PORTS OF CALL

England: "Land of Hope and Glory" (from *Pomp and Circumstance*); "Long, Long Ago"; "Drink to Me Only with Thine Eyes."

Scotland: "Flow Gently, Sweet Afton"; "Loch Lomond."

Ireland: "Last Rose of Summer"; "Believe Me, If All Those Endearing Young Charms."

Germany: "In the Time of Roses"; *Schubert's Serenade.*

France: "Depuis le Jour" (from Opera *Louise*); "Song of the Vagabonds" (from *If I Were King*); "Marseillaise."

Italy: Duet from opera, *La Forza del Destino;* "The Sextette" from *Lucia.*

Persia: "In a Persian Garden" (from *Rubaujet*).

Russia: "The Sleigh"; "The Volga Boatman."

Japan: Scene from *Madame Butterfly.*

INTERMISSION

Homeward Bound—"Goin' Home," Dvorak; "On the Ocean"; "America the Beautiful"; California chanty, "Blow Ye Winds Heigh-ho"; Arizona and Texas, "Home on the Range"; Southern Scenes: Negro Spirituals and Plantation songs ("Ole Man River," "Ezekiel Saw de Wheel," "Cornfield Melodies," "Lindy Lou," "Swanee River," "Southern Memories").

A flower garden of song.—*Setting*—A flower garden.

Personnel—Gardener with sprinkling can, girls dressed as flowers, musicians (singers and instrumentalists).

Music—(1) Piano solo—"Country Garden." (2) Solo—"Would God I Were a Tender Apple Blossom" (*Londonderry Air*). (3) Male quartet—"Bendemeer's Stream" (Ditson, "A Red, Red Rose," Scotch (Ditson), "Morning Glories," Dale (Presser). (4) Mixed octet—"Rosemary and Thyme," a cappella (Birchards). (5) Duet— "The Message of the Violet" from *Prince of Pilsen.* (6) Mixed quartet—"Honey You'se Mah Rose," Clark (Presser), "The Violet and the Bee," Caldicott, humorous (Presser), "In the Time of Roses," Reichart-Bliss (Presser). (7) Girls trio (dressed as roses) — "My Wild Irish Rose." (8) Mixed quartet—"Garden of Roses," Ritter (Presser). (9) Women's quartet—"Come Where the Lilies

Bloom," Thompson (Presser). (10) Solo—"The Last Rose of Summer."

The gardener appears with sprinkling can to water flowers. Girls dressed as flowers arise after he leaves and do some simple folk game figures to "Country Garden." "Come Let Us Be Joyful" could be used, especially since its lines are so suitable. All numbers are done in suitable costumes and setting. For at least one of the numbers the singers could appear behind a sheet, only their faces showing through holes. On the side of the sheet toward the audience giant flowers, made of cloth or crepe paper, could be sewn.

Away down South musicale.—*Setting*—Old South scene—front of old Southern home or plantation or levee.

Music—(1) Old Southern melodies—"Darling Nelly Gray," Stephen Foster songs, "In the Evening by the Moonlight," "Carry Me Back to Old Virginny." (2) Negro spirituals and plantation songs—"Water Boy," "Joshua Fit the Battle," "Standin' in the Need of Prayer," "Go Down, Moses," "Swing Low, Sweet Chariot," "I Got Shoes," "Ain't It a Shame to Work on Sunday?" "Deep River," "Hand Me Down My Silver Trumpet," "Nobody Knows the Trouble I See."

An excellent "Stephen Foster" program is published by the National Recreation Association, 315 Fourth Avenue, New York City. It contains suggestions for dramatic features.

When the curtains go up a group of cotton pickers is picking cotton as it sings softly in harmony "Old Folks at Home." Work out dramatic sequences. A wayward son returns to the plantation. While he was away Jeannie, whom he loved dearly, died. He is shocked and grieved. It proves a turning point in life for him. Later he sings Foster's lovely "Jeannie with the Light Brown Hair." This should be followed in a few moments by the plantation chorus singing softly "Swing Low, Sweet Chariot."

Somewhere in the program have some one call attention to the great contribution to the world's music which the Negro has made through the spiritual.

A community sing that's different.—One group presented a community sing program featuring dramatized versions of familiar old songs. In the list were "My Old Kentucky Home" (log cabin and cotton field setting), "Old Folks at Home," "When You and I Were Young Maggie," "Old Black Joe," "Jingle Bells," "Annie Laurie," "Reuben and Rachel," "Carry Me Back to Old Virginny," "Tenting Tonight," "School Days," "The Old Oaken Bucket," and "Perfect

Day." In between the dramatized numbers song slides were used and everyone sang such songs as "Juanita," "Row, Row, Row Your Boat," "The Quilting Party," "Coming Through the Rye," "Sweet Adeline," "Swing Low, Sweet Chariot," and "Taps."

Suggestions for an evening of Negro spirituals.—Antonin Dvorak, after studying the music of this country for his *New World Symphony,* came to the conclusion that our Negro music was the most typically American. In fact he claimed that it was the only original music to be found here. Therefore you will find the symphony based on Negro spirituals. The familiar "Going Home" is taken from this symphony.

Negro composers of note are Samuel Coleridge-Taylor, Nathaniel Dett, Harry Burleigh, and Carl Diton.

It may be of interest to note that the Fisk Jubilee Singers, of Nashville, Tennessee, were the first to travel over our own country and abroad presenting the spiritual. The beauty and simplicity of these songs soon popularized them, and added considerably to the fame of Fisk University.

PROGRAM

(1) *Group singing*—"Swing Low, Sweet Chariot."

(2) *Piano solo*—"I'm Troubled in My Mind." Coleridge-Taylor.

(3) *Solo*—"Go Down, Moses."

(4) *Choir or mixed quartet*—"Listen to the Lambs," Dett (G. Schirmer).

(5) *Solo*—"My Lord, What a Mornin'." Burleigh.

(6) *Male quartet*—"Good News, Chariot's Coming," "Couldn't Hear Nobody Pray," "Steal Away."

(7) *Group singing*—"Ain't Gwine Study War No More."

(8) *Female trio*—"Deep River" (Ditson).

(9) *Solo*—"Going Home." Dvorak.

(10) *Quartet*—"Standing in the Need of Prayer," "Keep a Inchin' Along," "O Mary, Don't You Weep."

Other books: Religious Folk Songs of the Negro. Hampton Institute, Virginia.

The Book of American Spirituals, and *The Second Book of Negro Spirituals,* James Weldon Johnson (Viking Press), containing more than sixty solo arrangements each.

Jubilee and Plantation Songs, Ditson.

The Dett Collection of Negro Spirituals, Books I, II, III, IV. Hall McCreary.

"A man should hear a little music, read a little poetry, and see a fine picture every day of his life, in order that worldly cares may not obliterate the sense of the beautiful which God has implanted in the human soul."—GOETHE.

An international song evening.—This can be made a colorful and attractive program of music. The solos, duets, and quartets ought to be presented in costume. Appropriate platform setting for the various numbers should be arranged. Some of the songs could be arranged for dramatic presentation. Colored lights will add effectiveness to some of the scenes.

Get a good song leader to lead the audience in singing some of the songs. Provide mimeographed song sheets containing the songs to be sung.

PROGRAM

Mexico: "La Paloma," "La Golondrina."

France: "Berceuse" from *Jocelyn,* "Because" (Teschermacher).

England: "Drink to Me Only with Thine Eyes."

Scotland: "Scots wha hae' wi' Wallace bled," "Roamin' in the Gloamin'," "Annie Laurie," "I Love a Lassie," "Comin' thru the Rye," "It's Nice to Get Up in the Morning," "Flow Gently Sweet Afton."

Ireland: "Kathleen Mavourneen," "Danny Boy," "Mother Machree," "My Wild Irish Rose."

Russia: "The Volga Boatman," "The Peddler," "My Little Cudgel," "Dark Eyes."

Germany: "Auf Wiedersehn," "Serenade," Schubert.

China: "Chinese Lullaby" from *East Is West.*

America: "When You and I Were Young Maggie," "Silver Threads Among the Gold."

Italy: "Funiculi, Funicula," "O Sole Mio."

American Indian: "By the Waters of Minnetonka," "Pale Moon."

Make the selections that suit you from the list of songs. Be careful not to make your program too long. Begin the program by singing some of the national anthems of various countries. Intersperse the special numbers with group singing. The following songs will offer a good selection for this purpose: "Old Folks at Home," "Old Black Joe," "Swing Low, Sweet Chariot," "Ain't Gwine to Study War," "Alouette," "All in a Wood," "Annie Laurie," "Roamin' in the Gloamin'," "I Love a Lassie," "It's Nice to Get Up in the Morning."

Heart songs around the world.— This program could be made a most interesting occasion. There should be plenty of variety, with solos, quartets, songs for everyone to sing, etc. Some of the numbers could be done in costume and some could be given a dramatic setting. The following are some suggested songs:

(1) "Love's Old Sweet Song." Everyone.
(2) "Annie Laurie." (Scotland.)
(3) "Believe Me, If All Those Endearing Young Charms," "Kathleen Mavourneen," "When Irish Eyes Are Smiling." (Ireland.)
(4) "Drink to Me Only with Thine Eyes." (England.)
(5) "Du Liegst Mir in Herzen," "Du Bist Wie Eine Blume," "The Loreley," "Auf Wiedersehen," "Hidden Love." * (Germany.)
(6) "In the Gloaming," "Sweet Genevieve," "Because," "Absent." (America.)
(7) "Indian Love Call," "By the Waters of Minnetonka," "Pale Moon." (American Indian.)
(8) "The Spanish Cavalier."
(9) "Rosemary." * (Poland.)
(10) "The Rada Song—Boy I Adore You." * (Czech.)
(11) "Cielito Lindo." (Mexico.)
(12) "The Kashmiri Song." (India.)

NOTE: Starred songs appear in the Botsford Collection of Folk Songs.

An American song evening.—Select some of the best songs of various periods for the program. If you can find a copy of Carl Sandburg's *An American Song-bag* in the public library it will give you some help. Arrange your program so as to give the crowd a chance to participate in singing some of the songs. Present some of the special numbers in costume and in dramatic fashion. Here are some suggested songs for the program:

Songs of the long ago—"Old Folks At Home," "Massa's in the Cold, Cold Ground," "Old Black Joe," "The Quilting Party," "Tenting Tonight," "When Johnnie Comes Marching Home," "When You and I Were Young Maggie," "Carry Me Back to Old Virginny," "My Old Kentucky Home."

The "Gay Nineties"—"The Bull-dog on the Bank," "Sweet Adeline," "Silver Threads Among the Gold," "Annie Rooney," "Eastside, West-side," "Juanita," "Rocked in the Cradle of the Deep," "The Levee Song."

Just Yesterday—"School Days," "Wait Till the Sun Shines Nellie," "Ah, Sweet Mystery of Life," "Gypsy Love Song," "Dear Old Pal of

Mine," "Moonlight and Roses," "My Wild Irish Rose," "The Rosary," "The Sunshine of Your Smile," etc.

Today—"Old Man River," "Indian Love Call," "Sylvia," "Home on the Range."

An evening of heart songs.—Say, how would you like to sing some of the good old heart songs? And how would you like some good music—something unusual in the way of a musical program? All right, what do you say? Let's plan "An Evening of Heart Songs."

First, we'll probably want to decide that everyone must have some part in this program. That will mean we'll have to have some mimeographed song sheets or some song slides. If you're going to have slides you can make them yourself by using radio-mats, obtainable at any photographic supply house at about three cents per mat. Here's a good list of songs from which we can select:

"Love's Old Sweet Song," "Annie Laurie," "In the Gloaming," "When You and I Were Young Maggie," "Sweet Adeline," "Let Me Call You Sweetheart," "Let the Rest of the World Go By," "Tell Me Why," "Silver Threads Among the Gold," and "The Silver Moon Is Shining."

We'll want some special numbers, solos, quartets, etc. The solo numbers are almost limitless. Look at this partial list: "I Love You Truly," "Sweetest Story Ever Told," "O Promise Me," "The Greatest Wish in the World," "Nuthin," "Little Grey Home in the West," "Smilin' Through," "Sorter Miss You," "Until," "Gray Days," "Toujours, L'Amour, Toujours."

The following suitable male quartet songs appear in *Twice Fifty-five Community Songs for Male Voices:*

"Jeannie with the Light Brown Hair," "Drink to Me Only with Thine Eyes," "How Can I Leave Thee," "Stars of the Summer Night," "Forsaken," "Soldier's Farewell," and Schubert's "Serenade."

Then, I wonder if we couldn't present some of the special numbers in dramatic fashion. Many of the numbers suggested lend themselves to that manner of presentation. For instance, a good dramatic cycle could be arranged with the use of "The Sweetest Story Ever Told," or "O Promise Me," "Soldier's Farewell," or "How Can I Bear to Leave Thee," "Sorter Miss You," and "Silver Threads Among the Gold."

Another suggestion would be that some of the songs be illustrated by tableaux, which are presented in a frame covered with blue gauze.

Select the best talent you can get for your program. Don't be satisfied with less than the best. Make this a never-to-be-forgotten evening of fellowship and song.

Trampin'

Oh, Lord I Want

Oh Lord I want two wings to veil my face;
Oh Lord I want two wings to fly away;
Oh Lord I want two wings to veil my face,
So the devil can't do me no harm.
My Lord, did he come at the break of day?   (No!)
My Lord, did he come in the heat of the noon?   (No!)
My Lord did he come in the cool of the evening?   (Yes!)
And he washed my sins away.

Won't You Sit Down?

1. Who's that yonda dressed in red?
   Must be the chillun that Moses led.
   O won't you sit down?
   Lord I can't sit down,
   O won't you sit down?
   Lord I can't sit down!
   O won't you sit down?
    Lord I can't sit down,
   'Cause I just got to heaven, gotta look around.

2. White .... Chillun of the Israelites.

3. Black .... Hypocrites turnin' back.

4. Pink .... Solomon tryin' to think.

5. Green .... Ezekiel in his flyin' machine.

6. Gray .... Sinners turnin' away.

7. Blue .... Chillun a-comin' through.

Cowboy Song

1. I can't play an accordeen,
   I can't pla-ay a fiddle;
   I can't play a guitar much
   But I can play a little.

2. Once I rode a longhorn bull,
   Once I rode a mulie
   When my work's done in the fall,
   I'm goin' home to Julie.

Skaal

OLD DANISH TOAST

Og dette skal vare (name) tiloere (til-air-e) hurrah!
Og skam for den some ikke (name) skaal vil drikke,
Hurrah! Hurrah den skaal var bra, Hurrah!

CHORUS:

Han skal leve, Han skal leve,
Han skal leve hojt hurrah;
Hurrah! Hurrah! Hurrah, hurrah, hurrah!
Hurrah! Hurrah! Hurrah, hurrah, hurrah!
Han skal leve, Han skal leve,
Han skal leve hojt hurrah!
Bravo, bravo, bravo, bravissimo,
Bravo, bravo, bravissimo.
Bravo bravissimo, bravo bravissimo,
Bravo, bravo, bravissimo!
Han skal leve, Han skal leve,
Han skal leve, hojt hurrah!

Han = he.   Hun = she.   De = they.
Leve = live.   Hojt = high or gloriously.

This is an old Danish toast. At the Boy Scout Jamboree in Stockholm some years ago fifteen thousand Boy Scouts from all over the world sang this song.

A free translation of the song as the following:

This is in honor of (name), hurrah!
Shame on the one who won't drink the toast
This toast is sincere
May he live; may he live high (gloriously)

When the Curtains of Night
(Old cowboy song—built on popular song of '70's)

When the curtains of night are pinned back by the stars,
And the beautiful moon leaps the sky;
When the dew-drops of heaven are kissing the rose,
It is then that my memories fly.
Go where you will on land or on sea,
I'll share all your sorrows and cares,
And at night when I kneel by my bedside to pray.
I'll remember your love in my prayers.

I Know the Lord's Laid His Hands on Me

CHORUS

O I know the Lord, I know the Lord,
I know the Lord's laid His hands on me,
O I know the Lord, I know the Lord,
I know the Lord's laid His hands on me.

1. Did ever you see the like before?
   I know the Lord's laid His hands on me;
   King Jesus preaching to the poor!
   I know the Lord's laid His hands on me.

2. O wasn't that a happy day,
When Jesus washed my sins away?

3. Some seek the Lord and don't seek Him right,
They fool all day and pray at night.

4. My Lord's done just what He said,
He's healed the sick and raised the dead.

Old Woman

1. **Men:**   Old woman, old woman,
Won't you card my wool for me?
Old woman, old woman,
Won't you card my wool for me?

Women: Speak a little louder, sir,
I'm so hard of hearing;
Speak a little louder, sir,
I'm so hard of hearing;

2. **Men:**   Won't you darn my socks for me?

Women: Speak a little louder, sir,
I can hardly hear you.

3. **Men:**   Won't you let me court you?

Women: Speak a little louder, sir,
I'm beginning to hear you.

4. **Men:**   Won't you let me marry you?

Women: (clapping hands) : Goodness gracious sakes alive!
Now I really hear you.

Hey-Day-Day

When early morning's ruddy light
Bids men to labor go,
We'll haste with scythes all sharp and bright,
The meadow grass to mow.
We mowers tra-la-la-lay,
We'll cut the lilies and the hay,
We cut and hey-day-day and hey-day-day
And cut the lilies and hay.

My Hat

My hat it has three corners;
Three corners has my hat;
And had it not three corners,
It would not be my hat.

Mein hut er hat drei Ecken;
Drei Ecken hat mein Hut;
Und hat er nicht drei Ecken;
Denn das ist nicht mein Hut.

Motions— (1) On "my" point to self.   (2) On "hat" touch top of head.   (3) On "three" raise 3 fingers.   (4) On "corners" touch elbow of left arm.

My Sins Are Taken Away

I Ain't Gwine Study War No More

Leader   down!

1. Gwine to lay down my bur - den, Down by the riv - er - side,
2. Gwine to lay down my sword an' shiel', Down by the riv - er - side,
3. Gwine to try on my long white robe, Down by the riv - er - side,
4. Gwine to try on my star - ry crown, Down by the riv - er - side,

Down!

Down by the riv - er - side, Down by the riv - er - side;
Down by tho riv - er - side, Down by the riv - er - side;
Down by the riv - er - side, Down by the riv - er - side;
Down by the riv - er - side, Down by the riv - er - side;

Leader   Down!

Gwine to lay down my bur - den, Down by the riv - er - side, to
Gwine to lay down my sword an' shiel' Down by the riv - er - side, to
Gwine to try on my long white robe, Down by the riv - er - side, to
Gwine to try on my star-ry crown, Down by the riv - er - side, to

REFRAIN

stud-y war no more. I ain't gwine stud-y war no more, Ain't gwine study war no

more, Ain't gwine stud-y war no more,............ Ain't gwine stud-y war no
stud- y war no more,

more, Ain't gwine study war no more, Ain't gwine stud-y war no more!...... no more!

Swing Low, Sweet Chariot

Swing low, sweet char-i-ot, Com-in' fo' to car-ry me home,

Swing low, sweet char-i-ot, Com-in' fo' to car-ry me home.

1. I looked o-ver Jor-dan and what did I see, Com-in' fo' to car-ry me home,
2. If you get there be-fore I do, Com-in' fo' to car-ry me home,
3. The bright-est day that ev-er I saw, Com-in' fo' to car-ry me home,
4. I'm some-times up and some-times down, Com-in' fo' to car-ry me home,

A band of an-gels com-in' aft-er me, Com-in' fo' to car-ry me home.
Tell all my friends I'm com-in' too, Com-in' fo' to car-ry me home.
When Je-sus wash'd my sins a-way, Com-in' fo' to car-ry me home.
But still my soul feels heav'n-ly bound, Com-in' fo' to car-ry me home.

The Old Ark's A-Movering

O the old ark's a-mov-er-ing, a-mov-er-ing, a-mov-er-ing,

The old ark's a-mov-er-ing, And I'm going home, O the I'm going home.

1. See that sis - ter dressed so fine? She ain't got
2. See that broth - er dressed so gay? Death's goin' to
3. See that sis - ter com - ing so slow? She wants to go to
4. Th' ain't but the one thing grieves my mind; Sis - ter's gone to

D. C. Sing before 1st and after 4th stanza

Je - sus in her mind. Th' old ark she reeled, The
come for to car - ry him a - way. Th' old ark she reeled, The
heav'n 'fore the heav - en doors close. Th' old ark she reeled, The
heav'n and a left me be - hind. Th' old ark she reeled, The

D. C.

old ark she rocked, Old ark she land - ed on the moun - tain top.

I've Got Shoes

Joyfully, but not too fast

1. I've got a robe, you've got a robe, All of God's chil-dren got a robe:
2. I've got a crown, you've got a crown, All of God's chil-dren got a crown;
3. I've got a shoes, you've got a shoes, All of God's chil-dren got a shoes;
4. I've got a harp, you've got a harp, All of God's chil-dren got a harp;
5. I've got a song, you've got a song, All of God's chil-dren got a song;

When I get to heav-en, goin' to put on my robe, Goin' to
When I get to heav-en, goin' to put on my crown, Goin' to
When I get to heav-en, goin' to put on my shoes, Goin' to
When I get to heav-en, goin' to play on my harp, Goin' to
When I get to heav-en, goin' to sing a new song, Goin' to

REFRAIN

shout all o - ver God's heaven.
shout all o - ver God's heaven.
walk all o - ver God's heaven. Heaven,* heaven, ev- 'ry -bod-y's talk-ing 'bout
play all o - ver God's heaven.
sing all o - ver God's heaven.

heav-en ain't go-ing there, Heaven, heav - en, Goin' to shout all o - ver God's

D. C. Ending for last stanza   *Repeat pendosi*

Heav-en, heav - en, Goin' to shout all o - ver God's heav-en.

* End "heaven" with a humming sound

Lord, I Want to Be a Christian

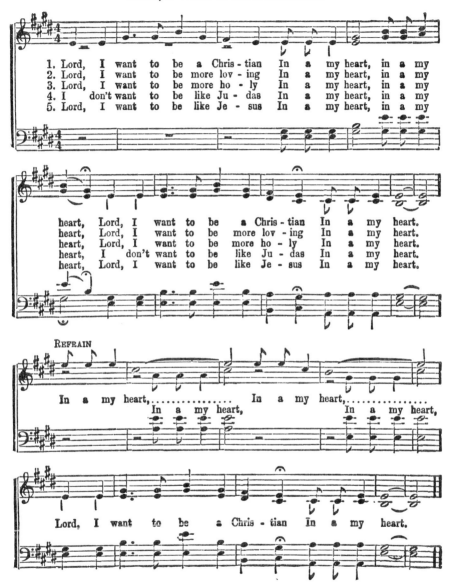

"If to this art of enjoyment can be added some ability as a performer of music, so much the better, for a true appreciation of musical values comes most surely through the actual experience of personal participation; and the real object of such personal performance is that of recreation and self-expression and a more intimate communion with beauty for its own sake."

—SIGMUND SPAETH in *The Art of Enjoying Music*.

No, Sir

1. Tell me one thing, tell me truly,
   Tell me why you scorn me so,
   Tell me why when asked a question,
   You will always answer, "No."

Chorus:

"No, sir; no, sir; no, sir; no."
"No, sir; no, sir; no, sir; no."

2. My father was a Spanish merchant,
   And before he went to sea,
   He told me to be sure and answer, "No,"
   To all you said to me.

3. If when walking in the garden,
   Plucking flow'rs all wet with dew,
   Will you be offended if I
   Have a walk and talk with you?

4. If when walking in the garden,
   I should ask you to be mine,
   And should tell you that I love you,
   Would you then my heart decline?

The old English folk song, "Oh, No, John," is very similar. It is altogether likely that it is somewhat kin to this American version. The music, however, is very different from its English cousin. It sounds very much like the old song, "The Gypsy's Warning," which started off "Trust him not, Oh, gentle lady."

It may be used as a dialogue between a boy and a girl. Or the men may sing one part of the song and the ladies the other.

Dr. John C. Orr, veteran minister and college professor, says that he remembers hearing this song sung when he was a student at Vanderbilt University back in 1882. A girl from old Ward College (now Ward-Belmont) sang it to the Vanderbilt boys, reaching a cresdendo on the last "No."

CHAPTER XIII
FUN WITH MUSICAL GAMES

FUN WITH MUSICAL GAMES

MUSICAL games have great values as socializers. There are also aesthetic and dramatic qualities that add to their value as recreational activities. When they are folk games they have the additional value of aiding in one's appreciation of folk of other lands. You cannot play "Chebogah" or "Marken Er Meyet" without feeling a bit friendlier toward the people out of whose culture the game originated.

Mrs. George Bidstrup, of the Campbell Folk School, Brasstown, N. C., got the following answers to the question, "Why do you like folk games?": (1) They are good fun. (2) I like the music that goes with them. (3) I enjoy the rhythm. (4) I like the social side. (5) They make you lose self-consciousness. (6) They make you more graceful. (7) Because they take team work. (8) Good exercise. (9) Because of the traditions that go with them. (10) They give you poise. (11) I like the pretty patterns of lines and formations. (12) They make you use your head. (13) Because they are artistic. (14) They don't take any equipment. (15) You can do them out-of-doors. (16) Folks will do them when they won't do anything else. (17) All share—no watchers.

TEACHING MUSICAL GAMES

1. Know thoroughly the game you plan to teach—words, music, and movement. Rehearse them when alone to develop confidence and certainty.

2. If possible, teach the games first to a small group. Have this group demonstrate each game before teaching it to the larger group.

3. In introducing these games to a new group use simple games at the beginning—"Looby Loo," "I Walk," "Chebogah," and "Susanna."

4. Do not allow your group to give up too easily before successful achievement has been attained. Where there are several movements, more or less difficult, teach the game one movement at a time. Offer words of encouragement from time to time.

5. Be more concerned about the joy to be found in the activity

than for meticulous precision. "We even had fun making mistakes," was the remark of one college student who was enthusiastic about the good time he had had doing folk games.

6. In teaching a movement new to the group it may be advisable to walk them through it several times. For instance, in teaching the grand right and left, which occurs in so many musical games, ask partners to hold right hands, with the man on the inside circle and the lady on the outside. Call attention to the fact that the man always moves with left hand in to center and lady with the right. This means the lady must reverse her direction of marching. Now suggest that all persons drop the partner's right hand and take the next person's left with the left. "Now keep on moving, right and left, weaving in and out until you get back to your partner." Some will get mixed. Patiently try it again. Then do the movement with music.

7. Introduce a folk game or two as part of some other program—a party, an entertainment, or an outing. One high-school teacher created a demand for a folk game party by introducing a game in costume as a feature of a banquet. The demonstration group had such a grand time that others began saying, "Why can't we do that sometime?"

8. All of the qualifications for leadership are called into play in directing folk games—enthusiasm, perseverance, tact, confidence, cheerfulness, friendliness, poise (not easily irritated by mistakes or by lack of complete co-operation), resourcefulness, insight, foresight, genuine interest in people, a genuine enthusiasm for and joy in the activity, the desire to be as inconspicuous as the effective discharge of his responsibilities will allow.

GRAND MARCH FIGURES

The following suggestions are made by Mrs. Harris ("Chris") Jesperson, of Viborg, South Dakota:

A grand march is an excellent beginning or a pleasant end to an evening of games. It can be used at any time whenever a large crowd must be set moving easily and pleasantly.

Be sure there are good leaders (the first couple) of the march who know the mechanics of the figures. The second couple should really be well versed also. The leader of the games should not join in, I believe, but be ready to straighten out possible missteps. In referring to the leaders later it means the first couple.

Sing or play any good quick marching song. It is not advisable to use popular songs as such. There are so many good marching songs. Have the tempo brisk, but not so fast as to be tiring.

The players line up as for any game and after securing their partners (boys with partners on their right) come up the center of the hall facing the front (where the leader or piano is placed).

I. Single lines.—

(1) The lines separate, girls going right, boys left. When they meet at the opposite end of the hall the girls go on the inside—boys passing on their left. Next meeting the boys go on the inside—girls passing on their left.

(2) When the lines move toward the back of the hall again the leaders make a sharp abrupt turn at the exact corner and head for the opposite corner. The lines meet and cross in the center of the hall in the form of an X—each lady passing in front of her partner. The leaders turn toward the back again and repeat, this time the boys passing in front of the ladies.

II. Couples.—

(1) Players join their partners and come up the center. At the front end of the hall the first couple goes to the right, second couple to the left, third couple right, etc. When the lines meet at the back the first couple and all couples behind them raise hands to make an arch, while the second couple and followers all pass under. Both lines keep marching. When they meet at the front end the second couple line makes the arch.

(2) *Zigzag*—All players link arms with partners and march forward with at least four feet between couples. Top couple with elbows linked cast off (swing about) to the right and go behind second couple, crossing over and around outside and behind third couple, and continue on zigzagging down the line followed at a short interval by the second and succeeding couples. This figure brings the players into a counterclockwise march which is customary.

(3) *Arch*—Players come up the center again in one line of couples. The first couple makes an arch, the second couple goes under, and also makes an arch. All follow, each in turn making an arch, till the line is all under when the first couple goes under repeating the figure.

(4) *Slide*—The second time the line goes under the arches the first couple steps back, followed in turn by each couple, till all the players are standing in two parallel rows, partners facing. First couple then clasps hands and with arms outstretched sideways goes

down along the line in a fast sideway slide or gallop. The others follow, but not too closely. *Variation:* Back to back, arms still outstretched.

III. In fours—three against one.—

(1) The players come up the center in couples, part left and right, then come up in fours. This time they part—three to the right side (the man on the left end going to the left alone). The second time the three go left (the girl on the right going alone).

(2) Players come up the center again in fours (part in fours right and left, come up in lines of eight (four couples). Halt at the front end and all mark time. The players clasp hands and the leaders begin to wind back between the lines—the last one in each line grasping the end player in the next line so that all face the same direction. The leaders continue back and forth down the hall till all are in a single line facing outward. The leaders go to the center and the line begins winding around them so that eventually all are standing in a spiral facing the center. The leaders now lead them out again—either by passing under the raised arms, straight out, or by unwinding, going back between the lines, which is slower. When the line is clear it breaks into couples and soon all are placed in the right position for another game or "Good-Night, Ladies."

Good songs to sing or play:

"On Wisconsin."
Iowa Song—"That's Where the Tall Corn Grows."
Minnesota Song—"Hat's Off to Thee."
"Stein Song."
"There's a Long, Long Trail A-winding."
"Pack Up Your Troubles."
"Glow Worm."
"Glory, Glory, Hallelujah."
"Happiness of Living."
"The Old Gray Mare."
"Parlez-vous."
"Tramp, Tramp, Tramp the Boys Are Marching."
"Marching through Georgia."
"Yankee Doodle."
"Dixie."
Yale's "Down the Field."
"Washington and Lee Swing."
"She'll Be Comin' 'Round the Mountain."

—MRS. HARRIS (CHRIS) JESPERSON, Viborg, South Dakota

The Organ Grinder Man

O the organ grinder man, the organ grinder man,
We will do the best we can to help the organ grinder man.

One player goes out of the room. The rest decide on something this player is to do. The player comes back into the room and starts around the circle of players or elsewhere in the room trying to discover where he is to perform. The only cue he gets is from the singing by the players of the above song. As he approaches the point where he is to perform they sing softly; when he draws away from it they increase in volume. At the point where he is to perform they sing very softly. After the player has located the place where he is to perform he begins trying various things. He may kneel before some player. He may pull his ear, pull a handkerchief from his pocket, remove his pen or spectacles. If the action is wrong the group sings loudly; if right they sing softly until the action is completed and then applaud. Try easy things at first. After a group has gotten the idea the players get amazingly expert at figuring out what action is required of them.

Popularity.—This is a good game where there is an overplus of either men or women. Players get partners through a grand march. Those who do not get partners go to center. If the ladies are in the majority the inside circle will be ladies. If the majority are men the inner circle will be men as the couples march around the circle. The extra players stand at center. At each blow of the whistle the inner circle reverses and marches in time to the music in the opposite direction. The outer circle always moves in the same direction it has been going. When the two circles are moving in opposite directions the extra players get in line and march with the inside circle. At the blow of the whistle the inside again reverses and marches in the same direction the outside circle is going. When they do this each person in the inside circle tries to get a partner.

The outside circle does not slow up or stop but keeps marching in time to the music. When done well the reverses will be done in perfect rhythm. Again players without partners go to center, excepting that the players in the outside circle do not go to center, continuing to march until some player on the inside circle notices that an outside circle player is without a partner.

The game continues until the group is well mixed. Added interest may be secured by having players shout "Howdy" when they meet and "So long" when they separate.

Squat.—The players march by couples at the direction of the leader. When he calls, "Men, three forward," the men leave their partners and march forward counting the next girl in front "One," then "Two," then "Three." Each player marches with the Number Three girl. On the command, "Ladies, four back," the ladies step back four and get new partners. When the leader blows a whistle all players scramble to find their original partners. They grasp both hands of the partner and squat. Last couple down is out of the game. The game continues until only a few couples are left marching.

I Walk Four Steps

Music, "Looby Loo"

I walk four steps in, I walk four steps out,
I take my partner by the hands and swing her about,
Here we go Looby Loo
Here we go Looby Light,
Here we go Looby Loo
All on a Saturday night.

Action—The players stand in a circle by couples, each man with his lady to the right. Then man walks in toward center four steps, reverses, and walks back four steps to his partner. Grasping his partner by the hands or just back of the elbows he circles with her eight walking steps. On the chorus partners take hold of hands, skating position, and they skip around the circle. Skating position is assumed by partners facing the same direction, lady to man's right, and holding hands, right to right and left to left.

The next time the ladies move four steps to center, but instead of coming back to the partner she had she moves to a new partner, taking the man who was on her right as she stood in the circle facing center.

Stop the game occasionally to allow partners to become acquainted.

—W. R. HAMMONTREE

Chum, Chummy Lou

This is a Virginia variation of "Skip to My Lou."

1. Get you a partner, Chum, Chummy Lou, (3 times)
   Chum, Chummy Lou, my darling.
2. I got another one good as the 'tother one, (3 times)
   Chum, Chummy Lou, my darling.
3. Can't get a biscuit, tater will do, (3 times)
   Chum, Chummy Lou, my darling.

Position—Players form a circle by couples, with a little space between couples. One odd player is in the center. Players sing, everyone keeping time by softly clapping the hands. The odd player skips over and takes someone's partner. The player whose partner was taken skips across and takes another. So it continues as long as desired. Several players may be used in the center of a large group.

—ELSIE DUDLEY

Smack Aunt Julie Down (Virginia)

(Music same as "Chum, Chummy Lou")

1. Sow your oats and reap your corn, (3 times)
   And smack Aunt Julie down.
2. Old Aunt Julie, smack her down, (3 times)
   And smack Aunt Julie down.

Position—Form circle by couples, girls to men's right. Each girl crosses her right arm over her left and takes right hand of her partner and the left of the man to her right.

Action—On 1, circle side skips to the left eight steps, then to the right eight steps. As soon as they finish this they drop hands in readiness for the next figure. At 2, partners take right hands for the grand right and left. Girls move clockwise, right hands to center. Boys move counterclockwise, left hands to center. Do grand right and left, girls singing "Old Aunt Julie" and boys answering with "Smack her down," all singing the last "And smack Aunt Julie down." Hold the partner gotten on this last "And smack Aunt Julie down." Repeat with new partner.

—ELSIE DUDLEY

Paa Vossevangen (Norway)

(English Version Translated by Anna Bergreen and Fred Smith)

Vossevangen is in Norway. It is here that the Saeter girls (cow-girls) go to live in the mountains each summer. They milk the cows and make butter and cheese while the men do the work in the valley.

'Tis Vossevangen that I will choose,
And live among the hills of clover.
There all the boys wear their polished shoes,
With jacket buttons silvered over.
Be-ribboned girls dancing there are found,
Their braids are almost reaching to the ground.
Believe you me, when I tell thee,
'Tis beautiful in Vossevangen.

Believe you me, when I tell thee,
'Tis beautiful in Vossevangen.

Danish words

Paa Vossevangen der vil jeg bo
Der vokser Klover over Hoje
Der gaar hver ungkarl med blanke sko
Og med en solver knappet troje
Der lansoe piger med baand i haar
De lange fletninger til jorden naar
Ja, tro du mig, Jeg siger dig
Der er det fagert at leve
Ja, tro du mig, Jeg siger dig
Der er det fagert at leve.

Formation—Partners join adjacent hands, the man with the left hand toward the center of the circle, and with the girl on the man's right.   Move in counterclockwise direction.   The count is waltz time, 1, 2, 3.

The Steps— (1) Step on left foot.
             (2) Cross right foot, and step on it.
             (3) Raise on toes, and lift left heel off floor.
             (4) Step on right foot.
             (5) Cross left foot, and step on it.
             (6) Raise on toes and lift right heel off floor.

At refrain in music, the partners drop hands.   Men join hands, making a circle with backs to center of circle.   Ladies join hands and face the center.   Repeat the step (1—6) once and bow to partner.   Repeat the step (1—6) again, and bow to partner.

                    —As directed by PETER OLSEN

You Must Pass This Spoon

You must pass this spoon from me to you, to you,
You must pass this spoon,
And do just what I do.

In a hotel ballroom on the floor at a National Recreation Congress in 1934 a small group of adults had a grand time playing this musical game. Sometimes shoes are passed instead of spoons. The game is credited to various countries, among them the Netherlands and Mexico. The Mexican version uses a different tune.

Action—The players are seated on the floor or around a table. Each player has a spoon in his right hand. As the song starts they tap the spoon on the floor or table in rhythm as they pass it to the right. In turn they receive the spoon from the left-hand neighbor and continue passing. On "and do just what I do" each player taps three times—to the right, to the left, and then back to the right. Anytime a player is caught with more than one spoon he is out of the game.

All Around the Maypole

1. All around the Maypole, tra la la la,
   All around the Maypole, tra la la la,
   All around the Maypole, tra la la la,
   I like sugar and candy.

2. Gotta make that motion, tra la la la, (three times)
   I like sugar and candy.

3. That's a very fine motion, tra la la la, (three times)
   I like sugar and candy.

Action—(1) The players circle around one center player, singing the first verse. (2) They continue to circle around singing the second verse. The center player performs with some step or motion of his own choosing. (3) On the third verse the players stop circling and imitate the action of the center player as he continues to perform.   Occasionally a center player should make the group perform some actions difficult enough to require a little effort.

—AL BROWN, Cleveland, Ohio

Daisy, Daisy

(1)   Daisy, Daisy, give me your promise, do,

(2)   I'm half crazy, all for the love of you.

(3)   It won't be a stylish marriage,

(4)   For I can't afford a carriage,

(5)   But you'll look sweet upon the seat
      Of a bicycle built for two.

Position—Double circle of partners, faced for marching, inside hands joined, outside hands on hips.

Action—(1) Take four change steps, or eight walking steps.   (2) Reverse, clasping opposite hands, and go back four change steps or eight walking steps.   (3) Partners face, shaking forefinger at each other.   (4) Fold arms, shake head, and look very sad.   (5) Swing partner, while singing the last two lines, eight counts.   On the last count leave the lady on the left, taking a new partner.

To do the change step, take a step with the left foot, bring right foot up behind and take another step with the left foot.   Then step with the right foot, bring up the left behind the right, step right foot again, etc.

—MRS. HARRIS (CHRIS) JESPERSON
Viborg, South Dakota

Chebogah (Hungarian Gypsy)

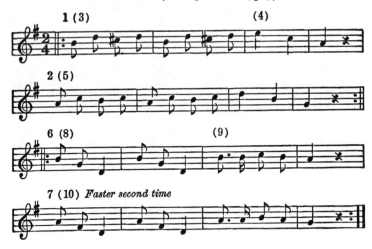

Left slide, left slide, here we go;
Right slide, right slide, to and fro.
One, two, three, STAMP,
One, two, three, STAMP,
Swing your partner, round we go.
Slowly, slowly, to the center go,
Ha-ha-ha-ha-ha-ha-ha—tra la la la la!
Slowly, slowly, Ha-ha-ha-ha-ha!
Swing your partner, merrily, tra-la-la-la-la!

"Chebogah" could be entitled "The Dance of the Moths." The moths circle the gypsy campfire, then fly in toward the flame, rejoice at their escape, and then try it again.

Action— (1) Players in a circle slide swiftly eight steps to the left. (2) Back eight slide steps to the right. (3) Four steps to center, stamping on the fourth. (4) Four steps back, stamping on the fourth. (5) Link right arms with partner and reel (turn) rapidly eight steps. The left arm is curved over the head in this movement, the forefinger nearly touching the top of the head. (6) Players step stealthily eight steps toward center. (7) Suddenly raise hands, and with head back, they laugh as they move backward to circle eight steps. (8) Four steps in the same manner to center. (9) Four steps back and laugh. (10) Link right arms with partner and reel very rapidly. Repeat from the beginning.

Ach Ja (German)

(1) When the mother and the father
Take the children to the fair

(2) Ach Ja, Ach Ja.

(1) They have little money
But it's little that they care.

(2) Ach Ja, Ach Ja.

CHORUS

(3) Tra la la, Tra la la,
Tra la la la la la la,

(4) Tra la la, Tra la la,
Tra la la la la la la,

(5) Ach Ja, Ach Ja.

Position—Double circle of partners, faced for marching.

Action— (1) Partners join hands, and walk four steps forward. (2) Face each other and bow on the first "Ach Ja." Then turn their backs and bow again back to back on the second "Ach Ja." (3) Face partner arms outstretched shoulder height, and slide four steps counterclockwise, while moving the arms up and down, windmill fashion. (4) Repeat slide step back. (5) Bow to partner, then step to left and bow to a new partner.

The family is on the way to a church fair. They have "no gold" but they plan to have a good time just the same.

Marken er Mejet, Mow the meadow (Danish)

VERSE 1

The grain field is mowed and the meadows are empty,
Going home are we at last with our day's labor done,
Harvest is plentiful, barns scarcely hold it—
Shocks of grain and hay in stacks, they greet the setting sun.

CHORUS 1

Children are dancing round,
Feet tripping on the ground—
The girls are gay, they sing this way:
Tra la la la la la.

(REPEAT CHORUS)

VERSE 2

Rake we the field lightly, old rite we honor,
Birds and poor must have some food wherewith to meet their
needs,
Barn lofts are decked with gay hollyhocks and foliage,
Dahlias, roses, flowers a-plenty, song of beauty breeds.

CHORUS 2

Tie the grain in wreaths so gay,
Shout hurrah for the country,
Harvest time is merry time,
Tra la la la la la.

(REPEAT CHORUS)

The harvest dance—This lovely tune is used at harvest time, particularly. The custom of sharing with the birds and poor, is one of the features of the harvest celebration.

Formation: Couples.

First part: with right-arm hook:
(1) Four Tyrolian steps in place.
(2) Eight run steps clockwise.

Change to left-arm hook:
(3) Four Tyrolian steps in place.
(4) Eight run steps counterclockwise.

Second part:
(5) Grand right and left.

Dance of Greeting (Danish)

Welcome, welcome, you are welcome,
Come and join us in our play.

Formation—Single circle of couples facing center.

First part—
(1) Clap twice, face partner and bow (curtsy).
(2) Clap twice, face neighbor and bow (curtsy).
(3) Face center, stamp twice, and turn in place with three running steps. Repeat from beginning.

Second part—
(4) All join hands in circle, face left and run around sixteen steps; repeat, turning and running sixteen steps in opposite direction.
Another version is:

Formation—Double circle of couples facing partners; men on inside.

(1) Clap hands.
(2) Clap hands.
(3) Turn around in place and bow (curtsy) deeply.
(4) Hop step with partner.

(1) Clap hands.
(2) Clap hands.
(3) Turn around in place and bow (curtsy) deeply.
(4) Grand right and left.

—As directed by PETER OLSEN

Svensk Masquerade (Swedish)

Formation: Couples.

Measures 1-4   March 16 steps counterclockwise.
                Turn on step 15-16.
       1-4   (Repeated). March 16 steps clockwise.
       :/: 5-12 :/: Tyrolian waltz. (Partners take adjacent

hands and swing away from one another, then to one another.

:/: 13-20 :/: Partners hold hands or arms at elbow and do hop-step in 2/4 tempo.

—Adapted from PETER OLSEN

Sisken (Danish)

Position—Circle. Couples, men back toward center.

Steps—Walk, hop step.

Measures 5-8—Walk forward to new partner to right, using hands in shoulder height, using the hands as pushing somebody away, while they sing, "Go from me, go from me, go from me again."

Measures 6-8—Walk forward to new partner to right, using hands as wishing them to come to you, singing, "Come to me, come to me, come to me my friend."

Measures 9-16—Forge. Clap own hands, partner's right, own hands, partner's left, own hands, partner's both, own hands three times, singing, "Tra, la la la, Tra, la la la la la, Tra la la la la la la.

Measures 17-32—Hop step with new partner.

—PETER OLSEN

Star Promenade

1. Six ladies in the center with the right hand crossed,
   Be careful that you don't get lost.
2. Back to the left and don't be afraid,
3. Pass your partner with the Star Promenade.

4. My old girl went back on me just because I went to sea,
   Because I went to sea, you see.
   My old girl went away last fall,
5. Break and swing and promenade all.

A circle game for six couples.

Action—Girls form circle at center crossing right hands with the girl opposite to form a star. The boys join hands around the girls, each boy behind his partner.

On 1, the girls circle left to position in front of partner. On 2, the girls form star with left hands and circle back to position. On 3, each girl gives the right hand to her partner, passes by his right, and on to the boy on her partner's right, with whom she promenades to end of musical phrase.

At 4, they promenade with new partner again. At 5, they break for a moment, then take position and swing, ending with a promenade.

Repeat until each girl has had every one of the boys for a partner.

The boys then go to center and the game is resumed. This time the group sings "Six Gents to the Center."

—From *"The Play Party in Indiana."* Used by permission of the publishers, Indiana Historical Bureau.

Tra, la, la, Ja sas (Norway)

Ud av alle som gaar i ringen
Jed velger dig eller ogsaa ingen
Ti jeg finder at det er umulig
At leve lykkelig foruten dig.

Tra la la la, Ja sas
Tra la la la, Ja sas
Ti jeg finder at det er umulig
At leve lykkelig foruten dig.

ENGLISH

I am waiting, I am hoping
That someone will join me in the ring,
Will you come and dance with me, my partner,
While our other comrades clap and sing?

Tra la la la, yes sir,
Tra la la la, yes sir,
Will you swing around and do as I do
Or shall I reverse and turn with you?

This is a Norwegian singing game and is played in a single circle.
During *A,* one or more odd players walk around inside the ring

and each chooses a partner. *B*—The partners walk, waltz, or skip around the circle. *C*—Each player turns a complete circle alone and bows to his partner. This is repeated. *D*—Partners swing each other vigorously by the right arm for six counts. This is repeated with the left arm for six counts.

The game is usually continued by having those chosen remain in the center while the others return to the circle, but all the players may stay in the center and each may choose a new partner. Using this method, a single circle of players may finish in couples.

—As taught by MAGDALENE L. HEIBERT

Home Demonstration Agent, Jamestown, N. Dak.

—English version by ELLA GARDNER

Recreation Specialist, Washington, D. C.

Six Little Girls A-sliding Went

Six little girls a-sliding went, a-sliding went, a-sliding went,
Six little girls a-sliding went,
So early in the morning.
   The ice was thin, and they broke in,
   And they broke in, and they broke in.
   The ice was thin, and they broke in,
The rest all ran away.

Position—Boys stand in circle. Girls join hands and form a circle inside, facing the boys.

Action—On 1, the girls circle left. On 2, the girls break line and each swings the first boy she comes to. On 3, all players get in position for the next game. Repeat, with boys and girls changing places.

—From *"The Play Party in Indiana."* Used by permission of the publishers, Indiana Historical Bureau.

The Paul Jones

This is always a popular musical social mixer. The music may be any lively march or two-step.

(1) Grand march in twos and fours.
(2) All join hands and circle to the left.
(3) Circle to the right.
(4) All forward to center and back.
(5) Right hand to partner and grand right and left all the way.
(6) Swing your partner. Take hold of hands and turn eight steps.
(7) Ladies to the center in a circle and gentlemen on the outside.
(8) Ladies circle to the left and gents to the right.
(9) Swing your partner.
(10) March by twos.
(11) March by fours.
(12) While marching four abreast in a circle the leader may call "Gents, four forward!" The ladies would stand still while the gentlemen advance four forward and take a new partner. The call may be "Ladies, two back!" or any other call the leader sees fit to give.
(13) Swing your new partner.

Waves of Tory (Irish) Victor Record No. 20991

(Can also be done to "The Galway Piper")

Formation—Sets of six to eight couples, men opposite the women as in the Virginia Reel.

Movement—(1) Men join hands. Ladies join hands. The two lines advance toward one another four fast running steps, hands raised on the fourth step, thus representing the waves. Back four steps.

(2) Repeat Number 1.

(3) Right-hand wheel in fours. Players cross and clasp right hands with the opposite. They move eight running steps around.

(4) Left-hand wheel in fours. Players reverse, clasping left hands with opposite. Eight running steps back to position.

(5) Couples clasp hands skating position. The head couple leads off to the right. All couples follow the head couple around and back up the middle to position.

(6) The head couple faces the group, the man holding the girl's right hand with his left. All other couples face the head, the man with his partner to his right. The head couple bridges Couple Number 2 and then goes under the raised hands of Couple Number

3. This is continued to the foot of the set and return. As soon as they pass Couple Number 2, that couple follows them. And so does each couple, in turn, go to the head, to the foot, and back to position. This again gives the effect of waves.

(7) Couples come back in position and cast off. That is, the head man leads off to the left, all of the men following him as he turns and runs just outside the line of men. At the same time the head lady casts off to the right followed by the ladies. When the head couple meets at the foot they make an arch and the other couples join hands and go through to position.

(8) Repeat with a new head couple.

We're Marching Round the Levee

1. We're marching round the levee,
   We're marching round the levee,
   We're marching round the levee,
   For we will win the day.

2. Go in and out the window, (3 times)
   For we will win the day.

3. Go forth and face your lover, (3 times)
   For we will win the day.

4. I kneel because I love you, (3 times)
   For we will win the day.

5. I measure my love to show you, (3 times)
   For we will win the day.

6. Goodbye, I hate to leave you, (3 times)
   For we will win the day.

As the players sing the first verse they march in rhythm around in the circle. Two or more players are in the center. On "Go in and out the window" the center players begin to weave in and out under the raised arms of the circle players, who stand still with clasped hands raised high. On the third verse each of the center players selects a partner, standing in front of some player in the circle. On the fourth verse the center players and the ones chosen kneel facing one another. On the fifth verse they clasp hands with arms outspread and sway in rhythm to the music. On the last verse the players chosen go to the center while the others return to the circle. The game proceeds with new players at center.

When older people play this game instead of kneeling the partners may bow, while the group sings, "I bow because I love you." On "I measure my love" the partners clasp hands, arms spread, while they do a side slip step around the inside of the circle.

The King of France

The King of France with forty thousand men,
Marched up the hill and then marched down again.

The players stand in two rows facing each other. Each row has a leader, who is the King. The players all imitate the motions of their King, marching forward on the first line of the song and back to position on the second line, indicating the motion set for them by the King.

The two lines alternate singing.

Other verses are as follows:

> Rode his horse up the hill and then rode down again.
> Filled his canteen up and then emptied it again.

> Drew his sword as he marched and then put it up again.
> Fired his gun up the hill and then marched down again.

The King may introduce any other variations that may occur to him. All of the players on his side follow suit each time.

I've Been Workin' on the Railroad

Oh, I've been workin' on the railroad,
All the live-long day. (Hey!)
I've been workin' on the railroad,
Just to pass the time away. (Hey!)
Don't you hear the whistle blowin'?
Rise up so early in the morn. (Hey!)
Don't you hear the captain shouting?
Dinah, blow your horn. (Toot! Toot!)

Formation—Couples face counterclockwise, man with his partner to his right. March in circle. Hold hands, skating position.

Action—Couples march counterclockwise on first line and stop. On the second line they reach the left foot forward, heel to the floor and toe up. The foot is quickly withdrawn and the right foot is extended in the same manner. On "all" the left foot goes forward. On "live" the right foot goes forward. On "day," "away," "morn," "horn," and "Hey!" bend the knees slightly.

The same action is repeated for lines 3 and 4 and 5 and 6.

On line 7 the players move forward as before, but on line 8 ("Dinah, blow your horn") the players stoop once, bending the knees slightly in rhythm (on "blow"). Then the man progresses to the lady just ahead, ending with a sharp "toot! toot!"

The game is then repeated with the new partner.

This game can be used on a hike, with no changing of partners being required.

Polly-Wolly-Doodle

1. O I went down South for to see my Sal,
Sing Polly-Wolly-Doodle all the day,
O my Sal she am a spunky gal,
Sing Polly-Wolly-Doodle all the day.

CHORUS

Fare thee well, fare thee well,
Fare thee well my fairy fay;
I'm a gwine to Louisiana for to see my Susie Anna,
Sing Polly-Wolly-Doodle all the day.

2. A grasshopper sittin' on a railroad track,
A pickin' his teeth with a carpet tack.

3. O I feed my pigs on candied yam,
They ought to be fatter than they am.

4. O I eat watermelon and I have for years,
I like watermelon, but it wets my ears.

MOVEMENT

Formation—Couples march in circle counterclockwise, man with lady to his right. Couples hold hands, skating position.

First verse—Couples march around circle on verse. **On chorus** odd couples (that is, couples 1, 3, 5, 7, etc.) turn and face even couples (that is, couples 2, 4, 6, 8, etc.). Each man grasps the right hand of the opposite lady (the other man's partner). In this position with hands crossed, the four people move around eight steps to position.

Second verse—Couples march as in Verse 1. On the chorus repeat the action for Verse 1 except that opposites take left hands and move around eight steps to the left.

Third verse—Couples march as in Verses 1 and 2. On the chorus do the grand right and left, getting a new partner on the final word, "day."

Fourth verse—On chorus all join hands and circle to the left eight steps and back to the right eight steps.

Boscastle

This English folk game is so similar to the Danish "Paul on the Hill," sometimes called "Paul with the Chickens," that it must have been an adaptation of the Danish game. Part 1 is exactly like the Danish version.

Formation—Each set or group is made up of two couples. All face forward, joining hands to form a hollow square.

Action—

Part 1—(1) Players move to the right in a step-slide, step-kick, that is, step to the right with the right foot, slide the left foot over toward the right, step to the right again and kick left foot over right. This action is repeated to the left. Four counts.

(2) The leading couple in each set drops inside hands, but holds on to hands of players behind them. In four hop or skip steps the head couple moves around to the rear. The rear couple moves

slightly forward in four hop or skip steps and becomes the front couple.

(3) Repeat the step-slide, step-kick figure with the new couple leading.

(4) Repeat No. 2.

Part 2—(1) Move forward, hands joined, four hop or skip steps.

(2) Keep hands joined. Rear couple forms an arch and head couple takes four hop or skip steps back under the arch. The rear couple moves forward four hop or skip steps at the same time, turning under their own arms (skin-the-cat style) without dropping hands. They become the head couple.

(3) Move forward again in four hop or skip steps.

(4) Repeat 2, Part 2.

Spanish Waltz

(Can be done to any good waltz music—"Missouri Waltz," "Blue Danube.")

Done in sets of four people—couples facing one another. The man has his partner to the right, the right hand of the man holding the left hand of the lady.

(1) Couples advance toward one another two waltz steps forward and two waltz steps back, raising clasped hands as they go forward, bringing them back down as they move backward.

(2) This is repeated except that as the couples move forward each person takes both hands of the person opposite, the lady passing in front of the man with a waltz step. In four waltz steps the man has a new partner to his right, and the couples are now facing from two different sides of the quadrangle.

(3) Repeat 1 and 2 with the new partner.

(4) This process is repeated until each person visits each corner of quadrangle and is back in his or her original position. This means that the figures in 1 and 2 will be done four times.

(5) The ladies clasp right hands across. The men clasp right hands across underneath the hands of the ladies. In this position all persons move around the circle in four waltz steps, moving in towards one another and raising hands as they do so. On the second step they move away from one another and lower hands. This is repeated for four steps.

(6) Reverse—take left hands and repeat steps back to original positions.

(7) Partners break hands and move forward to the opposite— the lady to the man opposite her and the man to the opposite girl. These opposites take right hands and take eight waltz steps around one another and through to another couple, the partners taking hold of hands again as they finish the circling of their opposites.

(8) Repeat the entire procedure with a new couple. Repeat as often as desired.

Betsy Liner

Music: "Ten Little Indians"

1. Bow down, old Betsy Liner, (3 times)
   Won't you be my darling?
2. Right hand swing, old Betsy Liner, etc.
3. Left hand swing, etc.
4. Both hands swing, etc.
5. Shake that foot, go all around her, etc.
6. Take her down, bring her back again, etc.
7. Swing that girl, old Betsy Liner, etc.
8. Girl wouldn't swing. I wouldn't have her.
9. Moon and stars shine all around you, etc.

Formation—Same as Virginia Reel, men on one side, ladies on the other. Six to eight couples to a set.

Action—Verse 1. Head lady and end man to center, bow and return. Then head man and end lady.

Verse 2. Same couples, one at a time, hold right hands high, turn at center and return to place.

Verse 3. Left hands same.

Verse 4. Turn with both hands.

Verse 5. Do-si-do. That is, head lady and end man move to center, arms folded over chest, pass around one another and return to place. Head man and end lady do same.

Verse 6. Head couple take hold of both hands and do a side-skip down and return.

Verses 7 and 8. Partners swing one another, holding right hands or locking right arms. The girl then swings the next man in line while the boy swings that man's partner or the lady at the end. In other words the swinging may be done with opposites or on the diagonal. Each time the partners come back to center and swing one another. This is continued until they have swung each person in the set.

Verse 9. Partners return immediately to the positions at the head of their respective lines and cast off, the lady leading her line around to the back, while the man leads his line around. At the foot the two leaders form an arch. The other couples meet and go through and back to position, leaving a new head couple. The former leaders take their place at the foot and the game continues.

This is a very popular version of the Virginia reel.

Phonograph Records of Folk Games

	Victor	Columbia
Ace of Diamonds (Danish)	20989	A3001
Black Nag (English)	20444	
Broom Dance (German)	20448	
Captain Jinks	20432	A3036
Chimes of Dunkirk (Belgian)	21618	A3061
Come, Let Us Be Joyful (German)	20448	
Crested Hen (Danish)	21619	
Chebogah (Cschbogar) (Hungarian)	20992	
Danish Dance of Greeting	20432	A3039
Gustaf's Skoal or Toast (Swedish)	20988	
Highland Schottische (Scotch)	21618	A3039
I See You (Swedish)	20432	A3031
Jolly Is the Miller	20214	
Klappdans (Swedish)	20450	A3036
Little Man in a Fix (Danish)	20449	
Looby Loo (English)	20214	100008D
Money Musk (American)	20447	
Muffin Man (English)	20806	

Norwegian Mountain March	20151	A3041
Oxdansen (Danish)	17003	
Pop Goes the Weasel (American)	20151	
Reap the Flax (Danish)	17002	
Ribbon Dance (English)	21619	
Roman Soldiers (English)	21617	
Seven Jumps (Danish)	21617	
Sicilian Circle (American)	20639	556D
Shoemaker's Dance (Danish)	20450	A3038
Tantoli (Swedish)	20992	A3054
Virginia Reel (American)	20447	5008D
Waves of Tory (Irish)	20991	

Wait for the Wagon

1. Will you come with me, my Phyllis, dear,
   To yon blue mountain free?
   Where the blossoms smell the sweetest,
   Come rove along with me.

It's every Sunday morning,
When I am by your side,
We'll jump into the wagon,
And we'll all take a ride.

Chorus:

Wait for the wagon, wait for the wagon,
O wait for the wagon, and we'll all take a ride.

Where the river runs like silver
And the birds they sing so sweet,
I have a cabin, Phyllis,
And something good to eat.

Come listen to my story;
It will delight your heart.
So jump into the wagon,
And off we will start.

Action—The players stand in square formation, each girl behind her partner. On "Will you come with me," the man turns to face his partner. While in this position he sings the first four lines. On "It's every Sunday morning" the boy steps to the left of his partner, taking her hands in skating position. In this position they promenade in line, tracing a rectangle by means of four sharp turns to the left.

During the chorus each boy swings his partner. On "We'll all take a ride" he takes a position in front of the next girl behind him, thus being in position to start over on verse two with a new partner.

CHAPTER XIV
FUN WITH DRAMATICS

FUN WITH DRAMATICS

The appeal of the ordinary dramatic performance is almost entirely to ego-centric interests, such as exhibitionism, self-assertion, power, desire to attract attention, to occupy the center of the stage, to make believe as an escape from reality. Again, the superficiality with which the youthful actors represent characters in play leads to half-learning and confusion. They do not acquire any understanding of the character's problems. They do not learn to appreciate his conflicts, or grasp the significance of the plot and dramatic situation. This type of dramatics encourages superficial thinking and unsympathetic response to others. Character education, on the contrary, ought to emphasize sincerity and honesty, thoughtfulness, insight, and sympathy—characteristics that are not engendered by mere impersonation.

In the light of these considerations play production is not a profitable activity for clubs of younger people, traditional club programming not withstanding. —From *Creative Group Education,* by S. R. Slavson, Association Press. By permission.

To become interested in dramatics is like visiting a labyrinth of never-ending loveliness, with surprises, thrills, variety, and new discoveries at every turn. Opportunities for varied activities— impersonation, manual arts (stage-settings, properties), color effects (lights, costumes, settings), design (costumes, settings), music, creativity, group co-operation—make this an ideal recreation.

At the same time, careful thought should be given to the dangers pointed out by Mr. Slavson in the quotation cited at the beginning of this chapter. A dramatic performance may easily become a painful display of peacock-strutting participants. The very dangers Mr. Slavson mentions make creative dramatics much preferable to exhibitionism for children, no matter how much it pleases doting parents to see their young hopefuls on display. And even with young people and adults these dangers are only averted by diligent and intelligent handling.

Common faults of amateur plays—

1. *Choice of Play*—(1) Lack of action, emotion, suspense, conflict, and climax in material selected. (2) Trivial and threadbare entertainment. (3) Moralizing and propaganda plays that bend the characters out of type. (4) Selecting a play not suited to the group's

ability.   (5) Plays and pageants too long and involved.   (6) **Satis-faction** with plays that lack merit.

2. *Acting*—(1) Poor casting.   (2) Players dropping out of character when they have spoken their lines.   (3) Poor voice production and poor enunciation so that lines cannot be understood.   (4) Satisfaction with mediocre performance and thus not enough rehearsing. Barrett Clark says that ninety-nine out of one hundred amateur performances are under-rehearsed.   (5) Using young people for mature parts.   (6) Poor make-up.   (7) Speaking with back to the audience. (8) Players stiff and self-conscious.   (9) Over-acting.   (10) Failure to learn lines.   (11) Superficial understanding of the characters portrayed.

3. *Staging* (costuming, setting, lighting, music) — (1) Costumes not historically accurate.   (2) Poor and inaccurate setting.   (3) Lack of appreciation of the values of good light effects.   (4) Poor co-ordination of telephone bells and other stage noises with action. (5) Music not in keeping with the time or theme.

4. *Directing*—(1) Making automatons out of the actors so that the performance becomes simply a live-puppet show.   (2) Losing sight of the fact that not what happens to the play, but what happens to the players is what counts most.

Play production.—It is a mistake to exclude serious drama when thinking of having fun with dramatics.   The preparation and production of a play like "The Servant in the House" or "An Enemy of Society" can be a most enjoyable experience.   If well coached it *will* be.   Plays dealing with social problems—war, economics, race, alcohol—can afford pleasant as well as profitable use of leisure time. The same may be said for plays definitely religious.

Comedy and operettas would naturally be included.   Cheapness should be avoided.   It is much more fun to produce a play of merit, whether it be comedy or tragedy, than to waste time on poorly conceived trash.   There is a certain satisfaction in producing a play or operetta of merit.   To do "The Mikado" is an experience that will be remembered with pleasure all of one's life.

Spontaneous drama.—In spontaneous drama the group decides on some conflict situation, selects characters, assigns parts, and begins immediately with the dramatization.   Each character says and does what he thinks the character impersonated would say and do under the circumstances.   In an alert group this can be loads of fun.   One group decided that the situation was as follows: A girl is trying to decide between a career and marriage.   Her love is insistent.   He wants her to abandon a career for a home. What a grand time the group had working out this play. Serious or comic situations may serve as the springboard for this sort of drama. It is possible to take certain problems and give them development in this manner. Follow a brief presentation with discussion.

Reading rehearsals.—Reading plays and discussing them is a fascinating exercise. Add to this the idea of assigning parts and giving them some dramatic interpretation and you have the reading rehearsal. It may be done with or without action. It is done without setting or costuming. We saw one group do the fourth act in Ibsen's "Enemy of the People" in this fashion. And what a grand time they had. The audience enjoyed it too. It was surprisingly effective. Another group did "Pawns" by Percival Wilde, in this manner, for a vesper hour. It was gripping.

Portions of plays may be read to serve as stimulators for discussion of certain problems. A few suggestions follow:

War—"The Enemy," Channing Pollock; "Bury the Dead," Irwin Shaw; "Paths of Glory," Sidney Howard; "Journey's End," R. C. Sherriff; "Pawns," Percival Wilde; "Wings Over Europe," Nichols & Browne; "Cavalcade," Coward; "R. U. R.," Capek; "The Terrible Meek," Kennedy; "No More Peace," Ernst Toller, translated by Edward Crankshaw.

Race—"Loyalties," Galsworthy; "In Abraham's Bosom," Green; "White Dresses," Green; "Porgy," Duboset and Dorothy Heyword; "The Color Line," Macnair.

Economics—"The Beggar and the King," Parkhurst, in *Atlantic Book of Modern Plays;* "The Fool," Channing Pollock; "Strife," Galsworthy; "Dead End," Kingsley; "John Withered's Hand," Mansfield; "Smoke," Dorothy Clark Wilson; "Bread," Fred Eastman.

Miscellaneous—"Our Town," Thornton Wilder; "Outward Bound," Sutton Vane; "The Passing of the Third Floor Back," Jerome; "Abraham Lincoln," Drinkwater; "Saint Joan," George Bernard Shaw; "The Blue Bird," Maeterlinck; "An Enemy of the People," Ibsen; "Green Pastures," Connelly.

Choral reading.—This ancient practice has recently come back into favor through the impetus given to it by John Masefield and Marjorie Gullan in England. Hundreds of years before Christ the Greeks produced drama with the parts spoken, not by individual actors, but by groups of people speaking as one voice. The Greek chorus murmured, swayed, chanted, spoke, and made live some of the greatest dramas of the ages.

Choric reading, sometimes called choral speech, or verse-choir speaking, is simply the reading together of poetry or prose by a group of people. Responsive reading is a form of choric speech.

Groups may be divided according to "light" or "dark" voices. In some cases voices are divided, according to timber, into much the same sort of ensemble as a singing chorus. Individuals or groups of five to ten persons may be assigned to read solo parts.

Some of the values of this form of activity that might be mentioned are speech improvement—consonants must be clipped, the vowels resonant, the tone pleasing, and the mood felt—and the appreciation of poetry, drama, and good literature. The same principles that underlie good dramatic production hold in choric speech.

Suggested material—Poetry (Masefield, Milne, Sandburg, Noyes, and others); the Bible (especially the Psalms and dramatic stories like the story of Elijah and the Prophets of Baal); great prose passages; drama.

Bibliography—Choral Speaking, Marjorie Gullan; *Poetry Arranged for the Speaking Choir*, by Marion Parsons Robinson and Rozetta Lura Thurston; *The Teaching of Choric Speech*, Elizabeth Keppie; *Lilts for Fun*, M. E. DeWitt; *Let Us Recite Together*, M. E. De-Witt; *Selections for Choral Speaking* (*Hiawatha*, arranged as a choral drama, Bible and other selections), by Agnes Curren Hamm.

DRAMATIC GAMES

Charades, dumb crambo, gestures, singing games like "I've Come to See Miss Jenny Ann Jones," "Did You Ever See a Lassie?" and many of the folk games come under this head.

Charades.—A charade is the dramatic presentation of a word with a view to a group guessing what the word is. Sometimes charades are done in pantomine. Sometimes they are acted out with dialogue. They may be simple or elaborate. The players choose a word, phrase, or sentence. Each part has a separate meaning. The audience is informed how many syllables or words are in the charade and in how many scenes it will be presented. The audience tries to guess what the word is. Most any group can work out its own interpretations. A few suggestions are offered:

Mis(s)-cell-any.—Four syllables. Presented in three scenes.

SCENE I—*Miss*—Old man enters. Sits down. Opens newspaper. Feels in pockets for his glasses. Doesn't find them. Makes gesture of disgust because glasses are missing. Enter young woman. Notes the evident discomfort of the old man. "What's the trouble, Grandfather?" "My glasses are missing." Young woman laughs gaily. "What's funny about that?" says Grandpa. "Oh, nothing. Only your glasses are on top of your head." Grandpa starts reading. A cat is heard off-stage. Grandpa goes to the corner, picks up a rifle and aims. Pretends to shoot. "Missed, by cracky."

SCENE II—*Cell*—Prisoner in jail. Jailer enters. "Say, Jailer, how long do they plan to keep me here?" "Maybe from now on." "What have I done?" "Didn't you sell the Brooklyn Bridge to an old man for twenty-five dollars?" "Yeah! It's worth that much, ain't it?" "Sure, but you don't own it." "Oh, I never thought of that."

SCENE III—*Any*—Cook working in kitchen. Boy enters. "I'm so hungry I could eat a wooden cow." Cook holds up a plate of apples. "Would these help?" "I'll say they will. Which one may I have?" "Any you want." "Any?" "Any."

Mend-i-cant.—Three syllables. Three scenes.

SCENE I—*Mend*—A repair shop. Workman repairing toys or garments. People bring in things to mend.

SCENE II—*I*—Optical shop. People come in to have eyes examined. One young fellow comes in. Boasts a lot while being examined. "I did this," "I did that." Examiner reports he has bad case of "eye" trouble.

SCENE III—*Cant*—Schoolroom. Pupils being quizzed by teacher. Invariable answer: "I Can't." Three pupils sing "I can't do this sum" when called upon by the teacher to work a problem. Scene closes with teacher saying that the most powerful word in the language is can and it is just can't with the "t" knocked out of it.

Sax-o-phone.—Three syllables. Three scenes.

SCENE I—*Sacks*—Cotton field. Cotton pickers going through field picking cotton. Singing "Swing Low." When halfway across stage, they pantomine throwing sacks over shoulders and carry them off.

SCENE II—*Owe*—Restaurant. Waiter comes in to wait on a couple. Brings meal. Brings check. Young man looks chagrined when he looks at the bill and exclaims, "Oh!" Pays bill and exit.

SCENE III—*Phone*—Girls sit on row of chairs. Imitate telephone exchange girls. All talking at once. "Number please!" "Line's busy!" "That phone is disconnected!"

Suggested words for charades.—Abridge, abate, abandon, acrostic, actuary, address, adhere, adhesion, adore, afford, airplane, background, bailiwick, Baldwin, balsam, bandanna, baronet. bastile, burlap, cabinet, canebrake, canvassing, counterpoint, courtship, dogmatic, drawbridge, earring, eyelash, farewell, father-in-law, footlight, footpad, furrow, gesticulate, hardware, heirloom, horse chestnut horsemanship, handsome, ideal, idol, incense, increase, indued, infer, indifferent, ingratiate, jack-pot, Jupiter, kidnaper, Kingfish, leapfrog, message, misunderstand, nightingale, outrage, parcel, penmanship, quarrelsome, quizzical, rainbow, restaurant, sausage, surprise, synthesis, tenant, teutonic, tidewater, transcendental, uproar, vacillate (vassal-ate), warden, youngster, youthful.

Gestures.—"Gestures" have been called "one-man charades." The game combines pantomime and guessing. Old and young enjoy it. It requires only two people—one to gesticulate and the other to guess what the weird movements represent. However, any number of people may play it. The more, the merrier. The players take turns acting out something perplexing for the others to guess. Songs, book titles, cars, names, words, familiar sights, famous sayings, words, etc., may thus be presented.

"Vanity Fair"—the player is a bit "snooty." He then becomes an umpire in a baseball game. After signaling a ball and a strike by first lifting the left hand and then the right umpire-fashion, he turns to watch a hard-hit ball sail to the outfield, and then waves the batter around the bases. It is a "fair ball."

A popular one was the holding of the hand to the back of the head. "An Indian looking backward" the actor explains, Patting a head that has lots of hair was described as "beating about the bush." When no one can guess what is being done the actor must tell what he is doing.

A variation of this game would be to divide into two sides. One side decides on a word to be represented by gestures. They whisper that word to one representative of the other side and that player tries to convey it to his group through pantomine. Three guesses are allowed. Then the other side takes its turn.

Dramatic adverbs.—One player leaves the room. The rest selects some suitable adverb. The player returns and tries to discover what the word is by asking questions and observing the manner of reply. In answering each player must act in such a manner as to suggest the word. For instance, suppose the word is "sadly." Each response must be in doleful manner until the player guesses the word. The player who furnishes the clue to the word leaves the room and the game continues. The questioner, perhaps, asks some such question as, "Can you give me a clue to the word?" The player asked assumes his saddest expression as he answers: "I am sorry, my dear friend. It grieves me beyond measure that I cannot disclose the word to you."

Suggested words are as follows: sweetly, excitedly, angrily, laughingly, crazily, haltingly.

Act it out.—A lot of fun can be had by giving to different players brief instructions for acting. (1) You are an old man (woman) eighty years of age. You lean heavily on your cane. Enter the room and sit down, greeting people in the room as you come in. (2) You are attending a church service. The sermon does not interest you. You get drowsy. You nod. You look about you to see if anyone noticed. You nod. You sleep. You awake with a start. You pretend to be wide awake. (3) You are at a picture show. Someone wants to get past you to get a seat. They tramp on your toe. You glare. Someone stands up in front of you and you crane your neck to see. The picture is exciting. It reaches a climax. The heroine is saved. You relax. You are pleased. (4) You are buying a hat at the millinery shop. The hat that pleases you costs too much. You finally buy another. Madame Albertini in her "Handbook of Acting" suggests numerous pantomimes. She has her actors imagining and reacting to the following situations: You hear an explosion near by and then far away: someone screaming in the next room; a favorite tune; a friend's voice. You see a flash of lightning; a rose, a violet, a daisy; a friend; someone you dislike; a child; a horse; a dog; a cat. For an evening's party this would prove capital entertainment.

Other Suggestions for Acting Out

1. *Act out vocations.* Cook, auto salesman, millinery saleslady, lawyer, doctor, dentist, preacher, politician, teacher, barber.

2. *Act out suppressed desires.* Actor, ball player, singer, orator, boxer, football star, jockey, auto racer, swimmer, etc.

3. *Act out proverbs.* Act out as charades such proverbs as "Make hay while the sun shines," "A stitch in time saves nine," etc.

4. *Act out Mother Goose rhymes.* (1) Pantomine the rhyme for the crowd to guess what it is. (2) Repeat the rhyme and then put on a dramatic version of it.

5. *Act out fairy stories.* See the "Fairyland Party." Clever parodies of fairy stories may be created such as "Red Riding Hood Up-to-date," "Sleeping Beauty Modernized." Satires on present-day customs could easily be fitted into these stories.

6. *Act out advertising slogans.* These could be done charade-fashion. "It never rains but it pours." "Ask the man who owns one." "Time to retire." "It floats." "Eventually, why not now?" "They satisfy."

7. *Act out songs.* Folk songs lend themselves to this use. "The Old Woman and the Pedlar," "O Soldier, Soldier," "The Generous Fiddler," "The Peddler" represent a few of the possibilities. See Chapter XII, Fun with Music.

8. *Act out a circus.* Present an impromptu circus. Assign parts —clowns, fat man or lady, tight-rope walker, bareback rider, ring-master, elephants, lions, monkeys, etc. Give the participants about fifteen minutes to improvise costumes (some forethought at this point would make it easier) and work out action. Then, on with the circus!

A List of Acting Out Suggestions

1. You are an auto salesman selling a prospect.
2. A man who does not cuss hitting his finger with a hammer.
3. A girl making up—compact 'n everything.
4. Peter Pan fighting his famous duel with Capt. James Hook.
5. Rip Van Winkle awakening from his twenty year's nap.
6. Little Black Sambo meeting the first tiger that wanted to eat him up.
7. The teacher when Mary brought the lamb to school.
8. A ball player striking out with the bases full.
9. A ball player hitting a home run over the fence.
10. A catcher catching a high foul.
11. A beggar panhandling.
12. A burglar trying to escape detection.
13. A man with a heavy burden on his back.
14. A mechanical doll walking.
15. A not-so-good golf player teeing off and then putting.
16. A girl receiving a box of candy from someone she likes.
17. A man reading a magazine and finding something funny.
18. A drum major strutting his stuff at the football game.
19. A rooter at a football game when a halfback on his favorite team tosses a forward pass which is caught by an end, who runs for a touchdown to win the game.
20. A concert pianist playing a grand finale.

Grecian statue.—One person, appointed or chosen by lot or as the result of a forfeit, stands on a chair, while any of the company may pose him. After three to five poses the model has the right to choose someone to take his place.

Stunts.—Dramatic stunts have lost much of their former popularity for three good reasons: (1) They have so often been pointlessly silly. *Good* burlesque is always clever. (2) The second reason for waning interest in stunts was the fact that players had the idea that stunts need not be given polished performance. Therefore, more often than not they proved shabby exhibitions with a minimum of entertainment value. It is true, of course, that stunts are better for having the element of spontaneity. A happy balance between spontaneity and polish makes the perfect stunt presentation. (3) A third reason for this waning interest was the fact that there was so much repetition of threadbare stunts. New ideas seemed scarce or nonexistent. When one appeared it was pounced on and worn to a frazzle in a season. The best stunts are original ones built around clever ideas.

Good stunts, well performed, can be lots of fun for both the participants and the audience.

One college group built a stunt night around the idea of the history of the drama. The possibilities here are immediately apparent. Greek drama, Shakespearean drama, melodrama, modern drama, drama a la Eugene O'Neil (with the characters saying what they think and then saying what they say). Perhaps Oriental drama could be done Cantonese—with one individual called "The Chorus" on the stage throughout explaining at the beginning of each scene what the action is to be and what the setting is, since the plays are done without scenery; and with the property man on the stage-left ready to provide whatever properties the performers need.

Other ideas around which stunts might be developed are the following: Scenes at the railroad or bus station; the schoolroom (this one has been overworked); dramatizing poems after the fashion of "Lord Ullen's Daughter"; dramatizing Mother Goose rhymes; dramatizing fairy stories; burlesquing historical incidents and daily happenings; dramatizing songs.

The photographer.—*Scene*—A photographer's studio.

Characters—Photographer, farmer, old maid, flapper, jellybean, newly-weds, take-offs on pastor and other notables.

Properties—A tripod, small box, large black cloth, toy balloon, pin.

Various characters enter, pose for pictures. The last person should represent some prominent member of the group. When the photographer attempts to take this picture there is an explosion, in which the tripod is upset and confusion reigns. The photographer shouts "You've busted my camera!"

Curtain. The explosion may be obtained by the photographer bursting a toy balloon under the cloth covering. Or a paper sack may be bursted off stage.

Bluebeard.—This stunt was originally presented at Randolph-Macon College, Lynchburg, Virginia.

DRAMATIC PERSONNEL

BLUEBEARD—His blue beard can be made of dyed rope or crepe
         paper.
FATIMA
SISTER ANN
SELIM
WIVES

BLUEBEARD: I have come to say,
               I find that I am called away.
               I've so much business to transact
               'Twill be a week before I'm back.

FATIMA: Oh, Bluebeard, dear, how sad you make me.
               Is that the way you would forsake me?
               I don't see why you cannot take me.

BLUEBEARD: Although I think so much of you
               I do not think that it would do,
               I fear that you would get the "Flu,"
               Perhaps you'll want a new hat too.

FATIMA: I declare I won't get the "Flu,"
               In business I'll be aiding you.

BLUEBEARD: Women in business should not roam,
               I say that you must stay at home.

(Enter Sister Ann)

BLUEBEARD: Sister Ann, prevent this strife,
               Come here and reason with my wife.
               If you'll but listen to my commands,
               I'll leave the house in your hands.

ANN: Why, Bluebeard, you're a perfect duck.
        I say, Fatima, we're in luck,
        Think of anything nicer if you can
        Than a whole quiet place without a man.

FATIMA: You wouldn't think so, I'm afraid
        If you were doomed to be an old maid;
        Eligible men are scarce enough,
        So grab 'em early and treat 'em rough.

ANN: Sure, Bluebeard, Kid, we'd love to stay;
        Suppose you slip those keys this way;
        Have you anything else to say?

BLUEBEARD: Yes, that I have—now listen here,
        Perhaps you'll think this slightly queer,
        But one room is forever hid;
        To open it, I you forbid.
        This key I give you, but don't unlock
        Or you will get an awful shock.
        And if you do I'll find out
        And so, my dear, you must mind out.
        Now fare you well—don't weep for me
        And mind you—*don't forget the key.*

        (Exit Bluebeard)

ANN: I'm so excited I could burst;
        What part shall we explore the first.

FATIMA: I don't know—now let me see;
        I can't forget that awful key.
        The thought of that but seems so funny;
        I wonder if it's full of money.

ANN: There's nothing there, men have no sense;
        Just like to keep us in suspense.

FATIMA: I know—I'll think of it no more;
        I wish I knew what's behind that door.

ANN: Oh, lots of junk, perhaps, who knows?
        Probably just his winter clothes;

I know when Papa goes away,
If he has any time to stay,
He locks his clothes with iron clamps,
For fear Ma'll give all to tramps.

FATIMA: But then they ought to be aired you know,
For in old clothes germs do breed so.
If this comes to Nurse ——'s eyes,
I'm sure she'd say to sterilize.
Do you really think Bluebeard would mind?
Ann, you'll do nothing of the kind.
I mean to be an old-fashioned wife
And obey my husband all my life.

ANN: But do you think he would refuse,
When we've got such a good excuse?

FATIMA: Ann, stop teasing. You've simply got to,
You know that Bluebeard said not to.

ANN: I'd rather be single
My whole life through
Than to be bossed around like you.

FATIMA: I hope you will be an old maid
I'll show you that I'm not afraid.
Give me the key and draw up near.
You listen, Ann, let's see what's here.
(Opens door and drops key)
O heavens, horrors, look, oh, dear,
I think that I will die with fear.
Oh, help me now my patron saint!
Ann, lock the door before I faint.

ANN: Oh, Fatima, what do I see—
And, Fatima, where's the key?

FATIMA: Don't speak to me, I think I'll die.
I dropped the key—Ann, oh, my!

ANN: Oh, Fatima, we're lost for good,
For see the key is smeared with blood.

FATIMA: Ann, this is more than I can bear;
He'll hang me up there by the hair
And when I'm withered up and dried
I hope that you'll be satisfied.

ANN: Fatima, be calm, don't take on so,
We'll wash it with Sapolio.

Curtain

Week elapses

ACT 2

(Enter Fatima and Ann)

FATIMA: Oh, Ann, whatever shall we do?
The blood is here as good as new.
Although we've scrubbed he'll surely see
Just how the blood got on the key.

ANN: Every cleaning thing we've tried it,
We'll simply take the key and hide it.
Make him forget—say how you miss him,
Beguile him with your charms—kiss him.

FATIMA: Oh, if Selim would come before
He gets my head behind the door.

ANN: He got our letter by last night's mail.
He'll come on, surely he'll not fail.
He can save us, he can surely do it,
The thing is, will Bluebeard beat him to it?

FATIMA: Poor little neck you feel so small,
Think of hanging on that wall.

ANN: They look funny hanging so
Like dried onions in a row;
Will it console you when you're dead
To know you'll have the prettiest head?

FATIMA: Oh, Ann, I think I hear his step.

ANN: Rush to him, don't lose your pep.

FATIMA: I didn't think 'twould be so quick,
               Here he comes, oh, I'm just sick.

               (Enter Bluebeard)

BLUEBEARD: Well, well, my dear, I'm back you see,
               And home looks mighty good to me.
               Come here and kiss your loving man;
               My! how I've missed you!   How're you, Ann?

FATIMA: Oh, Bluebeard, oh, dear, I'm so glad!
               The whole long week has been so sad.
               I know you're tired. Oh, what a pity
               Now tell me all about the city.

BLUEBEARD: Well, Bagdad's going pretty slow,
               No place like home after all you know.
               How's everything, been busy bees?
               By the way you haven't lost the keys.

ANN AND
FATIMA: Oh, no.

ANN: Now sit down, Bluebeard, sit down, do.
               Can't I get your pipe for you?

FATIMA: And some nice hot coffee, I'll light the taper
               So you can read the evening paper.

BLUEBEARD: You are most kind, too kind to me
               But first I'd like to have the key.

FATIMA: Why, certainly, I was just asking you,
               Did you see anyone in town we knew?

(to Ann)   I can't stand the strain and worry.
               Phone to Selim, make him hurry.

BLUEBEARD: I'll tell you later if you please
               But first, my dear, I want the keys.

FATIMA: (handing him all but one)
               Yes, here they are, now put them away;
               Let's talk of something else today.

BLUEBEARD:	Now, just a minute, not too fast. Where is the key I gave you last?
ANN:	Speak, Fatima, give him a hug.
FATIMA:	I think I dropped it under the rug.
BLUEBEARD:	Speak, Madam, speak, but don't evade me. I fear that you have disobeyed me. Stop hiding it—oh, yes, I see, Whence came the gore upon the key?
FATIMA:	Oh, Bluebeard, don't; oh, please forgive, I'll be so good, oh, let me live.
BLUEBEARD:	Don't plead with me, it's quite a bore, And useless too, with wives galore. Since you've a fondness for that door You may hang there forever more. My knife needs sharpening, while upstairs, I leave you here to say your prayers.
ANN:	Oh, Fatima, I feel for you, I really, truly, really do. I always stood for a single life; I'm glad I'm not Bluebeard's wife.
FATIMA:	Let this be a lesson to you, Ann, Never trust a man. If ever you approach the altar Think of my sad fate and falter.
ANN:	Oh, if Selim would only come And kill your Bluebeard, the old bum.
FATIMA:	Ann, look, I'm too scared to pray; Do you see anything coming this way? (Climbs on a chair and peers into the distance)
ANN:	I think I do; oh, me; oh, my. Oh, its just the milkman going by.
FATIMA:	Oh, look again, I think I'll die; Do you see nothing riding by?

ANN: Oh, yes, I see something, but, oh, the dickens
            I believe its just a flock of chickens.

FATIMA: Ann, Ann, my time draws near,
            Why isn't Selim hastening here?
            Don't you see someone? Ann, you must.

ANN: I see a little cloud of dust

            (Enter Bluebeard)

BLUEBEARD: Well, madam, I hope you are prepared;
            I'm sorry you could not be spared.
            But I feel after deep reflection
            I need a new head in my collection.
            It's my law you know and there's no repealing,
            But I hope you'll bear me no hard feeling.

FATIMA: Mercy, Bluebeard, mercy, pray!

BLUEBEARD: No, madam, no, just step this way.
            You must be punished, faithless wife,
            And feel the edge of this little knife.

            (Starts to kill her)

            (Selim enters)

SELIM: Down villain down and bite the dust
            My dagger in thy heart I thrust.

            (Kills him)

FATIMA: Oh, Selim, Selim, my noble lad,
            You've spared the only life I had.

ANN: Oh, Selim, Selim, you're simply great,
            Let's go somewhere to celebrate.

SELIM: Quite right. Put on your hat and coat,
            And we'll go get a chocolate float.

            (Curtain.)

What Fatima saw—Opens door or draws aside curtain, disclosing
gruesome sight of heads of two or three of Bluebeard's former wives,

seemingly detached from the body, and hanging suspended by the hair. Thus:

The heads are put through holes or slits in the sheets. Red ink blots appear below the neck. The faces are whitened to give them ghastly appearance. Eyes closed. The hair is tied to sheet, so as to make it appear that the head is hanging.

The use of this device will add to the effectiveness of the stunt.

The peanut stunt.—*Tune:* "We Won't Go Home until Morning" or "Farmer's in the Dell."

1. (Name of one of singers) has some peanuts,
   —————————————— has some peanuts,
   —————————————— has some peanuts,
   And he's going to give them to you.

2. —————————————— has some candy, (3 **times**)
   And he's going to give it to you.

3. —————————————— has confetti, (3 **times**)
   And he's going to give it to you.

4. —————————————— has some flowers, (3 **times**)
   And he's going to give them to you.

5. —————————————— has chewing gum, (3 **times**)
   And he's going to give it to you.

6. —————————————— has rotten eggs, (3 **times**)
   And he's going to give them to you.

Singers line up on platform and sing the song indicated with great eclat, whatever that is. As they come to the line, "And he's going to give them to you," the singer whose name has been mentioned tosses what he has to the crowd. The eggs are saved to the last. Sometime just before his turn this singer should drop one of the eggs "accidentally." It falls to the floor (on space covered with paper) and great is the fall thereof, for "all the King's horses, and all the King's men" can't put it together again. This egg is a real egg. The others are eggshells, the contents having been blown out. If desired they may contain a little water or better, confetti. There is some grunting, screaming, and ducking as the singer lets fly his handful of eggs in the crowd—one at a time in rapid succession. Or he may distribute to the other singers and they all throw at once.

The "ah" stunt.—*Characters*—hero, heroine, thief, cop, maid, father, mother.

Prologue—The heroine has been presented with a beautiful and costly jewel by her fiance. The jewel is symbolic of an editorial idea. (The stunt was worked out for use in an editorial group. It can easily be adapted to suit other occasions). The heroine shows the jewel to her parents. Her father doesn't seem to think much of it, but mother seems pleased. It is time for retiring and the heroine carefully puts the jewel away. A thief appears on the scene after all have gone to bed. He is about to appropriate the jewel when the maid appears on the scene and gives the alarm with an unearthly scream. The cop takes the thief in charge.

The only word spoken in the play is the word, "Ah." We trust you will enjoy this presentation and profit by the moral of the play. Don't steal another's idea, especially if it be an editorial idea, for they are few and precious.

Note: This stunt must be well done to be effective. Everything depends on the dramatic action and voice inflection. For the actors to walk about declaiming aimless and monotonous "Ah's" would be deadly.

Enter maid singing "Ah-ah-ah-ah-ah-ah-ah-ah-ah-ah-ah-ah-ah-ah" (to tune of "Auld Lang Syne"). As she dusts she hears the approach of the heroine and her lover and gives a disgusted "Ah." Exit.

Enter hero and heroine. Seat selves on divan, sighing "Ah!" Look in each other's eyes and both give romantic "Ah's." The hero draws a jewel case from his pocket, opens it, and offers it to heroine. She gives a delighted "Ah!" He arises to leave. Both express disappointment that the time has come to leave by their "Ah's." He leaves followed by a sighing "Ah" from the heroine.

Enter mother and father and heroine excitedly shows the jewel to them. Mother gives a pleased "Ah" of admiration. Father grunts a disinterested "Ah." Parents exit and girl stands admiring jewel. Decides to put it away for the night. Places it in a jewel box. Exit. Lights low.

Thief sneaks in. Discovers jewel. Gives satisfied "Ah." Hears approach of someone. Gives stealthy and frightened "Ah" as he attempts to hide behind a screen.

Maid enters. Sees thief. Screams "Ah!" Family rushes in. Variety of "Ah's." The thief tries to escape, but finds all exits blocked. Gasps frightened "Ah's." Enter cop. Sees thief and emits a knowing "Ah!" Thief gives a despairing "Ah!" Policeman nabs him with a satisfied "Ah." The thief leaves with the cop, exclaiming a disgusted "Ah." The family sigh together "Ah" of relief.

CURTAIN

A Russian drama.—The announcer makes an elaborate introduction, expounding the merits of Russian drama, mentioning names of Russian writers like Tchekohv, Dostoiviesky, and Tolstoy.

Characters—The hero—I. Strutsky.
The heroine—Ima Bugsky.

Act I

Scene—Chair, table. Strutsky sitting on stage with feet in pan of water. Wears bathrobe and has bandage about head. Face whitened. Evidently he does not feel well. He groans as if in misery.

The heroine stands in the foreground and announces solemnly between licks on a lollipop:

"The hero is sick."

The heroine is dressed and made to look ridiculous as possible. Perhaps her hair is brushed straight up and held in place by a huge ribbon. She looks awfully dumb, never changing the expression on her face as she says her lines. Curtain.

Act II

Same scene. Heroine solemnly announces, "The hero is very, very sick." Curtain.

Act III

Same scene. The heroine announces, "The hero is so sick we cannot give the show." Curtain.

An announcer should call out the various acts as the curtain is drawn.

The poor little match girl (a la Ruth Draper or Cornelia Otis Skinner) .—*Properties needed*—small table, a pillow, a man's cap, a man's hat, and scarf.

Characters—The little match girl, the hero, the villain. These parts are to be taken by one person, who indicates a change in character by changing headgear.

Action—The player places the pillow on the table kneels on it and then introduces the various characters as follows:

"The Little Match Girl." Player puts scarf on head.

"The Villain." The player pulls cap down over eyes and looks tough.

"The Hero." The player puts on man's hat and smiles and bows.

Scene opens with Match Girl shivering in the cold. She has a hand full of torn paper and tosses it up in the air to let the audience know it is snowing.

Girl: Oh, who will help me! Who will help me! I am so cold (Br-r-r-r) and I am starving. Who will help me!

Villain: "I'll help you, kid.

Girl: Oh, you will help me?

Villain: Yeh, I'll help you.

Girl: How will you help me?

Villain: I will marry you. That's how I will help you.

Girl (frightened) : Oh, you will marry me?

Villain: Yeh, I'll marry you.

Girl: But, I don't want to marry you. Oh, who will help me! Who will help me! I'm so cold (Br-r-r-r) .

Hero: I will help you, madam.

Girl (pleased) : Oh, you will help me? How will you help me?

Hero: I will marry you.

Girl (evidently delighted) : Oh, you will marry me?

Hero: Yes, I will marry you.

Villain: You will not marry her.

Hero: I will marry her.

Villain: I say you will not marry her.

Hero: And why will I not marry her?

Girl: Yes, why won't he marry me?

Villain: Because her father is a spy in the mint.

Hero: What, her father "a spy in the mint"? (looks dejected.)

Girl: Oh! Oh! Oh! Woe is me! Woe is me! My father is a mint spy (mince pie).

CURTAIN

The crooked mouth family.—*Scene*—A small town store.

Characters—Ma, Pa, Sue, Zeke, the customer.

When the play begins Pa and Ma are puttering around in the store. Finally Pa snaps his finger, and Ma looks his way inquiringly.

Ma (speaks with upper lip extended over lower lip throughout): "Whats the matter, Pa? Forgit something?"

Pa (speaks with lower lip extended over upper lip throughout): "I sure did. Fergot to stop by Lem Jones's house to get that five dozen eggs he has for me. Guess I'll have to go." Gets his coat and hat and leaves.

Ma (calls after him): "Don't get any more of that rancid butter from him."

Sue (enters lanquidly, nibbling on a cracker): "Hullo, Ma, Where's Pa?" She talks out of the left side of her mouth throughout.

Ma: "He's gone down to Lem Jones's to get them eggs. Now that you're here, I think I'll go on back to the house to get together my washing. You take care of the store."

Sue: "Aw, Ma." Ma leaves.

Customer enters.

Sue (perking up): "Anything I can do for you?"

Customer (speaking out of the right side of his mouth, which he does throughout the performance): "Yes. I want a box of matches."

Sue (indignant): "You quit making fun of me."

Customer (surprised): "I'm not making fun of you."

Sue (begins to cry): "Ma! There's a man out here making fun of me."

Ma (steps in and glares at the man): "What do you mean, making fun of my daughter?"

Customer: "I'm not making fun of her. I talk this way all the time."

Ma: "That's all right, then. Susie, get the man what he wants."

Sue waits on the customer. He holds her hand as she hands him the matches.

Customer: "Say, I like you! Why can't we get married?"

Sue. (excitedly): "Ma! This man wants to marry me!"

Ma (indifferently): "Wal, why not?"

Sue (turning to customer): "All right, mister. I'll marry you—

what's your name? Let's go get married now." They leave arm in arm.

Pa returns. Takes off coat and hat and hangs them up.

Ma (greets him) : "Sue's gittin' married."

Pa (shows little interest) : "Sure enough? Whut wuz the matter with the feller?"

Ma: "Nuthin', I reckon. He looked like he had good sense."

Pa goes over and lights candle in holder. Ma yells at him: "Blow that candle out. Wanta set this place afire?"

Pa blows, but with lower lip extended over the upper lip he is unsuccessful.

Pa: "I can't blow it out. You try it."

Ma tries, but since her upper lip extends over the lower lip she, too, is unsuccessful.

Ma: "I can't do it, pa."

Sue and her man return.

Ma: "Come here, Sue, and blow out this candle."

Sue tries, blowing out of the left side of her mouth. She fails.

Sue (to her new husband) : "Zeke, blow out this candle."

Zeke blows out of right side of his mouth. The candle still burns.

Zeke: "Shucks! missed it! I got an idee! Let's all blow together."

The entire family gathers round and blows and the candle is extinguished.

CURTAIN

Paying the rent.—This is a good stunt for the banquet. The leader or a small group could present it first. Then have everyone do it in unison. The players arrange the napkins to look like hair-ribbon bows. The lines are repeated in rhythm. All right, everybody! Let's go!

Landlord (deep, growling voice. Hold napkin to upper lip for mustache) : "I've come for the rent! I've come for the rent!"

Heroine (falsetto voice in distress. Hold napkin to side of head like a hair bow) : "But I can't pay the rent! I can't pay the rent!"

Landlord: "You must pay the rent! You must pay the rent!"

Heroine: "Oh, who will pay the rent? Oh, who will pay the rent?"

Hero (manly voice. Hold napkin to neck like bow necktie) : "I'll pay the rent! I'll pay the rent!"

Heroine: "My hero! My hero! My hero!"

Landlord: "Curses! Curses! Curses!"

The burial of Old Man Kant.—Someone steps to the piano and begins playing a funeral dirge. Enter five boys, one leading the way, the other four carrying a tiny coffin about two feet long. This coffin is made out of black cardboard and on it is written in big white letters, OLD MAN KANT. This is carried to the platform and the coffin is placed on the floor. The boy who led the way then proceeds to perform the burial ceremony. "I come not to praise Old Man Kant, but to bury him. He is an old and onery member of this group. He has made himself felt in our midst and in all of our activities through these many years. In consigning his body to the grave we do it with the hope that he shall never be resurrected. Dust to dust and ashes to ashes! May he never suffer from the cold where he is going."

The pallbearers weep bitter tears, wringing the water out of wet sponges which they have inside of their handkerchiefs.

Immediately following this ceremony a young man arises at one of the tables and calls, "Mister Toastmaster!" When the toastmaster recognizes him he says: "We have just buried Old Man Kant, we hope never again to be resurrected. We now wish to present our new emblem and motto." With these words he reaches under the table and draws forth a new tin can with large letters "WE" as he shouts "WE CAN."

This stunt was used successfully as a climax point of a banquet.

Suppressed desires.—A faculty group at a conference presented this clever stunt. One player claims to have power to help people realize their suppressed desires. Various people present themselves. One person has always wanted to be an opera singer. The magician makes a few passes over him and murmurs, "Abba ka dabba." The opera singer immediately swings into action with "La Donna e Mobile," singing:

> "Ho hum, Sapolio, high low fruit jello,
> Caviar, sarsaparilla, chocolate, vanilla,
> Hi ho, rutabagio, souffle potatio,
> Macaroni, spaghetti, ripe tomatio."

If the opera singer has a good voice so much the better.

Another has a suppressed desire to be a poet, another to be an orator, another to be an adagio dancer, another to be a great tennis player, another to be a magician. This latter person brings the stunt to its climax with a performance of magic which culminates in the tie feat. He explains that there has always been one trick he has seen that he has wanted to try more than any other. It is that of cutting a man's tie and then bringing it back whole. He calls for volunteers and a confederate comes forward. He takes hold of his tie and cuts it in two with a big pair of shears. He then proceeds to bring it back whole. This is done by his friend secretly having another tie the exact duplicate of the one cut. Usually ten-cent ties serve the purpose. After his success with the feat he invites someone else to come forward. A volunteer comes out of the audience. The tie is sliced so that just an inch or two is left below the knot. The "magician" makes his passes over it but to no avail. He finally looks distressed and then announces, "I'm sorry, but the power has left me. I cannot do it again." "What about my tie?" angrily demands the victim. "I'm sorry as I can be, but I tell you the power is gone." Curtain. (The victim is in on the hoax, of course.)

Mind reader.— (1) *Hindu mind reader*—Ushers go through the audience to collect questions people write on slips of paper. Each person must sign his name to his question. The ushers, unnoticed, pass the slips, or some of them to a confederate at the rear of the auditorium, and then come back to the front pulling the slips (fake ones) out of their pockets and putting them on a large pan. A match is struck and the slips are burned. The mind reader looks on but he never gets nearer than ten feet to them. To everyone's amazement the mind reader begins to call questions and names of people who have written them. He answers each question in some manner. The important thing, however, is that he reads the questions without any possibility of having seen them. The secret is this—the mind reader wears a turban and robe. Under the turban he has earphones connected up with wires which are plated on the soles of his shoes. Two small plates on the floor just beyond a rug are connected by wires with a phone connection in some room back of the platform. This is connected up with dry cell batteries. A confederate has received some or all of the slips from the ushers, unnoticed by the crowd. Those burned were phonies. The confederate picks out a few of them and phones them to the mind reader, who contacts the floor plates and listens, pretending to be in deep thought. The mind reader may stand or sit to get his message. This stunt should be tried out to make sure that everything is working perfectly.

(2) *The blindfolded mind reader*—One player is blindfolded and sits on the platform. His confederate goes through the audience, taking things from various people. The mind reader tells him what the articles are. All of the "tip-offs" are perfectly obvious. "Don't get stuck on this one. What is it?" "It's a pin," shouts the mind reader. "Watch your step this time." "It's a watch." "Right. Sign

on the dotted line with this one." "It's a fountain pen." "Right. Don't be *led* astray by this one." "It's a pencil." "Right."

Pulling off something.—"Everyone else is taking part in this show so we've decided to pull off something too." Whereupon they pull off their coats or ties.

The shirt stunt.—This is a favorite stunt to introduce fun in a magician's performance. He asserts that he can take off a man's shirt without taking off his coat and vest. He unbuttons the shirt at the neck and the sleeves and then catching it firmly by the collar jerks it off. The secret is that the shirt is not really on the confederate. It is only halfway on. The arms are not in the sleeves, just the cuffs being buttoned around the wrists. When these are unbuttoned it is a simple matter to pull the shirt off.

Pulling off the tie.—The performer catches hold of the tie and jerks it off without untying it. Here, again, the tie is only halfway on, a slender thread holding it around the confederate's neck.

The Saga of Little Nell.—A take-off on ye ole fashioned mountain tragedy.

CHARACTERS

Mammy—Costume—old-fashioned cotton dress, sunbonnet, and apron.

Pappy—Costume—overalls, ragged looking.

Little Nell, eldest daughter—Costume—ragged cotton dress, wig of long yellow curls.

Handlebar Hank—Villian, the bigger, the better. Costume—black coat and hat, high boots, black mustache.

Jack Dashaway—Hero, small. Talks in a high voice. Costume—Sissy outfit, small hat, riding pants, tight jacket.

Children—Use about six in addition to Nell. Ordinary clothes, very plain.

Properties—Table, loaf of bread, seven glasses of water, broken-down chairs, boxes, buckets turned over, etc., for family to sit upon.

SCENE I

Povery-stricken hut. It was Christmas Eve and bitter cold and snow was on the ground. Family is seated in room.

Mammy: "Well, Pappy, here it is Christmas Eve and this is our last bit o' vittles. If only our house was free of mortgage."

Pappy: "Yes, Mammy."   (Goes to door and peers out with hand over eyes.)   "'Taint a fit nite out for man nor beast, but Handlebar Hank will be here shore to collect that note."   (Paper snow is thrown in face from outside of doorway. Sits down beside Mammy.)

Mammy (desolately) : "Yes, and we have not a cent fer to pay with."   (Knock on door from off side.)

Second child: "Hark! I thought I heard a rapping at the door." (Goes to door.)

Enter the villain.

Handlebar Hank: "I have come for my money or little Nell." (Swaggers about stage.)

Little Nell: "O-O-O—"   (Waves arms, wrings hands—heavy acting —ends up on Pappy's shoulder.)

Third child: "'T's only a beast who would suggest such a plan."

Nell: "Do not fear little ones, Jack Dashaway will save us all."

Hank: "Ahar! Me proud beauty, I have ye in my power at last." (Sneering dirty laugh, flaunting note at Nell.)

Enter the hero.

Jack Dashaway: "I have heard all. Little Nell shall never become your wife. I will have the money here by midnite."   (Goes to door, peers out, snow is thrown in face.) " 'Taint a fit nite out for man nor beast."   (Plunges into the storm.)

Hank (Surveys all sneeringly) : "I'll return at midnite. 'Taint a fit night out fer man nor beast."   (Paper snow thrown in face.)

SCENE II (Same as Scene I)

Family shifts position to denote lapse of time.

Enter Hank.

Hank: "I've come for ye me proud beauty."   (Grasps Nell's arm roughly. Everyone wails—Nell demonstrates extreme agony.)

Child (In monotonous voice) : "Her bosom heaved."

Enter the hero.

Jack: "For shame. Release her instantly."   (Release.)   "Here's your money. Give me that mortgage."   (Gets paper. Family shows elation.)

Hank: "Curses; foiled again."

Jack: "Scram, you pop-eyed pole kitty."   (Climbs up on box and socks villain. Hank is sitting on floor in groggy condition.)

Pappy: "You've certainly done right by our little Nell."

Jack: "Come, Nell, let's away on our wedding trip."   (Nell registers joy, takes Jack's arm.)

Child: "She drew herself up to her full height."

Nell (Walks across stage with Jack and flaunts note under Hank's nose) : "We've got a deep lake on our farm. Drop in sometime."

Running time, 10 minutes. Slow motion for best melodramatic effect. May be given with one practice if characters are given copies previously in order to learn lines.

—HAROLD DOBBS and CATHERINE HOPKINS

Pearly Gates.—*Characters*—St. Peter, Satan, Angels, character who came up to the pearly gates.

Setting—The gates, in front of which sits St. Peter by a table. On the table is a pile of Victrola records. Back of the gates stand the angels (white sheets may serve as wings). To one side of stage stands Satan. In case a costume is not available, it can be improvised. A red bathing cap with imitation horns made of red paper. A red cap made of crepe paper. From the wings comes a red glow, and it is easy to imagine that this represents the fires of Hades.

Action—Various people appear at the pearly gates seeking entrance. The more prominent the people in the group the better. First comes a boy and girl. They explain to St. Peter that they desire to be married by some member of the faculty before entering. St. Peter asks them to sit down and wait. Others appear, and in between each entrance the couple gets up and reminds St. Peter that they are waiting to be married. He asks them each time to wait awhile longer. As the people come St. Peter says, "Let's see what your record is." Whereupon he selects one of the Victrola records and pretends to read from it. In one case he announces: "Oh, I see you're the one who gave fifteen cents to charity in 1930." That seems to end the record. Then he turns to the angels and says, "Angels, what shall we do with him?" The angels shout in unison, "Give him fifteen cents and let him go to the devil." Whereupon Satan, who has been showing keen interest in the examination and who may even have indicated in pantomime to the audience that he expects to get this one, prods the victim with his fork, and drives him over to his fire where he disappears with a yell. A dean, teacher, or preacher may be permitted to enter through the pearly gates because he has had enough hell on earth. Finally, the couple asks St. Peter when they can be married by a member of the ——— faculty. St. Peter appears confused, and then says, "I had hoped one of them might get up here, but it now looks as if they are all going in the other direction."

A historical stunt nite. — How about a "Historic Stunt Nite"? It will be such history as you have never seen or heard before, but history, nevertheless—that is, history plus imagination. What an opportunity for an ingenious group. Think of the dramatic possibilities in a burlesque of "Paul Revere's Ride," or of "Columbus Discovering America," or of "Washington Crossing the Delaware," or of "Pioneer Days!" or some group might like to present "The Landing of the Pilgrims" or "The First Thanksgiving." Such a program could be given in connection with the presentation of "The Courtship of Miles Standish," dramatized by Eugene Prebbrey. This play takes four characters and requires forty minutes for presentation. It can be obtained from Samuel French, 25 West 45th Street, New York. Make various groups responsible for the various stunts. The young people might even invite the adults to prepare one stunt. Imagine what an adult group that is alive could do with "Pioneer Days." The covered wagon (well, not such a big one), locating the camp site, the attack by the Indians, the battle (cap pistols and everything), victory, and the celebration with its songs and cheers. That's enough to give you an idea of what can be done.

A drama party.—A drama party could be sponsored by the Dramatics Club. Guests should come dressed to represent stage and screen stars or famous dramatic characters, such as "Cyrano de Bergerac." Play charades, dumb crambo, gestures, act out stunts, nursery rhymes, or fairly tales, and put on a reading rehearsal of a portion of some good play.

DRAMATICS FOR FUN

Acting Charades, Walter H. Baker, Boston.
Easy Blackouts, Fitzgerald Publishing Company, New York.
Diminutive Comedies, Theodore Johnson, Baker.
Let's Play Charades, Roger Wheeler, Fitzgerald.
Shadow Pictures, Sarah L. Stocking. T. S. Denison Company, Chicago.
Six Rehearseless Entertainments, Baker.
Stunt Plays, Owen Kelley. Old Town Publishers, New York.

CHAPTER XV
FUN WITH PUPPETS

FUN WITH PUPPETS

> "For in and out,
> Around, about, below,
> Life's nothing but
> A magic shadow show
> Played in a box,
> Whose candle is the sun,
> Round which we phantom
> Figures come and go."
> —OMAR KHAYYAM

Possibilities in puppets.—Puppetry is increasing in popularity as a recreation activity because of the many skills cultivated in working out any sort of puppetry project and because of the endless possibilities of developing originality and leading young people toward a creative attitude of mind.

Taught in connection with literature and drama in high schools, and quite inevitably bringing drama with it to the less formal entertainment and recreation projects in rural and city grade schools, more and more school instructors are turning to its use.

For summer playgrounds and for community theatre, P.-T. A., and club activities, the animated dolls capture everyone's fancy.

From experience in working with children of all ages it appears that there are three types of puppets that lend themselves most easily to amateur workers—the fist puppets of the old Punch and Judy kind, the clothespin puppets, and the stringed puppets, or marionettes. These last may be the rag doll kind made of cloth or the professional type constructed of wood and wire.

Marionettes, which are operated by strings attached to control sticks held in the operator's hands, are capable of uncannily intricate movements and can perform almost any kind of action, including many things that no other type of puppet can do. However, they require much more care and skill in their operation, and are so quickly made uninteresting by lack of proper manipulation, added to which their strings are so easily tangled by clumsiness, that only older children and young people should be encouraged to attempt their use.

Clothespin puppets, which are, as their name implies, ordinary clothespins dressed to suit the fancy of their creators, are manipulated from above by a single 16-inch (more or less) wire, one end of which is sewed firmly to the back of the doll's neck and the other end attached to a spool or small bit of wood to be held in the hand. Even preschool children can operate these on a stage made of a large cardboard box.

Hand or fist puppets are adored by smaller children, and, while the children cannot usually do all the work of constructing them, they are capable of manipulating this type of puppet with all the skill and dramatic fervor that could be desired.

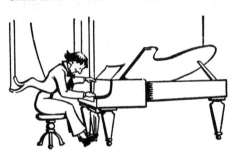

A Novelty Marionette

Plays, dialogs, and skits to be presented should be worked out by the puppeteers themselves. It is very nearly impossible to take a play of any kind, even one written for puppets, and present it without local modifications. A well-known fairy tale or story is the best foundation for first attempts at plays, and after several of these have been done the puppeteers may try out almost anything.

Several good rules for amateurs in planning their first puppet plays include the using of as few characters as possible, with no more than three on the stage at once except for a very short time, the use of plenty of entrances and exits of the characters, and the making of all dialog short and to the point, avoiding long speeches.

—JANE KEEN, Henry, South Dakota

Directions for making hand or fist puppets.—The following directions are for making cloth puppets: (1) Cut the head pattern out of cardboard. (2) Lay the pattern on peach colored broadcloth (for man, woman, or child), and mark around it. Cut the cloth, two thicknesses, about a quarter of an inch from the mark all the way around. (3) Backstitch or stitch exactly on the line leaving the neck open and an opening of about three-quarters of an inch on top of the head. (4) Turn material right side out and insert a tube two inches long and of size to get the finger into the neck. Gather and sew tightly, being sure that only about three-eighths of an inch of the tube is left outside the neck. Tubes may be obtained from the Meader Puppet Sales Company, 748 Goodrich Avenue, St. Paul, Minnesota. Or home-made tubes could be made

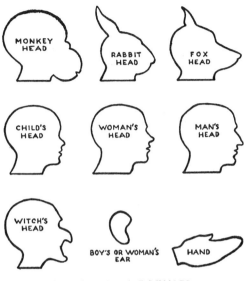

using cardboard and tape. (5) Stuff the head compactly with kapok or cotton from the top. Use an orange stick or pencil to push the ma-

Hand Puppet setting for "The Red Shoes," showing grandmother, Karen, and shoemaker.
—From photo by Minnesota WPA

terial tightly into the nose and chin. Fill the head until it is tight and hard. Then sew the top together. (6) Cut and sew two bags five inches long and two and one-half inches wide, leaving one end open. Stuff lightly with kapok and sew together. (7) Sew these bags to front and rear of the head. They give body to the puppet and give something for the unused fingers of the puppeteer's hand to grasp. (8) Use pattern for the hands and cut two pairs from peach colored broadcloth. Stitch around leaving the wrist open. Turn right side out and stuff lightly with kapok. Then stitch in fingers. (9) Cut two buckram cuffs. Fold cuffs to fit finger and thumb and sew to wrist of puppet hand. (10) Draw facial characteristics of puppet on the head with pencil. (11) Dampen face with clear water and blend in color for cheeks. Use a light purple or dark blue above the eyes for eye shadow. When the face is dry, outline features with black. (12) When the back is dry, color eyes, lips, nostrils, as desired. Show-card paints may be used.

Paper or pulp heads may be made. Ordinary toilet paper torn in bits, soaked in water, and then mixed with wallpaper paste makes a good pulp material. These must be allowed to dry thoroughly before attempting to paint features on them. Bake in an oven for several hours a day.

Dressing and operating hand puppets.— (a) Make loose gown-like garments that will drop down over the arm as the puppet is operated. Sew buckram cuffs and the hands into the sleeves so that the thumbs stand away from the body when the palm is out.

(b) Make a slit in the back of the puppet and place hand through that slit. In this kind of hand puppet the puppet may be given legs and shoes. It is harder, however, to hide the arm from the audience when operating it.

(c) Place the hand inside the thumb in one buckram cuff, and the small finger in the other. The forefinger goes up into the neck. The other two fingers drop down and take hold of the front sack. Some people prefer to use the second finger instead of the little finger. Follow the system that works best for you.

(d) Puppets who are talking should have their heads moving. A walking motion is achieved by turning the puppet slightly from side to side.

(e) Back drops with scenery painted with water colors or drawn in with colored crayons are quite helpful in creating the right atmosphere for the play. Tiny bits of furniture (one side) can be fitted to the puppet stage.

Theater.—A theater may be built as follows: three-ply wood may be used; also frame work covered with canvas. Use a manufactured building board four feet wide and six feet in length for the front, in which is an opening thirty-six inches wide and eighteen inches high; the bottom of which is fifty-two inches from the floor and use the same material for two wings, six feet high.

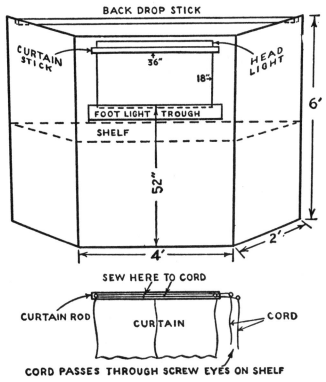

Strips—Fasten flush with all edges of the front and wings, strips of wood one inch by two inches. Also fix a strip entirely across the front between the border strips at the upper edge of the stage opening. Also strips flush with the other three edges of the stage opening. Nail, or better use screws, through the manufactured board into the wood. All strips are to be clear white pine.

Wings—Are hinged to either side of the front, enabling the whole to stand firmly on the floor. The hinges should be toward the inside edges of the strips on the front to reduce the crack between wings and front. The wings are spread to a convenient angle. They are held in position by a wood strip, extending between the top strips of the two wings, placed left to the rear of the front and provided at each end with an angle iron hook flatly over the upper edge of each wing. This strip serves also to support the back drops, being provided with six small right-angle hooks, placed eight inches apart, on its rear edge. The back drops are of cambric or similar semi-transparent fabric on which the scenes are painted but through which the puppeteer may see the puppets on his hands, directly in front of his face.

A shelf fourteen inches wide, angled at the ends to the spread of the wings, rests on horizontal strips across both wings, thirty-six inches above the floor. The shelf is notched at the corners to fit closely against the front. Holes to fit over upright round-headed screws in the strip supports hold the shelf in place and the wings firmly. It is for puppets, etc., not in use, and for the manuscript of the play.

Stage and footlight trough—The stage is a clear white pine board, one inch thick, four and one-half inches wide and thirty-eight inches long notched at the forward corners so as to easily go through the thirty-six-inch stage opening as far as the opening's front edge. This front edge of the stage is hinged to a trough thirty-eight inches long to contain footlights of any desirable dimensions, according to the electric lamps to be used, say three-inches to four-inches wide and of similar depth. By lifting one end of the stage and trough, they may be removed from the stage opening and the stage, if properly hinged, will then form a lid for the trough.

Headlights—May be supported by strip which supports the curtain rod. The electric lamps may be finger-shaped as show-case lights, ordinary bulbs, or Christmas tree lights adapted to the new use.

Property slot—Along the rear edge of the stage, place a strip of oak one-fourth inch by one inch, and thirty-eight inches long. This is attached at each end by a round-headed screw into the edge of the stage board but through a one-fourth-inch wood washer, forming a one-fourth-inch slot along the length of the stage, into which extensions of the various properties used in a scene may be slipped and firmly held in position. The tensions of the strip may be controlled by a second screw at each end, two and one-half inches from the other screws but omitting the washers.

Curtain—A metal curtain rod, extending from wing to wing, is held in position one and one-half inches to the rear of the long strip at the top of the stage opening and one-half inch above the opening by supports placed forty-two inches apart. These supports may be large screw-eyes, curtain hooks bent over the rod, or by other supports. On this rod ten curtain rings support each curtain, which is weighted by five lead weights along their lower edge. The curtains in length nearly touch the stage floor.

Curtain cord—For operating the curtains, place a screw-eye beyond the left support of the curtain rod at the level of the curtain top edge. Place two screw-eyes at the same level beyond the right support of the curtain rod. Place two two-inch round hooks, bent to almost form a screw-eye, upright in the right horizontal strip supporting the shelf —one extending up through a notch at the middle of the shelf's end and the second ten inches further towards the rear. Thread the five with a firm curtain cord that will not stretch, make it taut, and tie ends together. Sew the last ring towards the stage center of one curtain to one cord and that of the other curtain to the other cord— pulling downward on one cord, vertical at the right, will open the curtains and pulling downward on the other will close them.

The last rings at the opposite ends of the curtains tie to the rod supports—small pullies may be used instead of screw-eyes.

The theater built in this way may be foldable by removing drop-stick, shelf, stage and footlight trough, folding the wings on the front for storage.

Marionettes.—Marionettes are string puppets. The best size for average amateur operator is between fourteen and eighteen inches tall with a head about three inches in diameter.

Heads may be modeled from any plastic material, the best kind being unbreakable and light in weight. Bodies, legs, upper arms, and feet are sawed from three-quarter-inch soft wood boards. Forearm and hand are made from a piece of Number 19 iron wire (stove-pipe wire) bent to shape, padded, and wound with flesh-pink crepe paper. Neck, shoulder, and elbow joints are made with screw-eyes and hip and knee joints are formed by links of the wire. This is one of the simpler types of wood-bodied marionettes and is designed so that it may be constructed by children from twelve years of age up. After skill is gained in making these the more difficult kinds are carved, and shaped legs and bodies, also heads, modeled of papier-mache (not paper pulp), may be attempted.

The foundation for paper pulp or sawdust heads is a cooked flour and water paste. A cup of flour is enough for from three to five heads. Mix the flour with cold or warm water to a smooth paste, add hot water and cook until thick. It must be thoroughly cooked and quite thick. It may be used while warm or allowed to cool; stir into it enough sawdust or finely-torn-up newspaper or paper toweling to make a smooth, clay-like material. Paper, if used, should be torn into pieces no larger than one-fourth inch. Experience has shown that very fine sawdust is much the best and it is easier to use than to prepare torn paper.

Model the head on the end of a three-fourths-inch stick about a foot long. If the stick can be clamped in a vise both hands may be

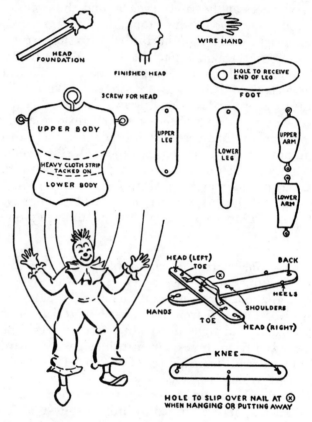

used. First, with a piece of the wire tie firmly on the end of the stick a ball of crumpled paper about the size of an egg. Drive a nail or staple over the wire and through the paper into the stick, so it cannot possibly slip off. Then plaster the modeling material onto this foundation, pressing it together as firmly as possible, until the head is the desired size and shape. Eyes are merely shallow hollows, and it is not necessary to try to model lips—they may be put on when the head is painted.

After the modeling is done a smooth surface may be achieved by rubbing with a paste-smeared finger, and the heads should be dried for a day or two in slow heat; if cracks appear they should be filled in smoothly with the modeling material. When thoroughly dry paint with tempera (show-card colors) or any water-color paint. Oil paint or enamel may be used on negro heads to obtain a gloss.

Saw the body and leg pieces out, and put together as indicated. The extra length of stick is sawed off the head, leaving a short neck; a screw-eye in this attaches it to the body. Screw-eyes for the neck and shoulder joints are spread open with pliers so they can be linked together, then closed again. Place screw-eyes for the control strings in the lower ends of the upper leg pieces, in the back of the shoulders, in the sides of the head just at the top of the ears, and, if desired, in the center of the lower back and in the heels and toes. Strings are attached to these and to the hands after the costume is on the figure.

Three sticks, almost any size, and about six, seven, and eight inches long, are needed for controls. Nail the short one across the long one about an inch from one end, and drill holes as indicated.

Begin the string process by attaching the head strings to the ends of the short crosspiece, holding the sticks so that the short piece is on top and the short end of the long piece is pointed forward. The length of these strings is such that the operators forearm is horizontal when holding the control in the hand with the puppet's feet on the floor. Then attach the shoulder strings. They are drawn through the costume and tied into the screw-eyes underneath, and are tied to the center of the control stick just back of the crosspiece. One long string is run through the hole in the front end of the stick, and each end attached to a hand. A string attached to the back is tied to the back end of the stick. The knee strings are tied to each end of the free control stick. All except the head strings are slightly loose, so the weight hangs from the head.

Black button and carpet thread is the easiest kind to use although fine fish line is the very best material.

Holding the crossed sticks in one hand, the operator sets the marionette's feet on the floor and catches the first finger around the shoulder strings; a slight pull on these will tilt the head forward. Other head and body movements are produced by movements of the hand. In the other hand is held the knee-control stick; tipping alternate ends of this lifts one foot at a time for walking and dancing. This knee-control stick is held with the fingers only, while the thumb is caught back under the hand strings and moves the hands in time with the feet. Toe strings, heel strings, and any other extra strings are tied to any spot on the crossed sticks that is most convenient.

An inexpensive puppet theater.—A heavy corrugated box, such as roll paper towels are packed in, makes an ideal beginning for an inexpensive puppet theater. Such a box is thirty-six inches by thirty-six inches by twelve inches and opens on the ends only. A smaller box can be used but makes the theater opening smaller.

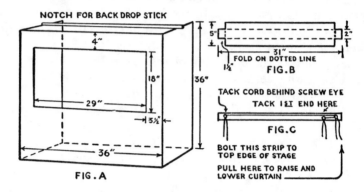

NOTCH FOR BACK DROP STICK

FIG. A

FOLD ON DOTTED LINE
FIG. B

TACK CORD BEHIND SCREW EYE
TACK 1st END HERE
FIG. C

BOLT THIS STRIP TO TOP EDGE OF STAGE
PULL HERE TO RAISE AND LOWER CURTAIN

First cut the stage opening on the thirty-six-inch square side or flat side. This is eighteen by twenty-nine inches and allows four inches at the top for curtains and supports. Next cut out all of the back and the top end. With strips such as lattice pieces, make a frame on the back of the stage opening, allowing the pieces at top and bottom of opening to extend the full thirty-six inches to give support. Put similar strips around the wing pieces at edges. These are fastened to the box by three-fourths-inch stove bolts, using washers on front and back of box so that the bolts will not pull through. Take the back-piece you have cut out and cut a piece thirty-one inches by five inches to make a trough for the footlights. Cut and fold this piece as shown in Figure B. Bolt to front and at bottom of stage opening. Line with asbestos and lay a Christmas tree string of white or yellow lights in trough to serve as footlights.

Cut a curtain twenty-four inches by thirty-one inches. Make a one-inch hem at bottom and two-inch hem at top. Make a narrow hem on each side before making top and bottom hem. Cut a strip of wood three-fourths inch by thirty-one inches by one-fourth inch (Figure C) and put in top hem. Now measure screw-eye at one end—put a one-fourth-inch iron rod in bottom hem for curtain roller and weight, using a heavy twisted cord; tack one end on back side of wooden strip opposite screw-eye away from third screw-eye. Run cord down under iron rod, then up and through screw-eye over and into third or end screw-eye down the iron rod back to third screw-eye and over to the remaining screw-eye, down under iron rod and back up and tack end to back of wooden strip and opposite to last screw-eye used. This makes a curtain that will roll up and down.

Now bolt at top and on front of the theater, being sure that your curtain just reaches the bottom of the stage opening. An electric-light bulb on an extension cord may be hung over a hook at center top of stage opening for a head light.

Shadow puppets.—The shadow puppet is of Oriental origin. As early as 121 B.C., Chinese literature tells a legend concerning their origin. The Emperor Wu of the Han Dynasty was made inconsolable by the loss of his favorite dancer. He commanded the court magician to bring her back from the "Land of the Shades." The penalty for failure was to be death. This stimulated his ingenuity and he cleverly contrived a shadow puppet likeness of the deceased out of fish skin. This he passed between a camp and a gauze curtain. The picture was so realistic that the Emperor was fascinated. From then on nightly performances were given at the palace. Here, then, was the forerunner of the modern moving picture.

The Chinese figures are made of donkey hide, treated by a secret process to make it transparent. They are carved with consummate skill and make the most colorful and artistic puppet in existence.

Setting and figures for Chinese Shadow perform-
ance of "The Elephant Child"—elephant, snake,
and crocodile.
—From photo by Minnesota WPA

The value of shadow puppetry as a recreational activity.—Shadow puppets have great possibilities as aids in visual education. In addition they offer opportunities for stimulating creativity, imagination, design, and sensitiveness to color harmony. Add to that the fact that they can furnish grand entertainment and you have recreation of high value. There are limitless opportunities for artistic skill in design, in color combinations, and in dramatic sequences.

How to make shadow puppets.—1. *The Materials*—(*a*) Dupont Pyrolin sheets fifty inches by twenty inches, gauge .0075 in various colors. Or use construction paper oiled with boiled linseed oil to make it translucent. (*b*) Black instant drying lacquer or crystalene. Finger-nail polish can be used for cheeks and lips. (*c*) Eastman Film Company adhesive. (*d*) Bessemer steel rods, 16 gauge, 12 inches long (from Meader Puppet Sales Company). (*e*) One-fourth-inch dowels for handles, cut in six-inch lengths. (*f*) No. 25 linen thread to sew parts of puppet together and to attach parts to rods. (*g*) Waverly white window curtain for screen. (*h*) Light box just back of the screen—twelve-inch lunaline bulbs would be best.

2. Cut out pieces in colors desired; glue together; sew hinged parts where puppet is to get action as shoulders, elbows, hips, knees; use razor blade to cut out intricate designs.

3. Attach steel rod to head and one or both arms with thread.

Technique of handling.—A skillful Oriental puppeteer can handle three puppets at one time. But the amateur will have his hands full handling one. The following simple rules must be observed: (1) Keep the puppets' feet on the ground. (2) Only the puppets speaking should move. (3) Keep puppet close against the screen. (4) When it is necessary for a puppet to turn keep one edge of the puppet against the screen, and pivot quickly. (5) Players should learn their lines as in any other dramatic performance.

Scenery—Remarkably beautiful scenic effects can be secured, since the material shows through in colors. Use oiled construction paper where color is desired. Where black shows in the setting use any heavy cardboard. Make light-weight wooden frames covered with Waverly window shades for the screen. Attach the setting to the back of this shade with Scotch tape.

Paper bag puppets.—Here is a stunt that will be lots of fun at the party, banquet, or for some special occasion. Make puppet heads out of paper sacks. Paint features on the sack with poster paint or tempera or mark features on with crayon. Blow up the sack. Tie with a string and attach a stick or pencil covered with a scarf, under which the hand operates the puppet. One group at a banquet, after putting on a brief paper-bag puppet show, had every person make such a puppet. A sack with all the necessary materials was provided for each person. Guests were grouped and required to plan and present a series of puppet shows.

Sock puppets.—White socks stuffed with kapok or cotton make good inexpensive hand puppets. Features can be painted on the puppet heads. Buttons can be used for eyes. One group had a grand time doing "Three Little Kittens" with sock puppets, with a choric speech choir reading the lines.

Rubber ball puppets.—Dig out a finger hole in a rubber or sponge ball. Paint features on the ball. Put a scarf over the hand and run the forefinger or a stick up into the finger hole.

Puppet Supplies

Hamburg Puppet Guild, 88 Hawkins Avenue, Hamburg, N. Y.

Helen Joseph Playfellow Shops, 2511 Overlook Road, Cleveland, Ohio.

Deborah Meader Puppet Shop, 748 Goodrich Avenue, St. Paul, Minn. (string, fist, and shadow puppet supplies).

Catherine Muller, 116 South First Street, Highland Park, Ill.

Master Marionettes, Duncan Mabley, Inc., 2063 East 100th Street, Cleveland, Ohio.

CHAPTER XVI
FUN WITH GENERAL PARTIES

FUN WITH GENERAL PARTIES

THE trend toward the informal type of recreation program is a wholesome one. It allows for more of spontaneity. It emphasizes a variety of possible activities and gives the participant an opportunity to choose what he *wants* to do. It releases the group from the rigidity of a theme program and makes it possible to follow the leads indicated by the moods and interests of participants. Sensing the value of this informal and varied program many groups have wisely swung to the open-house type of program with a wide variety of games and activities going on simultaneously, thus making it unnecessary to herd everyone into the same activity, whether or no.

However, in our enthusiasm for this freer type of program we must not lose sight of the values of the *theme party* as a useful agent in a well-rounded recreation program. A theme stimulates imagination, provides a basis for unity, suggests a decorative scheme providing atmosphere, makes it possible to avoid monotonous sameness, and assists the guests in remembering the occasion. This latter is more valuable than may be apparent. A good recreation occasion ought to be enjoyed three times—in anticipation, in realization, and in retrospect. In addition to its value at the time of the activity, the theme party has anticipatory and restrospective values not common to the themeless recreation occasion.

Characteristics of a good party.—Action, surprise, variety, spontaneity, balance (provided by "breathers" and the inclusion of a wide range of interests) , smooth continuous movement, unity, climax, and an atmosphere of friendliness are some of the essentials to be kept in mind in planning party programs.

THE GREAT GRINMORE CIRCUS

STUPENDOUS! COLOSSAL! MAGNIFICENT!

THE GREATEST SHOW ON EARTH!

COME ONE! COME ALL!

Starts Promptly at 8:01 P.M.

SEE THE MAIN SHOW!

SEE THE GREATEST COLLECTION OF FREAKS ON EARTH!

NO RAIN CHECKS ISSUED!

The barkers—Promptly at 8:01 a barker stood on a box or chair in front of each side show and began spieling for his particular performance. "Madame Utellum! Have your palm read!" "See the Teutonic Terror! He's plenty strong! Don't miss this great show!" "Hurry! Hurry! Hurry! There's a great show inside! Get in line, folks, get in line!" It sounded as if the State Fair had come back to town.

The crowd began pouring into the various shows. There were shouts of hearty laughter and countless broad smiles. The Great Grinmore Circus was on!

Side shows—Booths had been arranged. Posters advertised the mammoth exhibits. Large streamers spoke convincingly of the wonders inside.

The possibilities in side shows are limitless. Here are a few suggestions:

1. The legless, hairless dog. A weiner.
2. The Teutonic terror. A bit of limburger.
3. The wild baboon. A mirror inside shows the visitor this one.
4. The only red bat in captivity. A brickbat tied with a string.
5. A trip around the world. Roll visitor around globe map in wagon.
6. Wild man from Borneo. Painted and costumed.
7. "For ladies only." A hairpin.
8. "For men only." Suspenders.

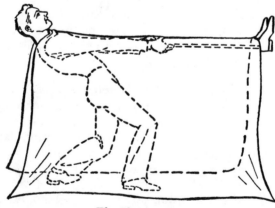

The Floating Man

Grand stage show—1. Marvelous exhibits. An announcer stands behind a screen and introduces each scene. If he can be provided with an amplifier so much the better. A clown walks on, performs appropriately, and exits.

(*a*) Remains of Ancient Greece. The clown carries a candle-stick which holds a much burnt candle.

(*b*) Ruins of China. The clown drops broken china. Then gets a broom and sweeps it up.

(*c*) Our own native land. Soil on garden spade.

(*d*) Yellowstone Park. The clown brings in a "Park Here" sign. Then he parks a yellow stone under the sign.

2. The floating man. The man lies, or appears to lie, on a table covered with a sheet or blanket. What appears to be his feet are really just two shoes fitted onto the ends of two poles or broom-sticks. He stands behind the cover, holding his head back. In his hands he holds the two poles with the shoes sticking out beyond the end of the cover. The magician makes a few mysterious passes over him and mutters the mystic words, "Abba ka dabba." The man moves off holding the sticks out in front of him. The sheet covers his body and gives the appearance of a man floating through the air. It might be well to tack the sheet to the poles so it will not slip, thus disclosing the man walking under it. Or this disclosure might be made part of the fun.

3. The Dancing Midgets. Two or more of these midgets could be arranged by taking an old sheet or outing cloth, cutting holes for the head, feet, and arms. Pin tiny costumes on the outside of the sheet. One person puts his head in the large hole in the sheet and his hands and arms (dressed in baby shoes and stockings) in the two

Midgets

holes for that purpose. Another person stands behind him and puts his hands out under the first person's armpits and through the arm holes, thus providing the midgets' hands. A table is provided on which the midgets dance. They may also talk, sing, and put on skit. Just the tiniest bit of imagination will disclose the possibilities in this stunt.

4. Puppet show. A puppet or marionette show would be appropriate. "Punch and Judy" would go over in great style.

5. Meller-drammer. A good take-off on melodrama would add to the fun of the evening. A suggested plot, a little threadbare but usable, that might do in a pinch is the following: Grandpa and Grandma; Little Nell—their pride and joy; the hero; the villain, who holds a mortgage on the old homestead and who threatens to foreclose unless he can get Little Nell. Naturally the hero appears just in the nick of time to pay the mortgage and to give the villain his just deserts.

The circus ring—The parade with the circus band and performers will announce the ring performance. There will be clowns, animals (and oh, what animals!), a strong man, a two-headed girl, Hiram and Mirandy who come to the circus, some real tumblers, and whatever goes with a circus performance.

Refreshments—Hot dogs and pink lemonade, served by the clowns.

Helpful books—"How to Put on an Amateur Circus," by F. A. Hacker and Prescott W. Eames (T. S. Denison and Co.). Detailed plans, how to make circus animals, photographs, drawings. For an elaborate circus this would be invaluable.

"Sorepaw and Fells Circus." Eldridge Entertainment House, Franklin, Ohio.

A HOBBY FAIR PARTY

What's your hobby? What's your hobby?
Share it friend, at the Hobby Fair!
It will be a party nobby;
Let's make it an occasion rare.

"Just jump on your Hobby, and ride him to our Hobby Fair Party. Turn in any material you have for the Hobby Exhibit to the Exhibit Committee."

What's your hobby?—Use a grand march to get the crowd into two concentric circles, with men on the inner circle. Have the two circles march in opposite directions. When the music stops marchers halt and face partners. Each person is given thirty seconds to talk to his partner about his hobby—the ladies first and then the men. When the music starts guests resume marching.

If preferred, the guests may be seated in a circle by couples. Partners are given a brief time to discuss their hobbies. When the leader rings a bell all of the men progress one partner to the right. With this new partner he again discusses hobbies.

Hobbyhorse ride—Several broomsticks are necessary. In a large group certain persons are picked for the ride. In a small group each person is expected to perform. The rider must prance over the room on his "steed"—bucking, leaping, trotting, galloping. Several riders may be on the floor at the same time. The crowd decides which rider shows the best riding form.

Hobbyhorse race—Two teams of five or more riders each engage in this relay race. The first runner takes his "horse" to the other end of the room and back, turning it over to his next teammate, who mounts and rides the same course. This continues until each rider has finished the course.

Hobbyhorse debate—One debater is selected for each side. The selections should have been made a sufficient time ahead to allow for preparation. Not more than five minutes should be allowed to each speaker both for direct argument and rebuttal. The subject is "Resolved, That it is better to ride a hobby than it is to ride a horse."

The hobby exhibit and demonstration—This is the principal feature of the party. Weeks should be spent in planning for it. The Exhibit Committee should carefully comb the community for interesting exhibits. Many people will be found who have hobbies that will fit in with the exhibit idea. Pictures, painted chinaware, old coins, stamp collections, old books, fancy work, quilts, wood carving, soap carving, leather work, doll collections, and the like. These should be arranged with the names of the persons, whose property they are, displayed along with the exhibit.

If along with the exhibits there can be some demonstrations, such as someone doing soap carving, spatter printing, leather tooling, making marionettes, putting on a marionette show, and wood carving, it will add greatly to the profit and enjoyment of the evening.

A FAIRYLAND PARTY

Put on "kid" clothes,
And goodness knows,
Follow your nose
To Fairyland Town.
There happiness grows
And joy supreme flows
So everyone goes
To Fairyland Town.

"The sugar plum tree"—In the first room the guests enter they find the "Sugar Plum Tree," a small bush on which hangs sticks of candy. Each guest is privileged to take a stick and eat it.

"The nursery"—Before entering "Fairyland" or "The Enchanted

Forest" the sticky hands must be clean.   Therefore, every guest must pass through the nursery where a nurse washes and wipes the hands.   If the crowd is large only a gesture is made by the nurse.

"Fairyland"—Vines, foliage, toy balloons, angel hair, animals peeping from behind the foliage.   Achieve a blue lighting effect by covering all of the lights with blue gelatin, cellophane, or crepe paper.   Over in one corner have a wishing well, which guests visit on entering.   Numerous strings hang out over the sides of this well.   At the end of each string is an answer to the wish of the one who pulls it.   Each guest is privileged to take hold of one string and pull it.

A scrambled fairy story—Each of several people is given the title of a fairy story.   One person is designated to begin the story and another to finish it.   Each tells a portion of the story given him at the time designated by the leader.   No person is allowed more than thirty seconds.   The sequences in this jumbled story promise lots of fun, as they skip from Little Red Riding Hood to the Little Red Hen to the Three Bears to Jack and the Bean Stalk, etc.

Fairy story rebuses—
1. ginleesp tubaye
2. hirendid doorg
3. thonew swi
4. seerg thip
5. hetneety yow tanmin
6. lentiled hert
7. baterep brit
8. delchet tha philnes
9. drersoe
10. cogdil klos

Answers: (1) Sleeping Beauty.   (2) Red Riding Hood.   (3) Snow White.   (4) Three Pigs.   (5) The Teeny Tiny Woman. (6) Little Red Hen.   (7) Peter Rabbit.   (8) The Elephant Child. (9) Red Rose.   (10) Goldilocks.

Fairy story dramatizations—This will probably prove the most enjoyable feature of the evening.   Divide the crowd into three or four groups.   Storytellers should be selected several days before the party.   They are asked to be ready with designated stories and plans for their dramatization, including materials and ideas for costuming. These storytellers are assigned to the various groups to act as advisers, as well as storytellers, in helping the groups plan their stunts. Both the storyteller and the group are allowed the privilege of giving their own interpretation to the story.

Red Riding Hood—One group had a lot of fun with this story.   A young man was made up as Red Riding Hood, wearing a red hood, a red dress, and white pantaloons.   The latter were achieved by pinning newspapers to his trousers. The wolf wore a dog false face. The storyteller and the actors collaborated in bringing the story to the proper climax.

The three bears—Small tables, benches, chairs, and bowls furnished the necessary properties. The tables and benches became "beds." Goldilocks enters. She tries out the porridge and eats with relish the porridge in the smallest bowl. She tries the chairs, and sits in the smallest. She tries the "beds" and goes to sleep on the smallest. The bears arrive. Deep-crowned hats of some of the ladies present had been borrowed. Heavy coats with fur collars were worn backwards. The baby bear came in holding to the mamma bear's coat-tail. From then on the dramatization moved with rapid pace to the climax when Goldilocks escapes.

These are enough to indicate the possibilities in working out these dramatizations.

In *Stunt Night Tonight,* by Catherine Miller, there is an excellent stunt that would fit into this party in "The Truth About Sleeping Beauty."

Children's games—In Fairyland it would be appropriate to play all sorts of children's games such as, "London Bridge," "Sugar-Loaf Town," "I Come to See Miss Jenny Ann Jones," "Looby Loo," and "Farmer's in the Dell."

Refreshments—Cotton candy, popcorn, pink lemonade.

A PIONEER PARTY

Advertise with a miniature covered wagon. A small grape basket, a bit of white crepe paper for the cover, and some heavy cardboard for wheels would do the trick.

If those who attend will agree to come in costume it will add to the fun.

Decorations—If some pioneer relics can be borrowed—a spinning wheel, an old musket, a tripod and kettle—it will assist in creating the atmosphere desired.

Pioneer music—As guests arrive have them gather around the piano to sing some of the old songs, such as "Oh, Susanna," "Camptown Races," "Old Folks at Home," "Juanita," "Silver Threads Among the Gold," "Love's Old Sweet Song," "The Old Chisholm Trail," "Sweet Alice, Ben Bolt," "My Old Kentucky Home," and "In the Evening by the Moonlight."

Pioneer games—Use some of the old musical games like "Jennie Cracks Corn," "The Old Brass Wagon," "Bingo," "Brown-eyed Mary," "Oh, Susanna," "Looby Loo," and "The Virginia Reel."

Other old games like "Going to Jerusalem" and "Wink" might also be used.

Pioneer charades—Work out charades on such words as pioneer (pie-and-ear or pie-oh-near), Standish (stand-dish), Davy Crockett (Day-vie-crock-eat), Daniel Boone (Dan-yell-boon), Samuel Houston (Sam-you-well-hue-stone).

Pioneer drama—Precious Priscilla.

1. PRECIOUS PRISCILLA, the pretty princess—All italicized parts are read by someone and the characters act out their parts. Priscilla flutters to the center of the stage, curtsies, bows, and exits.

2. PIOUS PAUL, a peppy pal—He is dressed in gypsy costume. He comes in taking long steps, tips his hat several times to the audience and exits.

3. PETRIFIED PETE, the Pawnee papa—He comes on the stage stealthily and scowls at the crowd.

4. PREVARICATIN' PAT, the Pawnee's partner—He follows just a few steps behind Pete and imitates him exactly.

5. PEGGY PERUNY, the poisonous prattler—Is indifferent to everybody.

6. PRIMITIVE POLLY, the plucky pet of the plains—She is snappy. Comes in with hands on hips. She may be a gypsy.

After all the characters have been introduced, the reader begins the story, being careful to read clearly and distinctly, so that audience will have no trouble understanding.

Precious Priscilla, the pretty princess, parts from the palace for the prosperous plains—She crosses the stage backwards throwing kisses toward the wings and runs into Pious Paul who has been watching her with interest. She shows surprise. He suggests walk, offers his arm, and the pair leave in the direction Priscilla was going.

Primitive Polly peers 'pon her pal and Precious Priscilla. Her poor pulse palpitates painfully—Polly enters and registers jealousy.

Petrified Pete and Prevaricatin' Pat plot to pounce 'pon Precious Priscilla and plunder the plains—Petrified Pete and Pat tiptoe stiffly to center stage. They plot together, scan the horizon together. They meet in center, go to opposite corners of the stage, and come back to center.

They park behind a pile of pebbles—They take two or three steps together and squat.

Precious Priscilla plods the plains plucking posies—She zigzags over the stage very elaborately breaking off flowers, reaching for them anywhere, occasionally smelling the bunch. She even goes so far as to pick some off Pete's head, absolutely ignoring the fact that Pete is there.

She sits on prickly pear—You know the action.

She perches 'pon peanut near pebbles—She assumes sitting posture beside Pete and Pat.

Pete and Pat pounce 'pon her—They creep up on either side of her and grab her. Priscilla registers screaming. They try to stop her. They gag her and swing her backward and forward as though wrestling.

They put her 'pon pony and part from plains—The three step back together, take high steps as though mounting and gallop off, Pete pulling reins, Priscilla screaming, and Pat slapping an imaginary horse.

Primitive Polly pears 'pon them and promptly protects Priscilla by persuading Paul to pursue—Enter Paul on horseback. He stops his horse and acts dismounting, listens to Polly, motions her up behind. They gallop off. They may use broomsticks for horses or even just imagine they are on horses. Height contrast is wanted here.

Pete and Pat progress—They gallop across stage left to right. Go in circles.

Paul's prancing pony is pricked by pointed posies and grows punk—Both hop heavily on right foot, dragging left.

Pete procures paddlewagon and proceeds—They paddle slowly together.

Paul and Polly procure another paddlewagon and resume pursuit—Paul in front takes long dignified strokes, Polly behind takes short, wild dashes, as they approach the center.

Paul's paddlewagon hits pesky protruding prong—On next stroke on the side of the audience, Polly goes over the side. Three short jabs, one long one, and then all is as calm as before.

Peruny is perched 'pon pallet perplexed over Pete's not producing the plunder—She comes in and squats at the back center.

Pete pitilessly pitches Precious Priscilla 'pon pallet. They produce poison and plan to poison her—Have large bottle labeled poison with water inside. They are trying to make her take the poison when—

Paul and Polly prevent poisoning by pitching pepper in Pawnee's eyes—Much sneezing and Pawnee falls over dead.

Primitive Polly, having played her part, plunges penknife into penetrable part of herself and pays the penalty—While the lovers embrace, Polly in center stage takes knife and with great deliberation stabs herself. She first tries to make it go in her head, and when she

finds it won't she stabs her heart, and falls over backwards. **Paul**
goes to her side, feels her pulse, and sees that she is dead. Returns
to Priscilla. They look regretfully at Polly. Paul takes off his hat
and Priscilla wipes a tear.

Curtain. —Written by ELIZABETH FORREST FARRIS

More pioneer music—An Indian camp scene. Indian music with
special soloists singing such songs as "Pale Moon," "By the Waters
of Minnetonka," "Little Papoose on the Wind-swung Bough" (3-
part song for women's voices by C. W. Cadman, published by
Ditson).

A white man has been in the scene all the time, seated upon a large
stone. The Indians now notice him and speak to him in friendly
tone. One Indian says, "And how is wife?" The white man bows
his head and answers softly, "Jeanie has gone far away to the Happy
Hunting Ground, but I dream of her constantly." Then he sings,
"Jeanie with the Light Brown Hair," by Foster (In *Sing* published
by C. C. Birchard).

A YEAR 2000 PARTY

Now use your imagination,
And out of your cogitation
Figure what will happen 2000 A.D.
Dress twenty-first century style;
Have a big time for a while;
A grand good party you can bet it will be.

Decorations—Futuristic pictures and other decorations. Have on
display some "relics" of the year of the party—a lipstick, an income
tax blank, etc.

Costumes—Guests may be asked to come in such costumes as they
think will be worn in the year 2000.

Passing fancies—Each guest is given a piece of paper and a pencil
and asked to write down what will be only a memory in A.D. 2000.
These are shuffled, and passed out. Each guest must then read what
the passing fancy is and suggest some substitute for it. Suggestions
for things that will be memories only in A.D. 2000—swing music, the
art of conversation, lipsticks, men's ties, battleships, college athletics,
newspapers.

Desired inventions—Have guests suggest the most desired invention
or discoveries by the year 2000.

Fashions—Give each couple bits of cheesecloth, scraps of cambric,
ribbons, old hat frames, plenty of newspapers, pins, some gummed
paper tape, and anything else available. Have each man dress his

partner in the sort of costume he thinks women will wear in A.D. 2000. In a very large crowd, the designs could be achieved by groups, each group selecting one person and dressing her to represent the group.

Rhythm design—Have each person experiment with rhythm design. Pans of water are made available. Someone starts gently to swirl the water until it is moving in circular fashion. Then a drop or two of India ink (or any ink that is oily) is dropped into the swirling water. Now persons drop white sheets of paper in the pan and then lift them out. All sorts of interesting designs appear. Care should be taken not to smear the ink either in removing the paper or after getting the design out of the water. Allow the paper to dry and then have each person develop whatever design he can from the pattern on his paper. Some exceedingly interesting designs will be created. It may be necessary to go on with some of the rest of the program while the papers dry, allowing the artists to finish their creations later in the evening.

The March of Time—Divide into groups and have each group dramatize in a two-minute sketch some typical daily happening in the year A.D. 2000.

Futuristic art—Give to each person a card, some confetti, and a dab of library paste. Allow three minutes for the creation of some futuristic design, achieved by sprinkling the confetti on the wet paste. Have each person label his picture and put it on display. "Sunset on the Beach," "A Storm," "Thoughts of You," and any other titles can be given to the pictures.

Looking backward—It would be appropriate for someone to give an interesting and brief review of Edward Bellamy's great book, *Looking Backward*, since his story pictures a man of the nineteenth century awakening in the year 2000.

Refreshments—Sandwiches, wafers, and bottles of chocolate milk wrapped in cellophane.

A PROGRESSIVE ATHLETIC CARNIVAL

This party can be used either indoors or outdoors. Divide the crowd into small groups of equal numbers—say four, or six, or eight to a group. Most of the games may be table games. Have table and play spaces arranged and numbered, so that it will be easy for the players to progress in order. The numbers and directions can be printed on cards and placed in standards.

All players at a table progress to the next game when the leader blows a whistle. Thus, during the evening, each person plays in each game. Even when a group has finished a game it does not progress until the leader signals for progression. Otherwise confusion will reign.

Scores are kept in each game, and noted by the player on a tally sheet. After each group has made the rounds, total high and low scores are announced for each group. Thus the evening's Champion and "Champ-nit" are discovered. Awards may be made to these two.

In selecting games for this party the committee, or leader, should select those that will require about the same time. The following are suggested:

1. *Basketball*—Bounce tennis ball into a wastebasket at distance of about ten feet. Point for each ball going into basket on first bounce. Five throws make a turn.

2. *Bowling*—Five ten-pins or long-necked bottles. Playground ball or baseball. Each player gets three throws for a turn. Limit game to two rounds.

3. *Markmanship*—Make target of soft wood. (Corrugated board or beaverboard will do.) Outer circle counts 1, next circle 2, then 3, 4, and 5 in center. If regulation darts are not available, make darts by using large corks, darning needles, and feathers or cards. Players cast darts at distance of ten or fifteen feet. Three throws constitute a turn.

4. *Quoits*—Use a "Dodo Board." Or drive a long nail into a piece of wood. The wood should be about three inches square. The nail serves as a peg. Use Mason jar rings for quoits. Two to five throws. Ringer counts three; touching peg counts two, and touching the wooden base counts one.

5. *Baseball*—A soft wood board about two feet long. A good knife with two blades at one end. The smaller blade is opened all the way; the other blade only half-way. Player touches this latter blade lightly to the board with forefinger under end of knife handle. He then flips the knife over. If the small blade enters the board, thus causing the knife to stick straight up with no other part of it touching the board, a home run is made and the player scores four points. If the small blade sticks in the board, but the other blade touches the wood, it is a three-bagger, and three points are scored. If the large blade supports the knife alone, a two-bagger and two points. If the large blade and the handle touch the board, then a single and one point. If the knife lands on its back and stands up in that position, no play; and the player tries again. If the knife falls over, no score.

6. *Marble shooting*—Three holes in a cardboard box, or a cigar box. Or just straight piece of board could be used. Center hole

about one inch in diameter. Two side holes about inch and one-half. Center hole counts five. Others count one. Players shoot with marbles as in regular game. If they prefer they may roll marble. Three shots count a turn. Any player getting two holes in succession gets extra shot.

7. *Jacks*—Need set of jacks and small rubber ball. Play as in regular game of jacks.

8. *Tennis rules*—Each player is provided with a sheet of paper and pencil. He then makes as many words out of the letters in "Tennis Rules" as he can, working at it until the whistle blows. No letter can be used in a word oftener than it appears in the two words given. Suggestions: Ten, net, leer, lure, utensil, etc. One point to each player for each word found.

9. *Football*—Cover a table with smooth piece of wrapping paper. Mark off football field, using chalk. Make football of empty eggshell. Paint and mark to look like football. By punching small holes in either end of the egg, and blowing into one of these ends you can force the contents out the other end. Each player takes his turn at blowing from behind one end of the field. The space into which he blows the football indicates the score. If the egg goes outside the field the count is made from the point at which it went outside. If a player blows the football all the way across the field he scores ten points.

A NAUTICAL PARTY

For 125 to 150 people, though a smaller crowd may enjoy it.

7:00 -730—"Over the Waves," Radio Program. This feature provides entertainment while the guests are arriving.

7:30-7:45—Instead of using a whistle as a signal for attention and for changing games, secure the assistance of someone who can play the cornet or bugle and use some simple military calls. Following the radio program the bugle sounds "Assembly" and the leader calls on the chaplain of the boat to give the invocation.

The guests are then given a word of welcome to the ship for the evening's cruise. The leader then calls on a helper to "weigh anchor." This is done by drawing it up by a rope to a balcony above if there is one available, or if not, it can be placed on scales in the middle of the floor and actually weighed. The anchor can be made from black cardboard. The mixer for the evening is a recruiting game. Copies of enlistment forms can be prepared on the mimeograph. These are given out and at a signal from the leader each one begins getting recruits for the navy. The one having the most at the end of the period receives a prize. A toy airship makes an appropriate prize.

NAVY RECRUITING FORM

Name	Address	Age	Weight	Health	Disposition	I.Q.	Married?
1.							
2.							
3.							
4.							
5.							
6.							
7.							
8.							
9.							
10.							
11.							
12.							
13.							
14.							
15.							
16.							
17.							
18.							
19.							
20.							
21.							
22.							
23.							
24.							
25.							

Navy Department, Washington, D. C.—Form No. 13

7:45-9:00—Crew Regatta. As each guest arrives he is given a program which has the name of one of the following eight ships on the back: Monitor, Merrimac, Old Ironsides, Pinta, Maria, Mayflower, Maine, Columbia. Lifesavers are made by wrapping old tires with white crepe paper and these are placed at regular intervals around the room. The names of the ships can be painted—one on each of the tires. At the time for the Regatta instructions can be given by the leader to gather at the lifesaver with the name of the ship on it which corresponds to the one on the back of his program. When each crew has gathered, instruct them to elect a captain for their boat. The Regatta will consist of a series of competitive games in which the winner will receive a prize. Do not announce all the games on the program, so that it may be changed or shortened if necessary.

1. *Walking the plank*—Have each crew select one boy and send him to center of room. A number of chairs are placed in various places on the floor. The boys are then blindfolded and lined up. At a given signal they are told to start and go as fast as possible to the other end of the room. Before they start, however, most of the chairs are removed noiselessly. If this is new, all of the chairs may be removed. First, second, and third places are recorded.

2. *Fish stories*—Have each crew select one member of their crew to tell a fish story. They are called on one at a time, given a limited time to tell the story (two minutes), and the judges award the places.

3. *A rush for the boat*—This is a relay. Line up each crew in single file with the leaders all on an even line. Place a chair at the other end of the room for each line of runners. Now place on the floor in front of each line a suitcase or handbag (preferably old ones). At the given signal (bugle blast) the leader of the crew picks up the bag and runs to the other end of the room, circles the chair, and comes back to the next person. The crew finishing first, of course, wins. Be sure there is the same number of players in each line.

4. *Ships and other ships*—This is a writing game. Each ship captain is given a sheet of paper and a pencil. Explain that at the signal of the bugle each crew is to begin to write all the words they can think of in which the word "ship" occurs, such as friendship, courtship, etc. At the end of the given time (two minutes) they are taken up and counted, awarding places to the three highest.

Grand flotilla review.—This will be the final of the crew competitions and is to represent a flotilla of ships passing in review. Each crew is to work out any form of formation or march step, maneuvers, etc., that they desire. After allowing about five minutes for this, have some good march music. The judges are seated where they may see each crew as it passes and they are to award places according to the following: General appearance, marching ability, historical representation (one crew marched as war veterans), good looks, and any other criteria desired may be used.

Salty symphonies—9:00-9:30. This is the formal or semiformal part of the program. The following numbers were used, but others can be substituted (A reading would be good):

Men's quartet—Medley of old sea songs.

Piano solo—

Male vocal solo—"The Mighty Deep."

Cornet solo—"Anchors Aweigh!"

Presentation of grand prize. A box of "Sea Foam" candy (can be made at home).

Refreshments—Doughnuts covered with powdered sugar, and cocoa with floating marshmallow. Carts were decorated with crepe paper to represent ships and were wheeled into room to center. Girls dressed in white middies and dark skirts, boys in white shirts and dark sailor trousers served in couples. Radio music during refreshments.

If a whistle with the sound of a boat could be obtained, it would be well to blow it just before the decorated boats enter the room as described above.

Vessel vespers—The entire group stood and sang together the old familiar hymn, "The Haven of Rest." This was followed by the benediction.

Decorations—We used the gymnasium which had a balcony running all around it. This made a good place for such a party, for we placed the tire "life savers" around the balcony against the railing, which resembled a ship's side. Then below the life savers at intervals around the balcony were placed portholes made by cutting out round gray disks of cardboard. The center of the disks were cut out, leaving just enough uncut to form a hinge so that the porthole door swung out. Blue tissue was pasted over the hole.

A blue and white color effect was worked out. A canopy of blue and white crepe paper streamers was placed over the entire room with a moon in one corner.

By calling at the nearest naval recruiting station we were able to secure a number of large posters and pictures of ships in various sizes and colors. These were placed on the walls around the room and added to the atmosphere. The lights were covered with a dark blue tissue paper which softened the bareness of the gym walls and gave a festive air to the room. Large size ropes were coiled and hung around the room. A gangplank was built from two planks with blocks under one end and upright pieces on the sides with ropes connecting them. This was placed in the door.

Properties—One anchor (black cardboard); one scales, or a rope if it is pulled up, recruiting blanks; eight sheets of blank paper; pencils, enough for group; eight old handbags or suitcases; eight blindfolds; grand prize (about a one- or two-pound box of Sea Foam candy); prize for mixer (toy boat or airship); score cards for the judges; radio, with good volume.

The party given above was put on by the boys of Asbury College,

Wilmore, Kentucky, in honor of the girls, which accounts for the absence of young ladies on the program. It also was worked up and given within forty-eight hours, so undoubtedly it can be greatly improved upon with a little more time put on it.

SHIP PARTY

This party has been used successfully with college groups where from 175 to 450 were present.

Place—Any place where there is one room large enough to accommodate the entire group, in addition to several smaller rooms or available spaces.

Suggested places—Gyms; Sunday-school buildings where there is a large assembly room or recreation hall; community buildings; schoolhouses; civic centers.

Decorations—Anything nautical such as: lifesavers; deck signs; paper pennants, etc.

The party may be a costume party where each will come dressed in sailor outfits. Passengers in a variety of costumes will lend atmosphere.

Preparation—Appoint decoration committee well in advance of party date as careful planning and decoration are important factors in determining success or failure of party.

Preparation will include: (1) Making of signs reading: "B-Deck"; "Promenade Deck"; "Look out for Sharks"; "Throw things off Lee Side Only"; "Swimming off Port Side—4:00-6:00 P.M."; "Ping-pong Tournament in Session"; "Ship News Out!" etc.

Place these signs where all can see them.

(2) Cutting and stringing of pennants: Cut tricornered pennants from colored paper of any kind (except crepe). Make enough for several strings across the ceiling. In other words decorate as a ship for the gala last night out.

(3) Printing of Passports: Make these tickets from scraps left from cutting pennants. (These aren't entirely necessary, but they add atmosphere to the party.)

(4) Arrangement: Of the smaller rooms or spaces to be used determine in which place a particular game or contest can best be played. Each room is to be named thus: Ballroom, Recreation Room, Lobby, Dining Salon, Pilot Room, Roost, Clubroom, Promenade Deck, Crow's Nest, etc.

Suggested games—

(1) Pencil games (such as making many words from one word, e.g., shipmate).

(2) Fortunetelling.

(3) Marble games.

(4) Dart baseball.

(5) Charades.

(6) Songs or games.

(7) Food game (good for dining salon). Set out several condiments such as cloves, pepper, vinegar, and anything with a distinctive odor that's connected with a dining-room or a kitchen. Blindfold passengers and let each smell the articles and try to guess what each is.

(8) Table games like anagrams, crokinole, logomachy, fiddlesticks.

At the party—Group may be divided into smaller groups according to size of group and number of games planned. A suggested way to divide a group is to give each passenger a passport to some country—for instance, give a certain number of green passports with Germany written thereon, and a certain number of yellow ones with France, etc. Then inside have large signs corresponding in color and name, on the wall around the big room. After the first get-together game or song each passenger will go to his or her color, and the rotation will start.

Passengers will be conducted by guides who have been previously instructed as to order of rotation. At the sound of ship's gong rotation will continue. Length of time in each game will be determined by number of groups and time allotted for entire party.

At a special signal on the gong (after the rotation is complete) all passengers will assemble in the largest room for grand finale. Grand finale might be mass participation in folk games; it might be just singing folk songs; or it might be planned entertainment by the ship's crew. Refreshments may or may not be served.

Suggested direction of groups at first gong—Germany to Ballroom; France to Roost; Italy to Pilot's Room; England to Dining Salon; Spain to Recreation Room; Denmark to Clubroom; Holland to Lobby; Switzerland to Promenade Deck.

Rotation might then be—From Ballroom to Roost to Pilot's Room to Dining Salon to Recreation Room to Clubroom to Lobby to Promenade Deck—then all back to Ballroom. This may be modified very easily.

A word about the crew—The master-of-ceremonies should be dressed as Ship's Captain, of course. His or her helpers as First Mate, Head Steward, etc. Guides, as "gobs," or in anything "sailorish." Ringer of gong as Ship's Page.

There will, of course, be one of the crew in each of the game rooms to direct play.   MARGARET TURNER

A RODEO PARTY

A rodeo party! Whee! Heap much fun!
A rodeo party! Ever see one?
Be on hand in costume gay;
Be ready to laugh, and romp, and play!
"Be round for the round-up at the Rodeo Party."

Some such invitation as this, written in a scrawling hand on wrapping paper, will give your crowd the cue for your fall rodeo party. Announce that the guests are to come in costume representing cowboys, cowgirls, and Indians. The cowboys ought to wear shirts of green, red, orange, yellow, or blue, with big bow ties of contrasting colors. A bright-colored vest should be worn, unbuttoned, over this shirt. Boots may or may not be worn. Sombreros are in style for headgear. Vests may be made by covering old vests with cheesecloth or crepe paper. The cowgirls could wear hiking clothes with bandana kerchiefs tied about the neck. A blanket and headpiece would answer for the Indians.

As each person arrives tag him with a name that is to be worn the rest of the evening. There would be "Hawkeye," "Deadwood Dick," "Sitting Bull," "Deer Heart," "Nell," "Flo," and others equally colorful. The guests are to be called by these names throughout the evening. There should be a penalty for using correct names.

Pony express.—Form two concentric circles with the girls in the inner circle. As the music plays, the boys march in one direction and the girls in the other. When the leader blows his whistle each girl grabs a boy for a partner and marches in the same direction that the boys are going. All extra girls go to the center of the circle and wait there until the whistle blows again. This time the girls again reverse their direction and march as at first. This process continues until the leader feels that the crowd has been fairly mixed. The music continues throughout. The boys do not stop or slow up when the whistle blows, but continue marching in time always in the same direction. As soon as the whistle blows each girl should immediately reverse her direction, keeping perfect time to the music.

Round-up.—Two leaders are appointed. The crowd endeavors to keep out of their way. The leaders begin by tagging some player, who then joins hands with the leader who tagged him. The two of them now endeavor to tag two others.   As fast as players are tagged, they join hands with the group doing the tagging.   Only end players can tag.   Players tagged while the line is broken are free.   If a line can encircle one or more players completely, they are considered tagged.   Each leader endeavors to round up the larger number of players.   When the game is played indoors, players are exempt from being tagged when they are touching any one of the walls of the room, but players may not claim this exemption for a longer period than ten seconds at a time.

Lariat race.—Ten players are selected to represent each side. They stand in single file.   The head player is provided with a rope, six feet or more in length.   At the signal to start he must jump this rope, passing it over his head in doing so.   The next player in line takes the rope from him and does the same thing.   So it goes to the end of the line.   The end player must then skip the rope to the head of the line and start it down again.   When the original top player is again at the head the team has finished the race.

Roping contest.—Two lassoes are provided.   These can be made easily by tying a noose in the end of a long piece of rope.   Each player is given an opportunity to test his skill at lassoing the leg of an upturned chair.   For each successful effort a point is awarded.

Stage.—Players are to stand or sit in a circle.   They number off by sevens.   All "ones" then become "cowboys," all "twos" "Indians," all "threes" "women," and "fours" "horses," all "fives" "stagecoach," all "sixes" "rifles," and all "sevens" "bows and arrows."   The leader then reads a story about the hold-up of a stage by Indians.   When the "cowboys" are mentioned they pretend to be driving a stage at a furious pace, and they shout a piercing, "Yip! Yip!"   The "Indians" war dance and yell.   The "women" scream.   The "horses" trot, beating a tattoo on the floor with their feet or on the knees with their hands.   The "stagecoach" turns completely around.   The "rifles" take aim and fire, "Bang!"   The "bows and arrows" drop to one knee or, standing, draw the bow and shout "Zip!"

Story for "Stage"—It was in the days of *stagecoaches,* and *cowboys,* and *Indians.*   Alkali Ike, Dippy Dick, and Pony Pete were three courageous *cowboys.*   When the stagecoach left for Rainbow's End they were aboard, as were also two *women,* Salty Sal and a doll-faced blonde.   The *stagecoach* was drawn by three handsome *horses* and it left Dead End exactly on time.

The most dangerous part of the journey was the pass known as

Gory Gulch. As the *stagecoach* neared this spot it could be noticed that the *women* were a bit nervous and the *cowboys* were alert, fingering their *rifles* as if to be ready for any emergency. Even the *horses* seemed to sense danger.

Sure enough just as the *stagecoach* entered the Gulch there sounded the blood-curdling war cry of the *Indians*. Mounted on *horses* they came riding wildly toward the *stagecoach,* aiming their *bows and arrows*. The *cowboys* took aim with their *rifles* and fired. The *women* screamed. The *horses* pranced nervously. The *Indians* shot their *bows and arrows*. The *cowboys* aimed their rifles again, this time shooting with more deadly effect. The leading brave fell and the *Indians* turned their *horses* and fled leaving their *bows and arrows* behind. The *women* fainted. The *cowboys* shot one more volley from their *rifles,* just for luck. The driver urged on the *horses* and the *stagecoach* sped down the trail.

If the leader desires he may divide the crowd into seven groups, designating each group. Thus all "cowboys," "Indians," etc., would be together. It would be well to practice each group once before proceeding with the story.

Indian war-bonnet race.—From four to ten players may represent each side. The teams line up in shuttle-relay style with half of each team at one end of the room and half at the opposite end. The first player on each team wears an Indian war bonnet. This may be made out of chicken or turkey feathers, if colored feathers are not available. At the signal to go this player hops to the opposite side of the room, where he doffs the headgear and hands it to teammate Number Two. This teammate dons the war bonnet and hops across to the next player on the other side of the room. So the game continues until each player has been over the course.

Stagecoach race.—Two girls represent each side. Two wheelbarrows are provided. One girl pushes while her teammate rides. When they get to the opposite side of the room, of course, the rider tumbles out and the pusher takes her place. The former rider then guides the "stagecoach" back to the starting point. The first team in wins.

Bucking contest.—All players form one big circle, the sides being evenly divided. In the center of the circle place a saddle or sofa pillow. When the leader's whistle blows each side begins pulling, endeavoring to make some player on the opposing side touch the saddle. To avoid it a player may jump. As soon as a player touches the saddle he must drop out of the circle. At the end of five minutes of strenuous pulling and bucking the team with the most players in the game is declared the winner.

Refreshments—Barbecue sandwiches, coffee, and ice cream cones will make an attractive and appropriate menu for your rodeo party.

A SLUM PARTY

Invitation—

> Dress in your rough clothes,
> Look kinda tough;
> Come to our Slum Party,
> But don't get rough.

The invitation might be decorated with the picture of a slum denizen.

Everyone is urged to come in appropriate costume.

Decorations—Boxes and nail-kegs for chairs; goods boxes for tables; candles stuck in bottles and lanterns furnish the only light.

Entertainment— (a) Begin the program by having everyone join in singing songs like "Sidewalks of New York," "Sweet Rosie O'Grady," and "My Wild Irish Rose." (b) Games. Tables arranged for chess, checkers, dominoes, logomachy, anagrams, and other table games. Have groups progress so that each person gets to play several different games. Bean bag and baseball boards, Japanola (c) Special musical numbers. A male quartet that sings "I've Been Workin' on the Railroad," "Sweet Adeline," and "Ain't Gonna Work No More."

> The poor man rides the street-car,
> The rich man rides a train,
> The hobo walks the railroad track
> But he gets there just the same!

> CHORUS:

> O, I ain't gonna work no more, no more,
> I ain't gonna work no more.
> I worked last night and the night before.
> But I ain't gonna work no more.

A duet sung by a boy and a girl. At the close of the duet someone rises from one of the tables and shoots both of them with a cap pistol.

Refreshments—Waiters, wearing white aprons, serve the crowd with hot-dog sandwiches and "pop."

BIG EXCURSION

The following clever announcement of a staff party for Boston Avenue Church, Tulsa, Oklahoma, could be easily adapted for use by either churches or clubs:

MEET US AT THE TRAIN

TUESDAY EVENING

8 P.M.

BOSTON AVENUE STATION

Everything free.—Round trip ticket, red cap service, Pullman, dining-car service, and accident insurance. Physicians will not be provided but if you have the "grip" the Baggage Master will check it. Get your sleep before hand as the Pullman cannot be used for "sleepers" on this train.

BE SURE TO COME AND BRING ALL THE FOLKS

(WIVES—HUSBANDS—SWEETHEARTS—KIDS)

NO PARROTS OR DOGS ALLOWED

Make your reservation by Friday noon at the "station." Phone 2-1217 or 3-9562.

"Excursion Train" will leave the "sheds" promptly at 8 o'clock Tuesday, May 12, Boston Avenue Standard Time.

This contract validated by,

BARBARA HARRINGTON

General Passenger Agent

GOOD FOR

ONE FIRST CLASS PASSAGE

ON

BOSTON AVENUE METHODIST UNLIMITED

LET'S GET ACQUAINTED RAILWAY

F & H LINES

FUN AND HILARITY

Subject to following conditions:

(1) This railway acts as the medium for your Good Fellowship Trip and expects you to be responsible for your own Good Time.

(2) This ticket is not transferable, but the spirit of the excursion is and should be taken advantage of at every opportunity.

(3) This ticket is void if you bring DULL CARE OR OLD MAN GROUCH with you.

(4) No Sleeper accommodations provided except for passengers from Cradle Roll Curve.

(5) No stops made at Backsliders Swamp and no passengers taken on at Kickersville.

(6) This ticket is not transferable, reversible, or salable. It must be signed by the person to whom it is assigned.

GENERAL SUPERINTENDENT

GENERAL PASSENGER AGENT

FROM
DONTNOEM STATION
TO
INTRODUCTION

(a) Require every person to get the signatures of at least 20 persons.
(b) Play some good mixing game.

FROM
INTRODUCTION
TO
CONVERSATION

Suggest topics for conversation.

FROM
CONVERSATION
TO
UNDERSTANDING

A chance to present matters of interest to members.

FROM
UNDERSTANDING
TO
CO-OPERATION

Some lively games.

FROM
CO-OPERATION
TO
BIGGER & BETTER THINGS

Refreshments.

RETURN TRIP VIA UNOEMNOW

_____

Name

_____

Position in Church School

_____   _____

Car No.   Seat No.

A SCAVENGER PARTY

This party was used successfully by one group. Meeting at the home of the recreation leader, where there was equipment for a campfire and plenty of yard space, the group was assigned to cars, about six in each one, and given a list of objects to be obtained from any place possible within a given time (one hour). When the time was up each group was to be at the starting point to display its booty. The group having the largest collection of the articles exactly as listed below, won a bag of candy.

Two ivy leaves, one celluloid collar, any live animal except dogs or insects, a punched railroad ticket, a corncob pipe that had been used, funniest thing you can find, an American flag, a raw carrot, a raw peanut, day before yesterday's paper, a chicken feather, old-fashioned nightshirt, three hairs from a horse's tail, a black silk stocking, worn overshoe, three smooth white stones, harmonica, a horseshoe, four needles threaded with red silk, white aster.

The scavengering was followed by a weiner and marshmallow roast around the campfire, and campfire gossip consisted mostly of how a nightshirt, the hairs from the horse's tail, and many other things were obtained. For the funniest thing, one of the girls brought a bottle of carefully preserved tonsils.

—MARY HUBBARD, Orlando, Florida

A KODAK PARTY

Look pleasant please, and come around,
For a Kodak Party has hit this town.

This party ought to follow a Kodak hike or a camera hunt. The pictures should be mounted and put on display or slides should be made so the pictures can be thrown on a screen.

Baby pictures.—The committee should gather baby pictures of many of those who are to attend the social, number them, and put them on display. Guests are given paper and pencils and asked to guess "Who's Who in Babyland." At the expiration of a given time the committee should announce the correct list. Players check upon their own lists.

Snapshots.—As each guest arrives he is taken to the photographer for a snapshot. The photographer takes his place behind the hood, the victim takes his pose in a chair, which is charged with electricity. As soon as he sits down the current is turned on and forthwith he arises.

Spirit pictures.—All guests are taken into a darkroom where they are told some spirit pictures are to be taken. Over in one corner of the room a light is flashed showing a ghost in pose. The light plays on the figure for just a moment and is then turned off. Again it flashes and a skeleton is seen standing there. The third time it flashes the head of a young girl appears apparently severed from the body and pinned to a white sheet by the hair. Beneath her head are splotches of what seems to be blood.

The skeleton and ghost should appear before a black background. The former is made by sewing to ordinary black cloth white cloth cut to represent a skeleton's frame.

The girl's head is stuck through a slit in a sheet. Her face is whitened to give it a ghastly appearance. The hair is drawn up and pinned to the sheet. Red ink is daubed below the slit in the sheet.

Spoon photography.—Two confederates are needed for this stunt. One of them goes out of the room. The other one remains and with a silver spoon professes to take the picture of some player in the circle. He does this by simply holding the spoon in front of that player's face. The player who went out of the room is called back and, after looking intently into the spoon, tells what player's picture was taken. The point is that he has a secret agreement with his confederate that he is always to take the picture of the person who speaks last before he leaves the room. Or it may be the person to the right of the talker, or some other signal that will easily designate the proper person, such as a secret confederate who assumes the identical position of the person whose picture has been taken.

Retouching.—Each person is provided with a paper spoon. On tables are crayons or water colors, pencils, crepe paper, and paste. Players make "Kodak Kuties," using red crayon or paint for the cheeks and lips, the pencil to mark the features, and the crepe paper for the dress. These "Kuties" may be used as souvenirs of the occasion.

Load the kodak.—Divide the crowd into two groups. Have each side represented by three players. The first one runs to a designated point and deposits a Kodak. He returns and touches off his next teammate. That player runs to the same point carrying a roll of films. On his return he touches off the third player who rushes forward, loads the Kodak, gets it ready for picture Number One, and returns to the starting point with it.

"Look pleasant, please"—Three to six players represent each side. They line up facing the crowd. While the leader counts ten slowly all players must hold a smiling expression. Immediately "ten" is counted the smile must fade out and a serious expression must take its place. This too is held until ten is counted by the leader. This is continued for three full turns. Whenever a player fails in his effort to immediately change his expression and hold it, he must drop out. The crowd may do its best to make a player laugh when he ought to appear glum. At the end of the three rounds the side with the largest number of players left standing is declared winner. When no players are left standing, one champion for each side may be selected to fight it out.

Focus.—Make a bean-bag board with a hole in it just big enough for the bean bag to go through. Line up both sides and allow each player one throw. One point is scored each time the bean bag goes through the hole. If desired, a board with three to five holes in it may be used, in which case the player ought to get as many throws as there are holes. It may be required that each time the bean bag must go through a different hole in order to count. Time will be saved by having bean bags for each side.

Mounting.—Line up five to ten players for each side. A small penny match box top is provided each side. The head player fits the match box on his nose. At the signal to start he must transfer it to the nose of the next player without using his hands. Thus it goes from nose to nose until the end of the line is reached. If the box falls the player whose turn it is must pick it up.

Framing.—Make a ring-toss board which you can hang on the wall. A board twelve by eighteen inches will do. Insert in the board five small screw-hooks, such as are used for curtains. Some fruit-jar rings complete your equipment. The center peg counts ten points. The four corner pegs each count five points.

Players stand at a distance of six feet and try to land the rings on the hooks.

For a large crowd each player should be given just one toss. Ordinarily, each contestant would be given five chances.

Silhouettes.—Stretch a sheet across the platform. Select players from each side to do some shadow posing behind the sheet. Judges should decide which side offers the best pictures. Short movies in shadow pictures may be offered instead of still pictures. Leaders may be appointed before the night of the party to work up suitable shadow-picture stunts. Costumes and paraphernalia that will likely be useful to the performers should be at their disposal. All lights should be off except the one back of the curtain. Performers stand between the light and the curtain.

Developing.—Players are furnished with paper and pencils. Each player draws a short line, curved, straight, crooked, or wiggly. He then passes his paper to the player to his right. This player must use the line in drawing something. It might be advisable to label each finished creation so others will be able to tell what it is.

Stunt.—*"The Photographer"*—Scene: A photographer's studio. Characters: Photographer, farmer, old maid, flapper, jelly-bean, newly weds, take-off on pastor and other notables. Properties: A tripod, small box, large black cloth, toy balloon, pin.

Various characters enter, pose for pictures. The last person should represent some prominent member of the group. When the photographer attempts to take this picture there is an explosion, in which the tripod is upset and confusion reigns. The photographer shouts "You've busted my camera!" Curtain.

The explosion may be obtained by the photographer bursting a toy balloon under the cloth covering. Or a paper sack may be bursted off stage.

Slides.—Slides may be made from the films of some of the best pictures and the program may conclude by showing these on the screen.

Enlarging.—The chairman may now announce, "We are going to give everyone a chance to do some enlarging now." That's the signal for the serving of refreshments.

There is probably too much material here for one evening's program. Select what you can use best in your group.

This party was written for "Journal Parties," and is reprinted by

AN INDOOR BEACH PARTY

Remember the "old swimming-hole" days when some playmate's upraised two fingers meant "the gang" was going swimming? Gee! Wasn't it thrilling? Well, whether it's the "old swimming hole" or the beach, there's an irresistible attraction about the water for most all of us. That suggests the idea that maybe an Indoor Beach Party would please the young folks immensely.

Posters may be used to advertise the party. One of them could bear the slogan: "Get in the Swim at the Indoor Beach Party." Another may play up this jingle:

> "Mother dear, may I go to swim?"
> "Yes, my darling daughter;
> Attend the Indoor Beach Party,
> And don't go near the water."

Appropriate pictures could be clipped from magazines to adorn these posters.

The decorations may be elaborate or not, as your time, money, ingenuity, and hard sense direct. The imagination of the guests will supply many details that are missing. You should have two or more beaches, depending on the size of your crowd. Say you have four—Atlantic City, Palm Beach, Ocean Grove, and Tybee. (Names of beaches of local interest may be substituted for any of these.) Atlantic City would occupy one corner of the room. When you think of Atlantic City you think of the "board walk." So by a stretch of the imagination you suggest this beach by improvising a board walk in front of it. Bright-colored bathing suits could adorn the wall to give it a bit of color. Palm Beach is easy if you can borrow a couple of palms. In a pinch palm-leaf fans could be used. Imitation oranges could be made out of crepe paper and tied to twigs adorned with artificial leaves perhaps. These could decorate the wall in the Palm Beach corner. The Ocean Grove corner could have a background of shrubbery. Heavily leaved branches of trees matted against the wall might give the desired effect. Or if a dark blue curtain drop of some sort could be secured for a background, some one could add to the effect by pinning a white paper sailboat on the sea of blue. Tybee, a beach near Savannah, could have numerous "B's" of varied brilliant hues strung across the front of its corner.

It might be of advantage to appoint a live leader for each beach before the night of the party. As the guests arrive they are assigned to one of the four groups. Different sorts of contests are now introduced. Each group, of course, should have its yells and songs.

The contests are as follows:

Board-walk race.—Two boys and one girl from each group. Boys walk or run, as decided, the length of the room and back, riding the girl between them on a piece of board about thirty inches long. Award points for first, second, and third places. This race could be run, all boys or all girls, in which case the runners would form a seat for the rider with their hands.

Swimming race.—One boy representing each beach. Each contestant would have before him a deep piepan filled nearly to the brim with water. At the bottom of the pan would rest four or five lozenges. These he must get out with his mouth. His hands must be folded behind his back so there will be no temptation to use them.

High dive.—One girl from each beach. Each is provided with a pitcher of water. On the floor at her feet is an empty tumbler. This must be filled at least two-thirds full from an erect standing position. Accuracy and not speed is the test here. The one who spills the least water on the floor is declared winner. Should there be a tie in the minds of the judges, then the matter of time consumed may be taken into account.

Life-saving feat.—One boy and one girl from each beach. The boy stands at a distance of five paces from the girl. She is supplied with ten "Life-Saver" mints. These she tosses to him one at a time. He endeavors to catch them with his mouth. The boy who catches the most in this manner wins for his group.

A clam dig.—One girl from each beach. A box of sand will be necessary. Hide ten peanuts in the sand for each contestant. Give each girl a spoon and a bowl. At the signal to go they run across the room to the sand pile, dig out their peanuts, put them in the bowl, and return.

Rowing race.—Five girls from each beach. Must stand in single file, close together, each girl grasping the forearms of the player in front of her by extending her arms on either side of that player. When the players have gotten in position, the signal to start the race is given, and they walk to a given point and back, working their arms like pistons all the way. The first team to cross the line wins.

Sailboat race.—Stretch as many strings across the room as you have contestants. On each string place a paper cornucopia. The contestant is to blow this "boat" from one end of the string to the other.

A scull (skull) race.—Each group is to work on the following contest as a group, turning in one paper each (the answers must be words beginning with "Sea" or "Se"):

(1) A sea that is insurgent. Sedition.
(2) A sea that is very old. Senility.
(3) A sea that denotes orderly succession. Series.
(4) A sea that is quiet. Sedate.
(5) A sea that entices to evil. Seductive.
(6) A sea that is choice. Select.
(7) A sea that follows as a result of something that has gone before. Sequence.
(8) A sea that is placid. Serene.
(9) A sea that is harsh. Severe.
(10) A sea that they say few women can keep. Secret.
(11) A sea that shuts itself apart. Seclusion.
(12) A sea that separates. Secession.
(13) A sea that adds flavor. Season.
(14) A sea whose schooldays are comparatively short. Senior.
(15) A sea that is safe. Secure.

Refreshments—Sandwiches (sand witches) and hot chocolate.

PANIC PARTY

Time—8 until 10
Place—Private home
Dress—The most disreputable looking rags that one can find.
Theme—Hard times . . . . everything is old and worn out.
Registration—Upon entering everyone must register at an improvised Employment Agency, giving name (this serves as the guest list for the paper), former position, and position now desired. These are read aloud as one of the amusements of the evening and are usually very funny.

Panic parade.—Immediately the "Panic Parade" starts. They march past appointed judges to the tune of "That's where my money goes." The King and Queen of Panic are chosen and escorted to their thrones which are soap boxes. Then the crowns are presented. These crowns are made of brown paper bags and are labeled King and Queen, in order. Then loving cups are presented to them and a bouquet to the Queen. The loving cups are aluminum pitchers and the flowers a bunch of wilted celery tied with long streamers and a huge bow. The "subjects" call for a speech and the said rulers must comply.

Stunts.—The next event is the punchboard of stunts. Everyone must punch and do the stunt appointed him. Or write out about a dozen stunts to be performed. Select a dozen individuals and have them draw for stunts to be performed. These individuals are given a few moments to get ready, and then they present their stunts.

Oratorial contest.—The "oratorial contest" of "twenty words—no more—no less" is next. One at a time they ascend the soap-box stage and speak on "Unemployment." The judges select the winning speaker and he is presented with a prize. In this case we have a gorgeous can of "Pork and Beans" to satisfy the said speaker until the next panic in which he might orate again on the same subject.

Charades.—Charades, gossip, and other well known games were played once through and after that, singing around the piano was enjoyed by all.

Bread line.—A "Bread Line" was formed and led to the "Relief Station." These were marked with posters and signs, where the table had a tablecloth of old newspapers. The punch was in a wash tub. (In the winter coffee served from aluminum pots would be ideal.) This was served in tin cups, and doughnuts from dime pie-pans.

After this a tin cup was passed around for contributions to defray expenses of the party.

Everyone enjoyed this party because it was unique and full of surprises. If the recreation leader can keep the plans secret it can be a success any time of the year.   —ELEY TAYLOR

A BACKWARD PARTY

1. Dress backward.
2. Greeting on arrival—"Goodbye," "Goodnight."
3. Refreshments.
4. Spelling bee. Words spelled backward.
5. Backward begging. Each girl is supplied with a stick of candy. Each boy must ask for it without directly doing so. Veiled and backward hints ought to do the work.

6. Backward race for girls. Walk backward to a given point.

7. Backward race for boys. On all fours and stiff-legged, contestants must back up to a given point.

8. Backward charades. Groups alternate in presenting charades of words containing the syllable "back" or "bac"—bacteria, baccalaureate, backfire, background, backset, backfield, quarterback, halfback, fullback, horseback, tobacco, backing, come-back, backboard.

9. Backward games. Play some familiar games with players being required to move backward—Going to Jerusalem, fruit basket, drop the handkerchief, for instance.

10. Sing greeting songs like "It's a good time to get acquainted" and "We're here for fun right from the start."

11. Say "Howdy" instead of "Goodnight" and back out.

A DATE SOCIAL

The date social idea lends itself to endless variations. Folk games may be played, or skill games, or there may be singing, musical numbers, dramatic skits, or a combination of all of these.

Each guest is given a card on which the days of the week are written. Guests proceed to make dates for each day of the week, writing the name of the partner opposite the proper day. No person is allowed to date any other person for more than one day in the week. When all of the dating has been completed guests hunt their partners for Monday and the program begins.

A sample program of activities follows: *MONDAY*—Squat; *TUESDAY*—Anagrams; *WEDNESDAY*—"Bug"; *THURSDAY*—Roselil; *FRIDAY*—"Sourwood Mountain"; *SATURDAY*—"Goodnight, Ladies"; *SUNDAY*—Community Sing and Refreshments.

A FINE ARTS FESTIVAL

Invitation—

"Art needs no spur beyond itself,"
So said Victor Hugo;
Here's hoping you will need no spur
To make you want to go
To the Fine Arts Festival.

This program will furnish an evening of worth-while entertainment, but it will require work. Plan carefully and thoroughly. Make it one of the most beautiful and elaborate things you have ever done.

Costumes and decorations—Guests may be asked to come representing some character or title in one of the four arts. The following are some suggestions: "The Village Blacksmith," "Robin Hood," "Romeo and Juliet, Mephisto (*Faust*), French peasants (from Millet's *The Angelus*), "The Mikado," "The Spirit of '76," "Macbeth."

Decorate the room with harps, flowers, tapestry, pictures, and wisteria bowers. Borrow, if possible, from local people some valuable paintings.

Four heralds will preside over the program of the evening, which is to be divided into four parts. These heralds may be dressed in symbolic costume, each representing one of the arts and presiding in turn.

"Music" wears a long, flowing robe, trimmed with harps and notes of the scale. She wears a head band of gold, with harp stick-up in front.

"Literature" has a dress covered with magazine covers and book jackets, or the conventional cap and gown.

"Drama" has a Shakespearean costume with long cape, or dress decorated in the typical false-face, symbolic of the drama.

"Art" wears an artist's smock.

The program—Each herald introduces his part of the program. Make such selections from the suggested program as are practical for your group.

Music—

> " 'Music hath charms to soothe the savage breast,'
> To woo the gentle maid, and set the heart at rest,
> Beloved by all, it holdeth full sway
> Throughout all the world, so hear it today."

Violin solo: "Ave Maria," by Schubert.

Vocal solo: "The Last Rose of Summer," "The Old Refrain," "Calm as the Night."

Vocal quartet: "Bendemeer's Stream."

Negro Spirituals: "Ain't Gwine to Study War no More," "Swing Low, Sweet Chariot," "Goin' Home," by Dvorak.

Literature—

> " 'The pen is mightier than the sword,'
> It sways the hearts of men;
> So here's to writer, philosopher, bard,
> Well skilled in use of pen."

A brief, interesting review of some good book.

Reading: "Trees," by Joyce Kilmer; "Abou Ben Adhem," by Leigh Hunt; "The Vision of Sir Launfal," by James Russell Lowell.

Drama—
           " 'All the world's a stage,'
             So in the drama of life,
             May each play well his part,
             And shrink not from the strife."

A reading rehearsal of a portion of some good drama, such as, "An Enemy of the People" by Ibsen.

Art—
           "The Master artist paints the hills
             In gorgeous hues and tints;
             Man at his best but copies him
             In feeble daubs and prints."

Plan an art exhibit. Arrange a display of some of the great pictures.

A brief closing worship service could be built around some picture such as Holman Hunt's, "I Am the Light of the World."

A MISSIONARY TRAVELOGUE PARTY

Passports were passed out to members a week ahead of time. On them were humorous pictures of the individuals to whom they were issued. Magazines and newspapers will furnish these pictures if you do not have a good cartoonist to do them.

Those invited were told to board the good ship (*name of club or group*) at an appointed place to make a cruise to many foreign ports, with interesting stop-overs.

The skipper—The president of the group may be the Captain or Skipper for the cruise. He should dress for the part.

Aboard ship—While aboard ship the group engages in a few games, listens to a good story about fishes, the sea, or travel, and then some music, perhaps.

Landing—The boat finally lands and the group goes down the "gang plank" into the social hall. Here they are divided into four groups, with guides for each group.

Foreign lands—Each group entered, respectively, (1) Africa, (2) Brazil, (3) Korea, (4) Japan. These were represented by certain rooms around the social hall. Curios, pictures, books, posters, and facts about these countries were on display. Someone may tell briefly about the customs, habits, and life of the people. At the sound of the gong the travelers move on to the next country. Finally, when each country had been visited the gong sounded to call all the tourists aboard, when refreshments were served.

A SONG-LAND PARTY

Guests are asked to come in costumes representing certain songs. Some suggestions are as follows: "My Bonnie" (girl in Scotch costume), "Robin Adair," "Marchita" (Spanish or Mexican girl), "Tramp, Tramp, Tramp" (three boys dressed as hobos), "The Last Rose of Summer," "Old Black Joe," "Spanish Cavalier," "Solomon Levi," "When You Wore a Tulip" (girl wearing a tulip and boy wearing a large red rose).

Grand march.—A grand march is staged and the judges decide on the three cleverest and most appropriate costumes.

Mixed quartets or octets.—Write words to the chorus of each of several well-known songs. Cut into slips of one or two lines each, and pass out or allow guests to draw. Slips are numbered so as to make it possible for people holding lines from the same song to get together. All the "ones," for instance, make the song "Love's Old Sweet Song" (chorus only). Each quartet, or octet, must sing its own song. Then all may be asked to sing at the same time.

Singing game.—Use any good musical game—"Roman Soldiers," "Brown-eyed Mary," "Bingo," or "Oh, Susanna."

A musical romance.—In the following romance the leader will read the story, with the pianist filling in the necessary pauses with a few bars of the song for which the story calls. The players may be required to write down in order the names of the songs played or they may be divided into two or more sides and the first side to call the correct song title scores a point. When a mistake is made a point is subtracted.

Song-land love.—In the *Long, Long Ago* when grandfather sang to grandmother *Just a Song at Twilight,* Dan Cupid was the same troublesome little fellow that he is today. *Sylvia* had been singing softly to herself *Just a Wearying for You.*

She called him *My Hero* because he was so brave. They had met *On the Road to Mandalay* and again down *By the Waters of Minnetonka.*

At Dawning. That's pretty early, of course, but Harry Lauder says *"Oh, It's Nice to Get Up in the Mornin' ";* so why bring that up?

"Who is Sylvia?" he had asked and *Robin Adair* had told him.

So he said, *"Let Me Call You Sweetheart."*

"That would be *A Merry Life*," she replied. "Get your car and you can *Carry Me Back to Old Virginny* for our honeymoon."

"*I Love You Truly*," he whispered softly. "We will *Let the Rest of the World Go By* while we live in my *Home on the Range*."

They were married down in *Dixie* more than a year ago, and a little stranger came into their home. Of course, he is not a stranger now, and when he decides to *Serenade* in the middle of the night papa gets up and sings *Lullaby and Good-night*. Now when he goes away on business he says, "*How Can I Leave Thee?*" And so they lived happily ever after in their *Little Grey Home in the West*.

The song shop.—Customers come seeking certain kinds of songs. The proprietor calls on certain ones to play and sing the songs wanted. In this way a clever and interesting musical program can be presented. The stage or platform should be set to represent a song shop.

1. The first customer says she wants a love song that has something about the sun coming up. She doesn't quite remember the title. This leaves the way open to introduce "At Dawning," "Sunrise and You," and "The World Is Waiting for the Sunrise." The customer decides that the last one is the song she is seeking. Different persons can sing these songs, if desired. One verse is enough.

2. The second customer wants to buy a good song for group singing. This opens the way for some singing by everyone. Stunt songs, ballads, or folk songs can be used.

3. The third customer wants some Spanish music. "La Paloma" or "La Golondrina" can be rendered.

4. The fourth may want something funny. Some humorous song or songs can be offered. "Lilac Tree," "April Fool," "Foolish Questions," "I Doubt It," and songs of that type would be in order.

5. The next customer wants some good love songs. "The Kashmiri Song" and "Jeanie With the Light Brown Hair" would answer.

6. The last customer wants a good-night song. "Good-night, Beloved," Pinsuti, by a quartet. Or the whole group could be asked to sing "Good-night, Ladies."

A DUMB PROGRAM FOR BRIGHT FOLKS

You are to say no word and utter no sound under any circumstances during this program. If you do, even if it's merely to whisper to someone, put a cross on the back of this sheet each time you make *any* noise. Be seated and *watch* the director after you read the first paragraph below. You are on your honor to read only one paragraph each time, between the director's instructions, when told to do so on this sheet. *Make no sound.* Now read Paragraph 1 and watch director.

1. Director will clap hands once. Immediately you will face your neighbor and grin as widely as possible until the director claps twice. Then you will scowl your worst until the director claps thrice. Then face front and resume your normal expression. If you laughed put down a cross for each chuckle. Now read next paragraph.

2. When director claps once, start to answer the following questions, putting the answer opposite each question. If you can't get first ones go on down until you strike some you can answer and then come back to first ones. *Be snappy* as the time limit will be short, but please don't write any answers until director signals as stated at first of this paragraph. When time is up the director will whistle and you are to stop work on these questions immediately, then read Paragraph 3, and watch director for signal.

My flower garden (Answer with names of flowers) —

(1) I planted a dairy product and a dish with a handle. What came up? Buttercup.

(2) Planted a happy facial expression and a tool used by a woodman? Smilax.

(3) Planted a lot of sheep? Phlox.

(4) Planted a dude and a ferocious animal? Dandelion.

(5) Planted a man's name and a feather? Jonquil.

(6) Planted a bird and something worn by cavalrymen? Larkspur.

(7) Planted a part of a train and all the people of America? Carnation.

(8) Planted a domestic animal and a pillow cover? Cowslip.

(9) Planted a country in Asia and a prominent New York family? China Aster.

(10) Planted some fragrant letters? Sweet Peas.

(11) Planted a falsehood and a door fastening? Lilac.

(12) Planted a Christmas decoration and a bird of prey? Hollyhock.

(13) Planted a rabbit and something that rings? Harebell.

(14) Planted a god of music and a groan? Pansy.

(15) Planted a couple of articles and a portion of the face? Tulips.

(16) Planted a liquid and a favorite Easter decoration? Water Lily.

(17) Planted an optic and a part of an arm? Iris.

3. Director will clap hands four times. Arise and sing first verse of "America" without making a sound, but saying words with lips. *Put your heart into it and sing with much feeling.* At finish you will resume your seat. Don't forget the crosses if you made any sounds! Now read paragraph four after you have acted paragraph three.

4. Answer questions below when director claps. Each division of the question between the commas indicates a syllable in the word that will answer that question; for instance, the first answer has three syllables. Don't start working on these until the director gives the signal, please. And don't forget the crosses if you do any whispering!

(1) The end of an arm, an optic, abbreviation for title of an army commander, equal a word meaning "hinder." What is it? Handicap.

(2) The atmosphere, a small valley, equal to the name of a breed of dog? Airdale.

(3) A mute, an attractive girl, equal a person not so attractive? Dumbbell.

(4) To approach, the word by which some children call their fathers, the abbreviation for New York, equal one or more guests? Company.

(5) Opposite of bitter, an examination, equal to what every real fellow says of his girl? Sweetest.

When you have answered all questions signal the director by raising your hand, and he will advise you what to do next. But don't make any noise!

Each question answered counted one point; each cross on back of sheet meant to subtract one-half point; 20 minutes allowed for first list of questions; four for last. Those finishing first were directed in a whisper to list all the slang words or phrases they knew on back of the sheet; as a penalty for their knowledge of slang a point was subtracted from their total score for every four slang words or expressions they had written! The prize was a small skull cap bearing the word "Champion." —LESLIE H. BROWDER

A HIGHBROW PARTY

What's your I Q? Do you rate
Genius or moron's fate?
No matter which, bet your pate,
You'll enjoy helping celebrate.

1. *An intelligence test*—As guests arrive they are put through this test. Use some of the brain teasers in the Chapter I, Home Fun, and

"A College Banquet" in Chapter IV, Fun with Banquets. Have ready cardboard "medals," two or three inches in diameter. These contain ridiculously low I Q ratings, a few high ratings, and a few normal ones. Guests are required to wear their ratings for the full evening. A large chart interprets ratings—I Q, 20-50, imbeciles; I Q, 50-70, feeble-mindedness; I Q, 70-85, very dull; I Q, 95-105, average intelligence; I Q, 120-145, superior intelligence; I Q, 180, genius.

2. *Modern art*—Ultra-modern—"A Storm" (splotches of paint), "Dawn of an Idea" (streaks of paint), "Freedom" (semicircular streaks of paint), "Peace" (straight lines).

The following exhibit may be used:

Art exhibit—Placards advertise "The Greatest Collection of Masterpieces in the World," "The Wonder Art Display," "Better than the Museum." The guests are given typewritten lists of art achievements on exhibit. Every exhibit is numbered. The guests must put the numbers beside the proper exhibits on the list. Following are suggestions for this "marvelous" display:

(1) Washington Crossing the Delaware. McNally. (2) The Peace Makers. Modiste. (3) A Perfect Match. S. Ulphur. (4) A Pair of Slippers. Yeswehaveno. (5) Rock of Ages. Lull Abi. (6) The Kids at Rest. G. Ote. (7) Old Ironsides. Bach Acher. (8) Voices of the Night. Thomas Katt. (9) Mustered In and Mustered Out. Keene. (10) A Young Man's Fear. Disputed. (11) My Own, My Native Land. O. U. Mudd. (12) Something to Adore. McKannick. (13) Can't Be Beat. A. Murphy. (14) One Hundred Years Ago. Al Manac. (15) Cause of the Revolution. Ole Bull. (16) Mementos of the Great. Cole. (17) "Samson Was Great! Lo, a Greater!" N. Meig. (18) Bonaparte Crossing the Rhine. Waterloo. (19) Horse Fair of '96. G. Raine. (20) The Skipper's House. A. Swiss. (21) The Four Seasons. Cooke. (22) The Great Commentator. P. Tater. (23) Crossing the Styx. Sharp. (24) Bridal Scene. Driver. (25) The Sun That Never Sets. Shanghai. (26) A Tearful Subject. Gardner. (27) A Swimming Match. I. Float. (28) The Tutor. U. Flatte. (29) Ruins of China. D. Washer. (30) A Drive Through the Wood. Carpenter. (31) Spring, Beautiful Spring. A. Wyer. (32) A Wayworn Traveler. P. Destrain. (33) An American Ruler. A. Foote. (34) A Marble Group. U. Shoot. (35) The Black Frier. Skill Lette. (36) The Tutor. U. Blow. (37) The Lamplighter. A. Taper. (38) Maid of Orleans. A. Sweet. (39) The Holy See. Alpha Bette. (40) We Part to Meet Again. A. Shearer. (41) De-

parted Days. Cal N. Derr. (42) Common Sense. Copper. (43) The Greatest Bet Ever Made. Abie See.

Articles— (1) Word "Washington" across map of State of Delaware. (2) Scissors. (3) Match. (4) Banana peels. (5) Cradle. (6) Kid gloves. (7) Flat iron. (8) Pictures of two cats. (9) Mustard inside and outside a cup. (10) Mitten. (11) Bit of earth. (12) Door-knob or lock and key. (13) An Irish potato. (14) 1840 (or date 100 years ago). (15) Tacks on tea. (16) Cinder. (17) Nutmeg grater. (18) Broken bone over rind. (19) Corn. (20) Piece of cheese. (21) Salt, pepper, vinegar, mustard. (22) Irish potato. (23) Sticks crossed. (24) Bridle. (25) Picture of rooster. (26) An onion. (27) Match afloat. (28) Toy horn. (29) Broken china. (30) Piece of wood with nail driven through it. (31) A spring. (32) Worn out shoe. (33) A foot rule. (34) A few marbles. (35) Black frying pan. (36) A horn. (37) A match. (38) Molasses candy. (39) Letter *C*, full of holes. (40) Scissors. (41) Last year's calendar. (42) A few pennies. (43) Letters of the alphabet.

3. *Modeling—*Clay or piece of chewing gum. Each person portrays his suppressed desire in a bit of sculpture.

4. *Illustrated lecture on child complexes—*Introduce Professor I. M. Dippy as a celebrated psychoanalyst, who can tell from a baby's picture what sort of person it will become. Baby pictures have been sketched or traced from magazine pictures. Or better get baby pictures of members of the group. Throw these on the screen by means of a reflectoscope. Or the pictures may be drawn with crayon on large sheets of paper. A good cartoonist would be invaluable here. The professor psychoanalyzes each baby. The babies hold tin horns, rolling pins, rattles, money, soap, and such things. The psychoanalyst interprets these to mean musical ability, domesticity, and the like. The fun comes from the fact that each picture is labeled with the name of some person present. A clever "psychoanalyst" can bring roars of laughter.

5. *Poetry and suppressed desires—*Each person is required to write a rhyme of not more than four lines about his suppressed desire. These are collected, shuffled, and players draw. They then read in turn. The group tries to guess who the writer is.

*Music memory test—*Piano, violin, or horn rendition of the following classical numbers, or portions of them: (1) Beethoven's "Moonlight Sonata"; (2) "Berceuse" from *Jocelyn*, Godard; (3) "Ave Maria," Schubert; (4) "Ave Maria," Gounod; (5) "Serenade," Schubert; (6) "La Donna e Mobile," from *Rigoletto*, Verde; (7) "Traumerei," Schumann; (8) "Lullaby," Brahms; (9) "Barcarolle" from *Tales of Hoffman,* Offenbach; (10) "Anvil Chorus" from *Il Trova-tore,* Verdi. When a number is finished the guests call the title and composer of the composition.

AN ARTISAN PARTY

The evening shift of laborers,
Dressed in overalls or smock,
On the evening of ————
At eight will punch the clock,
At our basement location,
In the south basement room,
Be on time and in your place,
Or "you're fired" will be your doom.

This party gives good opportunity for creative activity. It can be made a serious workshop party with the group making things for the gameroom or for Christmas. For instance, it could be a party in which the guests assume responsibility for outfitting the club gameroom, making shufflleboard courts, various game boards, and the like. Or gifts could be made for Christmas—block printing for Christmas cards, spatter printing, leather work, weaving, metal work, puppet making. There should be a variety of possible activities so each person could find something he would enjoy doing.

Or the party could be made purely a fun-making occasion. In this case, the following outline will indicate the possibilities:

Costumes—Overalls, smocks.

Perhaps some penalty could be required of those who fail to come in costume. Or a committee may be charged with the responsibility of dressing guests appropriately. Or those who fail to come properly garbed may be required to wash the dishes or serve.

Organization—Divide the crowd into four or more groups, each group to represent some labor union. Each group or union works on its job for about thirty minutes, and then displays its handicraft. If desired, a shorter time may be allowed, and the groups can rotate from one union to another, until they have had opportunities in several of the activities. In small groups the entire group each time would work at an activity and then take up another activity.

Four suggested unions for an evening of fun would be as follows:

1. *Carpenters' Union*—(*a*) Build a house out of cigar boxes or other material provided. (*b*) Make walks out of sand. (*c*) "Plant" trees, shrubbery, and grass. The miniature house would be put on display. Each person should have a hand in the finished product.

Materials—Cigar boxes, crates, scrap wood, brads, hammers, cellophane, sand, branches of trees, shrubs, flowers.

2. *Dress Makers' Union*—Make costumes out of crepe paper or newspapers.

Materials—Patterns, paper, scissors, pins.

3. *Molders' Union*—Use chewing gum on a card or modeling clay to fashion animals or people.

Materials—Chewing gum, cards, modeling clay, some knives.

4. *Newspaper Union*—Divide the group into sections—society news, sports, general news, advertising section, etc. Each section writes up part of the newspaper. The completed paper is read to the entire crowd.

Materials—Pencils, paper.

Other possible unions are the following:

5. *The Painters' Union*—Girls make up boys, using the usual cosmetics.

Materials—Rouge, lipsticks, eyebrow pencils.

6. *Cartoonists' Union*—Each person would draw a likeness of someone in the room.

Materials—Paper, pencils, colored crayons.

7. *Milliners' Union*—Make hats out of crepe paper to be worn by living models.

Refreshments—(1) Put lunch in buckets or boxes. (2) Wrap lunch in newspaper. (3) Have brick layers' union serve brick ice cream and layer cake.

A CLOWN PARTY

Just wrap up your gloom,
And throw it away,
Just sound sorrow's doom
And let us be gay;
A clown for a night,
A clown for a day,
A clown party, right!
It's coming our way.
Clown Party, Friday, 8:30 P.M.
COME IN COSTUME

Costume—Urge that everyone come in clown costume. Be prepared for those who fail to dress appropriately for the occasion. Have on hand clown hats and collars made of crepe paper, together with a supply of the reddest of red rouge. The committee should see that everyone is decorated in approved clown style, the face included.

Decorations—The room should be given a festive appearance with a plentiful supply of toy balloons, Japanese lanterns, serpentine and crepe paper streamers.

Four clowns in a row.—Give to each person present a sheet of paper marked off in twenty squares. In each square they must get someone present to write his or her name. That will mean that each person will get the signatures of twenty people, one for each square. Provide each player with fifteen or twenty small stickers. These may be obtained at any stationer's. If the committee could get white stickers and paint clown faces on them it would help.

Each one is now asked to write his own name on a small piece of paper the committee provides. These are placed in a hat. The leader draws the names from the hat, one at a time. As the name is called, the person bearing it responds with a lusty "Here," and raises the right hand. This serves as an introduction to the group. Each person who has that name on his paper puts a sticker in the square where it appears.

When any player gets four stickers in a row, either across, down, or diagonally, he shouts: "Four clowns in a row!" Some suitable award may be made to that player. Let him read the names of the four.

Surprise stunts.—(1) *William Tell Stunt.* The leader announces that two of the clowns are going to put on a "William Tell" archery exhibition. The two clowns appear. An apple is placed on the head of one of them with careful preciseness. "William" with his bow and arrow, then paces off about ten steps, and turns to aim. As soon as his back is turned the other clown removes the apple from his head and takes a healthy bite out of it. "William" patiently returns and places the apple back in position. Again he paces off, and again a bite is taken out of the apple. With a shrug of the shoulders "William" proceeds to again place it in position. This time the other clown removes the apple and hastily finishes it. He then rushes from the room with "William Tell" in pursuit. No words are spoken, the whole stunt being done in pantomime.

(2) *A Clown Duel.* Two clowns appear with stick swords. In the end of each stick is a pin. The swordsmen have several toy inflated balloons under their clown suits. Rapier thrusts are made which puncture the balloons one by one. When all the balloons are punctured, the clowns shake hands, embrace, and retire arm in arm. Much of the fun of the stunt will depend on the manner in which the clowns pantomime a burlesque duel.

Rollicking clown games.— (1) *Did You Ever See a Circus Clown?* This is an adaptation of the old game, "Did you ever see a lassie?" Instead of lassie substitute circus clown. On the second line the clown in the center of the circle goes through some clownish action. On the third and fourth lines everyone in the circle imitates that motion. The clown who is "It" then selects some one from the circle to take his place and the game continues.

> "Did you ever see a circus clown, a circus clown, a circus clown,
> Did you ever see a circus clown do this way and that?
> Do this way, and that way, and this way, and that way?
> Did you ever see a circus clown do this way and that?

(2) *Laugh, Clown, Laugh.* Divide the crowd into two groups. Line them up facing one another. The leader stands between the two groups and tosses up a cardboard clown. This clown is painted blue on one side, and is white on the other. When the blue side turns up, everyone in the blue group must laugh, while all in the other group assume solemn countenances, not even so much as smiling. When the white side turns up the action is reversed. Points are counted as follows: For each one who doesn't respond immediately with a hearty laugh when the clown indicates the group should laugh, one point for the other group; for each one who does not appear solemn when that's required, one point for the opposing group. Play rapidly for about ten turns.

(3) *Clown Chariot Race.* Ten contestants for each group. A chair to each group. Contestants stand in single file, the two lines being eight to ten feet apart. The head player in each line has a chair. At the signal he passes it over his head to the player back of him. That player passes it back overhead to the next, and so on to the end of the line. Immediately after the last player gets it he sits down, and the next two players just ahead of him drop back and carry him, chair and all, to the head of the line. The two carriers then hurry back to position at the foot of the line. The player who has just been carried to the head of the line starts the chair down the line again. So on it goes until every player has been carried in the chariot to the head of the line, and the original head player is back in position.

(4) *Clown Hat Pitch.* Two clown hats are placed on the floor, open side up. Each person is given three peanuts. From a distance of about fifteen feet, each in turn tries to toss his peanuts into the hat that belongs to his side. After all players have thrown, the peanuts in each hat are counted, and the side with the largest total wins.

(5) *Clown Volleyball.* A row of chairs across the room serves in the place of a net. Alternate them, first facing one way, and then the other. Two toy balloons, of different colors, are used as volley-balls. Both sides serve at the same time, thus putting both balls in play. The ball does not have to go over the net on the serve. The other players may help knock it across. A player may hit a ball twice or more in succession. The ball is in play as long as it is up in the air. It is out of play when it hits a chair or the floor. A side scores when a ball is grounded in the territory of its opponents. When one of the balls is grounded, the sides continue to play on the other ball. No serve is allowed until both balls have been grounded.

Any number of players may play.

A player fouls when he reaches over the "net" into his opponents' territory.

Fifteen points constitute a game.

(6) *Circus Ring Relay.* Ten to fifteen players on a side. Two circles. Players are seated in chairs facing out from center. One player on each side is designated as starting player. At the signal to go this player gets up and walks rapidly around his circle of chairs, seating himself in his own chair when he has completed his round. The player to his right gets up from his chair as soon as the leader passes him, and the player to that player's right follows the second, so that, by the time the starter is back to his chair more than half the circle of players is in motion. The side wins that first has all its players walk around the circle and get seated.

Next, try this with the players running.

For the third time try it with all the players carrying their chairs with them around the circle. All players must be seated before they can be considered as finished.

Clown capers.—End the evening's program with several short stunts. Place a time limit of five minutes on the stunts.

Refreshments—Serve clown cakes and pink lemonade. If a clown cake mold cannot be obtained, round cookies could be given clown faces by using white and red icing.

A GOLF TOURNEY

A Progressive Party—On arrival guests apply for tourney entrance score cards. These cards are arranged in groups. One group is numbered *One,* another *Two,* and so on up to *Nine.* Each group goes to the "Hole" indicated by the number on the score card. "Holes" are designated by large numbers on standards.

Ten minutes is allowed at each game. The starter's whistle indicates starting and quitting time for each round. Groups progress to the next hole after each game.

Hole 1—Driving. Tin can sunk in ground. Golf or broom stick. Golf ball, or large marble. Each person has turn to see how many strokes are necessary to put the ball in the hole.

Hole 2—Bean-bag Board. How many shots necessary to toss bean bag through each hole on the board.

Hole 3—Ring Toss. Chair legs. How many tosses to get ring on each of the four legs of the chair. A limit of ten chances to a person is allowed.

Hole 4—Table Games—peggity, crokinole, pick-up sticks.

Hole 5—Professor Quiz. Hand to all persons mimeographed tests with a row of horizontal numbers: 1, 2, 3, 4, 5, 6, 7, 8. The tests follow:

(1) If Florida is not South of the Mason and Dixon line, write the letter *R* under 4. If it is, write the letter *B* under 1.

(2) If a rabbit runs faster than a man, write the letter *N* under 6. If not, write *T* under 7.

(3) If iron cannot be made to float on water, write the letter *X* under 8. If it can, write *O* under 2.

(4) If frigidaires were invented in 1865, write the letter *Y* under 5. If not, write *O* under 4.

(5) If an airplane "takes off" against the wind, write the letter *G* under 5. If not, write *S* under 1.

(6) If cactus does not grow in Arizona, write *I* under 3. If it does, write *A* under 7.

(7) If blackberries are red when they are green, write the letter *L* under 3. If not, write *F* under 8.

(8) If "The Great Divide" is in the Catskill Mountains, write the letter *K* under 2. If it is in the Rocky Mountains, make a period under 8.

(9) If you like lots of what this spells, help yourself. If not, the same to you!

Insist that players work rapidly at these tests. After five or six minutes call time and read the correct answers. The game may be played by simply reading each test in turn and pausing a moment for players to write their answers on cards or sheets of paper they have before them.

Hole 6—Dart Board. Concentric circles, 1 at center, 2 next, then 3 outside circle. Missing the board counts 5. Small score wins.

Hole 7—Nail tin can or cup to stick, two feet long. Attach golf ball or rubber ball to string and tie to end of stick. Players toss ball into air and attempt to catch it in cup. Ten trials. Each miss scores one point.

Hole 8—Funnel catch. Players bounce a tennis ball against the wall and catch it on the rebound in a funnel. Ten trials. One point for each miss.

Hole 9—Players bounce rubber ball into a wastebasket or into a bucket. Five trials. One point for each miss.

A "caddie" is in charge of each "Hole." He gives instructions, keeps game moving, helps players with their scores, and sees that they move on to the next game as soon as the whistle blows. The smallest score wins.

—From suggestion by ALBERTA BAINES

SEVEN-DAY CHAUTAUQUA PARTY

A Seven-day Chautauqua makes a good "get-acquainted" party. Each person gets a new partner for each "day." Program cards may be used. Delegates sign up partners for each "day" of the week, no one being allowed to have the same partner a second time. For each "day" some entertainment is provided.

Monday — Community Sing; *Tuesday* — Grand Mixer (play "Daisy"); *Wednesday*—Hi-Klass Drammer (some stunt); *Thursday*—Concert (special musical numbers); *Friday*—Lecture (stunts—one does talking, another makes the gestures); *Saturday*—Debate (humorous); *Sunday*—Closing worship service (quartet, hymn, prayer, "Taps"). Infinite variety can be worked out in this type of program. Other features may be substituted for those listed: "The Sunflower Minstrel" (*Phunology*), "Grand Opery" take-off, sleight-of-hand, a short drama, etc.

A FETE OF MONTHS

Decorations—Twelve tables or booths representing the twelve months. Attendants in appropriate costume at each booth.

January—Cotton-batting icicles. Falling snow represented by small balls of cotton tied to thread. Table with snow mound. Sled on top. Figure of Father Time, if obtainable. Attendants dressed in costumes trimmed with imitation ermine. Cover cotton batting with mosquito netting and stripe with black muresco paint. Tiny calendar souvenirs.

February—Valentine decorations. White dresses trimmed in hearts. Candy heart souvenirs.

March—Green decorations. Girl and boy in Irish costumes. Shamrock souvenirs.

April—Rainbow colors. These colors fall about a large umbrella. Tiny umbrella souvenirs.

May—Maypole. Pink and green streamers from chandelier. Ends held by tiny dolls at farther edges of table. Attendants in party frocks and wearing garlands about their heads. Daisies for souvenirs.

June—A rose booth or table with bride as central figure. Large white wedding bell. Attendants in graduation dress. Roses for souvenirs.

July—Patriotic decorations. Uncle Sam and Miss Columbia in charge. Tiny flags for souvenirs.

August—Beach scene. Some sand, a large mirror or piece of glass, some tiny celluloid bathing dolls, etc. An amusing effect can be gotten by cutting some of the dolls in two. Some of them will appear then to be diving, and other to be standing waist deep in the water. Attendants in tennis costumes. Miniature fans for souvenirs.

September—Toy cardboard schoolhouse. Make miniature walk and fence. Tiny dolls carrying imitation books and slates. Attendants, school "marms" of the old type, or boy and girl dressed as school children. Souvenirs—small books, each with one conundrum inside.

October—Halloween. Attendants in Halloween costumes. Souvenirs—black-cat cut-outs.

November—Fall leaves, turkey, horn-of-plenty. Or a football field with dolls or peanuts representing the players. Attendants, football player in uniform, and girl rooter wearing sweater and carrying pennant. Small footballs or turkeys for souvenirs.

December—Green and red color scheme. Christmas bells, holly, etc. Santa Claus in charge. Christmas bells for souvenirs.

PROGRAM

Guests visit booths.

Guests mix around exchanging conundrums.

Have some features for each month.

January—All sing "Jingle Bells," or play "Jingle Bells." On the first part of the verse partners, who stand in circle, man to lady's left, skating position, slide four steps forward and in toward center and then four forward and out from center. On second part of the verse all join hands and take sliding steps to the left in one big circle. On the chorus partners face. Clap hands three times. Clap three times. Clap five times. Swing partner around once. Repeat. End by man taking lady back of him for a new partner.

February—Male quartet, "Love's Old Sweet Song."

March—An Irish song, or Irish joke-telling contest.

April—Solo, "April Fool," or April Fool quartet singing "Steal Away" or "The Lost Sheep." In the former the members of the quartet sneak out one after another after being announced to sing. In the latter they go through the motions of getting ready to sing, and then all give a plaintive "Baa-aaaa!"

May—Violin solo, "Spring Song." Play "All Around the Maypole" (Chapter XIII, Fun with Musical Games).

June—Riley's "Knee-deep in June," "The Hiking Romance" (Chapter IX, Fun with Mental Games).

July—All sing "America the Beautiful," Patriotic Tableau.

August—Everyone sing, "In the Good Old Summertime."

September—Spelling Bee.

October—Ghost story with lights low. Fortunetelling booths. Palmists. Invisible ink fortunes, etc.

November—Reading, "When the Frost Is on the Pumpkin," Riley. Table Football (page 62.)

December—All sing "Silent Night." Christmas tableau or play.

A LEMON SQUEEZE PARTY

Here is a novel party that will be lots of fun. Each guest is asked to bring one lemon. Extra lemons may be furnished by the committee for guests who forget. Ice, water, and sugar are provided. The group is organized so that everyone has some duty to perform. Some cut open the lemons, some squeeze them, others make the lemonade, while others prepare the ice. Two persons are assigned the job of putting the seeds in a jar after counting them. They keep their count secret. Others still are assigned to the job of cleaning all utensils used and of getting the glasses ready for serving.

Lemon bowling—Set up tenpins, duck pins, or pop bottles. Bowl with a lemon.

Lemons and lemonade—Guests pair off and hand one another "lemons," that is, remarks that are not so complimentary. The one to whom the remark is made is to come back with some interpretation that turns the point of uncomplimentary remark, thus making "lemonade" out of the "lemon." For instance, one young man says to his partner, "What a long nose you have." Immediately the young lady responds, "Oh, thank you. I appreciate the compliment. Long noses are signs of intelligence. But my, what big feet you have!" "Yeah! I have a pretty good understanding. All well-built structures have good strong foundations." After each exchange of "lemons" players seek new partners.

Lemon seed guessing—Have each guest except the ones who have counted them to write his guess as to the total number of seeds on a slip of paper with his name. Have the guest who guesses nearest to the correct number perform some stunt for the crowd.

Refreshments—Serve lemonade and cake.

COUNTY FAIR

Decorations—Booths, stands, side shows.

Advertising—Posters, handbills, phone committee to divide names of organization and friends and call.

HANDBILL

(NAME OF ORGANIZATION) COUNTY FAIR

EXHIBITS   SHOWS

FUN AND FROLIC

DON'T MISS THIS GRAND EVENT

COME YOURSELF

AND BRING YOUR FRIENDS

(DATE)

7:30 P.M.

---

1. *Exhibits*—Handcrafts, hobbies, sewing, needlework, old relics. Put someone in charge of this feature and work it up diligently. It can be made a feature of the evening's program.

2. *Dolls of many lands*—Together with a Doll Show in which children of the organization will be invited to put their dolls on display.

3. *Baby show*—Certain men and women of the organization made up to represent babies. Each baby will have a nurse or a fond mamma to stand proudly by while the nurse and doctor put the troupe through several tests. Weight Test—Piece of elastic placed under arms. Nurse pulls up and announces some ridiculous weight. Bawling Contest. Beauty Contest. Call someone up to pin the blue ribbon on the winner. Just as he stoops to perform this service all of the babies shout at him, "Da-da."

4. *Side shows—*

(1) Dancing Midgets. See "Great Grinmore Circus."

(2) Fat Lady. A fat man dressed up as the fat lady. Extra pillows, etc.

(3) Strong Man. Performs amazing feats with fake weights.

(4) Fortunetelling. Fortunes with lemon juice. Palmists. Book—*Fun with Fortune Telling*, Mrs. G. L. Henson, Eldridge Entertainment House, Franklin, Ohio.

(5) Concert—Some good musical numbers by members of a quartet. "Come to the Fair" would be an appropriate number for everyone to sing.

(6) "Swing Your Partner." A folk game demonstration in costume, if possible. A team of sixteen. "Weave the Wadmal," "Holdir-i-dia," "Jennie Cracks Corn," or any of the games in Chapter XIII, Fun with Musical Games, would do.

(7) Puppet Show. Marionettes.

(8) Athletic Carnival. Stunt events such as "Three-Legged Race" for men, "Nail Driving Contest" for women, "Cracker Eating Relay," etc.

(9) Strolling Musicians. Musicians (accordion, violin, harmonica, guitar—solo or group), who stroll along the midway playing at intervals, will add a lot to the enjoyment of the occasion.

Personnel—Besides performers, general committee (to make plans and keep things moving). The chairman could act as a general director.

Barkers—For side shows and other events. They would help move the crowd from place to place to see various features of the fair.

Announcer—For stage show. The Concert, Puppet Show, and "Swing Your Partner" events would be performed as part of the stage show.

Chairmen of various features—Exhibits, side shows, stage show.

CHAPTER XVII
FUN WITH SEASONAL PARTIES

FUN WITH SEASONAL PARTIES

JANUARY

A "BIG TIME" PARTY

START the New Year right by sending out invitations for a "Big Time Party." These invitations may be cut from cardboard in the form of little grandfather clocks. On the long narrow part of the clock write the verse:

> Eve had no wrist watch
> No watch had Adam;
> Didn't have a timepiece
> Nobody had 'em.
> Nobody had a Big Time
> You'd better believe
> But you can have a Big Time
> On New Year's Eve.
> If you come to our Big Time Party.

When the crowd arrives have them sing this song:

> Tune—*"SMILES"*
> **There are Times that make us happy
> There are Times that make us blue
> There are Times that make us snappy
> As Alarm Clocks mostly always do.
> There is Standard Time, and Daylight Saving
> And, Old Timers, there's another, too
> Do we hear you asking what that time is?
> It's the Big Time we're giving you.**

Timely tots.—To insure party getting off with a hilarious start, dress each guest regardless of sex, size, or protest in a baby bonnet made of crepe paper. Prepare the bonnets beforehand and let several help you put them on.

What time is it?—Now give each man a chance to get in the spotlight and show off his new bonnet. Have each one draw from a hat a slip of paper on which is written a word or phrase having to do with time. No two slips should be alike. The girls draw duplicate slips from another hat. Each man in turn steps forward and demonstrates his particular kind of time. His only chance of getting out

(617)

of the spotlight is to act so effectively that the girl with a similar time slip will recognize him as her partner. No one is allowed to show his card. Cards might have times that are easily acted such as—killing time, marking time, beating time, losing time, timely, timepiece.

Time to sing.—An impromptu singing contest is always fun. Select two leaders and let each in turn choose singers for his choir. Now tell them that you have given them five minutes to compose a suitable song, and then require them to sing the song with actions. One group originated the following:

> I wish I wuz a little clock that didn't have to chime,
>> Or strike, or nothin' all day long, but just be tellin' time.
> I'd run on slow time all my life, I'd never run on quick,
>> And if they didn't wind me up, I wouldn't even tick.

Big time riddles.—Each couple is supplied with one pencil and one sealed envelope containing a set of riddles. On the word "Go" all the envelopes are torn open and the riddles attacked, each couple working together:

1. What makes a striking present? Clock.
2. When is a clock dangerous? When it strikes one.
3. What day of the year is a command to go forward? March 4th.
4. When the clock strikes 13 what time is it? Time to have it repaired.
5. What is always behind time? Back of the clock.
6. I have hands but not fingers, no bed but lots of ticks. What am I? Clock.
7. What is time and yet a fruit? Date.
8. What does the proverb say time is? Money.

Set alarm clock and when time is up have it ring.

On plate with refreshments have a date to which is fastened with a toothpick a card or piece of paper bearing this query: "Will you make a date to meet with the (name of organization) Sunday evening at 6:30?"

March time.—Do some grand march figures. End by having them march around the room singing to the tune of "Jingle Bells":

> Wishing you, wishing you, wishing you, old dear,
>> The wish that you are wishing me—"A Happy New Year."
> Wishing you, wishing you, all along the line,
>> Lots of fun for everyone in Nineteen —————.

—ESTHER AHART

A PROPHECY PARTY

The announcement carries the suggestion that "we can help you see your finish at the Prophecy Party."

Prophecy exchanges.—Girls in outer circle, boys in inner. They march opposite directions to music. When the music stops players stop and face partners. Each one is given from fifteen to thirty seconds to tell the partner's future. In an exchange of experiences during the evening it may be discovered that some of the boys have told each girl the same story.

Prophecy web.—A web is made out of strings at one side of the room. Each player takes hold of a loose end and begins to unravel the web. He must follow his string to the end. It is tangled with other strings on the floor. The player must stop to untangle the strings. This makes the game a good mixer for other players are doing the same thing. The strings are wound around chair and table legs. They may go upstairs and downstairs. When the player comes to the end there is some sort of prophecy attached to the end of the string. This may be accompanied by some sort of trinket such as a toy hammer, or a horn, or a doll. With the hammer there would be a prophecy after this fashion:

A builder you will be
That's very plain to see.

With the horn there would be something like this:

In the orchestra you will play
At least it surely seems that way.

Ten years from now.—One player goes around and whispers to each person the name of a place. Another gives them the name of a person. A third person tells them something they will be doing ten years from now. Each player must then repeat what has been told him. It would be quite interesting to know that Miss Smith will be in Honolulu with Shirley Temple picking blackberries ten years from now.

Fortunetelling.—At this point introduce numerous fortunetelling devices. (1) Gypsy fortuneteller booth with palmist. (2) Invisible ink fortunes. Write with lemon juice and hold over lighted candle to bring out the message. (3) Candle fortune. Place six candles in a row. Label each with some prophecy of what is in store—misfortune, fortune, trip, a new friend, happiness, loss. The player is blindfolded, turned around, and given a chance to blow. The candle blown out indicates some future fate.   (4) Fortunes from cards.

Gypsy camp.—Decorate the platform with some branches of trees. Improvise a campfire. The gypsies enter single file humming "The Long, Long Trail." They group about the campfire and sing "Santa Lucia," "Gypsy Love Song," or "Marianina." Special musical numbers can be introduced, as desired—a violin solo, a vocal solo, duet, or quartet, a harmonica solo, etc.

An old gypsy fortuneteller makes her appearance, coming to the center where a tripod holds a kettle. From this kettle she draws prophecies for certain people in the group. This offers an opportunity to inject a lot of fun into the program. Some clever prophecies should be prepared.

As a closing number the entire group sings "Juanita." See "Gypsy Camp" musical program in Chapter XII, Fun with Music.

A FATHER TIME PARTY

Father Time would like to meet you,
In fact, we would like to greet you
At a party giv'n in honor of his name.
There'll be fun a bubbling over,
And you sure will be in clover;
If you miss it you will have yourself to blame.

Father Time.—Give two minutes for players to see how many words they can make out of the letters in "Father Time."

Baby days.—(1) Song, "When Mary Was a Baby."   (2) Milk drinking contest. Baby milk bottles.   (3) Stunt—Baby Show. Dress some of the crowd in baby caps. Have a committee decide on the prize baby, after putting them through various tests, such as weighing, using a piece of elastic under the shoulders, a bawling contest, tests for beauty, with the judges offering humorous criticisms.

Childhood days.—Play some children's game such as "London Bridge" or "Did You Ever See a Lassie?"

School days.—(1) Everyone sing "School Days."   (2) A spelling bee or living alphabet. (3) Anagrams.

Sweetheart days.—(1) Drawing for partners. A paper clockface is suspended in the doorway or from a chandelier. Through a hole in the center of it strings drop down on either side. Boys take hold of the strings on one side and the girls take hold of strings on the other side. At a signal from the leader they pull the strings and partners will be found holding the same string. (2) Partners work together on a time contest. The answers are parts of a watch, or timepiece.

(a) Used before. Second hand.
(b) Seen at the circus. Ring.
(c) Fifteenth wedding anniversary. Crystal.
(d) What we give new members. H-our Hand.
(e) Women love them for adornment. Jewels.
(f) A watering place. Springs.
(g) The palmist looks them over. Hands.
(h) Read by the secretary. Minutes.
(i) Supports a flower. Stem.
(j) Sometimes, they claim, it stops a clock. Face.
(k) A tight-rope walker is good at it; and a bicycle. Balance Wheel.

(3) Play any partner game such as "Roselil," "Bingo," "Brown-eyed Mary," or "Ace of Diamonds."

Parent days.— (1) Doll dressing contest. Each boy is required to dress a clothespin, paper spoon, or peanut as a doll. Crepe paper, paste, and crayons are furnished. Each girl supervises the work of her partner. (2) Tableau and song, "Little Mother of Mine."

Granddad days.— (1) Rocking chair relay. The crowd is divided into two sides. From five to ten players are selected from each side. Each contestant must run in bent-over position, holding the right hand on the back, to a rocking chair at the other side of the room. Here he must sit down, rock back and forth ten times, return to the starting line, and touch off the next teammate. (2) Play some old-fashioned games like "Going to Jerusalem," "Jennie Cracks Corn," "Wink." (3) Sing "When You and I Were Young Maggie," "Silver Threads Among the Gold," "Spanish Cavalier," "Solomon Levi," and other good old songs of granddad's day. (4) Special musical number, quartet or trio: "My Grandfather's Clock."

A STORYTELLER'S CONVENTION

A Storyteller's Convention makes a most interesting evening of fun and fellowship for either a large or small group. In some cases it might be advisable to invite the entire church membership to attend.

An atmosphere of informality should characterize the occasion. Have a carefully planned program but make it easy for spontaneous contributions to be made to the fun of the evening.

All stories used should be fairly short.

See six or seven people who are good storytellers and get them lined up for your program. Try to get a variety of stories—a fairy story or two; a mystery or ghost story with lights low; a funny story; a stunt story; and some beautiful story for a climax. Or the program may build about some special types of stories—such as Negro Folk Tales, Stories of Other Lands, Stories of American Indians, etc. An International Story Evening makes an interesting possibility.

Special features could be introduced such as the dramatization of a fairy story like "Little Red Riding Hood" or "Goldilocks and the Three Bears." See the "Fairyland Party."

A typical program for a Storyteller's Convention would be as follows:

1. Jokes, by several.

2. A pointless story like "What, no soap!"

3. A fairy story.

4. An Uncle Remus Story, "Tar Baby.

5. A fairy story.

6. Dramatization—"The Truth about Sleeping Beauty."

7. A good ghost story.

8. A Chinese story—"The Bell Maker," from *Chinese Ginger*, by Miller.

9. "The Happy Prince," from *Works of Oscar Wilde.*

The following sources of stories would prove helpful: *Uncle Remus, His Songs and His Sayings,* Harris; *East of the Sun and West of the. Moon,* Kipling (some good animal stories) ; *The Best Known Works of Oscar Wilde* ("The Happy Prince" and "The Selfish Giant") ; *Joy from Japan,* Miller (some good Japanese folk stories) ; *Chinese Ginger,* Miller (some Chinese folk tales, among them "The Bell Maker") ; *Grimm's and Andersen's Fairy Tales; Indian Why Stories,* Linderman; *Far Peoples,* Phillips (contains some good folk tales of various nations) .

OPEN SESSION OF "THE ORDER OF MOURNFUL OLD MAIDS."

The girls of the organization met at the home of one of the members to make plans for a party to be given the boys. The idea occurred to us that Leap Year had passed and many of us were without husbands, and of course we would have to go for four years before we would have another chance. Therefore, we should be mournful. So all the girls wore black dresses. Two young married women in the group and the pastor's wife were requested to wear bright colored dresses. Everything with reference to the party must carry out the idea that we were in mourning—black and white decorations, broken hearts, etc.

The following invitation was mailed to each and every boy of the organization:

Mr. John Smith
of the Order of Single Blessedness
BROTHER:
We, the Order of Mournful Old Maids, auxiliary of (name of organization), pray for your presence at our open session to be held at the home of our beloved Mournful Old Maid Sister, 719 Pizer, Saturday night (date), at 8 o'clock.
May the Lord be kind to us by not only giving you the desire to come, but by helping us in making this be our last meeting.

Hopefully we are,
THE MOURNFUL OLD MAIDS

To the married men we changed the first to read "of the Order of Married Bliss," and the last paragraph, asked that they come in such a happy and jovial spirit that the eligibles would want to become one of their number.

The girls were requested to come at 7:30, but not to come with the boys. Different girls with cars went after all the girls in order to be sure to have them there before the boys started arriving at 8 o'clock.

Arrivals—As each boy arrived he was met at the door, his name taken, called to the girls, passed on, then admitted to the room.

The meeting begins—At 8:30 the President took her chair at a table with the Secretary and called the meeting to order. Sister Ruth took her place at the piano. Sister Wilda led the singing. When the Chairman tapped on the table with the gavel twice, all stood and sang the following song to the tune, "Sweet Adeline":

> Oh, for a man, at his shrine we bow,
> We want him so, to be our beau,
> A sweetheart too, but that won't do,
> The desire of our heart's a husband true.

The President tapped the table once and all were seated.

The Secretary then read the minutes of the last meeting.

Reports—Then different girls were called on to give reports of their success, or failure, in trying to get a husband. Of course several of them were told before so that they could be prepared to give interesting reports. They should use the names of boys present, but should not use the name of any boy they had ever gone with or had been asked to go with.

Reports were called for from standing committees. Two offered some plans that might be used in trying to capture a husband.

The Sick Committee reported that one of our members was ill and unable to be present, and found that she was suffering from a broken heart.

New committees were appointed.

Then at two taps of the gavel all stood and again sang our Old Maids' anthem. The formal business being completed the group prepared to play games.

Games—Progressive Old Maid was then played. Tally cards were distributed. These we made ourselves. We used the regular Old Maid Cards. For score pads we got some comic Old Maid Valentines. Two hands were played before progressing. The two who had not held the Old Maid Card were the ones to progress. Of course if the same one held it twice another game had to be played.

Prizes were given to the boy and girl who were Old Maid the least number of times—the boy was given a diamond wedding ring from Woolworth's and asked to please use it shortly. The girl was given a little boy-scout doll, and with it a notation, "Bring up a husband in the way he should go."

Hot tea, crackers, and cheese, and pineapple salad, were the refreshments served. The cheese was melted on the cracker and while hot the top cracker placed on it. Pineapple salad was fixed by placing a slice of pineapple on lettuce, salad dressing, and a cherry.

Minutes of the meeting—The Order of Mournful Old Maids, auxiliary of (name of organization), met in regular session at the home of our beloved Mournful Old Maid Sister, ——— ———, 1234 Ashland Street, December 3rd, with our beloved Mournful Old Maid Sister, ——— ———, President, in the chair.

The meeting was called to order by the singing of our Anthem after which the Secretary read the minutes of the previous meeting.

As this was the first meeting of Leap Year the President urged that we stick strictly to business and see if we could not formulate enough definite plans whereby we could each secure a husband before the close of the year. Many a meeting we have had, but never has there been a meeting where there was as much interest and enthusiasm shown as there was at this meeting.

The President asked for reports from standing committees.

Mournful Old Maid Sister ———— reported that they had worked out a letter for each old maid to send to at least ten eligibles. The letter follows:

My dear and most respectful Sir,
I send you this, your love to stir.

'Tis you I've chosen first of all,
On whom to make my Leap Year Call.

Your heart and hand I ask—ah! and not in jest,
And pray that you will grant me this fond request.

'Tis you I've picked out on a hunch,
To be my husband—my darling honey-bunch.

Now send be back without delay,
Your answer pray, let it be "Yea," not "Nay."

But if your hand does not incline,
In wedlock clasp to join with mine,

Then you must the Leap Year Law obey,
And to me $100 pay.

Besides, kind sir, a handsome dress,
I'll take much more but nothing less.

Now you might think this letter funny,
But I must have either man or money.

So send to me your quick reply,
And let me be your wife until I die.

Now if for me there is no hope,
Send me back four yards of rope.

With love and lots and lots of kisses,
From one who wants to be your Mrs.

This letter was received with much enthusiasm, all feeling sure that no man could resist such an appealing letter.

Mournful Old Maid Sister ———— ———— was then called to make a report. She first asked that the minutes of the December meeting be read, wherein each member gave her requirements for a husband. She then said that she felt we were holding our standards entirely too high. In fact, she didn't think we could hold to any standards whatsoever, for she had watched all the eligibles and even the married men, and she could not find where any of them in any way came up to the requirements we had made. She urged that we forget our requirements and take the poor dumb men as they were.

Old Maid Sister ——— ——— was then called for a report. She said she had often heard that the way to a man's heart was through his stomach. So she suggested that we invite the desired ones to dinner, fix the very best, with the hope that maybe that would bring results. She, for one, thought it would and intended to try it anyway. Some thought this a very good plan and others were afraid that it might prove tragic.

No other suggestions were made, so the President asked for a report of the Sick Committee. They reported no very serious illness with the exception of Dollye, whose heart was breaking because ——— ——— refused to marry her.

The President then called for a report from the Nominating Committee consisting of Beth, Summa, and Dickie. Beth reported that they had been very unsuccessful in trying to get members to run for office. Sister Louise had refused to run as she hoped that she would have some success before the close of the year. All members were so hopeful and anxious to change from "Miss" to "Mrs." that all refused to run. It looked very bad, having an organization without even a president, so good-hearted Mournful Old Maid Sister Allena said that if the whistles at midnight December 31st found her still a Miss she would accept the position. Mary said she would accept the position of Secretary-Treasurer under the same conditions.

Our meeting place for February could not be decided on for all felt that with the helpful suggestions that had been made that they couldn't help but win a wedding ring if carefully and prayerfully worked out.

The meeting was then opened to a report from different members as to their luck during the past month. The reports were varied and interesting, but very mournful indeed.

We all stood and closed our meeting by again singing our Anthem.

—FLORENCE TERRY.

OLD TIMERS' PARTY

Get out the old-fashioned costumes. Drag out the old clothes. Buy some make-up, and dress up as an "old-timer." Borrow some old spectacle frames with the glasses knocked out. Powder your hair or make you a wig. Let's all be "old timers" for a night!

Here is a chance to allow play to the dramatic make-believe urge that's in most of us; to play some of the old games; to act and talk like real "old-timers."

Fun with make-up—It would be more economical if some make-up were provided by the group putting on the party. All the participants could chip in a few cents apiece and buy ample material for everyone—cold cream, old-age grease paint; brown, gray, white, and crimson liners; white powder. You can gray or whiten your hair by powdering with cornstarch. Crepe hair and spirit gum could be used for beards, sideburns, and mustaches. Ordinary hemp rope can sometimes be used for making beards. Teeth can be blacked out with black tooth enamel, or black wax, or even carbon paper. Ask local drugstore or write to M. Stein Cosmetic Company, New York City, for free pamphlet, or to Max Factor, Los Angeles, California, for a series of pamphlets on make-up.

How to make-up—Provide a make-up room and let part of the fun at the party be that of making-up. Encourage the young people to use their own creative ability in their characterizations.

Program—

1. Everybody make-up.

2. Grand Mixer. Guests will mill around getting acquainted with one another, each person to introduce himself under some assumed name. Some such get-acquainted game as Human Bingo could be used, if desired. Or a concentric circle mixer could be used, the players marching to music.

3. Play old-time games such as Charades, Wink, Going to Jerusalem, It, Old Dan Tucker, and Brown-eyed Mary.

4. Sing old-time songs. "Silver Threads Among the Gold," "When You and I Were Young, Maggie," "Annie Laurie," "Old Folks at Home," "Sweet Alice, Ben Bolt," "Old Black Joe," "Love's Old Sweet Song," "Juanita," "In the Gloaming," and other old favorites will never lose their appeal.

5. Refreshments. Lemonade and cake is an old stand-by that always pleases.

FEBRUARY

OUTLINE OF A SWEETHEART LAND PARTY

This party is presided over by the King and Queen of Hearts. A throne should be arranged at one end of the room. The Court Jester makes announcements and assists the King and Queen in directing the party. Decorate the room with hearts.

Invitation—

> In time of spring, the poets sing,
> That love must have its way;
> The same they say of Valentine's Day
> All Sweetheart Land will play

Program—

(1) Gathering of the Knights and Ladies of Sweetheart Land. A grand march—twos, double circle, men inside. Stop. Partners face, holding hands. Drop hands and step back two paces. Head couple holds hands, skating position, and skips inside the lane around circle and back to position. As soon as they pass the next couple, that couple falls in behind them. So it goes until all couples have made the circle. Then boy and girl of the head couple stand facing one another in the lane between the two lines of players, hands outstretched and clasped. In this position they do a side-skip around the circle and back to position. Each couple follows suit as soon as the couple next to them passes. When a couple completes the circle it must quickly drop back into position so the other couples coming can pass through.

(2) Entertainment fit for a king. Some dramatic stunt. See Chapter XIV, Fun with Dramatics.

(3) Music to a king's taste. Singing by the entire group of some such songs as "Love's Old Sweet Song," "In the Gloaming," "Annie Laurie."

Special musical numbers could be introduced as desired—solos, duets, quartets—vocal and instrumental.

(4) The knights and ladies play. Any lively games would fit in here.

(5) The Court of Love. Certain of the group should be brought

before the Court on charges of having broken the laws of Sweetheart Land. The King should render decisions on cases that concern the Ladies of the Court, while the Queen rules on cases involving the Knights. Have this part of the program well planned. Pick out well-known "Knights" and "Ladies" for trial. The prosecutor should name the culprit and the offense. The defendant has opportunity to answer the charges if he desires. A Knight may be charged with breaking the law of the Kingdom by remaining impervious, hard-hearted, and unmoved by the charms of the Ladies of the Kingdom. Or he may be charged with scattering his affections broadcast and refusing to concentrate, thus breaking one of the oldest laws of the Kingdom. A Lady of the Court may be charged with cold-blooded heart-breaking.

(6) "Goodnight Ladies." See Chapter XIII, Fun with Musical Games.

CUPID'S CARNIVAL OF HEARTS

February offers a number of themes around which to build a social. Yet it seems there is something about Valentine's Day that holds more interest for young people than any other. Hence the thought, why not have a "Carnival of Hearts"?

The Invitation—

Come one, come all, to the prodigiously produced and picturesquely presented

CARNIVAL OF HEARTS

Friday, February 14th
at 8 o'clock

———

Innumerable Innovations

———

Notable Novelties

———

A Full Evening of Fun,
Frolic and Fellowship

———

Come—bring your friends.

*Decorations—*Booths, which can easily be made by fastening thin posts to the front legs of tables, are placed around the room and appropriately decorated with hearts, cupids, and red and white crepe paper.

Each guest on arrival is given a small tally card on which to make the scores. The person having the highest score at the end of the evening is given some suitable prize.

Burr mixer.—As an opening "mixer" have small hearts (about two inches in diameter) prepared with various words printed on them, such as Love, Honeymoon, Courtship, Marriage, Acquaintanceship, etc. On the back of each heart fasten a half a burr or sticker with glue. These are stuck on the backs of the girls' dresses. The object of the game is for the girl to find out, by asking questions, what word is on her card. When she succeeds she may remove the heart and stick it on the back of someone else, who must repeat the process.

When a sufficient number of people have arrived the booths can be opened for business. The person in charge of each booth should have a good line of ballyhoo such as is exhibited by those conducting carnival or side-show attractions.

Booth 1—Heart darts.—Cut out of red cardboard a heart about two feet in diameter. On this mount small white hearts about four inches in diameter—these have the following inscriptions: (1) Single Blessedness; (2) Acquaintanceship; (3) Friendship; (4) Love; (5) Courtship; (6) Proposal; (7) Engagement; (8) Marriage.

In the center mount a black heart with the word "Refusal." The board is erected about seven feet back of the stand. Darts can be secured at most toy stores or can be made of a cork, pin, and paper.

Each person is given eight darts and permitted to try making the round of hearts up to "Marriage" without hitting the black heart. If a person succeeds the first time he is given twenty-five points and continues to another booth. The one doing it after one retrial is awarded ten points and if a player succeeds after a third trial, five points are awarded. No person is allowed to try more than three times. As an additional prize at this and other booths small baby dolls—of the chocolate candy variety—can be given.

Booth 2—Fortunetelling booth.—A girl dressed in a costume to represent the Queen of Hearts is in charge of this booth and reveals the fortunes of the guests, especially as pertains to love, marriage, etc.

Booth 3—Wheel of fortune.—A wheel is made of composition board and marked off in twelve sections named "Journey," "Success," "True Love," "Health," "Happiness," "Early Marriage," "Wealth," etc. This is fastened on an upright post with an indicator at the top of the wheel. The wheel should have a small spool at the center and be mounted on a flat-headed nail. For the point scoring—those spinning the wheel and getting "Matrimonial Bliss" or "Wealth" get twenty-five points; those getting "True Love" or "Happiness," ten points; and "Success" or "Early Marriage," five points.

Booth 4—Heart toss.—Make five heart-shaped rings of heavy wire. The hearts should be about four inches in diameter. Three upright sticks about a half-inch in diameter and six inches high are fastened on a board which is placed about six feet back of the position in which the player stands. One of the sticks is labeled "Happiness," another, "Wealth," and a third "Disappointment." Those throwing three or more hearts over the sticks receive twenty-five points. Two ringers earn a score of ten points, and five points are given to anyone throwing one ring over the stick.

Booth 5—Cupid's shooting gallery.—Secure a toy bow and some arrows. They can be purchased at a 5- and 10-cent store or any toy store. Make a large heart of composition board and mark smaller ones on it similar to the rings on a target. Those hitting the center are given twenty-five points. The next circles count fifteen, ten, and five respectively.

Booth 6—Cupid's fish pond.—Get a number of small metal novelties, such as a thimble, a wedding ring, engagement ring, coin, horn, button, etc. These are wrapped in red paper and tied with string. Each contestant is allowed to fish for one article (using a stick and string with a bent pin for fishing). In addition to receiving the article indicating his fortune, he is given twenty-five points if he secures a wedding ring, ten points for an engagement ring, and five points if he gets a coin.

Refreshment booth.—This booth is closed until most of the evening's program has been completed. Heart-shaped cookies with red and white icing can be served with grape juice punch or "pink lemonade."

Merry-go-round.—This is played the same as "The Jolly Miller" except for the substitution of these words:

> "Oh, have you heard of Dan Cupid and his bag of quills,
> How he shoots them around just as he wills;
> One hand on the arrow and the other in the pack.
> The girls step forward and the boys step back."

Heart race.—Cut four red hearts out of heavy cardboard. These should be about fifteen inches in diameter. The group is divided into two equal teams for a relay race and each team is given two hearts. The contestants must step from one heart to the other in racing to a given point and back. Each member on the team finishing the relay first receives twenty-five points on their score card. The losers each receive ten points.

For the "Midway Attraction" or "Free Acts" divide the crowd into two or three groups and give them each ten minutes to prepare some stunt around the theme, "How a modern man and maid became engaged."

DAN CUPID'S HOSPITAL PARTY

Invitation—

Dr. Dan Cupid, M.D., is opening an office at _____

_____

Hours 8-10:30 P.M.   Date_____

Invitations are placed in capsules.

Reception room—A doctor and a nurse in charge examine guests as they enter. Each person is assigned to some ward in the hospital.

Wards—The following wards are provided:

Broken-hearted ....Accident Ward.
Aching hearts ....Operating Room.
Misplaced hearts ....Sanitarium.
Lost hearts ....Emergency Ward.
Tender hearts ....Children's Ward.

If there is a large crowd divide into five groups as indicated and start each group in its particular ward. They then progress to the other wards in order, until they have visited every ward.

Accident ward.—Give each person a large heart cut in many pieces. Paste, needle, thread, etc., are provided. The first person mending his heart will receive five points. Each other person finishing before the group has to move on will receive two points.

Operating ward.—Scissors and paper are given to each person. The one who cuts out the largest number of hearts (well shaped) in two minutes will receive five points. All players making at least ten hearts will receive two points.

Heart's ease sanitarium.—Put a jar or wastebasket on the floor. Players are given twenty-five cardboard hearts to toss at the jar. Score five points for the winner and two points for each person getting as many as five cards in the jar. Players stand, or sit, at a distance of five or six feet.

Emergency ward.—Have guests make as many words as possible out of the letters in the words, "Lost hearts." Five points to the winner and two points to each person making as many as ten words.

Children's ward.—Suspend from the chandelier three wire hearts covered with crepe paper. Above each is a jingle:

> 1. Blow your bubble right through here,
>   And you'll be married within the year.
>
> 2. To be engaged within the week,
>   Number Two is the one you seek.
>
> 3. An awful fate for Number Three,
>   A spinster or bachelor you will be.

Guests are provided with a bubble pipe, fan, and bubble solution. The bubble must be thrown off of the pipe and then blown through a heart by means of the fan. Ten chances are given a player to get a bubble through one of the hearts. Two points are allowed for success.

Convalescing ward.—All guests are now invited into the convalescing ward where progressive hearts are played, or folk games may be played.

Some simple prizes may be awarded to persons scoring the greatest number of points in the ward visitation. An award of candy hearts can be made to the group with the highest group score.

Refreshments—The doctor may prescribe lemonade and cake or fruit punch.

A VALENTINE PARTY

Decorations—Decorations will do much toward making your party a success. Use festoons of red and white crepe paper. Strings of small red hearts cut from kindergarten construction paper and festooned about the walls or hanging from chandeliers are very effective.

Invitations—On hearts (about four inches in diameter) cut from white cardboard write the following invitation:

> Merry hearts, Fairy hearts,
> Fun and frolic galore!

A Valentine Party we're having,
A hearty time in store.

Date _____Place _____Time _____

Wherever the word "heart" is used paste a tiny red heart.

Finding partners.—A mixer—As the guests enter, give each, alternately, either a small red or a small white heart. On the back of each
heart is written the name of a famous lover, the names of the men
going to the boys and the names of the women, to the girls. (Suggestions: Romeo and Juliet, Punch and Judy, Jack and Jill, The
Prince and Cinderella, Priscilla and John Alden, Hiawatha and Min-
nehaha, Napoleon and Josephine, Jacob and Rachel, Ruth and Boaz,
etc.) Of course, Romeo must find Juliet; Punch, Judy; and so on.
If the crowd is large, or merely to make things more complicated, let
there be a duplicate list of names on red and white hearts. Then
Romeo who wears a white heart must find the Juliet who wears a
white heart. Romeo who wears a red heart must find Juliet who
wears a red heart, etc. As soon as partners have been found, it is
time for—

A love letter.—The letters of the alphabet are written on small
white hearts. Each couple is given a large paper bag containing one
alphabet. At a given signal the bags are opened and each player
is allowed to draw two hearts at a time from the bag. The couple
who first succeeds in drawing out the letters, "L O V E," wins and
five points are scored for their group (Red or White). Then comes:

A honeymoon trip.—A large map of the world is fastened to the
wall. Each couple selects the country which they would like to
visit on their honeymoon. They write the name of the place
selected on tiny red hearts given them. They are blindfolded and
holding hands must try to pin their hearts on the map as near as
possible the place selected. The couple who pins the hearts closest
the proposed destination gains five points for their group.

Lost arrows.—Small red and white arrows are hidden about the
room. On each arrow is written one of the following words: Love,
Friendship, Acquaintance, Deceit, Jealousy. The red arrows must
duplicate exactly the white arrows. Captains are elected for each
group. At a given signal the hunt for lost arrows is started. Members of the "Red" group must collect only red arrows and members

of the "White" group must collect only white arrows. At the end of three minutes the hunt is stopped and captains collect and count their arrows. The arrows score as follows: For each arrow marked Love count five points; for Friendship three; Acquaintance one; for each marked Deceit substract five points; for Jealousy subtract three. The winning side is given ten points in the count of the evening.

Heart and dart contest.—Cut a large red heart from heavy cardboard. Within this heart cut out three small hearts, each a different size. Above the smallest heart opening mark "15," above the next larger "10," and above the largest "5." Suspend the large heart in a doorway. A dart is made of a red feather and a needle stuck in a large cork. Each contestant is allowed three throws at the heart. His score is added to his group's score and the winning group at the end of the contest is allowed ten points.

Making valentines.—This game is played like the old game of Happy Hunter. In the place of the Hunter there is a Valentine Maker. Chairs are arranged in a row one facing one way, the next the other. There are equally as many chairs as players, excepting the Valentine Maker. Each player is given the name of some material or tool used in valentine making. (Hearts, arrows, cupids, colored papers, scissors, paste, rhymes, crayons, etc.) There may be several with the same name. The Valentine Maker starts marching around the chairs calling, as he walks, for the materials he needs in making his valentine. As he calls their names the players must rise and follow him. When he has all he desires, the Valentine Maker calls, "Posted," and everyone makes a jump for a chair. The one left standing is now the Valentine Maker and continues the game.

Building a love nest.—This is a drawing relay race. The blackboard is divided into two equal spaces. One space is allotted the "Reds," and one the "Whites." The captain of each group should get his contestants in a line facing the space of the board allotted them. Each captain is told to draw within this second heart the outline of a house; the third, the chimney on the house; the fourth, the windows and door; the fifth, the sidewalks; the sixth, the flowers in the yard; etc., until each has a definite part assigned in building the love nest. A piece of chalk is given each captain, the signal given, and the fun begins. The group which first succeeds in completing a recognizable "Love Nest" is winner with five points to their credit. It would add to the interest to provide each side with colored crayons. If desired the winner may be decided on the basis of the most artistic creation.

Cupid's heart exchange.—Players sit in a circle. Each has the name of one of the four kinds of hearts—Merry Heart, Contented Heart, Happy Heart, Broken Heart. One player stands in the center and, as Cupid, does the bargaining. Pointing to a certain player in the circle, he says, "I wish your heart." This player asks, "What will you give in exchange, sir?" Cupid must answer one of the four kinds of hearts he has in Exchange. If the player accepts, he says, "I'll take it." Then he and the players bearing the name of the heart mentioned must change places. In the mixup the center man seeks to secure a chair. If, however, the player does not wish to accept the bargain, he says, "Wait until Leap Year!" In that case everyone must change places. Of course, whoever fails to secure a chair is Cupid and must start the bargaining again.

At the end of the games a total is made of the points gained in all contests and the winning group awarded a box of candy hearts, or allowed to be seated and be served refreshments by members of the losing group. Refreshments consist of vanilla ice cream with tiny red candy hearts sprinkled over the top, and heart-shaped cookies.

—CLYDE KENNEDY

A HISTORICAL PARTY

Historic characters—Each person should come dressed to represent some historical personage—George Washington, Napoleon, Diogenes, Solomon, Nero, Florence Nightingale, Frances Willard, Lincoln, Lee, Lafayette, Betsy Ross, and others. Authors, artists, musicians, and people of the present day of note may be represented.

Guests, on arrival, should be greeted by George and Martha Washington.

Decorations—The room may be decorated with flags of different countries, or materials significant of various countries may be used, such as tapestries, Navajo blankets, Japanese lanterns, and curios.

Songs.—Folk songs of different countries, national anthems, and songs of various periods in our own history may be sung. In *Ten Folk Songs and Ballads,* published by E. C. Schirmer, appear such good ones as "Morning Comes Early," "The Keeper," "Tiritomba," "The Old Woman and the Peddler," and "The Golden Day Is Dying." Other songs that might be used would be "A Merry Life," "O Sole Mio," "Alouette," "Believe Me, If All Those Endearing Young

Charms," "Annie Laurie," "The Lorelei," "Oh, Susanna," "Long, Long Ago," "Santa Lucia," and some of the Negro spirituals.

What historical person?—Early in the evening guests should be required to tell a little about themselves, without disclosing names. The rest of the group guesses what character is represented. For instance Diogenes lifts his lantern and explains that he has been looking for an honest man without success. Betsy Ross explains that she has been hard at work on the American flag and exhibits her sewing basket. Florence Nightingale tells of her work among the wounded soldiers during the Crimean War.

Historical tableau.—Some very effective tableaux could be presented. "Penn's Treaty with the Indians," "The Cherry Tree Incident," and "John Smith and Pocahontas" are some suggestions.

Historical drama.—Divide the crowd into several groups and give each group ten or fifteen minutes to get up a dramatic stunt representing some period in American history. Or pass out slips suggesting the period assigned to the group. It would be well to have several persons prepared to make suggestions to the various groups. "The Making of the First Flag," "Paul Revere's Ride," "The Famous Cherry Tree Incident," "Pioneer Days," and "William Penn and the Indians," indicate some of the possibilities.

Folk games.—A fitting climax to the evening would be the playing of some folk games of ours and other lands.

A SKATING PARTY

Decorations—Balloons, crepe-paper streamers.
Favors—Paper hats of various colors.

Program—
  (*a*) Tag.
  (*b*) Only girls skate.
  (*c*) Only boys skate.
  (*d*) Couples. Change partners when leader's whistle blows.
  (*e*) Balloon skating. Furnish each person with a gas-filled balloon which is to be tied to the wrist. Play "Follow the Leader." Balloons in quantities may be ordered of Rubenstein's, 180 Park Row, New York, or Slack Mfg. Co., 124-125 West Lake Street, Chicago, Illinois.

Refreshments—Cold drinks could be served during an intermission and ice cream and cake at the close of the party.

VALENTINE PARTY GAMES

Furnish guests with red and white paper, scissors, colored magazine pictures, paste, and scraps of lace paper. Let each one make a fancy valentine. Send these to shut-ins and to hospitals.

Guess what?—Have two girls with powdered hair and valentine costumes meet guests as they arrive. On the back of each they pin a heart with a word appropriate to the season, such as "Honeymoon," "Courtship," "Marriage," "Rice," "Bride," "Groom." The guests are then required to guess what the "labels" are by the conversation addressed to them by other guests. "Was it a happy one?" "Where did you go?" "How long have you been back?" These were questions shot at the girl who had "Honeymoon" written on her back.

Hunting hearts.—Hearts of different colors are hidden about the room. Some are numbered and some are not. At a given signal all players hunt for the hearts. When all hearts are found players are privileged to trade for colors and numbers they think valuable. The values are unknown to the players until the trading is over. The leader then announces the values and players add up their scores.

> Each white heart ....1 point. 7 adds 50 points.
> Each green heart ....5 points. 11 doubles the score.
> Each blue heart ......2 points. 13 takes 20 from score.
> Each red heart ....10 points. 15 adds 75 points.

Valentine fashions.—Provide materials for a Valentine Fashion Show—yards of crepe paper in various bright colors, some newspapers, paper lace (perhaps cut out of newspapers), library paste, scissors, papers of pins, and ornaments of all sorts. Have each girl dress a man in becoming Valentine costume, or divide into small groups and have each group dress one person. Have a parade of the models.

Marooned.—Men form circle in one end cf the room and women another circle at the opposite end of the room. A large paper heart is laid out in each circle. Players march to music. When the music stops all players stop, and the man and woman on or nearest the heart in each circle are taken out to become partners for the next game. This continues until all players have partners.

Progressive fortune.—Give each player a piece of paper and a pencil. Tell each one to write his own name at the top and fold under toward himself. Then pass on to neighbor to right. Each player now writes on the next slip some future date and someone's name. Again he folds and passes it on. Then he writes on the next what will happen; then the name of a place; then something a person possesses; then how it was gotten; then the effect it has. When each one is unfolded it tells a strange story. Perhaps this is the story: "Earl Jones and May Martin on July 4, 1976, played the piano in Chicago. They had jewelry which they got by main force and awkwardness. They lived happily ever after."

Where's your heart?—Players sit in a circle. The first one turns to his right-hand neighbor and says, "Where's your heart?" The neighbor replies anything she pleases, such as, "My heart is in a sycamore tree." The questioner must now respond with something that rhymes with "tree," so he says, "Well, that's good enough for me." So it goes all around the circle. Any player who cannot respond with a rhyme might be required to perform some stunt.

Heart snatch.—Players form a circle and march to music. On chairs against the walls are paper hearts, one to each chair. There is one chair less than the number of players. When the music stops all players cease marching and rush for a chair first picking up the heart before sitting down. If two players arrive about the same time the one who gets the heart is the one who stays in the game. The player who fails to get a heart drops out of the game and sits on one of the chairs, thus eliminating one heart. This continues until only one player is left.

Eternal triangle.—Divide players into two sides facing one another. Each side decides whether it shall represent the coy maiden, or the lover, or the preacher. The coy maiden is represented by assuming coy expression with finger under the chin. The man holds one hand over his heart and extends the other hand beseechingly. The preacher stands with upraised hands in blessing. The maiden beats the man; the man beats the preacher; and the preacher beats the maiden. The whole side must do the representing. The leader will count three and immediately on "three" all members of both sides must assume the characters they have decided. The first side to score three points is winner.

Progressive conversation.—Each player dates up for five topics. One minute is given for each subject. The following topics are suggested: (1) My first date. (2) Why marry? (3) Qualifications of a good mother-in-law. (4) The best way to propose. (5) Shall the preacher kiss the bride?

Valentine jigsaw puzzle.—Paste valentines on pieces of stiff cardboard. Cut in a number of pieces. Be sure to keep each valentine to itself. Use envelopes for this purpose. Have each person or group put a valentine jigsaw puzzle together.

A GEORGE WASHINGTON PARTY

> In honor of George Washington
> The Father of our nation
> We've planned a party, lots of fun,
> And here's your invitation.

Crossing the Delaware.—Draw a winding river three feet wide across the room with chalk. The players march in a circle in rhythm to music from the piano. When the music stops players all stop immediately. Anyone in the river is out.

Independence day.—Each player gets a paper containing the following:

1. Henceforth, I declare my freedom of ....
2. Because ....
3. And I resolve to ....
4. At ....
5. On ....

Let each person write in of what he frees himself, and fold over. He passes the paper to the right and that player fills in No. 2, stating the reason, without knowing, of course, what the player to his left has declared. The papers are folded each time, No. 3 being a new resolution. No. 4 the place, and No. 5 the time. After all spaces are filled, the papers are unfolded and read. There will be some side-splitting combinations.

Shaking cherries.—One player is blindfolded and stands in the center of the circle. The other players move to the right in the ring as they sing to the tune of "I've Come to See Miss Jenny Ann Jones":

> "Oh, here's a tree with cherries ripe, cherries ripe, cherries ripe.
> Oh, here's a tree with cherries ripe,
> A tree both green and tall.

We'll shake it now with all our might, all our might, all our might,
We'll shake it now with all our might,
And watch the cherries fall."

One player steps into the circle while they are singing and gently shakes the blindfolded person. The "tree" tries to guess who shook it. If he guesses correctly the shaker takes his place and the game continues. If not, the game is repeated until the correct guess is made.

Cherry carry.—Each player dips his hand palm down in a bowl of cranberries. He carries as many cranberries as he can hold on top of his hand once around the room and back to the bowl. Where desired there may be two sides and two bowls for each group—one from which each player dips and another into which he drops all he returns. In this latter case the side wins that has the largest number of cranberries in the return bowl.

Artists' ensemble.—Divide the crowd into two or more groups. Each side is to draw a picture of George Washington's head, each person drawing one feature. Blackboards or large sheets of paper and crayon may be used. One person draws the forehead, another the nose, another the mouth and chin, another the hair, another the eyes or eye. The last person puts on the finishing touches.

Washington rhyme.—

George Washington, so history says,
Did always tell the (*truth*)
He cut down daddy's (*cherry tree*),
And 'fessed the job, forsooth.
He (*sword*) above all other men,
His courage did not (*flag*);
When others failed he'd (*hatchet*) out
Without a boast or brag.
An outdoor man, with (*coat*) of tan,
A (*dollar*) once he threw
Across the old (*Potomac*) span
A thing that few could do.
He crossed the (*Delaware*) one night
To fool the enemy.
He taught the colonists to fight,
Led them to victory.
And so they made him (*President*),
The first one in the land,
The (*Father*) of our country, too,
By popular demand.

Read aloud to the group and pause for them to fill in the par enthetic words.

Valley Forge.—Assign parts and have a reading rehearsal of se lected parts of Maxwell Anderson's great play, *Valley Forge* Published by Samuel French, 25 West 45th Street, New York City.

Things they missed in George Washington's days.—

1. No coal, no wood you need to burn
   To cook the meal to a brown turn.
   (Gas or Electric Stove)

2. No pen, no pencil, no ancient quill,
   But you can write lots if you just will.
   (Typewriter)

3. It sputters, roars, then down the road it speeds
   Two wheels, a frame, and a motor is what it needs.
   (Motorcycle)

4. It zips, it zooms, it sails thru the skies,
   Like a bird on the wing it dips and flies.
   (Airplane)

5. You can press your attire
   When it contacts a wire.
   (Electric Iron)

6. The one-hoss shay has passed away,
   The buggy is a relic.
   Their successor you dodge most ev'ry day,
   Or else you'll be angelic.
   (Automobile)

7. Nobody is there, but they walk and talk,
   And act so you think they're real.
   A gigantic business they've become,
   You've seen them a great deal.
   (Talking Pictures)

8. No need for brush, no need for broom,
   It's used a lot to clean the room.
   (Vacuum Cleaner)

9. No stairs to climb the difficult way.
   Up and down it goes all the long day.
                 (Elevator or Escalator)

10. You can talk to someone miles away,
    Whether or not you have much to say.
                  (Telephone)

11. It plucks melodies from the air,
    It brings voices from afar,
    Its programs here and there
    Can be heard right where you are.
                  (Radio)

12. It keeps it hot, it keeps it cold,
    Whatever 'tis you make it hold.
                  (Thermos Bottle)

13. No candle or oil lamp ever did glow
    Like Edison's invention which all of you know
                  (Electric Light)

14. Its bright penciled light illumines the way,
    A boon to the hiker who follows its ray.
                  (Flash Light)

15. (a) It puffs, it toots, it rides the rail,
    It carries most of the U. S. mail,
    (b) "Iron horse" the Indians called it,
    It races o'er the land;
    Streamlined, the modern way,
    It runs to beat the band.
                  (Locomotive)

16. The doctor uses it to see inside
    From its piercing eye you cannot hide.
                  (X-Ray)

17. It shoots you when you're looking,
    It shoots you when you're not,
    This candid instrument, indeed,
    Can put you on the spot.
                  (Camera)

18. A wedding, death, or house afire;
    A distant friend gets it by wire.
    (Telegraph)

19. No iceman comes now to your door,
    But cold your food it keeps in store.
    (Frigidaire)

20. It keeps you cool in weather hot,
    It keeps you warm in cold.
    In hotel and store and eating place
    It's not so very old.
    (Air Conditioning)

Washington's Birthday Drama and Readings

Washington and Betsy Ross, Percy MacKaye. Three men, two women. Forty-five minutes. Samuel French, 25 West 45th Street, New York City.

Washington Marches On, Olive M. Price. Fifteen scenes. Thirty-eight men, eleven women. Full evening. Historical. Samuel French.

Plays About George Washington, Theodore Johnson. Eleven short plays. Walter H. Baker, 178 Tremont, Boston, Mass.

Washington at Valley Forge, Esther W. Bates. Baker.

About Candlelight Time, Dorothy Allan. Three men, four women. Thirty minutes. Baker.

George Washington Anniversary Plays, Theodore Johnson. Eleven plays. Baker.

The Truth for a Day, Helen T. Darby. Six girls decide to tell the truth on Washington's birthday. Comedy. Thirty minutes. Eldridge Entertainment House, Franklin, Ohio.

Truthful Husbands, Palmer. Nine men, seven women. Laughable farce for Washington's birthday. Fifty minutes. Eldridge.

Washington's First Defeat. One man, two women. Twenty minutes. Washington at sixteen wooing his first sweetheart. Authentic. Samuel French.

Patriotic Pepper. Six girls. One act. Dramatic Publishing Company, 59 Van Buren, Chicago, Illinois.

Georga Wash, Nona Kehrberg. Italian dialect. Humorous reading. Wetmore Declamation Bureau, 1631 South Paxton Street, Sioux City, Iowa.

MARCH

A MARCH WIND PARTY

Invitation—

> Blow around to ——
> Friday evening, March ——, and enjoy the
> "March Wind Party." Bring along your raincoat.

When guests arrive have electric fans blowing streamers of crepe or tissue paper from the sides of the room. Have this room decorated with toy balloons, green paper and serpentine streamers.

Placards about the room will interest the guests as they arrive. Such messages as the following may appear on these placards:

"Blow yourself to a good time tonight."
"What city is known as 'The Windy City'?"
"Blow about your achievements as much as you like, but don't burst your bellows."
"Don't try to blow out the electric light."
"Blow your own horn, if you want it blown."

> Obituary:
> "A sad tale, alas,
> He blew out the gas."

> A Maiden's Prayer:
> "Blow him again to me."

> Heard from a Flat Tire:
> "Some blow-out."

Visit to Cave-of-the-Winds.—All who wish to enter the cave are asked to don their raincoats. A guide then conducts them through a dark passageway, after asking each one in the party to take hold of a rope the end of which he holds. This, he explains, is necessary in order that none might be lost. At one place in the dark passageway someone is stationed with an atomizer and a palm-leaf fan. The atomizer is filled with clear water and is sprayed on the visitors to the cave. Following the spray, a swoop of the fan adds to the peculiar sensation.

Entering the room that is fitted up as the Cave-of-the-Winds the visitors are introduced to the Wind King. This person has a long white beard and wears a flowing robe and a crown. Speaking through a megaphone he welcomes his guests after this fashion:

"Welcome to my Kingdom, children of the earth. Welcome, thrice welcome.

> I blow from the West,
> I blow from the East,
> From the North and South,
> On man and on beast.

"Let me introduce you to my assistants, the Four Winds of the Earth."

Immediately there steps forth four attendants in long flowing robes. Each holds a long horn to his lips and on the command of the King, "Blow ye Four Winds of the Earth!" they blow lustily. When they do, something surprising happens. The air is filled with a white mist and those visitors in front find themselves covered with white flour. If desired, the horns may be loaded with confetti instead of flour.

All visitors are now informed by the guide that it is time to depart from the cave.

If not possible to take all the people on this trip at one time, divide them into two parties, swearing the first party to secrecy.

The cave should be very dimly lighted, and electric fans should furnish a breezy atmosphere. A vacuum cleaner might be rigged up so that it would blow out instead of drawing in. It could furnish occasional gusts of wind.

Blowing contest.—Divide the crowd into two groups. Blindfold the players one at a time and give each three trials at blowing out a lighted candle. Count a point each time the candle is blown out. The side with the best score wins.

A breezy race.—Have from four to ten players represent each side. Furnish each player with a fan and ten tiny tissue-paper balls, all of one color for each side. At the signal to go all players start fanning their tissue-paper balls to the goal at the opposite side of the room.

Two large boxes several feet apart are placed so that the balls may be fanned into them. No player is allowed to scrape the ball in. He must use his fan to blow them along. At the end of one minute the side with the largest number of balls in their respective goals wins. No player may blow a ball into the goal provided for his opponent.

Feather blow.— (1) Fill jars with downy feathers, one for each contestant. The first who is able to blow all feathers out of the jar wins. (2) Furnish one downy feather to each contestant, one for each side. At the signal to start the players throw their feathers into the air and start blowing them toward a goal line. Ten points are allowed for crossing the goal line. Ten points are awarded the opponent each time the feather falls to the floor. When the feather does fall to the floor it must be picked up at the point where it fell, and started again, after the contestant has taken three long steps backward.

Windy words.—Each side is given one minute to write down all the words relating to winds they can recall. One player would act as clerk for each group and write down words as they are suggested by different ones. Some suggestions are breeze, gust, gale, blast, roar, cyclone, tornado, squall, whiff, puff, etc.

Blow-hard.—If a good get-acquainted stunt is desired it might be well to have the girls line up on one side of the room and the boys on the other. Both lines march to the end of the room, then to the middle, coming down the middle double file, and thus getting their partners. At signal the players stop marching and partners face one another in circle formation. Then for a few seconds each tells the other about his or her virtues. Both talk at once, and neither needs to feel confined to the realms of the truth. When the leader blows a whistle the boys move one step to the right facing a new partner. Again both start proclaiming their virtues. The leader should blow the whistle at short intervals, keeping the game moving rapidly. A few minutes of this will probably start your crowd off in good humor.

An added feature.—It would be appropriate to have someone give that old reading about the four people each of whom was afflicted with a different sort of distortion of the mouth. One talked out of the right corner of the mouth, another out of the left, a third had the lower lip extending out so that she could blow only up, while her husband's upper lip extended and he could blow only down. When the four of them try to blow out a candle there's lots of fun.

See "The Crooked Mouth Family" in Chapter XIV, Fun with Dramatics.

A SPRING PARTY

Invitation—

> "The flowers that bloom in the spring, Tra-la,
> Have nothing to do with the case,
> But at our Spring Party you'll laugh many a merry ha-ha,
> So bring your smilingest face."

*Decorations—*Flowers, green and white crepe paper.

Spring a joke.—Provide a number of magazines with joke pages. Let each person look up a good joke to "spring" on the crowd. If there can be one joke page for each guest it would help.

Another plan would be that of clipping the jokes out of the magazines and letting each of the guests draw one from a box.

Still another plan would be that of pinning the jokes on each person. Then form concentric circles and march the boys in one direction and the girls in another. When the music stops, they stop and face one another. Each reads the other's joke. Incidently, this might serve as a good mixer for a large crowd.

Spring a spring poem.—Give to each person an unfinished spring rhyme to which they are to add the last line. For a large crowd divide into groups and have each group present its poem.

Some suggestions are as follows:

(1) Spring is the season of the year
That some folk seem to hold most dear.
It looks so gay in color green,

_____

(2) The rose still blushes and the violets blow
The spinach still spins and the onions grow,
The lettuce still "lets" and the turnips "turn,"

_____

(3) When daisies pied, and violets blue,
And Lady-smocks all silver-white,
And cuckoo-buds of yellow hue,

_____

This third one is one of the beautiful things from Shakespeare's pen, and the last line reads,

"Do paint the meadows with delight."

If the person or group drawing it happens to know the last line, well and good. If not let them write one of their own. In the latter case be sure that the guests get a chance to hear it as Shakespeare wrote it.

It will not matter if many of the players get the same poem to complete.

Another variation to this feature of the program would be that of giving the different guests a chance to repeat the lines of some poem they have memorized.

Spring a spring bonnet.—Provide newspapers, crepe paper, scissors, pins, paste, and pictures of ladies' hats. Let each guest make a hat which he is to wear for a while, at least.

An award may be given for the best spring bonnet.

A variation of this feature would be to divide the crowd into groups and have each group make one or two models to be worn by persons selected from their group.

Spring a song.—Write the names of songs on slips of paper. There should be at least four slips for each song. Have the players draw the slips from a box. Then each player starts out to look for the rest of his quartet. As they find one another they link arms. Each quartet must sing its song. Then all of the quartets may be required to sing simultaneously, each singing its own song.

Spring a stunt.—Divide into two or more groups and have each group present some stunt. The general theme of the stunts could be "Signs of Spring." Appropriate subtitles that are suggestive are:

(1) In the Spring a Young Man's Fancy.
(2) Mr. Jones' Vegetable Garden.
(3) House-cleaning Days.
(4) Spring Fever.

If the idea of impromptu original stunts does not appeal then turn to Chapter XIV, Fun with Dramatics, for some ideas.

FARMER-FARMERETTE FROLIC

In one group putting on a party of this type two dummy forms were dressed up—one to represent "Willie, the farmer boy," and the other to represent "Nellie, the farmer girl." "Nellie," particularly made a striking figure in her gingham gown, apron, and bonnet. Her face was painted on a stocking. She held a cleverly designed poster—a sunbonnet girl on one side and a boy in overalls on the other. "Hay Farmer!" was the inscription at the top of the poster. Underneath that: "Better Kum to the Farmer-Farmerette Frolic." Date, time, and place were given in the following fashion:

"Where are you going, my pretty maid?"
"I'm going to the party, kind sir," she said.
"Where is this party, my pretty maid?"
"Down at St. Paul's, kind sir," she said.
"When is this party, my pretty maid?"
"Friday, March 8th, kind sir," she said.
"At what time, my pretty maid?"
"At 8:15, kind sir," she said.

Decorations—Corn shucks stacked in the corners. Branches of trees and vines should be used. A typical old-fashioned well with bucket, dipper, and everything, over to one side. A bale or two of hay.

Program—Girls wear calico frocks and sunbonnets. Boys come dressed in overalls and straw hats. Guests are greeted by Farmer Brown and his wife. An orchestra of stringed instruments plays "Turkey in the Straw" and other appropriate music as guests arrive.

Games—Farmer Brown and his wife suggest some games and the group starts playing "Farmer in the Dell." Following that comes "Betsy Liner," "Looby Loo," "Bingo," and "Oh, Susanna."

Spelling bee.—An old-fashioned spelling bee would be appropriate at this point. If possible, use an old blue-back speller.

Silhouettes and music.—A sheet is stretched at one end of the room. Arrange a light (candle, lamp, or electric bulb) so as to throw the proper sort of shadow on the sheet. For each silhouette there should be an appropriate song. For "I Was Seeing Nellie Home," sung by a quartet, several couples walked across the screen. Goodbye was said at a cleverly improvised gate. "The Old Oaken Bucket," "O Soldier, Soldier" (*Brown Book*), "Memories," and "School Days" could all be done effectively.

More games.—Play some of the old-fashioned games like "Going to Jerusalem," "Stagecoach," and "Charades." Do a grand march, bring the group down in sixteens, and then do "The Virginia Reel."

Refreshments—Serve lemonade from the old well.

Songs.—Close the party by singing such old favorites as "Old Folks at Home," "Old Black Joe," and "Goodnight Ladies."

AN IRISH PARTY

March 17 is St. Patrick's Day, the day when homage is paid to St. Patrick, who is said to have brought Christianity to Ireland, about A.D. 450. St. Patrick, legends say, drove the snakes out of Ireland, brought darkness upon his enemies, and performed many miracles. Why not make your March party, a St. Patrick's Day party?

Decorations—Shamrocks, cut from green paper, jonquils or other spring flowers, green candles in candleholders made from Irish potatoes by carving out a place for the candle.

Invitations—A shamrock, cut from either white or green cardboard may bear these words written in green ink, in limerick fashion:

> "Shure, won't you come to our party?
> You'll find a welcome that's hearty,
> Come Friday e'en,
> Wearin' some green,
> An Irish joke bring to our party."
>
> (*Date and time*)   (*place*)

Irish family assignments.—Before the guests arrive plan to divide the crowd into groups of ten each. Let each group be an Irish "family." Each member of a family may be given an Irish first name also. Suggested family names: Murphy, Mulligan, O'Shea, Maloney, O'Flaherty, Flannigan, O'Reilly, Kelly, O'Grady, Casey. The members of one family, for example, might be Ma, Pa, Pat, Mike, Bridget, Judy, Jo, Kathleen, Jerry, and Rosie. When the guests enter each one is given a slip of paper, tied with a bit of green ribbon, and on which is written a complete Irish name. Example: "Jerry Murphy." While the crowd is assembling each early comer will enjoy discovering the other members of his "family."

The Lakes of Killarney.—For this game a rough outline map of lakes should have been drawn previously upon the floor with chalk. A march is played upon the piano while the crowd marches in and out, and around the room. The music stops quickly, anyone standing in a "lake" must drop out of the game. The "lakes" should be drawn close together. This game may be played until all but a few persons have had to drop out.

The Irish family reunions.—Announcement is made that there are certain Irish families that are holding reunions tonight. Each family is asked to "get together" for group games.

1. Each family will hold a *Joke Contest*. Every member of the family is asked to tell the Irish joke he has brought to the party. The family decides which joke is best. Later in the evening, the entire group hears a representative from each family tell the Irish joke considered the best in the family.

2. *Limericks*. Limericks are nonsense poems said to have originated in Ireland, and received their name from the city of Limerick on the banks of the river Shannon. Limericks are read to the entire crowd and limerick structure is explained.

An often-quoted limerick:

> "There was a young lady of Niger,
> Who smiled as she rode on a tiger,
> They returned from the ride
> With the lady inside,
> And the smile on the face of the tiger."

A limerick consists of five lines, lines 1, 2, and 5 contain three poetic "feet" and rhyme, lines 3 and 4 contain 2 feet and rhyme. Each family is given the first line of a limerick and asked to complete the limerick.

Suggested first lines are:

  (1) There was an old man in a tree.
  (2) There was an old man in a boat.
  (3) There was a typist so pretty.
  (4) There was a young maid of Dallas.
  (5) A flapper down in Atlanta.
  (6) There was a young man from Mobile.
  (7) An aviator flew in the sky.
  (8) There was a small boy who went fishin'.
  (9) Susie went to a movie show.
(10) An old maid with a permanent wave.

Each family as a group recites its limerick before the other families.

3. *Irish stunts*—Each family is asked to plan an impromptu Irish stunt. By this time the crowd, no doubt, will enter into the "Spirit of the Irish" to such a degree that they will enjoy impromptu stunts. Give each family not more than five minutes to get its stunt ready. The stunts may then be given before the entire crowd by the families in turn. Charades, using the names of Irish towns, or Irish words, may be substituted for the stunts, if preferred.

Securing partners for refreshments—Cut two of one size of the following objects out of green cardboard: Shamrock, rose, pipe, snake, pig, Irish harp. By making variations in size or shape enough different objects may be made for your groups. The girls draw objects from one tray, the boys from another. Objects are then matched for partners for refreshments.

The refreshments— (1) A salad. Either potato salad on a lettuce leaf, or a green gelatin salad, containing yellow fruit, such as peaches, pineapple, or oranges. (2) Lettuce sandwiches, made of white bread cut thin, and in the shape of a shamrock. (3) Green mints. (4) Orangeade or tea.

Close the party with an "Irish sing" around the piano. Such songs as "The Wearing of the Green," "Mother Machree," "Kathleen Mavourneen," may be sung. The words to these songs may be found in most collections of old familiar songs. It may be necessary to have the words of the songs typed.

Reserve plans— It is always well to have some additional plans in reserve. The following are made as reserve suggestions:

(1) Irish songs played upon the victrola.

(2) Have someone prepared to tell an Irish fairy tale. Irish stories and poems by Padriac Colum may be found in most public libraries.

"Shure—we hope you'll enjoy our party."

—HELEN SWISHER

ADDITIONAL ST. PATRICK'S PARTY SUGGESTIONS

Going to Dublin.—Players are seated in a line or semicircle. The head seat is "Dublin." Players are trying to get to Dublin. Make the accompanying chart on a circular piece of cardboard and attach to it an arrow spinner. This can easily be done by cutting out a

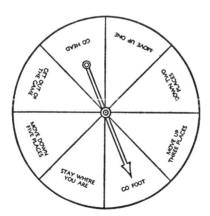

metal or cardboard arrow and punching a hole in it to allow it to spin around a pin placed at the center of the diagram. Perhaps a game with a spinner could be bought at the ten-cent store. The directions on the diagram could be pasted on it.

Each player, in turn, starting at the foot, spins the arrow and follows directions. Two or three times around could constitute a game.

Irish towns.—Read these aloud and pause for the answers:

1. What Irish town grows on a tree?
   It is very useful at the pharmacy.—Cork.
2. My first it rings,
   My second means speed,
   My whole it brings,
   An Irish town, indeed.—Belfast.
3. My first is England's greatest,
   My second rhymes with fairy,
   My whole is famed in music,
   You've guessed it.—Londonberry.
4. Three murderers in a row
   You'll guess them now, we know.—Killkenny, Killarney, Kildare.
5. Two cities breathe of royalty,
   They are easy, I'm sure you see.—Queenstown and Kingstown.
6. Multiply what you have by two,
   There ain't much use of troublin';
   You've guessed that one, I know that you
   Are shouting loudly.—Dublin.

Irish conundrums.—

1. Why would an Irish lassie never refuse an imitation diamond? Because it's a sham-rock.
2. What was the trick in driving the snakes out of Ireland? St. Patrick.
3. What Irishman is essential at the radio station? Mike.
4. When is a moving picture a dance? When it is an Irish reel.
5. What college dance is a reminder of St. Patrick? The snake dance.
6. What kind of knee does an Irishman like best? Blarney.
7. What color should be the carpet in an Irish church? Green to make the Emerald (a) Isle.

An optical illusion.—Draw and cut out of bright red paper a pig about four inches long. Mount him on a sheet of white paper. Mount a sheet on the wall. Stand with back to the light, and look the pig steadily in the eye while you say "poor piggy" twenty times. Then raise your eyes quickly and look steadily at the sheet. You're due for a shock! For there on the sheet is a green pig! Be sure to draw the eyes of the pig in heavy black lines.

Irish folk games.—Try "Waves of Tory" or some other good Irish folk game.

Irish music.—Special musical numbers: *Group singing* "Bendemeer's Stream," "Galway Piper," "When Irish Eyes Are Smiling," "My Wild Irish Rose," "Believe Me If All Those Endearing Young Charms."

APRIL

April Fool.—Around the world April Fool or what corresponds to it is observed. In *The Customs of Mankind* a brief poem reveals that this celebration is of ancient origin.

> "The first of April some do say
> Is set apart as All Fool's Day;
> But why people call it so
> Nor I nor they themselves do know."

In some ancient countries it was regarded with superstition. No one would dare plan an enterprise, and only the very brave or fool-hardy would venture to marry on that day. Napoleon married Maria Louisa on April 1, 1810, but the superstitious would point to him as Exhibit A.

The French call it *Poisson d'avril*—"April Fish." The inference is that they're easily caught. They have a French story of a woman who stole a gold watch from the home of a friend. When, after a lively chase, the police caught her, she cried, "Poisson d'avril." But the judge had a sense of humor also and he sentenced her to jail until the next "All Fool's" day.

In various countries all sorts of hoaxes are played on this day. It is the day for practical jokes. Neighbors and friends are sent on fool errands. Companions are tricked into doing foolish things.

AN APRIL FOOL'S PARTY

Invitation—

> For a cap and bells our lives we pay,
> But this is April first, they say,
> So don a dunce cap and bring a rhyme
> For we're going to have a grand old time.

The invitation must be written on highly colored paper, cut in the shape of a dunce cap and written backward so it will have to be held up to a mirror to be read.

A stuck-up reception committee—There should be a reception committee consisting of from two to four. In the right hand of each member of this committee there should be poured some glue. Those who shake hands with them get "stuck-up." Have a few towels handy so guests can wipe the glue off their hands.

Decorations and surprise hunt—For decoration use a large number of spring flowers, or perhaps artificial flowers and sprinkle with pepper. Have all sorts of foolish snares about the room, such as a coin glued to the floor, toy spiders, and hide under vases and every other conceivable place "Bingoes." A "Bingo" is a trick folder that can be placed under a plate, vase, or book. When the article is lifted "Bingo" explodes harmlessly. They may be ordered from any company handling novelties of this kind. Under these flowers and vases with the surprises hide pieces of paper numbered "One," "Two," or any other numbers you might care to use. Have surprises hidden with many of the numbers. After the guests arrive the leader explains that there are many things hidden in the room, and the one finding the largest number of them, or the one whose numbers amount up highest, gets a prize. The prize turns out to be a dunce cap which has to be worn all of the evening. The winner must also read backwards a paragraph given by the leader.

Foolish rhyming contest.—Each person is given a pencil and paper, and on the paper is written ten letters. Each must write a rhyme, each word beginning with the letters on the paper. The best one is read aloud.

A fool picture.—Now the guests form a single line. They are told they are to see a wonderful picture. Have them go singly past a mirror marked with the words "April Fool" written in soap.

Fool contest.—Then choose three or four guests to take part in the ten-second contest. Each person is to say, "What am I doing?" ten times in ten seconds. The crowd answers, "Making a fool of yourself."

False alarm.—Now the dinner gong will sound and someone will announce that "Dinner is not served."

"City Beautiful Club."—The leader now appears very serious as he says that he thought while they were all there together it would be a good time to organize a club he had been thinking of for a long time. He avers that he hates to break in on a party like this, but it is for the good of the community, etc. The club will be called the "City Beautiful Club," or something like that. He explains the purpose of the club. Nominations for president and other officers are called for. Go through the whole thing according to Hoyle, and at the end have all of the officers come forward. Then announce that these officers represent Exhibit A of "The City Beautiful."

Drawing the moon.—Form a circle. With a stick or the forefinger draw an imaginary picture of the man in the moon, putting in the eyes, nose, and mouth. Pass the stick on to the next one saying, "Do this." The trick is not in the drawing of the face but in changing the stick from the hand with which the picture was drawn to the other hand in passing the stick to the next person. Continue until each person solves the mystery and all can do it correctly.

Sleight of hand and April foolishness.—The guests may be asked to perform sleight-of-hand tricks. Each person present must endeavor to fool somebody else during the evening. The one who has *not* been fooled and the one who *has* been fooled oftenest will be called up before everybody and presented with tags, one labeled, "Wise Guy," the other, "April Fool."

Foolish eating.—Then choose two people from the crowd who will place each person there in an absurd position for the serving of the refreshments. They must eat in the position in which they are left.

—Lois Harper

April fool ideas.—

1. A metal pencil charged with electricity. Guests are told to register. In the midst of their writing someone turns on the juice. They'll probably never finish.

2. Require each person to April fool someone. Hand out cards as they arrive. On these cards are written such instructions as the following: "Tell someone he is wanted at the phone," "Tell John his shoestring is untied," "Tell Sue that Mary wants to see her." As soon as a person has fooled someone he turns in his card. At the end of a given time all persons who still hold their cards are required to perform some stunt for the crowd. It might be a good idea to arrange with someone to agree ahead of time to be the first to give a stunt, so as to get off to a good start.

3. Some high schools turn over the school chapel to students on "All Fool's Day." The students assume full authority and work out a fun program of some sort. One high-school group had a Mock Faculty Meeting with students impersonating the principal and teachers.

4. A "fish pond" with many joke packages and a few good surprises will be fun.

5. Have some member of the group tell about "The Biggest Fool Thing I Ever Did."

AN APRIL FOOL'S FESTIVAL

Invitations—The invitations may be written on lightweight cardboard. Invitations may be written backwards so that they will have to be held up to the mirror to be read.

Decorations—Decorate with green and white crepe paper and varicolored confetti. Arrange several April fool tricks around the room to entertain the guests upon their arrival. In some conspicuous place have an attractive bouquet of artificial flowers upon which black pepper has been sprinkled. A toy mouse might be suspended from a chandelier; a coin might be glued to the floor; a handkerchief tacked to the floor; a jack-in-the-box" or a "jumping snake" might be placed in a conspicuous place and labeled "Open for Inspection." Foolish signs and mottoes might be placed around the room.

Reception of guests—The guests should be met at the door by members of the reception committee dressed in clown suits and dunce caps. The clowns should reach out their hands as if they were going to shake hands with the guest and should suddenly withdraw their hands when the guest's hand is extended, and shake the hand of another clown.

Surprise handshake.—Secretly give trick prizes, such as small rubber spiders, to two or more people in the room (the number of prizes to be determined by the size of the crowd). Instruct these people to keep a count of the persons with whom they shake hands, and to give their prize to the thirteenth one. Then tell the crowd that there are some philanthropists in the crowd who will give wonderful prizes to the thirteenth person who shakes hands with them. This should be a signal for most vigorous handshaking, which should continue until all the prizes have been given out.

Laughing test.—Have a knife or piece of iron ready to use in this game. Anything that will make a noise as it hits the floor will do. Announce that everyone is to laugh lustily while the knife is thrown into the air but to stop laughing the instant it touches the floor. The knife should be thrown quickly and only a few times. The last time the leader only pretends to throw it up in the air. When the players laugh he holds the knife up to show them they've been tricked.

April fool race.—This game is the old favorite, the "Obstacle Race." Select two contestants. Place a number of obstacles in the race course—upturned chairs, buckets, ropes tied from one side to the other, etc. Let the contestants try the course first, walking through it with their eyes open. Then blindfold them and tell them they must make their way to the end of the race course. In the meantime someone has quietly removed all the obstacles from the course. This race will provoke lots of fun, especially if the contestants are not allowed to run and are told that every obstacle touched will count a point against them.

April fool conversation.—A long string is required. Two players who know the trick hold the ends of the string and prepare to carry on a "telephone" conversation. All the players are told to hold the string between their teeth if they wish to hear a most interesting conversation. After a short humorous conversation between the players holding each end of the string, one asks the other, "Where have you been?" The answer comes back, "I've been fishing." "Catch anything?" "Yes, here's a whole string of suckers."

April fool locomotion.—This is simply the "Kiddie Kar Relay" that always makes plenty of fun for any party. Choose as the contestants for this race the tallest, fattest, or most awkward members of your group. Use from two to four on each of two teams. The first one of each side is given a "Kiddie Kar" and at the signal sits down on it and without a push from anyone on his team, starts propelling his "Kar" toward the goal. If he gets back from the goal, he gives his "Kar" to the next member of his team, who goes through the same ordeal. This is continued until one side has won.

April fool music.—Tell the group that they are now going to be entertained with a most unusual musical number by a talented quartet. Explain that the talent of these singers has hitherto been undiscovered, but that on this occasion they have agreed to demonstrate to this appreciative crowd their ability to perform the great feat of singing a song backwards. The quartet which then appears is composed of two girls with aprons on backwards and two boys with their coats on backwards, who walk in backward, and with their backs to the audience, bow. They hold sheets of music behind them and turn the pages as they sing, singing such a song as "Yankee

Doodle" or "Three Blind Mice." At the close of the song they bow and walk off with backs to audience.

April shower race.—Several couples are needed for this race. They stand in line, with a closed suitcase and an umbrella in front of each couple. In each suitcase there are a pair of rubbers, and pair of gloves, a raincoat or cloak, and a hat. At the signal to start each young man grabs his suitcase, and, hand in hand, he and his partner rush to the opposite goal. When they arrive there, he opens the suitcase, hands his partner the rubbers, which she puts on, then hands her each of the other articles, which she in turn puts on. He then closes the suitcase and raises the umbrella, and holding the umbrella over his partner with one hand and holding the suitcase in the other, runs with her back to the starting point. When they arrive there he must close the umbrella, open the suitcase, help his partner take off her "rainy day apparel" and replace them in the suitcase and close it up.

An April fool tea party.—The use of this game in any form usually turns the thoughts of the players toward the "eats," so it is well to use it near the close of the party program. Players form a large circle. The one who begins this game is "on to the trick." He begins the game by saying, "My grandmother doesn't like tea, but she likes ————" inserting the name of some food or beverage that does not contain the letter *T*. Each player in turn repeats the sentence and inserts the name of some food. The fun comes in seeing who will be the first to "catch on to the trick." Grandmother doesn't like tea, and therefore she doesn't like anything with *T* in it.

Refreshments.—Give each person a copy of the following menu and tell them to choose three items from the list, indicating their choice by check marks:

Menu	*Item to Be Served*
Spring's Offering	Water
New England Brains	Boston baked beans
What We People Need	Bread
First Love	Candy kisses
Dates	Some calendar figures
Can't Be Beaten	Boiled egg
Honeymooners' Prayer	Lettuce alone
A Letter in the Alphabet	Tea
Hidden Tears	Onions
A Chip Off the Old Block	Toothpicks
Lover's Greens	Pickles
Sweet Sixteen	Sugar

After the orders have been filled according to the desires of the guests, the plates should be taken up and "real" refreshments should be served. Sandwiches and tea, with perhaps a pickle and a piece of April fool candy would be appropriate refreshments. Unpalatable April fool confections or food are not in good taste in more ways than one.

—From suggestions by Martha DuBerry

A PAUL REVERE COLONIAL PARTY

On the night of April 18, 1775, Paul Revere made his famous ride.

Invitations—The invitations are to be written on fire-crackers. Paste together two narrow strips of red cardboard with a piece of string representing the fuse, protruding at one end.

> Listen, my children, and you shall hear
> Of a party in honor of Paul Revere.
> A colonial party, a joyful affair,
> So dress up in costume; make sure to be there.

Decorations—Use the colonial colors, buff and blue. Crepe-paper streamers and flowers in these colors can be used effectively. Hang from chandeliers and doorways balls of tiny American flags. These can be made by sticking the flag-sticks into Irish potatoes.

If "Progressive Paul Revere" is played tables ought to be decorated to represent forts. On each table have a brick covered with red paper or cheesecloth. Tied at one end is a pennant bearing the name of the fort or town, and at the other is an American flag of suitable size. These are held in place by red ribbon. Suggested names—Fort Ticonderoga, Fort William Henry, Fort Duquesne, Boston, Medford, Charlestown, Lexington, and Concord.

Costumes—It would add much to the enjoyment of the occasion if all guests would come dressed in Colonial costume. If this seems impractical for your crowd, then have a committee dressed in Colonial style to receive the guests as they arrive.

Paul Revere in hiding.—Hide about the room cards on which are letters that appear in the name "Paul Revere," one letter to each card. There ought to be at least ten full sets of these cards, with numerous extra cards for each letter except one. This one will be the secret key letter and there will be just ten of that letter. For instance, there might be just ten "V's." That would mean that only ten persons could spell the name "Paul Revere." No player can take up a letter until he has the first letter in the name. Secrecy must be observed among the players. The first player to spell the name may be awarded some prize. The ten players to find "Paul Revere" are to be awarded crepe paper cockades, made in red, white, and blue. These are to be worn during the evening.

Historical art.—Each guest is given a piece of paper, a pencil, and five minutes in which to sketch an original drawing of some historical event. "Paul Revere's Ride," "Washington Crossing the Delaware," "The Spirit of '76," and "A Colonial Sentinel" are some suggestions. The more ridiculous the pictures the better. At the end of five minutes they are to be passed to the person to the right. After inspecting it this person writes below it the title of the picture according to his notion. No player is to label his own picture.

Take the town.—Players are divided into two equal groups. One group is named "The Yankees," and the other, "The Redcoats." The chairs are placed in a large circle, facing out from center. Players march around the room, as far from the circle of chairs as the space will permit. When the music stops the players rush for seats. No player is allowed to move a chair in order to get it away from another player. There must be less chairs than players. Each time the player left without a chair drops out one chair is removed, while the game continues until all players but one are eliminated. This one is declared winner, and is appropriately decorated with a cockade. Those "Yankees" and "Redcoats" who drop out are expected to "root" for their teammates who are still in the game. The side having the winner is credited with "taking the town."

Flag race.—Five girls represent each side. They are lined up single file. At the opposite end of the room are two potatoes with American flags stuck in them, one for each team. The first player runs to the flag, snatches it, and brings it back, handing it to the next player who takes it back, standing it erect in the potato. This player then rushes back and touches off her next teammate, who goes after the flag. Thus it continues until the last player has run. The team finishing first has its players decorated with cockades.

Bridling Paul Revere's horse.—This is played like the old game of "Pinning on the Donkey's Tail." The players are blindfolded one at a time and given a small bridle. The three to pin it nearest the proper place are awarded cockades.

Horse-race relay.—Five boys are selected as riders for each side. The horses are of the broom variety, one broom to a team. The first player rides his broom the length of the room and back, turning it over to his next teammate. Again the team finishing first is deco· rated with cockades.

Paul Revere relay.—Blackboard space for the two teams is needed. If the blackboard is not available, use two writing pads and have the players write with pencils. Thirty-three players for each side may be used, or the number of participants can be cut to suit the conditions. Players are to write the first five lines of Longfellow's poem, "Paul Revere's Ride."

Sides are lined up. The first player rushes forward and writes one word of the chosen excerpt on the board. He runs back and hands the chalk to the next player who rushes to the board and writes the next word. So it goes until the entire selection is written. If desired, fewer players may be used and the number of words per player increased. Or the selection may be trimmed to two lines. To refresh the minds of the players the poem may be read aloud several times.

> "Listen, my children and you shall hear
> Of the midnight ride of Paul Revere.
> On the eighteenth of April in '75,
> Hardly a man is now alive
> Who remembers that famous day and year."

The winning captain is decorated with a cockade.

"How?"—The "Yankees" and the "Redcoats" face one another in two lines about four or five feet apart. A captain is chosen for each side. Each player is given a name which denotes some action that can be pantomimed or demonstrated. These names are to be arranged in alphabetical order, there being one player for each letter, except that the less commonly used letters may be omitted, if desired. The names are whispered to the player by the captains in charge.

The game starts with the "Yankee" captain approaching the "Redcoat" lines and saying, "Paul Revere crossed the river tonight to Charlestown." The opposing captain asks, "How?" The "Yankee" captain responds *A*. The "Yankee" player whose word begins with *A* steps from the ranks and proceeds to act out his word, or name. If he can cross the intervening space between the two lines in this manner and gets back to his own line before the captain of the "Redcoats" can guess his name he is safe. For instance, *A* may stand for "anxiously," "awkwardly," "aimlessly," or some other word beginning with *A*. If the "Redcoat" captain guesses correctly, the player is captured, and takes his place behind the enemy's lines.

The "Redcoats" now take their turn. "I understand that Paul Revere threw some of the tea overboard in the Boston Tea Party," says the "Redcoat." "How?" asks the "Yankee" captain. *A* is again the answer. This time, perhaps it is "angrily," and the "Redcoat" with that name crosses "No Man's Land," registering anger by looks and actions.

So it goes on down the line. At the end of the game the side with the largest number of prisoners wins and the winning captain is decorated with a cockade.

The same statement may be made each time or it may be varied at the discretion of the captains. For instance, a captain may use, "Paul Revere made his famous midnight ride in '75." "How?" is invariably the comeback of the opposing captain. The letters are to be taken in order in answering this query.

Players may suggest to the captain the names of the performing player, but only the captain can capture a player by calling his name.

Following is a list of suggested names:

B—boldly, blandly, briskly.
C—courteously, cunningly, coldly, carefully.
D—devoutly, discreetly, dignifiedly.
E—earnestly, enthusiastically, excitedly.
F—fearfully, falteringly, facetiously.
G—genially, galloping, gallantly.
H—haltingly, haughtily, hysterically.
I—idiotically, idly, impassionately.
J—jauntily, jubilantly, jeeringly.
K—kindly, knavishly, knowingly.
L—lamely, lazily, lightly.
M—merrily, mincingly, magnificently.
N—noiselessly, nonsensically.
O—outlandishly, optimistically.
P—passionately, patriotically, pleasantly.
Q—quickly, quarrelsomely.
R—recklessly, revengefully, radiantly.
S—savagely, saucily, slyly.
T—tearfully, tenderly, thoughtfully.
U—uproariously, urgently.
V—vampirishly, vindictively, voraciously.
W—warily, weakly, whistling.
Y—yelling, yearning.
Z—zealously, zigzagging.

The winners—A count should be made of the number of cockades won by "Yankees" and "Redcoats" and the victorious group announced. The victorious army should be permitted to parade triumphantly about the room, the general leading the way on his trusty broom "charger."

Progressive Paul Revere.—Progressive Paul Revere may be played after the fashion of the familiar game of "Hearts." Wooden cubes can be obtained from some carpenter shop. The letters "R-E-V-E-R-E" should be printed with pencil or ink on the six sides of the cube. Six cubes make a set. For a small crowd there should be only four players to a table. Players draw slips or tally cards to determine how they shall be placed. For instance, "Company A, Fort Ticonderoga," or "Company B, Fort Ticonderoga," will each appear on two cards. These players immediately go to the table bearing a "Fort Ticonderoga" flag. See "Decorations" for the "Paul Revere Colonial Party" for the arrangement of these tables.

For larger groups, from six to a dozen players may be assigned to a table. In this case there should be several sets of cubes for each table so it will not be so long between turns for each player. If there are six players to a table, three players will form a company. The companies will remain intact throughout the play of the evening. That company with the largest score is declared winner. Winning teams at each table progress to the next table, moving clockwise.

Scoring is counted as follows: No score is allowed unless the player turns up at least the first three letters of the name, thus, "R-E-V." This counts ten points. "R-E-V-E" counts fifteen. "R-E-V-E-R" counts twenty. The player spelling the entire name is awarded thirty points. Any player who tosses three "V's" cancels his entire score up to that point for that game.

A bugle call announces the time for the winning companies to advance and attack the next fort or town.

Refreshments—Layer cake in red, white, and blue layers. Ice-cream mounds with tiny American flags stuck in them.

A CRAZY CARNIVAL

Invitations—Carnival posters. Crazy Cat invitations.

Decorations—Side shows, toy balloons, Japanese lanterns, crazy slogans, such as "A stitch in time saves embarrassment."

Crazy costumes—Ask each person who is invited to dress in some sort of crazy fashion. The arrangement of the hair, the wearing of unusual clothes combinations, and many other ways can be devised to make this feature add to the fun of the evening. A costume committee takes care of people who arrive at the party dressed normally.

Crazy introductions—Conduct a grand march to get the crowd into two concentric circles. Partners face one another and proceed with some sort of crazy introduction. "I am Olive Oyl." "And I am Popeye, the Sailor Man." "I am Snow White." "And I am Grumpy." When the music starts the circles get in motion again in opposite directions. A person may assume a new name each time he introduces himself.

Crazy spielers—Appoint spielers for each of the side shows. When ready for this part of the performance have each spieler mount a chair or box and begin "barking" for his particular side show in true carnival fashion.

Crazy side shows—"A Swimming Match" (a match floating in a pan of water), "The Boxers" (persons packing material in boxes), midgets, freaks, fortunetellers. For other suggestions see *Phunology*, "Circus Party" (pages 211-213); "Freak Exhibits" (pages 321-323); "High Class Vaudeville" (page 307); "Midget Ladies" (page 327); "Sunflower Minstrel" (pages 327 and 147); "The Dwarf" (page 313); "The Great Grinmore Circus" in this volume.

Crazy show—Present some well prepared stunts. Or present a program where the performers never do what they are announced to do, but always something else. The master of ceremonies proceeds as if nothing is amiss. For instance he announces that "Mr. Brown will sing for us" and Mr. Brown proceeds to recite a poem. "Miss Jones will give a dramatic reading" and Miss Jones sings a solo.

A PUZZLE PARTY

A puzzling intelligence test.—On arrival guests are given a puzzling intelligence test. Each person takes the test immediately upon arrival. Mimeographed sheets are provided with the following tests in order:

1. If blackberries are green when they are red write *H* at the right hand side of this test. If not, write *X*.

2. If black cows give white milk that makes yellow butter write *A* at the right hand side. If not, write *Y*.

3. If a regulation football field is just 90 yards long from goal to goal write *Z* to the right. If not, write *V*.

4. If paper is made out of wood, write *E* to the right. If not, write a zero.

5. If an airplane can travel faster than an automobile write *A*. If not, write the number four.

6. If summer is warmer than winter write *G* in the margin. If not, write *R*.

7. If Longfellow wrote "Twinkle, Twinkle, Little Star" write *S* in the margin. If not, write *O*.

8. If candy is sweeter than lemons write *O* in the margin. If not, write the number three.

9. If Beethoven wrote "Moonlight Sonata" write *D* in the margin. If not, write the number four.

10. If the climate in Siberia is warmer than it is in Florida write *X* in the margin. If not, write *T*.

11. If the printing press was first invented by an American write *Z* in the margin. If not, write *I*.

12. If New York City is the capital of New York State write *A* in the margin. If not, write *M*.

13. If baseball is a major sport write *E* in the margin. If not, write *O*.

When a guest has answered each of these tests correctly he has written *H-A-V-E A G-O-O-D T-I-M-E*.

Puzzling names.—Names of certain members of the group are written with jumbled letters, as for instance, REPTOR for POR-TER. Each person gets a list and tries to straighten out the names. At the end of five minutes, or whatever is the designated time limit, the leader reads a correct list and each player checks his own answers.

Jigsaws.—Tables are provided with jigsaw puzzles. Simple puzzles, Bible pictures, and difficult puzzles can be used. Work out plans so that each guest gets opportunity to work on the three types of puzzles. Four people or more work at a given table. Slips are drawn to determine who shall be at what table. Each group is allowed to work ten minutes and then the bell rings for all players to move to the second appointment. If a picture puzzle is incomplete it is left for the next group to finish. Plan so that each person will be with a different group on each move.

Puzzle teasers.—Have distributed about the room all sorts of puzzles to intrigue individuals and groups to add moments during the evening—the devil's needle, 33 hole solitaire, human checkers, lover's knot, various wire puzzles for the occasion.

Cross word puzzles.—One group worked out a clever cross word puzzle containing the name of the pastor. Or play "Cross Word Lexicon" or "Kan-u-go."

Puzzling refreshments.—Allow each person to order three articles from the menu of five. They order by number and no one knows what the numbers mean except the refreshment committee. People are served the three items they order. Of course, those that order the wrong numbers are later given some of the refreshments. Here's the menu key as held by the committee: one, empty plate; two, piece of cake; three, glass of water; four, ice cream; five, toothpick.

CRAZY INTELLIGENCE TEST

Each person is given a piece of paper upon which he writes his name. The group is then notified that they must answer the following questions with "yes" or "no," but must give the wrong answers. For instance, if the question were: "Is it hot at the South Pole?" The answer would be yes. About three seconds are allowed after each question then. Papers are exchanged and the leader reads the questions and answers.

1. Is it cold at the North Pole? No.
2. Is the moon made of cheese? Yes.
3. Are oranges black in South Dakota? Yes.
4. Does water flow up a hill in China? Yes.
5. Does a car use gasoline in the radiator? Yes.
6. Will paper burn upside down? No.
7. Can a dog bark after it is dead? Yes.
8. Are bananas good to eat in Siberia? No.
9. Are lemons sweet in California? Yes.
10. Is rain water good to drink in Honolulu? No.
11. Is gasoline inflammable? No.
12. Are green apples good for indigestion? Yes.
13. Is snow white on a coal pile? No.
14. Is gold valuable when lost? No.
15. Is a sweet potato a vegetable? No.
16. Is baking soda poisonous? Yes.
17. Is strychnine good for baby's colic? Yes.
18. Does kerosene taste good in milk? Yes.
19. Is the bottom of the ocean wet? No.
20. Does the sun set in the North? Yes.

In case there are ties the following questions are read to those who tied allowing about one second after each question.

1. Is the capitol of the United States in New York?   Yes.

2. Does the Mississippi river flow North?   Yes.

3. Is it nearer to Wisconsin than it is to New York?   No.

4. Does it ever snow in Nebraska?   No.

5. Will ten make a dozen in Florida?   Yes.

6. Can eggplants hatch in three weeks?   Yes.

7. Do kangeroos brush their teeth after shaving?   Yes.

8. Was George Washington born in Minnesota?   Yes.

9. Do natives eat crocodiles in Honolulu?   Yes.

10. Is molten lava good for toothache?   Yes.

—DAVIS WAGUESPACK

MAY

AN OLD CLOTHES PARTY

Wear old clothes—Each person is expected to come wearing old clothes—overalls, khaki, gingham, ragged clothes.

Names—As each one arrives, a patch bearing his name is pinned on his back. This is to be worn throughout the evening.

Grand march.—Line up girls on one side and boys on the other. Conduct a grand march to divide the group in two equal sides.

Dress-up contest.—This is similar to the old "Honeymoon Race" idea. Several boxes containing hats, coats, etc. One box with contents is given to each couple. On signal to go each couple must open box and dress in the garments found there. They must then run to a stated point, return, and remove the extra garments, putting them back in the box. The first couple to finish wins. Where there is a large crowd, representatives may be chosen for the two sides.

Clothespin race.—Have each side line up, single file. Give the first person in each line a double handful of clothespins. These are to be passed overhead, one at a time, till they reach the last person in line. This player then runs to the head of the line and starts the pins backward again. This continues until the original head player is back at that position. For each pin dropped, one point is scored for the opposition. The side which completes the round first is awarded three points.

Hanging clothes.—Five to ten players for each side line up single file at starting point. The starting player has a clothespin and a towel or handkerchief. At the far side of the playing space a clothesline has been strung. The first player must run to this clothesline and hang the towel or handkerchief with the use of the clothespin. The second player in line must run and remove the pin and towel, bring them back to player Number Three. So it continues until all the players have made the course.

Clothes grab.—This is similar to "Snatch" or "Bottle and Handkerchief Swipe." An old rag is placed on a book or stick or stone at a point midway between the two lines of players. The two lines of players "number off." The leader calls a number and the two players having that number rush out to the center. One of them finally grabs the rag and is pursued back to his line by his opponent. Two points are scored if he returns to his line without being tagged. One point is scored for the opposition if the player with the rag is tagged.

Clothes basket.—Played like "Fruit Basket." Players are numbered off by fours. The ones are "shoes," and twos are "hats," the threes are "coats," and the fours are "vests." "Clothes basket upset!" means everyone changes seats.

Old songs.—Have the party close with the singing of some of the old songs like "Silver Threads among the Gold," "When You and I Were Young, Maggie," "Annie Laurie," "Long, Long Ago," and "Old Folks at Home."

Refreshments—Wieners and buns.

A JIGSAW PUZZLE PARTY

Are you looking for some new fun for your party? Groups in search of new and interesting games to use in their recreational activities will find jigsaw puzzle contests fascinating and popular. The jigsaw puzzle, venerable parlor game of bygone days, still has an appeal. One group of folks became so fascinated in putting the puzzle pieces together that they were entirely unaware of the passing of time, and when they were finished it was much later than the parties usually end.

In recent years entertainment has become professionalized and artificial to a great extent and also quite expensive. When the spending capacity of the public is cut down people spend more time at home and employ their powers of imagination and resourcefulness to discover inexpensive forms of amusement and entertainment. Hence the comeback of the jigsaw puzzle.

In playing, divide your group into teams of two, three, or four, depending on the number of players. Seat each team at a small table on which the pieces of a jigsaw puzzle well shuffled have been previously placed, a different puzzle on each table. At a signal each team strives to be the first to solve the puzzle at hand, while judges or scorekeepers count the minutes. When every team has completed its puzzle and the winners have been noted the pieces are shuffled again and the players all move to the next table in turn to solve the puzzle on it while the judges again mark the time and note the winners. This continues until each team has solved all the puzzles in turn or until a specified time has been reached. If preferred, you can have several of the same puzzle, rather than different puzzles.

Jigsaw puzzles can be easily made by gluing an attractive picture or design to a piece of thin wood and sawing out more or less intricate pieces with a jigsaw. Old paintings, pictures that tell a story, and maps such as one of Treasure Island or the Holy Land, etc., make interesting puzzle subjects. They can be simple with as few as twenty-five pieces or exceedingly complex with five hundred to a thousand pieces.

A TENNIS PARTY

At least one tennis court should be available. Tables with games of anagrams, Kan-u-go, logomachy, and the like. From two to four persons will use the court for from one to three games. The rest will gather at the tables and play games. Pitchers of ice-cold lemonade or orangeade will be at hand for use as desired.

Mock tennis features.—*Balloon tennis*—A large, durable toy balloon will be the ball. Players will use their hands as rackets. As many players can play as can get on the court. The ball is put in play by one player near the net batting it high in the air. Players may hit the ball as many times in succession as they desire. When the ball hits the ground the play is over. Score as in regular tennis.

Serving blindfolded—Players are blindfolded, turned around, and made to serve. Any player getting the ball over the net scores a point. Another method would be that of having blindfolded players toss the ball over the net.

Getting partners—Strings are wound in and out through the meshes of the net across the court. There should be one string for each two persons. Players are told to take the end of a string and untangle it, the girls starting from one side and the boys from the other. When the string is untangled a boy and a girl will be holding it. These two are partners for refreshments or for some game.

A tennis romance.—Read this romance aloud and pause for the players to fill in the vacancies with words and phrases familiar in tennis.

He was considered a real good catch,
She first met him at a *(tennis match)*.
At *(forty all)* he knew did like him;
Her beauty with a jolt did strike him,
On him she looked with favored eye,
And decided he'd not draw a *(bye)*.
In a *(love)* game played by only two;
She felt that he was a lover true,
So she wasted no time, you can bet,
A-getting him fast into her *(net)*.
He'd seen her once at the church *(service)*
But now they'd met it made him nervous;
For he had a girl in ev'ry port,
Now her alone did he wish to *(court)*.
What if an old love-letter packet
Turned up to make an awful *(racket)*?
Or suppose some old flame played the *(deuce)*
And gossiped around town without excuse?
Those were the problems that made him halt,
Though his life was really without *(fault)*.
He soon decided he wouldn't fret,
But he'd try to get the stage all *(set)*.
Would she life's game with all its troubles
Play it *(singles)* or play it *(doubles)*?
She was a-tremble, her heart did burn,
But she soon gave him a quick *(return)*.
And wed they were as soon as her dad
Told him to proceed, it was his *(ad)*.

A MOTHER GOOSE PARTY

Adapted from suggestions by Mary Harvey Love in the Recreation Class at Lake Junaluska.

Invitation—Posters with Mother Goose pictures and rhymes. Special invitation with the following jingle:

"Hey, hey!" said Farmer Gray,
"There's a Mother Goose Party coming this way."
"Ray, ray!" said Mother Gray,
"I'll get our costumes ready right today."

Date_____   Place_____
(Please come in costume.)

Decorations—Celluloid dolls dressed to represent Mother Goose characters, such as Jack and Jill, Little Boy Blue (asleep under a haystack with toy cows and sheep near by), the Old Woman in the

Shoe, etc. Denison Manufacturing Company makes some "Mother Goose" crepe paper.

Throne for King and Queen of Hearts.

Red and white crepe-paper streamers for canopy.

Games and entertainment—The social committee should dress to represent the King, Queen, and Knave of Hearts, Old Mother Goose, and Old Mother Hubbard. These should serve as the reception committee.

Each person is required to go to the King and Queen, who give them slips of paper, one to a person. On these slips are instructions for later action. Each one is to keep his own instructions secret.

Mother Goose songs—The following Mother Goose numbers would furnish a good collection from which to choose some good special numbers:

John Church Company—(1649) "Old King Cole," Nevin (male quartet); "Jack and Jill," Jarvis (male trio); (1451) "Peter Piper," Jarvis (male trio); (1669) "Little Jack Horner," Ashford (male quartet); (1723) "Old Mother Hubbard," Ashford (male quartet); (2284) "Mother Goose," Bliss (male quartet); (1822) "Roundelay of Nursery Rhymes," Lovenberg (mixed voices).

Theodore Presser, Philadelphia, Pa.— (231) "Jack and Jill," Leason (mixed voices); (20243) "Old King Cole," Stults (mixed).

Oliver Ditson, Boston, Mass.— (9797) "Little Tommy Tucker," Bullard (mixed); (4556) "Dickory, Dickory, Dock," Allen (mixed); (6815) "Tom, Tom, the Piper's Son," Allen (mixed); (5053) "Old King Cole," Archer (mixed); (4320) "Jack and Jill," Caldicott (mixed); (4326) "Little Jack Horner," Caldicott (mixed).

Good collections of nursery rhyme songs can be found in most ten-cent stores. Some of these could be used for group singing as could also the familiar "Throw It Out the Window" song.

Guess who you are.—Pin the name of some Mother Goose character on the back of each person. As soon as one thinks he knows who he is he reports to the committee. If he is correct, the name is taken off. He guesses what character he represents from the remarks made to him by others.

Another way to use this idea would be to have each person, in turn, stand in the center of the circle of players. The players make remarks or ask questions appropriate to the character, until the player guesses whom he represents.

Grand march.—A pianist who can play a good march is needed. Put the group through several marching figures.

Impromptu stunts.—The leader stops the march and explains that at the sound of the whistle everyone is to follow the instructions on the slip of paper given earlier in the evening. Then strange things begin to happen—a tall "Simple Simon," perhaps, drops to his knees to propose to his partner. She, in turn, begins spinning around with her left arm crooked over her head, the fore finger touching the head. Everyone in the room is doing some crazy stunt. Allow this to continue for a few seconds only. If your crowd isn't loosened up by that time, they're hopeless.

Spider.—You know about Little Miss Muffett and the spider that sat down beside her. Well, you could play the old game of "Slide, Kelly, Slide," and call it "The Spider." The person who is "It" would be the "Spider," and the idea is to keep him from sitting down beside you. There is one vacant seat in the circle which the "Spider" tries to occupy. The crowd slides to the right to keep him out. If he gets seated, the person to his left is considered responsible and becomes the "Spider," in turn.

Jack Horner contest.—This is a blindfold marshmallow-feeding contest. Divide the crowd into two sides. Have a boy and a girl represent each side. Each of the contestants have five marshmallows on a saucer. These they must feed to one another. Of course there will be some missing of the mark.

Stealing the pig.—Just like "Tom, Tom, the Piper's Son." A handkerchief or bean bag on a stool midway between the two lines of players represents the pig. Players are numbered consecutively. Leader calls a number, and two players bearing that number rush out to get the pig or to tag the other player, when he touches it. The player who touches the "pig" must carry it safely to his line without being tagged by his opponent. He scores two points if he can do that. He scores one point if he tags his opponent who is trying to get back to his line with it. You can see it isn't a good idea to rush out and grab the "pig" immediately unless the opponent is asleep at the switch.

Blackbird pie.—Make a large crepe paper pie with strings dropping down from under the top crust. Each player takes hold of a string and at a given signal pulls. On the end of each string is a fortune written in white ink on a small, black paper bird.

Dramatizations.—Divide the crowd into two or more groups and have each group present a dramatization of some Mother Goose rhyme. If it's done in pantomime, the rest of the groups may try to guess what rhyme is being represented. It might be well for the committee to have some materials for costuming on hand, though costuming is not absolutely required.

Refreshments—Tarts and milk, or Humpty-Dumpty salad (an egg salad) and sandwiches. The refreshments may be served from Mother Hubbard's cupboard.

One such party had Mother Goose enter at the beginning of the party mounted on a large gander (two boys in costume).

A ROMANCE FOR MAY

The fillers-in in this story must all contain the name of May. Call them out as soon as you are sure you're right. One point for each correct answer. One point off for each mistake. Here goes!

> In the good merry month of (*May*),
> At least, that's what they all do say,
> The (*Mayor's*) sweet daughter (*Mayme*)
> Was to be the Queen of the (*May*)
> However, strange as it may seem
> That fact had brought no happy dream
> For (*Mayme's*) dear lover (*Maynard*),
> With anger his fierce eyes did gleam.
> (*Maybe*) he still was angry quite,
> (*Maybe*) he still was stern and sad,
> (*Maybe*) he'd still sternly refuse
> To make once more her sad heart glad
> But (*Maybees*) are such troubling bees,
> In fact, they nearly run one wild,
> So (*Mayme*) fell down on her knees
> And wept just like a little child.
> Oh, why had she refused to eat
> The (*Mayonnaise*) he'd freely sent?
> That was the thing that upset him,
> Filled him with glowing discontent.
> He taunted her with cruel speech,
> Before him trembling she did cow'r;
> He mocked her (*May-den*) pride because
> Her forebears were on the (*Mayflower*).
> She'd just as soon he'd maimed her sore,
> It filled her poor heart with (*dismay*).
> No (*Mayhem*) harsh could have been worse;
> It spoiled all that happy (*May Day*).
> But as she sighed the doorbell rang,
> 'Twas (*Mayflowers*) from her lover.

Again with joy her gay heart sang
And she thanked the God above her.
She warbled "Sweetheart" from ("*Maytime*"),
And "Oh, that we two were (*maying*)."
She skipped, she hopped, she leaped, she ran,
Like a happy colt at playing.
Her lover came to escort her;
They went down to the village green,
(*Mayhap*) the (*Maypole*) dance that day
Was the gayest one ever seen.
For sweet (*Mayme*) was the (*May Queen*)
And handsome (*Maynard*) was her beau,
And (*Maybe*) they will married be
Next (*May*) or in a month or so.

JUNE

A TREE PICNIC

Naturally, this will be an outdoor affair in a place where there are lots of trees.

Tree identification.—Pair off and provide each couple with a pencil and a card, which has a list of numbers corresponding to numbers on various trees about the place. Each couple is to identify the tagged trees, placing the name of each tree opposite its number on the card. When all have finished they return and the leader reads the correct list, each couple checking its own answers.

Tree leaves.—Couples change partners and scout the woods to find tree leaves. The couple to get the largest collection of different varieties of tree leaves is declared "Leaf Champions." They must be able to name the tree to which a leaf belongs before being allowed to count it.

Leaf identification.—The crowd now sits on the ground in a circle and the leader passes around a collection of leaves from various trees. Those leaves have numbers pinned on them. The couples write the names of the trees opposite their correct numbers. The leader reads the correct list.

Tree bark.—The same thing is done with bits of tree bark. It will add interest if a good woodcraftsman is present to explain how to identify trees.

Do you know your wood?—The same plan can be followed with polished pieces of wood—cherry, oak, maple, pine, gum, beech, hickory, walnut. It ought to be possible to get tiny samples from the lumber yard.

Spatter prints.—Have someone demonstrate spatter printing and have enough equipment on hand to give everyone a chance to print a few leaves on white sheets of paper. All you will need will be some showcard ink or tempera (green, red, blue), a number of old tooth brushes, and equal number of pieces of wire screen three by five inches, a few pins to hold the leaves and paper in place. See *Nature Crafts,* by Veazie (Woman's Press).

Tree anagrams.—Stand the group in line. The leader calls out a letter, for instance, *B.* The first person in line must call a word beginning with the letter. Perhaps he says "Beech." Then the next player says "Balsam," or "Banana," or "Butternut." When a player cannot answer with the name of a tree that has not been mentioned and some other player below him in the line can, the player must go foot while the successful player takes his place. Each player, must get his chance in turn. When no one can answer the leader calls another letter, and the game proceeds.

What good is wood?—Have the players seated in a circle. Each player, in turn, must mention some use man makes of trees. When a use has been named it cannot be called again. If desired, players may be required to drop out when they fail to respond. Some of the answers will be, as follows: For shade; to produce apples, peaches, pears, prunes, cherries, nuts; to build houses, sheds, stables, barns, chairs, tables, beds, etc.; to make fires, to make pencils, to absorb water, to prevent floods.

Tree poems.—Read some of the fine tree poems. Here are a few of the better ones: "A Psalm of Friendly Trees," Henry Van Dyke, in *Out-of-Doors in the Holy Land;* in *Quotable Poems*—"ABC's in Green," "Loveliest of Trees," "Good Company." ("Today I have grown taller from walking with the trees"), "Symbol"; in *Nature's Knap Sack*—"ABC's in Green," "God, When you Thought of a Pine Tree," "The House of the Trees," "The Trees," "What Do We Plant?" and others.

Solitude

"Have you breathed the faith of the fir trees, by the lure of campfire light?
Watched the wistful shadows creeping toward the restful lap of night?
Have you sent your thoughts a-homing to the source of space and time?
Felt the pulse of soul communion full and firm with the divine?
Sensed the wonders of creation? Gripped the purpose of the whole?
Then you know the mystic sweetness that comes stealing o'er the soul.
As on balsam boughs spread thickly on the mossy mountain sod
One with questioning eyes looks upward to the very heart of God."
—M. D. GEDDESS, in *Canadian Forest and Outdoors.* Used by permisison.

Bible references.—It would be interesting if someone is prepared to call attention to the number of references to trees in the Bible. Any good concordance will give this information. See Deut. 20: 19; Job 14: 7; Psalm 1: 3; Ecclesiastes 11: 3; Ezekiel 31: 1-9.

A vesper service.—A vesper service could be built around the verse, "He shall be like a tree planted by the river of waters." Psalm 1: 3. "Services for the Open," Mattoon and Bragdon (Century) has worship service on trees entitled "God's Sentinels."

Tree Songs

Sacred: "Into the Woods," Sidney Lanier.

Secular: Presser— (10252) "Away to the Woods," R. E. DeReef; (Z 0835) "The Brave Old Oak," A. Garland, 3-part chorus; (20108) "Where Cedars Rise," Lieurance; (20871) "Would God I Were a Tender Apple Blossom," Felton; (20707) "Gay October's Come Again," Baines, soprano-alto; (10347) "Voices of the Woods," Rubenstein, 3-part treble; (20691) "The Woods Are Calling," Baines, soprano-alto.

Birchard— (571) "The Birch Tree," Schubert (Arbor Day Song), soprano-alto; (478) "Cherry Ripe," Horn-Page, treble voices; (79) "In Vienna Woods," Strauss-McConathy; (931) "Flowering Orchards," Pillor's-Davison, a cappella male quartet.

E. C. Schirmer— (1149) "To Woodland Glades," Tessier, a cappella.

John Church— (2414) "The Woodland Sprite," Ardite, 3-part treble; (2573) "Trees," Hohn, 3-part treble; (1554) "The Wood Nymphs," Smart, 3-part treble; (2599) "The Arbutus Tree," Saar (Irish Folk Song), male quartet; (1497) "The Almond Tree," Schumann, male quartet; (1441) "The Drowsy Woods," Storch, male quartet.

Willis Music Co.— (1026-B) "The Lonely Pine," Rachmaninoff, soprano-alto; (1887) "Down in the Woodland," Edgar-Bliss, soprano-alto; (1013-B) "The Forest Fairies Call," Elliot, soprano-alto; (1845-B) "Singing in the Tree-Tops," Treharne, a cappella.

G. Schirmer— (7123) "Trees," Rasbach, mixed or male quartet, or treble.

All of these are chorus numbers unless otherwise indicated.

The familiar "Lilac Tree" makes a good encore solo and "All in a Wood There Was a Tree" is a good fun song for everyone to sing.

Tree story.—See "The Parable of the Trees" in *Greatness Passing By*, by Hulda Niebuhr, based on Judges 9: 8-13.

Books that will be helpful: *Talking Leaves*, King, obtainable at the ten-cent store. Your State Forestry Department will likely furnish you with a free book on state trees.

Tree Riddles.—

Which is the straightest tree that grows? Plum.
Which tree is made of stone? Lime.
Which tree is older than others? Elder.
Which tree languishes? Pine.
Which tree is found after a fire? Ash.
Which tree keeps milady warm? Fir.
Which tree is often kept in bottles? Cork.
Which tree is homely? Plane.
Which tree do you carry in your hand? Palm.
What tree reminds you of a couple? Pear.
What tree suggests your sweetheart? Peach.
What tree is sticky, but good to chew? Gum.
What tree suggests a color? Redwood.
What tree suggests clothes? Cottonwood.
What tree is an insect? Locust.

A TREASURE HUNT FOR THE BRIDE-TO-BE

The Invitation

You're invited to hunt treasure,
  With the bride-to-be;
Plan for frolic with good measure,
  Come right merrily.

This rhyme is written on a card with a pirate head or skull and crossbones adorning the upper left hand corner.

Hunting words—Give each person two minutes to find as many words as he can in the words "bride-to-be" or in the name of the lucky girl.

The bride's treasure hunt.—Explain to the bride-elect before the company that she is to start on a treasure hunt, following directions as she finds them. The hostess then hands her Card No. 1, which reads:

Look in the kettle where often there's fire,
And there you will find
What is next to transpire.

She goes to the fireplace and there finds in the kettle Card No. 2 which advises:

> Pick out the man who is to be your mate
> And he shall go with you to learn your fate;
> Next behind a picture on the dining-room wall,
> You may find just the way your fate will fall.

She takes the groom-elect with her to look behind picture frames in the dining room for Card No. 3.

> Not a Ford, nor a Packard,
> Nor a jitney alas!
> But it's down in the garage,
> And it travels with gas;
> Just look carefully
> Before going ahead
> For it may hold your fate
> When its message you've read.

The car in the garage happens to be an Oldsmobile.   There on the seat they find Card No. 4.

> We hate to delay you,
> But can't help it, my dears,
> The breakfast room holds
> A message for your ears.

In the breakfast room on a table they find Card No. 5.

> Right up the stairs
> In the room straight ahead
> You'll find some directions
> Displayed on the bed.

Card No. 6 reads:

> Pinned to a tree
> In the yard just below
> You'll find information
> About just where to go.

Card No. 7 gives the following instructions:

> Back to the house,
> To the living room go,
> Look back of the couch,
> And then you will know.

Behind the couch there is a little wagon or hamper with presents for the bride-elect and Card No. 8, which reads:

> Just like this hunt you'll find life to be,
> With its ups and its downs,
> And its uncertainty;
> In the end, if you stick,
> You'll find it is true,
> That success is attained
> By following through.

The bride reads all the treasure hunt directions to the guests, and then opens her packages.

Hunting futures.—Each person is allowed to select the end of a string. She must then follow this string to the end. It may tangle with other strings. She stops to untangle. It may go upstairs and downstairs. Or it may be just a short string leading into the next room. At the end is a fortune for the bride-elect. When all guests have gotten to the end of their strings, they reassemble and each reads her future for the bride-to-be. A few samples follows:

> Sunny days and honey days
> Your wedded days will be,
> Filled with golden happy ways
> And much felicity.

> When things seem to go wrong
> Don't bawl and cry;
> Just jack up your lower lip,
> Reach for the sky.

A MOCK TRIAL FOR THE BRIDE-ELECT

The trial is carefully planned and kept secret from the bride and groom. Two clever "lawyers" diligently coached their witnesses.

At the proper moment the judge took the stand and the clerk of court arraigned the culprit, the bride-elect, before the bar. She was charged with having forsaken her oath of allegiance to the United Daughters of Spinsterhood. For the prosecution, Witness Number One professed to be Secretary of the United Daughters. She testified that the bride-elect had been a member and had taken the oath to never marry. Witness Number Two testified that she had been persuaded to join by the defendant, much against her will. She wept bitter tears as she recalled how her hopes for wedded bliss were upset by a heartless woman who was only laying her plans to capture a man at the earliest opportunity. One or two other witnesses were offered. The defense offered a character witness or two, a girl friend who testified that the bride-elect was only fooling the bridegroom and really did not intend to get married, a former gentleman friend who testified that he did not believe she was going to get married. The judge's verdict was guilty and sentence was life imprisonment with the groom-elect as jailer.

A SHADOW SHOW FOR THE BRIDE-ELECT

Each couple must present a shadow picture of the bride-elect and her fiance. "The Proposal," "Her First Meal," "The First Goodbye," "Goodbye after Ten Years," "The First Quarrel," and "The First Shopping Trip" indicate some of the possibilities.

Hang a sheet over the doorway. Place a light behind the performers and turn out all other lights to get the shadow-picture effects.

A SILHOUETTE PARTY FOR THE BRIDE

Have each guest make a silhouette of the bride, who poses. First have them sketch the profile and head on white paper. Cut this out, place it on black paper, and outline. Cut out the silhouette and paste it on a white card. They will be good, bad, and indifferent, but it will be lots of fun.

ADVICE TO THE BRIDE, GROOM

Now have each person write a word of advice on the silhouette card to the bride and an additional word of advice to the groom.

SHOWERS FOR THE BRIDE

A recipe shower would be appropriate. Each guest must bring a favorite recipe written on cards of uniform size. These cards may be sent out with the invitations. They should be punched so that they can be tied together. An attractive cover might be improvised. At the party it would be fun to have the guests write novel recipes on various subjects, such as "Recipe for Keeping a Husband Contented," "Recipe for Keeping a Wife Happy," "Recipe for Keeping a Sweet Disposition When Hubby Comes Home Late," "Recipe for Keeping Calm When the Biscuits Are Burned."

Other showers for the bride could feature linens, handerchiefs, utensils, china, trousseau, and miscellaneous.

A GYPSY CAMP

Adapted from suggestions by Lucile Lewis in the recreation class at Lake Junaluska.

1. Divide responsibility. Appoint the following committees: Eats, Decorations, Games, Advertising.

2. The Decorations Committee found a deep rock pit for the Gypsy Camp. They fixed it up with old tents, old lanterns, a cauldron and tripod, and built a big bonfire.

3. Everyone is requested to come dressed as a gypsy. Old clothes, especially if colorful, and brilliantly-colored headpieces (scarfs) will do the job.

4. The Advertising Committee will get out special invitations with a picture of a gypsy on each one. Gypsy posters are also a possibility.

5. The Gypsy Bus. The crowd enjoys a hay ride to the Gypsy Camp. If it is impossible to get a truck, making it necessary to use cars, call this feature "The Gypsy Caravan."

6. Program:

(1) *Fortunetelling*—Try to get a clever palm reader. In lieu of a palmist, or in addition to that feature, have typewritten fortunes which are to be fished out of the gypsy cauldron.

(2) *Contests*—Divide the crowd into two gypsy tribes and engage in the following contests: (*a*) Weaver's relay. (*b*) Potato race. (*c*) Blindfold newspaper boxing match. Contestants lie flat on the ground holding one another's left hand. They take turns about hitting at one another with paper clubs. Every hit counts a point. "Ready Gypsy?" "Shoot!" (*d*) Cracker relay. (*e*) Talk fest.

Or in place of these contests, play folk games such as "Carrousel."

(3) *"All together!"*— (*a*) Laughing handkerchief. (*b*) Jacob and Rachel. (*c*) Songs: "Long, Long Trail," "Gypsy Love Song," "The Gypsy Trail," and "A Merry Life" (Funiculi, Funicula).

(4) *Gypsy witch*—A gypsy "witch" comes into the circle and stirs in the cauldron with a stick. Then she proceeds to take a message out of the cauldron and read. What she reads proves to be a prophecy for the group, particularly for certain members in the group. This should be carefully prepared beforehand.

7. Eats. The committee provides wieners, pickles, or sauerkraut, and rolls.

8. Taps.

> "Then good-night, peaceful night,
> Till the light of the dawn shineth bright;
> God is near, do not fear—
> Friend, good-night."

A NEWSSTAND PARTY

Invitation—Make a poster by cutting a jagged hole out of a newspaper and pasting it on a piece of poster cardboard. In this center print the announcement of the party.

Decorations—Rig up a newsstand in one corner of the room, displaying copies of magazines.

Stunts and Games.—*Newsboys*—Begin the program by having a couple of "newsboys" suddenly appear on the scene shouting "EXTRA!" They pass out mimeographed sheets containing the program of the party.

Newspaper hats—Each person makes a newspaper hat to wear during the evening. Furnish paper, pins, and as many pairs of scissors as you can get.

Advertisements—Cut out of magazines and newspapers familiar advertisements, deleting the name of the product advertised. Number these and place them about the room. Provide players with pencils and paper and have them guess what products are advertised. The "Extra" given out earlier in the evening may contain place for these articles to be written.

Newspaper doilies—Each player is given a page from a newspaper. He is given a few moments to tear out some design for a doily. The best of these designs may be put on display.

Newspaper tricks—Perhaps there will be some in the group who can teach the crowd some newspaper tricks, such as making "Jacob's Ladder," for instance. See "Fun with Paper" in Chapter I, Home Fun.

Newspaper race—Contestants are furnished two sheets of a newspaper. These they must place on the floor and step from one to the other as they race down the course. This means they will have to take a step and reach back for the sheet they have just left to place it ahead of them. Under no circumstances must they touch their feet to anything but the newspapers. Naturally, they will make slow progress.

Newspaper—Give five minutes for each person to make as many words as possible out of the letters in the word "newspaper."

Dramatization—Divide into several groups and have each group dramatize some incident reported in the daily newspaper. Each group would be furnished with a recent newspaper and the selection of the news item would be left to the group.

The comic strip—Each person would be given paper and pencil and required to sketch a likeness of the person sitting to the right. These cartoons are labeled with the names of the persons they are supposed to represent and passed around the group for each person to see.

Slips are passed out which assign the guests to different groups— "Sports," "News," "Editorials," "Advertising," "Society News," etc.

These groups are given from fifteen to thirty minutes to get up their respective sections of *The Daily Gossip*. This newspaper is then read, each group having someone read its particular section.

Newspaper costumes—(a) Pair off and have each boy dress his partner, consulting latest patterns on the wall, or using his own ideas. A whole newspaper and some pins are all that is furnished. (b) In a large crowd it might be advisable to have three or four groups dress some one person in each group. At one such party one group dressed their entrant to represent "The Gay Nineties." She had a muff, a bustle, a long dress, a cape, a clever hat—all made out of newspapers and all done without the use of scissors.

Newspaper refreshments—Serve the refreshments wrapped in newspapers. Or furnish newspaper napkins.

A JUNE PASSING-SHOW PARTY

Better go, don't you know,
To the June Passing-Show,
Don't be slow; ask your beau,
Or your belle; "Hey, let's go."

Suggest that all the boys come coatless. Girls should wear summer frocks in which they are not afraid to play.

Sing.—Begin the party with a rousing sing, using appropriate songs. We suggest "rose" songs, beginning the sing with "In the Good Old Summertime." Then follow with "Moonlight and Roses," "My Wild Irish Rose," "The Last Rose of Summer," and any other "rose" songs you may find. "Thank God for a Garden," and "Roses of Picardy" make good solo numbers. At the close of the sing have someone read Riley's "Knee-deep in June."

Under the rose arbor.—Have a grand march. Men form line on one side of room and girls on the other. The two lines meet and come down center as partners. At far end of room first couple goes to column left, second to column right, third to left, etc. March to other end of room. When two lines meet there the line of couples indicated by the leader forms a bridge by holding inside hands high. It will add to the effect if each player carries a rose, paper or real. The other line passes under this arbor. All players keep marching all the time. When the two lines meet again, the players bridged make an arbor for the others. Let each side form the arbor twice. The first time march around, the second skip it, keeping time to the music.

What I like about June.—At the end of the march have couples discuss for a few moments "What I like about June."

Rose garden.—Players should be seated in a circle. One player, who is "It," stands in the center. The leader has the entire group number off by fours. He then announces that all Ones are Red Roses; all Twos, White Roses; all Threes, American Beauties; and all Fours, Ramblers. "It" says, "I want a bouquet of Red Roses and Ramblers." All Red Roses and Ramblers have to change seats, while "It" endeavors to get a seat. The player who is left standing is "It" and the game proceeds, the player calling the names of any two of the kinds of roses named. When "It" calls out "Garden Gate," all players must change seats.

Rose relay.—The Red and White Roses combine against the Ramblers and American Beauties for all contests. Two teams of ten each are chosen for the relay. These two teams line up facing one another, their players placed at such intervals as to stretch out the line the length of the room. A rose is given to the player at the head of each line. At the signal to start this player must zigzag his way down his line and back to his position, passing the rose to the player next to him in line as he comes back to his position. That player immediately starts down the line in the same fashion. He must go to the foot of the line, the head, and back to position before passing the rose to his next teammate. The first team to have all its runners to complete the course wins.

Debate.—"Resolved, That the word 'obey' should be left in the marriage vow." A boy should present the affirmative and a girl the negative on this question. Limit speakers to five minutes for direct argument and rebuttal. Appoint judges to decide as to the winner.

Knot contest.—Five to ten players for each team. A string the length of the room containing as many tight knots as there are team representatives. Player Number One runs to the first knot, unties it, and runs back to "touch off" his next teammate. Number Two takes the next knot, and so on, the idea being to see which team can first untie every knot.

Matrimonial difficulties.—Two or three couples from each side. Tie ends of long pieces of string to the wrists of each girl. The boys then have a string tied to one wrist, looped under the girl partner's string, and tied to the other wrist. The idea is to see which side first has all its players get out of this double-handcuff without breaking or untying the string. It can easily be done by slipping one of the strings under the loop on the wrist of the other player, and then out over the hand, but don't tell them this until they have done a lot of amusing maneuvering.

Flag race.—Five to ten players for a side. A large Irish potato for each team on a table or chair at the opposite side of the room. A tiny American flag for each runner. Players must run to the potato, stick flag up in it, and rush back to "touch off" the next runner.

Flag pass.—Teams of from ten to twenty form circles, sufficiently far apart so as not to interfere with one another. A flag is provided each team. The tallest player should be made starting player. The flag must be passed around the circle, each player handling it cleanly, until it gets back to the starting player. Immediately he gets it he holds it high over his head and yells. The referee decides which side scores. This is continued until one side or the other makes six points.

Graduation exercises.—This stunt should be carefully prepared, the participants being coached and costumed for the occasion. The school teacher announces the graduation exercises of Hog Wallow School. "The school chorus will now be sung. Sing, children." Everybody sings lustily:

> "Twinkle, twinkle, little star,
> How I wonder what you are,
> Up above the world so high
> Like a diamond in the sky."

She then introduces "Willie Hopeless" to recite. "Willie" starts "Twinkle, twinkle, little star," and then forgets. After several bad starts he finally makes it with the help of the teacher.

Then the class poet is introduced to give a bit of original verse. She recites "Twinkle, twinkle, little star" with a decided lisp.

In turn, follow the cry-baby, who finished up in a good old-fashioned cry; the bashful girl, who recites with her finger in her mouth; the girl who stutters; the girl who plays on the piano, picking out the tune of "Twinkle, twinkle" with one finger; the tragedienne, who gives the same piece with dramatic gestures and deep emotional feeling; the singer who sings it a la grand opera. Each one uses "Twinkle, twinkle, little star," the teacher introducing them to give the class oration, the class prophecy, the valedictory address, a dramatic reading, etc.

"Goodnight, Ladies" and then refreshments.

JULY

A BALLOON PARTY

Lots of fun could be had at a balloon party. Old and young alike are thrilled at the sight of a balloon rising in the air and disappearing out of sight or catching fire and sending its hoop and blazing torch hurtling downward through the air.

Balloon-making contest.—With the proper sort of boosting quite a bit of interest could be aroused in a balloon-making contest, all the balloons to be made of tissue paper. Old and young might be interested in entering this contest. Ingenuity, beauty, and efficiency will be taken into consideration by the judges in rendering their decision. The efficiency will be rated by the ability of the balloon to function properly. This would be tested by actually sending the balloons up. Quite a feature could be made of this part of the program.

Fan ball.—Divide the group into two sides. Have teams of from five to ten players each to represent the sides. Each player is provided with a fan, and positions are taken much similar to those taken in basketball. The field is fifty by twenty-five feet. The referee starts the game by blowing his whistle and tossing the balloon in the air between the two centers, who leap high in the endeavor to knock it to one of their teammates. The idea of the game is to get the ball over the opponent's goal line.

After each score the ball is brought back to center and tossed up as before.

When the ball goes outside or touches the floor the referee blows his whistle and tosses it up between two opposing players at the point where it went out or touched the floor. If a balloon should burst, the referee should provide another, tossing it up at that point. All strokes must be made with the fan. No player may hit the balloon with his free hand, nor may he run with it. He must bat it through the air. Ping-pong paddles may be substituted for fans.

Ten points will be considered a game.

Balloon burst.—Get a number of large balloons. The watermelon type will be good for the purpose. Paint ridiculous faces on the ends. Have several representatives from each group contest. Each begins blowing up his balloon on the signal to start. The winner is the one who first bursts his balloon in that manner. Each player should continue to blow until his balloon bursts.

Balloon battle.—A paper balloon should be provided for each side. They hold them over the heat until they are filled with hot air. At the signal of the referee they let them go. When they have reached a reasonable height the referee blows his whistle. This is the signal for the players to throw rocks and clods of dirt at the balloons, the opposing sides each trying to bring down the balloon sent up by their opponents. Shouts of glee will follow a successful shot.

AN OUTDOOR PICNIC

Purpose—Recreation and devotion.

Time—Sunset through to moonlight hours.

Setting—A well-kept pine woodland, adjoining a grassy clearing to the left and away from the highway, afforded a natural playground. About seventy-five young people came directly from their day's work bringing sandwiches and salads to add to the wieners, to be roasted on long sticks over the fire. Marshmallows, cookies, and coffee were furnished also by the committee in charge of refreshments and so completed a well-balanced menu.

Supper—After the confusion of arrival, parking and exchanging of greetings, naturally supper was the first item on the program. A pine-log campfire supplied the center of attraction. The crowd was asked to sit on the ground in groups of ten or twelve. With some assistance the committee served plates of food and coffee cups were passed. Later the cups were gathered into a basket and the paper plates and napkins were thrown onto the fire so that a clean camp was left behind the party.

Games—The leader of games started at once on active games into which all could enter freely. "Snatch Ball" was played and then "Squirrel-in-the-Nest." Thirty minutes soon passed.

Songs—Gradually the group gathered about the fire again and song leaders began such familiar songs as "My Old Kentucky Home," "Way Down Upon the Swanee River," "Old Black Joe," and "Tenting Tonight on the Old Campground."

Story and worship—When musical enthusiasm seemed to blend with a desire for quiet, a reader stood within the light of the circle about the fire and beautifully told the story of a colored man and the loyalty, devotion, and love exemplified in his relation to his master in the reconstruction days following the Civil War. Closing the story with the suggestion, that all bow their heads in quiet meditation, and think upon every man's equality before God. A moment of perfect quiet was deepened into worship by the sweet strains of the Negro spiritual, "Steal Away to Jesus," followed by "Every Time I Feel the Spirit Movin' in My Heart, I Will Pray." (This was effected by two phonograph records played on a music box hidden behind the trees within easy sound range.) As the records ended, the whole group arose and sang, "Lord, I Want to Be a Christian."

All sang together in closing, "Abide with Me." Climbing into the cars, many groups sang as they rode happily homeward.

—Mrs. James V. Reid

A PROGRESSIVE ANAGRAMS LAWN PARTY

Decorations—Japanese lanterns and small tables. If necessary there may be a lighted candle on each table.

Plans—Tables are numbered and players draw tally cards, which are likewise numbered. Couple 1, Table 1, would indicate that the person drawing that tally would go to Table No. 1 to find his partner. There would be four players at each table. At the end of each game winners would progress toward the head table. Thus, the winners at Table No. 3 would move up to Table No. 2. Each time the players would change partners, except that the couple remaining at Table No. 1 would not change, necessarily. Losers at Table No. 1 go to the last table.

Anagrams can be bought at any store that handles games at prices ranging all the way from 10 cents to $1.00. Homemade sets could be made of heavy cardboard cut in three-quarters-of-an-inch squares. If a group plans to do this the following numbers of letters should be made for each set; A, E, I, O, 14 each; U, 6; S, 10; B, C, D, F, G, H, L, M, N, R, T, 8 or 9 each; J, K, P, V, W, Y, 4 each; Q, X, Z, 2 each.

One full set is needed for each table.

Score—One point is allowed for each letter in a player's possession at the end of the game. Partners would pool their scores.

Prizes—If prizes are awarded to the high scores they ought to be inexpensive toys or novelties that add to the fun of the evening.

A SOCIAL OF THE NATIONS

Guests are requested to come in costume representing some nation. A prize may be offered for the best costume.

Decorations—Flags of the various nations should be used, with red, white, and blue crepe-paper streamers festooned about the room. If the committee cares to do so some elaborate decorating—booths representing the different nations—may be arranged.

Refreshments—Swiss cheese sandwiches, rice cakes, and tea make a cosmopolitan menu for your social of the nations.

What's your nationality?—Each person is given a card and a pencil, the card shaped like the emblem of the organization, if desired. The guests are to scurry about and get the signature and ancestral nationality of as many persons as possible. The first person to get everybody in the room may be given some suitable reward.

National anthems.—The crowd is divided into two groups, each with a captain. Various national anthems are played. The first group to shout the name of the country whose anthem is being played is awarded a point. The whole group must shout the name together, directed by the captain, before the leader will award a point. Scattering yells from a group will not be recognized. Each side must wait until the music stops before yelling. In case both groups shout the name at the same time the leader will award a point to each.

National games.—Play games of various nations. Some valuable suggestions can be found in *Far Peoples,* by Phillips.

Hana, Hana, Hana, Kuchi (Japanese).—Let the two groups sit facing one another. The captain for one side stands and says, "Hana, hana, hana, kuchi," which means, "Nose, nose, nose, mouth." On the first three he taps his nose, while on the fourth, instead of tapping his mouth, he touches some other feature, as for instance, the eye. The idea of the game is for the players of the opposing side to do what their opponents' captain says, and not what he does. All players who make mistakes drop out, or, as the Japanese play it, submit to being daubed on the cheek with flour and water.

The other captain now takes his turn. If the idea of elimination is followed, the side with the player who stays in the game the longest is declared victor. If the other plan is followed, the fun will consist in artistically daubing the cheeks of opposing players with flour paste.

The names of the features are "Hana" (nose), "Kuchi" (mouth), "Mimi" (ear), "Me" (eye). The captains may agree to use only English.

Cat and mouse (Chinese).—This is very similar to our game. These differences may be noted: The circle revolves, with the mouse on the inside and the cat on the outside of the circle, the mouse seeking to keep as far away from the cat as possible. Suddenly the circle stops revolving, and as the cat rushes into the circle the mouse runs out. The cat must follow the mouse exactly as it does in and out of the ring. When the cat finally catches the mouse, a new cat and mouse may be chosen.

Tsoo! Tsoo! (also Chinese).—One player is blindfolded. The remaining players are chickens. The blindfolded player says, "Tsoo! Tsoo!" that is, "Come and seek your mother." The chickens run up and try to touch him without being caught. The player caught becomes blindman.

What Nation?

1. Is a lazy nation? Procrastination.
2. A resolute nation? Determination.
3. A cussing nation? Tarnation.
4. A nation much sought by travelers? Destination.
5. A scattering nation? Dissemination.
6. A ruling nation? Domination.
7. A growing nation? Germination.
8. The final nation? Termination.
9. A false nation? Hallucination.
10. An attractive nation? Fascination.
11. A bright nation? Illumination.
12. An unfair nation? Discrimination.
13. An explosive nation? Fulmination.
14. An expelling nation? Elimination.
15. A source nation? Emanation.

Instead of having guesses made by individuals read the questions and award points to first side answering correctly all together. A point is subtracted for an incorrect answer.

Drama.—Present "A Marriage Proposal," by Tchekoff, the Russian dramatist. "Stunts of All Lands," by Miller, would furnish good material for this part of the program.

Folk games.—Some of the excellent folk games of other countries would be appropriate. "Weave the Wadmal" (Danish) or "Gustaf's Toast" (Norwegian) in costume. These and others may be found in *Treasures from Abroad,* a section of Handy II. See Chapter XIII, Musical Games, in this book.

A PROGRESSIVE LAWN PARTY

The possibilities in progressive parties are almost limitless—skill-games, mental games (anagrams, logomachy, battleship, and the like), puzzles, creative activities (crafts, sketching, painting, informal dramatics), combinations of all of these, and numerous other activities.

Preparation—Mark each table or game with its number plainly in view. Type or hand print directions for each game when directions are needed. Place these directions where they can be easily seen. Provide tally cards, properly numbered to indicate groupings.

Methods of Progression.—

1. Four players at each activity. Two winners progress. Losers at Number 1 go foot. Change partners each time.

2. Even number at each activity. Half of the group progresses.

3. Entire group progresses to new game. In this case players are in one group all evening.

4. Entire group progresses, one-half of the group, moving forward to the next activity and the other half backward to the next activity behind, except Table 1. Half of Table 1 goes to the foot table and half to the table immediately behind them. Thus, if there are ten tables, half of Number 1 goes to Table 10 and half to Table 2. Also, half of the last table goes to Table 1 and half to table just ahead.

5. Time of progression. (1) At end of the game or activity. (2) When leader rings a gong. (3) When couple at the head table finishes an activity it rings a bell, thus giving the signal for all activity to stop at each table. Note "Progressive Bug Party."

Activities.—

1. *Miniature golf,* or *clock golf*—See Chapter X, Fun Outdoors.

2. *Bean bag golf*—Tossing a bean bag into cans, buckets, baskets, and boxes over a course—nine holes and return.

3. *Dart target*—See Chapter II, Fun in the Clubroom.

4. *Dodo*—See Chapter II, Fun in the Clubroom.

5. *Muffin pan toss*—Tossing linoleum disc into muffin tins at distance of six feet. Each pocket is numbered indicating the score. Discs may also be numbered in which case getting a disc in its proper receptacle doubles the score.

6. *Washer pitching*—Dig five holes—square and center—and sink five small soup cans. Players score ten points for tossing washer into center hole, and five points for each of the corners, tossing from a distance of ten to fifteen feet.

7. *Pole ring toss*—Drive broom-handle stakes into the ground so that they stand up about two or two and a half feet above ground. Make eight rings, seven to eight inches in diameter, of old bicycle tires, four red and four black. Players toss rings at distance of fifteen or twenty feet. Each ringer counts one point. Fifteen or twenty-one points as agreed constitute a game. Each player throws four rings, tossing alternately as in "Horseshoes."

8. *Hole bowl*—Holes are dug in the ground large enough to sink pound coffee cans (about five inches in diameter), one in each hole. There should be six holes, arranged in triangle shape, the apex toward the bowler. These holes are one foot apart, and are numbered: back row, three holes, 75, 100, 50; second row, two holes, 25, 35; front row, one hole, 10. Players bowl from a distance of fifteen feet, using croquet balls. If a player "calls his shot" and makes good he doubles his score for that shot. For instance, if he announces, "I am bowling for 100," and then proceeds to bowl the ball into 100, he scores 200 points. A player may not call the same number twice during a turn. Thus, if he calls 100, he cannot call it again that turn, even though he missed it the first shot. If a player "calls his shot" and misses, but goes into another hole, he scores whatever that hole allows. It would be advisable to erect a three- or four-inch-high backstop a foot or so back of the last can to stop balls that are tossed too hard.

9. *Chair-leg ring toss*—Turn a chair or stool upside down. Players try to ring the legs with rope rings five inches in diameter. Five points for each ringer. Toss from distance of six to eight feet.

10. *Bean bag board*—See Chapter II, Fun in the Clubroom.

AUGUST

A HIRAM AND MIRANDY PARTY

Three different plans are suggested for developing this party. Take your choice or make a combination of the three.

Invitations

Hiram, Hiram, I've been thinking
Just what great fun it would be,
If you'd bring Miss ——
Friday evening to see me.

Overalls, a red bandana,
Nary a necktie, a big straw hat,
Leave your city ways behind you,
Come prepared for a reg'lar bat.

———

Mirandy, Mirandy, I've been thinking
Just what great fun it would be,
If you'd come next Friday evening
With Mr. —— to see me.

Wear your apron and sunbonnet,
Lunch is needed, that's fact,
Leave your city ways behind you,
Come prepared for a reg'lar bat.

Plan I (Outdoors)

The group gathers at the place designated by the leader. Announcement is made that transportation will be provided for all. No one knows the destination of the group but the leader. When they are all assembled they are informed that each person's feet are to be the transportation provided. The group then follows the leader on a mystery ramble.

Mystery ramble—When they have gone some distance they are stopped, lined up single file, and given instructions to proceed without conversation, and with as little noise as possible. Thus they follow, single file, until the leader brings them to a spot where a campfire is burning. Seats have been arranged, council fashion.

Discoveries—After they are seated one of the leaders explains that they are in a strange land, weaving a fanciful story of romances, Indians, pirates, treasures, etc. Each one is then given fifteen minutes to go out and bring in some memento significant of those adventurous days. Ingenious and imaginative hunters find some remarkable exhibits. One comes back with a knob off of the ark, another with a leaf from the Garden of Eden, another with a feather from the bonnet of Pocahontas, another with the stone David used to slay Goliath, another with a jewel from Captain Kidd's treasure.

At the end of the allotted time the leader blows a whistle and all return. Each person is required to display his trophy and tell its story. He explains what it is, how it came to be in this place, how it came into his possession, and something of its history. This gives promise of some "fairy tales" that will rival Hans Christian Andersen.

Plan II (Indoors or Outdoors)

Howdy, Hiram! Howdy, Mirandy!—The stock greeting for the evening and the only one used all evening as couples meet, or as friend greets friend, is "Howdy, Hiram!" "Howdy, Mirandy!"

Games.—

1. *Pinning the tail on the donkey*—This old one needs no explanation.

2. *"Farmer in the dell"*—Another familiar old-timer.

3. *Farmer Brown*—One player starts it by saying something like this:

> Farmer Brown went to town
> Riding on a pony;
> Came back home, all alone,
> With a lot of Bologna.

This is correct for the person's name is Baker. It begins with a *B* and so does Bologna.

It should be explained that each player is expected to answer in rhyme, when at all possible. If he cannot answer in rhyme he is to tell what Farmer Brown brought from town at any rate. It will add to the fun if the players are not warned that the articles mentioned must begin with the players last initial. When they answer incorrectly they are informed that they are wrong.

Suggestions—

> *A.* Farmer Brown went to town
> With a Ford he grapples;
> Came back home all alone
> With a load of apples.

> *B.* Farmer Brown went to town
> Up and down the wide streets,
> Came back home all alone
> With a dozen red beets.

C. Savages, cabbages. *D.* Wishes, dishes. *E.* Legs, eggs. *F.* Hour, flour. *G.* Train, grain. *H.* Tow sack, hardtack. *I.* Nice, ice. *J.* Lakes, Johnny cakes. *K.* Lout, kraut. *L.* Wrather, leather. *M.* Sunny, money. *N.* Bag, nag. *O.* Bargain, organ. *P.* Sizes, prizes. *Q.* Princes, quinces. *R.* Steeds, reeds. *S.* Spots, scots. *T.* Measure, treasure. *U.* Yellow, umbrella. *V.* Ran, van. *W.* Rig, wig. *Y.* Barn, yarn. *Z.* Hero, zero.

4. *Number change*—Players are seated in a circle and number off in fives, 1-2-3-4-5. There are just enough seats for the players except one. The player who is "It" announces that the numbers represent farms and that the numbers he calls must change locations. "It" will try to get a farm (seat) in the scramble. Because there are several people with the same number there will be four or more players changing each time. The player left without a farm becomes "It" in turn.

5. *An old-fashioned spelling bee*—Divide into two equal sides and conduct an old-fashioned spelling bee.

Ten difficult words—Here are ten difficult words that are likely to trip even the best of spellers: rarefy, liquefier, supersede, naphtha, sacrilegious, paraffin, kimono, tranquillity, picnicking, battalion. Try them on some of your friends.

Fifty hard spells.—Here is a list of fifty words that are likely to trip the best you have:

appendicitis	capillary	ghoul
asafetida	chrysalis	gnome
acetylene	columbarium	gnomology
baccalaureate	ecclesiastic	geranium
believe	eclectic	hauteur
caoutchouc	fossiliferous	hautboy

hallucination	oleomargarine	stationery
isobar	onyx	stereopticon
innuendo	periphery	sycophant
latitudinarian	pharmaceutical	synagogue
mademoiselle	personnel	synchronous
marvelous	physiognomy	syzygy
maraschino	psychology	tautological
meningitis	puissance	toxic
mignonette	punctilious	turquoise
miscellaneous	receive	valetudinarian
nonchalance	rendezvous	

Plan III

Use play-party games like "Oh, Susanna," "Bingo," "Jennie Cracks Corn," "Old Brass Wagon," and "Paw Paw Patch," and such games as you will find in Chapter XIII, Fun with Musical Games.

A GLOBE-TROTTER'S PARTY

The crowd assembled at the church, and some 125 young people enjoyed a thirty-minute fellowship period while waiting for everyone to come. The group was then divided into four smaller groups. Each group was led by a previously appointed leader. Each leader distributed to his group mimeographed papers that disclosed concise but clear directions. It was a responsibility of each of these leaders to have already secured enough cars to care for his crowd, and it was this time that everyone found his place in one of them. Each of the four groups went to one of the four different houses prepared for the party. It was also a responsibility of the leader to keep his crowd on schedule; twenty minutes was allotted for time spent at each house.

First house—Japan.—Hostesses in costume. Each guest removed his shoes before going in, and sat on the floor.

Decorations—All furniture removed and pillows placed on floor around walls, lanterns, etc.

Program—"Madame Butterfly" was read; music on portable victrola.

Refreshments—Tea and crackers served.

Second house—France.—Hostesses in costume.

Decorations—Small tables with checked coverings, cabaret style.

Program—Short musical program.

Refreshments—Ginger ale or punch.

Third house—Mexico.—Hostesses in costume.

Decorations—Few Spanish shawl drapes.

Program—Mexican fortunetellers and Mexican music on guitar and piano.

Refreshments—Hot tamales and crackers in small portions.

Fourth house—Fairyland.—Two little girls dressed as fairies greet guests.

Decorations—Nursery. All furniture removed. Toys.

Program—Played jacks, blocks, checkers, etc., on floor.

Refreshments—Lollipops and blow gum.

Church—Dixie.—Watermelons served in abundance. Songs. The party was over by 11 o'clock.

Why it was a success: (1) Cost, only $10.00. (2) Committees—composed of sixteen, and everyone really worked. Three weeks spent in preparation. An attempt was made to visualize and eliminate all difficulties that might be encountered. (3) Advertisement —letters, phone calls, announcements in church publications, short skit on Sunday morning preceding the party. Just as few details as possible disclosed ahead of time.

—MARY BLANTON

A BOHEMIAN PARTY

Costume—Each person should wear a smock during the evening's entertainment. That includes the males present.

Decorations—Odd lanterns and candlesticks, including old bottles. Weird, funny, and senseless pictures. A few daubs of various brilliantly colored paints in futuristic design may be given the title "Peace at Dawn." All but one of these pictures should be titled. That one is the "unnamed picture." Artist's easel.

Games and entertainment.—*Sketching*—Have each person sketch person to the right, using pen or pencil. Write name of person sketched and of artist. Pass around for crowd to see.

Chewing gum sculpture—Give each person a card and a stick of chewing gum. They are to chew the gum and then mold some "work of art" on the card. These should be placed on exhibit.

Naming the picture—Have each person write a title for the unnamed picture at the beginning of the evening. By this time the committee will have had time to look the titles over and select certain ones to suggest to the group for its decision as to the best.

Poetry—Give four rhyming words such as "shove," "dove," "love," "above," and ask each person to write a poem ending the lines with these four words. They can take them in any order that suits them. For a large crowd divide into three or more groups and let each group present a poem.

Soap carving—Ask each person to bring to the party a bar of Ivory soap and a pocket knife. Write to the manufacturers of Ivory soap, Proctor and Gamble, Cincinnati, Ohio, for several of their booklets on Soap Carving. Let those who desire consult the book for models. Have a supply of magazines on hand so the sculptors may consult them for models. Put the results of the modeling contest on display. If someone who is expert at soap carving could be gotten to give a demonstration, offering the group some instruction in the art of soap carving, it would add interest and value to this feature. Be sure to cover the floor with old newspapers to protect it.

"Bohemian Girl"—Get several of the best soloists available to present some numbers from *The Bohemian Girl* opera. "I Dreamt that I Dwelt in Marble Halls" makes a good soprano number. "Then You'll Remember Me" calls for a good tenor voice. "Heart Bowed Down" is a good baritone solo. If these can be presented in costume so much the better.

Bohemian orchestra—The players use dish mops and pans, a scrubboard, a floor mop, and other such articles. The pianist strikes up some melody and all the players keep time. The pianist gets faster and so do the players. As the pianist slows down so do the players. The tempo gets slower and slower until the climax when the whole group of players yawns and drops off to sleep.

Bohemian chorus—The party could close with the playing of "Come, Let Us Be Joyful" which can be found in *Twice Fifty-five Games with Music*, or in *Treasures from Abroad*.

Or there could be a good rousing sing, using songs like "Du Liegst Mir in Herzen," "Alouette," "Old Folks at Home," and "Long, Long Trail."

Refreshments—Orangeade and wafers served at tables.

A NOMAD PARTY

Oh, would you be a roamer,
And with the roamers roam?
Then hie yourself to Funland,
And to our party come.

Guests should be requested to attend in gypsy costume. A bright-colored head-piece and sash will answer the purposes. The boys should doff their coats for the evening.

Souvenir programs—Mimeographed programs in decorated covers should be provided each guest on arrival. Some of your young people who are clever with water colors should be pressed into service in the making of these covers. Landscapes, campfire scenes, gypsy heads, or magazine picture cut-outs may be used to decorate them. The name of the party, organization, place, and date should be indicated. The programs should be attached to the covers with ribbon or fancy cord. These will serve as excellent mementos of the occasion.

The Program

1. The Gypsy Trail.
   "We're not stringing you."

2. The Gypsy Fortuneteller.
   "Sees all! Knows all!"

3. Gypsy Frolic.
   "Be lively and gay."

4. Gypsy Tents.
   "Scoot!"

5. A Gypsy Daisy.
   "Daisies sometimes tell."

6. The Gypsy Court.
   " 'S a secret!"

7. The Gypsy Camp.
   "Watch for the witch!"

8. Gypsy Sing.
   "Now, everybody."

9. Gypsy Partners.
   "Knife 'em!"

10. Gypsy Treasure.
    "Oh, boy!"

The gypsy trail.—Each guest selects the end of a string from a bunch of strings at the porch, and follows this string until he comes to the other end. It crosses and tangles with other strings, zigzagging back and forth until it leads the holder to his goal. On the end of the string he finds some fortune, which indicates his future fate.

The gypsy fortuneteller.—Fix up a gypsy fortunetelling tent on the lawn. If you can get someone who knows something of palmistry much of the success of the evening's program is assured. On arrival guests can be sent to the tent. After the "Gypsy Trail" guests can also visit the fortuneteller. If a palmist is not available, have the gypsy provided with slips of paper on which are written fortunes in invisible ink (lemon juice). These she passes over a lighted candle until the heat brings out the message.

Gypsy frolic.—The players form a circle with two or three players in the ring. These players walk about the inside of the circle as everyone sings the verse of the song indicated below. As they come to the chorus they stand in front of some player and courtesy. They then grasp that player's hands, skating position, and on the chorus skip about the inside of the circle together. All players forming the circle remain stationary, but all sing. As the next verse is started partners drop hands and again walk about inside the ring. This time, on reaching the chorus, each new player on the inside also takes a partner. And so the game continues until all players have been taken from the outer circle.

> As I was walking down the street,
>   Heigho-heigho, heigho-heigho!
> A gypsy (girl) (boy) I chanced to meet,
>   Heigho-heigho! Heigho-heigho!
>
>   CHORUS:
> Rig-ajig-jig, and away we go,
>   Away we go, away we go!
> Rig-ajig-jig, and away we go,
>   Heigho! Heigho! Heigho!

Gypsy tents.—Players form in groups of three. Two of these players hold hands, while the third player gets inside, as in "London Bridge Is Falling Down." The two players form the tent, while the third is a gypsy. There ought to be several extra gypsies. When the leader blows his whistle that is the signal for every gypsy to get out of his tent and scoot for another one. The extra gypsies endeavor to get a tent in the scramble. Play rapidly for about five minutes.

The gypsy court.—A throne has been arranged by draping two chairs. The committee has selected a King and Queen of the Gypsies. The court is called to order by the leader who explains what the players shall do. He announces that in the possession of the Queen is a red bandana handkerchief. Some boy whom the leader selects is required to go to the throne, make obeisance before the Queen, and receive from her that handkerchief. He must then do with it what she whispers to him to do! For the time, he must keep this order a secret, simply obeying her wishes. For instance, the Queen may tell him to give the handkerchief to the prettiest girl at the party. Without a word, he makes his selection, and proceeds to tie the bandana handkerchief loosely about the girl's neck. The girl then must go to the throne and bow before the King. He whispers into her ear that she must give the handkerchief to the boy present who will make the best husband. When she has decided, she ties the bandana about his neck and he appears before the Queen. So it goes until many of the players ought to be given this privilege. Then the leader announces that the first player, and then each player in turn, must tell to whom he gave the handkerchief, and why he gave it. There may be some blushing, and much laughter, but each player is required to tell his secret. The handkerchief may be given for the "prettiest eyes," "the best conversationalist," "the smartest," "the sweetest," "the biggest ears," "the loudest," "the hungriest," "the most lovable," etc. The girls always go to the King, and the boys to the Queen.

A gypsy daisy.—The Gypsy Queen has been provided with a beautiful wand. The wand is made of a light stick about two and one-half feet long, on the end of which has been tacked or glued two cardboard discs about four inches in diameter. The rod is covered with green crepe paper, and the discs with orange or deep yellow. Each disc is covered separately for there must be space between them for the insertion of the daisy petals. Each petal is double. Between its folds is folded a slip of paper containing a fortune or fate. The petals are inserted between the two discs and held in place by a pin. One at a time, players appear before the Queen. She extends her wand, and the player pulls one of the petals. He is required to read it to the entire group. If the crowd is too large to allow everyone present to have a chance in "The Gypsy Court," then the players left out are to be given first chance at the "Gypsy Daisy."

The gypsy camp.—If a real campfire is not possible, then one should be improvised with the use of a flashlight, some red crepe paper (or theatrical gelatin), and some sticks. Six or eight "gypsies" then come slowly marching into the court singing softly "There's a Long, Long Trail," or "Gypsy Trail." They form a circle with plenty of space between the members of the group, seat themselves, and hum the chorus. The chief of this gypsy band may then suggest that since "Nita," the witch, has not yet arrived they might have some entertainment. This can serve as the setting for one or more special musical numbers. "Gypsy Love Song," "Gypsy Trail," "Wraggle Taggle Gypsies," or other songs may be used effectively. Banjo, guitar, and ukulele numbers would also be appropriate. At the conclusion of this program, three knocks on the porch announce the approach of the witch. The gypsy band assumes an expectant attitude, and the witch slowly approaches, finally entering the circle and moving toward the campfire over which a cauldron is hung. She makes a few mysterious passes over this cauldron, muttering some unintelligible gibberish, and then looks intently into it.

Then, in a firm voice, that can be heard by everyone she begins to prophesy for the group, and for individuals in the group. "I see across the years into the year 1960. John ——— is still a lonely old bachelor, etc." If the committee, or the witch, will take the time to work up some clever prophecies, this stunt can be made to add tremendously to the entertainment of the evening.

Gypsy sing.—Get the entire crowd to singing some of the old songs, and maybe, some new ones. Such songs as "Juanita," "Spanish Cavalier," "In the Gloaming," "Love's Old Sweet Song," and "Gypsy Love Song" might be used. The words to some of these could be included in the mimeographed program.

Gypsy partners.—After a short sing announce that all the men are going to knife their partners. Have the men gather to one side. Write the name of each girl on a slip of paper. Place these slips on the ground. The leader selects some man to step forward. He is given a long-bladed, sharp-pointed knife, and told to stick a name by dropping the knife from waist height on some slip. Slips are turned face down so no man can tell just what names are on them. Each man thus "knifes" his partner.

Gypsy treasure.—Each man and his partner is now given a map directing them to find a "gypsy treasure." They follow directions on this map and finally come to the place where the treasure is hid, probably under a rock, or porch corner, or piano cover. The treasure proves to be a tiny match box, in which is a slip of paper which tells the couple to present this slip to the refreshment committee and receive a reward. The reward is some ice cream and cake. No couple should be served until it finds its treasure, or makes an earnest effort to do so. Several special treasures should be arranged, so as to add interest to the search. Ten-cent store necklaces would make splendid treasure to stimulate the interest. Members of the committee should carefully draw the charts as they hide the treasures. This will save confusion.

Note: Should this party be held indoors a pine board, or an old pine-top table, will have to be provided for the "knifing" of partners.

When held outside, plenty of Japanese lanterns should be used to give light and color. Written by the author for the *Journal Party Book,* and used by permission of the *Ladies' Home Journal.* Copyrighted by Curtis Publishing Company.

SEPTEMBER

A POPULAR PARTY

Invitations—

> Pop calls and pop concerts
> Are popular with some;
> We're having a popular party
> And want you to come.

Append your address and specify the date and the hour. Decorate the house in strings of popcorn. For favors, buy the penny all-day suckers on sticks and mold popcorn balls around them, using any good recipe for sugar syrup.

When the guests arrive, give each a small paper bag and require him to blow it up and pop it. Anyone taking two claps to pop the bag must pay a forfeit. This helps to start things off immediately. Another way to place guests on terms of comradeship is to pin the name of some popular actor or author on the back of each and require the other guests to call him by the first name—the guest to guess the full name. It adds to the fun if the girls are given the names of men, and young men the names of girls.

"Pop the question."—Play this after the order of "Cross Questions and Crooked Answers." Line up the girls and boys. Give out slips with proposals to the young men and answers to the girls—the more mixed, the merrier. Each young man must step forward and pop his question, and the girl must answer without laughing, or else pay a forfeit.

"Poor popper."—Play it this way. Give out numbers and each boy must kneel before the girl holding his corresponding number and say this rhyme:

> There once was a kind-hearted papa,
> Who told his wife a big whopper;
> He said she could kiss
> Like a pretty young miss,
> Then nothing in reason could stop her.

The girl must pat him on the head and say three times, "Poor Popper," without smiling or laughing.

"A Pop Contest"

What pop is a flower? Poppy.
What pop is a tree? Poplar.
What pop is a toy? Popgun.
What pop is a cloth? Poplin.
What pop is a muffin? Popover.
What pop is a utensil? Popper.
What pop is a member of the People's Party? Populist.
What pop is the whole number of people in a place? Population.
What pop grows in a field? Popcorn.
What pop is a species of parrot? Popinjay.

Give a popgun to the young man having the greatest number of correct answers, and a can of unpopped corn to the girl.

Pop-sack relay.—Players stand in two equal lines, single file. Each has an unopened new paper sack. At signal to start the last player in each line blows up his sack and pops it on the back of the one in front of him. As soon as the sack is popped the next player blows up his sack and pops it in the same manner. The head player pops his sack on his knee.

Other pop-sack contests can be used, such as each player in turn running to a chair where the sacks are, blowing up one, popping it, and returning to touch off his next teammate; putting sacks under foot on the floor, and conducting the same sort of relay as described in the first paragraph; tying blown-up sacks to ankles of girls and expecting their escorts, who have linked arms with them, to protect them. The men try to pop sacks on the ankles of other girls, by tramping on them, while each man tries to protect his own partner's sack.

Pop goes the weasel.—Play "Pop Goes the Weasel." See Chapter XIII, Fun with Musical Games.

For refreshments serve soda pop, sandwiches, and popcorn balls.

A FUN-SCHOOL PARTY

Come to our party, a Big Fun School,
Don't bring your books along, it's against the rule.

Sculpture.—On arrival each person is furnished with a piece of Ivory soap. If desired, you may ask them to bring their own soap. A knife is also necessary. Models are placed about the room, and each person is required to carve some bit of statuary. As the pieces are finished they are placed on display. Some award may be given for the best. Be sure to have plenty of newspapers on hand so that the carvers can keep their shavings off of the floor.

Arithmetic.—*Numberology*—To the ancients numbers had great significance. Even down to our day this superstition about numbers persists. Thirteen is unlucky. Some hotels have no thirteenth floor, because so many guests refuse to be placed on that unlucky floor. Thus they skip from the twelfth to the fourteenth floor. In baseball there is the "lucky seventh" inning when every rooter stands and expects something to happen. Lower seven is considered the lucky berth on the Pullman.

Numberology is an old form of fortunetelling by numbers.

Each guest is given an opportunity to work out his own fortune. Or, in a small crowd, someone may do it for them, announcing the result to the group.

Each letter has a significance, as follows:

1	2	3	4	5	6	7	8	9
A	B	C	D	E	F	G	H	I
J	K	L	M	N	O	P	Q	R
S	T	U	V	W	X	Y	Z	

Now write your full name. Say it is:

6 9			
John Smith	15	1 plus 5	6
	—	—	—
1 85 14 28	29	2 plus 9	11

Each letter has a numerical value. The values of the vowels are placed above the name, the consonants below. They are added, and then the digits of the result are added. The final resultant indicates the fortune. If it should amount to more than thirteen, then add the two digits again. Thus you reduce the name to the key numbers. These indicate the character reading of the person using Numberology.

The key: (1) Creative ability. (2) Action. (3) Executive ability. (4) Love of detail. (5) Strength of character. (6) Thinker, meditative. (7) Aggressive. (8) Care of others; unselfish; domestic.   (9) Emotional power; dramatic ability.   (10) Kindness; considerate of others.   (11) Artistic sense.   (12) Imagination.   (13) Troublemaker.

Thus, "6" shows John Smith to be a thinker, and meditative, and "11" shows that he is a man of artistic sense.

Living numbers—The crowd is divided into two or more sides for the various events that are to follow.   In Living Numbers players are furnished with numbers from 0 to 9, one number to each player. The sides face one another.   The leader calls out certain problems in arithmetic, such as, "How much is 2 plus 2?"   The first side to have "4" step out in front of his line is awarded a point.   "How many cakes in a baker's dozen?"   This time 1 and 3 must stand together in front of the line.   More difficult problems may be given. Or the leader may throw in questions regarding historic events, such as "When did Columbus discover America?"

Reading.—One or two persons are elected from each group.   The leader has written the names of certain nursery rhymes on slips of paper.   The readers draw one slip each.   They are then required to recite the particular rhyme omitting every fourth word.   The rhyme must be recited without undue hesitation, and, if a reader puts in a fourth word, that is counted against him.   Thus, "Mary had a little lamb" would be recited in this fashion:

> Mary had a —— lamb,
> Its fleece —— white as snow,
> —— everywhere that Mary ——,
> The lamb was —— to go.

The reader might be required to whistle where each fourth word should come.

Dramatics.—The groups present the names of states in charades, taking turn about.   Easy ones are Pennsylvania (pencil-vain-you), Tennessee (Ten-S-see), Arkansas (Ark-and-saw or R-can-saw), Illinois (Ill-eye-noise), Maryland, Colorado.   As each charade is presented the others try to guess what state is represented.

History.—Each group is given some historic event to illustrate by a drawing on the blackboard.   The other groups try to guess what event is represented by the drawing.

The leader has slips of paper with various events written on them. The groups draw one slip each, and then plan to illustrate the events in turn. The crowd tries to guess the event portrayed. Suitable events would be:

> Washington Crossing the Delaware.
> Lindy Crossing the Atlantic.
> Paul Revere's Ride.
> George Washington and the Cherry Tree.

Geography.—Fifteen bean bags are needed. On each bean bag is pinned the name of some metropolitan city. The idea is to get each city in its own state by tossing the bean bag from a distance of about ten feet. A miss means that the player has to throw over until he gets the city in the proper state. The group having the lowest score for the fifteen states wins.

The states are blocked off in eight-inch squares. If the bean bag lands on a line between two states it shall be counted as being in state which holds the most of it.

English.—Take some writing contest like the familiar "Motor Romance" (*Phunology*, page 227, or "A Hiking Romance," page 272 in this book), and read it aloud. The words are to be filled in by the groups shouting them. A point is awarded to the first group having someone shout the proper word. If there is a tie a point is awarded to each group. For instance, in the "Motor Romance," it starts off—

> "Alice and her beau one day
> Went riding in his ——."

The reader pauses for a moment, and the first group to have someone shout "Chevrolet" gets a point. If no response is made, he may read again, and may even offer hints. A good reader can make this sort of contest a "howling" success.

We think you'll find this a pleasing variation from the old type of writing contest.

Spelling.—Use the familiar "Living Alphabet."

Or use "Discovered Words." Words are written out and then cut into single letters. Letters in a given word are numbered alike. Thus, in the word "Quarrel," each letter is numbered "1." That makes it possible for all the players in this word to get together. Their next job is to discover what the word is, for none of the words are announced. They then present the word to the crowd in dramatic form. The rest of the players try to guess what the word is.

Suggested words are: football, baseball, automobile, chorus, opera, quartet, movies, propose, airplane, school.

Refreshments—Have lunch-men serve refreshments. Eskimo pies or ice-cream cones could be served.

A GIVE-AWAY PARTY

The invitation should request that everyone who comes to the party should bring some discarded garment or garments, things that they are willing to give away—hats, shoes, dresses, suits, caps, sweater, etc. These should be wrapped and tied up. At the close of the party they are to be turned over to the proper committee to be distributed to the needy or given to the Goodwill Industries.

Give away.—When the party starts each person is told to carry his bundle in the grand march that is to follow. The girls form a line on one side of the room, and the boys a line on the other side. As the music plays they march down the sides of the room and across to middle, coming down the middle by couples. They march around by twos into a circle. When the leader's whistle blows the inner circle reverses and marches in the opposite direction, the outer circle continuing as before. When the leader's whistle blows a second time the two circles stop and face one another. Each person in the inner circle must pair off with one in the outer circle. The leader then announces that each person is to give his package to his partner.

Players immediately open their packages and they are required to wear the garments received for the rest of the evening.

It's just too bad if Mary Jones gets a pair of large oxfords that used to grace the big feet of Bob Brown. Imagine the hilarity of the group when husky Ed Clark opens his package and dons a cute little baby cap.

Another plan of distribution would be to have the committee collect the packages as they arrive and distribute them later to the group, being careful to see that no one gets the package he brought.

Follow this feature by playing give-away games. Some of the following would do well:

1. *Poison penny*—Pass article or articles to right, giving them away as fast as possible. When the music stops or the whistle blows players holding the "poisoned pennies" drop out of the circle.

2. *"You must pass this spoon"*—See Chapter XIII, Fun with Musical Games.

3. *Secret handshakers*—One or more persons in the crowd are secretly given pennies. They are instructed that the fifth person

who shakes hands with them must be given the pennies. They may continue until the leader blows his whistle. At the end of that time the players holding the pennies may keep them.

4. *Give-away beans*—Each player is given ten beans. Whenever a player can get another player to answer any question with "Yes" or "No" he hands that player a bean. The idea is to get rid of all ten beans by giving them away to others.

5. *Percolate*—One player goes out of the room. The others select some verb such as "sneeze" or "snore" or "smile" or "sing" or "cook." The player sent out of the room comes back and tries to discover what the word selected is. He must do this by asking questions to which the players are required to answer truthfully "yes" or "no." In framing these questions he must use the word "percolate" for the verb selected by the group. "Do you percolate?" "Do you percolate at night?" "Do you percolate frequently?" "Do you like to percolate?"

The player who "gives it away" by his answer is selected to go out next.

6. *Who's the leader?*—("Look for the give-away")—One person leads the group in what it is doing, another player in the center of the circle tries to discover who the leader is. Players stand in a circle and clap their hands, jump, wave, or do whatever the leader does. It will add to the fun if the game is played to music.

7. *Pinchee—no laughee* ("Don't give it away")—Players are seated in a circle. The leader turns to the player to his right, pinches both cheeks of that person, and says solemnly "Pinchee—no laughee." That person turns to the player to his right and repeats the action. On the next round the players put the forefinger of one hand under the chin of the person to the right and say "Chuck-a-luckee." On the third round they run the fingers down the face of the person and say "Cootchie-cootchie."

The trick is soon apparent to all but one of the players. One player has his fingers smutted. When he gets through he leaves black soot marks on the face of the player to his right.

8. *Give away packages*—Several players are given packages which they are told they must try to give away to other players. A player does not have to take the package and can only be made to do so by being inveigled into answering "yes" or "no" to some question. After the game has been played a brief time the leader should have gotten one of the packages. He should proceed to open his package and start eating it, for it contains a piece of candy, or a sandwich, or something of the sort. Then players who passed up any of the packages will be sorry.

OCTOBER

HALLOWEEN SOCIAL

About two weeks before Halloween the following invitation should be sent out: (It may be written or typed in black on orange paper which has been cut or traced for cutting after typing into six and one-half-inch discs. On the front a black cut-out of witch riding a broom should be pasted and the invitation written on reverse side.)

Another invitation may be made by cutting the outline of a bony hand in white and mounting on black drawing paper post card size, the invitation written across the hand.

> "The spectral hand of Halloween,
> With eerie and uncanny mien
> Bids you a welcome to its fete
> Where ghosts and witches you will greet
> And much, I'm sure, to your surprise,
> They'll penetrate through your disguise
> And guide you through the secret pass
> That leads you to their haunt, Alas!
> Enough is said—do not delay
> By eight at ——
> They'll hold full sway."
>   (Date ——)

Decorations—A meeting place should be decided upon a short distance from the party. This may be at the church, on someone's front porch, or in a side or back yard. The meeting place should present a spooky appearance, no lights except weird ones. Jack-o'-lanterns or alcohol lamps should be used, and moss, greens, and branches of trees or cornstalks should be used in corners and over doorways and arches. Moss hung from lines should extend from one end of the room or yard to the other.

For the party—The home or assembly room in which the party is given should be appropriately decorated in orange and black with long orange crepe-paper strips forming curtains and valances upon which have been pasted black cut-outs—bats, cats, owls, and witches. This gives the room a cheery atmosphere. To divide rooms apple portieres may be used to advantage, later using the same for bobbing, the tall ones taking the short strings and the small persons the longer strings. Corn shucks, branches, and vines fill the corners and may be converted here and there into witches, spooks, or scarecrows. Cover the lights with orange crepe paper upon which have been pasted bats, etc.

Weird jack-o'-lanterns should hang from everywhere. In a corner of the room the witches' cave can be made by turning a kitchen table over with the top to the wall and covering the legs with gray crepe paper to form the sides and draping with vines and leaves. The top of the cave may be extended or lowered by fastening a string to the middle of a sheet or canvass which has the four ends fastened to the table, and raising it above, tent fashion, by attaching string to ceiling. One whole room could well be devoted to various fortune booths or dens.

The program—At the place designated as the meeting place, the crowd should be met by several ghosts and witches who hand out to each person a small Halloween cut-out upon which has been written Group 1, 2, 3, or 4. These slips should be evenly divided before being given out so that there will be about the same number in each group. The guests are told to assemble in their various groups and await instructions, each group is given a slip of paper, apparently blank, but by holding the slip over a lighted candle which the ghosts will furnish them they will find instructions such as "Make a wild dash for the drugstore," "Stop when you reach second and third streets," "Beware lest you tarry at the Big Oak." These instructions have been previously written in lemon juice or milk on each slip of paper. As soon as the different directions are read the groups start out to the given spot. Here they receive instructions from another ghost or witch stationed there to go farther, making as many stops as you deem necessary for the various groups to reach the goal which is the Halloween Party itself, each group taking a different course to get there. The first group to reach the house is presented with a small sack of candy chicken corn.

Upon arrival at the party, each guest is presented one at a time to the "master ghost" who shakes hands and to their horror the hand comes off as they clasp it. This can be done by stuffing a white rubber glove with wet corn meal leaving the wrist unstuffed in which to poke the hand of the ghost. Tie a long string around the arm at the elbow and sew to edge of glove. This will leave the hand dangling when released and prevents having it carried off.

Dance of the witches.—*Equipment*—March music, whistle, broom. *Formation*—Two concentric circles. Boys on outside, girls on inside. If more girls than boys, extra girls pair off half on outer and half on inner circle. One player marches in center of circle with broom in hands. A lively march is played as couples march around. When whistle blows the inner circle reverses and both circles continue to march to the music until the player in center drops the broom and makes a dash for a partner. The player left out is "It" next time.

Pumpkin plunking.—A row of ten pumpkins cut out of cardboard decorated and graduated in size are strung up. The largest pumpkin is at the beginning of the row and smallest at the end. Explain that each pumpkin counts for the number of points marked on it. The largest 5, 10, 15, and so on until the smallest which counts for 50. Use the four groups already assembled or group them to make only two sides according to your crowd. A line is marked off twenty feet away. Arrange the two sides in parallel lines behind the mark. Give a small ball to the first in line who tosses it and returns the ball to the first in line of the second group and so on both groups alternating. The side having the largest score is awarded a bundle of crepe-paper caps, one for each member. If four groups are used, play two at a time running off the final for the two winning teams to determine the victors.

Ghost treasure.—Draw one small circle in center of floor with four large circles equally distant from center. Let each of the four original groups occupy one. This is their home base. A pile of candy or peanuts is placed in the center circle. Cut the numbers 1, 2, 3, and 4 from a calendar and pin on back of each member of corresponding group. Upon the signal to start, all players run out to get the treasure, carrying away one piece at a time. If a player's number is taken off by an opponent while outside of home base he is "dead," and out of the game. If more than one peanut is taken the guilty group is disqualified. Count the treasure to determine winners. All the spoils going to winning group.

Apple race.—Four contestants from each group. Draw two lines ten feet apart. Half the players from each group line up on opposite sides making four parallel lines with teammates facing each other. Give all contestants a toothpick and place an apple before the first runner of each team. The toothpick must be held in the mouth and the apple pushed to the teammate on opposite side who returns it to the other side, Number 2 having stepped up to front of line. Number 2 returns it to second teammate who returns it to original position. If the toothpick breaks the runner must start over. The victors receive a box of "goblin teeth" (marshallows).

Ducking and bobbing apples.—It wouldn't be Halloween without large tubs of water with apples for apple ducking. This should be preferably out of doors. Apples may also be strung on clotheslines out of doors with small sacks of flour hung here and there to add to the fun. The player's hands should be tied behind his back.

Fortune booths.—A real-looking gypsy fortuneteller (unknown to the crowd) can prove a big hit by putting common sense and a few hints given beforehand together to make some startlingly real fortunes. She instructs her visitor to touch one of the articles on the table before her and learn his fate:

A pile of gold dust denotes wealth.
A needle—spinsterhood or bachelorhood.
Rice—a wedding.
Fan—romance.
Dime—an inheritance.
Torn rag—poverty.
Scissors—a short life.

Have other fortune booths presided over by witches, melting lead —the guests pour melted lead (or paraffin for convenience) through the end of a key into a glass of ice water. The shape taken by the lead when cold denotes the fortune of the inquirer. Quick thinking and ingenuity in interpreting the shapes make these fortunes very popular.

Fortune wheel.—Divide a cardboard wheel into six colors providing cardboard indicator and hang on wall. Make up suitable rhymes for each color and post on wall near by. Each person spins the indicator around and when it stops the color foretells fortune.

Bluebeard's den.—Decorate a back room or garage as spookily as possible and drape to resemble "Bluebeard's Den." To the back of the room, hang a sheet or brown curtain behind which seven girls stand with their heads thrust through holes in sheets as though hanging on wall. Streaks of red extending from the heads to resemble blood. When a victim is led in, the heads should shake and groan at intervals. Two ghosts walk silently about the room tickling the victims with feathers or dropping ice snow on them. The grim tale of the fate of Bluebeard's wives is recited as the victim is shown about the dimly-lighted room—first, the clothes, food (untouched), shoes, jewels, beads hanging on the wall, and finally the storyteller, an Oriental, offers to show them the fatal key and allows them to hold it in their hands, telling them to take special precaution not to drop it as it will mean harm to them. The trick is that the key is connected with an electric battery which gives the victim such a shock that he drops the key. He is then hurried out lest Bluebeard return, and the next person is called.

Refreshments—Nut cookies, candied apples on sticks, and witches brew (fruit punch) would be appropriate.

—Mrs. R. P. Jackson

HARD LUCK HOBO PARTY

Invitation—

> Yoo-Hoo! Hoo-Doo! Hobos!
> Want to change your luck?
> Come to Hoo-Doo Hall
> Next Friday the thirteenth at 8:13
> On time is good luck;
> Late is bad luck!

Decorations—Use bad luck emblems for decorations; guests walk under ladder upon entering. Artificial campfire in center of room. Guests sit on logs and boxes.

Lucky scramble—At 8:13 leader blows whistle and scatters candy kisses on floor. Late comers miss scramble, their bad luck!

Lucky scrawl—Contestants given pencil and paper and instructed to get autographs and phone numbers. First to get "thirteen" wins simple prize.

Hobo's pot luck—Hobos given five beans and engage in conversation. When he receives yes or no for answer, he is paid one bean. First to get thirteen beans is winner.

Lucky handshake—Three people given small luck charms. Hobos instructed to shake hands with each other, not knowing who has charms. Person holding charm, gives it to the thirteenth person whose hand he shakes.

Hobos pack their kit—Circle formation. Leader begins by saying, "When I pack my kit, I shall take my comb." Second person repeats first object and adds one of his own. This continues around circle, everyone who forgets object drops out.

Hobos go to court.—The cast for this moot court should have been secretly appointed days before the party so that everything can move with precision. You will need a judge, a clerk of court, prosecuting attorney, an attorney for the defense, a defendant, and at least two witnesses for each side. Encourage the two sides to work up their presentations carefully. The charge against the defendant is that he has been guilty of working. In one such trial one of the witnesses testified that he had seen the defendant working. He was leaning out the window holding a lighted candle so his mother could see to chop the wood. A jury selected from the group weighs all evidence and brings in a decision. The judge renders the decision of the court.

Hobos view the remains.—Use "A Halloween Stunt" appearing on page 819.

March to victory—Hobos march before judges. Best boy and girl costumes receive red bandanas as prize.

Strolling fiddlers appear—Musical program presented.

Hobos feast—Hot dogs and coffee or hot chocolate.

A HALLOWEEN CAMPFIRE

Guests are notified to meet at some central point dressed for a hike. No one knows the route except the leaders. There are surprises at certain points. Finally, the group comes upon a campfire. Here, a ghost announces a nut hunt. Peanuts are hidden all about the place.

The group is then led to a second campfire where a near-by tree is decorated with sacks containing bacon, wieners, buns, eggs, and pickles. Coffee is prepared over the campfire. Songs, jokes, and stunts are enjoyed.

The group then proceeds to a third campfire where there is a delicious pot of molasses candy. A sticky time will be enjoyed by all.

GRAVEYARD TRAIL PARTY

It is hard to get something different each year for Halloween, when you work with practically the same crowd year in and year out. However, this year we handled it as a sort of "Follow the Leader over the Graveyard Trail." We met in a certain spot in the park in our neighborhood with instructions that no one was to speak a word when we met there. You can realize what a task this was. It was absolute misery for some of those folks. We introduced the visitors in pantomime.

We then proceeded to the home of one of the girls in the neighborhood. We were met at the door by a ghost who shook hands with everyone as they entered. He held a hot potato in his hand and it made a rather warm welcome.

The lights were turned off after the guests were all seated on the floor in a circle. A ball of yarn of various colors and lengths was started round the circle with the request that each one add to the ghost story started by the leader. It was weird and woeful as it went along.

We went from there to another home in the neighborhood where entrance to the house was gained by climbing a ladder to a sleeping-porch and entering an upstairs door. No lights were on in the house and each guest had to find his way downstairs in the dark. Along the way we stationed three boys; the first one threw water from a brush in the face of each person; a little further along a sheet of paper was caught in a quickly buzzing electric fan as each approached, making a terrible sound, and then on the stair landing a boy stood with a bucket of salty ice water. Into this he dipped his hands (he had on a pair of kid gloves), pressing them quickly upon the face or hands of each one as they passed by. They fell all over one another in their fright getting downstairs.

A game or two was played in the living-room and the party then went back to the park, where the cars had been left, and drove to a creek bottom where a wiener roast was already started by a couple who went out early. Jack-o'-lanterns were hung about the trees and ghosts were hidden in the shrubs and trees.

They bobbed for apples and roasted the wieners and marshmallows, and were ready for home about eleven o'clock. Everyone said it was a "keen" party, and they really seemed to enjoy it.

—MILDRED A. JONES

GYPSY HALLOWEEN PARTY

Decorations—Branches of trees, cornstalks, a cauldron, and camp-fire. All lights covered with blue noninflammable crepe paper. Have a gypsy tent for a fortuneteller.

Invitation—The gypsies gather for their annual festival Tuesday, October 31, in the church social room. Wear gypsy costume. Boys wear red bandana handkerchiefs around head. For those who fail to come dressed in costume let the committee have pieces of red crepe paper.

Gypsy broom frolic.—Boys line up on one side of the room, the girls on the other. As the music plays they march forward toward one another four steps, then back to place, and repeat. An extra player roams up and down between the two lines carrying a broom. When the lines have marched forward and back twice the leader blows a whistle and every player rushes for a partner. The rover drops his broom and also tries to get a partner. The couples skip about the room in time to the music, the player left without a part-ner picking up the broom and skipping with it. After one time around the boys again line up at one side of the room and the girls on the other, and the game proceeds as before.

"Come, let us be joyful."—This fine old German game may be found in *Twice 55 Games with Music,* published by C. C. Birchard, or in section "Treasures from Abroad," from *Handy II.*

Gypsy circle.—Form circle about campfire, asking everyone to be seated. Musical numbers can be introduced at this point.

Songs for everyone to sing—"Merry Life," "Juanita," "Long, Long Trail."

Specials—"Gypsy Love Song," "Gypsy Trail."

Violin solo—"La Paloma" or "La Golondrina."

Following some number an old gypsy witch makes her way to the center of the circle. She reaches into the cauldron and draws out slips of paper from which she reads the fortunes of certain persons in the group.

Gypsy fortune room.—Each person is required to go through this experience. The room is dark, and there are weird noises—the rattling of chains, groans, a sudden blood-curdling scream. Then there is a disappearing skeleton. This is achieved by dressing some boy in black, with phosphorescent white strips of cloth sewed on the front of his costume to represent the bones of a skeleton. Against a black background in the dark this will be all the victims will see. When he turns his back to them he disappears.

WITCH PARTY

Invitations—Black cardboard cats and bats written on them in white ink is the following invitation:

"THE OLD WITCH WILL GET YOU IF YOU DON'T SHOW UP AT THE WITCH PARTY." "DID YOU SAY WITCH PARTY?" "YEAH, WITCH PARTY."

Giant witch.—A giant witch greets each just outside the door. The giant effect is achieved by having a girl stand on a chair. The flowing robes cover the chair and lead to the floor. This witch simply motions the direction guests are to go.

Witch greeter.—If possible the group should be sent upstairs and through a dark passageway at the end of which an old witch stands with hand extended. Each person is required to shake hands. The arm and hand are artificial, the latter being a glove stuffed with cold wet sand.

Witches' graveyard.—The guests are led into another dimly lighted room. One side of the room is decorated with what appears to be tombstones. These may be made by dropping white pillow cases over primary chairs. A witch explains to the group that—

> "Many a witch once young and gay
> Has passed along Death Valley's way.
> Their restless spirits roam and rave;
> Their bodies lie in the cold grave.
>
> Just now we'd like to hear from you
> Some epitaphs you think will do,
> Or some you've seen, or some you've heard,
> When you're ready, you just say the ward."

It might be well to have some persons primed with some good humorous epitaphs like:

> "Here lies the body of Susan Proctor,
> She died before they could get a doctor."

> "Here lies the body of Sally Lonn,
> Her motor stopped but Sal went on."

> "Here lies the body of Hattie Howe,
> She lied in life, she's lying now."

> "Here lies the body of Johnny Ray,
> Who died maintaining his right of way;
> He was right, dead right, as he sped along;
> But he's just as dead as if he'd been dead wrong."

> "Here lies the body of Bobby Bains,
> The road was slick, he had no chains."

Murder.—The witch now announces that a "murder" is to be committed on the spot. Each person draws a slip of paper from a box. What is on it is kept secret. Only one slip is marked and it carries the one word "murderer." The lights are turned out and the group mills around in the room until the "murderer" selects his victim. He does this by putting his hands loosely about the throat of some person. That person screams (the most blood-curdling, the better), and falls to the floor. The lights are flashed on. The prosecuting attorney, who has been selected previously, requires every person to take the witness stand. Each person, except the guilty party must answer truthfully any question asked by the attorney. When the questioning is finished the crowd votes on who they think the "murderer" is. Then the "murderer" confesses. A good prosecuting attorney can make this a most interesting feature.

Witches' den.—The witches' den is a booth made out of cornstalks. Guests are allowed to visit one at a time. Inside is an old witch who reads palms. If it is impossible to get a palmist use some other fortunetelling device.

Witches' paradise.—The lights in this room should be covered with blue paper or blue spotlights may be used. The room is decorated with cornstalks, pumpkins, hanging black cats and bats, stick candy and apples hanging by strings. Persons are allowed to help themselves to the apples and candy if they can get them without the use of their hands.

Broom dance.—Players line up in two equal lines facing one another, men on one side and girls on the other. If there are more girls than boys it will be necessary to have some of the girls act as boys. They ought to be designated in some way so there will be no confusion during the game. For instance, they may wear handerchiefs on their arms to indicate they are taking the part of men. The pianist plays some song like "Oh, Where, Oh, Where, Is My Little Dog Gone." The two lines sing the song marching forward between one another four short steps and returning. This is repeated a second time. The player with the broom marches up and down between the two lines. When the group has marched forward and back twice the pianist plays faster and each player rushes for a partner. The player carrying the broom drops the broom and also tries to get a partner. Players and their partners skip about the room in time to the music. The player who is left out must pick up the broom and skip with it. The game continues. It ought to make a good mixer.

Witches' race.—Witches straddle broomsticks and race the length of the room and back.

Shadow shows.—The crowd is divided into two or more groups and each group is requested to get ready to present a shadow show. All arrangements have been made by the committee for this by putting up a sheet behind which they place a light at the proper distance to throw the picture shadows on the sheet. Suggestions for shadow show stunts are as follows:

Operation—A patient is brought in and put on a table. A nurse puts a large funnel over the patient's face. The patient slowly loses consciousness. The doctor gets his tools ready. He carries a saw, a hatchet, butcher knife, and various other implements. He begins to work with the knife while the patient groans. He lifts out a string of wieners, a toy dog ("hot dog"), and various other things. Then he begins to saw off a leg. The sound of the saw can be heard as it cuts through the wood. In a moment he lifts up a part of the leg with a shoe on it. This is achieved by having a stuffed leg ready. All of this looks extremely funny in shadow pictures.

Courting—The arrival, the courting, "Pa" on the scene, and the climax where "Pa" boots the young man out.

Many other suggestions for Shadow Pictures can be gotten from the *Shadow Pictures, Pantomime, Charades, Tableaux*, Stocking.

Witch is witch?—Conundrums. Ask that the group be seated and have an exchange of conundrums. This ought to be informal so that everyone could feel free to participate. Announcement ought to be made ahead of time for this feature so various members of the group could come prepared to take part in it.

Ghost stories.—Have one or two good storytellers tell some thrilling ghost stories. Lights low for this feature.

Refreshments—Witches' punch and cake.

A PARTY FOR HALLOWEEN

Invitation—

> The Black Cat bids you come
> Next —— eve at eight,
> Unto his mistress's home
> Prepared to stay quite late.
> Your fortune will be told,
> Perhaps you'll get the ring;
> And please do bring some stunt
> To speak or act or sing.

These are written on white paper, folded, and hung on the neck of a black cat, cut out of cardboard.

The decorations—Decorations may consist of green branches, autumn leaves, and moss. To secure a weird effect, hang gray paper cut in strips between lights or at intervals around the room, with a lighted pumpkin placed here and there. All lights should be dim.

Refreshments and place cards—Little paper horns make attractive little witches for place cards. Dress up the horn in full skirt, make arms of wire, make a broom from a toothpick and straw.

For refreshments, doughnuts, punch, and apples are easy to serve, although hot coffee and "hot dogs" might be welcome on a chilly night.

Suggested Games

A Halloween party is always more successful if the guests are masked for at least part of the evening. Since it is often difficult to have the guests come masked, why not have them make their masks after they arrive? This can easily be done by giving each guest a large paper sack and some colored chalk or pieces of crayon. The sack is to be used as a hood, with holes torn out for the eyes. The chalk is used to decorate the masks. After all masks have been completed, the lights should be turned out. Each guest then puts on his paper sack and moves to a different position. When the lights are flashed on again, each guest tries to identify as many people as possible. As each person is identified a mark is put on his mask by the person who recognized him. As a surprise finish to this game, give a small prize to the guest who has the most marks on his mask, for being so well known.

Skull ball.—Guests sit or stand in a circle. One of the players is the witch and stands in the center. Someone in the circle has a ball painted to look like a skull. At the starting signal the skull is passed around or across the circle rapidly. If the one in the center catches the ball while it is in the air, the person who threw it becomes the witch and takes the place in the center. If the witch can touch the skull while it is still in some player's hand, that player becomes the witch.

Witch's hunt.—Cut a number of cats, bats, and owls out of cardboard and hide them around the room before the party. The players march around in a circle while music is played. When the music stops the players find as many cats, bats, and owls as they can. When the music begins again all must stop hunting and march in the circle until the music stops again. The game continues until all the cut-outs have been found. Cats count one point, bats count three points, owls count five points. Person having the most points wins.

Retrieving the witches' broomstick.—A small pumpkin is placed in the center of the floor. The players are divided into two equal sides, and are numbered. The leader calls a number and the player from each side having that number comes to the front. These players are stationed at an equal distance from the pumpkin holding a broomstick between them. At the signal each one pulls and the player who pulls his opponent past the pumpkin wins. The game continues until all have tried it.

Bats, goblins, and elves.—The players are divided into two equal sides—each side at opposite ends of the room. Each side sends a player to the center. These are the "elves." One side is the "bats," the other is the "goblins." The elves call "bats change," and all bats run to the opposite side of the room. The elves catch all they can. Those caught stay and help. With "goblins change," the game continues. At the end of four or five minutes, the side having the most players left wins.

Game of the three fates.—Guests sit in a circle. Three Fates are chosen. The first whispers to each person in turn the name of his or her future sweetheart. The second Fate follows, whispering to each where he will meet his sweetheart, as, "You will meet on a load of hay." The third Fate reveals the future, as, "You will be separated many years by a quarrel, but will finally marry." Each guest must remember what is told him by the Fates and each in turn must repeat his fortune. For example: "My future sweetheart's name is Obednego. I shall meet him next week, and we shall be married on a moonlight excursion."

A good stunt with which to close the party is "The Ghosts' Minuet," by Evelyn Price. This stunt is to be found in a collection called *Successful Stunts,* edited by Katherine Ferris Rohrbough.

—Alberta Baines

A BLUEBEARD PARTY FOR HALLOWEEN

Decorations—Cover all the lights with blue. If possible have blue floodlights at several vantage points in the room. Use the usual Halloween decorations—shocks of corn, black cats, witches, ghosts, jack-o'-lanterns, etc. The jack-o'-lanterns can be decorated with blue crepe-paper beards. A suspended stuffed ghost or two, with skeleton face and hanging by the neck, would add to the effect.

Hemp-rope beards—Give to each person a six-inch piece of hemp rope and have each one make a beard to wear. A prize may be given for the best. If this does not seem practical for your group, make crepe-paper beards of blue for each one, and have them put them on as they arrive at the party.

Bluebeard's key.—The players stand or sit in a circle. A door key is placed on a string that goes around the circle. The players hold the string in both hands and keep their hands moving along the string constantly, passing the key from one player to another, moving it in either direction. One player, who is "It" stands inside the circle and tries to discover which player has the key in his possession. Whenever he touches a player's hand that player must open that hand to show whether or not he has the key. If he has, he takes "Its" place, and the game continues.

Bluebeard's knife.—A wooden knife tipped with red ink is used for this game. Bluebeard and his wife preside. Some boy is selected to appear before the wife. She hands him the knife as she whispers to him, "Give it to the girl who you think could be most easily trained to be a good wife." He makes his selection, and the girl presents herself before Bluebeard, who whispers some directions to her. She hunts up a boy and gives him the knife. And so the game proceeds. When enough of the players have been before Bluebeard and his wife, the players are asked to tell why they presented the knife to those selected. Begin with the first one called, and then they come in order. It might be well to rule that no person is eligible to receive the knife more than once, especially if there is a large crowd.

Bluebeard lock and key.—Players are taken into a booth or another room and given a chance to unlock Bluebeard's lock. A key is provided, and the person inserts it in the lock. But does he unlock it? He does not. With a howl he lets the key go in a hurry. The "catch" is that the lock is connected with a battery. As soon as the key is inserted someone throws on the switch. The electricity does the rest.

Bluebeard chamber of horrors.—In this horrible place have rattling chains, giant ghosts, moving skeletons, weird noises, wet and clammy stuffed hands with which everyone has to shake hands, etc. The lights are very dim. Over in one corner the curtains are suddenly drawn and three gruesome-looking heads appear to be hanging in front of a sheet. The faces are white and ghostly. Red ink is splashed on the sheet just below the heads, and the hair of the heads is tied to give the head the appearance of hanging there, detached from the body. These are three of Bluebeard's wives, so you are told as someone flashes a light on the sight. The girls' heads appear through holes in the sheet.

In coming out of this room the guests are required to step down into another room which is dark. As they step down they land on a bed spring, which is covered with a piece of carpet. If both rooms are on the same level, fix a step so they will have to come down on the bed spring from an elevation. In this dark room have tiny ghosts painted with phosphorescent paint flit across the room. This can be done by having a wire stretched across the room, one end higher than the other, the ghosts can be attached to bent pins and placed on the wire. They'll scoot across as if they are flying through space. There may also be a skeleton or two moving about. Dark suits covered with strips of cloth painted with phosphorescent paint and skeleton false faces will do the work here. A person standing in a dark corner with a lighted flashlight held just below the chin looks awfully weird.

Bluebeard bean bag.—Make a bean-bag board out of wood or beaverboard. Divide into four sides and let them contest to see which can make the largest score. Any throw that goes over his head takes ten off. The holes should be about four inches in diameter.

Why Bluebeard killed his wives.—Ask each of the four groups to present a three-minute stunt on this subject.

A Bluebeard stunt.—Select your cast for this stunt and have them rehearse so that it may be well presented. Costuming will add to its effectiveness.

Characters

Bluebeard   May Knott, the maid
Lessee, his wife   Salvo, the hero

Scene—A room in Bluebeard's castle. If there is no door at the back of the stage or platform suitable for use, a curtain may be drawn across to hide from view the gruesome scene of the heads of Bluebeard's wives. The same sheet and the same girls used in the Chamber of Horrors can be used here.

Scene 1

Curtain rises with Mrs. Bluebeard and the maid on the stage. The maid is arranging the furniture. Mrs. B. is sitting in a rocking chair, reading. The maid is singing softly some song.

LESSEE: "You have a beautiful voice, May, and I like to hear you sing. Sing another for me."

MAID: "Thanks, Mrs. Bluebeard." (Starts to sing.)

Enter Bluebeard in a hurry. Glares at the maid and growls: "What's the matter with you? Sick? Sounds like static on a stormy night." Then turns to Mrs. B. and says: "My dear, I'm going away on a business trip."

The maid glares at him behind his back, and makes a face.

MRS. B.: "I'm so sorry. I don't know what I'll do without you."

B.: "Well, it has to be. And I'm leaving right away. Take this key, and keep it for me till I return. It's the key to my secret room. See that no one enters that room. Whoever opens that door I'll kill." (Draws his finger across his throat with a significant gesture.) "I must be gone." (Hurries to door, stops there for a moment, turns and repeats the significant gesture, as he says): "Remember!" Exit.

MRS. B. (Stands looking at the key. Muses): "I've always wanted to see what is in that room."

MAID: "Well, why not open the door?"

MRS. B. "Oh, I'm afraid. Did you see his look when he made his threat?"

MAID: "Sure, but his face looks terrible any time. He'll never know. Come on. You're his wife. You have a right to know what's in that room."

MRS. B. "Well, just one peep." (Unlocks door—throws it open and both the maid and Mrs. B. let out unearthly screams. The open door, or the screen drawn aside, discloses the gruesome view of the three suspended heads. The door is immediately shut and locked. The key is dropped in the excitement, and picked up off the floor.)

MRS. B.: "Oh, what'll I do? How can I explain this blood on the key. It won't rub off."

MAID: "Tell him you cut your finger and got blood on it. And you'd better send for Salvo, your former sweetheart. He'll protect you against this human devil."

MRS. B.: "Go and send word to Salvo to hurry to my aid." (Maid exits as Scene 1 ends.)

Scene 2

Mrs. B. is pacing up and down much disturbed. The maid enters excitedly, announcing, "Mr. Bluebeard is just driving up."

MRS. B.: "Oh, what shall I do? What shall I do?"

MAID: "Just keep a stiff upper lip, and stall him off until Salvo can arrive."

BLUEBEARD: "Well, I'm back. Where's the key?"

Mrs. B.: "I'm so glad you are back, dear. Did you have a good trip?"

B.: "Never mind the trip. Where's the key?"

Mrs. B.: "Oh, the key? I'll get it for you directly."

B.: "You'll do nothing of the sort. You'll get it now. Hand it over."

Trembling, she hands him the key. He looks at it, sees the bloodstains, and shouts) : "So you've disobeyed me, have you? Well, that's the end for you, and for that loud-mouthed maid. Wait till I sharpen this knife." Strides out. Sounds of grinding a knife are heard. He comes in occasionally to try it out on a piece of paper or a hair. Seems dissatisfied and goes back. Finally seems satisfied. Gets ready to work on Mrs. B.

In the meantime, Mrs. B. is walking up and down, wringing her hands, and pleading with the maid to see if she can't see Salvo coming.

The maid has climbed up on a chair, or stepladder, and is peering into the distance.

Maid: "Ah, I see a cloud in the distance. It draws nearer, nearer, nearer. Oh, it's only Mr. ——— on his way to the golf course." (After a pause) : "The moon is coming up over the hill. Oh-h-h-h, it's just Mr. ———'s bald head." (Pause) "There's a strange speck on the horizon. Well, well, it's only Mr. ———'s mustache." (Pause) "Oh, there he comes! There he comes! He's riding like the wind. Courage, madam, Salvo is on the way. He's here! He's here! We're saved!"

B. has gotten ready for the slaughter, but as he advances on the cowering women, Salvo dashes into the room, riding a hobbyhorse. He draws a wooden sword, and engages B. in combat. After a very brief struggle B. falls mortally wounded. Salvo stands with one foot on B. and takes Mrs. B. in his arms as she rushes to him.

Curtain.

Refreshments—Orange punch and Bluebeard cakes. The latter can be made by using blue icing to make faces and beards on round cakes.

HALLOWEEN HAIRDRESS

> Come wearing your hair in different style,
>   And if you happen to have no hair,
> Then come along with your very best smile,
>   And a ribbon or wig you may wear.

By the above invitation it may be seen that guests are to be asked to change the style of their hairdressing for the party. A committee of helpers (?) inspects persons on arrival, and if not satisfied, it has the privilege of making more drastic changes. A supply of headbands and brilliantly colored pompons is at hand to use as the committee desires. These may be placed at awkward angles, at the committee's discretion.

The basement trail.—The guests are led single file to the basement door, through which they enter, one at a time. Each guest, as he goes through, shuts the door behind him. The doorknob is charged with electricity. Guests must hold onto a long rope after stepping inside, for it is pitch dark. Various surprises are arranged —a sewing machine motor which is so connected that it is set in motion when the victim steps on a certain plank, over which he has to go; a vacuum cleaner that blows out instead of drawing in; ghosts; piercing screams; the drip, drip of water falling down a height into a metal bucket; luminous skeletons.

Musical Jonah spots.—There are five such spots in the room, one each for five times. The music plays and couples march around the room, keeping time to the music, but not being required to move in any certain direction. When the music stops all couples stop. The couple nearest Jonah Spot Number 1, which the leader now announces as being "the chandelier," must perform some stunt. After the stunt, all guests change partners and march again. This time the Jonah Spot is the piano. And so it goes until five couples have performed by singing a song; enacting a skit such as a couple at a baseball or football game; a movie; or in a boat; dancing a jig; or pantomiming some familiar activity, such as a tennis match; buying a hat; or directing traffic.

Halloween faces.—Each guest is given a large paper sack which will fit over the head. Charcoal or crayons are provided. Each person punches eyes, nose, and mouth in his sack, and draws a face on it. He must then drop it over his head. When all guests are properly adorned with sacks they mill around shaking hands with one another. When a person recognizes the guest with whom he is shaking hands he is privileged to make a black cross mark on that person's sack. When three or more persons get as many as ten crosses on their masks the leader requires them to perform some stunt for the crowd.

A HALLOWEEN HIKE

If you live where an old fort, a tower, a lighthouse, or an

old church is available, an interesting Halloween hike could be planned. Arrange for all sorts of surprises along the way and at the place of destination—ghosts, weird noises, and the like. At the place of destination play "Who Am I?" requiring that all characters selected be dead. A good ghost story would furnish a fitting climax.

A HALLOWEEN PARTY THAT IS DIFFERENT

We located a house in another part of town. None but the leader knew its location. It was decorated with the usual black cats, streamers, candies, etc. The meeting place was the church. The guests were asked to come in costumes of some kind and a varied group presented themselves that night at the church. No instructions were given; they were bundled into machines and told to "keep mum" and follow their leader.

A circuitous route was made through strange streets, turning many corners, through dark alleys till finally they drew up to a large residence in total darkness. They were met by a ghost who, with pointed finger, directed them through a tangle of bushes, tall grass, and low-hanging trees, till they passed before a dark and forbidding cellar door, surmounted by a blinking skull. "Abandon all hope" read a sign in luminous paint over the door. A chorus of groans and moans issued from the cellar. They were directed down the steps by the ghost and told to "follow the rope." Inside all was pitch dark. Turning a corner there suddenly appeared before them a luminous skeleton.

"Nothing but a picture," said someone; but suddenly the skeleton raised its arms and started toward them. A loud scream was heard but strange hands pulled them away from the grasp of the specter. On all sides one could see other skeletons, large and small, dancing up and down and screaming. It was truly a dream of the lower regions. Some of the guests were so frightened they had to be led past the scene.

The screams and groans died out now as we turned another corner and beheld a man lying in a coffin. A ghastly green light in the coffin lid lit up his features in a truly gruesome manner. "Oh, nothing but a dummy," said someone and poked his finger at the dead man. Instantly the dead man opened his eyes and without warning raised up in his coffin. The inquisitive one jumped back in alarm and was warned by the specter to "let the dead man lie!"

The rope trail led through the cellar, up through the kitchen and then to the dressing rooms. In the darkened kitchen a noise was produced by allowing a small stream of water to fall into a metal tub.

When the dressing rooms were reached, a draped ghost directed the boys to one room, the girls to another. Here they regained their scattered senses in the dismal light of grinning skull heads over each light. Everyone then assembled in the main room where the usual Halloween games were played.

"Beheading of the Ghosts" proved an exciting stunt. The victims were led, one by one, into the death chamber where a boy dressed as a devil carried a huge cardboard axe over his shoulder. Each one was led by a ghost to a wooden block and made to kneel before it with his neck across it. The axman then raised his axe and as it descended, apparently on the victim's neck, the lights were extinguished and a resounding whack was heard, followed by a scream. When the lights were again turned on, the victim was gone and the axman stood waiting for the next victim. In the meantime his assistant had struck a heavy block of wood with a real axe and then pulled the victim away before the lights were again turned on. This stunt should all be done in full view of the rest of the crowd, while the assistant hides behind a curtain.

A good way to end the party is to have a ghost story told at exactly 12 o'clock. Everyone should sit in a circle upon the floor while a burning pan of alcohol (to which salt has been added) is placed in the middle. Let a witch tell a story and time it so the alcohol burns out just as the most exciting part of the story occurs. At this point more excitement may be secured by letting the several luminous skeletons walk around the room dragging chairs behind them.

The luminous skeleton idea is very simple. Secure a picture of a skeleton, block it off into squares and then enlarge it to life size, drawing it on sign-painters cloth. This may also be done by enlarging a lantern slide to life size and then drawing it off. Paint over the lines with luminous paint which can be bought at art or paint stores. Then cut off the arms, legs, and head and pin it together to the clothes of the boy who is to take the part. Now expose the skeleton to a strong electric light for about ten minutes. In the dark this figure will now stand out like purple fire and remain luminous for about a half hour. One of the arms should be detached from the body and then float around the air, approaching people, then dodging off in the distance. Many stunts will suggest themselves when these skeletons are finished. The small skeletons can be secured as cut-outs, having movable legs and arms. Paint these as was done with the larger figures.

To make the dead man in a coffin, place a man on a table and lay cardboard boxes over him, cut and formed so as to resemble a coffin. Cover with black crepe paper, place two green bulbs inside near the face, and you will have a coffin fit for any ghost. The room should be in total darkness, therefore the lower part of the coffin need not be made since it cannot be seen.

HALLOWEEN SUGGESTIONS

Walnut boats.—Open a number of English walnuts, remove the meat, and in each half-shell fasten short pieces of differently colored Christmas candles. These are each to be named for a member of the party, and, after lighting, set afloat in a large pan or tub of water.

The behavior of these tiny boats reveals the future of the youths and maidens for whom they are named. Two may glide on together as if talking to one another, while one may be left alone—out in the cold. Again, two may start off and all the rest may follow in close pursuit. The one whose candle first goes out is destined to be an old bachelor or old maid.

Blind fate.—Blindfolded players walk through a doorway in which are hung, a few inches apart, various objects such as a candy heart, a thimble, an irregularly shaped stone, a toy steam engine. As the blindfolded one approaches the doorway both hands must be extended and the objects touched will indicate the future—the candy heart, a new sweetheart; the rough stone, a hard road to travel, etc. It will be easy to supply the ten or twelve different objects needed. Of course, just one article should be touched.

Saucers.—Seven tiny saucers, each with different articles, presided over by a gypsy. The seeker is blindfolded and touches one of the saucers. The contents of the saucer tell the fortune, as follows:

Moss—A life of luxury. Money and worldly goods.

Thorn or scrap of brier—Unhappy love. Disappointment.

Red cloth—Military profession, military husband, a military man as rival.

Blue cloth—Navy for profession, or husband whose profession is navy.

Forked stick—Widow or widower.

Clear water—Single blessedness.

The murderer's dagger.—All the players are seated in a circle. The first player hands a dagger-shaped paper knife to the person on his left saying, "Take that!" to which the question is asked, "What is it?" Answer, "A dagger." The second player then hands it to his left-hand neighbor with the same remark. This is repeated

around the circle. After it has reached the original player it continues around again, but this time the second player on receiving it
says, "There is blood on it," to which the reply is "Sh!" The next
time around is added the question, "Who did it?" and the answer
is a very expressive shrug of the shoulders. The last time after the
shrug the second player asks, "How did he do it?" to which the first
player with much realism makes the motion and a noise indicative of
cutting his throat.

It is very necessary to the success of this game that the first two
players know how to do it well.

A HALLOWEEN HARD-TIMES PARTY

Decorations—Cornstalks, jack-o'-lanterns made out of cardboard
boxes.

Hard-luck clothes—Each guest is asked to come dressed in the most
delapidated costume available.

Hard-luck experiences—Guests must greet one another with "hard-
luck experiences," such as "I need 17 cents more to have enough to
pay my bus fare home where I have a sick child (wife, husband,
mother) , etc."

Bobbing for apples.—Interest could be added to this old favorite
by placing a penny in one apple, a thimble in another, and a ring
in another. The penny will prophesy wealth; the thimble, single
life; the ring, marriage within the year.

Spider-web fortune.—Draw a large spider web on smooth yellow
paper. In each section write some fortune. Players spin a spool top.
The space on which the top stops, after spinning, indicates the fortune.

Hoop fortunes.—A barrel hoop, stick candy, slices of bread, red
peppers, small candles, and strong cords are needed. Cut the cord
different lengths and tie the articles into the hoop. Suspend the
hoop from the ceiling or chandelier. Twist the cords holding it and
spin it merry-go-round fashion. Then the bite tells, for each guest,
in turn, endeavors to grasp one of the articles in his teeth. If he
bites the candy, sweet and rosy is the future. Bread portends plenty
to eat, but an even humdrum existence. The red pepper foretells
trouble and a "hot time" generally. The candle indicates a short
honeymoon.

Flame fortunes.—A plate of alcohol. Fortunes written on paper and wrapped in tinfoil. The alcohol is lighted and guests are allowed to snatch a fortune from the flaming dish.

Threading needle.—Guests are required to sit on a milk bottle (side down), with feet touching and in the air. In this position each one tries to thread a needle. The first one to do so will be the first one married.

Apple fortunes.—After ducking for apples each person breaks or cuts his apple in half, and counts out his fortune in this fashion: (1) Disappointment in love, (2) early marriage, (3) legacy, (4) wealth, (5) a voyage, (6) fame, (7) attainment of one's most cherished wish. If there are more than seven seeds the count goes back to number one.

Following this stick two of the seeds on the forehead. The one that sticks longest indicates the fortune. The player can name them for two persons to decide which will be his mate, or he can call one "riches" and the other "poverty," or one "Get my wish," the other "Don't," etc.

Poorhouse.—Place chairs in a circle facing in toward center. Leave four openings three or four chair-spaces wide in the circle of chairs. There should be enough chairs in the circle so that all but two players can be seated. For the two left over there are two chairs in the center of the circle. The players seated there are in the "Poorhouse." As the music plays all guests except the two in the "Poorhouse" get up and march on the outside of the chairs. When the leader blows a whistle they all rush inside the circle and try to get chairs. The "Poorhouse" couple also tries to get seats in the circle. The two players left out take the seats in the "Poorhouse" and the game proceeds. Players are only allowed to enter the circle through the four original openings. It is illegal to step over the chairs or to move a chair out to save the time and trouble of getting in through the regular openings. If desired, chairs may be arranged in two's and players may be required to move in couples, holding hands.

Canned beans.—Nail five tin cans to a board—one in each corner and one in the center. Give each player five tosses with a bean bag. Center can count twenty-five; top cans count ten each; and bottom cans, five each.

Hard-times food—Sandwiches wrapped in newspaper and coffee.

SPOOK SHIP PARTY

Invitation—Skull and crossbones ship cut-outs.

"Davy Jones and all the crew,
Together are inviting you
To come aboard the good spook ship
And take a thrilling spooky trip."

Davy Jones' crew—The Recreation Committee dressed in pirate costume. This crew serves as a directing committee.

The gangway—Guests should be required to enter the ship (room) through some narrow passageway. This may be darkened and the usual Halloween scares provided—rattling chains, groans, ghosts, and the like. "All Aboard!" The party is on with some good mixer. Some folk game like "Ach Ja," "Chimes of Dunkirk," or "Bingo" would do.

Ship games—Divide into groups to play shuffleboard, bean-bag board, dart board, anagrams, skill games of various sorts, crokinole, dominoes, and the like. Ducking for apples and various other familiar Halloween games can be introduced here.

Ship concert—Here group singing can be enjoyed. Special musical numbers may be introduced. "The Goblins'll Get You if You Don't Watch Out" would make an appropriate pianologue.

Ship ghost story—Some good ghost story, such as "The Phantom Ship," would fit in nicely.

Mess call—The bugle blows mess call and that is the signal for everyone to get ready for refreshments. Doughnuts and sweet milk are suggested.

HALLOWEEN DRAMA

"The Ghost Hunters," Watkins. Four men, two women. Thirty minutes. A mystery comedy. Baker.

"Ghoses or Not Ghoses," Long. A debate on the subject, "Resolved, Dat Dar Ain't No Ghoses." Black-faced comedy. Twenty minutes. Four participants in the debate in the presence of seven officers of the club and as many judges as desired. Eldridge.

"The Ghost Story," Tarkington. Five men, five women. A young man is trying to propose when friends arrive. He strives to get rid of them by telling a ghost story without success. The young lady, however, does the work by going into hysterics. Baker.

NOVEMBER

A USHARIT PARTY

There's a great big party a coming this way,
So get yourself ready, and keep your spirits gay.
Put on your old play clothes, bring a game or two;
Usharit with us, and we'll share with you.

Everyone is requested to bring at least one game, or idea for one. The game is explained to the crowd, and the person suggesting it may lead them in playing it. If desired, someone else may lead the crowd in playing the games suggested. Some people don't mind telling about a game, but they would be embarrassed if asked to direct a crowd in playing.

In a large crowd it would be impossible to play all the games suggested. Therefore, it might be necessary to divide into four or more groups with a good leader for each group. Those groups will meet for a few minutes and each will plan for fifteen minutes or more of the program. Each person is supposed to suggest a game to the group of which he is a member. The group decides which games it will use.

Let them vie with one another to see which group can furnish the best time.

They will draw for the order in which they are to come in the program. This drawing may be done by leaders of the groups, so each group can better arrange its part of the program.

If the leader thinks there is any chance whatever of failure because the individuals will not respond with suitable games, then it might be well to have a preliminary meeting of the leaders, and map out plans which will do in case the groups should fall down in game ideas. Often a suggestion from the leader of the group will start the individuals of that group off to making some suggestions that will make a glorious evening of fun.

All those who are invited to the party may be urged to look up some game in some recreation book. If the church has a recreation library, put the books where they will be easily available.

Each person may be asked to bring some refreshments, with a limit of twenty-five cents, or less, being placed on the expenditure per person. All refreshments are turned in to a committee, which sees that they are served.   Thus, each shares his refreshments with the others.   If a person desires, he may trade what is served him to someone else who would rather have what he happened to get.

Another plan would be that of making the girls responsible for preparing and serving cake, while the boys are responsible for ordering and serving ice cream, or Eskimo pies.

A KNOXEM COLLEGE FOOTBALL PARTY

Invitation—On yellow cardboard or paper footballs.

> "You are requested to report for football practice at the church gym on Friday evening, November ——. No excuses accepted."
> Signed: Athletic Committee, Knoxem College.

Decorations—Have a fake tackling dummy rigged up in one corner of the room.   Use a lot of "Knoxem College" pennants made of crepe paper.   Post slogans around the room.   Here are a few suggestions:

"A strong line aids a weak plunger.   What's your line?"
"Tackle low, but don't dig up our grass."
"Many a full-back is seen on sun-tan days."
"They shall not pass."
"Pass the ball.   Don't pass the buck."
"A straight arm gaineth more ground than a crooked character."
"Be sure all your side-stepping is done within bounds."

Program.—
1. *Scrimmage*—See "Squat."
2. *Testing of wind*—Paper-sack-burst relay or blowing up toy sausage balloons until they burst.
3. *Falling on the ball*—Use bean bag on a piano stool.   Players line up in equal sides.   Each player is numbered.   Leader calls a number and the two players with that number rush out to get possession of the bean bag.   If a player can get back to his line with the bean bag without being tagged by his opponent he scores two points.   If he is tagged, the opponent scores one point.
4. *Forward passing*—Two long lines of players.   Pass toy balloons overhead down the lines.   End player receiving runs to head of line and passes down again.   This is continued until original head player is at the top of his line.
5. *Tackling*—Play "Going to Jerusalem."
6. *Interference*—Select about six couples.   Tie toy balloons to

the ankles of the girls with strings twelve to eighteen inches long. Each girl links arms with her partner. When the whistle blows the battle is on. Each boy endeavors to protect his partner's balloon, and at the same time he tries to burst the balloons of his opponents by tramping on them. Fast and furious for a few moments.

7. *Signals*—All players are seated in a circle. They number off, each player remembering his own number. A center player also takes a number. This player is "It." He proceeds to call signals, calling from four to six numbers. No one moves until he yells "hike." Then all players whose numbers are called must find other seats. "It" tries to get a seat in the grand rush. The player left out is "It" for the new turn.

8. *Eggshell football*—

Refreshments—If one hard-boiled egg in the shell for each guest could be worked into the refreshment scheme the crowd could have a lot of fun egg-plugging. Pair off. Winners pair off again. And so on until one player is left with an eggshell unbroken. This player is recognized as the "Champion Plugger."

SUGGESTIONS FOR A THANKSGIVING PARTY

Thanks.—For a group of thirty-six you would write the word "Thanks" six times. Cut these into single letters and give each person one letter. Then tell them they are to try to find enough people to spell the word "Thanks." As they discover players with the letters they want they link arms and search for others until the word is spelled. This goes on until each person has found a group to spell the word. Some award may be given to the first six to spell the word. *T* will look for *H* and link arms with him. Then they will look for *A*. It may be in the meantime that *A* has already found *N* and linked arms with her. No player can link arms with players other than those who have the letter immediately preceding or following theirs in the word "Thanks." Sticks of candy would do for the award.

Shouting proverbs.—Each group of six now decide on some proverb of six words, such as "A stitch in time saves nine." Each player is assigned one word in this proverb. The leader counts "One, two, Three" and each player in the group of six shouts his word at the same time. The other groups try to guess what proverb has been shouted. Then try it over until some group guesses it or they all give up. Then another group shouts its proverb. "All that glitters is not gold," "Make hay while the sun shines" are some of the other proverbs that may be used.

You have a face.—See Chapter V, Fun with Games for Small Groups.

Thanksgiving.—Each person is given a piece of paper and told to write down as many words as he can find in the word, "Thanksgiving." Proper names are excluded. Give about five minutes for this and then let each player count his own list. Have the winner read his list.

Turkey or Thanks.—Make as many sets of cubes as you will need for "Progressive Turkey." Some lumber yard or carpenter shop can make these for you. Six cubes will be necessary for a set. On the six sides of each cube write the letters (with pencil, crayon, or ink) of the word "Turkey," one letter to a side. The word "Thanks" may be used in the same manner.

For thirty-six people nine sets of cubes will be necessary.

Play as in the game of "Hearts." Four players to a table. Each player tosses the six cubes out on the table. If he gets a "TH" he scores five points. If he gets a "THA" he scores ten points; "THAN," fifteen; "THANK," twenty; "THANKS," twenty-five plus ten for getting them all. Any player throwing three "T's" cancels all his score up to that time. After each player has had three times around, the two winners at each table should progress to the next table. Players keep their scores and the girl and boy ending the evening with largest score declared winners.

FOOTBALL PARTY

Decorations—Hang school banners and pennants around in room, carrying out two school names and two color schemes. Place goal post at each end of room. Give each person a novelty football on ribbon, as they enter.

Helmets—Give all who come pieces of brown paper and pins and let them make football helmets to wear throughout the evening.

The referee—Consider your leader the referee and have him wear white knickers and white shirt.

Football spell.—Divide group into two teams and have each elect a quarterback as their leader. Play animated alphabet using football terms for words to spell. The following words are suggested: Yard, Tackle, End, Half, Jump, Down, Reverse, Forward, Guard, Back, Kick, Punt, Umpire, Timer, Quarter, Linesman, Veterans. Wedge, Expert, Victory, Zero, Zigzag, Zone.

Eggshell football.—Play eggshell football. See "Table Football," page 62.

Forward pass.—Each player is given three peanuts. A basket is provided for each side. Players stand at ten feet distance from the basket and try to toss peanuts into it. The side having the largest number of peanuts in the basket after the last player has thrown wins.

Touchdown.—Players are seated in two circles, faced out from center, an equal number in each circle. When the "referee" blows his whistle the leader on each team starts walking around his circle. As soon as he passes his teammate, who sits next to him on the right, that player follows. And so it goes until all the players have been all around the circle and have become seated in their original places. Next let the players run it. The third time have the players pick up their chairs and carry them with them.

Player guess.—Have a leader read out names of prominent football players and give prize to person that names the correct school for which players play opposite the players' names.

Refreshments—Popcorn, peanuts, and Coco-Colas.

"THE HOBOS' CONVENTION"

Advertising and invitations—This is a very important part of any social. Use posters, church notices, newspapers, circular letters, the telephone, etc. Have your social advertised two or three weeks in advance so that there will be plenty of time for careful preparation. Do not divulge too many particulars regarding the program if you want to arouse keen interest and more active participation.

Decorations—This is another very important part of any social and one which is often neglected. By using evergreen foliage, plants, corn, etc., a woodland setting can be secured. An artificial campfire adds an effective touch. Have the lights not too bright and use boxes and planks for seats.

Costumes—This social is much more successful if all wear tramp clothes. A prize may be offered for the best tramp costume.

Program—This is the real part of the whole social, of course, and is much more interesting if the theme is followed closely. Here is a suggested program for "The Hobos' Convention."

The hobo's pot luck.—So that there may be no delay for those who arrive on time or even sooner, this game can start as soon as there are two present. Each one, as he arrives, is given ten white beans with full instructions on how to play. He then engages the others in conversation and every time he gets "Yes" or "No" as an answer to one of his questions he is paid one bean. Should he say "Yes" or "No" to someone else he must forfeit a bean. This game may be played until all have arrived. The one having the most beans at this time wins.

The hobo's introduction.—In order to become a member of the Grand Order of Hobos one must be formally introduced. Two lines are formed facing each other about two feet apart. Everybody then crosses his arms and takes the hand of the person standing on the right and left of the one directly opposite. When in this position all hands are raised and lowered six times, everybody repeating aloud his name each time. By adding to the above this may be made into a real funny ceremony.

The hobos hike and are arrested.—Every boy gets a partner and all form a line and march around to music. Some three or four large circles are marked out on the floor and over these the line must pass. The circles represent places of ambush where policemen are in hiding. The music stops at intervals and when it does so, anyone found in a circle is arrested and is out of the game. The last couple on the floor wins.

The hobos hunt for dinner.—Having arrived at the meeting place, the hobos plan to secure some food. For this purpose the group is divided into a number of "gangs" each of which chooses a leader and is given a name and call such as Cat—"Meow," Dog—"Woof woof," Goat—"Baa," etc. Previous to the social, peanuts have been hidden in various places about the room. The "gangs" then search for them but no one is allowed to touch a peanut except a leader. When a peanut is found the one finding it must give the call of his "gang" until the leader comes and gets it. When all the peanuts have been collected they are put in one pile in the center of the floor.

The hobos divide the spoils.—There being much quarreling among the tramps as to the disposition of the spoils it is decided to divide the peanuts in this way. Around the pile the hobos form a large circle. Those in charge then go to each one and whisper in his ear the word "Monkey" telling him, at the same time, to keep it secret. This same word must be given to everyone without letting anyone else know. The leader then announces that he has given to everyone the name of some animal found in Africa **and that he is** going to tell a story of a recent trip to that continent during which he will mention various animals which he saw there and that when he does so, those who have been given that name will run to the center for the peanuts. Stating that more than one person may have the same names he makes a rule that only the first one to the center gets a peanut and stresses the need of quick action to share in the spoils.

The leader then proceeds with his story, and after a few preliminary remarks, he mentions the word "monkey." The ensuing scramble will reward your very best efforts to make this game interesting.

The hobos pack their kits.—It becomes necessary for some of the hobos to leave so it is decided to pack. Seated in a circle the leader begins by naming something which he is going to take as, "I am taking a comb." Following around the circle each in turn names some thing which he is taking. When it gets around to the leader again he tells what he is going to do with what he is taking as "I am going to comb my hair with my comb." This is repeated by everyone in turn except that the name of the article each is taking is substituted for the word "comb." After going around the circle the one next to the leader tells what he will do, etc. Note: Do not play this game too long for best results.

The hobos catch a freight.—Having packed their kits, those who are leaving decide to go by freight in this way. The hobos sit in a circle leaving no empty seats and having one hobo in the center. The leader gives to each one the name of some city. The one in the center then says something like this, "All hobos going to Chicago, Minneapolis, and Portland take this freight." Those have those names must change seats while the one in the center tries to get a seat for himself. Should he succeed, the one who is left must be "It."

The hobos in the barnyard.—While prowling around in search of food the hobos find themselves in a barnyard and the following occurs: Someone is blindfolded, given a short stick and put into the center of the circle. Stretching the stick before him he touches someone in the circle who must then imitate some barnyard animal or fowl. The blindfolded one is given three guesses to name whom he is touching. Should he guess right, the one touched must go to the center.

The hobos have their questions answered.—At this time the hobos get down to the real business of the convention and decide to have their problems solved in a very unique way. Slips of paper have been prepared on which is written "What would you do if ——?" These are numbered from one to twenty-five and are passed around to the hobos who are told to fill in the blank space with whatever they wish. After they have been gathered another set of slips is passed around. These are also filled in with answers which should not be answers to what each wrote before. When all are gathered both sets are passed out. Be sure to see that no person gets two slips with the same number on each. The one having Question Number 1 then stands and reads it to be answered by the one having Answer Number 1. Continue until all are read.

The hobos write home.—Everyone is supplied with a pencil and paper. Ten letters are called by anyone and everyone writes them on his slip of paper, leaving some space between each as A——C——J—— P—— (Do not use X). Using these ten letters as the initials of ten words the hobos are told to write a telegram. A time limit is set after which all are read aloud.

A hobo tells a story.—One of the hobos, who is already prepared of course, then announces that he is going to demonstrate a conversation which he overheard between President Coolidge and King George. That they may understand better he asks them all to listen in on the line. A long string is held up and all stand in a line along the string with the string in their mouths. Two hobos, representing the two parties concerned, take one end each and a conversation occurs something like this: "Hello, Cal!" "Hello, George!" "How are you feeling, Cal?" "I'm fine, George, how are you?" "Have you been fishing lately, Cal?" "Oh, yes, George, I was out the other day and had great success." "Is that so? What did you get, Cal?" "A whole string of suckers, George. They are on the line now."

By adding to this conversation and bringing in jokes of local interest and about local people it may be made into a real stunt.

A strolling fiddler appears.—Someone who can sing or play here renders several selections. While this is going on the "eats" can be prepared.

The hobos dine.—Hot dogs and coffee or beans and bread make good eats for this occasion. Self-serve style saves a lot of work at this time.

The hobos make merry.—Conclude with a real good sing song. Include folk songs, old-time favorites, favorite hymns, and close with "Blest Be the Tie That Binds" or "Taps."

To those who attempt to put on the above allow me to point out one or two things. First, as to the order of the games. Those, you will notice, are not put in at random but follow an accepted plan as follows: first comers; get acquainted; active games; quiet games; pencil and paper games; mental games; stunts; music; eats; and sing song. Second, a further word as to advertising. When announcing this social, the reading of the headings over each game will serve to arouse much curiosity and interest.

By A. E. GARWOOD. Copyright by the International Society of Christian Endeavor. Used by permission.

DECEMBER

A CHRISTMAS PARTY

Invitations—Tiny, green-paper Christmas trees. The invitation is written on a slip of paper and passed through two slits in the tree.

Christmas caps.—Divide your crowd in two groups. Give one group red crepe paper, the other green. Pins and string should also be furnished. The paper may be cut in strips large enough to fit about the head. Each group is given ten minutes to make caps to wear. At the end of the time limit they parade before the judges' stand. The judges decide which group best expresses beauty and originality in its headgear. An award may be also made to the individual with the most clever creation. These caps are to be worn during the evening.

Christmas bell trade.—Each player is provided with a small paper bell. One of the players is given a gold bell. The rest are all red. Players walk about with closed hands and introduce themselves to other players. As they do so they extend their clenched hands and tap one of the extended hands of the other player. If the player happens to have his bell in the hand tapped he must trade with the player who has introduced himself. At the end of three minutes the leader blows a whistle and the player holding the gold bell is given a large stick of candy as a prize.

Jolly is Saint Nicholas.—This is an adaption of the familiar game, "Jolly is the Miller." Couples march around the circle hand in hand, the ladies at the right and on the inside. On the last line the girls step forward and the boys step backward to meet new partners. In the confusion "Jolly Saint Nicholas," who has been standing in the center, endeavors to get a partner. Whoever fails to get a partner becomes the "Jolly Saint Nicholas" for the next game. Players sing the following song as they march:

> "Jolly is Saint Nicholas, who lived up North,
> He gives us a good time for all we're worth;
> And we like to see him coming, with his pack on his back;
> The girls step forward, and the boys step back."

Telegrams to Santa.—Players keep the partners they have at the close of "Jolly Saint Nicholas." Each couple is given three minutes to write a telegram to Santa Claus, using in order the letters S-A-N-T-A C-L-A-U-S. In small crowds these telegrams may be read and the best decided by vote. The winning couple may be given two small dishes of ice cream and two spoons. The spoons, however, are tied together with a piece of string about six inches in length.

Where the crowd is large it would be best to let the Green Caps contest against the Red Caps in writing the telegrams. Each side may be allowed to write three. Judges would decide as to the cleverest.

Gift exchange.—Each person has been notified in the invitation to bring some gift, for which not more than twenty-five cents has been paid. These gifts are to be wrapped in Christmas packages in such style as may suit the whim of the donor. All players stand in a circle, and as the music plays packages are passed around the circle to the right. When the music stops each player keeps the package he happens to have at that time. He unwraps it, and, after seeing what it is, if he is not satisfied, he may rewrap it, and endeavor to swap with some other player. Players endeavor to disguise the nature of the gift by the manner of wrapping it. A time limit of ten minutes is laid on the swapping period. At the end of that time each player must keep the present he has.

Christmas swipe.—A large sack containing candies and trinkets of various sorts is hung in the center of the room. Players from the Red Caps and Green Caps take turns in being blindfolded, turned about, and in being given an opportunity to bring the sack down with a swipe of a wand. If a Red Cap brings down the sack, then his teammates are privileged to scramble for the contents. If it is brought down by a Green Cap, then only the Greens have that privilege. Players are not allowed to coach a contestant.

Christmas present relay.—From four to ten players represent each side. The runners must run to a chair or table, untie, unwrap, rewrap, and tie up a Christmas package. They then run back and touch off the next teammate.

Christmas stocking contest.—Two or more red stockings are hung up, the number depending on the number of contestants you desire to allow for each side. Each contestant is provided with a teaspoon and three apples. These apples must be picked off the floor with the spoon, carried to the stocking, and dropped into it. It may be run as a relay, each runner putting in just one apple, returning and handing the spoon to the next runner. The apples must be gotten into the stocking without the aid of the extra hand.

Christmas trail.—Each player selects a string from a mass of strings in one corner of the room. This string he then follows to the end. It passes along the floor and is tangled and tied with strings of other players. It is wound around chair legs, posts, and what-not. It may lead upstairs and back. When the end is reached a sack containing candies and fruit, or some sort of noise-making toy may be found. The players now form a line, and march about the room playing their instruments. The color of the girls' strings and that of the boys may be different. Partners for refreshments could be matched by tying the ends of the string together.

A SANTA CLAUS PARTY

This party can be given for either a large or small group. The committee should carefully go over all the plans and arrange all the details of the party.

Pinning on Santa's pack.—The old game of pinning on the donkey's tail adapted. The one who pins his pack in the most nearly correct place should be given some sort of award. As persons arrive at the party they should be tried at this stunt.

Debate.—"Resolved, That There Ain't No Santa Claus." Have one or two speakers on each side. Appoint the debaters a week or so in advance. Limit speeches to five minutes.

Santa's pack.—Give all the players the names of certain things that would likely be in Santa's pack—doll, horn, knife, candy, orange, gun, tie, etc. The crowd is seated in a circle with no vacant chairs. The player who is without a chair starts walking around the circle telling a story about Santa filling up his pack before starting on his journey. "He put in a pretty little doll, a scout knife," etc. As he mentions the names of articles the people bearing those names get up and follow him around the circle putting hands on the shoulders of the person immediately preceding. When the player who is telling the story mentions "Reindeer," each player makes an effort to get a chair, the storyteller among them. The player left without a chair starts another story, and the game continues.

Santa Claus letters.—Each person is given a pencil and a piece of paper and asked to write a "Santa Claus" letter for the player to the right. If the crowd is small each player then reads what he has written. If the crowd is large, the letters are collected, and a committee selects the ones that are to be read to the group.

Santa's bag of stunts.—Write certain stunts to be performed on slips of paper. Put them in a sack, and have the players draw one slip each. Each person is to perform the stunt drawn. Some suggested stunts are the following:

(1) Select a partner and pose for one of those old-time photographs, the girl sitting and boy standing beside her chair, hat held stiffly across his chest.

(2) Propose to anyone of the opposite sex in the room, just to show how it is done.

(3) Laugh in three keys—first low with a "Ho, ho, ho!" then in middle register with a "Ha, ha, ha!" and then in high pitch with a "He, he, he!"

(4) Pantomime a baseball player striking out, swinging on the first two, and having the third strike called by the umpire.

(5) Dramatize the actions and expression of a small boy at an exciting "Wild West Show."

(6) Pantomime the actions and expression of a teen-age girl at a picture show when a romantic picture is being presented.

(7) Give your own explanation of how the custom of allowing a lady to precede a gentleman on entering a door came into vogue.

(8) Briefly state three reasons why you think men are superior to women, whether you believe what you are saying or not.

(9) Briefly state three reasons why you think women are superior to men, whether you believe what you are saying or not.

(10) Dramatize the rocking of a baby to sleep.

Santa's gifts.—Ask each person to bring some inexpensive Christmas present. The cost may be limited to ten cents. These packages are handed to the committee on arrival, and they number them in consecutive order. Players draw numbers from a hat, one number to each player. The packages are given to Santa and he calls the numbers written on them. The player with the number called gets the package. If one is not satisfied with what he gets he is privileged to trade, "sight unseen," or otherwise, if he can find anyone who wants to trade.

Refreshments—Eskimo pies.

A CHRISTMAS CAROL FESTIVAL

Christmas carols.—Christmas caroling was widely popular in the Middle Ages, being especially associated with English traditions. In 1525 we find a specific prohibition was entered against "carols, bells, and merrymaking" because of the illness of King Henry VIII. To this good day it is the custom of England for troops of men and boys to go about the villages several nights before Christmas, singing Christmas carols.

In America, too, caroling is a feature of the Christmas season in many cities and towns. Usually the carol groups go out on Christmas eve and sing wherever a lighted candle appears in the window. It is a beautiful custom, and worthy of perpetuation.

Program

1. Song, "Joy to the World."
2. Reading, Luke 2: 8-20.
3. Song, "There's a Song in the Air."
4. Christmas Story, "The First Christmas Tree," Van Dyke.
5. Hidden quartet and tableaux, "Silent Night."
6. Song, "Hark, the Herald Angels Sing."
7. Play. Some good short Christmas play or the dramatization of some carol.
8. Song, "O Come All Ye Faithful."
9. Games. (*a*) Christmas Greetings. (*b*) Illustrated Christmas Gifts. (*c*) Human Christmas Trees.
10. Closing. One verse of "Silent Night" by everyone.

"Silent Night"—While the hidden quartet sings this beautiful Christmas song present tableaux on the platform. For the first verse, the manger and Mary. For the second verse shepherds assume reverent attitude before the manger. On the third verse a lighted cross appears at the back of the platform. Mary and shepherds kneel, facing the cross.

Christmas greetings.—Each person is given a card at the top of which is attached a sprig of holly. Ten minutes is given for each one to get as many Christmas greetings written on the card as is possible. An award of some sort is made to the one who gets the most. The greeting in all cases will be the same, "Merry Christmas," with the initials of the writer underneath the greeting.

Drawing Christmas gifts.—Have the crowd paired off in couples. Arrange chairs in two rows, back to back, with couples seated back to one another. Each couple is furnished a pencil and piece of paper. One of the partners describes some Christmas gift he would like to have, without naming the gift. The other tries to draw what is described. The one giving the description must not look until the leader calls time on the group. The name of the article described is written beneath the drawing, and the works of art (?) are passed around for inspection. Give ten minutes for the artists to work.

Human Christmas trees.—Have three or four girls to act in this capacity. They are to wear tight-fitting, green crepe-paper caps with red tassels on top. These girls are to be placed at a sufficient distance from each other to allow the groups space in which to work. The crowd is divided into as many groups as there are "trees." Each tree is numbered. The players draw numbers, and then gather about their trees. A decorating committee is appointed by each group, and tinsel, crepe-paper streamers, popcorn, needle and thread, etc., are provided. The trees are then decorated and presents are hung on them, or placed about the foot of the tree. When the job is finished the trees are put on display. Then the leader announces that each person is to find the tree on which is his present, and help himself to that present. Fifteen or twenty minutes is allowed for decoration of the trees.

Presents are provided for all. Each person is asked to bring some toy or trinket, not to cost over ten cents. As guests arrive they are required to register at the door and leave their presents there with the committee. The committee places names on the presents and hands them over to the tree-decorating committees.

A parade of the group, following the distribution of gifts, will be quite interesting, especially if some noise-making toys have been provided.

Closing—Have the crowd sing one verse of "Hark, the Herald Angels Sing" before singing a verse of "Silent Night" as the closing feature of the social.

Excellent suggestions for the dramatizing of carols may be found in *The Christmas Book,* published by the National Recreation Association, 315 Fourth Avenue, New York City.

OTHER CHRISTMAS SUGGESTIONS

Bridgeboard.—From a large sheet of cardboard, cut a series of arches, each arch large enough to admit a ball. Number each arch "5" "10," etc. Attach this cardboard to the sides of a doorway so that the arches will rest on the floor. The players in turn try to roll balls through the numbered arches. One person is appointed to act as scorekeeper, to stand at the door and record the number of the arch through which each ball rolls; another is a hall man to return balls sent through the arches to the next room. The player making the largest count wins.

Safety stars.—Stretch a piece of paper about four feet high around the walls of the room and on it at different places and different heights paste large stars. These are safety stars. The players march slowly to music around the room, not being allowed to touch the wall. When a whistle is blown and the music stops, every player to be "safe" must have his hand on a star. The players left without stars are given seats in the center of the room and five or six stars are taken down from the wall. This is repeated until only one star is left to be contested for by two or more players.

"Rompiendo la pinata."—This is a Mexican Christmas game. A large paper bag is filled with nuts and candy wrapped in wax paper. The mouth of the bag is tied and hung from the ceiling with a cord. The bag is dressed to represent a boy or a girl, using either tissue paper or old clothes.

The guests, each in turn, are given a stick, and with eyes blindfolded, they try to break the pinata. Only one stroke is allowed, and the player is not permitted to grope for the pinata. When someone finally breaks the bag and the contents are scattered, the players scramble for them.

Sometimes a bit of novelty is introduced into the game by preparing three pinatas—the first filled with flour and rice, the second with a pair of old shoes, and the third with the sweets (dulces) .

Hunting Christmas presents.—The guests are told that hidden about the room are Christmas presents, one for each guests. No guest is permitted to disturb a present intended for someone else, nor is he expected to tell another where he has seen a package with his name on it. Each guest must hunt until he finds the package addressed to him.

Making Christmas presents.—Provide patterns—a clown, a horse, a teddy bear, a Santa Claus. If the toys can be made to move by pulling a string, so much the better. Ask each guest to bring along with him cardboard (a suit box or hat box or heavier material if possible) , scissors, crayola or water colors, pencil, an old safety razor blade, and cotton for Santa's beard. The committee should have on hand brads and paste. Lots of fun can be had making these toys. There will be some in the group who will do an artistic job, no doubt. Perhaps the toys can be taken to some children's hospital. A shadow show could be put on with some of the articles made. See Chapter XV, Fun with Puppets, for suggestions regarding shadow puppets.

CHAPTER XVIII
FUN WITH CHILDREN

Chapter XVIII

FUN WITH CHILDREN

Beware of him who hates the laugh of a child.
—LAVATER

The child is trained by play not merely to make a living but to fulfil all the essential relations of a human life.
—JOSEPH LEE in *Play in Education*

CHILDREN live in a world of play. The early Greeks recognized this, and therefore they built their educational system around the play idea. Froebel recognized it when he initiated the kindergarten idea. Parents and other adults who deal with children must recognize it and be sympathetic toward the child's desire to play. Joseph Lee in his *Play in Education* insists that the grammar school, high school, and college, as well as the trade school, should make "deliberate provision for the development in every boy and girl of some form of expression" outside of their expected occupation.

Suggestions are offered in this chapter of things to do with children in their play time. See also Chapter I, Home Fun; Chapter III, Fun with Hobbies; Chapter XV, Fun with Puppets; and other sections of this book.

DIRECTING GAMES FOR CHILDREN

1. Get attention before trying to explain the game. Don't shout directions above the noise of the group. Talk in normal voice. To get quiet, adopt some method that works for you. Different leaders use different techniques. Some can get attention by simply standing quietly before the group. Some use the lifted hand, with the children lifting hands, one by one, as they observe the leader's lifted hand. This is the recognized signal for silence. Some use a whistle. Many leaders, however, consider a whistle irritating.

2. Appeal to the imagination. Children are always responsive to the imaginative touch. A ball can become a fox, or a rabbit. A handkerchief can become a snake, with the greatest of ease. You

---

Note: Much of the material in this section of the book will be useful to young people and adults in their recreation.

(759)

should see the eyes of the seven-year-old sparkle as we play **Dwarf Hide-and-go-seek.** Imagination gets a play there.

3. Get into position to play a new game before explaining it. The explanation becomes more simple and intelligible then.

4. Do more demonstrating than talking. Children want action.

5. Do not try to teach a game of which you are not sure yourself.

6. Have all necessary equipment ready before beginning a game.

7. Use children as leaders wherever possible. Encourage them to share their knowledge of games.

8. Do not permit certain aggressive children to monopolize the game.

9. Once rules are established, see that they are observed. Build up a healthy respect for their observance.

10. Enjoy playing yourself. Children are quick to sense it when a leader carries about with him a "This-is-a-pain-to-me" attitude.

Counting Out

1. Eeeny, meeny, miny, mo,
   Cracka, feeny, finy, fo,
   Mamma woocha, papa doocha,
   Rick, bick, ban, do.

2. Eeeny, meeny, miny, mo,
   Catch a bad boy by his toe;
   If he hollers make him pay
   Fifty dollars every day.

3. Wire, brier, limberlock!
   Three geese in a flock!
   One flew east. One flew west.
   And one flew over the cuckoo's nest.
   O-U-T spells out,
   And out go you.

4. One, two, three, four, five!
   I caught a hare alive.
   Six, seven, eight, nine, ten!
   I let him go again.

5. **Eeenie, meenie,** dixie, deenie,
   Hit 'em a lick and John McQueenie,
   Time, time, American time,

Eighteen hundred and ninety-nine.
O-U-T spells out,
And out you go.

6. Hic-up, snick-up,
Isaac, Jacob,
Two-cup, penny-cup,
Good for the hic-ups.
O-U-T spells out,
And out you go.

7. Apples, peaches, pears, and plums,
Tell me when your birthday comes.
(Tell the date of birthday of person it counts out on,
Then count out that number.
Example: October 12—count to 12.)
And out you go.

8. (Have group of children put out doubled fists.
Then count around) —
One potato, two potato,
Three potato, four,
Five potato, six potato,
Seven potato more.
The fist that "more" comes out on goes behind the back. When both fists are behind the back, step out of counting. Last fist out is "It."

FUN WITH GAMES

Bowing dolls.—Straighten a hairpin. Bend one end until it resembles a shepherd's crook. Hang this end on the edge of the table and it will swing back and forth like a pendulum.

Fix several of these pins. Then look through magazines until you find just the pictures you want—men, women, animals, of a size just a little longer than the pins.

Thrust the hairpins through these paper dolls and hang the bent edges of the pins over the table edge or over the edge of a book cover.

Blow slightly on these and watch them bow politely, bobbing back and forth in amusing fashion.

These tiny actors will make a great deal of fun for the children. Try it and see.

Singing tag.—This starts the same as ordinary tag with "It" chasing the runners. However, if "It" is very fleet of foot and is just about to tag you, you may save yourself, if you have breath enough to burst into song. Just so long as you keep singing you may not be tagged. Once you stop, however, "It" may tag you and you must then chase the runners. If "It" is wise enough to stand and hear all of your song until you get out of breath and stop, or burst out into laughter instead of song, you may be tagged. Grown-ups play this singing tag, too. That is, provided they don't believe in the saying, "Laugh and grow fat," for this game is certainly a breeder of laughter.

I spy.—One player leaves the room. The rest hide an object in plain sight, but in an unusual place. The child returns to the room and tries to find the hidden article, which may be a knife, an eraser, a ball, a book, etc.

Variations– (1) More than one player may be sent out. As soon as one of them finds the article he takes his seat, but does not disclose the hiding place to anyone else. So it goes until all players are seated. If desired, a new group may be sent out after three hunters are captured.

(2) Hide the object out of sight. The children who know where the object is hidden help the searcher by telling him he is "cold," "warmer," "very warm," "hot," etc. When he is far away they tell him he is "cold." When he is right at it, they say "hot." As one little boy shouted excitedly, "You're red hot."

Who is knocking?—Children sit quietly. One child is chosen to sit on a stool in the front of the room. He must shut his eyes tightly and hold his hands over them.

Another child (chosen by the leader) goes up and knocks on the floor behind the player on the stool.

"Who is knocking at my door?" calls the child with the closed eyes.

"It is I," the child who knocked must answer immediately, though he may disguise his voice.

The child on the stool must guess who it is that knocked. He has three guesses. If he guesses correctly, the two players exchange places and another knocker is selected.

Animal blind man's buff.—One player is blindfolded. He stands in the center of the circle of players. In his hand he holds a stick or cane. The players dance around him until he taps on the floor. At that signal they must stand still. The "blind man" then points his cane at some player. That player must take the other end of the cane in his hand. The "blind man" commands him to make a noise like some animal such as a cow, a cat, a dog, a lion, a donkey, a goat, a duck, a parrot, a hog. The "blind man" then tries to guess who the player is. If the guess is correct, they exchange places. If not, the game proceeds, with the "blind man" trying again with some other player.

Players may disguise their voice, and thereby make some rather peculiar animal sounds. Often, the player also disguises his height by stooping or standing on tiptoe before answering.

With a large crowd two or more "blind men" may be used at once.

Imaginative hunting.—This is a mental hide-and-go-seek and it may be played in a number of different ways:

One player decides on a place of hiding. Bounds have been set by common agreement, such as "in the house," "in the room," "in the yard." "Guess where I am hiding." The player who guesses correctly has the privilege of hiding next time. If the bounds are confined to the room, the player may hide in a vase, in a desk drawer, behind a flower pot, etc., since this is an imaginative game.

Geography hide-and-go-seek.—Use a map. "I am thinking of a river in Brazil. It begins with an *A*." Of course that's "Amazon," but the player calling it must not only name it; he must locate it on the map. "I am thinking of the capital of Kentucky." The hunters must locate Frankfort on the map. If one of those large picture maps is available, such questions as "I am thinking of a state that has the most wheat (or corn, or cattle, or cotton, etc.) ." This would be a simple way for children to pick up a lot of geography. This writer can still remember the fun he had in the seventh grade with this simple, but interesting game.

Hidden object.—"Guess of what object in this room I am thinking, it begins with the letter ———."

Nature hunting.—"Guess of what tree I am thinking." "Guess what bird." "Guess what animal." "Guess what insect." Cues may be given to help the group locate the particular subject. For instance, the hider may say, "The bird I have in mind has a red stripe on a black wing. I am often seen on swaying cattails in swampy land."

Vacation trip.—"I am going on a vacation and the place I am to visit is noted for its mountain scenery (or for its bathing beach, or as a land of sunshine, or as the home of the Aztec)." The guessers must locate the place on the map.

Bible hunts.—With a large map of Bible lands the hunt could be built around Bible questions.

Locating quotations.—"Guess where this quotation is found, 'pulled out a plum'." Nursery rhymes, fairy tales, familiar poems, and stories may be used.

I see.—The leader begins the game by saying, "I see something that is blue" (or "red," or "yellow," or any color). The children try to guess what it is. The one who guesses correctly continues the game by choosing something and saying, "I see something that is black," for instance.

Players may say, "I see something made of wood" (or "iron," "brass," or "glass"), or "I see something, the first letter of which is 'a'," or "I see something in a tree."

This is a good game to help children distinguish colors, identify materials, and spell words.

Who has gone?—The children stand or sit in a circle. One player is "It." He closes his eyes and puts his hands over them. The leader motions for some player to leave the room. That player does so quietly. The player who is "It" then opens his eyes and tries to guess which child has gone from the room. If he guesses correctly the player who went out becomes "It." If not, "It" continues until he does guess correctly.

Huckle, buckle.—One group of players leave the room. The rest hide some object, leaving it in plain sight, but where it will not be likely to be seen easily, for instance, on top of a picture, in a corner of the room, behind a vase. After the object has been hidden the players who went out are recalled. They begin the hunt. When a player discovers the object, he goes immediately to his seat, saying, "Huckle, buckle, bean stalk!" He tries not to tip off the other hunters where he discovered the object. The hunt continues until all the players have been successful. Then the player who first found the object has the privilege of hiding it as a new group of players are sent out of the room.

Cowboys and Indians.—The players are divided into two even sides. The cowboys are supposed to be in the woods. They fall fast asleep with one cowboy to stand guard. The Indians are hidden in the bushes, behind trees, etc. They come from their hiding places and approach the cowboy. If they can tag a cowboy before he gets up he is captured. However, they are not likely to be able to do this, for the watchman sounds the alarm. At his call the cowboys get up and rush after the Indians before they can get back to their "wigwams." Every Indian captured becomes a cowboy. The Indians may then be allowed to go to sleep while the cowboys slip up on them.

Pretty girls' station.—This old game is variously named, "Lemonade," "New York Town," "New Orleans," "Sugar-loaf Town," and "Georgia Town." The players are divided into two even sides. Boundaries are decided. One group approaches the other, each group having its players arranged in a straight line. The following dialogue takes place:

> "Here we come!"
> "Where from?"
> "Pretty Girls' Station!"
> "What's your trade?"
> "Lemonade!"
> "Go to work!" or "How's it made?"

Immediately the players, who have approached, go through motions that represent some activity, such as sweeping, picking cotton, churning, washing clothes, ironing, sewing, driving nails, being a soda fountain jerker, etc. As soon as the opposing side guesses correctly the pantomimers must dash to their goal line with the guessers in pursuit. All players tagged go over to the other side and the game continues with the other side pantomiming.

Variation—Instead of chasing and running, points may be allowed for a correct guess in three trials.

Modeling.—Give each child a stick of chewing gum, a white card, and two toothpicks. After the gum has been chewed to the proper consistency, each person proceeds to mold an animal, a bust, or whatever his imagination dictates. The result is mounted upon the card, the modeler's name is signed to it, and it is put on display with the creations of others.

Resemblances.—Divide into two even groups. The two groups stand in line facing one another. On one side each player is given the name of an animal—fox, hippopotamus, elephant, donkey, horse, dog, cat, rhinoceros, hog, etc. Players on the other side are given the names of flowers—rose, violet, daisy, petunia, pansy, chrysanthemum, carnation, dahlia, iris, gardenia, orchid, etc. The first players on the side step out in front of their lines facing one another. The player on the flower side must say, "Do I not look like a pansy?" "No," comes the answer from the player on the animal side, "You look like a donkey." This dialogue must be repeated three times without either player smiling or laughing. Of course, all the other players may laugh at will, but the two concerned must keep solemn countenances. If a player laughs or smiles on his turn, he is out of the game. The game continues with two more players stepping in front of their lines and repeating this process, the "flower" speaking first in each instance, and the "animal" answering.

Variation—Have the "animal" side ask the question, with the "flower" side responding. "Do I look like a horse?" "No, you look like a petunia."

What'll I do?—Players line up in two groups facing one another. One person whispers to each player on one side some predicament, such as "I burned my hand," or "I fell off of a horse," or "I smashed my fender," or "I stumbled over ——'s foot," or "I snored in church." The other person gives each person on the other side some answer, not knowing what predicaments are being whispered to the opposite side. Number One player on one side then says, "I lost my hat, what'll I do?" Number One on the opposite side offers the following puzzling solution, "Use Vick's Salve."

The sea.—The players are seated in a circle, except one who represents the "Sea." That player stands outside the circle. Each person is given the name of some fish or denizen of the sea—whale, shark, porpoise, star, sail, sword, buffalo, perch, cat, etc. The "Sea" walks slowly around the outside of the ring, calling one fish after another to follow. When all of the fish, or a goodly number of them have their seats, the "Sea" begins to run about, exclaiming, "The Sea is troubled!" "The Sea is troubled!" Suddenly the "Sea" sits down in one of the chairs, which are arranged back to center. All "fish" follow the "Sea's" example, as long as seats are available. The player left out becomes the "Sea" and the game continues.

My lady dresses.—All players but one are seated in a circle with that one standing at center to represent the "Lady's Maid." Each player takes the name of some article of dress—shoes, skirt, blouse, coat, hat, ribbon, comb, bracelet, necklace, brooch, stockings, etc. The "Lady's Maid" calls out "My lady is up and wants her shoes." The one or ones with that name must immediately jump up and shout "Shoes!" They then sit down. If a player does not rise as soon as he is called, he must pay a forfeit. The "Lady's Maid" calls for other articles of apparel, and then suddenly shouts, "My lady is up and wants her whole outfit." At this all players jump up and exchange seats. The "Lady's Maid" also seeks to get a seat so it is likely that someone else will be left without a chair, since there is always just one chair short of enough for all of the players. The person left without a chair becomes the new "Lady's Maid."

The blind musician.—Blindfold one player who stands at the center of the circle of players. He holds a wand or baton (a pencil will do). The players dance around humming some familiar tune. The blind musician beats time with his baton. When the group stops singing, he points the wand at someone. That player must start humming the tune, disguising his voice as best he can. If the blind musician guesses correctly who is humming, the two players exchange places.

Button, button, who's got the button?—The players sit in a circle with one player at center. In the circle of players is a button which the players pass back and forth. All players keep their hands in constant motion as if they are receiving or passing the button. The center player tries to guess who has the button. When he does, that player takes his place.
Variation—Pass a thimble or coin.

Knight of the whistle.—Several players, who do not know this game, are sent out of the room. They are recalled one at a time. On entering the room, the candidate is presented to the High Commander of the Order of Knight of the Silver Whistle. The Commander instructs the candidate as to requirements. He explains that certain conditions must be met in order for the candidate to prove he is worthy of the honor about to be bestowed upon him. The victim is blindfolded while one of the Knights hides the insignia of the Order, a silver whistle. This the candidate must find. On finding it, he is received into full membership.

When the candidate consents to being blindfolded he is taken to the center of the room. The others crowd about him. While he is being blindfolded, the whistle, which is attached to a short piece of string, is fastened to the back of his coat. The string has a bent pin hook on one end. The whistle may be blown once or twice to give him an idea of which way to look. Then the bandage is removed and the hunt proceeds. At intervals, when his back is turned, players blow the whistle. The player turns swiftly, but then he hears it blow back of him again. This goes on until he discovers the hoax. Upon this discovery, he is made a full-fledged Knight. Then another candidate is ushered into the room.

Knee sitting.—The players are seated close together in a circle or half-circle. One player is blindfolded. Each player sits with his knees well out. After the player is blindfolded, all of the others change seats. The blindfolded player now sits down on someone's knee, saying "Um." The player on whose knee he is sitting must answer with an "Um," disguising his voice. The word is repeated until each of the two have said "Um" three times. The blindfolded player then must guess on whose knee he is sitting. If he fails all of those seated change places and the blindfolded player tries again. When he guesses rightly, the person on whose knees he sat, becomes blindfolded. The blindfolded player must not touch the players seated with his hands in any way.

Loo K'bah Zee.—This is a game which is played in far-off Burma. One boy, who holds a stone or other small object in his hand, walks up and down behind all of the players, who stand in a row, their hands held open behind them. As he walks up and down he pretends to put the stone in their hands (something like the way we play "Button, Button"). Finally he drops the object in someone's hands. The boy who gets it runs out of the line trying to avoid being caught by the boys on either side of him. They may not move out of their places, but must catch him as he leaves his place. After he is caught he changes places with the boy behind the row. If he is not caught he goes back to his own place and the play continues, the first boy behind the line continuing his job of walking up and down and depositing the stone in someone's hands until a boy is caught to take his place.

Testing the cloth.—Circle formation with players facing center. All elbows linked. By all players pulling back, the circle becomes taut. Players keep pulling attempting to break the circle. When a break is made, the two players at the point of the break drop out of the game. The circle is renewed and the process repeated until the circle can no longer be broken. None of the players are allowed to release hold to take a rest. If they do they drop out. At the command of the leader the circle will relax and move to center and then back swiftly. This sudden and hard pull is likely to break the circle at some point.

Wild bull.—A dozen players or so form a circle with hands firmly clasped. One player, at center, is the bull. He tries to break through the ring. He walks around examining the arms and hands, and selects a place to try to break through. If he gets through he runs and the others give chase. The one who tags him, becomes the bull for the next game. The bull often breaks through by some surprise move. Just as two players relax because he has passed them, he turns suddenly and makes a vigorous assault.

Tommy Tucker.—Players stand in a circle. Tommy Tucker walks around inside the ring. He holds his right hand out between two players and repeats, "Tommy Tucker, run for your supper!" As soon as he has finished the two players run around in opposite directions outside the circle. The one who first gets back to the vacant place becomes the new Tommy Tucker. The game may be varied by players being required to skip, walk, gallop, fly, or hop. No player must move until Tommy Tucker finishes his announcement. At the word "supper" they may run, but not until then.

Blind neighbors.—Half the players have sacks over their heads so they cannot see. The chair to the right of each blind player is vacant. The other players sit in these chairs and at a signal from the leader they perform in various ways. For instance, they say "Howdy!" "Hello!" crow like a rooster, quack like a duck, sneeze, cough, sing, bleat like a sheep, etc. As soon as the blindfolded player recognizes his neighbor to the right of him, he may take off his sack.

My father's store.—The players sit in a circle. It is better if several players are familiar with it. The game continues until all of the players discover the catch. The secret lies in the fact that the knowing ones mention objects they are actually touching at the time. As far as possible, this touching should be done as naturally and unconcernedly as possible.

The leader turns to his right-hand neighbor and says, "My father has a store."

"What does he sell?" the second player must inquire.

"Chairs," says the leader.

The second player turns to the third and the same dialogue continues, with the second player mentioning some other article the father sells, "carpets" for instance.

If a player is unfamiliar with the catch he is likely to answer incorrectly, in which case he is told that there must be some mistake, since his father could not possibly sell the mentioned article. Shirts, collars, ties, stockings, dresses, suits, coats, watches, pencils, pens, tables, vases, and jewelry are a few of the things that may be mentioned.

Peas porridge hot.—Two children sit or stand facing one another. They clap their hands as indicated as they repeat:

> Peas porridge hot,
> Peas porridge cold,
> Peas porridge in the pot
> Nine days old.
> Some like it hot,
> Some like it cold,
> Some like it in the pot
> Nine days old.

Action:

First line— Clap both hands to thighs,
Clap own hands.
Clap right hand with partner.

Second line— Repeat first two movements and on third word,
Clap left hand with partner.

Third line— Repeat first two movements,
Clap right hand with partner,
Then, clap own hands together.

Fourth line— Clap left hand with partner.
Clap own hands.
Clap both hands with partner.

Last four lines—Repeat action on first four lines.

Bubble blowing.—*Equipment*—A large bowl of soapy water. Add a little glycerine to give the bubbles a prismatic effect. Clay pipes or regular soap blowing pipes.

Stunts—

1. See who can blow the bubble that goes the highest.

2. The bubble that lasts the longest.

3. The largest bubble.

4. The most bubbles from one dip.

5. Have two blow one bubble together, holding their pipes close together and allowing their bubbles to merge into one bubble. Try three or four blowers on this stunt.

6. Fan bubble through hoop or wicket.

7. *Play bubble tennis,* requiring the players to fan their bubbles over a table tennis net. A bubble that lands on the table on the other side of the net shall be regarded as scoring a point. Opposing players do not try to prevent the bubble from landing.

8. *Play bubble croquet,* by fanning bubbles through wickets on a table. Use only seven wickets like this:

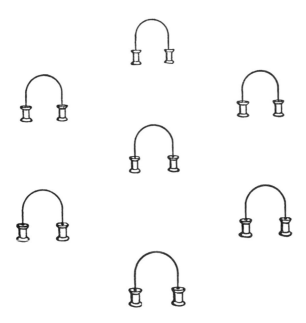

Wickets can be made of pieces of wire stuck in spools. A player blows a bubble and fans it through the first wicket. If successful, he blows another bubble and fans it through the second wicket. He continues until he is unsuccessful. Then another player takes his turn. The player wins who first gets a bubble through each wicket in turn.

Weathervanes.—Any number of players may play. The four sides of the room are named after the four points of the compass, North, South, East, and West. One player impersonates the Wind and stands at center. When the Wind points to one side and calls that point, all of the vanes must immediately face in the opposite direction. For instance if Wind calls "North!" the vanes must immediately face South. If he shouts "Variable!" then they must raise on their tiptoes and sway backward and forward, from heel to toe and toe to heel. If he shouts "Storm!" they must spin around three times. Any player failing to obey immediately must pay a forfeit to be redeemed by some humorous "stunt."

Fisherman.—Players gather around a table or sit on the ground. One player is the Fisherman. He has a short stick to which a piece of string is attached, the twine being tied in a loop at the end. The Fisherman drops his line in such a way that the loop lies on the table, near center. When he says "whose fish?" all the players put the tips of their forefingers on the table inside the circle formed by the twine. Suddenly the Fisherman calls "My fish!" and pulls in his line. Players try to withdraw their fingers before they are caught in the loop. The Fisherman must pull in his line very quickly in order to catch anything. Each player is Fisherman in turn.

Swapping farms (Moving day).—Arrange chairs in two rows, train fashion, with an aisle between them. The seats in a schoolroom would answer the purpose admirably. In this latter case all unoccupied seats would be marked in some way—by a book, a piece of paper, etc. For the purposes of the game there must be one less seat than there are players. The extra player walks up and down the aisle or "road" between the farms. At a signal from the leader—a raised hand, a whistle, clapping of the hands—all farms change owners. That is, every child must leave his seat and find another. He may move across the "road" or "straight ahead. The "buyer" who is walking the "road" may get himself a "farm" in the ensuing scramble.

If there are a number of children, there may be more than two rows of "farms," with a "buyer" roaming each "road" or aisle.

Variations—(1) If played as "Moving Day" the extra player is a "renter." At signal all tenants must move.

(2) If desired, the rules may not require each "farmer" to move each time. Players may signal one another—by a wink of the eye, a nod of the head, or some other gesture—that they are willing to "swap" when the leader signals for "Moving Day," or "swapping time," they must get up immediately to exchange. If played in this way, it may be required that no "farmer" can stay on his "farm" longer than "three years"— that is three signals from the leader.

Chinese holdup.—Players are seated in a circle. One player starts the game by holding his hands to both of his ears. He catches the lobes between his thumbs and forefingers. Immediately the persons to the right and left of him must hold the ear nearest the player holding both ears. The last one of these two players to comply with this requirement of the game is out. He gets up and stands behind his chair. The player who started the game immediately "casts" to another player in the circle by pointing in his direction. The player to whom he "casts" holds both ears and his neighbors must hold the ears nearest him. Again a player is eliminated and stands behind his chair. Thus it goes until only two players are left. The players should keep the game moving rapidly by "casting" quickly from one player to another.

In a large crowd have several players start the game simultaneously. "Casters" will operate in certain sections of the circle to avoid confusion. When the circle is trimmed down sufficiently, go back to the plan of one "caster." Or, divide into several circles and play the game.

Trades.—One player is the "King" or "Boss." Each player selects for himself some trade or profession. They all announce what they will impersonate. The King selects some trade or profession no one has chosen.

All players now begin to pantomime their trades. The doctor holds his own wrist as if feeling the pulse; the carpenter planes or hammers; the blacksmith beats an imaginary anvil; the trombone player plays an imaginary trombone; the cook kneads dough; the painter welds the brush; the housekeeper sweeps; the preacher makes familiar gestures; the traffic cop directs traffic; and the gas station worker fills the tank with gas.

The "King" pantomimes his trade, whatever it is. He is, however, privileged to discontinue it suddenly and take up the trade belonging to some other player. When he does that player must immediately do what the "King" had been doing, while all other players remain inactive. As soon as the "King" goes back to his own trade, all the players immediately return to their own trades. The "King" should be sudden in his changes, taking up first one and then another trade, until it becomes difficult to follow him. Anyone making a mistake by not responding correctly, immediately must pay a forfeit, for which some stunt will be required after the game is over.

Frog in the middle.—The players form a circle. One player is the frog and he sits at the center. The other players crowd around the frog, teasing him by various means, but trying to keep from being tagged by him. The frog is not permitted to move from his position in the center of the floor. If he touches a player, that player changes places with him. The children may taunt him, calling "Frog in the middle, can't catch me." In a large group of players, divide into two or more circles with a frog for each circle. Or there may be from two to five frogs. The space in the circle may be a sea, pond, creek, or river. The players who are not frogs may be grasshoppers or animals of various sorts, sometimes the players shout: "Frog in the sea, can't catch me."

Feeding the elephant.—Use a megaphone, or cardboard funnel. Put it in a bucket or wastebasket. The children are each given ten peanuts. These they try to toss into the elephant's mouth (the

funnel). If two large elephant ears, cut out of paper, can be pinned to a chair back of the funnel, it will add to the effectiveness of the game.

Snatch the bean bag.—The players are lined up in two equal lines with about twenty feet between the two lines. At the center of the space a bean bag is placed on a stump, on a stool, or on the ground.

At the signal to go the four end players (two from each side) run to center. If a player gets back to his line with it without being tagged, he scores two points. If he is tagged the other side scores one point. Players may feint at snatching the bean bag, but if a player touches it at any time, he is liable to be tagged. When a player finally snatches the bag, he runs for his line. Anywhere in the line is safe. His teammate may try to prevent the opponents from tagging him by keeping in their way, warding them off. However, he must not trip an opponent, nor shove him hard. No blocking, such as in football is allowed. The four players take their places at the middle of their respective lines, leaving four new end players.

Variation— (1) Play the game with a football. The four players rush out from their sides and try to fall on the ball so as to gain possession of it. One point is scored.

(2) Feint and snatch as with the bean bag. This time football blocking is permissible. A player must be tackled and brought down to complete his capture.

Hurricane.—A ping-pong ball and a fan for each player are necessary. The room is cleared of chairs and other obstacles. It would be better if the floor is uncarpeted. Outside lines and goal lines are determined by the size of the group.

The ping-pong ball is placed at the center of the playing space. At the signal to start the players try to blow the ball toward the goal line of their opponents. This must be done by the breeze of the fan. In no case must a player hit the ball with his fan, nor may he touch it with his hand. Each goal counts one. The first team to score five points wins.

Jackstraws.—This old game requires steadiness of nerves. Jackstraws may be made of matches, or tiny sticks or twigs, anywhere from two to six inches long. It would probably be better for all sticks to be of uniform length. A match with a bent pin hook in the end of it will do for a lifter. A player holds a handful of jackstraws in his closed fist. He drops them from a distance of ten inches to the table. Then the first player takes the lifter and tries to lift one of the "straws" without disturbing any of the others. He continues to play until he fails. Then another player takes his turn. The one with the most sticks wins.

Grass snap.—Each child gets himself a blade of grass. He holds both ends of this blade, making a loop. Another child loops his blade of grass through this one, and they both pull. The child, whose blade breaks, hands the winner the two pieces. As long as a child wins he continues to take on the others, in turn. When his blade breaks, he hands over the two pieces of grass and drops out. At the close players count broken pieces. The child with the most wins. Players get other blades of grass and continue the game, as long as desired. This game comes from Japan.

Red rover.—This is similar to "Pom Pom Pullaway." Players stand at one side of the playground. One player who is "It" selects a player to come over instead of having the whole crowd come at once. Say he selects Jim. Then he calls:

"Red Rover! Red Rover!
Let Jim come over!"

Jim must leave and try to get past the Red Rover to the opposite side goal. If he is caught he helps catch the others.

Black Tom.—Two parallel lines thirty feet or so apart. Players, except one, stand behind one of these lines, just as in "Pom Pom Pullaway." The middle player, who is "It" calls "Black Tom! Black Tom! Black Tom!" At this all the players must dash across the opposite goal. Any player caught must help "Black Tom."

The player who is "It" may fool the runners by calling "Green Tom!" or "Blue Tom!" or "Brown Tom!" Any player who starts to run at this bit of trickery is considered captured, as is also any who start to run or leave the base before "It" calls "Black Tom!" three times. Still another way to trick the runners is to have someone besides the player who is "It" call "Black Tom!" Players only run at the call of "Black Tom" himself. The first player caught is "It" for the next game.

Ham! Ham!—This game is played exactly as "Black Tom," except that "It" calls "Ham! Ham! Chicken, Ham and Bacon!" No player must start until the word "bacon" is called.

Blowing out the candle.—The candle is placed on a table. The players are blindfolded one at a time and turned around three times. They must then try to blow out the candle. The chances are that many of them will blow in any direction but in the direction of the candle.

Sniping.—Two blankets or sheets are required for this game. The players are divided into two equal sides. Each side selects a player to hide. Two teammates are selected to hold the blanket in front of the player chosen so as to hide him from the player chosen by the other side. Each player tries to find out who is behind the other blanket without being discovered himself. They may push one another and chase each other, but they are not allowed to touch the other with the hands. The one who first guesses who the other player is scores a point for his side. Two other players are then chosen.

White elephants.—Each child is asked to bring some plaything of which he has tired. These may be wrapped as the child sees fit. It is lots of fun to see someone get a large package and then see the look of surprise as at the end of the unwrapping he finds a very small article. As the children arrive, they leave their packages in a huge box or basket. When ready the hostess or teacher has the children stand in a circle. Each child is given a package. Then, as the music plays, they pass the packages to the right. When the music stops, each child holds onto the package he has. Thereafter, the Swapping Market is open and players try to trade packages. This swapping may continue until the leader blows a whistle, when each child must keep whatever it has. Then, and not until then, the packages are opened. Again the Swapping Market may be opened and children may swap to their heart's content.

Dwarf hide-and-go-seek.—In their imaginations the players may make themselves as small as they desire—a half-inch tall, three inches, six inches. They then hide in or behind anything in the room—a vase, a thimble, a hat, a book, a picture, etc. One youngster hid up his daddy's sleeve. The one who is "It" tries to discover where the "dwarf" is hidden. If the hunter is having trouble the one who has hidden may give him some cues, such as "I am hidden on that side of the room." This is a grand game for a parent and an imaginative child. If you have recently been reading *Gulliver's Travels* you could imagine you are Lilliputians when you are hiding and that you are Gulliver when you are hunting.

Pig.—Players are seated about a table, six or eight players to a game. Rook cards are dealt face down. An extra set of like cards lies face down on the table. Players begin trying to match what they have, from the extra deck, working as fast as they can and taking no turns. All players work at once. If a player gets a card he does not need he puts it face down on the table immediately. No player tips off what progress he is making in matching. When a player completes his set he quietly lays the cards down and puts his hands under the table. This is the signal for all players to do the same thing—that is, cards down, hands under the table, and complete silence. Most of the players will likely be so intent on finishing out their sets that they will not notice what is happening. The last to follow suit is the "Pig." Pigs may be required to pay forfeits which must be redeemed.

The wild hunter.—Players, except one, are seated in chairs. These chairs may be arranged in a line as for "Going to Jerusalem," or they may be in a circle facing center, or they may be in a circle facing out from center. If facing center, the extra player is inside the circle and leads the group around inside. This extra player is the "Hunter." All of the players have taken the name of some part of a huntsman's equipment—gun, jacket, knapsack, cap, boots, dog, shirt, compass, shells, rabbit, bird, etc. As the "Hunter" starts around the chairs he calls for various parts of his equipment. If he calls "Gun!" the child with that name gets up and follows him, taking hold of his hand. The next child takes hold of the "gun's" hand, and so on. After all players are up and moving around, the "Hunter" suddenly shouts "Bang!" This is the signal for all players to scramble for a chair. The player left out becomes the new "Wild Hunter."

It may add to the fun if the hunter carried with him a blown-up paper sack. Instead of saying "Bang!" he would pop the sack as the signal to be seated.

In a large crowd there may be several sets playing simultaneously. Or the same designation could be given to several players.

Whisk broom catch.—Players are seated in a circle. One player in the circle has a whisk broom. Outside the circle stands one player while at center stands another. The players in the ring toss or pass the broom around the ring while the center player tries to intercept it. When he does he tries to toss it to his confederate outside the ring. The ring players try to prevent but they must not leave their seats. When the two players succeed in intercepting and passing the broom outside the circle the last player in the circle to have it must take the place of the outside player. That player moves to center and the center player takes his seat in the ring of players.

Variation—Use a sponge instead of a whisk broom.

Feather volleyball.—Two downy feathers and a piece of string are necessary. The string is stretched across the room or across the doorway. The crowd is divided into two sides. Each side is given possession of a feather. At the signal to start each side tries to blow its feather over the string into its opponent's territory. Play is fast and furious with two feathers in the air and each side trying to prevent a feather from dropping in its territory. No player must touch the feather with any part of his person, else it is counted down. When a feather falls to the floor or touches a person or object, it is down and a point is scored by the opposition. A player must stay on his own side of the net. Bounds may be determined, but it would perhaps be better to consider everything within the field. Players may relay the feather from one to the other as often as they desire, even on the serve. The idea is to keep it up in the air. Therefore, there is no three and over as in regulation volleyball.

Fruit basket.—Each player gets the name of some fruit. They are seated in a circle with one player at center who is "It." This player calls the names of any two or three fruits. Players with those names must get up and find another seat. In the scramble "It" finds a seat. The person left out takes his place. Players who are "It" must call names loudly so everyone can hear. Suggested fruits: apples, pears, peaches, plums, bananas, pineapples, raspberries, strawberries, prunes, currants, grapes, oranges, lemons, kumquats.

Variations—Number all players off by fours. Announce that all Ones are raspberries, all Twos are lemons, all Three are peaches, and all Fours are prunes. This will add to the interest in a group where there are twenty-five or more players.

Fruit basket call.—This is very similar to "Fruit Basket," except that as a player's name is called, he must stand and shout the name of his fruit three times before the center player can count to ten. In this game the player who is "It" calls only one name at a time.

Variation—Allow "It" to call as many as two fruits at one time. In this case both players called must stand and shout their fruits three times before the center player counts to ten.

Toe ball.—Players stand in a wide circle. Each player has on the floor or space in front of him a small circle about eight or ten inches in diameter. This circle may be made of a cut-out piece of newspaper, wrapping paper, or cardboard. Two rubber balls of tennis ball size or as large as a volleyball, are provided. The balls are

put in place at the center of the ring. After that they are kept
moving. The players push, not kick, the ball with the toe, trying
to keep it away from the circlets they are protecting, and at the same
time trying to send it across the circlet of some other player. As the
balls are constantly in motion, the players must keep watch in all
directions. As a ball approaches the circlet, the player protecting it
toes it away. Each player starts the game with ten points. When a
ball crosses his circlet he loses a point. When he loses ten points he
is out of the game. The game continues until most of the players
are eliminated. The player with the most points intact is winner.

Partner pussy wants a corner.—The players are divided into
couples. Each couple holds with one hand to a handkerchief, the
boy holding one end and the girl the other. A short piece of string
or a switch will do. They must not let go for any reason. From
there on out the game is played exactly as the regulation game of
"Pussy Wants a Corner."

Variations—(1) Play as singles and force players to hop instead
of run. (2) Play on roller skates.

Bounce the ball (Yemari).—This Japanese game is a good one for
fun and exercise. The word "Yemari" means "handball," but the
game is very different from our handball. The ball is usually about
two inches in diameter. The players stand in a circle. One player
tosses the ball to the floor so that it will bounce straight up to him.
As it rebounds he strikes it back with his open hand. He continues
this as long as the ball is within reach. However, he may not move
from his place in the circle. When the ball moves near another
player, then that player must strike it and continue to do so as did
the first player. So the game continues until some player fails to
hit it on the rebound. If a player misses he drops out and the circle
draws in closer. This continues until only one player is left. A
larger rubber ball may be used, if desired.

Variation—Each player bounces the ball until he misses, being allowed to move to any position to keep up with it. Count the number of times the ball is hit on the rebound. The player with the
highest score wins.

Bookkeeper.—The leader stands in the center of the circle. Each
player holds out his hands, palms upward, and upon them a book is
placed. The leader goes around the circle catching up the books in
turn and trying to strike the hands with it before they can be withdrawn. The players try to withdraw the hands before they are

struck. The leader continues until he strikes someone's hands. When he does, that person must take his place. The leader may feint at taking the book off a player's hands. In this case, if the player withdraws his hands and the book topples off, it counts as a successful blow by the leader, and the guilty player is "It."

Statue race.—Players form in a line facing a goal—a fence, a line, a walk, a post, a tree. A leader stands between the line of players and the goal, facing the goal. This leader counts aloud to ten, keeping his eyes covered or looking straight ahead. When the leader calls "ten," he uncovers his eyes and turns around. Immediately everyone must be perfectly still, holding whatever position they have at the time "ten" is called. If the leader discovers anyone moving that player must go back to the starting position and begin over. Players will often be caught in interesting and ludicrous poses. These they must hold until the leader again faces the goal and starts counting.

The player that first reaches the goal line wins the race. The leader is not entered into the race and no player must get ahead of him. The winner becomes the new leader for a continuation of the game.

Aviator's test.—How many have ridden in an airplane? How many of you would like to ride in one? How many of you would like to drive one? All right, if you can pass the following tests in co-ordination you have made the first step in becoming a full-fledged aviator.

1. Place knuckles of both hands together with right palm on top. By rotating the hands turn left palm to the top, still keeping knuckles together. "Remember that both ends of your automobile stop when you shut off the gas and apply your brakes; both hands will turn around."

2. Close left fist and extend tips of right fingers on the little finger side, both palms up. Now reverse the process and extend the fingers of the left hand to the little finger side of the closed right fist, palms up. Repeat several times, increasing the speed with each change.

3. Place tips of fingers of both hands together; close fingers of right hand into cluster and place in palm of left hand; tips together again. Then close fingers of left hand together and place in palm of right hand. Repeat this several times, increasing in speed with each repetition. Remember to place finger tips together after each change of palm.

4. How many are right-handed? All right, how many can always find what you look for? How many know where your nose is? Not sure. Well, try this: Place your right hand on your nose, and your left hand on your right ear, crossing your arms in front. On the command of "Change!" release your hands and quickly clap them together in front of your face. Then immediately grasp your left ear with your right hand and your nose with your left. "Ready! Go! Change!" There, I see one person with both hands on his nose, and another with a hand on each ear. Now let us do it five times in succession. (Suppose we give you more time between changes. This time clap your hands, revolve them around one another, and then change.)

5. Have your group stand with arms hanging loose at the side, and not leaning on anything or anyone. Close both eyes, raise on tiptoes and stand still; now raise the right foot from the floor and stand still. Not so easy as you might believe.

6. With the group still standing, try this one. Make a clockwise circle with the right foot on the floor. At the same time describe the figure "6" in the air with the right hand.

7. Face each other in couples—one person with hands held in front, palms up. The other person rests his hands, palms down, on the palms of the first player. The first player, by jerking his hands out, tries to slap the backs of the hands of the second player. If he succeeds he scores one point, and he tries again. If he misses, the second player tries the same thing. The game continues until one player scores three points.

8. The leader secures some object, such as a penknife or a ball. He tosses it into the air. The players are told to shout as long as the object is in the air. But the instant it is caught they are to stop. After three or four times the leader can make as though he is going to throw the object into the air and then not do so. Some will be sure to yell and this will always bring a good laugh.

9. Solo flight. Now we are ready for our first solo flight. Place tips of forefingers and tips of thumbs together so as to form a diamond. Raise the right thumb to the tips of the right and left forefingers. Then extend right forefinger upward. Raise left thumb to tips of left forefinger and right thumb. Extend left forefinger to tip of right forefinger, thus forming a second diamond. Proceed on upward in this fashion until your arms are extended in the air as far as you can reach. By reversing this procedure you can come back to normal position.

Note—Start all of these movements slowly, gaining speed as you progress.

—R. BRUCE TOM

Flies and spiders.—The spiders stand with their backs to the flies. The flies move slowly and quietly toward them. When the leader thinks they are near enough he shouts, "Look out! The spiders are coming!" The spiders turn immediately and chase the flies back to the starting line. Those flies who are caught become spiders. The game is continued with the flies doing the chasing.

The sides may be named Dogs and Cats, or Hounds and Rabbits, or Brownies and Fairies.

Chase the rabbit.—The players stand or sit in a circle. A rag, a ball, or a handkerchief (representing the rabbit) is started around the circle, players passing it from hand to hand as rapidly as they can until it gets back home. After they have practiced a bit with the rabbit, announce that the next time a hound will chase the rabbit. Start the rabbit and then start another rag (the hound) after it. Players pass the hound as fast as they can, trying to overtake the rabbit. At the same time they try to keep the rabbit from getting caught.

Jump the creek.—Players line up single file. Two lines are drawn to represent the banks of the creek. The players run, one at a time, and try to jump the creek. If a player misses he must drop out to get his feet dry. Each round the creek is made a little wider. Thus it may be determined who is the best creek jumper. There may be several creeks and files, graded according to size or ability.

Tiger.—The players hold hands in a circle. In the center is an Indian club, or bottle, or a sharp-pointed stick driven just far enough in the ground to make it stand erect. The players pull and push until one player knocks down the club. That player immediately becomes the tiger. He chases the others. Players may run only in a specified play area. When caught a player becomes a tiger and helps to tag others. This continues until all players are caught. The circle may be formed again and the game continued as long as desired.

Railroad.—Similar to "Stage Coach." Players are given the names of the equipment and personnel of the railroad—the stationmaster, engineer, fireman, brakeman, conductor, porter, engine, coach, Pullman, whistle, etc. The leader tells a story that takes these in, and the various players get up and perform. The engine "choo-choos";

the coach goes "rattle, rattle"; the Pullman sleeps and snores; the stationmaster calls stations; the conductor calls "All aboard!" the engineer pulls the throttle and says "Toot! Toot!" the fireman shovels coal, etc.

Hunt the key.—A key is hung on a long piece of twine. The players form a circle, holding the twine and keeping the hands constantly in motion. One player stands inside the circle and tries to discover where the key is. When a player is caught with the key in his possession, he becomes "It." This is similar to "Ring on a string."

Fire.—The person in the center of a ring of players points his finger at one of the players. As he does, he shouts either "Earth!" or "Air!" or "Water!" or "Fire!" and counts to ten.

The person to whom he points must answer appropriately before "It" can count to ten. If "Earth" was called, then he must name some quadruped (horse, cow, dog, mule, etc.). If "Water," it must be some denizen of the deep (whale, shark, perch, turtle, etc.). If "Air" is called, it must be some bird or flying insect.

If "Fire" is called, the player must remain silent.

Variation—A ball or knotted handkerchief may be thrown to the player who is called on to respond.

Quack! Quack!—This is a variation of "Blind Man's Buff" that may afford lots of fun. The players form a circle with a blindfolded player at center. They march around him until he taps a cane or stick on the floor. Then they stop. The blind man points his cane, the player to whom he points must say, "Quack! Quack!" The blind man tries to guess who the quacker is. If he guesses correctly they exchange places. If not, the blind man tries again. The quacker may be required to imitate "Donald Duck."

Hare and turtle.—Even sides. Players line up in two lines, facing one another and alternating players from the two sides. Two bean bags of different colors are provided, one to the head player on each team. The red bean bag may represent the hare, while the blue one represents the turtle. At the signal to start the leader on each side tosses the bean bag diagonally across to his first teammate on the opposite side. The bean bag zigzags back and forth across the intervening space between the lines until it has gone down the line and is back in possession of the leader. The first one to get back is the winner.

Crow.—Two equal sides. They line up in two single files back of the starting line. The first player in line on each side is the farmer. The second is the crow. The third is a farmer. The fourth is a crow. And so on it goes. Each team is provided with five or more bean bags. The farmer places the bean bags in a straight line about two feet apart, the last bean bag resting on a line or marker previously determined. He rushes back and touches off the next player in his line. This player is a crow and he must hop over the bean bags until he has hopped over the last one. He now may hop back on the other foot, picking up the bean bags as he comes. He hands them to the next player in line and that player, a farmer, plants the seed again. The next crow comes along and picks them up. And so it goes until each player in line has finished the course. The team finishing first wins. This game is very similar to "Chinese Hop."

Beetle goes around.—The players form a circle, facing center. They hold their hands back of them. One player walks around outside the ring carrying a knotted towel in his hand. After walking or running a short distance, saying, "Beetle is out! Don't look about!" he puts the "beetle" (towel) in the hands of some player, shouting "Beetle move!" He then takes that player's place. The one receiving the "beetle" strikes the player to his right. This player, trying to avoid the "beetle," runs around the outside of the circle and back to his place. If the player to the right is caught, he becomes the new "beetle." The game continues until all players have had a chance to have the "beetle."

Enforce a ruling that there shall be no hitting above the shoulders. Under no circumstances allow a belt to be used for the "beetle." The danger of injury is too great. A sock or stocking stuffed with soft rags would make a good "beetle."

Hawk and hen.—A file of ten or twelve players (the hens) stand behind each other, hands on the shoulders of the player in front. The first player raises his arms shoulder high to protect those behind him. A player known as the "hawk" tries to catch one of the hens. It cannot be the first or second hen. The first hen tries to keep facing the hawk through all of his movements, in order that other hens can be kept out of the hawk's reach. This means that all the other hens must keep moving so as to keep in line with the leader. When a hen is caught he is out of the game. Both the hawk and the first hen take their places at the end of the line and the next players in line become the new hawk and first hen.

Hunter, fox, and gun.—This game is kin to "Jam-kem-po." Two lines of players stand facing one another. The players in each line consult to determine whether they will be the "hunter," the "gun," or the "fox." To save the necessity of consultation each time they may decide on what they will be for three successive times. They should be sure that everyone in the line thoroughly understands. At the same time they are careful to keep the secret from the other side. The leader counts "One, two, three!" On three each side begins to perform. For instance, if one side has decided on "hunter," each player in that line poses with one foot forward, shading eyes with right hand. At the same time he says, "Aha," three times. The "gun" stands in position as if aiming with a rifle, and shouts "Bang!" The "fox" puts thumbs in his ears and wiggles his fingers. He barks with a sharp "Yip, yip, yip!"

Scoring is done on the following basis: The "fox" beats the "hunter," the "hunter" beats the "gun," and the "gun" beats the "fox."

Muffin pan polo.—*Equipment*—A muffin pan and six one-inch wooden cubes.

The game—Players stand at a distance from five to ten feet, depending on the skill of the group. The pan is placed on a chair or table. Each player tosses all six cubes, trying to land them in the muffin pan compartments. For each cube that remains in the pan, ten points are allowed. More than one cube may rest in a single cup. It might add to the interest of the game to number the sides of the cube—0, 5, 10, 15, 20, 25. In this case when a cube rests in a cup, the score for the particular cube is indicated by the top side. The total score for the throw would be the sum of the sides facing up within the cups of the pan.

Peg placing.—Each boy secures a peg about eight inches long. A line is drawn on the ground, or some marker is arranged. From this line each player, in turn, gives one hop. Then without touching the other foot to the ground, he leans forward and sticks the peg into the ground just as far as he can reach. He must then stand erect without moving the ground foot from its position. The peg must stand up in order to count. The player placing his peg at the farthest point wins.

Back to back push.—Two players stand back to back with elbows locked. Goal lines are marked approximately six feet in front of each contestant. At the signal to start each player tries to push the other over the goal line he (the opponent) is facing. Contestants are not allowed to lift and carry. Pushing only is permitted. The one pushed over his own goal line loses the bout.

Back to back pull.—The idea is the same as in "Back to Back Push" except that this time the contestant tries to drag his opponent in his direction and over the goal line he faces.

Wibblety-wobblety.—Each player stands in a circle with the toe of his right foot against a soft ball on the ground. The leader starts the game by calling, "Wibblety-wobblety—Joe! Pop!" The player named Joe gets possession of the ball. All of the other players scatter in different directions. As soon as the player whose name was called gets the ball he calls, "Stop!" The players all stop wherever they happen to be. Joe, or whoever is "It," then tries to hit some player with the ball, throwing from home base. A player may move his body to avoid the ball, provided he does not move his feet. When "It" succeeds in hitting some player they all return to home base. The game starts again with the player who was "It" acting as the caller this time. If he misses he is charged with one "punk." Three "punks" put a player out, and he has to crawl through the "greasy barrel." The other players stand single file with feet spread far apart. The loser must crawl through their straddled legs while they paddle him with their hands.

It would be well to limit the playing area.

Affinity tag.—This tag game may be adapted for use in several different ways, depending upon the way the group is dressed, the available playing space, and the ages of the players.

For lawn or gymnasium floor: In order to be safe each player must find a "soul (sole) mate." To do this, players must sit facing each other on the ground with soles of shoes touching. If in a room they may sit in chairs with soles of shoes touching.

Variations—(1) Players must sit on chairs with backs to one another. (2) Stand back to back. (3) Stand face to face and hold hands.

If players are inclined to stay too long with the same "sole mate" the leader can break up the group by a signal, such as calling, "New sole mates!" or by the blast of the whistle. In the scramble "It" may tag any player not with a mate.

Bung the bucket.—*Equipment*—An old tin can or bucket. A circle from ten to twenty feet in diameter. The can or bucket is placed within the circle.

This game is a combination of "Hide-and-go-seek," "Prisoner's Base," and "Tag." By a counting-out process one player is chosen to be "It." The other players hide while "It" is not looking. As each player is caught he is put in prison with the tin can. While "It" is out hunting, any player who is still hiding may run in and "bung the bucket," that is, kick the bucket or can outside the ring. This releases all prisoners and they may hide again. "It" must return the bucket to prison before he may look for the hiders. If a player who is trying to bung the bucket is tagged by "It" before succeeding in getting the bucket outside the circle, he is captured and must stay in prison. The game continues until all players are in prison. "It" may tag any player who is outside the circle, thus making prisoners of them. The game may be repeated as often as desired with a new person being selected as "It" each time.

Tip cat.—*Equipment*—A piece of broom handle about six inches long, tapered to a point on each end like a "dainty." A paddle or bat about two feet long, including the handle, and about six inches wide in the paddle part. Shingles or three-ply wood make satisfactory paddles.

The game—The players select two captains to choose sides. After sides are chosen another choice may be decided to determine which side will get to bat first. Players on each side number off for their turns at the bat.

The only base required is a home base. This is a circle on the ground about six feet in diameter. The fielders scatter about over the playing field. Batter Number One steps into the ring and bats the "cat," as the pointed stick is called, out into the field.

Players in the field may attempt to catch the "cat." If a player succeeds in catching it, the batter is out and Number Two comes up to bat.

If the "cat" is not caught a fielder throws it toward home base. If he succeeds in throwing it so that it lands within the limits of the circle, the batter is out. If not, the batter has the privilege of tipping the "cat" by striking it on one of the pointed ends so that it will fly into the air. While it is in the air he strikes it with his paddle, knocking it as far as he can. He repeats this two more times.

Scores are made by taking the number of paces or lengths of the paddle from the position of the "cat" to the center of home base.

The batter usually guesses at this. If any of his opponents doubt his guess, the distance is measured. If the actual paddle lengths are more than the guessed distance the batter is safe, and his score counts as he guessed it. If the actual paddle lengths are less than the guessed number the batter is out and he gets no score whatever. After three outs, the other side comes to bat. Nine innings may be played. See the game of "Dainty."

Chuckwallah.—This game is similar to "Tip Cat." *Equipment*—Two paddles eighteen inches long and eight inches wide. Round the corners on one end and shave the other end down to a handle about six inches long. Smooth the edges so that the handle will fit the hand.

Take a piece of wood one inch square and six inches long. Sharpen both ends, leaving about one inch of square space at the middle. On the square sides mark the figures from one to four.

The game—Two or more players play the game. Each player has a paddle. Players stand in circles six feet in diameter. These circles must be at least four feet apart. One of the players serves the chuck by hitting one of the pointed ends and batting it with the flat side of the paddle while it is in the air. He tries to knock it into the circle of an opponent. If it lands in the circle of any one of the other players, the server scores the number of points marked on the top side of the chuck. If it lands outside a circle, it counts one against the server. Players take turn about serving. No player may hinder a batted chuck from getting into a circle.

Hunting for diamonds.—This is a form of paper chase without the objectionable feature of littering the woods with paper.

Preparation—A day or two before the hunt select two players to act as trail layers with the understanding that they will furnish the trail markers consisting of "pathfinders" and "diamonds." Instruct the trail layers to prepare a large bag of paper torn into three-fourth-inch squares. Mark with colored pencil or crayon numbers from two to ten on about half of the squares. The plain squares are called "pathfinders." The marked ones are "diamonds."

The game—The trail layers precede the hunters by three minutes or more. They lay a very clearly defined trail, using a liberal supply of paper. The hunters follow, picking up the "pathfinders" and "diamonds." When the trail is lost the players scatter. The one who finds it is on his honor to yell, "Trail! Trail!" before he picks up a single marker. When the trail layers exhaust their paper they indicate the fact by placing their bags in the center of the trail. Then they hide separately somewhere within one hundred paces of the spot at which the bags were dropped. Upon discovering the bags the hunters scatter and hunt for the trail layers. Points are counted, as follows: Twenty points for discovering a trail layer; one point for each "pathfinder"; the sum of the numbers on whatever "diamonds" have been found.

Pipety-pop.—Players stand or sit in a circle. The player who is "It" takes his place inside the circle. He points his finger at some player and says either "Pipety-pop" or "Popety-pip." If the word "Pipety-pop" is used the player at whom he is pointing must respond by saying "Pip!" before the word "Pipety-pop" is completed by "It." If "Popety-pip" is hurled at the player he must shout "Pop!" before "It" can complete "Popety-pip." Thus it can be seen that the first syllable of the word must be given by the player addressed. If "It" succeeds in saying his word before a player responds correctly they exchange places.

For variety the player who is answering may be required to say the last syllable of the word instead of the first. In other words, if "It" says "Popety-pip" then the player must shout "Pip" before "It" can do so.

Ten fine birds.—The group sits in a circle. One player starts the game by saying, (1) "A good fat hen." This is repeated by each player in turn. When all players have said "A good fat hen," the starter begins again. This time he says, (2) "Two ducks and a good fat hen." This is repeated by each in turn again. As others are added the reciting becomes a bit more difficult. Players always begin with the last bird mentioned and repeat them in order back to "a good fat hen." (3) Three squawking wild geese. (4) Four plump partridges. (5) Five pouting pigeons. (6) Six long-legged cranes. (7) Seven green parrots. (8) Eight screeching owls. (9) Nine ugly turkey buzzards. (10) Ten bald eagles.

On the last round, therefore, each player would be saying, "Ten bald eagles, nine ugly buzzards, eight screeching owls, seven green parrots, six long-legged cranes, five pouting pigeons, four plump partridges, three squawking wild geese, two ducks, and a good fat hen."

All of this must go around the circle every time, being repeated separately by each person. If a player leaves out anything or makes a mistake he must pay a forfeit.

Cricket.—The players seat themselves in a circle on the grass, on the floor, or on chairs. Provide one player with a metal cricket, such as is used by drillmasters. One of the players is chosen as a "Frog." He stands inside the circle. The cricket is passed around the circle, the players trying to hide its location from the "Frog." The holder of the cricket watches an opportunity to snap it when the "Frog" is not looking. He then hastily passes it on to another player. If the "Frog" finds the cricket, then the player who has it in his possession becomes the "Frog."

Crambo.—One player begins the game by saying, for instance, "I am thinking of something in the room that rhymes with "fair." The others ask, "Is it chair?" "Is it hair?" "Is it pear?" and so on until they guess it. The one who guesses correctly starts another. The game may be varied by enlarging the boundaries so that one is not confined to the room for his thought. Or the limits may be determined by some classification, such as nature lore, geography, etc.

"More sacks!"—Two even sides are chosen. The players of one side bend over, hands on knees or grasping ankles, leapfrog fashion. Each player has his head between the legs of the teammate in front of him. The front player of the side that is down braces himself against a tree, post, or wall. The players of the other side line up single file. The first man runs and leaps through the air, landing astraddle the opposing team and as far up toward the front player as possible. As he does so he yells "More sacks!" The next player in line then leaps in the same manner. And so it goes until the benders break or fall under the impact. The score is one point for each opponent carried without breaking. The sides take turns at bending over for the other side to jump.

Boot the pin.—*Equipment*—Volleyball or rubber play ball. Two Indian clubs, tenpins, milk or pop bottles.

The game—Divide players into two even sides. Each group forms a circle with approximately eight feet between each player in the group. A tenpin, bottle, or can is placed at the center of each circle. The players attempt to kick the ball so as to knock down the pin. All kicking must be done from the circle. Each group tries to knock over its pin first. The team that succeeds scores one point. Ten points constitute a game.

Hop, step, and jump.—Players do a hop, a step, and a jump from a given starting line to see who can set the farthest mark. It may be a standing or a running hop, step, and jump. In the latter case the player takes a short running start to the line before taking off on his hop. The step follows in the same momentum from where the hop ends, and the jump in the same manner from the step.

Going to market.—This is a good game for the motor trip. One player starts it by saying, "I am going to market and I am going to buy (at this point he mentions some article beginning with the letter '*a*') some apricots." The next player then says, "I am going to market and I am going to buy (using the next letter of the alphabet) some bananas." The third player, perhaps, mentions "a carpet," the fourth "a doorstop," the fifth, "an egg," and so on. Each letter of the alphabet must be used in turn. The persons who fail to comply with requirements may be required to pay forfeits, such as to make three uncomplimentary remarks about themselves, or answer truthfully any questions put to them, or make some extravagant statements about their own abilities or the abilities of certain members of the group, or spell some short words backwards.

License tags.—Another auto trip game would be that of making words out of license tags. Usually the tags have certain designating letters, at the beginning, such as, 1 D, 1 B, 3 J, etc. Each player puts down these letters from ten or more tags and then tries to make words out of them. Players use pencil and pad. A time limit is determined before starting.

Here 'tis.—On the motor trip this one helps to entertain the little ones, and the big ones too, for that matter! The idea is to pick out something a short distance ahead, such as a red barn, a church, a house, a silo, etc. The player calls the object and then shuts his eyes. When he thinks the car is just passing in front of the object, he opens his eyes and says, "Here 'tis!" The persons in the car take turns.

Signboard.—Pick out one outstanding word from each of ten or more billboards and road signs along the way. Then make up a story containing these ten words. Or compose a telegram with the ten words.

Fishing.—Here are thirty well-known fish. How many can you catch? Try to identify them from the clues offered. Ready! Here goes!

(1) A struggling fish. (2) A fraudulent or cheating fish. (3) A

fish of precious metal.   (4) Man's best friend.   (5) A royal fish. (6) A heavenly fish.   (7) A fish in the band.   (8) An animal almost extinct.   (9) An ugly old witch.   (10) A household pet.   (11) A fish in a bird cage.   (12) Good with hot biscuits.   (13) A sharp point in the center of a shield.   (14) A member of the barber shop quartet.   (15) A deep gutteral sound.   (16) Some boats have them. (17) Useful in summer.   (18) Used by a fencer.   (19) Seen at night.   (20) Anemic.   (21) Good with bread and butter.   (22) An evil fish.   (23) Colorless.   (24) Floats through the air.   (25) A favorite with dairymen.   (26) A rosy biter.   (27) A popular alphabet code for stores that deliver purchases.   (28) A process for refining metal.   (29) A gloomy fish.   (30) Warms the earth.

Answers— (1) Flounder.   (2) Shark.   (3) Goldfish.   (4) Dogfish. (5) Kingfish.   (6) Angelfish.   (7) Drumfish.   (8) Buffalo.   (9) Hagfish.   (10) Catfish.   (11) Perch.   (12) Butterfish.   (13) Pike. (14) Bass.   (15) Grunt.   (16) Sailfish.   (17) Fantail.   (18) Swordfish.   (19) Starfish.   (20) Weakfish.   (21) Jellyfish.   (22) Devilfish.   (23) Whitefish.   (24) Balloon fish.   (25) Cowfish. (26) Red Snapper.   (27) Cod.   (28) Smelt.   (29) Bluefish.   (30) Sunfish.

Circus.—When sides are chosen, the two leaders seat themselves facing each other about four feet apart, the members of each side sitting as near their respective leaders as possible.

One leader begins by mentioning the name of an animal commencing with the letter *A*, and then counts ten (not too fast). Before he has finished the other leader must mention another animal beginning with the same letter, and so on until neither can think of any more animals whose names commence with *A*, then they take all begining with *B*, then with *C*, etc.

The sole duty of the other players is to think of new names and suggest them to their respective leaders; also to suggest the names to their leader while the opposite leader is counting.

If either side fails to give a name before the ten count has expired, the opposing side has a choice from among their number.

The wee bologna man.—A leader stands before the group and repeats:

> "I'm the Wee Bologna Man.
> Always do the best you can
> To follow the Wee Bologna Man."

The players then all imitate the leader. That individual goes through the motions of playing some instrument in a band—a fife, a drum, a trumpet, a cornet, a piccolo, a trombone, a piano, a violin, a bass drum, cymbals, or he imitates an orchestra or band leader, or a drum major.

A good leader will put the group through at a brisk pace. The leader repeats the rhyme each time he changes to another movement.

Variation—Players may stand in several lines, single file. Or the game may be played in the schoolroom. In this case the head person in the first line would be the leader for some one motion. When he finishes, he goes to the rear of his line. Then the head player in line two becomes leader. Gymnastic movements may be introduced, such as hopping on one foot in place, running in place, doing arm exercises, bending and touching the floor, whirling the arms windmill fashion, etc. As soon as a player finishes each time, he runs to the rear of his line and another leader takes his place immediately. This may continue until each child has had a chance to be leader. The action should be fast, with no long delays between the time one leader ends and another begins.

The toy shop.—One child acts as shopkeeper. Another goes out of the room. He represents the customer. All the rest of the children decide what toys they will be, each child representing one toy. When the customer comes in he asks for certain toys with the idea of buying. If he asks for a top, the person who is a "top" spins around. If he asks for a bugle, the "bugle" blows imitating the sound of the instrument. Thus it goes—the doll walks stiffly and says, "Ma-ma!"; the violin plays; the scooter "scoots"; the "skates" "skate"; the football runs signals or kicks; the "doll dishes" pretend to eat; the "bracelet" looks admiringly at the wrist.

Hen and fox.—One player represents the "Hen." Another is the "Fox." All the rest are baby chickens. The "Hen" leads the chicks around and the "Fox" leaps out from unexpected places. The 'Hen" tries to anticipate the "Fox's" presence, and warns the chickens. They immediately fall to the ground. If the "Fox" catches one of them before he gets down, that player drops out. So it continues until all of the chickens are caught. The last one caught becomes the "Fox" for the new game.

Variation—Instead of Hen, Chickens, and Fox, the players may represent Bear, Cubs, and Tiger.

Egg hunt.—Real or candy eggs are hidden about the grounds. The children have paper sacks or tiny baskets and at the signal to start they begin to hunt for the eggs. Certain extra points may be allowed (if points are used at all) for a gold egg or a silver egg. The children should be encouraged to share with others who do not get any eggs or who get only a few.

Variation—Peanuts may be hidden in this same manner. It adds to the fun if the children are divided into groups and given names of animals or fowls. In this case, a child cannot pick up the peanuts. If he is a "Cat" he mews when he discovers a cache of peanuts. His captain or keeper comes a-running and picks up the discovered treasure. The "dogs" bark, the "ducks" quack; and the "sheep" baa-aa-aa.

Follow the leader.—Players form single file behind a leader and imitate everything he does. They hop, they jump, they walk stooped over, they strut, they play a trombone or fife or drum or some other musical instrument, they sweep, they walk around looking like a monkey, they fly like a bird, they skip, they walk backward, they spin, they shake the head, they wave, they clap their hands, they sing, they climb, or jump over obstacles, they do difficult stunts, or they act as if looking at an airplane. In fact, anything the leader does, everyone does. When a player fails to perform the required action he drops to the foot of the line. Play for a few moments. Send the leader to the foot and let the next player in line be leader.

Smuggle the geg.—The "geg" may be a pebble, a marble, a knife, a key, or anything of the sort. The players are divided into two even sides. Which side shall be the "Outs" and which side shall be the "Ins" is decided by the toss of a coin.

A den four by six feet is marked off at the center of the playing space. Boundaries are decided.

The "Outs" get the "geg." They get into a huddle and hide the "geg" or "treasure" on one of their players. Or they stand in line and pass it from hand to hand behind their backs until the one upon whom they have decided has received it. The "Ins" stand by the "den" while the "smugglers" run and hide themselves. Before they are finally hidden, the "smugglers" must shout "Smugglers!" The "Ins" then try to find and tag them. The object of the "Ins" is to find the player who has the "geg." Since they probably do not know which player that is they will have to challenge every player captured. If the custodian of the "geg" can return to the "den" without being caught, the "Outs" win and they remain in possession of the "geg" for the next game.

When an "In" finds and captures an "Out" the latter is not a prisoner until he takes off cap of the captive and places the palm of his own hand on the prisoner's head. At this, the "Out" must cease struggling. Then the "In" demands "Deliver up the 'geg'!" If the player has it he must surrender it at once. This fact is then shouted aloud, and all players return to the "den." If the player caught does not have the "geg," he goes free. When the "geg" is found the two sides change places.

This game originated in Scotland.

Map hunters.—This game can make geography fun. One player selects a river, city, state, or country on the map. "I have selected a city in Russia whose name begins with an *"M."* The other player or players would search the map to find Murmansk or Moscow or whatever city the first player had in mind. "Here it is! It is Moscow!" "No," answers Number One. "Well, then here it is; It is Murmansk!" "Right." Then that player selects some place and the others guess and locate it. And so the game continues.

The hunting could be limited to a state or country, if desired.

Ring the stick.—Each player has a short stick. Players toss embroidery hoops wound with tape at the catcher who tries to catch them on the stick.

Variations—(1) Players toss the hoop from stick to stick. When a player misses he drops out. (2) Use teething rings instead of embroidery hoops. (3) Play by sides as in deck tennis. Players may toss from player to player before sending the hoop over the net.

Pebble chase.—One player, who is the leader, holds a small pebble between the palms of his hands, while the others stand grouped around him, each with his hands extended, palm to palm. The leader puts his hands between the palms of each player, ostensibly to drop therein the pebble which he holds, as in the game called "Button, button." The player who receives the pebble is chased by the others, and may only be saved by returning to the leader and giving the pebble to him. This chase may begin as soon as the players suspect who has the pebble. Each player should therefore watch intently the hands and faces of the others to detect who gets it, and immediately that he suspects one starts to chase him. It is therefore to the interest of the player who gets the pebble to conceal that fact until the attention of the group is distracted from him, when he may slip away and get a good start before he is detected. He may do this whenever he sees fit, but may not delay after the leader has passed the last pair of hands. The leader will help to conceal the fact of who has the pebble by passing his hands between those of the entire group, even though he should have dropped the pebble into the hands of one of the first players.

If the pebble holder gets back to the leader and gives him the pebble before being tagged, he continues with the group. If the pebble holder is caught before he can get back to the leader he must pay forfeit or change places with the leader, whichever method is decided on before the game opens.

In a crowded playground it is well to require that the chasers follow over exactly the same route as the pebble man. Under such conditions the game is more successful if limited to ten players to a group.

Lady of the land.—One of the players takes the part of a lady and stands alone on one side. Another represents a mother, and the balance are children, from two to eight in number. These the mother takes by the hand on either side of her, approaching the lady, repeating the following verse; the children may join with her if they desire:

> Here comes the widow from Sandy Land,
> With all of her children at her hand;
> The one can bake,
> The other can brew,
> The other can make a little white shoe,
> The other can sit by the fire and spin,
> So pray take one of my children in.

The lady then advances and chooses one of the children, saying:

> The fairest one I can see
> Is ———, she's the one for me.

Then Mother:

> I leave my daughter safe and sound,
> And in her pocket a thousand pound,
> Don't let her ramble,
> Don't let her trot,
> Don't let her carry the mustard pot.

The mother then departs with the other children, leaving the daughter chosen with the lady. This daughter stays behind or beside the lady. As the mother departs the lady says under her breath so that the mother may not hear:

> She shall ramble,
> She shall trot,
> She shall carry the mustard pot.

This is repeated until all of the children have been chosen and left with the lady. The mother then retires, but after a time comes back to see her children. The lady tells her she cannot see them. The mother insists and then is taken to where they are sitting. The mother comes to one child and asks how the lady is treating her:

> She cut off my curls and made a curl pie,
> And I have none of it, not I!

The mother asks the next child, who says she cut off her finger, ear, etc., and made a pie, not getting any of it. When all have told the mother what the lady has done to them, they rise up and chase the lady; when she is caught she is led off to prison.

Guess who.—When there are more than twenty players it is desirable to have them separated into several groups. Each group has a leader and lines up side by side, with the leader in the middle. The odd player stands in front of the line facing it, and asks, "Have you seen my friend?" The line answers "No."

PLAYER: Will you help me find him.

LINE: Yes.

PLAYER: Put your finger on your lips and follow me.

The odd player then runs to another part of the room followed by the players in the line, each with his fingers on his lips. When he reaches the place he stands with his back to the line which is arranged in different order by its leader. The leader chooses one of the players who now comes forward and asks, trying to disguise his voice, "Guess who stands behind you." If the odd players guesses correctly he retains his position, turns about to face the line, and the dialogue begins over again. If he fails the one who stood behind him takes his place.

Gipsy.—One player is chosen to be the mother, another is to be the gipsy. All of the other players represent children. The gipsy remains in hiding while the mother talks to her children, pointing to each one as she repeats the following:

I charge you children every one,
To keep good house while I am gone,
You and you, and especially you,
Or else I'll beat you black and blue.

The mother then goes away to blind her eyes. While she is gone the gipsy comes forth and sends the children away, one by one, to hiding places. Then the mother returns, and finding her children all gone searches for them. When they are all returned they chase the gipsy. The one successful in catching her becomes mother for the next game. The former mother becomes the gipsy.

Panjandrum.—A small space is marked off at one end of the ground as a "home" or "goal"; one player is chosen to be "Panjandrum," an important person who needs a bodyguard. Two other players are chosen to be the guard. The game starts with these three players in the "home" ground and the balance of the players at large. The three go forth with the two players who act as bodyguard, clasping each other by the hand, preceding the "Panjandrum." The object of the game is for the players at large to touch the "Panjandrum" without being tagged by the guards. Whenever a guard succeeds in tagging a player the "Panjandrum" and his guards return at once to the "home"; thereupon the player tagged changes places with the "Panjandrum," and the game continues as before.

Buying chickens.—One player is chosen to be market man and another buyer. The rest of the players are chickens. They stoop down in a row, clasping their hands under their knees. The buyer approaches the market man asking, "Have you any chickens for sale?" The market man answers, "Would you like to see and try them?" Whereupon the buyer goes up to different chickens and tries them by laying over the head his clasped hands and pressing downward on them. The buyer pretends to be dissatisfied with some of the chickens, saying, "This one is too fat." "This one is too lean," etc., until at last he finds one that suits him. The chickens bought are supposed to go through this ordeal without smiling.

When a chicken is found to be right the buyer and the market man take him by the arms, one on either side. He remains in his first position with hands clasped under his knees, swinging him forward and backward three times. Should he stand this test without loosening his clasped hands he is supposed to be right and the buyer puts him off to the opposite side of the ground or floor. The game continues until all of the chickens are sold. All that smile have to pay a forfeit.

Circle race.—The players stand in a circle a considerable distance apart and face around in single file in the same direction. At a signal all start to run, following the general outline of the circle, but each trying to pass on the outside the runner next in front of him, tagging as he passes. Any player passed in this way drops out of the race. The last player wins. At a signal from the leader the circle faces about and runs in the opposite direction. As this reverses the relative position of runners who are gaining or losing ground, it is a feature that may be used by a judicious leader to add much merriment and zest to the game.

Flowers and the wind.—This game is suitable for little children. The players are divided into two equal parties, each party having a home marked off at opposite ends of the playground with a long neutral space between. One party represents a flower, deciding among themselves which flower they shall represent, as daisies, lilies, lilacs, etc. They then walk over near the home line of the opposite party. The opposite players (who represent the wind) stand in a row on their line, ready to run. They try to guess what the flower chosen by their opponents may be. As soon as the right flower is named the entire party owning it must turn and run home, the wind chasing them. Any players caught by the wind before reaching home become his prisoners and join him. The remaining flowers repeat their play, taking a different name each time. This continues until all of the flowers have been caught.

Slicing flour.—Fill a medium-sized bowl with flour and press it compactly. Turn it out on a large plate, placed in the center of a table. On top of the mold thus formed lightly lay a small ring.
The object of the game is to slice as much flour from all sides of the mound as possible, without disturbing the ring. Each player has a broad-bladed knife, and each in turn removes a thin slice of flour, until finally only a slender column is left with the ring on top. Whoever causes the ring to fall must pick it up with his teeth.

Shaking Quaker.—The company sits in a circle. One begins the game by patting his hand on his knee and saying to his left-hand neighbor: "Neighbor, neighbor, how art thou?" to which Number Two replies: "Very well, thank thee." Number One then asks: "And how is the neighbor next to thee?" to which Number Two responds: "I don't know, but I'll go see." Number Two then turns to Number Three and asks the same question, and so the questions pass around the whole circle until they come back to Number One, who, after replying, repeats the questions to Number Two, patting both knees with both hands. This form is then gone through with by the whole company. Number One then taps his right foot while both hands are patting knees, then adds left foot. The next time he shakes his head, then stands up, keeping all the motions going at the same time.

This is a very amusing game for small children, making noise enough, and yet not being boisterous.

Hold fast.—All the players stand up, taking hold of the sides of a handkerchief. The leader says: "When I say 'hold fast' let go; when I say 'let go' hold fast." He then says, "Let go" or "hold fast," as he may feel inclined. When he says, "Let go," those who do not hold fast pay forfeits; when he says, "Hold fast," all who do not immediately let go are punished in like manner.

Rat hunt.—All the players seat themselves in a circle, one of them being supplied with a stick, toy, or other implement with which to make a scratching noise on the floor. The player who acts as "cat," stands in the center. The holder of the toy watches an opportunity to scratch on the floor with the toy, when the "cat" is not looking in his direction. The latter turns quickly around to detect, and if possible, to seize the instrument from the scratcher.

The scratcher, however, passes the toy to another, and so on, the person holding it sounding it whenever the "cat's" attention is turned in an opposite direction. If the "cat" succeeds in detecting a player and seizing the toy from him they change places, the detected scratcher becoming "cat" in his turn.

Silent Quaker.—The company seat themselves so that each one can whisper to his next neighbor on his right. When all are ready the whispering begins. Each one tells his next neighbor to do some absurd thing. When everyone has received a commission the leader announces, "The meeting has begun." All join hands and solemnly shake them after which no one must speak or laugh. Each one in turn performs his commission with solemnity. Anyone who laughs or speaks pays a forfeit.

Suggestions for commissions—One might be ordered to make a pantomime speech, another told to dance a jig, another commissioned to sing by action. A gentleman might be told to play barber or dentist, another might be told to play a violin, etc.

Promenade concert.—The players seat themselves in a circle, each adopting a musical instrument on which he is supposed to be the performer. For instance, one chooses the violin, and draws his right hand backward and forward with a vigorous action, as though he were drawing the bow across the instrument. Another takes the cornet, and puffs out his cheeks to the utmost extent. A third chooses a clarinet and rolls his eyes painfully. Another beats an imaginary drum, while another, strumming with his hands upon his knees or a table (the latter real or imaginary), shows that the piano is his choice. The banjo, jewsharp, comb and paper, triangle, cymbal, tambourine, hand organ, may all be represented. Every player must imitate the actions and, as closely as possible, the sound peculiar to his adopted instrument, selecting any tune he may think best calculated to display his powers. No two players are allowed to play the same tune, and the greatest enthusiasm must be thrown into the performance. Or all may be required to play the same tune.

Gravity is indispensable (because next to impossible) and the slightest violation of it costs a forfeit.

The conductor takes his place in the center of the circle, sitting cross-legged on a chair, with his face to the back of another chair on which he beats time. When the music (?) is at its height, and the greatest confusion prevails, the leader suddenly singles out one of the performers and asks him why he is at fault. The person thus unexpectedly pounced upon must immediately give some excuse for his want of accuracy, which excuse must be in keeping with the nature of his instrument. For instance, the fiddler replies that the bridge is broken and he couldn't get across; the pianist, that he has left one of the keys of his instruments at home on his dressing table, etc. Any delay in this, or repetition of any excuse already given, costs a forfeit.

Jacks.—This game is played with five jacks and a rubber ball. It has been a favorite with children for many years. The jacks are tossed upon the ground. Then the player must pick them up in the following fashion: He tosses the ball into the air. While it is still in the air he picks up a jack and then catches the ball before it hits the ground. He continues this until he has picked up each jack. After the ones he does the twos, picking up two jacks, two jacks and one jack, though not necessarily in this order. Then he picks up three and two; then four and one; and for fives he picks up all five jacks.

For the game of elevens the ball is thrown into the air. One jack is placed in the left hand, the ball being allowed to bounce before catching it. This is kept up as in the ones until fifteen is reached.

For the game of twenty-ones the ball is tossed into the air, the jack being picked up in right hand, allowing the ball to bounce once. The jack is then swiftly placed in the left hand, the ball being allowed to bounce again before the player catches it. Twenty-five is the score to be reached.

Knock at the door.—The ball is thrown up, the player picks up a jack, knocks on the floor with his knuckles, and catches the ball before it hits the ground.

Around the world.—The ball is thrown into the air, the player must pick up a jack and with the jack in his hand go around the ball while it is in the air. The ball is then allowed to bounce once before being caught. This is continued until the fives are reached.

Rock the baby.—This is done in the same fashion as "Around the World" except that the player puts his arms together as if rocking the baby before catching the ball.

Scrub the floor.—Same as "Around the World" except the pantomime of scrubbing the floor is substituted for going round the ball.

Bow wow.—The players form a large circle. One player who is "It" runs around outside the circle. He suddenly taps some player in the circle and keeps on going. The tapped player leaves his place immediately and goes the opposite way around the circle. When the two players meet they must go down on all fours and say "Bow wow!" three times. Then each goes on around the circle trying to get to the vacated place first. The one left out is "It."

Mrs. Grundy's kitchen—All players sit in a row, except one. That player goes to each child in succession, and asks him what he will give for equipping Mrs. Grundy's kitchen. Each answers whatever pleases him—a cakepan, a strainer, an egg beater, a piepan, a dishpan, a saucepan, a skillet, a coffeepot, a mouse trap, spoon, etc. When all of the replies are in, the questioner returns to the first player and puts all sorts of questions. These questions must be answered by the article he contributed to Mrs. Grundy's kitchen. No other word may be used. For instance, he asks, "What is your favorite food?" "Fly swatter," comes the reply, because that person agreed to furnish a fly swatter to Mrs. Grundy's kitchen. Any other question may be asked, at the discretion of the questioner, such as "Who is the best looking girl in this room?"; "What do you like to wear best on your head?"; "Who did you see at church last Sunday?"; etc. The object of the questioner is to make the answerer laugh. When he succeeds in making some player laugh, that person must pay a forfeit. Or the two may change positions.

Washer line-toss.—A line is drawn about ten feet away from the players. Each player has a washer. In turn, they toss these washers at the line. The one who lands closest to the line scores a point. Players may slide the washer or toss it through the air. Ten points may constitute a game. If played on the sidewalk the crack between concrete blocks may serve as the line.

Here I bake.—Players join hands in a circle. One player inside the circle is the captive. He endeavors to find freedom by trickery and force. Touching one pair of clasped hands he says, "Here I bake!" Passing around the circle he touches another pair of hands, saying, "Here I brew!" Suddenly, in a place least suspected, the prisoner whirls around, springs at two clasped hands, and tries to break through. As he does he shouts, "Here I mean to break through!" The prisoner endeavors to catch two players off guard. The two players responsible for the prisoner breaking through draw straws to determine which one of them takes the prisoner's place.

Who has the ring?—The players stand or sit in a circle or straight line. One player has a ring which he carries. The other players hold hands clasped in front of them. The player who has the ring passes along from player to player, tapping the closed fists as if putting the ring in their possession. He actually may give it to the first player visited. But he goes to each, in turn, pretending to deposit the ring with them. As he does he repeats:

"Biddy, Buddy, hold fast my gold ring,
Till I go to London and come back again."

Each child, in turn, is called on by the leader to guess who has the ring. If successful he takes the leader's place. Forfeits may be required for failure to guess correctly.

Driving piggy to market.—*Equipment*—A pop bottle, milk bottle, or Indian club, and a short stick for each contestant or team. For the stick an umbrella or cane will do.

At the signal to start each contestant starts pushing his "pig" toward a designated goal. He then brings it back in the same manner. The player is allowed to use only one hand, holding the other back of him.

If done as a relay the two teams line up single file. As soon as a player gets the "pig" over the line back home the next player in line drives him to market and back.

It will be found that the "pig" is not always easy to control.

Air route.—The players are seated, preferably in a circle. Each one is given the name of some city or airport or country. One player has no chair. He stands inside the circle and calls "All aboard for plane from Oklahoma City to Boston! All aboard!" As soon as he has finished the two players representing Oklahoma City and Boston must change seats. The starter or caller tries to get a seat in the scramble. The player left out is the caller, and the game continues. Clipper service may be offered in this game by the starter calling "All aboard the Clipper! New York to Bermuda (San Francisco to Tokyo, etc.). All aboard!"

Falling in the lake.—This game may be played with or without chairs. A space six or eight feet wide is marked off on the floor. If chairs are used they are placed in a circle and they face out from center. The players march around the circle to music. When the music stops all marchers must stop where they are. If a player is in the space marked off as the lake, he is considered to have fallen into the lake and is out of the game. He takes a seat on one of the chairs. All players are required to walk through the lake, and all players must stay in line. In a large group there may be more than one lake. The game may be continued until only one player is left.

Feel and pass.—Players are seated at a large table, hands under the table. At one end of the table is a big wastebasket. The leader requests that the players receive and pass to the right articles as they come to them. From a covered basket articles are started, one at a time, under the table. The last player in line drops them in a basket provided for that purpose. No player must look to see what the articles are. From twenty to fifty articles may be passed. It would be advisable if none of them are breakable. Among the things passed may be an apple, a turnip, a ball, a thimble, a penknife, a clothespin, a pencil, a top, a corkscrew, an onion, a marble, a spectacle case, a pear, a penholder, a peanut, a walnut, other kinds of nuts, a screw, a bolt, a key, a stopper, an old doorknob, a hammer, a pair of pliers, a nail file, a spoon, etc. After all articles have been passed and the basket containing them put aside, all players are given ten minutes or so to write a list of all of the things they remember handling.

Variation—Work this as a relay with two sets of articles and two teams. The object will be to see who can finish passing the articles first, and then which group or team can make the most complete list.

Mother Goose quiz.—Someone starts this game by asking some question about a Mother Goose rhyme. For instance, he queries, "Who stole a pig?" The first player to shout "Tom, Tom, the piper's son" is allowed to quote that rhyme. Then he is permitted to ask the next question. However, if he could not quote the rhyme the player who did may be allowed to ask the question. Each player thinks up his own question.

Stir the soup.—Players are seated about the room. One player stands at center with a cane, umbrella, or stick. There are just enough chairs for all of the players except the one at center. The seated players gather round the one in the center. They walk around in a circle saying, "Stir the soup! Stir the soup!" The one in the center goes through the motions of stirring the soup. Suddenly, when no one is expecting it, he taps on the floor three times, drops the stick, and runs for a seat. This is the signal for all of the players to sit down. The player left out is the new soup stirrer.

Wheel of fortune.—Draw a wheel upon a tablet or piece of paper. Between the spokes write numbers, one number for each space— one, two, three, five, ten, etc. Each child, in turn, takes a pencil, twirls it in the air, saying,

> "Tit for tat,
> Butter for fat,
> If you pet my dog,
> I'll pet your cat."

On the word "cat," the player brings the pencil point down on the wheel. The number written on the space touched indicates the score. If the pencil lands on a line or outside the circle no score is made. Then the next player takes his turn. Twenty-five or fifty points may be considered as a game.

Witch's cage.—One of the players is the witch. Each of the others chooses a tree or post or large rock as his home. The witch marks off on the ground as many "cages" as there are players. The children run out from their homes and the witch pursues them. When she catches a player she puts that child in one of the "cages." The only way the captured player may be freed is to be touched by one of the other players. After being freed he is privileged to return to his home unmolested. The player who freed him, however, may be caught by the witch. When all of the players are caught a new witch is selected.

Giant tag.—One player is the giant. He hides behind a bush, tree, chair, or something else. Another player is the mother or father. The rest are children. The children call to their parent:

> "Mother (Father) may we go out
> If we behave?"

The mother (father) answers:

> "Yes, but don't go near
> The giant's cave!"

The children then leave the home base and walk or run around until the mother shouts: "Children, come home!"

At this signal the giant leaves his hiding place and starts in pursuit of the children. He growls as he does so. The children run for home base, screaming as if frightened.

All of the children the giant tags become giants to help him catch the others the next time.

Japanese crab race.—The children go down on all fours. In this position they move backward toward the goal line.

Crab and monkey relay.—The race may be run as a relay, in which case all players on a team would be lined up single file behind the starting line and the players may come back as monkeys. That is, on the return, they may move face forward on all fours.

Blind bag tag.—The players mill around promiscuously at the center of the playing area. One player has a big paper bag such as is gotten at the grocery store with a large order of groceries. The mouth of the sack is folded back several times to make it easier to handle. Suddenly the player with the bag claps it over the head of one of the players so that it covers his entire head and he cannot see. All of the other players scatter. The player over whose head the bag has been placed counts, "One, two, three! Stop!" Immediately all players must stop where they are. The blind player then moves about, hands out, until he touches some player. He asks this player to imitate some animal by putting some such question as this to him, "How does a rooster crow?" The captured player must answer appropriately, trying to disguise his voice, of course. If the blind man guesses correctly as to who the captured person is that player has the bag clapped on his head and the group scatters again until the new blind man shouts, "One, two, three! Stop!" If he does not guess correctly he tries again.

Hit 'em tag.—*Equipment*—A soft rag ball, tennis ball, sponge ball, or small play ball. One player is "It." The rest scatter as "It" tries to hit one of them with the ball. If he misses, the player near whom it lands picks it up and tosses it back. "It" keeps trying until he hits someone.

Chinese junket.—The children sit or stand about the room in a circle, or in any position so they can all see one another. One of them starts the game by saying:

> My Chinese junket's in with a cargo of tea,
> And plenty of presents for you and for me.
> She's brought me a fan! Oh, joy! Oh, bliss!
> I fan myself every day just like this.

On "like this" the player starts fanning and all the other players follow suit.

Another child now takes up the lead and has the junket bringing something else, the player making his own choice of what the junket brings. Each time all of the children join in the action, such as playing the piano when a piano is brought in by the junket, or sweeping the floor for a broom, or sneezing for a handkerchief. Other things that may be brought might include a drum, a horn, a fife, a trombone, a doll, a bicycle, a hoe, a hammer, a baton, etc.

Bird-cage tag.—All of the birds are in a "nest" at one side of the playing space. The "nest" is a space marked off in some way on the ground or floor. The cage is across the playing space, it being a space marked off in similar fashion to the "nest." The game is very similar to "Pom Pom Pullaway."

One player is the "Hawk." He stands in the space between **the** lines where the "nest" and "cage" are located. These two, by the way, are at the corners of the two base lines.

The players are divided by a counting off process into four groups. Each group selects the kind of bird it will represent and tells the leader or bird keeper. Where two or more groups want the same name, adjustments must be made. The leader then announces to the "Hawk" what birds are in the nests—robins, redbirds, bluebirds, sparrows, for instance.

The "Hawk" calls to the bird keeper, "I want a bluebird." The bird keeper calls, "Bluebirds fly, but don't let the 'Hawk' catch you."

Immediately all of the bluebirds must leave the nest and run across to the opposite side. The "Hawk" tries to catch them. Those he catches must go to the space marked off for the "cage." The birds are safe when they cross the opposite line. The "Hawk" then calls for another bird, the robin, for instance. This continues until he catches all of the birds. In a large group there may be two or more "Hawks."

The birds run lightly because they are birds. A word of reminder to the children will probably get the desired results at this point.

Third degree.—The players are divided into two equal groups. They go to different rooms. Or, if outdoors, they are separated by some distance. Each group selects one of its own number to represent them. The two players selected get together outside and decide on some object—a tree, a chair, a piano, a book, a flower, a vase, a chandelier, etc. Each goes now to the opposite group. The idea is to see which side can first guess the object by means of questions which can be answered by "yes" or "no." The side which guesses first keeps the one who came to them and, in addition, gets its own member back. Two more players are chosen and the game continues.

Bean bag go-foot.—All children stand in line facing a leader a few few away. The leader throws the bean bag to the child at the head of the line. That player must catch it and toss it back. The leader then throws it to the second player in line, and so on it goes back and forth until all players have caught the bean bag and tossed it back. If a player in line, or the leader, fails to catch the bean bag or tosses it back with a wild throw, that person goes to the foot and players below him move up one.

Blindman's buff catch.—A blindfolded player is led to the center of the room. Here he is taken by the shoulders and turned about three times, with the following rhyme being chanted by the children:

"Blind man, blind man, do you think you're able?
How many horses in your father's stable?"
"Three have I; they're black, white, and gray."
"Turn about, and turn about, and catch whom you may."

After this ceremony the blind man tries to catch and name some child. In a large space limits will have to be determined beyond which the players may not go to avoid being caught.

Washer woman.—Players stand in couples in two lines facing one another. Couples clasp adjacent hands. They swing their arms slowly and gracefully, first three times toward the right and then three times toward the left. As they do this they sing to the tune of "Miss Jennia Jones":

"This is the way we wash our clothes, wash our clothes, wash our clothes, wash our clothes."

Then they unclasp their hands and rub them together as washwomen do in rubbing their clothes, singing:

"This is the way we rub our clothes, rub our clothes, rub our clothes."

In the third movement the couples again clasp hands. The line on one side stands with arms raised in an arch and the couples on that side slip through the other line so that the two lines stand back to back. Immediately the other side repeats the movement so that the couples are again face to face. This is done quickly, three times in succession, while the players sing:

"This is the way we wring our clothes, wring our clothes, wring our clothes."

Then suddenly they stop and clap their hands while singing:

"And hang them on the bushes."

Puss in the corner.—The four corners of the room are occupied by four pussies. The other children stand in a group in the middle. The pussies raise their fingers, beckon to each other, and call, "Puss, puss, puss!" The object is to change corners so quickly that no one from the waiting group can get a chance to slip into the vacated corner, and so become a pussy.

Animal silhouettes.—Provide each child with a pair of scissors, a sheet of white or dark paper, and a pencil. The leader then calls out the name of some animal—an elephant, for instance. Each child must then cut out an elephant. Three to five minutes may be allowed. The names are written on them and they are put on display. Next a pig may be silhouetted. Then a dog, or a cat, or any other animal. If the animals can be pasted on a dark background if cut out of white paper it will help.

Letting out the doves.—Players stand in groups of three. One in each group, usually the smallest, represents a dove. One, a hawk, is larger than the dove or swifter. The third player in the group is the owner of the birds.

The dove stands in front of the owner, who holds her by the hand. The hawk stands behind the owner, and is also held by the hand.

The owner throws the dove from her with a gesture of the hand, first toward herself and then away, as a dove might be tossed for flight in the air. The dove sails away, with arms extended like wings. When the dove has a sufficient start, so that the hawk may not catch her too easily, the owner throws the hawk in the same fashion. The hawk, too, runs with extended arms, as though flying. She tries to catch the dove, but she must run over exactly the same route as the dove. At her discretion the owner claps her hands, or gives some other signal, for the birds to return to her. The dove tries to get back without being caught by the hawk. The clapping is usually done with hollow hands to make a deep sound. This signal is usually given when the dove reaches the farthest point to which the owner thinks it best for her to go. The dove may not come home until the signal is given.

Master of the ring.—A circle is drawn on the ground. The players stand shoulder to shoulder, inside the circle, with arms folded either on their chests or behind their backs. When the signal is given players try to push one another out of the circle. When a man steps on the circle he is out. He is also out if he unfolds his arms or falls down. The last player to remain is master of the ring.

Old woman from the wood.—The players are divided into two equal groups. The two lines face one another with only a short distance between them. One line advances toward the other saying, "Here comes an old woman from the wood." The second line answers, "What can you do?" At this the first line responds, "Do anything!" The second line then says, "Work away!" The players of the first line now imitate some occupation in which an old woman might engage. They have previously agreed among themselves as to what this shall be. So they iron, or wash, or sweep, or churn, or sew, or dig in the garden, or pick weeds, or pluck flowers, or knead dough, or stir cake, or whip cream, or knit, or phone, or anything the old woman might do. The other side tries to guess what is being done. If they guess correctly they become the old woman. If not, the first line tries again.

Ringmaster.—This one will be fun for young children. One is chosen for ringmaster. If he can flourish a whip like a real circus ringmaster, it will increase interest. The other players form a circle around the ringmaster without holding hands.

The ringmaster turns and moves around in the circle, snapping the whip, and calling the name of some animal. The players in the circle immediately imitate the animal, both as to its movements and cries. For instance, for an elephant they droop their shoulders, stooping over, and walk swinging their hands like a trunk. For a bear, they run on all fours and growl, or they stand and claw. For a frog they hop and croak. Other animals that may be suggested are a barking or yelping dog, a mewing or purring cat, a humped and swaying camel, a snarling and springing tiger, a roaring and nervous lion, a balking and braying donkey, a scratching and cackling hen, Ferdinand the bull, smelling flowers, a mooing cow, a neighing and galloping horse, a strutting and noisy peafowl, a chesty and crowing rooster, etc.

The ringmaster, at his discretion, may announce, "We will all join the circus parade!" At this, each player chooses some animal he would like to represent and gallops around the circle in characteristic movements.

High windows.—All of the players but one join hands in a circle. The extra player stands inside the circle. Passing around, he tags one of the players in the circle. Then they both run around the outside of the circle, the vacant place being left open. The one who was tagged tries to tag the center player before he gets around the circle three times. If he fails to tag him the players call "High window!" and raise their clasped hands to let both players inside. Should the one who is being chased enter the circle without being tagged, he takes his place with the other players, and the game continues.

How many miles to Babylon?—The players form two lines and stand facing each other, there being about eight feet between the lines. The players number off by twos. A dialogue takes place, the players of each line speaking in unison. They sway back and forth in time to the words, swinging clasped hands by couples and shifting the feet rhythmically, as they sway. The tempo should be fast.

FIRST LINE: "How many miles to Babylon?"

SECOND LINE: "Only a bare three score and ten."

FIRST LINE: "Will we be there by candlelight?"

SECOND LINE: "Yes, you will, and back again."

FIRST LINE: "Open your gates and let us through."

SECOND LINE: "Not without a beck and boo (bow),
Not without a side and sou."

FIRST LINE: "Here's a beck and here's a boo,
Here's a side and here's a sou.
Open your gates and let us through."

SECOND LINE: "We'll open the gates and let them through."

At the words, "Here's a beck and here's a boo," the players of the first line suit the action to the words by placing the hands upon the hips for a "beck" and making a bow. On "Here's a side and here's a sou," they stand erect and turn the head to the right. Then the partners clasp hands and run forward eight steps in the same rhythm as the dialogue just given. Each couple of the first line passes under the upraised arms of the opposite couple of the second line. Having taken the eight steps, the running couple turns around in four running steps, facing the city gates from the other side. The couples in the second line, the gates, also turn in four running steps, and the group is in position to repeat the game with the side that has run through now representing the gates.

If music is desired the game could be done to "Country Garden."

Wiggums.—The players are seated in a circle. One player starts the game by passing some object (an ornament, a pencil, a knife, a book, etc.) to his right-hand neighbor. As he does so he introduces himself, as well as the article, thus: "My name is George. And this is Wiggums." The second player turns to the third and announces as she hands over the article: "My name is Mary. George says that this is Wiggums." The third player hands over the object to his right-hand neighbor, saying: "My name is Dick. Mary says that

George says this is Wiggums." So each player has to announce the names of all of the players that preceded him, and in proper order. Aften ten or more persons have handled the article this isn't so easy. Players making mistakes may be required to pay forfeits.

Bottle answer.—A milk bottle or pop bottle will do for this one. This mysterious bottle always tells the truth.

Players are seated in a circle. One player takes the center and spins a bottle on its side. Just before doing that he asks the bottle a question, such as, "Who is the best looking in this room?" or "Who will be married first?" or "Who is the most brilliant?" The bottle answers when it stops by pointing its top at some person. This person then takes the center, asks the bottle another question, and spins it. Thus the game continues.

Variation—The person toward whom the bottle points may be required to do some stunt.

Homemade ring toss.—Take an old shoe box or any other cardboard box. A box a foot square would be even better than a shoe box. Punch holes in the bottom of the box and stick clothespins in them so that the pins will stand straight up, a couple of inches above the box. Mark the center hole twenty-five; the holes around the center, ten; and the other holes with varying amounts, from one to five. Numbers may be cut from calendars and pasted on the box. Use Mason jar rings. Outside pins can be slipped over the edge so that they clamp onto the box. Pins in toward center can be stabilized by using short strips of cardboard. Slip these between the legs of the clothespin and bend them in opposite directions on either side of the pin. Each player gets five tosses with the rings. One hundred points may constitute a game.

Heads.—The answers contain the word head. The leader may give an example if he feels it is necessary.

1. A head that glows.
2. One that brings woes.
3. A head the football player knows.
4. A head that pains.
5. A head that gains.
6. A head that marks the dead's remains.
7. A head that's food.

8. A head that's rude.

9. A head that usually is nude.

10. A head for the printer.

11. A head that is center.

12. A head that seats the crowd for dinner.

13. A head that flows.

14. A head that goes.

15. A head that every woman shows.

Answers—1. Headlight. 2. Headstrong. 3. Headgear. 4. Headache. 5. Headway. 6. Headstone. 7. Headcheese. 8. Heady. 9. Head hunter. (Someone suggested "baldhead" for this one. That checks one hundred per cent.) 10. Headline. 11. Headquarters. 12. Head waiter. 13. Headwater. 14. Head race. 15. Headdress.

Feet.—The answers in this game are words containing the word "foot."

1. A foot to buy a barefoot guy.

2. A foot that tells someone's close by.

3. A foot on a page.

4. A foot on a stage.

5. A foot that when friendly is good for any age.

6. A foot that steals.

7. A foot that feels.

8. A foot that woe to cattle wields.

9. A foot that's tired.

10. A foot that's hired.

11. A foot by grandma oft desired.

12. A foot that is free.

13. And one we will agree
Is a very good game
That we like to see.

Answers—1. Footwear. 2. Footfall. 3. Footnote. 4. Footlight. 5. Footing. 6. Footpad. 7. Footsore. 8. Foot-and-mouth disease.

9. Footworn. 10. Footman. 11. Footstool. 12. Foot-loose. 13. football.

Hands.—In this one the word "hand" is the keyword.

1. A hand for the acrobat.
2. A hand for the monkey.
3. A hand for which you'll never
   Have need of a donkey.
4. A hand for the criminal.
5. A hand that's for play.
6. A hand for measuring.
7. Or the wedding day.
8. A hand for the creative.
9. One for those who toil.
10. A hand for letters.
11. A hand you often spoil.
12. A hand that's good looking.
13. A hand for the bike.
14. A hand that is useful
    On hammer, spade, and pike.
15. A hand that's improvident.
16. A hand that supports.
17. A hand that advertises.
18. One useful in jobs and sports.

Answers—1. Handspring. 2. Hand-organ. 3. Handcart. 4. Handcuff. 5. Handball. 6. Handbreath. 7. Handmaiden. 8. Handicraft. 9. Handwork. 10. Handwriting. 11. Handkerchief. 12. Handsome. 13. Handle bar. 14. Handle. 15. Hand-to-mouth. 16. Handrail. 17. Handbill. 18. Handy.

Bogeyman.—One player is called the "Bogeyman." He stands at one goal. The other players are lined up at the opposite goal. The Bogeyman steps out and shouts, "Are you afraid of the Bogeyman?" At this the other players run toward his goal, while the Bogeyman tries to tag him. The players caught must go with the Bogeyman to the opposite goal to act as aids in catching the rest of the runners.

The last player caught becomes the new Bogeyman.   Or it may be decided that the first one caught shall be "It."

Hickory, dickory, dock.—Small children will enjoy going through the simple movements of this game.   They recite the nursery rhyme as they act out the words.

Hickory, dickory, dock,
  (Move arms to right, to left, pendulum fashion.   Stamp foot.)
The mouse ran up the clock.
  (Run four steps forward.)
The clock struck "One!"
  (Pause a moment to listen, hand to ear.   On "One!" clap hands.)
The mouse ran down.
  (Run four steps back to place.)
Hickory, dickory, dock.
  (Move arms to right, to left, pendulum fashion.   Stamp foot.)

Jack be nimble.—Place a small object eight to ten inches high upright on the floor to represent a candlestick.   The players run in single file and jump with both feet over the candlestick, while they recite:

> Jack be nimble,
> Jack be quick,
> Jack jump over the candlestick.

All of the action is in rhythm.   Players try to avoid knocking over the candlestick.

Seesaw Marjorie Daw.—This simple game adds the dramatic to the fun of the rhythm.

Seesaw, Marjorie Daw,
  (Arms sideward raise.   Sway body to left and right.)
Jack shall have a new master.
  (Partners join hands.   Skip forward four steps.)
But he shall have a penny a day.
  (Step left.   Point right toe forward, shaking right forefinger at partner.   Left hand on hip.)
Because he won't work any faster.
  (Join both hands with partner.   Skip around in place four steps.)

The leaves.—This is an old English rhythmic game. The players stand in a circle. During the first three and one-half lines they run around the circle, hands stretched high over head. On "Come down together" they drop to the floor or ground.

> The leaves are green, the leaves are brown,
> They hang so high they will not come down.
> Leave them alone until frosty weather,
> And they will all come down together.

Round and round.—Players form a circle, hands joined. Stepping in rhythm around the circle, they recite the following rhyme, bobbing down quickly on the word "sank":

> Round and round went our gallant ship,
> Round and round went she;
> Three times round went our gallant ship,
> Till she sank to the bottom of the sea.

Ring around the rosy.—The players join hands in a ring and skip around reciting, sing-song fashion, the following lines:

> Ring around the rosy,
> Pocket full of posy,
> Fall down and break your nosey!

On the last line all children drop to the floor. Sometimes it is recited:

> Ring around the roses,
> A pocket full of posies,
> With a curtsy here and a curtsy there,
> And a curtsy all together.

Curtsy to the right, to the left, and to center.

Fingers out.—This Chinese game is fun. It requires no equipment and may be started at any time. Two players engage in it. In a large group pair off players and everyone can play at once. Players count play at once. Players count "One, two, three!" and on "three!" they put out their right hands simultaneously, either closed or with one or more fingers outstretched. At the same time they shout some number which they guess will be the number of fingers out for both hands. The player who guesses the correct number of fingers, or the nearest to it, scores a point. Five points may constitute a game.

Variations—(1) Allow players to walk about playing "Fingers Out!" with first one player and then another, but with no player twice in succession. The first to score ten points in this fashion yells "Ten and out!" as soon as he completes the tenth score.

(2) Play the game with three players instead of two.

A Halloween stunt.—(This game should only be used with older children. Even then it would be well to guard against any child being unduly frightened.) Dim the lights so that no one can see clearly. Have a helper stand at each end of a row of children. The leader, using a flashlight, reads a story of a man named Brown. As he reads, parts of the body are passed by the helpers. The players pass the articles from one to the other until the helper at the other end gets them. The reader pauses long enough each time for the article to pass the full length of the line, before reading the next item.

Once upon a time in this very town
Lived a miserly man whose name was Brown.

Alack and alas, on a Halloween night
He was terribly murdered because of spite.

And ever since then he has roamed the earth
To warn and to haunt the place of his birth.

Tonight we have some of his restless remains,
So we'll make you acquainted at once with his brains.
(Wet sponge.)

And now your shuddering touch will know
The victim's hair has continued to grow.
(Corn silk or yarn.)

He heard too well the tinkle of gold,
It's a powerful ear that now you hold.
(Dried apple or dried peach.)

His hand is clammy, cold, and still,
No longer can it shoot to kill.
(Cold rubber glove filled with sand.)

His eyes were small, but very keen,
Though the kind deeds of earth they've never seen.
(Hulled grape.)

He talked a lot when he was young;
Now you're feeling of his tongue.
(A raw oyster.)

He was sly and cruel from the start,
So now you'll feel his bleeding heart.
(A piece of raw liver.)

The tendons which helped his strong right arm
We pass to you. Keep them from harm.
(Cooked spaghetti.)

The meals he ate were coarse and dry,
So his teeth were strong. They'll never die.
(Kernels of corn.)

But wait! He comes and stands within.
He's hunting for some friend or kin!
Listen closely and above his moans
You'll hear the rattle of his bones.

A ghost moves slowly through the darkness rattling a bunch of clothespins tied loosely together. Exits with a moan. Lights on!

Do as I do.—The players may be seated or standing. They may be in rows, in a circle, in a semicircle, or arranged promiscuously. The leader calls, "Do as I do." Every player must be where he can clearly observe the leader for every action of eye, hand, feet, head, or body, and must be imitated exactly. The leader may sneeze. Everyone sneezes. He may wink his eye, or wag his head, or beat time, or jump up and down, or wave. Whatever he does everyone must do immediately and all together. A good leader will soon have a crowd "in stitches" over the antics they must do. When he shouts "Present Arms!" each player must stretch out his right arm toward the leader. At the next command, "Fire!" he pushes the player nearest him, being careful only to unbalance him without hurting him. Each player pushes another in the same fashion. When done indoors, care must be taken not to push people against sharp-pointed surfaces. If done outdoors, the third command could be "Left foot, raise!" The pushing in this case would have players picking themselves up from the grass.

FORFEITS

(1) Put one hand where the other cannot touch it. After the player tries unsuccessfully, have him put the right hand to the left elbow.

(2) Say "Quizzical Quiz, Kiss me quick" six times running without drawing a breath in between.

(3) Ask a question which cannot be answered in the negative. The question is, "What does 'Y-E-S' spell?"

(4) For a boy: Imitate a girl. For a girl: Imitate a boy.

(5) Hop across the room on one foot.

(6) Pose as a football player kicking a goal.

(7) Pose as a football player warding off a blocker.

(8) Pose as a football player about to make a forward pass.

(9) Pose as a baseball pitcher who is getting the catcher's signal.

(10) Pose as a baseball pitcher who has just delivered the pitch.

(11) Pose as a fielder who is waiting for a fly ball to drop into his hands.

(12) Stand with back against the wall and try to pick up a handkerchief two feet in front of you on the floor.

(13) Bow to the wittiest, kneel to the prettiest, and salute the one you love the best.

(14) Yelp like a dog that has been whipped.

(15) Mew like a cat putting on a back-fence serenade.

(16) Say three times with increasing speed: "Eleven elephants elegantly equipped stopped Eleanor's equipage."

(17) Read rapidly: "Esau Wood sawed wood. Esau Wood would saw wood! Oh, the wood Wood would saw! One day Esau Wood saw a saw saw wood as no other wood-saw Wood-saw could saw wood. In fact, all of the wood-saws Wood ever saw saw wood Wood never saw a wood-saw that would saw wood as the wood-saw Wood saw saw wood would saw wood, and I never saw a wood-saw that would saw wood as the wood-saw Wood saw until I saw Esau Wood saw wood with the wood-saw that Wood saw saw wood."

(18) Read rapidly three times with increasing speed:

"I saw Esau kissing Sue
In fact we all three saw.
I saw Esau, he saw me,
And she saw I saw Esau."

(19) Repeat rapidly three times: "Neddy Noople nipped his neighbor's nutmegs."

(20) Repeat rapidly three times: "Peter Piper picked a peck of pickled peppers, and put them on a pressed pewter platter."

(21) Repeat rapidly twice: "Sam Slick sawed six slim slippery slender sticks."

(22) Repeat rapidly three times: "Sheep soup! Shoot sheep!"

(23) Perform the following dramatic interlude along with some other person who has to redeem a forfeit:

The two people are given lighted candles and are told to approach one another slowly, with solemn countenances, while they recite in slow and dismal manner the following dialogue:

FIRST SPEAKER: "The King of Hunky Bunk is defunct and dead."

SECOND SPEAKER: "Alas! Alas! How died his Majesty?"

FIRST SPEAKER (*dolefully*): "Just so! Just so! Just so!"

SECOND SPEAKER: "How sad! How sad! How sad!"

If they laugh they must pay another forfeit.

(24) Sing a song.

(25) Recite a poem.

(26) Sing "Way Down Upon the Swanee River," counting the words as you sing, thus: "Way (one) down (two) upon (three) the (four) Swanee (five) river (six) ."

(27) Lisp "Twinkle, twinkle, little star."

(28) Kick the box. Place a penny match box on the floor, end-up, just exactly three lengths of your own foot from your toe. Stand on one foot and try to kick the match box over with the toe of the other foot. You must not change the position of the balancing foot, or lose your balance. It sounds simple, doesn't it? Well try it!

There are many other suggestions in this book that can be used for forfeits, such as the "Act it out" suggestions in Chapter XIV, Fun with Dramatics.

FUN WITH MARBLES

Holding steady.—A circle about eight feet in diameter. A dozen or more marbles are bunched at center. Players may shoot their marbles at a line to determine the order of playing. The nearest to the line is first, the next nearest second, and so on. In shooting players must hold their hands to the ground either on or outside the circle. The shot must be made without the hand being moved from that position. The idea is to knock the marbles outside the circle. Each one so struck is a point. If a player hits a marble and knocks it out he continues shooting. A favorite trick is to knock a marble out at such an angle that the taw, or shooting marble, rides to a position within the circle near to another marble. If a player's taw stays in the circle, after knocking out a marble, he shoots from where it stops. As soon as a player fails to knock out a marble, he loses his turn and the next player shoots.

Hunching Boston.—A circle about ten feet or more in diameter is used. The players usually use heavy taws to shoot. They are allowed to shoot from the ground or standing and they may hunch or move the hand as much as they please as they shoot. This motion of the hand as the marble is delivered gives it greater force. The same rules, otherwise, obtain as in "Holding Steady."

Cincy.—The players make a circle about four feet in diameter. Across the middle of this circle and parallel with the shooting line a line is drawn. On this line the marbles are placed several inches apart. The players shoot from a line ten to fifteen feet away to start the game. Order of shooting is determined by tossing or shooting the marble from the shooting line to the circle. The one nearest the line of the circle is first. The rest come in the order of their nearness to the line. After the first shot players play from wherever their taws stop. If a player hits another player's taw with his own, the player hit is out of the game and all of the marbles he has shot out of the circle up to that time are put back in the circle. Each marble a player has when the game is over is a point.

Fats.—Anywhere from five to ten marbles are put in the center of a small circle about fourteen inches in diameter. Sometimes one or more marbles are placed for each player in the game. There is a dead line three feet from the circle. The shooting line is from ten to fifteen feet away from the circle. A player's first shot must not hit the ground on his side of the dead line. In all other respects the game is the same as "Cincy," except that any player, whose marble rests completely within the circle, is in "fats" and is eliminated from the game. All marbles he has gained must be put back in the circle when a player is thus eliminated.

Chasers.—Ground limits are determined. The first player shoots his marble, and the others follow in turn. When a player hits another marble that player is out of the game. The player who hits is permitted to shoot again until he misses. The players try to keep out of one another's way so as not to be "killed," and at the same time they try to keep in position to hit some other player. The game continues until only one player remains.

Picking plums.—Two straight lines are drawn parallel to one another, from four to eight feet apart. Each player places two or three marbles on the far line. These are the "plums." They are about one or two inches apart, depending on the skill of the shooters. The players knuckle down as in "Holding Steady!" on the near line and shoot, in turn. The marbles knocked off the line are taken by the shooter. But he is not allowed to shoot again until the next round. If a player fails to hit a "plum" he must place a marble on the line, adding it to the row. When all "plums" have been picked, players get one point for each marble or "plum" in their possession.

See also "Marble Plug" and "Marble Golf" in Chapter VI, Fun with Active Games.

OTHER GAMES FOR CHILDREN IN THIS BOOK

* Indicates rhythmic game.

Ach Ja*
Advancing statues
All around the Maypole*
Anagrams
Animal antics
Animal chase
Apple bite
Aunt Dinah
Auto trip
Back to back tag
Barrel hoop race
Battledore and shuttlecock
Battleship
Bean bag boards
Bear and guard
Bear in the net
Betsy Liner*
Birds have feathers
Birds, fish, and animal
Bird in a nest
Black and white tag
Blind pig
Blindman's buff
Bombardment
Bowling skittles
Box hockey
Broken hearts

Bug
Bull board
Bull in the ring
Burying white horses
Cat and rat
Catch tag
Center dodge
Chain tag
Charley over the water*
Chebogah*
Checking mail boxes
Chicken market
Chinese checkers
Chinese hop
Chum Chummy Lou
Ciel
Circle touch ball
Clap in, clap out
Conundrums
Croquet
Croquet ball bowling
Crows and cranes
Dainty
Daisy, Daisy*
Do you know Jim Crow?
Dodo
Dodo baseball

Dogs and chickens
Drop the handkerchief
Duck pins
Fan mien
Finger painting
Finish the alphabet
Fish in the sea
Flower garden
Flying feather
Fox and geese
Garden scamp
German bat ball
Ghost walks
Goosey, goosey, gander
Grocery store
Guarding the treasure
Guessing blindman
Hangman
Have you seen my sheep?
Hawk
Hearts
Hill dill
Hindu tag
Hole bowl
Hop Scotch
Hot cockles
Hul gul
Hurly burly
I am very, very tall
I spy
In the pond
Indian baseball
Indoor shuffleboard
I've been workin'*
Jacob and Rachel
Jacob's ladder
Jan-kem-po
Kick the can
King of the castle
King of France*
Lame wolf
Loose caboose
Magic music

Man, gun, rabbit
Man, gun, tiger
Marshmallow race
Mumblety-peg
Musical telepathy
Mystery tag
Nature sounds
Net tag
Nose and toe tag
Number call
Odd or even
Oracles
Organ grinder man*
Paper bag puppets
Paper tree
Parlor dodgeball
Pass it
Pick a peach tag
Pig in a hole
Ping-pong
Poison
Poisoned bean bag
Poisoned circle
Polly wolly doodle*
Pom pom pullaway
Pop sack races
Puppets
Pussy wants a corner
Queen's headache
Rabbit and dog
Ring on a string
Rubber ball puppets
Run sheep run
Sack baseball
Sack race
Safety zone ball
Sardines
Score ball
Shinney
Sit and see
Six little girls*
Skittles
Slap Jack

Sock puppets
Softball touch football
Spatter printing
Square dodgeball
Squirrel in a tree
Squirrel tails
Stagecoach
Still pond
Stone, paper, scissors
Stop ball
Stormy sea
Straddle ball
Swimming snake
Table caroms
Table football
Table polo
Table shuffleboard
Table steeplechase

Tag games
Three-legged race
Testing five senses
Three deep
Throw the club
Tip-tap-bat
Tit-tat-toe
Touch football
Triangle ball
Two deep
Uncle Ned
Up Jenkins
Water sprite
We're marching*
What did you see?
Wheel tag
You must pass this spoon
Who's the leader?

FINGER PLAYS

There are numerous kinds of finger plays. One of the oldest and most familiar is "This little pig went to market." Remember it?

"This little pig went to market;
This little pig stayed at home;
This little pig had roast beef;
This little pig had none;
This little pig said, "Wee,wee-e-e.""

Ten little squirrels.—The individual doing this holds up all ten fingers, palms out. As he mentions each little squirrel he wiggles the particular fingers on each hand—thus, the two thumbs, the two forefingers, the two second fingers, the two third fingers, and for the fifth two squirrels, the brave ones, the two small fingers. On "Bang went the gun!" clap hands together suddenly. On "Away they run" move hands out from body with the fingers wiggling.

Ten little squirrels up in a tree.
The first two said: "What's this we see?"
The second two said: "A man with a gun!"
The third two said: "Let's run! Let's run!"
The fourth two said: "Let's hide in the shade."
The fifth two said: "Shucks! We're not afraid!"
Bang! Went the gun! And away they run!

After saying this over once, get the group or the individual child to do it with you. Repeat it and try to get some dramatic touches in it—surprise, shock, fear, stealthiness, bravado.

Church and Steeple.—Another old one is this one.
This is the church.   (Interlock fingers on both hands.)
This is the steeple.   (Straighten out two forefingers with the ends of the two fingers touching to make the steeple.)
Open the door.   (Pull thumbs back.)
And see the people.   (Turn palms up, fingers intertwined and sticking up.)

Monkey on the stick.—See "Solo Flight" under "Aviation Test" in this chapter.

Three blue pigeons.—Hold up three fingers and sing to the tune of "Three Blind Mice":

> Three blue pigeons sitting on a wall,
> Three blue pigeons sitting on a wall.

Then the leader announces, "One flew away."   He moves the right hand away from his body with the fingers wiggling.   All of the others do likewise with a disappointed, "Oh!"
The group now holds up two fingers and sings:

> Two blue pigeons sitting on a wall,
> Two blue pigeons sitting on the wall.

"And another flew away!"   Again the movement with the right hand, fingers fluttering.   "Oh-h-h!"   Register increasing disappointment.
Now hold up one finger and sing:

> One blue pigeon sitting on the wall,
> One blue pigeon sitting on the wall.

"And the last one flew away!"   The movement with the right hand.   Register deep sorrow with a tearful "Oh-h-h-h-h-h!"
Slowly and dolefully sing:

> No blue pigeons sitting on a wall,
> No blue pigeons sitting on the wall.

Excitedly the leader announces, "Then one came back!"   The crowd shouts a joyful "Hurray!"

They sing cheerily, "One blue pigeon, etc." "A second one comes back!" Then the third one returns. The "Hurrays" register increasing joy and excitement, as does the singing each time.

FUN WITH DRAWING AND PAINTING

Before man knew anything about an alphabet he wrote his messages in pictures. Even to day the apt illustration makes the written or printed word more vivid with meaning. Thus the child's response to pictures need cause no wonder. Sketching and painting, however crude, become an important part of the child's education. Encouraging him to draw some of his own ideas not only will afford him a lot of fun but it will help him to get better acquainted with the world in which he lives. Add color by furnishing him with water colors and crayons and you enhance the values of this sort of creative play.

A few simple suggestions are offered for helping the child find fun in the use of pencils, crayons, and paint.

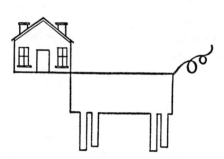

Johnny's dog.—The storyteller draws as he tells about the dog. Johnny lived in a house that looked like this. It had two windows and a door at the front. It had two chimneys, one on either side. (The storyteller proceeds to draw the house.) Johnny had a dog, but he couldn't find him. So he said: "Maybe my dog is over at Sue's house." Now Sue was Johnny's friend and she lived close by. Johnny had a special path that he followed to get to Sue's. So he started down this way, then turned sharply, and went this way. He fell in a hole, but got up. He fell again. In fact he fell four times. Then he came to a corner and started right up to Sue's house. When he got there the smoke was coming out of the chimney. (All of this time the storyteller is drawing the route that Johnny followed. At this particular point he draws the smoke coming out of the chimney.) He called Sue and said: "Sue, have you seen my dog?" "Yes, I have," Sue replied. "He has just gone home." So Johnny went straight home and sure enough there was his dog.

Johnny's goose.—O n e d a y Johnny lost his goose (or duck, or whatever you want to make it. This dot represents Johnny. (Put a dot on the paper.) Johnny lives in a little round house. (Draw a small circle around the dot.) Near his home is a pond. (Draw a large oval.) From Johnny's house to the pond there is a short path. (Draw a line from the small

circle to the oval.) Johnny took the path and looked around the pond for his goose. He went back in the bullrushes but found no goose. He went back again four times in different directions. Still no goose. Each time he retraced his steps. (Draw four lines at the end of the oval.) Johnny started back but decided to go way down from the lake—way down. (Draw a long line from the bottom of the oval.) But he came to a dead end. So he retraced his steps a short distance and tried again. But he had no better luck. (Draw a short branch out from the long path.) Again he tried on the other side, but again he had no luck. (Draw another short line from the main path.) So he went back to the pond and started out on another path. (Draw another long line from the bottom of the oval.) But again he came to a dead end. Again he retraced his steps a short distance and started out on a short bypath. (Draw a short line.) But he did not find his goose, so he came back and took a short path out from the other side. He had no better success. (Draw another short line.) He went back to the main path and returned to the pond. Brokenhearted he went around the pond and up the path to his house. He went to the front door, opened it, and walked out a very short distance. (Draws a short line from the front of the house.) And what do you think? There was his goose! He ran back to the house overjoyed. (Draw another short line back to the house.) "What a goose you are," he said to himself, "that you did not look for your goose out front, rather than all around the lake. There it is!" And sure enough there it was!

Wiggles.—This is a grand game for two players. It develops ingenuity and creativity, and gives expression to whatever of artistic ability the player has. One does not have to be a skilled sketch artist to get a lot of fun out of it.

One player draws a short wiggle line. The other player must take this line and make something out of it, using the line as a starting point.   The paper may be turned sideways, upside down, **or any-way** the artist desires.   He may draw a house, a bird, an animal, **a** person, or anything he pleases.   When he finishes he makes the wiggle part of the picture stand out in heavier or blacker line than the rest.

If done at a party each player may be required to write his name **on** his creation.   The various pictures may be placed on display.

Funny faces.—Each player draws the funniest faces his imagination and artistic ability will allow.   If desired, bodies may be added. Suggestions may be offered regarding portraying certain moods— happy, glum, angry, surprised, frightened.   Encourage the child to use his own ideas in making his sketches.   An example or two drawn by an adult may be helpful.   Or the child and the adult may alternate in drawing faces.   Here are a few examples:

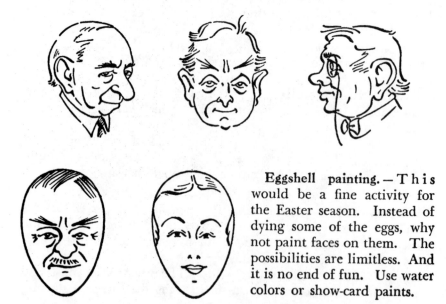

Eggshell painting. — T h i s would be a fine activity for the Easter season.   Instead of dying some of the eggs, why not paint faces on them.   The possibilities are limitless.   And it is no end of fun.   Use water colors or show-card paints.

Egg head sketching.—Provide each sketcher with a sheet of paper on which there are egg-shaped ovals. Have them sketch faces, using the oval for the head. If desired, crayons could be furnished so that the pictures could be colored.

Picture letters.—Letters which say most of what they have to say by pictures are fun both to the writer and to the reader. The parent who writes to his children will find his letters of more interest to them if he can illustrate them with sketches. Theodore Roosevelt used to do this in the letters he wrote to the members of his family. One does not have to be an artist to do this. The illustration here demonstrates the puzzle type of picture letter. Try it sometime. As a part of a party stunt you might have each guest write such a picture letter. If you think it will help you might call it a Chief Wahoo letter.

(Dear Tommy:
I will be home Sunday. I can hardly wait 'till then to see you. That's all for today!)

Finger painting.—See "Finger Painting" in Chapter III, **Fun with Hobbies.** Here is fun galore for the child and the adult.

Drawing animals.—Each player is given a slip of paper and a pencil. On this paper write at the top the name of an animal. **Turn** this under so that the name will not be seen by the others. **Then** try to draw a picture of that animal. When finished each person exhibits his work of art. After others have guessed at what it is turn back the flap so they can see what you have tried to draw.

Variation—Pass the slips to the right. Each player draws whatever is indicated on his slip.

This is a good one for the family group.

MARCHING FIGURES FOR CHILDREN

March down middle by twos. Separate into two equal groups by couples alternating in marching to the right and the left. Come down middle by fours. Separate, with first four going to the right and second four to the left. Meet at end of the room and come down by eights and halt.

Serpentine.—Line one winds around, going by line two and in back of it. As the last player in line one passes the first player in line two he takes his hand and they follow the winding march between the remaining lines. The last player in line two catches the hand of the first player in line three and so on until the entire group is marching. No line moves until the line ahead takes it along. Wind in and out and finally bring the whole group out in a large circle or square formation.

Criss-cross.—Two equal lines march down opposite sides of the floor. At the end of the floor each line turns sharply and marches diagonally to the center of the floor and on across to the opposite corner at the other end of the hall. The marchers alternate in crossing through one another's line. At far corner turn abruptly and march straight ahead to middle to meet other line and march down middle by twos.

Arbor march.—March down middle by twos. At far end of floor separate into single files, partners leaving one another. One line thus moves off to the right and another to the left. The two lines march around the hall. When they meet at the middle from which they started the first two marchers in each line take hold of hands, facing one another and forming an arch. The next two meet, go through the arch and immediately raise their arms to form an arch also. Each couple, in turn, follows suit until all are in line in one long arch. The first couple then lowers arms and passes under the arms of all the rest. Each couple follows, in turn, until the arch is dissolved.

Hour glass.—The marchers may come down the side single file or by couples. At the end corner of the room they turn sharply and march diagonally to center. Here they turn sharply again and march out diagonally to the far corner of the same side from which they started. At this point they turn sharply again and march straight across to the opposite side. Here they repeat marching to center and then on to the corner on that side. Then they go straight across to the point from which they started. Thus the group marks off a perfect hour glass by its maneuvers.

Variety.—The marchers walk, skip, hop, march stooped, skate, and trot as directed.

Walking.— (a) Stamp feet as they march.

(b) Clap hands as they march.

(c) *Dwarfs*—March in squatting position, making self as small as possible.

(d) *Giants*—March on tiptoes, hold hands high in air, reaching up as high as possible.

(e) *Dolls*—March stiff legged and with bodies rigid like dolls.

(f) *Rooster*—Walk like a rooster with knee lifted high and leg stretched forward.

(g) *Kangaroo*—Walk like a kangaroo, elbows close to body, forearm up chest high, and hands drooping. In this position move with short jumps.

(h) *Band major*—Strut with high knee action like a drum major.

FUN WITH SINGING GAMES

Looby Loo

1. Now we dance loo - by loo,   Now we dance loo - by

light,...... Now we dance loo - by loo,......

All on a Sat - ur - day night..... night.....

I put my right hand in,.... I take my right hand out,   I

give my hand a shake, shake, shake, And turn my-self a - bout. Oh,

2. Left hand.
3. Right hand.
4. Left foot.
5. Whole self.

Action—Players skip or walk with springing step counterclockwise on first verse.

On second verse they stand still and extend right hand toward center. They give it a vigorous shake.

On "whole self" they move toward center and back.

Between each verse they move around the circle singing, "Now we go Looby Loo."

The Farmer in the Dell

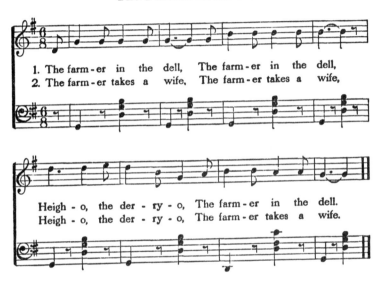

1. The farm-er in the dell, The farm-er in the dell,
2. The farm-er takes a wife, The farm-er takes a wife,

Heigh - o, the der - ry - o, The farm-er in the dell.
Heigh - o, the der - ry - o, The farm-er takes a wife.

1. The farmer in the dell, the farmer in the dell,
   Heigho! my dearie, Oh, the farmer in the dell.

2. The farmer takes a wife, etc.

3. The wife takes a child, etc.

4. The child takes a nurse, etc.

5. The dog takes a cat, etc.

6. The cat takes a rat, etc.

7. The rat takes the cheese, etc.

8. The cheese stands alone, etc.

There are many versions of this song. "The farmer in the well." "High-O-my cherry-O," and "High-O-merry-O" are some of the variations.

Action—Players join hands and walk around in a circle. The farmer stands at center. As the song indicates he chooses a partner for a wife. Each player, in turn, selects another to represent the "child," the "nurse," the "dog," the "cat," and the "cheese." During the last verse they all gather around the "cheese" and clap their hands.

The "cheese" becomes the "farmer" for the next game.

Did You Ever See a Lassie?

Action—Players join hands in a circle with one player at center. They circle around, singing the first two lines of the song. While they are doing this the center player demonstrates some movement which he means for all the players to imitate. As they reach the lines beginning "Do this way," the players stop circling, drop hands, and imitate the movements of the center player, while he goes through the action with them. The center player may decide to sweep, or row, or bat, or play tennis, or shoot a rifle, or skate, or prance like a horse, or bow, or skip, or swim, etc.

If a girl is at center the players sing "lassie"; if a boy, "laddie."

Pop Goes the Weasel, No. 1

Formation—Line up facing partners. Number off by threes. This will make three couples to a set. Each set should have some room between the sets.

Action—(1) Each Number One player turns toward the outside (casts off) and skips down back of his line and returns to place. Sixteen counts. This means both partners.

(2) Each Number One player joins hands with partner, facing one another. They skip sideways down and back. Sixteen counts.

(3) Couple Number One now join hands with player Number Two on the left. This makes a ring of three. They skip around in a circle for twelve counts. On "Pop goes the weasel" the two Number One players raise their arms and pass Number Two under their arms and back to place. They repeat this action with the other Number Two. Again they do the same action with both Number Threes. This brings them to the foot of their set. The new head couple begins over with the first figure.

After playing this game you will see the wisdom of having only six players in a set. It is rather vigorous.

Pop Goes the Weasel, No. 2

Formation—Circle of threes-abreast promenade counterclockwise, usually one boy and two girls. The player in the middle takes a position slightly in front of his two partners, taking their outside hands. These two partners then join their inside hands behind his back, thus:

All around the cobbler's bench,
The monkey chased the weasel,
The monkey thought 'twas all in fun,
Pop! goes the weasel!

A penny for a spool of thread,
A penny for a needle,
That's the way the money goes.
Pop! goes the weasel!

You may buy the baby clothes,
And I will buy the cradle,
That's the way the money goes.
Pop! goes the weasel!

Round and round the cobbler's bench,
The monkey chased the weasel,
The farmer kissed the cobbler's wife.
Pop! goes the weasel!

Action— (1) Players skip in promenade formation sixteen beats.

(2) On "Pop!" they stop and on "goes" they snap the center player under their raised hands to the next two players behind.

(3) Repeat from the beginning.

Miss Jennia Jones

"We've come to see Miss Jen - ni - a Jones,
Miss Jen - ni - a Jones, Miss Jen - ni - a Jones.
We've come to see Miss Jen - ni - a Jones,
And how is she to - day?"......

CHILDREN: We've come to see Miss Jennia Jones,
Miss Jennia Jones, Miss Jennia Jones,
We've come to see Miss Jennia Jones
And how is she today?

MOTHER: She's washing.

CHILDREN: We're very glad to hear of it,
To hear of it, to hear of it,
We're very glad to hear of it,
And how is she today?

MOTHER: She's starching.

CHILDREN: We're very glad to hear of it, etc.
And how is she today?

MOTHER: She's ironing.

CHILDREN: We're very glad, etc.
And how is she today?

MOTHER: She is ill.

CHILDREN: We're very sorry to hear of it, etc.
And how is she today?

MOTHER: She is dead.

CHILDREN: We're very sorry, etc.
May we come to the funeral?

MOTHER: You may come.

CHILDREN: We're very glad to hear of it, etc.
And may we come in red?

MOTHER: Red's for soldiers!

CHILDREN: We're very sorry to hear of it, etc.
And may we come in blue?

MOTHER: Blue's for sailors!

CHILDREN: We're very sorry, etc.
And may we come in yellow?

MOTHER: Yellow is for jealousy.

CHILDREN: We're very sorry, etc.
And may we come in pink?

MOTHER: Pink is for babies.

CHILDREN: We're very sorry, etc.
And may we come in white?

MOTHER: White is for weddings.

CHILDREN: We're very sorry, etc.
And may we come in black?

MOTHER: Black is for mourning.

Action

VERSE ONE: One child represents the mother. She stands with her skirts spread, hiding Miss Jennia, who kneels behind her.

The children form a straight line facing the mother. They march forward four steps and back four steps as they sing.

The mother announces "She is washing." She goes through the motions of washing as the group sings, "We're very glad to hear of it."

Next she dips clothes in starch. Next she irons. Then she looks troubled as she announces Jennia is ill. Next she pretends to wipe the tears away as she announces her death. Jennia stretches out at this point.

After the verse on mourning the children crowd around, pick up Jennia, carry her a short distance, and lay her flat on the ground. Then they sing:

"I dreamt I saw a ghost last night,
A ghost last night, a ghost last night,
I dreamt I saw a ghost last night,
Under the apple tree."

At this point Jennia gets up and chases the children. The first two she catches become the mother and daughter for the next game.

This is the way the writer played this game when a child back in Kentucky. Some versions have the mother singing her replies. Our group never did. The mother always spoke.

Oats, Peas, Beans

1. Oats, peas, beans, and bar - ley grow; Oats, peas,
2. First the farm - er sows his seed, Then he
3. Wait - ing for a part - - ner, Wait - ing

beans, and bar - ley grow, Can you or I or
stands and takes his ease, Stamps his feet and
for a part - - ner, Op'n the ring and

an - y - one know, How oats, peas, beans, and bar - ley grow?
claps his hands, And turns him round to view his lands.
choose one in, While we all gai - ly dance and sing.

4. Now you're married you must obey, etc.
   You must be true to all you say.

5. You must be loving, kind, and good, etc.
   And help your wife to chop the wood.

Action

VERSE ONE: One player at center. The rest join hands in the circle and walk around as they sing.

VERSE TWO: Stand in circle and imitate seed sowing. Stamp right foot and clap hands. Turn about and with backs to center shade eyes with the right hand as if peering into the distance.

VERSE THREE: Center player chooses a partner of the opposite sex. They join both hands and pull back, skipping around in place during the remainder of the verse. At same time the players in the ring skip around.

VERSE FOUR: The couple in the center kneels together as the others sing as they walk around the circle, hands joined.

VERSE FIVE: The group sings to the couple, pointing finger at them, and standing in place.
The farmer joins the ring while the chosen partner stays at center to begin the game again.

London Bridge

1. Lon-don Bridge is fall-ing down, fall-ing down, fall-ing down,
2. Build it up with i-ron bars, i-ron bars, i-ron bars,

Lon-don Bridge is fall-ing down, my fair la-dy.
Build it up with i-ron bars, my fair la-dy.

3. Iron bars will rust away, etc.
4. Build it up with pins and needles, etc.
5. Pins and needles rust and bend, etc.

6. Build it up with penny loaves, etc.

7. Penny loaves will tumble down, etc.

8. Build it up with bricks and mortar, etc.

9. Bricks and mortar will wash away, etc.

10. Build it up with gold and silver, etc.

11. Gold and silver will be stolen away, etc.

12. We will set a man to watch, etc.

13. Suppose the man should fall asleep, etc.

14. We will set a dog to bark, etc.

15. Here's a prisoner I have got, etc.

16. What's the prisoner done to you, etc.

17. Stole my watch and broke my chain, etc.

18. What'll you take to set him free, etc.

19. One hundred pounds to set him free, etc.

20. One hundred pounds we have not got, etc.

21. Then off to prison you must go, etc.

Action—Usually, as played in America, children use only one or at most two verses.

Two players hold their joined hands as high as they can, thus forming an arch. This represents the bridge. Each of these two players have previously secretly chosen some object he is supposed to represent—a rose or a lily, a pearl or a diamond, a gold crown or silver slippers. If they desire they may choose to be animals or birds—such as an elephant or a horse, a robin or a cardinal. The two players agree between them what they are to represent, but do not let the other players know.

The children march around in a circle and through the arch as they sing the song. On "my fair lady" the bridge comes down on some player. The two children forming the bridge whisper to the captive, "Which would you rather be, a lily or a rose?" The child makes his choice. Not until then does he know which of the two children is what. Perhaps, it would be well for the two players to take the captive aside so others may not hear. The player makes his choice and then is told to stand behind the one he has chosen. The game continues until each child has chosen. The game ends with a tug of war between the two teams. The two head players hold hands and pull as their teammates grasp one another about the waist and help.

Itiskit, Itaskit

I sent a letter to my love, I thought I put it in my glove,
But on the way I dropped it, I dropped it, I dropped it,
But on the way I dropped it.
And some of you have picked it up.
And put it in your pocket.

Itiskit, itaskit, a green and yellow basket,
I took a letter to my love, and on my way I lost it,
I lost it, I lost it.

This game is familiar under the name of "Drop the Handkerchief." All form in a circle, excepting one player. While they
sing the stanza given above, one person skips around the outside
of the ring and drops a handkerchief behind one of the players.
The persons in the ring are allowed to look behind them once after
each circuit which the handkerchief-dropper makes.

As soon as the person behind whom the handkerchief has been
dropped, discovers it, he picks it up and runs around the circle in
pursuit of the one who dropped it. If he succeeds in catching him,
the dropper must stand in the center of the ring, "the mush pot."

The second person then continues skipping around the circle

while the stanza is sung again. On the other hand, if the person behind whom the handkerchief is dropped does not discover it until after the dropper has come back to him, he goes in the "mush pot."

So the game goes on until all are in the "mush pot" excepting two players.

Sometimes a way is provided for an alert player to get out of the "mush pot." If he can snatch the handkerchief before the person behind whom it is dropped discovers it, he becomes "dropper," and the slow one takes his place in the "mush pot."

In a large circle two "droppers" may be used. In this case they would move around the circle in opposite directions.

Here We Go Round the Mulberry Bush

Here we go round the mul - berry bush, The mul - berry bush, the mul - berry bush; Here we go round the mul - berry bush, On a cold and frost - y morn - ing.

2. This is the way we wash our clothes,
   Wash our clothes, wash our clothes.
   This is the way we wash our clothes.
   So early Monday morning!

3. This is the way we iron our clothes,
   Iron our clothes, iron our clothes,
   This is the way we iron our clothes,
   So early Tuesday morning.

4. This is the way we scrub our floors, etc.
So early Wednesday morning.

5. This is the way we mend our clothes, etc.
So early Thursday morning.

6. This is the way we sweep our floors, etc.
So early Friday morning.

7. This is the way we bake our bread, etc.
So early Saturday morning.

8. This is the way we go to church, etc.
So early Sunday morning.

Action

VERSE ONE: Join hands in a circle and dance around as they sing.

VERSE TWO: Motions of washing clothes.

VERSE THREE: Motions of ironing.

VERSE FOUR: On knees scrubbing floor.

VERSE FIVE: Sewing.

VERSE SIX: Sweeping.

VERSE SEVEN: Kneading dough and putting loaf into the oven.

VERSE EIGHT: Slowly walk around circle.

Sometimes for Saturday they sing:

Thus we play when work is done, etc.
So early Saturday morning.

The action is for each child to frolic around as he pleases—he may skip, dance, play leap frog, etc.

King William

1. King William was King George's son,
   All around the race he'd run.
   He wore a star upon his breast.
   Choose the one that you love best.

2. Go choose to the east, go choose to the west
   Choose the one that you love best.
   If she's not here, go take her part,
   Choose another with all your heart.

3. Down on this carpet you must kneel,
   Sure as the grass grows in the field.
   Salute your bride and kiss her sweet,
   Sure as the grass grows under your feet.

The game shows evidences of English origin. There are different versions in various parts of the United States. This one was the one used in Kentucky in the writer's boyhood days. One version goes:

> "King William was King James' son,
> Who from a royal race did come.
> Upon his breast he wore a star,
> Like the points of the compass are."

Action—Players join hands in a circle. One boy stands at center. On the second verse he chooses a girl. They kneel together. On the third verse he bows to her, and kisses her hand. They take their places in the circle. The game continues with a new King William.

On the Bridge at Avignon (French)
(Sur Le Pont D'Avignon)

1. On the bridge at A - vi - gnon, They are danc - ing,
1. Sur le pont d'A - vi - gnon, L'on y dan - se,

they are danc - ing, On the bridge at A - vi - gnon,
l'on y dan - se, Sur le pont d' A - vi - gnon,

FINE

They are danc - ing in a ring. The gen - tle - men go
L'on y dan - se tout en rond. Le beaux mes - sieurs font

D. C.

this way, And then a - gain this way.
comm' - ça, Et puis en - core comm' - ça.

Words and action—

1. The gentlemen go this way (Le beaux messieurs comm'-ca) —
Bow.

2. The ladies fair go this way (Les belles dames font comm'-ca) — Curtsy.

3. The soldiers brave, etc. (Les braves, soldatz, etc.) —Salute.

4. The organ man, etc. (Le joeur d'orgue, etc.) —Turn handle.

5. The boys and girls, etc. (Les garcons et filles, etc.) —Dance in ring.

FUN WITH STORYTELLING

All of the world, old and young alike, respond to a good story. Here is an art as old as the human race. Sagamen, rhapsodists, bards, and minstrels have handed down much of our literature.

To the child stories are important. They satisfy the craving of his imagination. They serve to introduce him to the world in which he lives. They are his first introduction to literature. Thus good stories are an essential part of his development.

Pointers for the Storyteller

1. He should have a real enthusiasm for the stories he tells.

2. He should tell the story with appreciation for its dramatic qualities.

3. He should build the story to its proper climax.

4. He should not point out the moral of the story. A good story is its own excuse for being told. The storyteller would do well to remember Henry Van Dyke's prayer: "Grant, Lord, that I may never tag a moral to a tale, or tell a story without a meaning."

The Part of the Child in Storytelling

Angela Keys in *Stories and Storytelling* (D. Appleton-Century) list the following as the part of the child in storytelling: listening, being silent, commenting, asking questions, joining in the telling, retelling, telling other stories, inventing stories, playing the stories, and growing by the story.

Using Poetry

The child makes a natural response to rhythm. As soon as he can understand anything he begins to repeat the nursery rhymes. The five-year-old will delight in the poems of James Whitcomb Riley, particularly those about little boys and girls, and those about animals. Riley's famous "Bear Story," "Out to Old Aunt Mary's," and "Howdy, Mr. Hoptoad," are particularly popular. Almost invariably, as we came to the refrain in this latter poem, "Howdy, Mr. Hoptoad, Howdy Do!" the five-year-old joined in with gusto, his eyes sparkling with delight. The hoptoad became a friend ever thereafter.

A. A. Milne's poems and stories also get a good response. "James, James, Morrison, Morrison, Weatherby, George Dupree," who took good care of his mother though he was only three," is a favorite. How the five- or six-year-old chuckles at the presumption of the three-year-old James!

Try some good poetry on the child. It needs to be part of his fun heritage.

A List of Stories

For children one to three years of age:

This Little Pig Went to Market.
The Three Bears.
The Three Pigs.
The House That Jack Built.
Rumpelstilzkin.
Snow White and Rose Red.
Mother Goose.
Fairy Stories.

For children three to six years of age:

Stories about animals, birds, flowers.
Stories of home and play.
Fairy Stories.
Peter Rabbit.
Pinnochio.
Peter Pan.

Just So Stories—"The Elephant Child," "How the Whale Got His Throat," "The Cat that Walked by Himself," etc.
Alice in Wonderland.
Little Black Sambo.

For children six to nine years of age:

Fairy Stories.
Stories of Great Men—Washington, Lincoln, Livingstone.
The Ugly Duckling.
The Gingerbread Boy.

Stories on Inventions, Industries, etc.
Aladdin and His Wonderful Lamp.

For children nine to twelve years of age:

The Story of Midas.
The Great Stone Face.
Ruskin's "King of the Golden River."
Robin Hood.

Thirteen to seventeen:

Stories of Romance, Adventure, Altruism.
King Arthur and the Knights of the Round Table.
Stories of "Beowulf," Siegfrid.
Homer's "Iliad" and "Odyssey."

Play stories that carry many a chuckle.—"The Little Red Hen," "Chicken Little," "The Fox without a Tail," "Epaminondas," "Why the Bear Has a Stumpy Tail," "The Elephant Child," "Billy Goats Gruff," "Puss in Boots," "Uncle Remus Stories" (especially the famous "Tar Baby"), "Teeny Tiny Woman," "East of the Sun and West of the Moon," "Raggedy Ann and Raggedy Andy."

Fun Acting Out Stories

The child's unspoiled imagination makes story dramatizations unforgettable experiences. With the nursery and kindergarten children everybody can be everything in the story. When the elephant comes on the scene every child can walk across the room as the elephant. They can trot as horses. They can droop as flowers. They can be "Ferdinand" smelling the flowers, or sitting on the bumblebee, or raging about after that experience.

In the home the child may be allowed to select the story to be dramatized. He may even select the cast. He should be allowed, at least, to make suggestions regarding the story, the cast, and the setting.

Most any good story will lend itself to simple play-acting. A few that are particularly good are the following: "The Three Bears," "The Three Pigs," "Little Black Sambo," "Dick Whittington and His Cat," "The Hare and the Tortoise," "Nicodemus and His New Shoes," "Little Red Riding Hood," "The Fox and the Grapes," "Tar Baby," and "Hansel and Gretel."

For the informal dramatization of Bible stories see Elizabeth Miller's book, *Dramatization of Bible Stories* (Chicago University Press).

STORYTELLING HELPS

For additional materials see bibliography at end of this book.

BRYANT, SARA CONE. *Best Stories to Tell to Children.* Houghton-Mifflin.

HOLBROOK, FLORENCE. *Book of Nature Myths.* Houghton-Mifflin.

IRVING, WASHINGTON. *The Legend of Sleepy Hollow.* W. R. Scott.

——. *Rip Van Winkle.* McKay.

MELCHER, MARGUERITE FELLOWS. *Off Stage.* A book on how to make plays from books you read for ages 8-12. Knopf.

SETON, ERNEST THOMPSON. *Famous Animals.* Tudor.

——. *Wild Animals I Have Known.* Grosset.

WRIGHT, LOUISE. *Story Plays.* One hundred story plays classified and described. A. S. Barnes.

SOME STORIES

How the Sun, Moon, and Stars Got into the Sky

Long, long ago the Indians had no fire and no light. They suffered much during the cold of winter and they had to eat their food raw. They also had to live in darkness because there was no light.

There was no sun, moon, and stars in the sky. A great chief kept them locked up in a box. He took great pride in the thought that he alone had light.

This great chief had a beautiful daughter of whom he also was proud. She was much beloved by all of the Indians of the tribe.

In those days the raven had the powers of magic. He was a great friend of the Indians and wondered how he might make life more comfortable for them.

One day, as he saw the daughter of the chief come down to the brook for a drink, he had an idea. He would change himself into a pine needle on a tree that spread out over the brook.

So the next time the maiden came to drink he dropped into the brook and was swallowed by her.

As time went on he was born to her as a son. The old chief was delighted and as the boy grew his grandfather became devoted to him. Anything he wanted he could have.

So one day he asked the old chief for the box containing the stars. Reluctantly the old chief gave it to him. The child played for a while by rolling the box around. Then he released the stars and flung them into the sky.

The Indians were delighted. This was some light, though not enough.

After a few days the child asked for the box containing the moon. The chief demurred but by insistence the boy got what he wanted.

Again, after playing awhile with the box, the boy released the moon and flung it into the sky.

The tribesmen were overjoyed. But still there was not light enough. And anyway, the moon disappeared for long periods.

So, finally the child asked for the box with the sun. "No," said the old chief, "I cannot give you that." But the boy wept and pleaded. The old chief could not withstand his tears and finally gave it over to him.

As soon as he had a chance the child released the sun and cast it into the sky.

The joy of the Indians knew no bounds. Here was light enough and heat as well. So they ordered a feast of the sun and all the Indians celebrated it with great jubilation.

And the old chief was happy. He had not known the sun, moon, and stars could mean so much for the comfort and happiness of his people. And for the first time he, himself, enjoyed them.

How Old Man Made the Races

(A Cree Indian Story)

Once upon a time Old Man lived all alone, except for the animals. Their companionship was something, but it was not satisfying. So Old Man was lonesome and he longed for company. So he said, "I'll make man."

He built a great big earth oven and built a fire in it. Then he took some clay and molded it into the form of a man. He put this into the oven. Directly he took it out, but it did not satisfy him. It was not done. It had not stayed in long enough. This clay man became father of all of the white races.

Again the Great One made a clay man and put it into the oven. This time when he took it out it was burned black. It had stayed too long. This clay man became father of the black races.

With great care he formed a third man of clay and put it into the oven. This time he watched it carefully and took it out just when it had baked to a perfect brown. It was just right.

This third clay man became the father of the Red Man, or Indian.

The Fable of the Scorpion

(An African Story)

Since the scorpion hides its head it seems to have no face. Do you know why he has no face?

In the beginning of time God created all of the animals. The last thing he did was to give each of them a head and face.

One day it was appointed that all of the animals should report at a certain spot, where the distribution of heads was to be made. All of the animals started out on the journey.

But the scorpion was slower than the others, so as he labored along the road the other animals passed him. When he was still not more than halfway he met the screech owl coming back. And what a sight he was! His face looked like it had been shoved in and not pulled out again.

The scorpion stopped him and looked at him in amazement.

"Hello," greeted the screech owl, "You had better hurry or you'll get there too late to get a face."

"Well, what is that you've got on your shoulders?" asked the scorpion, looking puzzled.

"Oh, that's my head and face. Isn't it handsome?" said the screech owl.

"Goodness gracious!" exclaimed the scorpion. "Is that what they're giving out?"

"Why, yes!" responded the screech owl. "Everyone gets one."

"Well, excuse me," said the scorpion. "I don't believe I want one and I'm not going."

The Camel and the Jackal

(A Hindu Story)

In the long ago when animals could talk there was a camel and a jackal who were good friends.

Now the camel loved sugar cane and the jackal dearly loved crabs.

Just across the river was a fine cane field and near by there were lots of crabs and other delicacies that tickled the palate of the jackal.

"I cannot swim," said the jackal, "but how about taking me across the river on your back. There's plenty of juicy sugar cane over there."

So the camel let the jackal hop on his back and away they went.

The jackal jumped off as soon as they were across and fell to on the crabs. He was a fast eater and he had stuffed himself with crabs and fish before the camel could get a good start on the sugar cane.

Then he began jumping and running about yelping and making a terrible racket.

Some men in the village near by heard the noise and sounded the alarm. So many men came running. They couldn't catch the jackal but they did catch the camel and they beat him unmercifully.

When the men had left the jackal ran up to the camel and said, "Let us go home."

"I guess we had better," groaned the camel. "Climb up on my back and let us start."

When they had gotten where the water was deep the camel said, "Why did you make such a racket before I had hardly gotten a mouthful of sugar cane?"

"Oh," answered the jackal, "that's just an old habit of mine. I always sing after I have been well fed."

The water was getting deeper and deeper and in another step the camel would be compelled to swim.

"You know," said the camel, "I fell like taking a roll."

"Oh, don't do that," exclaimed the jackal. "You know I can't swim."

"Well, I guess I'll roll," again said the camel.

"Please don't!" begged the jackal. "Why in the world would you want to roll."

"Well, you see," answered the camel, "It is just an old habit of mine. I always like to roll after dinner."

And roll he did, and you can guess what happened to the jackal. Some say he drowned. Others say the camel finally pulled him out and left him exhausted on the shore, coughing up water, and trying hard to get his breath.

Why Dogs and Cats Hate Each Other

(Chinese)

Once upon a time a Chinese dog and a Chinese cat lived with an old Chinese man and woman. The old man and woman had a magic wishing ring which meant everything to them. But the ring had been stolen by robbers and they were very sad.

It seems the robbers had gone across the river in a boat, and they were in hiding on the other side. So the cat said to the dog, "I cannot swim, but if you will carry me across the river on your back, maybe we can find the robbers and get the ring back."

At that time the dog and cat were good friends. Therefore the dog answered, "Why certainly. By all means we must get the ring back to our heartbroken masters." So he took the cat on his back and swam across.

They soon found where the robbers were in hiding. Then they discovered that they had hidden the ring in a wooden chest. So the cat caught a mouse and the mouse gnawed a hole in the chest so the cat could bring out the ring. Then the dog took the cat on his back and swam back across the river.

They started for home but the cat left the dog and climbed over the roofs of houses. The dog had to go around through the streets and alleys, because dogs cannot climb, you know.

Therefore the cat reached home first with the ring. He never told what part the dog had in its recovery. The old Chinese man and woman were delighted. They petted and patted the cat and gave her cream to drink.

When the dog got home, they scolded him for being away so long and for being wet and muddy. The old woman took the broom to him.

So the dog chased the cat up a tree. And ever since dogs and cats have been enemies.

The Bell Maker

(Chinese)

In the long ago a certain province in China was famous for its bells. Now the average Chinese bell is not like ours in that it is struck with a gong rather than by a swinging clapper. The fame of the bells of this province was due to the skill of one particular bell maker. He even achieved official distinction because of the richness of a tone sounded by the gongs from the metals he was able to produce from his molds.

One day the Ruler of the Province summoned the bell maker to his court. "Make me," he said, "a bell that shall have in its tones the mellowness of gold, the music of silver, and the depth and resonance of brass. (These qualities vary in different versions.) "Furthermore," he added, "the sound must be heard for at least three miles."

The bell maker went home sad at heart for he feared the could never fulfil this command. Nevertheless he set his men to work and finally the day of the test came. The Ruler of the Province was there with his retinue. The molten metal poured through the runway into the mold and all awaited the final proof when the gong should sound forth the magic tones. None in the great crowd watched more anxiously than Kong Gay, the bell maker's lovely young daughter. But it was as the bell maker had feared. His efforts were in vain for this was no magic bell with the mellowness of gold and the music of silver and the resonance of brass.

The ruler was angry and declared that he had been made to "lose face" before the whole world for he had boasted of the skill of one who had proved himself unworthy. The bell maker plead for another chance and finally his plea was granted.

Alas, the second trial was no better than the first. This time the Ruler was so infuriated that he threatened to execute such an inferior artisan. Finally, however, he was persuaded to grant one more trial but if that should fail, the bell maker's life should be the forfeit.

Poor little Kong Gay realized the hopelessness of her father's case. Twice he had tried and twice he had failed. Something must be done or he would lose his life. Under cover of night she slipped away to consult a soothsayer. Perhaps he could help her to find some way to save her father.

When the fortuneteller heard her story, he was silent for awhile, then said: "The only thing which will make a bell with such a miraculous tone is for human flesh to be molded in the metal of it, and this would mean the sacrifice of a life to make it possible." Kong Gay returned home without telling anyone what she had heard.

The morning of the great day arrived when the last run of molten metal was to be poured from the immense cauldron. Above this runway a platform had been constructed and on it stood the bell maker, his daughter, Kong Gay, her Amah, and other attendants.

As the red hot molten liquid came streaming beneath them, Kong Gay suddenly cried out, "For you, my father," and leaped downward into the fiery stream. As she sprang, the Amah screamed and tried to hold her, but all she caught in her hand was a tiny silken shoe.

The father in his horror tried to leap after her and only the combined efforts of his attendants restrained him from plunging off the platform.

The metal cooled and a silent audience waited the sound of the great gong. Suddenly it rang forth, sounding out across the miles a magic tone which had in it all the mellowness of gold, all the musical peals of silver, and all the strength and resonance of brass. But that was not all! There was a distinct sound of a plaintive voice as if calling "Kong-g- Gay-y-y! Hai Yai!"

"Ah!" the listeners cried. "It is Kong Gay. She is calling for her slipper. It is Kong Gay, calling for her little silken shoe."

And today if you go to that province and to that city you will hear the great bell. The children on the streets stop their playing as it sounds forth at noon. "Listen," they will tell you. "Listen to Kong Gay. She is calling for her little silken shoe."

Note: Mrs. Sadie Wilson Tillman, former missionary to China, uses this version of this famous Chinese story. She writes: "This is one of the traditions of Chinese folk lore—one of the many illustrative of filial piety. I have heard it in varied forms. Sometimes it is located in Soochow, and at other times in an interior city and province. The official status of the characters vary, too, in different versions."

Clappertown

(A play story)

In Clappertown everyone claps when the words "Doctor" and "Drake" are mentioned. If they are mentioned together they clap twice. They are very careful not to clap at any other time.

The storyteller will tell a story about "The Duck's Lament" or "The Duck's Distress," or something of the sort, making the story up as he goes along.

The players must clap at the right place, and refrain from clapping at all other times on penalty of paying a forfeit.

Perhaps the story may run like this:

Once upon a time a duck took a cold, or what he thought was a cold. "I must go to a doctor" (clap once), said he. "What doctor" (clap once) "shall it be?" "Try Doctor Drake" (clap twice) advised a friend. So he went to Doctor Drake (clap twice).

The doctor (clap once) looked him over carefully, made him say "ah" while he looked down his throat, thumped his chest, looked stern, and then said, "Hmm! You've got the epizoodic."

"The what?" said the duck.

"The epizoodic, no more nor less," answered Doctor Drake (clap twice).

This made the duck angry. "What a doctor!" (clap once) he stormed. "I'll go to a quack doctor" (clap once) "and he will fix me as good as new."

"Suit yourself," said Doctor Drake (clap twice).

So the duck went to see a quack doctor (clap once). "Hmm! Looks like the epizoodic," said the quack doctor (clap once).

"The what?" said the duck.

"The epizoodic, no more and no less," replied the quack doctor (clap once).

"Aw, go chase yourself," said the duck. "I'll go to another doctor" (clap once).

So he went to a famous eye, ear, and nose specialist. This doctor (clap once) looked serious, put an electric light bulb on his forehead, made the duck open his mouth, peered down into it, shook his head, and said, "Hmm! It looks like you have the epizoodic."

"The what?" said the duck.

"The epizoodic, no more and no less," answered the doctor (clap once).

"What will I do?" said the duck.

"There's only one doctor" (clap once), "that can cure that," answered the doctor (clap once).

"And who is that?" asked the duck.

"Doctor Drake" (clap twice). "Yes, Doctor Drake" (clap twice) "is the great epizoodic specialist. You'd better go to Doctor Drake" (clap twice).

So the duck hurried to Doctor Drake (clap twice) and Doctor Drake (clap twice) cured him.

CHAPTER XIX
FUN AS A HOSTESS

Chapter XIX

FUN AS A HOSTESS *

The beauty of the house is order;
The blessing of the house is contentment;
The glory of the house is hospitality;
The crown of the house is godliness.
—UNKNOWN

Believe it or not, being a hostess *can* be fun. It all depends upon the hostess. If she is all that is implied in the term, *"charming hostess,"* it *will* be fun.

WHAT IS A "CHARMING HOSTESS"?

A "charming hostess" is marked by the following qualities: modesty, sincerity, poise, sympathy, tact, perfect manners, ingenuity, and good taste.

Modesty—She is not afflicted with "I" trouble. All that she does is done with becoming modesty.

Sincerity—She is genuine. There is no veneer. When she invites people into her home it is because she wants them. She isn't trying to "keep up with the Joneses." She does not pretend.

Washington Irving put it correctly when he said: "There is an emanation from the heart of genuine hospitality, which cannot be described, but is immediately felt and puts the stranger at his ease."

Poise—She remains calm under every circumstance. The fact that company is coming does not get her all a-jitter. She plans well ahead and then lets things take their normal course.

Sympathy—She is concerned for the welfare of her family and for her servants.

Tact—She uses good judgment in inviting her guests. If Mrs. A. and Mrs. B, both good friends of hers, have certain incompatabilities that make it a risk to invite them in the same group, she keeps that in mind. She knows how to make the timid forget to be self-conscious. She fits people into situations that suit them.

---

* The material in every chapter of this book will be helpful to the hostess.

(863)

Perfect manners—She knows the correct things to do on all occasions and she does them with never failing courtesy.

Ingenuity—She cultivates ingenuity. That is, she is always on the alert to capture clever ideas that will bring joy to her friends. She uses intelligence in planning social events in her home. If she does not have a new idea she searches until she finds one.

Good taste—Coarseness, vulgarity, and cheapness find no place in her home. The activities, the food, and the decorations all show evidences of good taste.

Inviting Guests

Formal invitations would read as follows:

MR. AND MRS. THOMAS JONES

REQUEST THE PLEASURE OF YOUR COMPANY

FOR DINNER, 6 P.M., OCTOBER 20.

R.S.V.P.

MR. AND MRS. THOMAS JONES

INVITE

MR. AND MRS. HARVEY COOK

TO A DINNER PARTY, OCTOBER 20,

6 P.M.

KINDLY SEND REPLY TO A7 STERLING COURT

MR. AND MRS. THOMAS JONES

AT HOME

THURSDAY EVENING, DECEMBER 6

6-11 P.M

THE FAVOR OF AN ANSWER IS REQUESTED

In some cases invitations may be issued over the phone.

In inviting guests make it clear when you expect guests to arrive.

For informal affairs the hostess may work out clever devices for inviting friends to the home. Seasonal symbols may be used—bunnies, sprigs of holly, turkeys, hearts, etc.

On one invitation a stick of chewing gum was held in place by a bit of glue or a clamp. Then there was this rhyme:

> Wrigley's, Dentine, or Beechnut,
> No matter what the kind,
> *Wax* warm with an acceptance,
> Don't let it slip your mind.
> We're inviting you to visit
> Our home in Hilltop Court,
> Please *choose* (chews) to come and see us.
> By gum! What's your report?
> 8-11 P.M.   MRS. AND MRS. EARL BROWN
>   3 Hilltop Court

FORMAL DINNERS

Emily Post warns that no novice as a hostess should begin her social career with a formal dinner any more than an inexperienced swimmer should try a three-mile swim in a rough sea. Needless to say all plans should be made with the greatest of care, any who are to assist being carefully instructed as to procedures.

INFORMAL DINNERS

A Do-it-yourself dinner.—When the guests arrived they were given assignments. "Slice the bread," "butter the rolls," "serve the salad," "**pour** the coffee" or "fix the ice tea," "serve the plates," "fix the ice water and pour it," "arrange the table," etc.

One husband who had to bring a five-year-old boy, was given the assignment of "Chief Entertainer," and, my, was he kept busy!

Each guest had a job, and what a good time they had! The whole affair was so carefully planned that there was not the slightest confusion.

Buffet style.—The food is arranged on a large table "smorgasbord" style. Guests walk around and help themselves. Then they find a comfortable seat out on the porch, or in the living room, and go to it.

Picnic style.—The party is held in the yard or out at the park. Everything is served picnic style. See "Picnic Plans" in Chapter X, Fun Outdoors.

Family style dinner.—There is an utter lack of formality. The company becomes part of the family. Everyone relaxes. That's when a meal can be fun! Memory recalls several graduate students in a large university visiting in a home where they felt very much at home. What a grand time they had bringing a book of etiquette to the table, reading aloud what it had to say, and then doing just the opposite!

ANNOUNCEMENTS AND SHOWERS

(See also Chapter XVII, Fun with Seasonal Parties, especially the parties for June.)

A stunt party.—One girl announced her engagement in a clever way. She invited a dozen or so of her intimate friends to a "Stunt Party." Each one was requested to come prepared to do some brief stunt. A sister had worked up a clever monologue in rhyme which introduced the news of the engagement. She came at the close of the program and proved a fitting climax to a grand evening of fellowship.

Clever announcement plans—(1) In miniature suitcases—"A case worth investigating."

(2) In match boxes—"A match" has been made—announcing the engagement of ————————.

(3) Nut shells—"In a nut shell, ———— and ———— are engaged to be married."

(4) Daisies—"Daisies sometimes tell"—announcement of engagement.

(5) *Planter's prospects*—

If I plant a woman's foot what flower will come up? Lady's slipper.

If I plant a boat what will come up? Leeks.

If I plant a cow what will come up? Milkweed or cowslip.

If I plant an infant what will come up? Baby's breath.

If I plant a menagerie what birds, beasts, or reptiles will come up? Adder's tongue, dandelion, snakeroot, wolf's bane, foxglove, pussy willow, larkspur, ragged robin.

If I plant a bee what will come up? Honeysuckle.

If I plant a history what will come up? Dates.

If I plant a lively boy what will come up? Johnny-jump-up.

If I plant a theologian what will come up? Jack-in-the-pulpit.

If I plant an orange tree what will come up? Orange blossoms.

Just put the last four together and you will understand that we are announcing the engagement of —— to ——.

WEDDING ANNIVERSARIES

First year—Paper wedding.—The "Newsstand Party" would give some ideas for this occasion.

Second year—Cotton wedding.—Use cotton string in manner similar to the suggestion made in "The Cobweb Party." A "King Cotton Festival" could be worked out. Cotton snowballs. Cotton boll invitations.

Third year—Leather wedding.—Try some of the Quizzes in Chapter X and hang leather medals on the smart ones.

Fifth year—Wooden wedding.—See "Tree Picnic" and tree stunts and games for ideas for entertainment.

Tenth year—Tin wedding.—Well, "Spin the Plate" could be done at this one. A kitchen shower would be appropriate.

Fifteenth year—Crystal wedding.—The various marble games could be played at this one—Chinese checkers, wari, gomoku, etc. An amateur fortuneteller might do some crystal ball gazing and tell futures.

Twentieth year—China wedding.—Chinese decorations. Chinese stories. A play done Chinese fashion—sans stage setting with one person designated as "the chorus" to explain the setting and action. Chow mein.

Twenty-fifth year—Silver wedding.—A "Twenty-five Years Ago Party" with displays of books and songs popular twenty-five years ago. Interesting photographs of that period. Things of twenty-five years ago we miss.

Fiftieth year—Golden wedding.—

A Married Couple's Party

Only married people were invited to this party. The announcement informed Mrs. John Doe that she was invited to a husbands and wives social. "Bring your matrimonial exhibit along with you. Tell him this is not formal."

Some of the features of the party were the following:

(1) The ladies of the party got together and worked out suggestions on "How to manage a husband." At the same time the men were preparing a list of suggestions on "How to manage a wife." The assignments may be reversed. At the end of fifteen or twenty minutes each group read its suggestions.

(2) Progressive anagrams were played.

(3) Dramatizations. Familiar domestic situations were dramatized by groups of two to six persons, depending on the size of the crowd. "What to do when the biscuits burn," "How to act when hubby's late for dinner," and "The first domestic quarrel" are suggestions for this dramatic feature.

Folk games may be played and old songs enjoyed.

Seating Guests at the Table

(1) One hostess hit upon the plan of using a nursery rhyme to seat guests. Each guest got a portion of the rhyme. As they stood near the table in the dining room, the hostess took her place and read, "Old King Cole was." A guest read "A merry old soul" and took the place to the right of the hostess. Then followed each in turn until all were located at the table. At this point they all sat down and the dinner began.

(2) Guests are given conundrums. The answers are at the table. Each finds his answer and is seated.

(3) Guests find place cards with their names. On each place card is a rhyme about the particular person.

(4) The place cards are written in the form of conundrums. Thus, "a traveling necessity and a meadow" was Bagley (Bag-lea). These may be done in rhyme. Guests have to locate themselves.

(5) Guests may be required to match hearts, hatchets, rabbits, or something else of the sort, suitable to the season or occasion.

(6) Guests are given one line of a nursery rhyme before going into the dining room. They find the completed quotations at their places at the table.

(7) Guests draw numbers. Find duplicate numbers at the table and be seated.

(8) Guests draw pictures of birds or animals from a box and find miniature animals at each place at the table.

(9) Guests draw circus assignments. The clown hunts the place at the table where there is a clown; the lion or menagerie finds the place appropriately marked, etc. Later on in the evening an impromptu circus may be a part of the evening's fun. See 'The Great Grinmore Circus Party" and "Clown Party" for suggestions.

(10) For a Christmas dinner guests could be given cards on which are written the names of various toys. Find the place at the table where these toys or their miniatures are.

(11) One hostess had the guests draw typewritten slips containing a tell-tale cue to some nursery rhyme. The person who drew "sat on a wall" looked until he found a Humpty Dumpty place card. "Lost her sheep" looked for "Little Bo Peep." And so each guest found his place at the table.

Fun with Conversation

Some years ago Joseph Lee stood before a National Recreation Congress and made the statement that the art of conversation was a lost art. Any hostess who can stimulate and make easy the practice of this art is rendering a distinct service to her guests.

Conversation can be fun—fun that will bring more than temporary satisfactions, if the talkers have some interests and ideas and a willingness to share them.

One does not have to be a high-brow to be a good conversationalist. Briefly here are a few rules that govern the art of conversation.

(1) A good conversationalist is a good listener. He really listens to what the other fellow is saying and weighs what he says. He is not thinking all the time the other fellow is talking of what he, himself, will say next.

(2) He has interests and ideas. He knows what is going on in the world because he reads, observes, and listens.

(3) He knows that there are times when "silence is golden," and that a good conversationalist is not a chatterbox.

Plans for Encouraging Conversation

Fireside chats.—One minister invites young people to the parsonage after the Sunday evening service for an informal chat. The young people suggest questions, problems, and subjects for discussion and the group goes to it in the most informal way.

Talk fest.—How about a hostess inviting a few friends to a "Talk Fest." She may suggest that they come prepared to present as a subject for conversation their pet peeve, or their favorite dish, or book, or poet, or hobby, or song, etc., or the best magazine article of the month according to their judgment. No speeches, no presider, no debate! Just a good time talking about things of common and uncommon interest!

Humorous stimulators—

(1) Progressive conversation. Pair off the group. Announce subjects for conversation. Allow one or two minutes per subject. Then shift to a new partner and discuss another subject. This may continue as long as desired.

(2) Concentric circles. March to music. When music stops face a partner and converse on an announced subject.

(3) Guests have names of famous people pinned on their backs. Each guest must find out who he is. Only two questions may be asked of each person. "What made him (her) famous?" "Is it ——?" The person asked must pantomime what made the particular character famous. For instance, for George Washington the cherry tree is chopped down. For Paul Revere, there is the midnight ride. Betty Ross makes a flag. See "The Dummy Line" in the chapter on "Fun with Icebreakers."

(4) Capitalize on some such wisecracking fad as the "Confucius say" stuff to center attention on some of the things Confucius really did say. Let them get a few "Confucius say" wisecracks off of their chests. There are really some good ones, such as the following:

"Confucius say 'The man who shaves swiftly loses face.' "
"Confucius say 'The man who sits down on a tack is better off.' "
"Confucius say 'Pay more for your stockings and get a longer run for your money.' "

After a few of these discuss some of the things that Confucius really did say.

Brain teasers.—Use brain teasers as stimulators. See the brain teasers in Chapter I, Home Fun. It is likely that your guests will suggest others. Here are a few good ones:

Railroad crew.—A railroad train had a crew of three, and three passengers, traveling between Chicago and New York. The train crew is made up of an engineer, fireman, and a guard. Their names are Smith, Jones, and Robinson, but not necessarily in that order.

The passengers are Smith, Jones, and Robinson but will be referred to as Mr. Smith, Mr. Jones, and Mr. Robinson.

Mr. Robinson lives in New York, Mr. Jones' annual salary is $5,000.00. The guard lives halfway between New York and Chicago and his namesake lives in Chicago. The guard's closest neighbor is one of the passengers and his annual salary is exactly three times that of the guard.

Smith beat the fireman at billards.

The problem is: What is the name of the engineer?

Answer—The guard could not have been named Robinson, for Mr. Robinson lives in New York. Since his "closest neighbor" is one of the passengers that means he could not be located in either Chicago or New York. He is an equal distance from both of these. It is likely that Mr. Jones' annual salary of $5,000.00 could not be exactly three times that of the guard since a third of $5,000.00 is an uneven fraction, and it is not likely that the guard's salary could be $1,666.66⅔. That means Mr. Jones must have lived in Chicago. That would make the guard's name Jones.

Smith beat the fireman at billards. Therefore the fireman's name could not be Smith. If the guard's name is Jones, then the fireman's name must be Robinson.

By elimination that makes the engineer's name Smith.

Indians and white men.—Three Indians and three white men traveling come to a river which they must cross. There is no bridge and the river is too deep to wade and too wide to swim. In looking around they find a boat that will carry only two people. In what manner can these six persons transport themselves across the river so that there is always an equal number of whites and Indians, or more whites than Indians on the same side? *Note:* To have the Indians outnumber the whites at any time would be fatal to the white men. Use three boys and three girls to represent Indians and white men. Mark lines on floor or ground to represent river.

Answer—Two Indians go over and one returns with the boat and takes the third Indian over. The Indian again returns with the boat and two white men go over; one Indian and one white man return in the boat and the two white men go over. This leaves three white men and one Indian on one side and two Indians on the other. The one Indian goes over and returns with one of his comrades and then goes back after the other and last one.

Fox, goose, and corn.—A fox, a goose, and some corn are on one side of a river with their owner; the boat on the river will carry only the owner and one of his possessions at a time. If he takes the fox, the goose will eat the corn; if he takes the corn, the fox will eat the goose. How can he get them across without losing any of them? Use boys and girls to represent the farmer, the fox, the goose, and the corn.

Answer—He takes the goose over, goes back and takes the fox over. He then brings the goose back with him and leaves it while he takes the corn over. He returns for the goose.

The Ideal Hostess

She gleans how long you wish to stay;
She lets you go without delay.

—GRENVILLE KLEISER

The Ideal Guest

She is not difficult to please;
She can be silent as the trees;
She shuns all ostentatious show;
She knows exactly when to go.

—GRENVILLE KLEISER

CHAPTER XX
FUN WITH MAGIC

FUN WITH MAGIC

By E. L. Crump

HINTS TO THOSE WHO WOULD HAVE FUN WITH MAGIC

The secret of success in magic is, of course, keeping the spectators from knowing how the trick is done. In order to do this the performer must practice each trick thoroughly many times before a mirror in order to perfect his technique. He must also learn how to evade the questions of his friends as to how the tricks are done. For just as soon as he tells one friend the news will spread until everyone knows the secret of the trick and immediately it will cease to be fun to the crowd. Several rules might be set down for the magician to follow strictly:

(1) Practice before a mirror each trick until it becomes natural and easy.

(2) Never repeat a trick.

(3) Never tell the audience what you intend to do.

(4) Never tell how you did a trick.

(5) Practice misdirection with your eyes. Your eyes should always look where you want the audience to look regardless of what your hands are doing.

(6) When something goes wrong, laugh and turn it into a joke, and the audience will laugh with you instead of at you.

(7) Work up some interesting patter to go with your tricks as it not only helps in the misdirection but adds to the interest of the effect.

If you wish to keep up with current magic it would be well to subscribe to some of the magic magazines of note. Four of the best are as follows:

Genii, 705 South Hudson, Pasadena, California.

The Sphinx, Sphinx Publishing Corporation, 130 West 42nd Street, New York.

The Tops, Abbott's Magic Novelty Company, Colon, Michigan.

The Dragon, Vernon, East Lux, Mount Morris, Illinois.

It is impossible to cover much of the field of magic in a work of this nature. The reader, if interested, should secure some of the many fine books on magic which are available today. The following are suggested:

200 Tricks You Can Do and *200 More Tricks You Can Do,* by Howard Thurston.

How's Tricks, by Gerald Lynton Kaufman.

Greater Magic, by John Northern Hilliard.

Modern Magic, by Professor Hoffman.

Magicians Tricks, How They Are Done, by Henry Hatton and Adrian Plate.

Houdini's Magic, by Walter B. Gibson.

See Bibliography, page 945, for other books. publishing house.

Jumping peg.—A small paddle is constructed so that it has two holes going all the way through it, and two other holes, each one of which goes halfway through from each side. See figure. Holes 2

TOP VIEW   SIDE VIEW
   A   *B*

and 3 go all the way through. Holes 1 and 4 go only halfway through from opposite sides. A small peg which fits snugly into one hole is made to jump about from place to place, going from end to end. This trick depends upon the trick construction of the paddle and a special move which apparently shows both sides of the paddle, while really only showing one side. Suppose the little peg is placed in Hole 2. If the *A* side of the paddle is shown it will appear to be in the hole nearest the handle, but if the *B* side is shown it will appear to be in the center hole. Turn the paddle so that the *A* side is up and peg appears to be in hole nearest handle. Hold paddle between thumb and forefinger with paddle in horizontal position pointing away from the body. Paddle is now swung up and back by twisting the wrist so as to reveal the *B* side, yet the peg is still apparently in the hole nearest handle. This is because the same side of paddle is shown. As it was swung up and back the handle of the paddle was given a half turn between the fingers and thumb. The turning movement of the paddle is unnoticeable since the whole paddle is in motion. Actually the same side of paddle is shown twice. Then the paddle is given a shaking motion while held horizontally again and it is turned over revealing the fact that the peg has jumped from one hole to another. Actually the spectators are seeing the other side of paddle. The peg may be removed by hand and apparently placed back in the middle hole. But actually the paddle has again been turned and the middle hole from side *A* would be No. 3, which when turned over to show side *B* would make the peg appear to have jumped to the extreme hole. Many simple routines can be worked out with this paddle after the one twist is mastered.

The paddle may be constructed in a very few minutes from a little wooden stick such as doctors use to depress tongues while they look into mouths, or from the stick which often forms the handle to the ice creams sold on a stick. The little peg may be a piece of match or toothpick, or any little piece of wood. Both ends of the peg should obviously be alike.

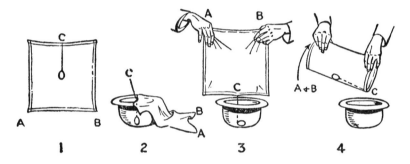

The invisible hen.—The performer shows a handkerchief and a hat. He folds the handkerchief and shakes it repeating the words "cluck, cluck," or "kit-kit-ki-dat-cut," and an egg drops from the handkerchief into the hat. May be repeated many times and hat shown empty at close of trick.

Hat may be borrowed, but the handkerchief and egg are prepared. A wooden egg may be used, or the shell of an egg from which the contents have been blown out. This is fastened to the end of a black thread and the other end of the thread attached to the center of one hem of the handkerchief as shown in Figure 1 at the point *C*. The thread should be long enough to allow the egg to hang just about the center of the handkerchief. At the start of the trick the borrowed hat is shown to be empty and then the handkerchief with egg concealed is placed over the borrowed hat so that the egg is within the hat. Grasping the handkerchief by corners *A* and *B*, it is raised above the hat and shown on both sides, the egg remaining in the hat during this showing. The handkerchief then is laid back on the hat and both hands are shown empty. This time the handkerchief is picked up with one hand at the point *C,* being careful that the egg falls behind the handkerchief. The other hand may show the hat to be empty if desired (first time only). Then putting the hat down the hands double the handkerchief around the egg and hold it over the hat and shake it as shown in Figure 4 and the egg drops out into the hat as the magic words are said. Again the same moves may be repeated (with exception of showing the hat empty) and apparently several eggs will be "laid" in the hat. The hat is then returned to its owner and to his surprise he finds it empty for the eggs have all disappeared.

Removing ring from loop of string on fingers.—Tie the ends of string together forming a loop. Thread a finger ring on the double string, and slip the ends of the loop over the forefingers of a spec-

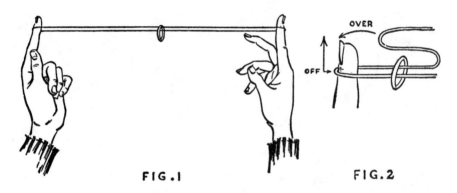

FIG.1   FIG.2

tator, as seen in Figure 1. Without removing the string from the fingers, you can remove the ring from the string. To do this, slide the ring up close to one finger. Then one of the strings (as indicated in Figure 2) over the finger and remove the loop already there. The ring will immediately fall, yet the loop of string is still over the fingers.

Rope release.—Magician has his two arms tied together at the wrist with a large handkerchief. A long piece of rope is now looped between the arms and around the handkerchief, and a spectator is asked to hold both ends of this rope and to pull hard. The magician is able to free himself from the rope without untying the handkerchief. It is done this way: Work some slack in the long rope the ends of which the spectator is holding. Pull the rope toward the fingers through the loose place in the handkerchief next to one wrist. This loop is then slipped over the hand and the magician may step backward free from the long rope.

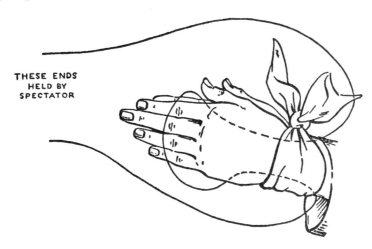

THESE ENDS
HELD BY
SPECTATOR

Cut and restored string (Chewing method).—A string two or three feet long is tied to make a circle or loop. It is then twisted to make a double loop and audience is advised that if it were cut in any place it would form two pieces of string, each having two ends. String is then opened out and in the act of doubling it into double loop again an extra half twist is given so that it takes on the form shown in figure. The performer covers up the twisted portion to prevent the spectator seeing same and asks him to cut the string at X which is the part held between the hands. When the string has been cut the performer gives the spectator the two ends of the long piece and places the two short ends in his own mouth, keep-

ing these covered with his hands all the while. The performer apparently causes the two ends to be chewed together for when the string is pulled from the mouth it is whole. What actually happens is that while the string is in his mouth the performer removes the short piece of string and tucks it under his lip with his tongue, or disposes of it with hands before he shows the string "chewed together" again.

Restored string (Drinking straw).—A drinking straw is shown with a string running through it. The performer bends the straw and cuts right through the center of it.   Apparently the string is cut

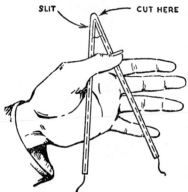

but when the sections of the straw are placed together and then again separated the string is found to be restored.

Secret—With a razor blade cut a slit in the center of the straw about an inch or more running lengthwise of the straw.   When the straw is bent the string is pulled by the protruding ends down into the fingers and the center of the straw is cut above the hidden string.   Thus the string is not cut with the straw.

Coin and match box.—A match box is shown empty inside.   It is closed and upon reopening a coin is found within.   The trick has been arranged beforehand.   The drawer of the match box must be opened half way and a coin wedged between the cover and the end of the drawer.   In this position the box may be shown apparently empty, but when it is closed the coin drops into the drawer and appears there when the box is reopened.

Removing ring from string.—A ring is passed for examination, after which it is threaded on a string, the ends of which are held by spectators.   While the ends are being held firmly the ring is covered with a handkerchief, a special knot is tied and one of the spectators is allowed to remove the ring.

The secret—Two rings, exactly alike, about one inch in diameter or slightly larger, are required to perform the trick.   The string should be about three feet long.   Have the duplicate ring concealed in your left hand before the trick begins.   Now have one of the spectators thread the ring onto the string, and give each end to one of the spectators.   Throw the handkerchief over the ring and under cover of the handkerchief grasp with the right hand the ring that is actually on the string, covering it.   Now take the duplicate ring, which has been concealed in the left hand, and place it on the string as follows: Tell the spectators to give you a little slack so that you may tie a special knot.   Pull the string through the duplicate ring in left hand as seen in the figure below:

Having pulled the string through the ring as in Figure 1, pass it over the ring as in Figure 2, until it reaches the position when

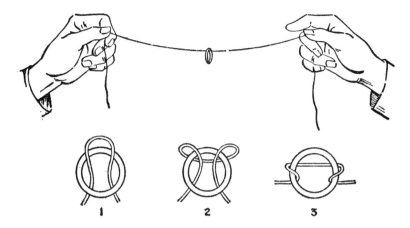

the string is tightened as in Figure 3. The performer now has spectator on his left remove the handkerchief, and turning to spectator on right tells him he is going to allow him to remove the ring from the string magically while the ends are held. He tells him to take the ring in his left hand and the loop of string in his right and remove the ring. As he does this the performer, still concealing the original ring under his right hand slides it along the string as if to take the string from the spectator on his right while he uses both hands to free ring in center. As soon as he slides the ring off the end he hands the string to a third spectator to hold it while the ring is being removed. During this time he has ample opportunity to pocket the original ring. With a little practice this trick will bewilder the most intelligent audience. It is well worth the time it takes to learn it.

Two thieves and five chickens.—In this clever little mystery seven little paper balls or pellets are used. The performer says that two of them represent thieves and the other five are chickens. Holding one pellet in each hand he states that each hand is a barn in which a thief is hiding. The thieves steal the chickens, one by one. First one hand picks up a ball of paper, then the other, and so on, alternately, until all the paper balls have been gathered. Hearing a noise, and thinking they are about to be caught, the thieves put back the chickens. The hands deposit five paper pellets on the table, one by one, alternately. Again as the noise subsides the thieves steal the chickens, picking up the pellets alternately. But hearing the farmer coming to inspect his chicken house they escape to the other barn. To the surprise of everyone the hands are opened and the two thieves are found in one barn while the five chickens are found in the other. One hand holds two paper balls while the other holds five.

The secret—The trick is accomplished by a very simple system. When the five pellets are picked up the first time, start with the right hand—pick them up as follows: right, left, right, left, right. In replacing five pellets on the table start with the left hand—left, right, left, right, left. Practically everyone will think that you put back the same five which you picked up. They will believe that each hand now contains one paper ball, whereas the right hand really holds two, and the left hand none. (Be careful to keep the left hand closed, however, as if it really contained the one they think is in it). In picking up the pellets the second time begin with the right hand as before: right, left, right, left, right. Then when you open your hands you will have five paper balls in the right hand and only two in the left.

The magic moth balls.—This little mystery will cause much wonder on the part of the group for a long time although it is a simple experiment in chemistry rather than a trick of magic. Fill a quart jar about three-fourths full of water. Stir into this about a spoonful of soda from the kitchen and about an equal amount of citric acid crystals which are inexpensive at any drug store. Then drop in six or eight round moth balls and watch the fun begin. It will be more entertaining to put the jar in front of a light or an open window. The balls will go to the top of the water, turn over, and descend again continually for hours in a very orderly fashion. Of course when the action slows down it may be speeded up again by the addition of a little more soda or citric acid.

Small articles vanish (The French Drop).—For vanishing a small article or transferring it from one hand to the other the French

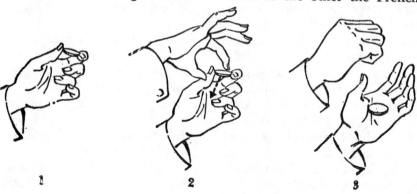

1   2   3

Drop is a very useful move that should be mastered by all magicians. First, the coin is held between the thumb and forefinger of the left hand which is extended in a horizontal position. See Figure 1 above.

Next the right hand moves forward as if to take the coin from the left hand, but just as the right fingers cover the coin the left fingers release it and let it drop into the left palm, which should be turned at such angle as to hide it from the spectators. As the coin drops into the left hand, the right hand is closed which causes the audience to believe the coin is in the right hand. The left hand, however, which contains the coin, drops naturally to the side and after the coin is shown vanished from the right hand the left hand may produce it from some other position by letting the coin slip from the palm to the finger tips. The whole action must be blended into one quick movement.

Making a ruler or other long object stick to the hand.—The laws of gravity are apparently defied as the performer makes a ruler stick to the palm of his hand. The Figures below show how it looks and how it is done.

Place the ruler across the palm of the left hand, which is held in a horizontal postition. Grasp the left wrist with your right hand and slowly raise the left arm, placing the index finger of the

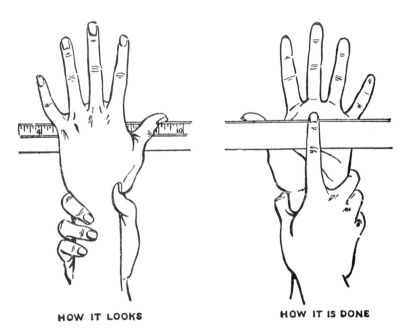

HOW IT LOOKS   HOW IT IS DONE

right hand over the ruler and keeping the back of the left hand turned toward the audience. The ruler will appear to be sticking to the left palm.

Which hand conceals a coin?—The performer turns his back and asks someone to hold a coin in one of his hands. He tells this person to close both hands and hold them palms down. The person holding the coin is then asked to raise the hand holding the coin to his forehead and concentrate upon the coin for a moment and then to lower the hand at the same time saying "Ready." The performer, turning around quickly, will note that the hand holding the coin is whiter than the other one since while it was held to the forehead the blood circulation was retarded. So he will know easily that the coin is in the whiter hand.

Traveling coins.—Four coins and two filing cards or envelopes are needed for this trick which is one of the best small impromptu tricks ever performed. With proper showmanship it can really be made a masterpiece although it is extremely simple. The coins should be placed on the four corners of an imaginary square, which should be on a bed or soft chair or cushion of some sort. The soft surface is needed in order to prevent the coins "rattling" or "talking" when they are laid down, as well as to make it easier to pick up the first one with the fingers.

1

2

3

4

The object of the trick is to cover the coins with the cards, yet to cause them mysteriously to travel until all four come to Position 1 (see Figure 1). Start by placing the coins in positions marked 1, 2, 3, and 4. With one card in right hand and other card in left hand cover coin at 3 with card in left hand, and coin at 4, with card in right hand. Hold the cards over the coins, do not lay them down as yet. State that the coins cannot be seen when covered with the cards because the cards are opaque. Then by crossing the hands reverse position of hands holding cards so that the right hand now covers No. 3 and the left hand covers No. 4. Announce that the coins cannot be seen when covered in this manner for the same reason. Immediately without stopping continue the covering by placing right hand card over No. 2 and left hand card over No. 1. At this point the right forefinger goes under coin at No. 2 and picks it up under the card. Left hand brings the card over to cover coin at No. 2 (which has been picked up under cover of card in right hand), and just as it covers the place where coin No. 2 was the card in right hand concealing coin No. 2 carries it over and places it down with coin No. 1. Both cards are laid down at this point and coin No. 3 is picked up and vanished with a throwing motion toward card covering two coins now at No. 1. (The French Drop, described elsewhere herein would be a good vanish for the coin, leaving the vanished coin in the left hand.) When card now at No. 1 is picked up it has two coins under it. One has apparently gone there magically. In placing card back down it is switched to left hand which holds vanished coin and the coin is placed down with the other two under cover of the card with left hand. The coin now at No. 4 is likewise vanished and apparently found under card at No. 1 with the other two. When card is replaced again it takes the last coin and adds it to the other three under cover of replacing the card. The spectators still think a coin is under card at positon No. 2, so you apparently take a magic hair and push down through the card and get the coin invisibly and take it over and put it through the card at No. 1. Immediately all will want to see the result of this so will eagerly watch as you pick up the card at No. 1 revealing all four coins, and the card at No. 2 revealing none. All movements in this trick should be memorized so that they might be done without a moment's hesitation. It is a clever trick and will be well worth the time it takes to master it.

Multiplying currency.—In preparation for this mystifying trick fold up a few dollar bills into a neat wad and place between the folds of your sleeve in the crook of your elbow. Having shown hands empty borrow a dollar bill as a starter, and as you show it, remark that there is nothing up your sleeves. To prove this pull up the sleeves to give audience a look. When pulling up the sleeve that conceals the money in its folds pick up the wad of bills off your elbow. The audience will not see you do this as they will be watching your sleeves, which you should also do. Pretend to roll up the borrowed bill into a little ball, of course adding the wad, and presently start taking out of hands many bills to the surprise of the spectators.

Right side up match box.—A box of safety matches when flipped into the air always lands right side up on the table for the magician. *Secret*—A half-dollar was placed between the bottom of the container and the outside shell of the box. This gives just the right weight to cause the box to land right side up or label up. The coin is of course secretly removed by the magician before he challenges someone else to try the trick.

Vanishing coin (Confederate).—Several persons are allowed to feel a coin which has been placed in a handkerchief in order to prove it is really there. Finally the handkerchief is shaken out and the coin is gone. The secret lies in the fact that you have a confederate in the audience and he comes to feel the coin last and removes it from the handkerchief unknown to the audience. After he has removed it of course the handkerchief may be shown empty as desired.

Smelling out the coin.—Have a row of pennies on the table. While you step outside the room ask someone to take one of the pennies and hold it tightly above his head and concentrate on its position in the row. After a brief moment he is told to put it back in place and the performer comes and smells the coins and tells the one that has been touched. The secret is in the fact that as the performer pretends to smell the coins he actually allows his nose to touch the coins as he goes from one to the other. Since copper is a good conductor of heat and the nose is very sensitive to heat changes it will be very easy to tell the coin that is the warmest of the group, and after a few sniffs at it the performer announces which coin was held.

Suspending a coin to the wall.—With a pocketknife, unknown to the audience, cut a small nick in one edge of a coin. A good coin to use for this is the quarter (25-cent piece). The little sharp edge may be pressed into the wood of the wall and the coin will remain suspended.

Heads or tails.—While various members of the group spin a coin on the table the performer, who is on the other side of room and cannot see, announces each time correctly whether the coin falls "heads or tails." The secret is in the fact that the coin has a small nick in one side near the edge (the above coin will work satisfactorily). When the coin falls so that the nicked side is down it will have a flat sound and will stop spinning almost immediately. When the nicked side is up the coin will spin much longer and have a gradually diminishing ring to it. A few tries will make it very easy, since you will know what to listen for.

Vanishing coin (Wax).—Coin placed in hand vanishes when hand is closed and reopened. Put a small piece of soft soap on the finger-nail of second or third finger. Put the coin in the palm where this finger will contact it when hand is closed. Show coin there, then close your fist, letting the coin adhere to the soap. Open your hand and the coin has disappeared. It is stuck to the back of your hand and cannot be seen from the front. Be careful not to turn hand over.

The broken match restored.—Insert a match into the hem of a gentleman's handkerchief (unknown to audience). Have a match marked and placed in the center of the handkerchief. It is then folded into the handkerchief and apparently broken, yet when the handkerchief is shaken out the match falls to the floor completely restored. The secret, of course, is in the fact that the match in the hem is folded into the center and broken by the spectator, while the performer holds the marked match safely in the folds of the handkerchief, and shakes it to the floor, disposing of the handkerchief while the match is being examined.

The ring that climbs.—A borrowed ring is dropped over a pencil which the performer holds vertically in his hands. At his command it rises or falls or jumps completely off the pencil. The secret is in the fact that the pencil has a fine black thread fastened to its top and this thread is wound round a button on the performer's vest. As he moves his hand away from him the thread tightens and causes the ring to ascend. The thread will be invisible at short distance especially if the performer wears a dark suit. If the pencil is reversed and the end to which the thread is fastened is placed down in the hand, then by moving the hand back and forth the pencil itself may be caused to rise and fall. In this latter case no ring would be used. The thread may be fastened to the end of the pencil simply by cutting a slit in the end and passing the thread tightly through it.

The magnetized cane.—A yardstick or walking cane or similar object is placed upright on the floor between the legs of performer who is seated. It will move about and respond most readily to his commands. A fine black thread is fastened to each leg of his trousers just below the knee. It should be long enough to allow the performer ease in walking, yet it will not be seen against a dark background. After several attempts to get the cane to stand the performer gets it against the thread and then by slight movements he may cause it to obey his commands.

Magic writing, or invisible ink.—An apparently blank piece of paper may be shown the audience. The paper may be passed for examination or even signed by one of the spectators. Yet upon holding it over a lighted candle a message mysteriously appears on it. *Here's how*—Before the program starts you make "ink" out of lemon juice and write any message desired on the paper. The writing will be invisible until the heat of the candle is applied to it. The heat brings it out and reveals the secret message.

Many a miss (Fifteen matches).—Put down fifteen matches in a row. One player begins at one end and another at the other. Each is privileged to pick up one, two, or three matches in his turn. The object of the game is to force the opponent to take the last match. It sounds simple but there will be many a miss to those who do not know the trick. *To win* of course the performer must pick up the fourteenth match. In order to be sure of this he must get the tenth match. It will be well for him to try to get the second, the sixth, the tenth, and the fourteenth matches picked up. If he will count them as they are picked up he will have no trouble winning, no matter who goes first.

Bottoms-up mystery.—Three glasses are put in a row—the two end ones being upside down and the middle one right side up. The object of the trick is to pick up the glasses two at a time and turn them over three times, finishing with all three glasses right side up.

Explanation—When the moves are made rapidly it will be very hard for anyone to follow. Numbering the glasses 1, 2, 3, in their order from left to right, first turn over Numbers 2 and 3, next Numbers 1 and 3, and last, Numbers 2 and 3. (You will note that No. 3 is turned each time.) An interesting follow-up to this is simply to turn over the center now so that it is upside down and ask someone to duplicate your feat. Not one in a hundred will realize that you are starting with the glasses reversed to the way you started, and even though he catches your moves he will end up with the glasses all bottoms-up instead of upright.

Unbuttonhole.—A string which has been tied into a circle is threaded through a buttonhole of performer's coat or shirt, so that a loop of the string is on either side of the buttonhole. The ends of these loops are now caught over the thumbs (which are pointing forward and upward). The object of the illusion is to get the string out of the buttonhole and still have it on the thumbs. It is accomplished as follows: With the little finger of each hand reach over and catch the opposite top string from the under side: and holding these strings on little fingers bring hands back to first position. With the strings hooked around each thumb and little finger in this manner you let go of string with the right little finger and the left thumb; pull on the string quickly and as the string comes clear the left thumb is slipped into the loop on left little finger as the left little finger is removed. This last move is made so quickly that the spectators do not notice the change of fingers, and when they try it, they fail.

This same method may be used to pull the string through the neck, although a longer loop of string will probably be required.

Contact telegraphy.—This little magic stunt is performed by two people, the magician and his assistant. Assistant goes out of the room while the audience gives the magician a number which he is to transmit. When the assistant returns he places his hands on each side of the magician's head so that his fingers are on the magician's temples. A few seconds later the assistant announces the number. It appears to be mind reading, although there is really no mind reading to it. The magician signals by slightly tightening his lower jaw causing his temples to press slightly against the assistant's fingers. Suppose the number were 273. The magician would press his jaw twice, signifying two; then after a brief pause, seven presses; and after another pause, three presses. Zero is transmitted with ten presses on the jaw.

The rising ruler.—A small foot rule is held in the magician's hand. Upon command it rises. *Secret*—A rubber band is slipped around the first two fingers of the right hand; and the ruler is pushed down into the loop of the band inside the hand. Pressure of the fist holds the ruler in place. When the pressure is released it will rise slowly, or even jump from the hand. Care should be taken not to push the ruler so far down that the audience sees the rubber band.

Grandmother's necklace or the Indian beads.—This is a favorite trick of the Hindu magicians. Three beads are strung on two cords. The ends of the cords are held by spectators, yet the magician removes the beads without damage either to them or to the cords.

The secret of this trick will be easily understood by referring to the figure below. Examine this illustration closely for the manner of threading the beads on strings. Show the three beads threaded

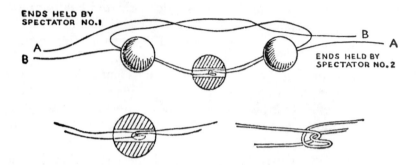

on the strings and ask spectators to take the strings at each end and to hand you one string for each end in order to tie the beads on securely. (This is really done to reverse the ends of strings.) Then under cover of hand or handkerchief pull the strings out of beads and they will come off and all may be examined.

Mysterious paper bands.—Take several strips of paper about fifteen inches long and one inch wide. Glue the ends of first strip together to form a ring as in Figure 1, make one complete twist with one end of the second strip as in Figure 2 and glue the ends together to form a ring, then make two complete twists with one end of the third strip as in Figure 4 and glue the ends together to form a ring.

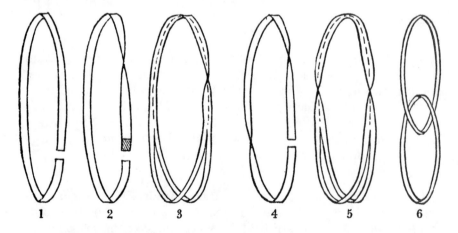

Punch a small hole in the center of these three strips and cut them lengthwise with scissors. The first one will form two bands, of half width, disconnected. The second will be cut as in Figure 3 and will form a paper ring twice as large as the original. The third one will be cut as in Figure 5 and will form two bands linked together in a chain as seen in Figure 6. Larger bands might be made according to same plans and used in cutting contests.

The pencil in the buttonhole.—A small wooden stick resembling a pencil with a loop of cord through its butt end is looped into a buttonhole. The loop of string is so much shorter than the pencil that it seems impossible to loop it, yet the magician does it very easily. First put the entire loop over the cloth around the buttonhole, and pull the material through the loop. Then put the point

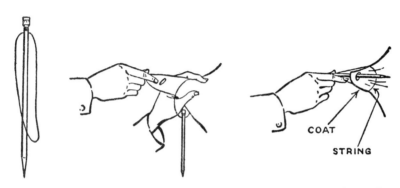

of the "pencil" through the buttonhole, pull the pencil through and slip the loop of string off the cloth. All you need to do to remove the "pencil" is to reverse the moves by which you put it on. You should learn to do this so quickly that no one will notice the method and then see if anyone can take the "pencil" off after you have put it on.

Magic dealers.—To those who wish to secure professional magic equipment it is suggested that you secure a catalogue of magical supplies and literature from some of the following dealers:

Thayer's Studio of Magic, Los Angeles, California.
Kanter's Magic Shop, 1311 Walnut Street, Philadelphia, Pennsylvania.
Frank Lane and Company, 5 Little Building, Boston, Massachusetts.
Abbott's Magic Novelty Co., Colon, Michigan.
Max Holden's Magic Shops, 220 West 42nd Street, New York City; 120 Boylston Street, Boston, Massachusetts; and 117 South Broad Street, Philadelphia, Pennsylvania.
National Magic Co., 119 South State Street, Chicago, Illinois.

Martinka Co., 304 West 34th Street, New York City.
Silk King Studios, 25 Sheehan Avenue, Cincinnati, Ohio.
Atlanta Magic Co., 924 Courtenay Drive, N. E., Atlanta, Georgia.
For Magic Books, Leo Rullman, 203 West 81st Street, New York
  City.

Magic catalogues generally contain some valuable information not only about the prices and descriptions of effects but some magic secrets. Consequently they are seldom supplied free. A small charge is made to cover expense of publishing and distributing but it is always well worth it to the one interested in Fun with Magic.

CHAPTER XXI
FUN IN SHARING FUN

Chapter XXI

FUN IN SHARING FUN

A good recreation leader makes himself dispensable.

Training for vocation is relatively simple. Training for leisure is pretty difficult, and it requires for its fullest success the co-operation of home and school, and the school that overlooks sowing the seeds of a proper use of an obtainable leisure has done only part of its work.
—NICHOLAS MURRAY BUTLER, President of Columbia University, in *Recreation*, December, 1933

The whole end and object of education is training for the right use of leisure.
—ARISTOTLE, 384 B.C.

The person who plans, organizes, and administers leisure programs for the future should be something more than an athlete; he should be, in fact, a fit representative of the best in our cultural life. Since it will be a part of his task to restore to human dignity the losses incurred through our present use of the machine, he should be a personality of dignified proportions, that is, an educator of the first caliber.
—EDUARD C. LINDEMAN, in *Annals of the American Academy of Political and Social Science*, November, 1927

SHARING VERSUS LEADERSHIP

FUN, like many of the best things of life, grows as we share it with others. This truth can be easily demonstrated by anyone who will take the time to try it. You share a song with a comrade, or you share a game, or a book, or an idea, or a skill, and you both are richer for it. So it is appropriate that this book close with a chapter on sharing fun.

It is this idea of sharing that we have in mind when we talk about the recreation leader. We are not thinking of the traffic-cop type of leadership, *directing* the leisure-time traffic into proper avenues, or frantically endeavoring to do so. Dr. E. Stanley Jones criticized leadership training *pitched on this basis*, and charged that it was developing a lot of "fussy managers of other people's business." We need to train, as someone has suggested, not so much for leadership as for "functioning membership."

This book emphasizes, therefore, the recreation leader *not* as a

(895)

director, though there will be many times when he will direct; not as a *coach,* though he may coach; not as *guide,* thought there may be times when he will point out the way; but as a *sharer.* He is one who has something to share with others. Being a sharer he assumes not the teacher-pupil, or leader-follower, or counselor-counselee attitude, but the attitude of a comrade and friend.

This theory of leadership would do several things.

For the leader.—

1. He would make himself as inconspicuous as possible.

2. He would not be seeking the limelight, though he would not be afraid of it if he *had* to take it.

3. He would make himself dispensable to the group and would be delighted whenever they gave evidences of being able to proceed without him.

4. He would not be bossy.

5. He would not be so likely to be self-conscious.

For the members of the group.—

1. Their own ideas, skills, and talents would be drawn out in this sharing process.

2. Their self-directive powers would be developed.

3. Their skill and interest range would be considerably enlarged as they caught the idea of sharing.

4. They would develop a program of wider and more varied range than would otherwise be possible.

THE RECREATION LEADER'S ATTITUDES

Attitudes toward others.—

1. Co-operative. Knows how to work with other people.

2. Sympathetic. Is sensitive to difficulties of others.

3. Considerate. Takes into account all factors involved in one's behavior. Does not jump to conclusions quickly, but is inclined to give the benefit of the doubt to others.

4. Unselfish. Does not crave the spotlight. Is willing to suffer discomfort for the sake of others.

5. Patient. Corrects mistakes without losing temper, and without embarrassing the mistake maker.

6. Encourages players by words of commendation and helpful advice.

7. Believing. Has faith in people. Believes they will respond to what is good if given sufficient opportunity. Believes they are co-operative. Believes they have capacity and ability.

Attitudes toward leisure.—

1. Believes heartily in the necessity and benefits of play.

2. Considers the use of leisure time of prime importance in the development of character and personality.

3. Sees in the wise use of leisure time the means for achieving abundant and radiant living.

4. Is able to properly evaluate activities in terms of those of marginal and central importance, of temporary and permanent values, of cheapness and its various shades, and of worth in its varying degrees.

Attitude toward life.—

1. A cheerful and confident attitude toward life, rather than a cynical one.

2. Feels he owes the world a good return for the investment it has made in him rather than that the world owes him something.

3. Believes in the good life and desires that it be made available to everyone.

CHARACTERISTICS OF THE RECREATION LEADER

(These characteristics are adapted from the chart, "The Characteristics of Human Beings," published by Character Education Institute, Chevy Chase, Washington, D. C.)

Intellectual character.—

1. Accurate, not indefinite. Does not guess. Digs for facts, sources.

2. Alert, not indolent. Not afraid to spend mental and physical energy.

3. Retentive memory, not forgetful. Develops memory by practice.

4. Keen perceptions, not unobserving.

5. Discerning, not superficial. Discriminating judgment and insight.

6. Ability to make accurate analysis, not scatterbrained.

7. Inquisitive (in best sense), not lacking in the keen desire to know.

8. Judicious, not lacking good sense. Wise and sound in his decisions.

9. Thorough, not slipshod.

10. Inventive and constructive, not lacking in initiative.

11. Open-minded, not dominated by prejudgment.

12. Sincere, not diverted by personal interests. When he does not know he says so. He makes no pretense.

13. Keen sense of values, not unresponsive to real worth.

Working character.—

1. Artistic and neat, not slovenly.

2. Co-operative, not individualistic.

3. Adaptable, not slow to fit into new situations.

4. Teachable, not stubborn.

5. Work by design (definite and planned), not haphazard.

6. Attentive to details, not careless.

7. Decisive, not procrastinating.

8. Self-directive, not dependent.

9. Industrious, not lazy.

10. Prompt, not dilatory.

11. Reliable, not irresponsible or negligent.

12. Thrifty, not wasteful, nor extravagant.

13. Cautious, not reckless.

14. Persistent, not vacillating.

15. Cheerful, not complaining.

Personal character.—

1. Conscientious, not unscrupulous.

2. Magnanimous, not small-minded and petty.

3. Self-controlled, not weak.

4. Self-respecting, not dissipated.

5. Independent, not suggestible.

6. Thoughtful, not merely impulsive.

7. Prudent, not foolhardy.

8. Refined, not coarse.

Social character.—

1. Faithful, not unmindful of obligations. Community-minded, not narrow.

2. Helpful, not self-centered. Shares, not a social-sponge.

3. Loyal, not treacherous.

4. Trustful toward others, not suspicious.

5. Just, not unfair.

6. Honest, not disposed to cheat.

7. Honorable, not sneaking.

8. Mindful of rights of others, not overbearing.

9. Sociable, not exclusive or snobbish.

10. Congenial, not unfriendly.

11. Courteous, not rude.

12. Genuine, not affected.

13. Harmonious, not antagonistic or wrangling.

14. Patient with others, not irritable.

15. Respectful, not imprudent nor flippant.

16. Tactful, not brusque nor priggish.

Emotional character.—

1. Courageous and self-confident, not timid nor shirks responsibilities.

2. Ambitious, not self-satisfied.

3. Buoyant, radiant, cheerful; not morose, dull, and moody.

4. Hopeful, not pessimistic.

5. Progressive, not opposed to change.

6. Earnest, not trifling.

7. Determined, not easily discouraged.

8. Idealistic, not content with low standards.

9. Responsive to beauty, not unappreciative.

10. Friendly, not lacking good will.

11. Grateful, not inattentive to kindness.

12. Sympathetic, not absorbed by self-interest.

13. Poised, not excitable, hysterical, or melancholy.

14. Humble, not conceited.

15. Sense of humor, not upset by trifles.

16. Forgiving, not vindictive.

17. Sportsmanlike, not envious.

18. Generous, not stingy.

19. Alive to truth, not complacent.

20. Tolerant, not angry over difference of opinion.

Physical character.—

1. Developed body, not undernourished.

2. Muscular control, not clumsy.

3. Grace of figure and carriage, not slouchy.

4. Expressive face, not stolid.

5. Strong musical voice, not choked or rasping.

6. Vital, not sluggish.

7. Endurance, not easily tired.

8. Healthy, not sickly.

THE RECREATION LEADER'S SKILLS

There is a total of forty-three points in these skills. A score of twenty-five points would be considered as FAIR, thirty as GOOD, thirty-five as VERY GOOD and forty and over as EXCELLENT.

Skills in leadership of music.—

1. Ability to lead a group in singing 1

2. Ability to train a choir or chorus 1

3. Ability to train an orchestra 1

4. Ability to play a musical instrument 1

5. Experience in doing solo, duet, quartet, or chorus singing 1

6. Ability to arrange programs of music 1

7. Ability to recognize at least ten classical selections 1

8. Knowing at least twenty folk songs 1

                                                         —
8

Skills in leadership of dramatics.—

1. Ability to direct a dramatic performance 1

2. Ability to act a part in a performance 1

3. Directing a group in the reading and discussing of a play.. 1

4. Knowledge of and experience with workshop activities— stage-lighting, making sets, arranging stage setting 1

5. Familiarity with a wide variety of plays 1

6. Ability to evaluate the value of dramatic materials 1

7. Knowledge of and experience with informal types of dramatic experiences, such as charades, spontaneous drama, act-it-out, etc. 1

                                                          —
7

Skills in social fellowship.—

1. Ability to plan and direct a party 1

2. Ability to teach and lead folk games 1

3. Planning and directing other group games 1

4. Ability to show a group how to plan a social evening 1

5. Knowledge of the best source materials 1

6. At least twenty-five social games at finger's tip for ready use in emergency 1

—
6

Skills in sports.—

1. At least one sport in which one is proficient 1

2. A working knowledge of all sports 1

3. Ability to map out and direct a field-day or track meet ... 1

4. Ability to instil in participants the idea of playing for the fun of playing 1

5. Accurate knowledge of the field dimensions and rules for sports that are popular in the particular region 1

—
5

Skills in outdoor recreation.—

1. Ability to plan and promote a picnic for large or small groups 1

2. At least elementary knowledge of nature lore—birds, trees, flowers, stars, etc. 1

3. Ability to plan and direct interesting hikes and treasure hunts 1

4. Some knowledge of outdoor cookery 1

5. Ability to plan and direct campfires of various types—the council ring, the campfire sing, etc. 1

6. Knowledge of games suitable in the out-of-doors 1

7. Knowledge of camping 1
                                                       —
                                                       7

Skills in uses of good literature.—

1. A love of good literature that creates enthusiasm for it .. 1

2. A repertoire of good stories and ability to tell them 1

3. A knowledge of good poetry and ability to create interest in it 1

4. Ability to plan literary programs—book reviews, book discussions, poetry evenings, etc. 1

5. Ability to plan and conduct forums on interesting and timely subjects 1
                                                       —
                                                       5

Skills in hobbies.—

1. Adeptness in at least one creative hobby 1

2. A wide knowledge of possible hobbies 1

3. Ability to plan and conduct a hobby fair 1

4. Knowledge of how to proceed in arranging for a hobby school 1

5. A sound philosophy of hobbies that discourages piddling and fadism, and that encourages creativity 1
                                                       —
                                                       5

This skill rating scheme would indicate the versatility of the recreation leader. It would not necessarily mean the ability to do a great variety of things well. If the leader should want to rate himself both with regard to versatility and efficiency he would check each item *E* (Excellent), or *V.G.* (Very Good), or *G* (Good), or *P* (Poor) according to his proficiency or lack of it. This would give him a good idea of the points at which he needs to improve.

GENERAL REQUIREMENTS OF RECREATION WORKERS

The National Recreation Association in *Standards of Training, Experience, and Compensation in Community Recreation Work* has worked out the following "General Requirements for Recreation Workers."

Social attitude.—

1. Sense of the worth and dignity of every human being and desire to serve the group.

2. Understanding of people with insight into processes of life; comprehending the hungers, needs, and aspirations of people; sensing the wholeness of life.

3. Personal realization of the joy of life, of life's rich meanings and possibilities, of the art of living.

4. Sense of humor, at least enough to prevent one's taking himself too seriously.

An adequate social attitude will require familiarity with such fields of study as sociology, psychology, philosophy, education, history, biology, and physiology.

Creative Attitude.—

1. Concerned with growth and development of individuals.

2. Concerned with the stimulation of the creative impulses in others—initiative, freedom of expression, productive activity.

An adequate creative attitude will require a developed constructive faculty and creative imagination.

Scientific attitude.—

1. Understanding of the scientific method.

2. Hospitality to different points of view and diverse personalities.

3. Keen interest in research and experiment.

4. Especially concerned with human engineering.

Capacity and zest for learning.—

1. An understanding mind.

2. The ability to think; i.e., skill in using the mind in analyzing, in selecting what is significant and in making concepts which will serve human purposes.

3. Insatiable curiosity, especially with reference to discovery and solution of social problems.

Ability to lead democratically.—

1. Belief and enthusiasm for self-government, for democracy in recreation.

2. Understanding of co-operative, democratic recreation procedure as distinguished from arbitrary control.

3. Skill in the techniques of group discussion and group determination of policies.

4. Character and personality (not the dominating type).

5. Organizing ability.

6. Productive energy (as distinguished from mere health, implies manner of use).

Technical skill.—

1. Possessing skill in the particular field in which recreation worker is going to lead, i.e., as executive, supervisor, specialist, group leader, or other type of worker.

2. Possessing skill in dealing with people to be served according to age and group interests.

A STANDARD FOR RECREATIONAL LEADERS

A recreational leader is very patient. He maintains his poise through the most trying circumstances.

A recreational leader is very kind. He is particularly concerned for the slow, the careless, the indifferent.

A recreational leader knows no jealousy. He is quick to pay tribute to another's skill.

A recreational leader makes no parade. He never boasts of his exploits and he makes himself as inconspicuous as the occasion permits.

A recreational leader gives himself no airs. He never pretends. He never struts.

A recreational leader is never rude. He respects human personality too much to treat people with anything but the greatest courtesy and considerateness.

A recreational leader is never selfish. Not "How am I doing?" but "Are the folk having a good time?" is his chief concern.

A recreational leader is never irritated. He knows that if he loses his temper, he has lost the play spirit; and if the leader loses the spirit of play how can he lead others to find it?

A recreational leader is never resentful. He holds no grudge against the umpire, or the other team, or the players who, by their carelessness, or indifference, or horseplay, have made it difficult for him.

A recreational leader is never glad when others go wrong. He does not gloat when another recreation leader pulls a "cropper"; nor does he seize upon mistakes of those playing as occasions for holding them up to ridicule.

A recreational leader is gladdened by goodness. He inspires good performance by encouraging remarks and by his evident joy in what is good.

A recreational leader is always slow to expose. He sees all, hears all, and knows all because he is alert. If someone needs discipline or help he gives it in such a way as to best benefit the individual.

A recreational leader is always eager to believe the best. He looks for the best in people and always finds it.

A recreational leader is always hopeful. He is not easily discouraged. He embodies radiant optimism.

A recreational leader is always persevering. He never gives up. He endures because he believes so firmly in the thing he is doing.

The above is adapted and enlarged from an outline by Mr. R. C. Sidenius, Recreation and Young People's Leader of Hamilton, Ontario. It was given as a part of the worship service at a Recreation Leaders Conference held at Hamilton, Ontario, February 27, 28, 1937, which was sponsored by 4 F-Recreational Guild. Read I Corinthians 13: 4-8.

METHODS OF THE RECREATION LEADER

Choice of activities.—

1. Activities should be selected with the following considerations in mind: age range; sex; prejudices, if any; experience, ability, and capacity of the players; size of the crowd; available play space; time alloted for play; consideration of what precedes and what follows the play period, if anything; theme, if any; weather conditions.

2. The leader's own knowledge and ability is a determining factor, except where he has the ability to co-opt helpers who are expert in specific activities.

3. Games and activities are selected with a view to giving the players a sense of successful achievement. Therefore, they must be in their skill range.

Arrangement of program.—

1. Start with activities that are easy.

2. In the early part of the program, particularly, make it easy for people to get acquainted. Break down stiffness. Create an atmosphere of friendliness and warmth.

3. Arrange program in logical sequence as far as is possible. Each game or activity ought to leave players in position for the game that follows. This is not always possible, but it is highly desirable.

   For instance, the leader may work out a sequence of games that require three players in a group or a multiple of three. The following program might then be used:

   (1) Squirrel in a Tree.

   (2) Spoke Tag.

   (3) Loose Caboose.

   (4) Four Deep.

   (5) Pop Goes the Weasel.

   (6) The Wheat.

   (7) Come, Let Us Be Joyful.

   (8) The Crested Hen.

When breaking from one pattern into another do so with as little jolt as possible. For instance, if the group is doing circle games and it is desired to do a line game like the Virginia Reel or Betsy Liner, swing the players into a grand march. March them around into groups of eight couples each, and then space them for the line game.

4. Arrange for "breathers." Balance the program so that the players will not be exhausted by unbroken strenuous activity.

5. Build to a fitting climax. The fun should reach its height in the closing activity.

Getting attention.—

Always get attention before beginning to explain an activity. Under no circumstances try to shout directions over the noise of an inattentive group.

1. Stand where you can be seen easily and where you can see the crowd. The center is usually a poor position because part of the group is in back of the leader.

2. Wait for the group to get quiet before attempting to speak.

3. If necessary, use some signal for getting attention.

   (1) Hands up! A successful method for some leaders is that of raising the right hand. As players observe this their hands go up. It is understood that this is the signal for quiet.

   (2) "Shushers' Club." "When my left hand goes up every member of the 'Shushers' Club' goes 'Sh-sh-shush!'"

   (3) Piano chord.

   (4) A whistle. If you use a whistle let it be thoroughly understood that its sound is the signal for silence. Too frequent use of a whistle is annoying. Therefore many leaders prefer to do without it except where the game requires it. Some leaders prefer a whistle with a soft musical sound, rather than the shrill type.

   (5) Start a song with the aid of the group close around the leader. The others will likely join in the singing, especially, if the song is familiar and tuneful. At the close of the song or of a series of songs tell the group what you want it to do.

4. Don't dally. The moment you have the attention of the group move with precision and snap. Delay may prove deadly.

5. Create an air of expectancy. The leader can do this by his manner—his enthusiasm, a merry twinkle in his eye, his evident pleasure in anticipation of the fun, the introduction of surprises, and his method of directing the activity.

Presentation of games and technique during their progress.—

1. Get group into formation before explaining the game. This makes it easier for the players to understand. It also eliminates to some extent other difficulties, such as those you have with the "I-don't-want-to's" and the "I'm-not-sure-I-want-to's." They are enjoying the game before they know it. Make this getting into formation part of the fun.

2. Lose as little time as possible getting into the actual playing of the game.

3. Give explanations clearly, briefly, and correctly.

4. Demonstrate. Often the very best possible explanation of what you want done is to take a partner or a group and show just what to do.

5. Where the game is intricate or where it involves several movements, teach it movement by movement, or let the players learn it as the game progresses. Explain necessary details as you come to them.

6. Encourage the players now and then by words of commendation.

7. Where mistakes are made be patient in pointing them out and, if possible, make them part of the fun. "We even enjoyed making mistakes," said one enthusiastic college student in telling about the good time he had at one party. Call attention to mistakes but not to the persons making them.

8. Direct attention to the game and not to self. A good leader merges himself with the group.

9. Encourage everyone to play, but do not insist on them doing so. If people do not play take it for granted that they have valid reasons that are satisfactory to them.

10. When a game or activity does not "take hold" for some reason (the mood of the group at the time, inability of certain players to "catch on," lack of time to master it) move quickly from it to some other game or activity. Care must be taken, however, not to destroy interest in a good activity by a poor and unsatisfactory experience with it.

11. When a game fails to interest, the leader should first examine his own technique in trying to determine the cause of the failure.

12. Stop the game when interest is at its height.

13. Be firm, but kind, in enforcing rules.

14. Write out an outline of the things you plan to do on a small card or slip of paper. Keep this in the palm of your hand where you can refer to it, if needed.

15. Have extra material ready for use in case of emergency. The leader may find that certain games or activities are impractical under the circumstances, or they may not fit the particular mood of the group. He is ready with suitable substitutions. The man who gets credit for being resourceful is very often the man who has had foresight enough to prepare for such emergencies as arise.

16. Have all properties ready for use when needed, but never give them out before time for their use.

17. Be thorough, but do not insist on meticulous precision in such a manner as to destroy the fun of the activity. Joy in the activity may be means of *making* the participant *want* to know how he can approximate perfect performance.

18. Never "boss," scold, or ridicule.

19. Never allow the program to drag. The leader must be "on his toes" all the time, and yet he is so poised that he works with ease in keeping things moving.

20. Enjoy the activity yourself.

TEN COMMANDMENTS PLUS THREE

(By Eugene T. Lies, National Recreation Association)

For those who toil in the recreation vineyard.—

1. Thou shalt not regard thy labors as a mere job but rather as an ever-present opportunity for fine human service.

2. Thou shalt not permit thyself to get into a rut but shalt ever be alert for new ideas the other fellow may offer unto thee and which a book may present unto thee; remembering what Mr. Matthew said of yore: "If the blind lead the blind, both shall fall in the ditch."

3. Thou shalt not forget that prompting of mere imitative motions in thy fellowmen is not in very truth, recreation, but that evoking their inner spirit into satisfying activity is.

4. Thou shalt remember in all thy doings, all of the people within thy gates, the old as well as the young, the rich as well as the poor, for all these thy brethren are in sore need of the blessings of creative expression. Deny them not, lest they shrivel and die.

5. Thou shalt open wide not merely one or mayhap two gates of opportunity, but many—yea, all the gates through which the human mind and soul doth crave to enter in search of nourishment, understanding, and sheer delight.

6. Thou shalt never exploit innocent little children to gain vainglory for thyself nor for thy department. Neither shalt thou stir within the breasts of babes and sucklings feverish longings to gain fame and fortune in ye place called Hollywood; when rather, thou shouldst provide them with nice rattles, rag dolls, and teddy bears. They are clay in thy hands, O potter!

7. Thou shalt love thy neighbor as thyself, honor the work of other well-doers in thy community, grasp their hands with cheering warmth, join with them in mind and purpose, for the greater good of all the people in thy midst—and in the doing thereof, thou shalt be mindful even of the worthy burgomaster and his trusty crew. Yea, thou shalt love, honor, and obey those whom the burgomaster hath placed over thee to guide thy footsteps and to keep thee within thy pesky budget. Yet, thou shalt be permitted to remind them gently that hope deferred maketh the heart sick!

8. Thou shalt ever keep an eagle eye on those of low repute who for filthy lucre would corrupt the bright imaginings and aspiring ideals of childhood and youth. With others, thou shalt up and at them, lash them hip and thigh, with a whip of thorns and put them into outer darkness now and forevermore. Thus wilt thou bring blessings unto thy people.

9. Thou-who art in high place, sometimes called boss, shalt ever lend a helping hand to the younger toilers in the vineyard lest perchance they grow sore in spirit, tread wrong paths, step unwarily into lurking quagmires or fall into bottomless pits; neither shalt thou smite them too rashly when they err, forgetting never that thou too wast once like unto these, just a stumbling creeper, and that in Ecclesiastes it sayeth that "Anger resteth in the bosom of fools."

10. Thou shalt not swipe the golden nuggets of thy brother's brain, over which, mayhap, he hath burned the midnight oil and hath sweat much gory blood. Nay, when thou wouldst use any such brain child of him who hath given it birth, thou shalt openly avow the debt and tell his name unto all the people and thou shalt set the nugget in little marks, fore and aft.

11. Thou shalt ever, O brother, take heed of thine acts, especially when thou art in the market place where the populace may look upon thee, lest thou givest cause to thy brother to stumble and also bringest sore reproach upon thee and upon thy works. For a wise man hath said: "If you can't be glad, be careful."

12. Thou shalt ever remember the larger relationships of the work thou doest to the work like unto it which goeth on beyond thy gates in state and nation. Yea, thou shalt cherish and strengthen such bonds lest thou soon findest thyself standing alone, weak and bereft, and topplest over.

13. And last, though not least, beloved brethren of the flock, when doubts assail thee and those of little understanding cast ridicule upon thy works, and difficulties sorely afflict thee and thou growest weary of well-doing,— oh, forget not those sources from which cometh help, refreshment, and strength of heart; for they beckon thee ever, spurn them not but diligently use them.

PLANNING A RECREATIONAL EVENT

Preparation

Research—Examining books, pamphlets, and magazines for ideas.

Properties—Getting all of the necessary materials together.

Decorations—For some events decorations will be necessary to give color, atmosphere, a festive appearance. Or exhibits may be required. Or it is necessary to locate a suitable spot for an outdoor event and get it ready. All of this requires forethought and planning.

Publicity—The publicity will depend on the group you want to reach. Interesting newspaper accounts of the coming event, letters, posters, telephone calls, announcements, and special invitations may be part of the plan.

Helpers—Have all who are going to help in any way with the event meet and discuss what is to be done. Especially is this important where a large crowd is to be handled. Such a meeting may have to resolve itself into an instruction session.

The crowd—Condition the crowd for what is to come, if at all possible. Arouse interest; pique curiosity; create an atmosphere of expectancy. And then make good by fulfilling all of their anticipations, and more.

Know their likes and dislikes, and the reasons for them. Know their needs, felt and unfelt. Know their background. Keep all of these things in mind while planning whatever the event is.

Guiding Principles

1. *Unity*—The event should have unity. This unity will be easier to achieve if it is clear what the aim of the particular program is. For instance, one college wanted to interest its students in a varied campus social program. One of the events they used to achieve this purpose was "A World Play Day" held in connection with a homecoming celebration for old graduates. There was a variety of activities during the day—speeches, folk games on the athletic field, a football game, etc. But in it all they kept the main purpose in view and thus the day's program was a unit. Sometimes unity is achieved by using a theme around which the whole program builds. It is a Hobby Fair, or a Circus Party, or a Nature Hike, or a Council Campfire, or an Evening of Indian Music, or a Drama Festival.

2. *Variety*—Not only should there be variety in particular events, such as parties, but the group should be given a variety of experiences over a period of time. A chance to enjoy experiences with drama, music, parties, forums, sports, hobbies, and all of those interests that make up part of a well-rounded life, should get into the picture at one time or another.

Someone has suggested facetiously that the reason a lullaby puts a baby to sleep is because of the dreadful monotony of the thing. Certainly no group can afford to lull its crowd to sleep with a monotonous sameness in the events it promotes. There must be the element of surprise, the lure of new ventures, the tang of an occasional new idea, the pull of opening horizons.

3. *Climax*—The event, whether it be a banquet, a musicale, or a party, should reach a fitting climax at its close. The best at the last is a good rule. A banquet feature that caps the program for the evening. A musical number that marks the interest peak for the

night. A game or stunt that finds the fun at its highest level. Sometimes a surprise can serve as this climax. Sometimes a sing can do it by drawing the threads of fellowship and unity together in a closing moment of harmony. Sometimes some lovely experience, such as a beautiful story that fits into the theme or a brief worship experience, marks the climax. Whatever it is, build to a climax and stop.

WORKING WITH A COMMITTEE

Usually recreation plans are most successful when they represent the pooled thoughts of a committee. "Everybody knows more than anybody does." The combined thinking of a group is likely to result in bigger and better plans than anyone in the group could think out alone.

Important rules for successful committee meetings.—

1. Be prompt in beginning and closing committee sessions.

2. Stick to the business to be done. Don't wander off into more or less interesting bypaths that are unrelated to the job that the committee is expected to do.

3. Move with precision in the committee meeting. When a point of progress has been made clinch it and move on to the next item.

4. Where ideas of different members of the committees are at variance try to find some points of agreement and move on from there.

5. Encourage every member to participate in the discussions. Give respectful consideration to every suggestion offered. Even weak suggestions can often be used to mark progress by pointing out whatever of good there may be in them and by building on that. Never ridicule any suggestion given in good faith.

6. Discourage any attempt on the part of any person to dominate in the decisions of the group. The chairman will have to be particularly careful not to abuse the authority of his position in committee deliberations.

7. Often the committee meetings can be occasions of good fellowship. Some light refreshments, a trying out of some of the materials to be used later in programs, or a meeting in connection with an attractive meal, can serve to put the members

of the committee in the mood to do some good work. Care needs to be taken, however, to see that the social aspects of the meeting do not interfere with the serious business at hand.

Three kinds of chairmen.—The chairman has much to do with the successful functioning of a committee. He needs to be fair, alert, thorough, systematic, humble, open-minded, and tactful.

There are three types of committee chairmen. For two of them success is impossible unless members of the committee take things in hand.

There is the empty-headed chairman.—He has given the committee meeting no previous thought. He has no ideas. If the others in the committee are like him the session reaches a stalemate. "Well, we've got to do *something!*" And the result is a flat, stereotyped plan.

Then there is the rubber-stamp chairman.—He has everything all planned. He *tells* the committee. He does not receive suggestions cordially unless they coincide with his own prepared plans for the committee. The committee is used merely as a rubber-stamp. Its members feel that their time has been wasted. The chairman could have done as well without them.

The good chairman gives serious thought to the committee meeting long before it meets. He jots down an agenda of things that need to be done. He has encouraged members of the committee to bring to the meeting ideas to throw into the hopper. He may even put some material in their hands so that they may examine it for suggestions. He has some ideas of his own, but he does not insist on them. He thinks with the committee, not *for* it. Whatever plans are worked up are the committee's plans.

CRITERIA FOR EVALUATING THE PROGRAM

1. Did the program grow out of democratic participation of the group involved in determining what shall get into it?

2. Did it take into account the potential as well as the present interests of the group?

3. Did it over-emphasize the value of temporary interests as over against the value of permanent interest?

4. Did it set in motion any new and growing interests?

5. Does it provide any means for following up such interests?

6. Is there definite advancement in skills and appreciations as a result of the activities promoted?

7. Are the people who participate in the program becoming more skilful and versatile in the arts of leisure so that they are no longer easy victims of stereotyped and fruitless patterns of play?

8. Are the creative abilities of the participants challenged and given opportunity to develop?

9. Does the program develop a spirit of friendliness? Is anyone left out of the circle of friendship?

10. What contribution, if any, has the program made toward the development of well-rounded personality in the participants?

11. What disintegrating personality factors, if any, has it set in motion? Was any bad feeling aroused? Jealousy? Bitterness? Division? Desire for self-display? Inflated ideas of one's own importance?

12. Does the program make the best use of the equipment, leadership, and time that are available; and does it challenge the talents and capacities of the participants?

GETTING PARTICIPATION

Individuals are different.—Fingerprint experts testify that no two people have identical fingerprints. It is doubtful if any two people are exactly alike in all of their attitudes and responses. The recreation worker must remember that he is dealing with individuals. To a certain extent people can be classified in groups, but within each type there will be individual differences. It is important that this be kept in mind in trying to solve the problems that are related to getting participation. The recreation leader must study the individual.

Often communities and neighborhoods are different.—Recreation plans that "strike fire" in one community often "backfire" in another. Mental, physical, and moral background, traditional attitudes, and past experiences are factors in making these differences. The recreation leader must take them into account. He must, therefore, study the individual's environment.

The recreation leader is interested in more than getting people to engage in the activities he promotes. He wants them to find their own best selves through the release and enrichment that comes from these activities.

Certain types are fairly common in the experience of the recreation leader. A few of them are noted here, with an effort to offer suggestions for helping them.

THE TIMID—BACKWARD, BASHFUL

The problem.—

1. Refusal to participate.
2. Restrained participation preventing spontaneous play.
3. An appearance of being unsocial when one really would rather be friendly.

Condition that give rise to problems.—

1. Lack of experience in the activity and consequent fear of embarrassment through mistakes and clumsiness.

2. Self-consciousness that makes it difficult to mingle with social groups.

3. Unsympathetic persons in the particular group who think it clever to make "smart" remarks about participants, or who make the timid the butts of their alleged jokes.

4. A leader who is constantly playing "tricks" on participants.

Ways of helping.—

1. Find something the timid individual can do well and put him at it.

2. Seek occasions for him where he will not be conspicuous.

3. Offer an encouraging word occasionally.

4. Always be sympathetic. Never make him the victim of a "goat stunt."

5. Develop a friendly spirit in the group, thus making it easier for the timid and inexperienced to participate without embarrassment.

6. Encourage small group socials to help "break the ice."

THE LOVELORN

The problem.—

1. They prefer to "sit out."

2. They resent being separated in the games.

3. They are extremely unsocial.

Conditions that give rise to problems.—

1. Cozy corners in the social room that invite "sitting out."

2. Fear of not showing up well in the eyes of one's beloved.

3. A sort of "superiority complex" that sometimes characterizes lovesick couples.

4. A desire to impress one another with the idea that their company is all in the world that's desirable or necessary to their complete happiness.

5. Lack of program continuity that makes it necessary for them to entertain themselves.

6. Automobiles that make it easy to "sit out" or to leave for a ride during the social.

Ways of helping.—

1. Eliminate all cozy corners, as far as possible.

2. Keep the program moving.

3. Use games that will mix the group.

4. Use clever devices for getting partners, but allow no partner arrangement to last for more than one or two games.

5. Create sentiment against the use of automobiles during the progress of the social.

6. Plan such an interesting party that everyone will want to participate.

THE DIGNIFIED

The problem.—

1. Prefer to look on.

2. When they do participate, they do so reluctantly and with that "I'm doing you a big favor" air. Restrained.

3. Have a depressing effect on the rest of the group.

Conditions that give rise to problems.—

1. The feeling that "play is silly" and intended only for children.

2. Fear that the estimate of the group of them would be lowered if they "let loose" in spontaneous play.

3. The feeling that play is unbecoming in one who has serious purposes in life.

4. An exaggerated personal pride that objects to engaging in anything in which one does not excel.

Ways of helping.—

1. Educate in the importance of play.

2. Seek to arouse the play spirit by finding something they like to do. For instance, maybe they like to sing, or debate, or act.

3. Develop programs of such high quality that they are forced to see the values in them.

THE RELIGIOUS DYSPEPTIC

The problem.—

1. Refuse to participate.

2. Look with disfavor on harmless fun, and sometimes are very critical.

3. Have a depressing effect on the rest of the group.

Conditions that give rise to problems.—

1. Young people in the group who do things that are subject to criticism.

2. A committee that allows objectionable features to creep into the socials.

3. The feeling that play is an evil, a sinful waste of time, and that it is dangerous to the spiritual life to indulge in it.

4. Commercialized amusements and other agencies in the com-

munity offering harmful types of recreation and thus arousing an antagonism toward all forms of leisure time activity.

Ways of helping.—

1. Educate in the values of wholesome play.

2. Demonstrate these values by actual promotion of such recreation.

3. Have respect for their sincere convictions.

THE KNOW-IT-ALL

The problem.—

1. Lessen interest of players by disparaging remarks. "Oh, I know that"; "That's an old one"; "Why don't we try something new?"

2. Take edge off of a game by explaining it to players around them while leader is trying to tell the group what he wants done.

Conditions that give rise to problems.—

1. A committee or leader using too much "old stuff."

2. An exaggerated case of "ego" that resents having it appear that anyone knows anything he doesn't know.

3. The existence of a clique with which the "know-it-all" has influence.

Ways of helping.—

1. Use them in places of leadership, if possible.

2. Use new material in your programs.

3. Don't assume a "know-it-all" attitude yourself. The more one knows about any subject the more conscious one is that there is much to be learned.

4. Make them victims of "goat stunts" occasionally. Never do this with malice, however.

THE BLASE

The problem.—

1. If they participate at all, it is with a bored air.

2. Assume a superior attitude and prove a deterring factor in the games or other activities.

Conditions that give rise to problems.—

1. An excessive enthusiasm for social dancing so that nothing else appears worth doing.

2. A desire to appear sophisticated.

3. Lack of variety in programs.

4. The use of too much "kid stuff" in programs.

Ways of helping.—

1. Use new material in programs.

2. Make the party programs lively and interesting.

3. Don't coddle.

4. Introduce surprises in your programs.

5. Occasionally use some of this group as the victims for "goat stunts."

THE GRANDSTAND TYPE

(Desire to be the center of attraction)

The problem.—

1. Their desire to be prominent in all the activities makes it difficult to get general interest.

2. They sometimes seek to start something else while the leader is directing some activity.

3. Inclined to make "smart" remarks, and prove to be a disturbing factor in the social or games.

Conditions that give rise to problems.—

1. Lack of continuity in the program which gives the "grandstand" players opportunity to take the reins.

2. Leadership which allows a few of the more aggressive to "hog" the program.

3. A feeling of dissatisfaction on the part of the group with the leadership and the program.

Ways of helping.—

1. Have a well-planned program with no awkward pauses in it.

2. Strive to give everyone a chance in the games.

3. Occasionally give the "grandstander" some responsibility in putting the program over.

4. Use him as the victim in "goat stunts.'

OBJECTORS

(Some people seem to have been born in the "objective case.")

The problem.—

1. Opposition to the plans of the committee or to suggestions of the leader.

2. Dissipate the play spirit of the group by disparaging remarks. "Oh, let's not do that. Let's do so-and-so."

Conditions that give rise to problems.—

1. Lack of confidence on the part of the leader in himself and in his crowd.

2. Lack of enthusiasm on the part of the leader.

3. Lack of friendliness in the group. Ill feeling or envy always gives rise to a flock of problems.

4. The desire on the part of the objector to "boss" or dominate the group.

Ways of helping.—

1. Consult with the committee in planning the program so that it does not represent only the leader's ideas. Maybe the objector has much to be said in his favor.

2. If the objector's suggestion seems to be a good one, it may be possible to use it. The leader ought never to carry about with him that "I'm infallible" air. Sometimes the leader says, "All right. Let's play this one now, and then we'll play the one you suggested."

3. Always be courteous, but don't spoil the plans arranged by

the committee by acquiescing in every suggestion that comes after the games get started.

4. Sometimes it is advisable to ignore the chronic objector.

THE LAZY

The problem.—

Do not participate, or do it so lifelessly as to prove a hindrance to the spirit of the game.

Conditions that give rise to problems.—

1. Programs too strenuous.

2. The idea that recreation means simply resting or loafing.

3. Hard work that leaves the energies too depleted for much physical activity in play.

4. Poor health.

Ways of helping.—

1. Adapt the program to the physical needs of the group.

2. Encourage them to play, but don't nag.

THE SUBNORMAL

The problem.—

1. They don't know how to play.

2. The weakened mental state is often accompanied by physical weakness, depleted energies, and lack of interest. Therefore it is difficult to arouse a spontaneous play spirit.

Conditions that give rise to problems.—

1. Those in charge may not know the value of play as a mental and physical stimulant.

2. Unsympathetic leadership.

Ways of helping.—

1. Use simple games.

2. Have infinite patience.

3. Find something the subnormal person can do well and proceed to build on that.

4. Experiment with the uses of music in participating and non-participating programs. (See *The Influence of Music on Behavior,* by Diserens, published by the Princeton University Press.)

GENERAL SUGGESTIONS

1. Never be overly insistent on any person participating.

2. Have confidence in the power of suggestion. The play spirit is contagious. Often it is best to go ahead and play, ignoring any special problems.

3. Always remember you may be mistaken in your analysis of the situation. The player you classify as "lazy" may be "run down" physically. The person you tag "grandstand" player may be simply interested in making the program go.

4. Don't offer public criticism of any player.

5. Maintain your poise under any conditions. The slogan for a successful recreation leader is, "Say it with a smile."

6. Be sympathetic with the players in any difficulties they may have.

SOME QUESTIONS FOR THE LEADER TO ASK HIMSELF

1. Am I friendly and congenial with other people?

2. Have I tried to discover my own interests and abilities, and do I try to develop those interests and abilities?

3. Do I refrain from unnecessarily hurting the feelings of anyone?

4. Am I familiar with the rules of common courtesy and good manners?

5. Do I watch for every chance to do favors unasked?

6. Do I recognize my obligation to my organization?

7. Do I put co-operation before competition?

8. Do I respect the other fellow's viewpoint?

9. Do I suggest rather than command or demand?

10. Do I try to remedy a bad situation rather than just finding fault?

11. Do I conceal unpleasant feelings?

12. Do I give credit where and when credit is due?

13. Do I take advantage of opportunities to develop self-confidence?

14. Do I read widely?

15. Do I endeavor to overcome objectionable mannerisms?

16. Do I make an effort to understand the situation or problem with which I am confronted?

17. Do I try to foresee possible results?

18. Do I try to avoid prejudice or bias in my thinking?

19. Do I recognize the value of facts?

20. Am I always on the alert to improve my plan?

21. Do I take advantage of opportunities to learn more about my field?

22. Do I remain poised * under criticism, and do I profit by criticism?

23. Do I check on myself when there has been failure or only partial success to discover whether or not I was at fault?

24. Do I look at myself objectively to discover my strong points and my weak points, and do I do anything about what I find?

25. Do I plan my work carefully or do I simply trust to the inspiration of the moment?

* Poise or self-control—to be unexcited, unruffled, undisturbed, both on ordinary occasions and in emergencies.

—Adapted from BRUCE TOM

THE RECREATION LEADER'S CALENDAR

January

1. New Year's Day.

6. Twelfth Day, or Twelfth-tide in England. Previous evening, Twelfth Night celebrated as Christmas in Spain.

7. Gregory XII. 1502. (Our present calendar known as Gregorian calendar.)

17. Benjamin Franklin's Birthday. 1706. American statesman, philosopher. Printer. Journalist. *Poor Richard's Almanack.*

19. Edgar Allan Poe. 1809. Poet. Writer.

19. R. E. Lee's Birthday (observed in Alabama, Arkansas, Florida, Georgia, Mississippi, North Carolina, South Carolina, Tennessee, and Virginia). 1807.

20. Presidential Inauguration Day, beginning 1937, and every fourth year thereafter.

25. Robert Burns, 1759. Scottish Poet.

31. Franz Schubert, 1797, Composer. "Serenade," "Ave Maria," "Unfinished Symphony," etc.
National Drama Week.

February

2. Ground Hog Day. (The groundhog is a marmot or woodchuck.) Candlemas.

3. Sidney Lanier, 1842. Poetry.

7. Charles Dickens, 1812. Fiction. English Writer. *David Copperfield, Oliver Twist, Tale of Two Cities, Christmas Carol,* etc.

11. Daniel Boone, 1735. American Pioneer. Thomas Edison, 1847. Inventor.

12. Abraham Lincoln's Birthday, 1809. "Rail Splitter." United States President.

14. St. Valentine's Day.

22. George Washington's Birthday, 1732. First United States President.

27. Henry Wadsworth Longfellow, 1807. American Poet. *Evangeline, Tales of a Wayside Inn,* etc.

March

6. Michelangelo, 1475. Art. Italian sculptor.

7. Luther Burbank, 1849. Nature. Arbor Day in California.

16. Florence Nightingale. English philanthropist. Organized

Crimean War hospital service. Laid foundation of modern scientific nursing.

17. St. Patrick's Day.

21. First Day of Spring.

24. Fannie Crosby. 1820.

April

1. All Fool's Day.

3. John Burroughs, 1837, Nature. Washington Irving, 1783. Writer.

6. Robert Edwin Peary discovered the North Pole, 1909.

11. Arbor Day and Bird Day. (In the south Arbor Day comes in winter.)

13. Thomas Jefferson's Birthday, 1742. (In Alabama.)

14. Pan-American Day. (On that date in 1890 was held First International Conference of American States. At that time the Pan-American Union was organized.)

18. Paul Revere's Ride, 1775.

23. Shakespeare, 1564. English writer. *Hamlet, Othello, Romeo and Juliet, Midsummer Night's Dream,* etc.

May

1. May Day. Also Labor Day in Philippines.

4. John J. Audubon, 1780. Birds, Nature.

9. Richard E. Byrd flew to North Pole, 1926.

21. Charles A. Lindbergh flew the Atlantic, 1927.

22. Wilhelm Richard Wagner. 1813. German Composer. "Creator of modern musical drama." *Tannhauser, Lohengrin, Meistersinger, Parsifal,* etc.

24. Queen Victoria. 1819. England.

25. Ralph Waldo Emerson, 1803, Poetry, Essays.

30. Memorial Day or Decoration Day (all states and possessions except Alabama, Arkansas, Florida, Georgia, Louisiana, Mississippi, North Carolina, South Carolina).

Mother's Day (second Sunday). Mothers and Daughters Week.
National Music Week (begins first Sunday of the month).

June

5. Rose Festival.

14. Flag Day, 1777. Stars and Stripes adopted by Continental Congress.

17. John Wesley, 1703. Founder of Methodist Church.
Father's Day (third Sunday).

July

1. Dominion Day in Canada. (Dominion established that date, 1867.)

4. Independence Day, 1776.

14. Rembrandt. 1607. Art.

August

6. Alfred Tennyson, 1809. *In Memoriam, Idylls of the King, The Princess,* etc.

9. Izaak Walton, 1593. English Writer. *Compleat Angler.* Great fisherman.

15. Sir Walter Scott, 1771. Scotch poet and novelist. *Ivanhoe, Lady of the Lake, Rob Roy,* etc.

17. David Crockett, 1786. Frontiersman. Defender of the "The Alamo."

29. Oliver Wendell Holmes, 1809. Poet.

September

15. James Fenimore Cooper, 1789. Author. (Indian stories, pioneers.)

17. Constitution Day, 1787.

22. Emancipation Proclamation, 1862.
Labor Day (first Monday).
American Indian Day (fourth Friday).

October

7. James Whitcomb Riley, 1853. American poet.

12. Columbus Day. (America discovered—1492.)

23. Frances C. Willard Day. Temperance reformer. Organized W.T.C.U.

27. Roosevelt Day (Theodore Roosevelt, 1818). President of the United States, writer, naturalist, athlete, statesman.

29. John Keats, 1795. English poet. *Lamia, The Eve of St. Agnes, Isabella,* etc.

31. Halloween.

November

2. Daniel Boone, 1734. American pioneer.

3. William Cullen Bryant, 1794. *Thanatopsis.*

10. Oliver Goldsmith, 1728. Irish poet and writer. *She Stoops to Conquer, Vicar of Wakefield, Deserted Village,* etc.

11. Armistice Day, 1918.

13. Robert Louis Stevenson, 1850. Scottish novelist. *Treasure Island, Kidnapped, Dr. Jekyl and Mr. Hyde.*
General Election Day, first Tuesday after first Monday.
Thanksgiving Day (last Thursday).
Father and Son Week.

December

9. John Milton, 1608. English poet. *Paradise Lost.*

17. John G. Whittier, 1807. Charles Wesley, 1708.

21. First Day of Winter, shortest day of year. Forefather's Day (landing on Plymouth Rock, 1620; celebrated by New England societies everywhere).

25. Christmas Day.

31. New Year's Eve.

SUGGESTIONS FOR A YEAR'S PROGRAM

January

Possible parties—See January (Chapter XVII). Other possibilities: "Calendar Social"; "New Year's Jamboree"; "Season Social"; "A New Year's Masquerade"; "Twelfth Night Party."

Music—A Franz Schubert Evening; A "Hits of the Ages" Musical Program.

Outdoor sports—Skating, tobogganing, sleighing.

Indoor sports—Basketball, volleyball, indoor baseball, track.

Literature—A Poetry Evening (Poe and Burns); "Modern Fiction," Book Discussion Club.

Drama—Dramatic Festival; Drama Party; Organization of Dramatic Club.

February

Possible parties—See February (Chapter XVII). Other possibilities: "A Cupid Party"; "A Hatchet Party"; "A Pioneer Party" (Daniel Boone); "Heart Banquet."

Music—"Heart Songs Around the World."

Outdoor sports—Skating, tobogganing, sleighing.

Indoor sports—Baseketball, volleyball, indoor baseball.

Literature—"Southern Poets" (Lanier); "The World's Greatest Novels" (*Les Miserables; Don Quixote;* Dickens), Book Discussion Club; "A Longfellow Evening."

Drama—"A Marriage Proposal," Tchekoff. A farce for two men, one woman. Thirty minutes.

March

Possible parties—See March (Chapter XVII). Other possibilities: "A Pat Party"; "A Pig Party"; "Circus Party"; "Fine Arts Party" (Michelangelo).

Music—"An Evening of Irish Songs."

Outdoor sports—Hobo Hike; Nature Hike (Burbank).

Indoor sports—Basketball, volleyball, indoor baseball.

Literature—Review of some book on nature lore.

Drama—Stunt Nite; preparation for an Easter play.

April

Possible parties—See April (Chapter XVII). Other possibilities: "Rainbow Party"; "Color Party"; "A Spring Millinery Party"; "A Pan-American Fair."

Music—"Evening of Negro Spirituals."

Outdoor events—"Tree Picnic" (Arbor Day); "Bird Hike"; baseball, softball.

Literature—"Stories of Washington Irving."

Drama—Easter Drama (*The Rock*, by Hamlin).

May

Possible parties—See May (Chapter XVII). Other possibilities: "A Flower Show"; "A May Day Party"; "Mother and Daughter Banquet."

Music—May Music Festival or Costume Musicale (Music Week).

Outdoor events—Picnic, "Bird Hike," baseball, softball, badminton, tennis.

Literature—"An Evening With Ralph Waldo Emerson," "Some Modern Fiction," Book Discussion Club.

Drama—Operetta, *The Mikado*, or some other Gilbert and Sullivan opera.

June

Possible parties—See June (Chapter XVII). Other possibilities: "A Flower Social"; "A Garden Festival"; "A Flag Party"; "Outdoor Book Costume Party"; "Father and Son Banquet"; "Recognition Party for Graduates."

Music—"An evening with the Wesleys," A Community Sing.

Outdoor events—Picnics, boat fiesta, baseball, softball, badminton, tennis, deck tennis, croquet, clock golf.

Literature—Book Trail (John Masefield's poems).

July

Possible parties—See July (Chapter XVII). Other possibilities: "Trip Around the World," Storytellers' Convention."

Music—"International Music Fiesta."

Outdoor events—Fourth of July picnic, a cook-out, camping, baseball, softball, badminton, tennis, deck tennis, croquet, clock golf.

Literature—Book Trail ("Old Man Adam and His Chillun").

August

Possible parties—See August (Chapter XVII). Other possibilities: "A Freeze-up Party," "A Watermelon Feast."

Outdoor events—"Moonlight Picnic," "A Camera Hike," "A Hayride," picnics, baseball, softball, badminton, tennis, deck tennis, croquet, clock golf.

Literature—Book Hike (*A Daughter of the Samurai*, Sugimoto, or *Where the Blue Begins*, by Christopher Morley).

September

Possible parties—See September (Chapter XVII). Other possibilities: "Big Bluff College," "An Auto Party," "An Indian Party," "A Welcome Party for Students."

Music—"An Evening of Old Songs."

Outdoor events—Treasure hunt, an Indian Campfire (Indian stories), baseball, softball, volleyball, tennis, deck tennis, croquet, clock golf.

Literature—"The American Indian in Literature"; "Looking Backward," Bellamy.

Drama—Reading rehearsal of fourth act of Ibsen's "An Enemy of the People."

October

Possible parties—See October (Chapter XVII). Other possibilities: "Halloween Frolic," "A Goblin Party," "A Black Cat Party," "A Discovery Party" (Columbus).

Music—"Gypsy Camp Musicale."

Outdoor events—Nutting Hike, Lantern Hike and Campfire.

Indoor sports—Volleyball, indoor baseball, shuffleboard.

Literature—"A World Story Evening," "An Evening with James Whitcomb Riley."

Drama—"An Old-Fashioned Mother," by Walter Ben Hare.

November

Possible parties—See November (Chapter XVII). Other possibilities: "Harvest Home Social," "A Pilgrim Party," "A Harvest Home Banquet."

Music—"A Stephen Foster Evening."

Outdoor events—Football, touch football, hunting.

Indoor sports—Volleyball, indoor baseball, shuffleboard.

Literature—"An Evening with Robert Louis Stevenson."

Drama—"The Courtship of Miles Standish," Prebbrey (French); Discussion of Pollock's "The Enemy."

December

Possible parties—See December (Chapter XVII). Other possibilities: "A Star Party," "A Christmas Tree Party," "A Watch Night Party."

Music—"A Carol Festival." Tableaux.

Outdoor events—Skating, tobogganing, sleighing, caroling.

Indoor sports—Basketball, volleyball, indoor baseball, shuffleboard.

Literature—Dickens' "Christmas Carol."

Drama—"Fiat Lux," Falkenberg.

REGULAR LONG-PERIOD EVENTS

1. **Once-a-week open-house program.**—Informal participation in table games, floor games, social games, folk games, music, dramatics, etc.

2. **Hobby night or workshop night.**—A once-a-week program that runs for a definite period, such as ten or twelve weeks in the autumn and winter, and for the same period in the late winter and spring. Woodwork, carving, leather work, and all sorts of hobbies and crafts. One church ran a three-months "Hobby School."

3. **Interest group night.**—A once-a-week program for adults and other young people that runs for a period of ten weeks. Book reviews, current events, music appreciation, dramatics, study classes, etc.

4. **Forum nights.**—A series of from six to ten forum periods on hot-spot problems.

BIBLIOGRAPHY

BIBLIOGRAPHY

SIGNIFICANT POINTS OF VIEW

BENNETT, ARNOLD. *How to Live.* Garden City Publishing Company. 1910.
A plea for a better use of time, especially in Book I, on "How To Live on 24 Hours a Day."

BURNS, C. D. *Leisure in the Modern World.* Century. 1932. 314 pp.
A careful analysis of the whole problem.

BOWIE, WALTER RUSSELL. *On Being Alive.* Scribner's. 1931.
Life comes from enriching interests.

BREITIGAN, GERALD. *Dare to Live.* Falcon Press. 1934. 229 pp.

CABOT, RICHARD C. *What Men Live By.* Houghton. 1914.
Work, play, love, worship.

CALKINS, ERNEST ELMO. *Care and Feeding of Hobby Horses.* Leisure League of America. 1933.
The basic pamphlet of the Leisure League series.

CUTTEN, GEORGE B. *The Threat of Leisure.* Yale University Press. 1926.
Points out the necessity for the intelligent use of leisure.

DALE, EDGAR. *How to Appreciate the Movies.* MacMillan. 1933.
Standards for evaluating the movies.

DIMNET, ERNEST. *The Art of Thinking.* Simon and Schuster. 1929.

———. *What We Live By.* Simon and Schuster. 1932. 303 pp.
The true, the beautiful, the good.

FOREMAN, HENRY JAMES. *Our Movie-Made Children.* MacMillan. 1933.
A startling picture of the effect of the movies on behaviour.

HAMBIDGE, GOVE. *Time to Live.* McGraw. 1933.
An indictment of standardized leisure.

HARBIN, E. O. *Recreational Materials and Methods.* Cokesbury Press. 1931.
The church's stake in the leisure-time problem and techniques of leadership.

HEATON, K. L. *Character Building Through Recreation.* University of Chicago Press.
Case studies in the effects of recreation on character.

JACKS, L. P. *Education of the Whole Man.* Harper's. 1931.

———. *Education Through Recreation.* Harper's. 1932.
The necessity for educating people for the use of leisure.

JOAD, C. E. N. *Diogenes; or, the Future of Leisure.* Dutton. 1928.

LIES, EUGENE T. *The New Leisure. Challenges the Schools.* National Recreation Association. 1933.

LUNDBERG, KOMAROVSKY, McINERY. *Leisure.* Columbia University Press. 1934. 389 pp.

MAY AND PETGEN. *Leisure and Its Uses.* Barnes. 1928. 268 pp.
A study of the uses of leisure in foreign countries with interesting comparisons.

MITCHELL AND MASON. *The Theory of Play.* Barnes.

NEUMEYER, MARTIN H. AND ESTHER S. *Leisure and Recreation.* Barnes. 1936.
A study of the social aspects of leisure and recreation.

NASH, JAY B. *Spectatoritis.* Barnes.
A plea for active as against passive recreation.

OVERSTREET, H. A. *We. Move in New Directions.* Norton. 1933. 275 pp.
An interesting discussion of escape and fulfillment activities.

———. *A Guide to Civilized Leisure.* Norton. 1934. 220 pp.
A discussion of constructive uses of leisure.

PAGE, KIRBY. *Living Creatively.* Farrar and Rinehart. 1932.
Suggests the budgeting of one's time.

PITKIN, WALTER. *Life Begins at Forty.* McGraw. 1932.

RUGG, HAROLD. *Culture and Education in America.* Harcourt. 1931. 401 pp.
The necessity for the schools developing "creative craftsmen" with inner integrity and a social point of view.

SLAVSON, S. R. *Creative. Group Education.* Association Press. 1937.
A severe indictment of over-emphasis on competition.

SOCKMAN, RALPH. *Morals of Tomorrow*. Harper's. 1931.
Aspects of the age in which we live.

STEINER, J. F. *Americans at Play*. Recent Trends in Recreational
and Leisure-Time Activities. McGraw. 1933.

ACTIVITY BOOKS

Archery (See Archery in Chapter XI, Fun with Sports)

CRAFT, D. AND C. *The Teaching of Archery.* Barnes.

LAMBERT, A. W., JR. *Modern Archery.* Barnes. 1929. 306 pp.

REICHART, N. AND KEASEY, G. *Modern Methods in Archery.* Barnes. 1937.

ROUNSEVELLE, PHILLIP. *Archery Simplified.* Barnes.

ROUNSEVELLE, PHILLIP. *Student's Handbook of Archery.* Barnes.

STEMMLER, L. E. *The Archery Workshop.* L. E. Stemmler Company, Queens Village, L. I., N. Y.

Art (See also "Handcrafts" and "Hobbies")

BAILEY, HENRY TURNER. *Famous Paintings.* Art Extension Press. Five volumes.

BARNES, A. C. *Art of Painting.* Harcourt. 1923.

BLAKE, V. *Way to Sketch.* Oxford. 1925.

GARDNER, HELEN. *Understanding the Arts.* Harcourt. 1932.

GEEN, E. *Pencil Sketching.* Pitman. 1930.

GOLDSTEIN, H. I. AND V. *Art in Everyday Living.* MacMillan. 1932.

HECKMAN, ALBERT W. *Paintings of Many Lands.* Art Extension Press.
An appreciation course.

LUTZ, E. G. *Practical Pen Drawing.* Scribner's. 1928.

NICHOLLS, BERTRAM. *Painting in Oils.* The Studio Publications, Inc., New York.

ORPEN, SIR WILLIAM. *The Outline of Art.* Putnam. 1938.

RUCKSTULL, F. W. *Great Works of Art and What Made Them Great.* Garden City Publishing Company. 1925. 547 pp.

STEARNS, MYRON M. *Drawing for Fun.* Leisure League of America. 1938.

Athletics—Sports (For other books see Chapter XI, Fun with Sports)

GREGG, ABEL J. *Basketball and Character.* Association Press. 1934.

McCORMICK, OLIVE. *Water Pageants—Games and Stunts.* Barnes.

MITCHELL, E. D. *Sports for Recreation.* Barnes. 1936.

NATIONAL RECREATION ASSOCIATION. *Recreative Athletics.* Barnes.

REYNOLDS, H. A. *The Game Way to Sports.* Barnes.

SPAULDING ATHLETIC LIBRARY. Booklets.
Write for list to American Sports Publishing Company, 45 Rose St., New York, or see any good local sporting goods house.

Camping, Hiking, Outings

ALLEN, HAZEL K. *Camps and Their Modern Administration.* Woman's Press. 1930.

BOY SCOUTS OF AMERICA. *Hiking.*

DIMOCK AND HENDRY. *Camping and Character.* Association Press. 1929.

DIMOCK, H. S. *Character Education in Summer Camp, I.* Association Press. 1933.

——. *Character Education in Summer Camp, II.* Association Press. 1934.

GRAHAM, ABBIE. *The Girls Camp.* Womans Press. 1933.

NATIONAL RECREATION ASSOCIATION. *Picnic Programs.*

——. *Suggestions for Hiking.*

SETON, ERNEST THOMPSON. *The Birch Bark Roll of Woodcraft.* Barnes.

SOIFER, MARGARET K. *Firelight Entertainment.* Furrow Publishing Company. 115 Eastern Parkway, Brooklyn, N. Y.

SOLOMON, BEN. *Hikers' Handbook.* Leisure League of America.

STONE, WALTER. *Camp and Trail Craft.* 1938.

Dramatics

ALBERTI, MADAME EVA. *A Handbook of Acting.* Samuel French.

ATKINS, ALMA N. *Drama Goes to Church.* Bethany Press. 1931.

BOLESLAVSHI, RICHARD. *Acting; The First Six Lessons.* Theatre Arts. 1934.

COOKSON, MRS. NESFIELD. *The Costume Book.* McBride.

DESEO-PHIPPS. *Looking at Life Through the Drama.* Abingdon. 1931.

GRIMBALL AND WELLS. *Costuming a Play.* Appleton-Century.

EASTMAN, FRED AND WILSON, L. *Drama in the Church.* Willett-Clark. 1933.

HAIRE, FRANCES H. *The Folk Costume Book.* Barnes.

HOBBS, MABEL F. *Play Production Made Easy.* National Recreation Association. 1933.

JONES, LESLIE ALLEN. *Painting Scenery.* Baker.

KNAPP, JACK S. *Lighting the Stage with Home-Made Equipment.* Walter H. Baker. 1933.

LEEMING, JOSEPH. *The Costume Book for Parties and Plays.* Stokes. 1938.

MILLER, CATHERINE. *Stunt Night Tonight.* Harper's.

———. *Stunts of All Lands.* Harper's.

NELMS, HENNING. *Lighting the Amateur Stage.* National Theatre Conference, 119 W. 57th St., New York.

ROHRBOUGH, KATHERINE. *Successful Stunts.*

SELDEN, SAMUEL AND SELLMAN, H. D. Stage Scenery and Lighting. Crofts. 1934.

SMITH, MILTON. *The Book of Play Production.* Appleton. 1926.

WARD, WINIFRED. *Creative Dramatics.* Appleton.

WELLS, CHARLES F. *Drama Clubs Step By Step.* Walter H. Baker. 1933.

WILSON, DOROTHY CLARKE. *Twelve Months of Drama for the Average Church.* Baker. 1933.

WHORF, RICHARD. *Time to Make Up.* Baker.

Folk and Musical Games

BIRCHARD AND COMPANY. *Twice 55 Games with Music.*

BURCHENAL, ELIZABETH. *Folk Dances and Singing Games.* G. Schirmer. 1933.

————. *Dances of the People.* G. Schirmer. 1934.

CAMPBELL FOLK SCHOOL, Brasstown, N. C. *Singing Games.*

CRAMPTON, C. WARD. *The Folk Dance Book.* Barnes.

————. *The Second Folk Dance Book.* Barnes.

DEARBORN PUBLISHING COMPANY, Dearborn, Mich. *Good Morning—* A Manual of Old American Dances. 169 pp.

GIRL SCOUTS OF AMERICA. *Skip to My Lou* (17 singing games)

HINMAN, MARY WOOD. *Ring Dances and Singing Games.* Barnes.

HINMAN, MARY WOOD. *Group Dances.* Barnes.

ROHRBOUGH, LYNN. *Handy II.* Sections on "Play Party Games, Treasures from Abroad, and Quadrilles."

SCHWENDENER, N. AND TIBBELLS, A. *Legends and Dances of Old Mexico.* Barnes.

SPICER, DOROTHY GLADYS. *A Book of Festivals.* Woman's Press.

Handcrafts * (See Chapter III, Fun with Hobbies, for additional books)

BECHDOLT, JACK. *The Modern Handy Book for Boys.* Greenburg. 1933.

COLLINS, A. FREDERICK. *Making Things for Fun.* Appleton-Century.

COUCH, OSMA PALMER. *Basket Pioneering.* Orange Judd Publishing Company. 172 pp.

DURST, ALAN. *Wood Carving.* The Studio Publications, Inc., New York.

FAULKNER, H. W. *Wood-Carving as a Hobby.* Harper's.

GRISWOLD, LESTER. *Handicrafts.* Colorado Springs, Colo., 1100 Glen.

JACKSON, JAMES. *Handicraft of Wood-Carving.* Pitman.

NATIONAL RECREATION ASSOCIATION. *Handcraft.*

PERKINS, DOROTHY. *Handbook of the Use of Crafts.* Woman's Press. 1934.

REYNOLDS, H. A. *Complete Book of Modern Crafts.* Association Press. 1938.

TAYLOR, STEWART. *Clay-Modeling for Schools.* Pitman.

TURNER, HERBERT. *Artistic Leather Craft.* Pitman.

* Handcraft suggestions and materials may be gotten from the following firms: American Handcrafts Company, 2124 S. Main, Los Angeles, California, 193 William St., New York; American Reedcraft Corp., 130 Beekman St., New York; Camp Fire Girls Outfitting Company, 197 Greene St., New York (Catalog); Graton and Knight (leather), Worchester, Mass.; Fellow Crafters (all crafts), 739 Boylston St., Boston; The Handcrafters, Waupun (all crafts); Industrial Arts Co-operative Service, 519 W. 121st St., New York (catalog, 10 cents); National Handicraft and Hobby Service, 201 N. Wells St., Chicago (all crafts); Manual Arts Press, Peoria, Ill. (books); Universal School of Handcrafts, Inc., Rockefeller Center, R. K. O. Building, New York (all crafts).

Hobbies

(See also "Art," "Handcraft," and other Activity Lists)

CALKINS, ERNEST ELMO. *Care and Feeding of Hobby Horses.* Leisure League of America. 1934.

GREENBIE, MARJORIE. *The Arts of Leisure.* McGraw-Hill.

GUPSTILL, ARTHUR L. *Sketching as a Hobby.* Harper's. 1936.

LAMPLAND, RUTH. *Hobbies for Everybody.* Harper's. 1934.

MOORE, NORMAN. *How to Draw What You See.* Hillman-Curl, Inc 1938.

SHAW, RUTH FAISON. *Finger Painting.* Little, Brown, & Company. 1934.

SOAP SCULPTURE. National Sculpture Committee, 80 E. Eleventh St., New York; Proctor and Gamble, Education Department, Cincinnati, Ohio. Pamphlet material from the latter.

STRONG, WILLIAM M. *Photography for Fun.* Leisure League of America. 1934.

TANGERMAN, E. J. *Whittling and Woodcarving.* Whittlesley House 1936.

TAUSSIG AND MEYER. *The Book of Hobbies.* Minton-Balch Company. 1934.

THACH, STEPHEN D. *Finger Painting as a Hobby.* Harper's. 1937.

WILLOUGHBY, WALTER. *Drawing for Fun.* Leisure League. 1938.

WOODWARD, AGNES. *Whistling as an Art.* Carl Fischer. 1938.

Home Play

MARRAN, RAY J. *Fun at Home—How to Make Indoor and Outdoor Games.* Appleton-Century. 1938.

LAWSON, ARTHUR. *Fun in the Backyard.* Crowell.

MEYER, JEROME S. *Fun for the, Family.* Greenberg. 1937.

———. *More Fun for the Family.* Greenberg. 1938.

Home Play. National Recreation Association.

Home Play and Indoor Playroom. National Recreation Association.

Leadership

HARBIN, E. O. *Recreational Materials and Methods.* Cokesbury Press.

HEATON, K. L. *Character Building Through Recreation.* Chicago University Press.

POWELL, WARREN T. *Recreation for the Church and Community.* Abingdon. 1938.

SMITH, CHARLES F. *Games and Recreational Methods.* Dodd, Mead. 1924.

———. *Games and Game Leadership.* Dodd, Mead. 1932.

Magic and Tricks

GIBSON, C. R. *Chemical Amusements and Experiments.* Lippincott. 1928.

GIBSON, W. B. *New Magician's Manual.* Blue Ribbon Books.

HOFFMAN. *Modern Magic.* McKay. 1933. A gold mine of ideas.

HUNTER, N. *New and Easy Magic.* Pearson, London, Eng. 1938.

KAUFMAN, G. L. *How's Tricks.* Stokes. 1938.

LEEMING, JOSEPH. *Tricks Any Boy Can Do.* Appleton-Century. 1938. Ryerson Press. (Canada).

——. *Magic Made Easy.* Doubleday-Doran.

Mental Games and Tests

COLLINS, A. F. *Fun with Figures.*

HEATH, ROYAL V. *Mathemagic* (fun with figures). Simon and Schuster. 1933.

HIRSCHBERGER, ARTHUR. *Can You Solve It?* Crowell. 1928.

LICKS, H. E. *Recreation in Mathematics.* D. Van Nostrand Company, New York. 1917.

STREETER, R. A. AND HOEHN, R. G. *Are You a Genius?* Stokes. Series I, 1932. Series II, 1933.

Music

(For additional books see "Fun with Music")

ANNESLEY, CHARLES. *The Home Book of Opera.* The Dial Press, N. Y. 1938. (Stories of 300 operas.)

C. C. BIRCHARD AND COMPANY. *The Brown Book, The Green Book, Sing, Rose Book* (for ladies' voice), *Blue Book* (for men's voices).

BOTSFORD, FLORENCE H. *Collection of Folk Songs.* G. Schirmer. 1930. Three volumes.

BOTSFORD, FLORENCE H. *The Universal Folk Songster.* G. Schirmer. 1938.

COLEMAN, SATIS. *Creative Music in the Home.* Myers, Valparaiso, Ind.

CLARK, KENNETH. *The Cowboy Sings.* Paull-Pioneer Music Corp., New York.

——. *Everybody Sing.* Paull-Pioneer.

——. *Keep on Singing.* Paull-Pioneer.

ELSON, ARTHUR. *The Book of Musical Knowledge.* Houghton-Mifflin. 1827.

FAULKNER, A. S. *What We Hear in Music.* Victor. 1931.

HAMPTON INSTITUTE. *Religious Folk Songs of the Negro.*

HARBIN, E. O. *Parodology.* Cokesbury Press.

NATIONAL RECREATION ASSOCIATION. *Songs for Informal Singing.* Sets I, II, and III.

PARKHURST, WINTHROP AND DEBEKKER, L. J. *Encyclopedia of Music and Musicians.* Crown Publishing Company, Inc., New York, 1937.

PEYSER, ETHEL. *How to Enjoy Music.* Putnam. 1933.

E. C. SCHIRMER CO. *Ten Folk Songs and Ballads.* Sets I, II, III, IV.

SPAETH, SIGMUND. *The Art of Enjoying Music.* Whittlesley House. 1933.

———. *Music for Everybody.* Leisure League. 1934.

SURETTE AND DAVISON. *The Home and Community Book.* E. C. Schirmer.

TOBITT, JANET AND WHITE, ALICE. *Dramatized Ballads.* Dutton. 1938.

YOKOM, J. H. *Introduction to Music Enjoyment and Appreciation.* Ryerson Press. 1937.

ZANZIG, AUGUSTUS. *Assembly and Community Singing.*

Nature Lore

BAKER, L. H. *When the Stars Come Out.* Viking Press. 1934.

JOHNSON, GAYLORD. *Discover the Stars.* Leisure League. 1935.

INGALLS, A. C. *Amateur Telescope Making.* Scientific American, 1933.

KING, JULIUS. *Talking Leaves.* Harter Publishing Co., Cleveland, Ohio.

PALMER, E. L. *Nature Games.* Comstock Publishing Co. 1925.

———. *Camp Fire Nature Guide.* Comstock Co. 1925.

PEATTIE, DONALD COLROSS. *Green Laurels.* Garden City. 1938. (Lives of Great Naturalists.)

VINAL, W. G. *Nature Games.* Comstock. 1926.

WOOLWORTH. Woolworth's Five and Ten Cent Store gets out a series of ten-cent booklets on birds, flowers, trees, and stars.

Palmistry

HAMON, L. *Language of the Hand.* McClelland, Toronto. **1938.**

VEQUIN, CAPINI. *Hands Up.* Stokes.

Puppets and Marionettes

(See Chapter XV, Fun with Puppets)

ACKLEY, E. F. *Marionettes.* Stokes. 1929.

BUCHLER, ANNE K. *Marionette Making.* Fellowcrafters. 1930.

BUFANO, R. *Be a Puppet Showman.* Century. 1933.

COLLINS, E. A. AND CHARLTON, A. B. *Puppet Plays in Education.* Barnes.

FICKLIN, BESSIE. *Handbooks of Fist Puppets.* Stokes.

JOSEPH, H. *Book of Marionettes.* Viking Press. 1929.

McPARLIN, P. L. *Puppet Heads and Their Making.* McParlin. 1931.

MILLS AND DUNN. *Marionettes, Masks, and Shadows.* Doubleday-Doran.

————. *Shadow Plays and How to Produce Them.* Doubleday-Doran. 1938.

NELSON AND HAYES. *Trick Marionettes.* McParlin.

MILLIGAN, DAVID A. *Fist Puppetry.* Barnes. 1938.

ROSSBACH, C. E. *Making Marionettes.* Harcourt, Brace. 1938.

SARG, TONY, AND STODDARD, ANN. *A Book of Marionette Plays.* Walter Baker.

SOIFER, MARGARET. *With Puppets, Mimes, and Shadows.* Furrow Press.

TREASURE CHEST PUBLICATIONS. *Series of four booklets on Marionettes.* 62 W. 45th St., New York City.

Socials and Games

BANCROFT, JESSIE. *Games for the Playground, Home, School, and Gymnasium.* Macmillan.

BREEN, MARY J. *Partners in Play.* Barnes.

BOWERS, ETHEL. *Recreation for Girls and Women.* Barnes.

DEPEW, A. M. *The Cokesbury Party Book.* Cokesbury Press.

DRAPER, GEORGE O. *Games.* Association Press.

FORBUSH AND ALLEN. *Games.*

HARLEY, BRIAN. *Chess for the Fun of It.* McKay.

HARBIN, E. O. *Phunology.* Cokesbury Press.

LAWSON, ARTHUR. *Home Made Games.* Lippincott.

NATIONAL RECREATION ASSOCIATION. *Games for Boys and Men.* 1938.

MARSHALL, F. J. *Chess in an Hour.* Leisure League.

MITCHELL, D. *A Guide to the Game of Chess.* McKay. 1933.

MITCHELL AND MASON. *Social Games for Recreation.* Barnes. 1935.

———. *Active Games for Recreation.* Barnes. 1935.

ROHRBOUGH, LYNN. *Handy I; Handy II.*

RYAN, WILLIAM F. *Scientific Checkers Made Easy.* The New Checkergram, 2258 Preston Avenue, New York.

WOOD, CLEMENT AND GODDARD, GLORIA. *The Complete Book of Games.* Halcyon House. 1938.

STORIES AND STORY-TELLING

How to Tell Stories

KEYES, ANGELA. *Stories and Story Telling.* Appleton. 1925.

LYMAN, EDNA. *Story Telling.* McClurg. 1923.

SHEDLOCK, MARIE. *The Art of the Story Teller.* Appleton. 1926.

WYCHE, RICHARD T. *Some Great Stories and How to Tell Them.* Newson. 1910.

Story Collections

ALDEN, R. M. *Why the Chimes Rang and Other Stories.* Bobbs-Merrill. 1930.

ANDERSEN, HANS CHRISTIAN. *Andersen's Fairy Tales.* Rand. 1916.

BAILEY, CAROLYN SHERWIN. *Stories from an Indian Cave.* Albert Whitman. 1924.

BAYS, ALICE. *Worship Programs and Stories.* Cokesbury. 1938.

FIELD, RACHEL. *American Folk and Fairy Tales.* Scribner's.

GRIMM. *Grimm's Fairy Tales.* Rand. 1913.

HAWTHORNE, NATHANIEL. *Great Stone Face and Other Stories.* Houghton. 1935.

HARRIS, JOEL CHANDLER. *Uncle Remus—His Songs and Sayings.* Appleton-Century. 1921.

——. *Tales from Uncle Remus.* Houghton-Mifflin.

HEAL, EDITH. *Robin Hood.* Rand. 1928.

KIPLING, RUDYARD. *Just So Stories.* Garden City Publishing Co.

——. *Jungle Book.* Doubleday-Doran.

KOMROFF, MANUEL. *Great Fables of All Nations.* Tudor Reprint.

LEE, F. H. *Folk Tales of All Nations.* Tudor Reprint. 1937.

LIEBER, M., AND WILLIAMS, D. C. *Great Stories of All Nations.* Tudor.

LINDERMAN, FRANK B. *Indian Why Stories.* Scribner's. 1915.

———. *Indian Old Man Stories.* Scribner's.

MVKERJI, DHAN GOPAL. *Hindu Fables.* Dutton. 1929.

NIEBUHR, HULDA. *Greatness Passing By.* Scribner's. 1936. (Bible and Other Stories.)

PYLE, HOWARD. *Some Merry Adventures of Robin Hood.* Scribner's. 1935.

RAND. *Arabian Nights.* Rand. 1914.

SLY, WILLIAM JAMES. *More World Stories Retold.* Judson Press. 1937. (Included Bible Stories.)

STEWART, MARY. *Tell Me a Story of Jesus.* Revell. 1913. (N. T. Stories.)

———. *Tell Me a True Story.* Revell. (Bible Hero Stories.)

ORGANIZATIONS PUBLISHING
RECREATION MATERIALS

ORGANIZATIONS PUBLISHING RECREATION MATERIALS

AMERICAN ASSOCIATION FOR HEALTH, PHYSICAL EDUCATION, AND RECREATION (formerly American Physical Education Association), 1201 16th Street N. W., Washington, D. C.

AMERICAN NATURE ASSOCIATION, 1212 Sixteenth St., S. W., Washington, D. C.

AMERICAN SPORTS PUBLISHING COMPANY, 45 Rose Street, New York.

BOY SCOUTS OF AMERICA, 2 Park Avenue, New York.

CAMPFIRE GIRLS, 41 Union Square, New York.

CO-OPERATIVE RECREATION SERVICE, Delaware, Ohio.

FOUR-H CLUBS, Extension Service, U. S. Department of Agriculture, Washington, D. C.

GIRL RESERVES, Y. W. C. A., 600 Lexington Avenue, New York.

GIRL SCOUTS, INC., 570 Lexington Avenue, New York.

LEISURE LEAGUE OF AMERICA, 30 Rockefeller Plaza, New York.

NATIONAL ASSOCIATION OF AUDUBON SOCIETIES, INC., 1006 Fifth Avenue, New York.

NATIONAL BUREAU FOR THE ADVANCEMENT OF MUSIC, 45 W. 45th Street, New York.

NATIONAL RECREATION ASSOCIATION, 315 Fourth Avenue, New York.

SPORTSMANSHIP BROTHERHOOD, INC., 342 Madison Ave., New York.

WOODCRAFT LEAGUE OF AMERICA, INC., Santa Fe, New Mexico.

Y. W. C. A., 600 Lexington Avenue, New York.

Y. M. C. A., 347 Madison Avenue, New York.

PERIODICALS IN THE RECREATION
FIELD

PERIODICALS IN THE RECREATION FIELD

Amateur Astronomer. Quarterly. Museum of Natural History, 77th and Central Park, New York.

American Checker Monthly. American Checker Association, Box 623, Abilene, Texas.

American Chess Bulletin. Monthly (November-April). Bi-monthly (May-October). 150 Nassau Street, New York.

Archery Review. Monthly. Archery Review Publishing Company, P. O. Box 361, Tulsa, Okla.

British Chess Magazine. Monthly. Whitehead and Miller, Ltd., 15 Elmwood Lane, Leeds, England.

Camping. Monthly. Camp Directors Association, Ann Arbor, Mich.

Design. Ten times a year. Columbus, Ohio.   (Art and art appreciation.)

Educational Screen. Monthly (September-June). 64 E. Lake Street, Chicago. (Movies.)

Educational Music Magazine. Bi-monthly (September-March). Educational Music Bureau, Inc., 434 S. Wabash Avenue, Chicago.

Enigma. Monthly. National Puzzlers League, Inc., 1325 E. Gibson Street, Scranton, Pa.

Etude. Monthly. Theodore Presser Company, 1712 Chestnut Street, Philadelphia, Pa. (Music.)

Field and Stream. Monthly. Field and Stream Publishing Company, 578 Madison Avenue, New York.

Home Arts Needlecraft. Monthly. Needlecraft Publishing Company, 420 Lexington Avenue, New York.

Home Craftsman. Bi-monthly. Home Craftsman Publishing Company Corp., 63 Park Row, New York.

Industrial Arts and Vocational Education. Monthly. Bruce Publishing Company, 524-544 N. Milwaukee Street, Milwaukee, Wis.

Junior Arts and Activities. Ten issues. Chicago. (Creative activities for elementary teachers.)

Kit, The. Quarterly. Lynn Rohrbough, Delaware, Ohio.

Leisure. Monthly. 683 Atlantic Avenue, Boston, Mass.

Magazine of Art. Monthly. American Federation of Arts, New York. (All arts.)

Mechanics and Handicraft. Monthly. Better Publications, Inc., 22 W. 48th Street, New York.

Mechanix Illustrated. Monthly. Greenwich, Conn.

Minicam. Monthly. Cincinnati, Ohio. (Photography.)

Model Craftsman. Monthly. Model Crafts Publishing Company, 205 E. 42d Street, New York.

Musical Quarterly. New York.

Music Supervisors Journal. Six times a year. Educators National Conference, 64 East Jackson Boulevard, Chicago.

Musical America. Monthly. 113 West 57th Street, New York.

National Geographic Magazine. Monthly. National Geographic Society, 16th and M Street, N. W., Washington, D. C.

Nature Magazine. Monthly. 1214 Sixteenth Street, N. W., Washington, D. C.

Outdoor Life. Monthly. Popular Science Monthly, Inc., 381 Fourth Avenue, New York. (Fishing, hunting.)

Popular Astronomy. Ten issues. Northfield, Minn.

Popular Homecraft. Six times a year. General Publishing Company, 737 North Michigan Avenue, Chicago, Ill.

Popular Photography. Monthly. 608 South Dearborn, Chicago, Ill.

Playthings. Monthly. McCready Publishing Company, 381 Fourth Avenue, New York.

Popular Mechanics Magazine. Monthly. Popular Mechanics Company, 200 East Ontario Street, Chicago.

Popular Science. Monthly. Popular Science Publishing Company, Inc., 381 Fourth Avenue, New York.

Recreation. Monthly. National Recreation Association, 315 Fourth Avenue, New York.

School Activities. Nine months. School Service Company, Topeka, Kan.

School Arts. Ten months. Worcester, Mass.

Scientific American. Monthly. Munn and Company, 24 West 40th Street, New York.

Social Chess Quarterly. Empire Chess Association, 4 Homegarth, Leftwich, England.

Story Art. Six copies. National Story League, Marie Hopkins, 93 West Frambes Avenue, Columbus, Ohio.

Theatre Arts Monthly. Theatre Arts, Inc., 40 East 49th Street, New York.

Travel. Monthly. New York.

Walking. Monthly. Walking Publishing Company, 158 West 44th Street, New York.

MAGAZINES ON COLLECTING HOBBIES

American Philatelist. Monthly. American Philatelist Society, 104 Academy Avenue, Federalsburg, Md. (Postage stamps.)

Collectors Club Philatelist. Quarterly. Collectors Club, 30 East 42d Street, New York. (Postage stamps.)

Hobbies: The Magazine of Collectors. Monthly. Lightner Publishing Company, 2810 South Michigan Avenue, Chicago.

Hobbies. Five times a year. Buffalo Museum of Science, Buffalo, N. Y.

Philatelic Journal of Great Britain. Monthly. International Philatelic Union, Pemberton and Company, Ltd., 12 South Molton Street, London, England. (Postage stamps.)

INDEXES

ALPHABETICAL INDEX

(965)

CLASSIFIED INDEX

Children's Games

Homemade Games

Musical Games

Nature Games

Party Plans

Sports (Athletics)

Stories

Water Games

793
H
HARBIN, E.O.
  The fun encyclopedia

DATE DUE			
22			
			ALESCO